POLITICS, LAW, AND SOCIAL CHANGE

Politics, Law, and Social Change

SELECTED ESSAYS
OF OTTO KIRCHHEIMER

EDITED BY FREDERIC S. BURIN

AND KURT L. SHELL

COLUMBIA UNIVERSITY PRESS

NEW YORK AND LONDON

1969

PREFACE

OTTO KIRCHHEIMER died at the age of sixty on November 22, 1965, at a time when he impressed his friends by the vigor and profundity with which his mind was striking out in new directions, enlarging further the already broad range of subjects to which he had devoted his life as a scholar.

His work as a thinker and scholar extended over almost four decades. Most of its results were published on both sides of the Atlantic in periodicals some of which are almost inaccessible today. Upon learning of his sudden death, we were convinced that the best tribute we could pay our late friend's memory would be to bring together in one volume a selection from his work reflecting the wide scope of his scholarly efforts.

In our choice of items from the large number of Otto Kirchheimer's articles and essays we were guided, first of all, by the consideration that material he had published in his major work, *Political Justice* (Princeton University Press, 1961), should not be included. Hence the present volume does not adequately reflect what was perhaps his major interest: the areas where law and politics intersect. Subject to this qualification, our second consideration was to present a balanced cross-section of the work he undertook in various phases of his life and intellectual development. Third, we had been tempted initially to weight the volume quite heavily with items from the earliest period of

Kirchheimer's scholarly work, particularly as these had appeared in German periodicals now defunct and as none of them had been previously translated. Yet in the end we decided to exclude the majority of them, both in the interest of balance and because many of his early pieces deal with specific issues and conflicts of German politics of the declining period of the Weimar Republic which are today of interest mainly to specialists. Fourth, though his more recent writings are accessible, we regard them as of such importance for their insights into the development of mass democracy that we included them with few exceptions. Thus the contents of the volume came to represent a compromise among the above-mentioned considerations.

We have thought it best to reprint all items without editorial changes, except for minor stylistic adjustments and the addition of a few explanatory editorial footnotes. Professor Kirchheimer's original footnotes were modified, where necessary, to provide a uniform style throughout the book and to conform to American usage.

Professors Erich Hula, of the Graduate Faculty of Political and Social Science of the New School for Social Research, and John H. Herz, of the City University of New York, long-time colleagues and close friends of Otto Kirchheimer, immediately and enthusiastically responded to our initiative, readily agreed to write the introduction, and were generous with their advice and assistance throughout the preparation of the volume. To Professor Arnold H. Heidenheimer of Washington University (St. Louis) who, as a friend of Professor Kirchheimer and to honor his memory, undertook the onerous task of translating from the German the long essay "Weimar—und was dann?," we likewise extend our sincere thanks. We are deeply grateful as well to Mrs. Anne Kirchheimer who at the inception of our work on this collection helped us greatly by preparing an exhaustive bibliography of her late husband's writings and by making available to us a large number of reprints, saving us by her cooperation much tedious labor. Professor Philip E. Mosely, Director of the European Institute at Columbia University, as soon as we informed him of our plan, obtained for this volume from Columbia's School of International Affairs a commitment of financial assistance which rendered feasible its publication. To both Professor Mosely and Dean Andrew W. Cordier of the

School of International Affairs we wish to express our profound gratitude. Except for "Weimar—and What Then," the translation of
those articles (five in number) of which there had been no previous
version in English is the work of Mr. and Mrs. John H. Paasche of
Washington, D.C. Mrs. Paasche attended to the typing connected with
these translations. We greatly appreciate Mr. and Mrs. Paasche's devoted contribution to preparing the manuscript for publication.

FREDERIC S. BURIN
KURT L. SHELL

OTTO KIRCHHEIMER

— — —

AN INTRODUCTION TO HIS LIFE AND WORK

BY JOHN H. HERZ AND ERICH HULA

I

IT MAY BE STRANGE to start the analysis of a great achievement with a seemingly negative statement: Otto Kirchheimer was not a systematic thinker. Many social scientists, especially in Europe, consider system-building the hallmark of scholarly creativity. Otto Kirchheimer's life-work proves cogently that this is not necessarily so. His creativity lay elsewhere; above all, in his superb and at times almost uncanny faculty to sift from the limitless data furnished by history that which is relevant and to analyze it in highly original fashion. His business, as he once put it, was "to uncover the basic mechanisms of political order and disorder." [1] In doing so, he was often able to lay bare what subsequent, more systematic analysis would confirm or enlarge upon. Thus he was above all an initiator, instinctively at the frontier of knowledge.

His rich lifework, mirroring his fate as an exile, a wanderer between worlds and cultures, was written in several languages, German, English, and French. Even his one great treatise, a comprehensive volume, really constitutes a collection—integrated, to be sure, through one common problem area, that of the use of legal procedures for political purposes—of a number of article-like essays. Our chief purpose, there-fore, in writing this Introduction has been to trace the development of

[1] See his preface to his collection of essays *Politik und Verfassung,* in the pocketbook series "Edition Suhrkamp" (Frankfurt/M., 1964).

Kirchheimer's mind and ideas in this maze of publications, and especially the ones brought together in the present volume.

Kirchheimer's specific talent, his sensitivity to the historically relevant and the uniquely political, can be observed throughout his life, straight from the beginnings of his scholarly efforts in the late 1920s. In trying to discern "epochs" or "stages" of his mind's development—an enterprise he most likely would have deprecated as too "pedantic" or "systematic"—we may perhaps distinguish four periods. The first would be his German period, the springtime of his life as a young, politically committed socialist intellectual. It comprises the five years from 1928—the year his doctoral dissertation was published in the form of a lengthy periodical article [2]—to 1933, when the last of his articles forming an astonishing series of publications containing a searching and critical analysis of the political and constitutional drama unfolding in Germany at that time appeared when the regime responsible for his exile was already in power.[3] There is a freshness, a flavor of commitment and enthusiasm, that peculiarly distinguishes these early writings. There is the urgency of the subject matter, of topics actually dealing with matters of life and death of a political community. There is also a tendency toward theoretical extremism, possibly reflecting the influence of his chief teacher, Carl Schmitt; an inclination to place findings into somewhat doctrinaire, "either-or" conceptual strait-jackets, as for instance when, in his dissertation on the political doctrines of socialism and Bolshevism, he characterizes both liberal democracy and Russian communism as "non-states," the one being an "empty legal machine" (*Rechtsmechanismus*), the other, a world-wide "interventionist movement"; or when, in his "little *magnum opus*" of this period, the essay "Weimar—und was dann?",[4] in a peculiar amalgamation of Schmittism and Marxism, democracy to him means mere

---

[2] "Zur Staatslehre des Sozialismus und Bolschewismus," *Zeitschrift für Politik*, XVII, 1928, 593 ff., translated in this volume as "The Socialist and Bolshevik Theory of the State," pp. 3–21 below.

[3] "Marxismus, Diktatur und Organisationsformen des Proletariats," *Die Gesellschaft*, X (March, 1933), 230–39, here reprinted in translation as "Marxism, Dictatorship and the Organization of the Proletariat," pp. 22–32 below. Almost all his articles of this period appeared in *Die Gesellschaft*, the theoretical organ of the German Social Democratic Party (SPD).

[4] Berlin, 1930, here reprinted in translation as "Weimar—and What Then?," pp. 33–74 below.

"bourgeois" rule unless and until it becomes the political form of a homogeneous society after the victory of the working class. There is also a tendency to subject political phenomena to legal analysis which reflects the then prevailing continental attitude toward state and politics and his own legal training.[5] Among the younger German social scientists of that time few were as intrinsically political-minded and, in this sense, political-science-oriented as Kirchheimer. His legal background, however, explains not only the large number of subsequent legal writings and analyses (especially during his exile in France and during his first years in the United States) but also his lasting interest in the functions of law and the functioning of its practitioners within the political framework. In his "German" period this concern is reflected in a second large essay, dealing with problems of expropriation.[6]

His second period comprises the long years of exile. These included the initial three years spent in France and the early years of his life in the United States, through the war, and even the first postwar years until he began really to sink roots in America and things American. This is not to imply that he was entirely uprooted during this time. To be sure, to a man so deeply immersed in German culture and so deeply committed to the cause of what he considered to be the most valuable, the most forward-looking movement and class of the German people, the victory of all he detested forcing him to leave his country was a deeply shocking experience. But he quickly struck roots in a "community of the uprooted," a group of German exiled scholars that rallied around the Institute of Social Research (transferred from Frankfurt to New York). It was the common purpose of his colleagues and subsequent friends there, scholars like Franz Neumann, Herbert Marcuse, and Arkadij Gurland, to account for what had happened in Europe and to analyze the trends of society and politics in the new age. Some of Kirchheimer's writings of this period show traces of being *œuvres d'occasion*, reflecting the fact that now he could not choose his topics as freely as before and had to write to make a living. But even

[5] In the light of his later career as an eminent political scientist, it is strange to see that Kirchheimer, in reviewing one of the earliest German treatises on "politics," expresses his doubts as to the justification of such an enterprise and even as to the existence of political science as a discipline. See his review of Adolf Grabowsky's *Politik* in *Die Gesellschaft*, X (1933), 173.

[6] *Grenzen der Enteignung* (Berlin, 1930).

these writings (e.g., a study of the fate of small business under the Nazi regime, written for a U.S. Senate Committee in collaboration with Neumann and Gurland [7]) betray his talent for incisive political analysis. There was found in his papers an unpublished manuscript—apparently commissioned by a Jewish organization in the late 1930s—on "The Policy of the Catholic Church toward the Jews," which, in tracing the history of Catholic doctrine and attitude toward Judaism, illustrates Kirchheimer's genius for understanding ideological trends in their relatedness to historical events; it still makes exciting reading today.

His most "pragmatic" period was that spent in government service during the war and early postwar years. But analyzing German affairs for his employer, the U.S. government, did not constitute a case of *trahison des clercs*. He could at that time still identify his political aims and ideals with those of a country fighting fascism and ostensibly working for the restoration of democracy in all of Europe. Kirchheimer had never given up his expectation of an eventual victory of democratic socialism. The ties he established, or reestablished, either in his official capacity or privately, with influential Germans as soon as contacts could be made again—with trade union leaders, members of the judiciary, politicians, scholars—attest to his expectation and concern. Many of his postwar writings, from empirical analyses of election results and legislative bodies to searching investigations of the West (and also the East) German political scene, date from and illustrate this period, which also served as incubation time for the last two stages of his development.

These stages comprise the ten remaining years of his life from the termination of his government service through his teaching at the New School for Social Research and, finally, the years he spent at Columbia University. The New School period is distinguished by an ever broader range of interests and concerns. Where, previously, he had dealt either with specific regimes and specific institutions or legal problems, or else grappled with the more abstract problems of "the State" or "sovereignty," his writings and research now showed an increasing

---

[7] *The Fate of Small Business in Nazi Germany.* Memorandum written for the U.S. Senate Special Committee on Small Business (Washington, D.C., 1943), with A. R. L. Gurland and F. Neumann.

emphasis on the over-all social and political trends of the changing industrial and technological society as expressed in transformations of its political movements and institutions: political parties, parliaments, trade unions, and so forth. His *magnum opus, Political Justice,* ranging widely into history and over systems and countries, likewise testifies to his steadily broadening grasp.

His fourth, and last, period, if one were to distinguish it from the third at all, remained, alas, unfinished. Kirchheimer now crossed the boundary of what had hitherto been his chosen areas within political science.[8] Though already apparent in his major work with its emphasis on the political role of law and justice, there now emerged an even greater concern with the condition and role of the individual in society. His approach now became more sociological, as, for instance, in one late article, "Private Man and Society," [9] with its bold analysis of working men's (now called "executants") isolation and frustration in a mass society made up of consumers; or more philosophical, as in his probings into problems of the philosophy of history (relation between historical change and restraint, superstructure and base, the "political" and the "socioeconomic") in "Confining Conditions and Revolutionary Breakthroughs." [10] At the very end he was ready to branch out into studies of foreign policy and the international environment, which, as he had come to realize, had now become vital for the survival and transformations of domestic systems and institutions.[11] Notes he left reveal that he had embarked on a study of hegemonial and alliance relationships. At this point his life was cut short.

---

[8] It is interesting to note that in those years he also became more cosmopolitan in his personal attitudes and sentiments. Thus, in an essay of 1964, he reflected on "how little it matters in which geographical sub-department of industrial society one spends his waiting time." See his contribution to Hermann Kesten, ed., *Ich lebe nicht in der Bundesrepublik* (Why I Don't Live in the Federal Republic) (Munich, 1964).

[9] *Political Science Quarterly,* LXXXI (1966), 1–24; reprinted below, pp. 453–77.

[10] *American Political Science Review,* LIX (1965), 964–74; reprinted below, pp. 385–407.

[11] The impact of international affairs on intrastate matters is emphasized in almost all of his late writings. See, e.g., "The *Rechtsstaat* as Magic Wall," in Barrington Moore, Jr. *et al.,* eds., *The Critical Spirit* (Boston, 1967), pp. 287–312, reprinted below, pp. 428–52; or "The Transformation of the Western European Party System," in J. LaPalombara and M. Weiner, eds., *Political Parties and Political Development* (Princeton, 1966), pp. 177–200, reprinted below, pp. 346–71.

II

"Weimar—und was dann?" constitutes the most impressive of his earlier German writings. It still is not only readable but one of the most incisive and instructive analyses of the Weimar system. According to Kirchheimer, constitutions usually ratify victory or defeat of a social class. Weimar, in contrast, was a "constitution without decision." Its formal democracy stood for nothing but rendered possible everything. One's attitude toward such a constitution depends on what one wants politically. Constitutions are not "good" or "bad" per se, no more than are specific governmental institutions and procedures, such as election systems. This statement reflects Kirchheimer's activist attitude toward politics and government.

When interpreting the control over the "directive sphere" of government—which Kirchheimer here distinguished from the "distributive sphere" and which, according to him, Weimar for the most part had left in the hands of old-regime officers and officials—as "rule of the bourgeoisie," Kirchheimer overlooked the split between "bourgeois" and feudal-military forces in Germany. The difference between formal-bourgeois democracy and "old-power" authoritarianism or new-style dictatorship was soon to become apparent to him.

In his early essay on socialist and Bolshevik political doctrines Kirchheimer had developed a theory of democracy that merged ideas of Schmitt and Marx. Democracy presupposes homogeneity of the underlying "people," but while this people, for Schmitt, was conceived as a "nation" (soon thereafter to become a "racial community"), for Kirchheimer it could only be the classless and hence homogeneous society of a future socialism. He realized that real, or socialist, democracy was not likely to be attained by the peaceful progress envisaged, and the parliamentary means advocated, by the socialist reformists. Was he, then, a Leninist? Although in the essay mentioned there may, perhaps, be perceived an underlying, unexpressed admiration for Lenin's politics free from compromise and illusion, there is also a strong criticism of violence, a criticism which, in the last article he managed to publish in Germany before his exile, he developed into a still valid critique of Bolshevik theory and practice.[12] He uncovered a

[12] See above, footnote 3.

basic contradiction in Lenin's glorification of revolutionary violence and his insistence on an authoritarian structure of the revolutionary party, on the one hand, and his "naive democratism" that expected the functioning of a noncoercive, cooperative democracy after the revolution. In postrevolutionary reality this contradiction was resolved in favor of violence: Lenin's party doctrine (*Parteitheorie*) supplanted Lenin's doctrine of the state (*Staatstheorie*), and "soviet" democracy was transformed into rule of the authoritarian party, thus illustrating the impact which the prerevolutionary organization of a political movement can have upon postrevolutionary state and government.

Kirchheimer's criticism of authoritarian-dictatorial socialism reflected a change in his attitude toward liberal democracy. In his early essay he had asserted that liberalism vastly exaggerates the true importance of constitutions and "rule of law" (*Rechtsstaat*) concepts and institutions. In "Weimar—und was dann?" he was still skeptical. But in the series of articles in which he analyzed the process and the successive stages of the dissolution of Weimar democracy we encounter an increasing awareness of the importance of democratic rules of the game and of political rights of citizens, elected parliamentary bodies, and parties even for a socialist labor movement intent on replacing the existing social and economic system with a new one. Growing authoritarian and dictatorial trends now made him aware of the practical, instrumental value of "formal democracy." Thus, in "Legalität und Legitimität"[13] he defines liberalism as "the way in which a class-divided nation can be organized in practice." And in "Verfassungsreform und Sozialdemokratie"[14] he recognizes the importance, for the functioning of a constitutional system, of the observance of the rules of the game by *all* groups. Disregard of these rules by authoritarian or fascist groups may, in turn, absolve a democratic labor movement from observing "constitutional legality" and force it into civil war. In a polemic with those in the Social Democratic party who advocated a constitutional reform that might have "legalized" the presidential-authoritarian system of that period,[15] Kirchheimer argued that it was

---

[13] *Die Gesellschaft*, IX (1932), 8–20.
[14] *Die Gesellschaft*, X (1933), 20–35.
[15] His "Verfassungsreform und Sozialdemokratie" was written in response to an article published under the same title by Ernst Fraenkel. See Ernst Fraenkel, "Verfassungsreform und Sozialdemokratie," *Die Gesellschaft*, IX (1932), 486 ff.

not the duty of socialists to see to it that the constitution should "function" more smoothly; their interest, rather, was in promoting or defending that which benefits the socialist labor movement, and not in enabling a bureaucratic-militarist regime to rule somehow within limits of an amended constitution.

In this respect Kirchheimer clearly underestimated the advantages which even an authoritarian rule of civil servants and military entailed as contrasted with what was to come: Nazi totalitarianism. Indeed, to the end, that is until 1933, he was not quite aware of the raw and brutal force of a rightist totalitarianism based on extreme nationalism. But the polemic revealed him again as an activist, a genuine heir of Marx trying to "change the world" while interpreting it. This commitment to πράχις, contrary to the impression he gave to some in later life, never left him. It not only motivated him in subsequent writings on the Nazi system, which combined distinguished scholarship with strong critical thrust.[16] It not only continued into the period of his wartime government service and is not only to be found in his postwar writing on and activities in the new Germany. In a less apparent but more profound way this motivation was present in his research into and concern with the general transformations of the postwar social and political landscape. Overstating it only a little, one might say that his ingenious analyses of parties, of the "waning of opposition," of the "decline of ideology," [17] in a way were merely a new version of his early battle against the lack of militancy and the indecisiveness of German socialism and labor in the twenties. Being a political realist, he saw that fundamental structural changes had rendered the attainment of his political ideals infinitely more difficult. He knew (as is apparent from one of his last articles) that technological as well as socioeconomic developments were making obsolete the very concepts of classes and class consciousness and, consequently, institutions such as "issue parties" and "opposition of principle." Perhaps he saw that, in a society

---

[16] A curious piece should be mentioned in this connection: There was found among his papers an essay, dated 1935 and ostensibly published under the auspices of "Staatsrat" Carl Schmitt (a title Schmitt had acquired under the Nazis) by "Dr. Hermann Seitz": *Staatsgefüge und Recht des Dritten Reiches*. This pungent analysis was written by Kirchheimer in exile and smuggled into the Third Reich as underground literature.

[17] See below, pp. 292–318, 346–71.

becoming "homogeneous" through mass consensus on the lowest common denominator of material affluence, the function of the critical analyst would constitute the last refuge of πράχις.

Let us return to his earlier writings. In a witty, short autobiographical note appended to an article justifying his "not living in the Federal Republic of Germany" [18] Kirchheimer characterized the period between the termination of his university studies and his leaving Germany with these few words: "exercised the trade (*das Handwerk*) of a law trainee (*Referendar*) and a critic of the administration of justice (*Justizkritiker*)." It shows the importance he attached to this aspect of his life and activities. His criticism of the way in which law and courts operated in the Weimar Republic is not only found in numerous newspaper articles he contributed to the socialist press. In more theoretical fashion it came to the fore in the striking theory of property and expropriation he developed at that time.[19] Taking Carl Schmitt's theory of institutions (*Institutionenlehre*) for a starting point, he traced the evolution of the concept and practice of expropriation since the French Revolution; he showed how and why in the classical liberal-constitutional period expropriation had the limited function of protecting bourgeois "rule over specific pieces of property" (*Sachherrschaft*) against expropriation without indemnification; he then demonstrated how and why this limited purpose, in the late period of capitalism (e.g., under the jurisdiction of the German Supreme Court in the Weimar period), began to yield to the much vaster purpose of protecting everything and anything possessing exchange value (*Tauschwert*). This, he believed, was contrary to the specific intentions of the Weimar Constitution. To him this development indicated abuse of the law by a biased judiciary, permitting an unrestrained capitalism to defeat the communal tasks of organized society. In addition to his observation of judicial bias in more directly political cases (decisions in treason cases of the *Reichsgericht*, with its pro-rightist, anti-leftist

[18] See the collection of essays edited by Hermann Kesten quoted above, footnote 8. In the article itself, Kirchheimer typically does not waste time in dealing with the question asked but indignantly comments on the then topical *Spiegel* case.

[19] Besides *Grenzen der Enteignung*, referred to above, see also "Eigentumsgarantie in Reichsverfassung und Rechtsprechung," *Die Gesellschaft*, VII (1930), 166 ff.

coloration, etc.), the trauma created by this early discovery of justice turned into the handmaiden of politics or class interest never left him. Eventually it was to lead him to conceive of the idea of a comprehensive analysis of the "use of legal procedure for political ends" (*Political Justice*, 1961).

This concern—in addition to the fact that he was a legally trained social scientist—explains the large interest he invested in legal subjects after he left Germany, and especially during his French and earlier American years. These studies, however, are never purely legal in content and significance. They either have some constitutional—and thus political—relevance (as, for instance, an article on double jeopardy), or they investigate sociologically certain aspects of the law (for instance, his analysis of "the historical and comparative background of the Hatch Act"), or they deal with certain legal aspects of a particular political system, this way elucidating the system itself. The system which preoccupied him most at that time was, naturally, the Nazi system (he dealt with it in articles on criminal law under Nazism and, more generally, on "The Legal Order of National Socialism").[20]

In regard to the second of these categories, the sociological, Kirchheimer in this period emerged as a criminologist—another one among the many facets of his scholarly career. Outstanding among his criminological writings is *Punishment and Social Structure*,[21] a book which, as the title indicates, traces the relationship between punishment (types of penalties, etc.) and the respective social structure from the Middle Ages to fascism (the earlier period being dealt with by Kirchheimer's co-author). Punishment is understood "as a social phenomenon freed from both its juristic concept and its social ends," and Kirchheimer's conclusion is that "the crime rate can really be influenced only if society is in a position to offer its members a certain measure of security and to guarantee a reasonable standard of living. The shift from a repressive penal policy to a progressive program can then be raised out of the sphere of humanitarianism to constructive social activity" (p. 207). The study combines most careful analysis of

[20] *Studies in Philosophy and Social Science*, IX (1941), 456–75; reprinted below, pp. 88–109.
[21] George Rusche and Otto Kirchheimer, *Punishment and Social Structure* (New York, 1939).

the statistical and historical material with interpretations and conclusions based on the author's socioeconomic theory.

Besides these legal-sociological studies, Kirchheimer's most significant writings in this period of his life and work concern the analysis of political systems and regimes. He now had a chance to branch out into areas beyond Germany, and the first country to which he could apply insights gained from German experience was his initial way-station in exile, France. His study of decree powers in the Third Republic [22] traces the decline of that system as reflected in the replacement of parliamentary government by executive rule. Here we have the companion piece to his study on the corresponding developments in Germany at the time of the Brüning chancellorship ("Legalität und Legitimität," see above). With the wisdom of hindsight he now could interpret such developments as transitional stages from parliamentary democracy to totalitarianism. As he expressed it in a footnote to this article appended after the fall of France, "the French example, coming eight years after the German *Präsidialregierung* of Brüning and Papen, shows that the unlimited decree-rule of a constitutional government with a dubious popular or parliamentary basis serves only as an intermediary station on the road to complete authoritarianism." [23]

As the Nazi regime unfolded in its various ramifications, Kirchheimer subjected some of its most characteristic features to critical search. We have mentioned already his studies of what became of law and the administration of justice under the system. In the article on "The Legal Order of National Socialism" he perceived of the "technical rationality" of a smoothly functioning legal machinery combined with total incalculability of the law itself as the fundamental characteristic of this aspect of the total state. But how was this state itself, the political system of Nazism, to be interpreted? In close agreement with the theory developed at that time by Franz Neumann,[24] Kirchheimer saw in the regime not one coherent unit but rather a coalition of separate, quasi-autonomous forces (of which the state machinery and

[22] "Decree Powers and Constitutional Law in France under the Third Republic," *American Political Science Review*, XXXIV (1940), 1104–23; reprinted below, pp. 110–30.

[23] *Ibid.*, p. 1123.

[24] *Behemoth: The Structure and Practice of National Socialism* (New York, 1942).

its bureaucracy was only one), more or less integrated through political compromise.[25] In contrast to Neumann, he did not question the ultimate authority of the group centered around the Führer; but the Führer's position as arbiter of intergroup differences was rendered possible only through a program of imperialistic expansion: "It is this interdependence between the unquestionable authority of the ruling group and the program of expansion which offers the characteristic phenomenon of the compromise structure of the Fascist order." [26]

His essay on "sovereignty" [27] is one of Kirchheimer's relatively rare ventures into the more general theory of state and society. That he considered it one of his major pieces is clear from the fact that he chose it with only three others for inclusion in a volume of his articles published in Germany one year before his death. The essay reflects his observation of things American and the overwhelming impression made on him by this country's pluralism and, more generally, by the role interest groups play in modern society and politics.

He might have called this article "The Waning of Sovereignty." He begins with a recognition as well as a critique of pluralism. Groups make up society and make politics, but the result is not, as pluralists tend to assert, some kind of conciliation of conflicting interests through compromise, a peaceful settlement in which public power plays the role of arbiter; all this is ideology and rationalization. As far as the really important big groups and interests are concerned, their discord most likely results in domination and control, or else in the perpetuation of conflict. The state can no longer be the arbiter, a role that—through parliament, judiciary, etc.—it could play when interests still were smaller and more scattered. Nowadays, exactly as consumers are left only with a choice between brands of equal value (or worthlessness), the voter is left with a choice between teams preestablished and presented by those in control of the big organizations. Accordingly, he has as little "sovereignty" as has a state bureaucracy dominated or penetrated by, or subservient to, the big interests.

[25] "Changes in the Structure of Political Compromise," *Studies in Philosophy and Social Science*, IX (1941), 264–89; reprinted below, pp. 131–59.

[26] *Ibid.*, p. 288.

[27] "In Quest of Sovereignty," *Journal of Politics*, VI (1944), 139–76; reprinted below, pp. 160–93.

Only when—as under fascism—"practitioners of violence" manage to organize the total state, sovereignty in some fashion emerges again. The fascist state perpetuates that "state of emergency" the control over which, according to Carl Schmitt, conveys "sovereignty" upon the controller. But even there, political control is based, on the one hand, upon the suppression of certain "undesired" groups and their interest organizations, such as trade unions, while, on the other hand, it is exercised in common with, if not in subservience to, the big economic interests which under fascism are organized as appendices of the state itself and share in the imperialistic exploitation of the countries and regions into which fascism expands. Since at the time this article was written (that is, toward the end of the war), the process of Nazi-fascist expansion was on the point of failing, controls were bound to revert to the monopolistic and other dominating groups again; sovereignty was to remain, or to become again, *introuvable*.

The summary of a piece by Kirchheimer like this one might convey the impression of rather abstract and even dogmatic argument. No summary can render the flavor of the inimitable Kirchheimer style: nor can it convey the wealth of specific insights and particular comments which one invariably encounters in the course of his major arguments. To mention just one of these, we would like to refer the reader to the few paragraphs on "rackets" in his essay on sovereignty.

III

Kirchheimer repeatedly returns to the topic of interest groups in his later writings. Their role in society and state is a recurrent theme, especially in the many articles on political parties which, together with the treatise on *Political Justice*, form the bulk of his publications in the fifties and sixties. This is not to imply that he saw in the political party just one among the innumerable associations over which the state is presiding in the industrial society of today. Indeed, the very first essay devoted to the discussion of political parties opens with a firm rejection of this view, widely held for a long time, particularly by German authors, and of the underlying tendency to assign to the party a low rank of legitimation. Its political function, Kirchheimer insists, sets the party clearly apart from other intermediary social bodies.[28] But he was, of course, interested in, and anxious to clarify, the relationship between political parties and those other groups as well as the respective relations of both of them with the several organs of public power.[29]

The geographical range which these disquisitions on political parties cover is as broad as Western and Central Europe. This is true, in particular, of the first article just mentioned, of "The Waning of Opposition in Parliamentary Regimes," [30] and of one of his last essays, "The Transformation of the Western European Party System," published posthumously in 1966.[31] They no doubt were intended to exemplify "a truly comparative approach" to the study of politics, leading to at least "a modicum" of valid and meaningful generalizations.[32] But the emphasis throughout these essays is on current trends in the party systems of Central Europe, or, more precisely, of Austria and Germany. Kirchheimer's many contributions that appeared in the volumes of *World Politics* and another of his posthumous publications, "Germany: The Vanishing Opposition," [33] are devoted exclusively to the German scene.

In these writings Kirchheimer concentrated his attention not merely on a particular geographical area but also on a particular type of politi-

28 "Parteistruktur und Massendemokratie in Europa," *Archiv des Öffentlichen Rechts*, LXXIX (1954), 301–25; reprinted below as "Party Structure and Mass Democracy in Europe," pp. 245–68.

29 One "interest group" particularly close to Kirchheimer's heart and mind were the trade unions. Some of his essays are entirely devoted to an analysis of their structure and prospects in the postwar world (see, e.g., his contribution on "West German Trade Unions" to the volume *West German Leadership and Foreign Policy*, ed. Hans Speier and W. Philips Davison [Evanston, Ill., 1957], pp. 136–94). Indeed, one has sometimes the impression that what he missed in the functions of the increasingly "catch-all" socialist parties he hoped—although, realistically, without too much confidence—might be supplied by the unions: a shield from complete alienation for the working man, and more socially meaningful alternatives to the policies of a capitalist consumers' society.

30 *Social Research*, XXIV (1957), 127–56. It was this brilliant piece that put Kirchheimer in the front rank of political scientists engrossed in the current problems of political parties.

31 See above, footnote 11.

32 See Kirchheimer's comment on the symposium *Modern Political Parties*, ed. Sigmund Neumann (Chicago, 1956), in "The Party in Mass Society," *World Politics*, X (1958), 289–94.

33 In Robert A. Dahl, ed., *Political Oppositions in Western Democracies* (New Haven, 1966), pp. 237–59.

cal party. In describing and analyzing political developments in the postwar period, he was chiefly concerned with the transformation of the former Marxist class-oriented mass-integration parties into what he felicitously called the "catch-all parties" of today and with the concomitant phenomenon of "the waning of the opposition of principle." In his characteristic fashion he based his thesis on close observations of slowly emerging facts. In the essay "Parteistruktur und Massendemo-kratie," [34] written in 1954 at a time when only the first symptoms of the new trend were discernible, he touched upon it only cautiously. When the trend became clearly manifest in Austria, he made it the starting point of his article on "The Waning of Opposition in Parliamentary Regimes" three years later. When finally the symptoms of the same process multiplied in Germany, he elaborated on it in discussions that culminated in his posthumously published contribution to *Political Oppositions in Western Democracies*. The consummation of the trend —which he had so acutely analyzed—in the coalition formed in 1966 between the Christian Democratic Union and the Social Democrats would thus not have come as a surprise to him.

The reasons for Kirchheimer's concentration on the problems of present-day political parties are not far to seek. Familiar though he was with the "political culture" of all Western countries, he had passed his years of scholarly and political apprenticeship in Germany and in the German socialist movement. The experience of his earlier years now turned to the advantage of his analysis of current developments. In fact, as already suggested, the lines of thought and the postulates of the young Kirchheimer reappear in this late critical research into the changing nature of political parties and its most characteristic feature, the de-ideologization of politics. But the will to "change the world" while interpreting it is now much less powerful than it was in the past. As he put it himself in the preface to *Politik und Verfassung*, the *Wünschbarkeiten* (wishful thoughts) become in his later writings subordinate to a critical analysis of reality. Rather than expressing revolutionary fervor, his later publications show traces of resignation and even of nostalgia for the past. "We may yet come to regret," he concludes one of his last essays, "the passing—even if it was inevitable—of the class-mass party and the denominational party, as we already re-

[34] See above, footnote 28.

gret the passing of other features in yesterday's stage of Western civilization." [35] The transformation of the party systems was for Kirchheimer merely one aspect and one symptom of the general process of rationalization of the modern social world and of its consequence, the growing alienation of the individual, about which he showed such deep concern during the last phase of his life. A direct line leads from his disquisitions on political parties to the meditations in his posthumously published article "Private Man and Society," which centers on the phenomenon of alienation. But what then is the essence of his writings on the metamorphosis political parties in Western Europe are going through currently?

Kirchheimer, like most students of European constitutional government, saw in the British parliamentary regime, the British party system, and especially the British type of opposition party the "classical" model. The continental forms of government and parties are more or less far-reaching deviations from this model. The most outstanding feature of the British type of parliamentary regime is the "game of alternation," the smooth transfer of the machinery of government from one party to the other. The basis and the presupposition of this game is the existence of two parties that offer to the electorate more or less clearly defined policy alternatives but at the same time keep the pursuit of their divergent ideas and interests within strict limits. They agree "on major objectives or, at least, on the mutually permissible range of change." It is this agreement on fundamentals, combined with the presentation and execution of meaningful policy alternatives, that makes for the classical government-opposition pattern of the British system. Kirchheimer shows that, and tries to answer the question why, this pattern never did "implant itself more firmly into the mores of the major continental countries of Europe," and least of all of Central Europe. He distinguishes two different types of deviation from the British government-opposition pattern, the one prevailing in Central Europe during a period extending down to World War II, the other in the postwar period. He characterizes the first deviation as the "opposition of principle," and the second as the "waning of the opposition."

The description, explanation, and evaluation of the "opposition of principle" make fascinating reading. It is here that Kirchheimer's per-

[35] "The Transformation of the Western European Party System," p. 200.

sonal experience shines through most clearly. His involvement of earlier years in the German Marxist movement, once the very prototype
of an opposition of principle held together by strong ideological ties,
enabled him to appreciate the positive side of the mass-integration
party of the old style. Yet he was no longer blind to the dangers it
posed to the operation of parliamentary democracy, especially since
the "opposition of principle" was now chiefly represented by Communist parties. "Bent not only on wrenching power from the government of today but on ending once and for all the system on which that
government rests," the "opposition of principle" excludes itself from
participation in the game of alternation. In fact, its very existence is apt
to make altogether impossible the game in which Kirchheimer in his
later years had learned to see a guarantee of the most basic human
rights and freedoms. This danger may be insignificant as long as the
"opposition of principle" is weak. But once it has sufficiently grown in
size and strength to pose a serious threat to the existing order, it may
force the other parliamentary parties into "abdication of their power
into the hands of other institutions—the army, the police, the bureaucracy." A democratic regime confronted with a large opposition of
principle is, Kirchheimer remarks, by far the weakest of all types of
democratic government.[36]

But quite apart from such extreme contingencies, the *Weltanschauungspartei*, be it of the Marxist or of a denominational kind,
integrates its members not into the all-comprehensive political community but into what Rousseau called a "partial association" formed at
the expense of the "great association" and thus renders a democratic
consensus impossible. In fact, the more powerful it is as an instrument
of partial integration, the greater might be its disintegrating effect
upon the political community as a whole. The tendency particularly of
Marxist parties to guide and shape the spiritual and material life of
their members from cradle to grave, to isolate them in their social
activities from any outside influence, and to enforce upon them strict
discipline by tightening the organization of the party has often been
described. Kirchheimer did not hesitate to recognize that the Marxist
opposition party of principle anticipated many features of the totali-

[36] "Majorities and Minorities in Western European Governments," *Western
Political Quarterly*, XII (1959), 492–510.

tarian parties of the twentieth century. He also recognized the difficulty of the task of the former ruling powers to cope with this type of
opposition party. But he also saw the other side of the picture. The
very same parties that prevented the integration of the workers into
the great association of the bourgeois state and society protected them
against the consequences of the atomization effected by the rise of
capitalism. They not only concerned themselves with the social welfare of their members but also provided them with a "spiritual shelter"
and the vision of a better life in a more just political and social order.
Time and again Kirchheimer emphasized that the class-mass-integra-
tion party of the old style functioned as a kind of "secular chapel" as
well, uniting the faithful in the pursuit of common ideals. That the
party has recently lost this ennobling function made Kirchheimer
wonder whether its transformation during the postwar period into
the "catch-all people's party" of today was an "advance" or a
"reduction."

What, then, were the positive aspects of this transformation recognized by Kirchheimer? The catch-all party, being interested primarily
in immediate electoral success by broadening its following among all
groups of society, social and denominational, is a type of mass-integration party that is no impediment to, but rather an instrument for,
making its "members previously outside the official political fold full-
fledged participants in the political process." The catch-all "people's"
party does not integrate its members and followers "into its own ranks
against the official state apparatus" but "into the existing political
community" as a whole. It performs the function of "political integration" proper. The new opposition party, inspired by pragmatic rather
than ideological motives, thus is fully qualified to participate in the
game of alternation. It no longer frustrates but is apt to ensure the
smooth operation of parliamentary democracy. The emergence of the
new type of opposition party is, moreover, the symptom and the consequence of a wholesome change in industrial society itself: the improvement of the social condition of the workers and, resulting from
it, the weakening of the antagonism between the classes of modern
society. Diminished social polarization makes for diminished political
polarization as well. True, Kirchheimer held it was premature to speak
of "a unified middle-class society" in which the rule of man over man

had been—or soon would be—replaced by the mere "administration of things" in the sense of Engels' and Lenin's utopian prediction. But he did not deny that in the postwar period society, particularly in Central Europe, was actually moving in that direction. As a matter of fact, he saw in this trend one of the reasons for the waning of opposition, the second type of deviation from the nineteenth-century British classic model of the parliamentary regime. The parties in present-day Western Germany agree not only on the fundamentals spelled out in the Bonn Basic Law but on many issues of practical policy, domestic and foreign, as well. The Social Democratic party, after a brief initial period during which, in accordance with the classical conception of opposition, it considered as its chief duty the presentation to the public and the government in power of more or less sharply drawn policy alternatives, has, much to Kirchheimer's regret, abandoned this function. "In a sound and developing democracy," Willy Brandt proclaimed in 1961, "it is the norm rather than the exception that the parties put forward similar, even identical demands in a number of fields." The area of disagreement between parties was to be confined to "the question of priority, of the rank order of tasks to be solved, and of methods and accents." [37] Opposition has been reduced to its competitive elements. In the process the opposition party necessarily has lost much of its importance as an organ controlling and criticizing the ruling party.

Kirchheimer realized the extent to which the transformation of the German party system was due to special conditions prevailing in postwar Germany. But he also attributed it to general reasons operative in practically all highly advanced industrial societies and, accordingly, was inclined to think that similar patterns are likely to emerge in other countries as well. But, needless to say, he was far from being dogmatic about the general significance of the trends he discerned so clearly in Austria and Germany. The picture he drew of other party systems in the Western world was not excessively simplified in the pursuit of generalizations but reflected most vividly the rich variety of all local factors bearing on the character and the functions of the respective parties. Nor did he overlook the limitations upon the operation of

[37] Quoted by Kirchheimer in "Germany: The Vanishing Opposition," pp. 246–47.

those trends in Central Europe itself. He did not even rule out the possibility of a reemergence of an opposition of principle, conceivably of a right-wing coloration.

Rather than playing the role of a "futurologist" trying to predict the unpredictable, Kirchheimer preferred to confine himself to the role of a political observer describing and analyzing the relevant aspects of the transformation of political parties already accomplished. He shows how what is now their overriding concern, namely the winning of a maximum of votes among all social and ideological strata of the population, weakens their inner coherence on the one side, and necessitates the rationalization of their structures and procedures on the other. He examines and illustrates the reciprocal permeation of parties and interest groups and the arbitral function of the parties in harmonizing conflicting interests within their ranks and conveying the claims of the groups concerned to the legislature, the political executive, the bureaucracy. In discussing the traditional specifically political functions of the party and the impact on them of the process of transformation, he singles out "the nomination of candidates for popular legitimation as officeholders as the most important function of the present-day catch-all party." The role the political party plays today in Western industrial society is, he concludes, "more limited than would appear from its position of formal preeminence."

But, to repeat once more, Kirchheimer's deepest concern in all his writings on political parties was the effect of the recent changes in the party system upon man's role as a citizen. This concern is apparent in the wider context of his essay on "Private Man and Society," devoted to a general discussion of man's participation, or lack of participation, in the affairs of society and state, with special emphasis on the position of the industrial workers. By calling the workers "executants" he indicates that in the technological society of today they are confined to a more or less passive role. Indeed, after having introduced finespun distinctions and carefully weighed the evidence supporting optimistic and pessimistic views on the degree to which there exists for the workers the possibility of meaningful participation in the operation of society on its several levels, he concludes that at best they have a chance of escape from being irrevocably engulfed by mass society. He sees no chance of their taking the initiative in reshaping it. Kirchheimer takes an equally dim view of the practical significance of the workers' contribution to the political process. "The executant is unlikely to disturb the political process, but, if called upon, he makes his legitimizing gesture" in the form of casting his vote. He states here succinctly what he stated more elaborately in his earlier disquisitions on political parties.

It is because of the modest part the citizen actually plays in and through the catch-all party of today that Kirchheimer wonders whether its emergence was not a step backwards rather than an advance. "To the older party of integration," he says, "the citizen, if he so desired, could be closer. Then it was a less differentiated organization, part channel of protest, part source of protection, part purveyor of visions of the future. Now, in its linear descendant in a transfigured world, the catch-all party, the citizen finds a relatively remote, at times quasi-official and alien structure." Such influence on politics as the citizen exerts, he exerts through interest groups rather than political parties. Kirchheimer realizes, of course, that this political alienation is by no means only an aspect and a consequence of the transformation of the political parties. The transformation itself is a part and a result of profound changes in the economic and social system, due mostly to technological development. Kirchheimer welcomed the wholesome effects of those changes but deplored the price to be paid for them. He never ceased to look back ruefully to a more idealistic and heroic past, and never ceased to fear that modern industrial society, "this *terrible simplificateur*," with its concomitants of a consumer-oriented attitude and the privatization of its members, might be ushering in an era of "new boredom."

Even though Kirchheimer, at that time, devoted so much of his interest and efforts to parties, he by no means gave up his concern with the political structures of entire countries and regimes. In this respect we have already mentioned his writings on West Germany, and we should mention here another article dating from this period which illustrates his power to gain insights into the character of entire political systems: his essay on the transition from the French Fourth to the Fifth Republic.[38] The article, besides testifying to his continued inter-

[38] "France from the Fourth to the Fifth Republic," *Social Research*, XXV (1958), 379–414; reprinted below, pp. 212–44.

est in countries outside Central Europe, contains a double analysis: of the nature and the process of dissolution of the Fourth Republic through what he calls a "process of migration of political substance" and the "reversion of the citizen to the status of a private individual, minding his own business and regarding the apparatus of public power as an alien phenomenon with which he has intercourse only through the agents of interest-group ambassadors" (in this way alluding to the over-all process of alienation and anomie he will describe in his last articles); and second—a real tour de force, considering that he wrote the article at the very beginning of the new regime—a searching and prophetic analysis of the nature and the functioning of the Gaullist system, which he predicted would be one of "authoritarian technocracy rather than of plebeian totalitarianism," with an "ascendancy of the administrative personnel over the political professional."

IV

"The use of legal procedure for political ends" which Otto Kirchheimer so magisterially described and analyzed in his *Political Justice* [39] had been one of his foremost preoccupations throughout his life. Into this volume went the rich fruits of lifelong studies in the fields of philosophy, history, and jurisprudence. Kirchheimer's erudition stands out in this, his *magnum opus*, even more impressively than in his other writings. As early as 1955 he had contributed to a *Festschrift* dedicated to Max Horkheimer an essay on "Politische Justiz" [40] that foreshadowed the essential theses of the book published six years later. Thus the work on *Political Justice* had been progressing during the very same years in which Kirchheimer was engaged in his analyses of the postwar development of Europe's political parties. In fact, the theme of opposition and of the different types of opposition parties figures prominently in *Political Justice* as well.

The area covered in the book is much broader than the title suggests.

[39] *Political Justice: The Use of Legal Procedure for Political Ends* (Princeton, 1961).

[40] *Sociologica: Aufsätze, Max Horkheimer zum 60. Geburtstag gewidmet*, Frankfurter Beiträge zur Soziologie, I (Frankfurt/M., 1955), 171–99. The English version, "Politics and Justice," *Social Research*, XXII (1955), 377–98, is reprinted below, pp. 408–27.

True, Kirchheimer concentrates upon the use of judicial procedures for political ends, but such use is for him only one aspect of the relationship between government and opposition in general. Accordingly, the discussion often widens into a treatise on the historical patterns of this relationship beyond the role of courts in domestic strife. This is not to imply that the book is a comprehensive and systematic history of those patterns or, for that matter, of political justice in particular. Kirchheimer himself denied that he had wanted to write a history of political justice. But he culled from his wide reading in political and legal history enough material to show the endurance of the forms and problems of political justice throughout human history as well as their significance in the never-ending struggle between justice and law on the one side and power on the other.

It is characteristic of the pragmatic bent of Kirchheimer's mind that he immediately plunges into a discussion of concrete questions and cases relating to the subject matter he proposes to investigate. Many another scholar, especially if of German origin, would have first probed the deeper meaning of such basic concepts as justice, politics, and power, only to become bogged down in his preliminary exploration. Not so Otto Kirchheimer. He is content with defining the sense in which he, following a continental tradition, uses the term "political justice," namely as connoting judicial devices, court proceedings in particular, employed for the purpose of bolstering established or creating new power positions. Nor does he display much patience with those authors who deny that political justice is a phenomenon partaking of the spheres both of law and of politics, and who assert that therefore the very term "political justice" is a *contradictio in adjecto*. They fail to realize, Kirchheimer argues, that the rulers of practically every regime have the desire to see the exercise of their power legitimized by legal formalities. Nor do they sufficiently realize, he suggests, that even under a constitutional regime the rule of law is by no means immune to political infection.

It would be a mistake, indeed, to assume that it was primarily the experience of the totalitarian regimes of the twentieth century that aroused Kirchheimer's interest in the problem of political justice. As mentioned previously, his lifelong trauma of justice turned into a handmaiden of politics originated in his experience with the administration of criminal justice in the Weimar Republic. It would be equally mistaken to expect that the use of judicial devices for political ends in totalitarian countries is at the center of this great work. The theory and practice of political justice under totalitarianism are, to be sure, repeatedly expounded throughout the volume and systematically treated in one of its most brilliant chapters,[47] for which the illustrative material was mostly drawn from the various Communist systems. Kirchheimer shows that the political trials of the Stalinist type have in common with genuine judicial proceedings only their outward forms at best. He analyzes the means of mechanical and ideological coordination between the policies of the party leadership and the actions of the judicial functionary (who no longer is a judge proper) by which the aleatory element, inherent in genuine court proceedings, is completely eliminated. He indicates how in the Stalinist political trial the defendant is made to cooperate in the presentation of "a prefabricated and alternative reality," and how its image-creating effect serves the purpose of manipulating and rallying public opinion. Kirchheimer thus was far from neglecting the totalitarian version of political justice. In writing his treatise he nevertheless concerned himself chiefly with the question of political justice within the pale of constitutional government.

In discussing the operation of justice in political matters under nontotalitarian regimes, Kirchheimer goes far back into the beginnings of modern constitutionalism. The picture he draws of its development is anything but encouraging. It is a history of regress rather than of progress; more precisely, it is a history of a period of initial progress followed by a period of regress. World War I, the overture to our revolutionary age, formed the watershed between these two periods.

The gradual recognition in the eighteenth and nineteenth centuries of the right to political dissent opened up a new chapter in the history of the relationship between rulers and opponents and, concomitantly, also of political justice. In the era of constitutionalism advocacy of political change began to be considered permissible. Legal restrictions upon political dissent were increasingly limited to the use of violence in attempting to change the constitutional order and to the use of language inciting to violence. Kirchheimer shows in detail how the

[41] Chapter VII.

new conceptions affected the principles of criminal law in relation to political matters. He points out particularly the tendency to distinguish between offenses against internal security and offenses against the external security of the state, and, most importantly, the tendency to differentiate between political and common offenses. "The state, it was reasoned, had to safeguard itself against its foes, but this did not necessarily imply a need to stamp one's foe as a dishonorable man and scoundrel." Political trials became more and more judicial contests, to be sure not of equals, but conducted by the judge in accordance with the rules of chivalry. The generosity of the rulers of the nineteenth century expressed itself also in the kind of punishment meted out to political offenders. Summarizing this development, Kirchheimer speaks of "the receding tide of offenses against the state" and characterizes the period as "the halcyon days of receding absolutism, constitutional monarchies, and liberal democratic regimes." No doubt, he saw in this trend that was to be reversed after World War I another of those features in yesterday's stage of Western civilization the passing of which, as he says in his study on "The Transformation of the Western European Party System," we may yet come to regret.

Kirchheimer was no romantic. He clearly realized the darker sides of "the halcyon days" as well. In a chapter on the "legal represssion of political organizations" he subjects the nineteenth-century record of repression to an incisive and critical analysis. He had no illusions about the past but refused to look at the complex pattern of the constitutional government of the nineteenth century, both its more or less authoritarian and its more or less liberal type, through the oversimplifying glasses of the democratic absolutist. With his keen appreciation of the variety of contradictory elements in political reality he recognized that a government's resort to repressive measures did not preclude its being devoted, nonetheless, to the constitution and to the principle of the supremacy of law; and that such a government might honestly try to apply those measures in accordance with preestablished substantive and procedural rules. In other words, he realized that a policy of repression might in some cases be mitigated by adherence to the rule of law.

Contrary to the democratic absolutist, Kirchheimer also was ready to concede that the widening of the basis of government from a small minority to a large majority, accomplished by the adoption of universal suffrage, does not necessarily have a beneficial effect upon the relationship between rulers and principal opponents of the existing constitutional order and, for that matter, upon political justice. Indeed, the victory of mass democracy in the twentieth century coincides with a reversal of the trend that prevailed during the two preceding centuries. The subtlety of Kirchheimer's mind again kept him from oversimplifying matters and from overlooking the host of factors which in our turbulent age are primarily responsible for wiping out most of the advances made prior to World War I: the rise of revolutionary totalitarian movements cutting across national boundaries with the attendant military and political risks to internal and external security; the broadening of the basis of public opinion and the (rather problematic) success of the mass media in making opinion "more uniform, less alert, and more uncritical"; and last but not least the emergence of secular political orthodoxy, as intolerant toward the political heretic as religious orthodoxy had been toward the religious heretic. "The internal deviant and potential foreign foe are considered *hostis generis humani.*" Democratic faith is no automatic protection against such a conception. In fact, the aura of democratic legitimacy facilitates its adoption. It is no accident, as Kirchheimer points out, that the distinction between political and common crime has not found favor with American democracy. Be that as it may, in the years following World War I most countries of the Western world, not to speak of others, have been engulfed in a swelling tide of what they consider offenses against the state, obliterating the refined notions and distinctions criminal jurisprudence had worked out in the course of the nineteenth century. The author vividly illustrates this retrogression by many case histories.

Space does not permit us even to touch on other important questions raised, though not necessarily answered, in Kirchheimer's volume. We can suggest the richness of its content only by briefly commenting on the general character of Kirchheimer's discussion of political justice and pointing out one or two specific topics covered by him. The work is, among other things, a study in political sociology concentrating on the ends and techniques of political justice and relating them to the different types of society and constitutional order. It describes the

forces and pressures working upon the courts which emanate both
from government and from public opinion, and the reaction of the
courts to the influences brought to bear upon them as well as the
general ground on which they base their decisions. It defines in detail
the role not only of the judge but also of the jury, the police, the
prosecutor, the defendant, the defendant's lawyer, and the witnesses.
The exposition concludes with a penetrating analysis of asylum and
clemency, devices which usually are not considered integral parts of
political justice. Kirchheimer rightly thinks there is "an inner logic and
necessity" that ties them "to the chariot of political justice." Given
the problematic character of the latter, there is, he argues, an imperative need for "institutionalized ways of escaping and mitigating its
impact."

The tenuous basis of justice in political matters is the theme running
through all parts of Kirchheimer's treatise. The actual balance between
law and politics in court proceedings calling to account persons or
groups challenging public authority differs from period to period,
from country to country and from case to case, but everywhere and
always it is precarious. It is the more favorable to the accused the more
generous the law to be applied, the stronger the guarantees of the
procedural rights of the defendant, and the larger the "judicial space"
within which the judge is free to decide in strict accordance with law;
in other words, the more closely the political trial approximates a
genuine judicial contest involving risks for the prosecution if it fails to
prove its case. Kirchheimer is by no means optimistic as to the likelihood of these optimal conditions prevailing. Political justice is by definition for him a method of making justice serve politics. But he also
thinks that even under conditions less favorable to the accused—dis-
regarding, of course, totalitarian regimes—the powers that be cannot
apply this method with complete success. The judiciary is by its very
nature not altogether malleable. "As long as the institution persists," he
remarks, "the 'judicial space,' though it may be reduced, cannot be
completely abolished." At any rate, political justice also has its merits
which we should not overlook in spite of all the reasons we have for
denigrating it. Compared with its appalling alternative, political arbitrariness without benefit of access to courts, "it is one of the more
civilized of political games."

Kirchheimer wrote *Political Justice*, as a reviewer of the book rightly observed, "with cosmic objectivity, but with a feeling for the human beings involved—both judges and judged." [42] The sympathetic feeling for the judged is expressed throughout the text, and most impressively in the dedication of the book "to the past, present, and future victims of political justice." The inclusion of the future victims proves that Kirchheimer could not bring himself to believe in the possibility of de-politicizing political justice. If he ever shared the Marxist expectation of the final triumph of justice in a classless society, *Political Justice* does not testify to such an expectation. It rather indicates that Kirchheimer in his later years was convinced of the abiding weakness of justice in the complexity of human affairs. Political justice is one of the perpetual forms, and not even the worst one, of the never-ending struggle within society. This view enabled him to weigh with detachment also the role of the antagonist of the victims of political justice. In the concluding passages of the treatise Kirchheimer pictures both the defendant and the judge as involved in a tragic conflict with the question of guilt suspended until the judgment of history is delivered. "And may not Clio refuse a clear-cut answer, marking them both as fools whose efforts were neither necessary nor salutary for whomever they were appointed to serve?" In the very last words of the volume he suggests that we should pray for "both potential brethren in error," and recites verses from *Dies irae, dies illae*, that stirring sequence in the mass for the dead: "God, we beg, be kind to them." The request to pray for both parties to the political trial is indeed a moving testimonial to one of the most prominent traits of Kirchheimer as a human being, his magnanimity.

Kirchheimer turned once more to the problems of law and the individual in his posthumously published essay on "The *Rechtsstaat* as Magic Wall." [43] He asked whether the concept of "rule of law" as developed in England and Germany in the nineteenth century was still serviceable under the conditions of advanced industrial society and arrived at a qualified affirmation of the question. Denying that the extension of state activities to an increasing number of fields was in-

[42] Thomas I. Emerson, in *Political Science Quarterly*, LXXVII (1962), 269.
[43] See above, footnote 11.

compatible with the rule of law, he maintained that, on the contrary, it might open new legal opportunities to the citizen. If so, "the *Rechtsstaat* is transformed into the *Sozialrechtsstaat*." But he was aware of the ever-present danger that the execution of the mandate may lag behind the mandate itself. In yet another of those flashes of brilliant insight with which his work abounds, he illustrated this possibility by what one may call a case of "negative political justice," namely, the various failures and omissions by German public agencies in the prosecution of Nazi criminality.

"Confining Conditions and Revolutionary Breakthroughs" [44] is another posthumously published article that testifies to the endurance of Kirchheimer's scholarly interests. The relationship between political action and the structure of society, a chief concern of his "Weimar—und was dann?," is the main theme of this late essay. But the scope of the questions posed and of the material tested has now become vastly extended. Kirchheimer ranges far and wide through the history of revolutions from the days of the French Convention in 1793 through the revolutions wrought by the American Civil War down to the revolutions of our century with a view to exploring whether and to what extent revolutionary movements and their leaders were capable of transcending the confining conditions that surrounded their access to and maintenance of power. Recognizing that, for certain reasons, capacity to transform society has increased in the twentieth century, Kirchheimer yet emphasized the limits set to this capacity. "Every revolution," he concludes, "is both phenomenon and epiphenomenon."

Is it possible to assess the conclusions Kirchheimer, at the end of his life, reached concerning the future of man and society? Reading over and over again the last paragraphs in "Private Man and Society," "*Rechtsstaat*," and "Confining Conditions," one is struck by their ambiguity and their almost sibylline character. Yesterday's air is "both fragrant and pestilential"; man is being "engulfed by mass society," but not "irrevocably." Thus past and future both beckon and repel. Although to the end Marxism remained for him "the best method of analyzing reality," no Marxian utopia about things to come guided him any longer; yet it is not likely that he had given up all hope in man's

[44] See above, footnote 10.

chance to break through confining conditions as long as he remains conscious of his present inability to control reality. Such consciousness, especially on the part of the "executant," seemed to take the place of the "class consciousness" of yore as prerequisite of, and pathbreaker toward, a better world. Is this what he wanted to convey? He was not granted the time to elucidate. As he had said in "Private Man and Society": "The human supply of time runs out rather quickly."

CHRONOLOGY

1905	Born November 11 at Heilbronn, Germany
1924	Graduated from *Gymnasium*
1924–28	Studied law and social sciences at universities of Münster, Cologne, Berlin, and Bonn. Principal teachers: Max Scheler, Carl Schmitt, Rudolf Smend, Hermann Heller
1928	Doctor Juris at Bonn University
1930–33	Lecturer at German trade union schools
1932–33	Member of the Berlin bar
1933	Left Germany for France
1934–37	Research at the Paris branch of the Institute of Social Research (formerly in Frankfurt)
1937	Came to the United States
1937–42	Research associate at the Institute of Social Research in New York
1943	Visiting lecturer at Wellesley College
1944–45	Research analyst, Office of Strategic Services, Washington, D.C.
1945–50	Research analyst, Department of State, Division of Research for Europe
1950–55	Chief, Central European Branch, Office of Intelligence Research, Department of State
1955–62	Professor of Political Science, Graduate Faculty, New School for Social Research
1957–58	Rockefeller Foundation fellow
1961	Fulbright professor, University of Freiburg, Germany
1961	Publication of *Political Justice*
1962–65	Professor of Public Law and Government, Columbia University
1964–65	Fellow, Social Science Research Council
1965	Died November 22 at Washington, D.C.

CONTENTS

PART THREE. MAN, VICTIM AND MAKER OF SOCIETY

PART ONE

UNCOVERING BASIC MECHANISMS OF POLITICAL ORDER AND DISORDER

THE SOCIALIST AND BOLSHEVIK

THEORY OF THE STATE

LIBERALISM, while concerned with keeping the cultural areas of life outside the framework of the state, has confined itself to conquering within it a position of power commensurate with the economic status enjoyed by the forces liberalism represents; it has not, however, tried to annihilate the state. The struggle was always fought in a spirit of respect—even of unavowed admiration—for the powers representing the state. During the battle, the weapon wielded by liberalism was the constitution. The insufficiently political orientation of bourgeois liberalism was its undoing: in France this twice caused its defeat at the hands of a Napoleonic power drive, while in Germany, before and under Bismarck, it surrendered its autonomy vis-à-vis the state-power time and again.

What liberalism expected from the constitution, and from the concept of the constitutional state in general, was far in excess of their true significance. They were to be used by the liberal forces for assigning to the ruling nobility a specifically circumscribed sphere of competence. This process was rather drawn-out because the only weapon the liberal forces could bring to bear in the contest was their economic position of strength. The delay led to the last phase of the battle being fought while the working class, by now a political factor, was already pressing forward.[1] Thus, as a result of their common front against

This translation of "Zur Staatslehre des Sozialismus und Bolschewismus" is published by permission of Carl Heymanns Verlag KG. The original article appeared in *Zeitschrift für Politik*, XVII (1928), 593–611.

[1] This process is concisely described in F. Engels, Introduction to Karl Marx, *Klassenkämpfe in Frankreich*, p. 5. An adversary is of the same opinion: Lorenz von Stein, *Der Sozialismus und Kommunismus im heutigen Frankreich*, p. 145.

feudal semi-absolutism, the working class was brought into closer contact with liberalism. In view of the inevitable gap between them,
caused by their contradictory economic interests, the joint struggle of
liberalism and Social Democracy for political and ideological freedom
was a welcome factor making for cohesion. For liberalism continued
this struggle, which had been part of its tradition, even in such countries as Germany where in other respects it had surrendered its freedom of political action almost entirely, while in Western Europe the
struggle of Social Democracy for political freedom has remained a
durable element. The fight for political liberty carried on by the loyal
liberal parties for the sake of realizing their claim to power in the
political arena was relatively devoid of danger so long as the political
unity of the state was guaranteed by a common national basis. However, that common basis no longer existed when the struggle was
terminated for the time being by the achievement of political democracy. Owing to the concerted pressure of the working class, the struggle had been propelled beyond the political aims of liberalism, and the
political equality attained was complete, with the right to vote no
longer restricted by property qualifications. At that point had disappeared those underlying values which are needed by a democracy even
more than by any other system, regardless of what ideas are reflected
in such a democracy.[2] For democracy means the participation of all
individuals in a whole brought about by the integration into the nation
of all those who share the common values. And democracy loses this
original meaning as soon as any major segment ceases to recognize the
common values as its own and clashes with them.

The nineteenth century was the arena of the battles for, and the final
victory of, democracy. Under the impact of that grim struggle people
failed to ask themselves what should be the possible and ever changea-
ble content of the new popular sovereignty.[3] The failure to do so
appears adequately explained as the result of the complete equation,
soon after resorted to, between people and democracy on the one hand
and liberalism and the bourgeoisie on the other. For thereby the con-

[2] For problems relating to the structure of democracy, see W. Becker in
Schildgenossen, September, 1925.
[3] As regards the changeability of prevalent ideas in the realm of democracy,
Proudhon complains movingly in his *De la Justice dans la Révolution et dans
L'Église*, I, 10.

tradiction was transposed from the purely political aspect and acquired a social content, so that from then on the term "democracy" became an expression for specific ideas of social homogeneity. Democracy taken in this sense is hailed even by socialist writers. Yet this accolade is weakened by the too-pronounced generality, amounting to a catch-all, of the values in whose name socialism claims to be "democratic." For as a result of the very demand for social equality which socialism makes on democracy, the latter is already conceived as a transition to the classless society, that is, to the condition of statelessness. However, the component characteristics of a democracy based on values do not include a standard of value defined *a priori*, but only one that goes beyond mere political equality. This sharply differentiates value-based democracy from the type of "democracy" which was achieved in Germany after World War I and elsewhere.[4] The latter variety merely designates conditions of general political equality, ignoring all considerations of substantive value. The hallmark of such formal [5] democracy is the absence of values which could be confronted by counter-values, unless one considers such absence of values a value in itself.[6] This kind of democracy provides a crucible for the crosscurrents and encounters of classes and their value systems, in which, to be more precise, the antagonistic forces are lined up at a particular stage of the class struggle. This poses the question as to how government is at all possible under such conditions and who decides on the wielders of governmental power. In the case of a democracy characterized by agreement on fundamental values, a majority vote amounts to a decision on the best way to concretize these common values.[7] In the ab-

---

[4] This clash between "formal democracy" and "value democracy" also pervades the entire work of Max Adler, *Politische oder Soziale Demokratie* (Berlin, 1926), where the terms "political democracy" and "social democracy" amount to a narrowing-down of the contrast between "formal democracy" and "value democracy." Yet the expression "political democracy" is unfortunate, since all forms of democracy are political, it being an emanation of governmental activity. This shows up the inevitable dilemma to which purely socialist concepts are exposed: even when a nonpolitical thought is to be arrived at, the political prerequisites for such thought cannot be avoided.

[5] Only formal democracy is meant by Karl Renner in his disquisition in *Die Gesellschaft*, December, 1926.

[6] Thus Hans Kelsen in *Sozialismus und Staat*.

[7] See the *locus classicus* in Rousseau, *Contrat Social*, Book IV, ch. 2, Des Souffrages: "Quand donc l'avis contraire au mien l'emporte, cela ne prouve autre chose, sinon que je m'étois trompé et que j'estimois être la volonté générale, mais ne l'étoit pas." In complete agreement is Max Adler, *op. cit.*, p. 85.

sence of such basic agreement it is by no means self-evident why the majority should have the power to decide, for in that case majority rule is tantamount to passive submission of the minority to its political opponents. This is best illustrated by the habit of socialist authors to define as dictatorship such a long-term submission without struggle. In so doing they pay less attention to the concept of dictatorship as such, which designates an emergency situation,[8] than to the absence of a formal act of submission.

The following are the prerequisites of democracy in the formal sense: an approximate state of equilibrium among the conflicting classes and, as a result, a tacit agreement to let the outcome of each election decide, so long as the equilibrium lasts, who shall take over the government.[9] A government originating in this way does not have a free hand, however, since the loser of the election is protected by the system of detailed constitutional safeguards inherited from the liberal era. In this context it is of a certain significance which class or ideological group has succeeded in incorporating parts of its own program into the constitution, that is, into the procedural rules of this system of constitutional safeguards. For, given the two-thirds majority requirement for constitutional change, a group can by so doing shield its vital interest positions from temporary disturbances of the equilibrium as well as from any real attack, so long as the system remains in operation. Instructive examples can be gleaned from an explanation of the Weimar Constitution from this point of view. Thus, the concept of the *Rechtsstaat*, emerging out of the mental horizon and the hands of the bourgeois-constitutional parties and entering the broad battleground of people against propertied classes, has gradually undergone profound changes of function.

[8] Cf. Carl Schmitt, *Die Diktatur* (Munich, 1921) and *Politische Theologie* (Munich, 1922).

[9] In the monarchical age the equilibrium problem presented itself as a problem of social balancing. In his *Politische Geschichte der französischen Revolution*, II, 44, Aulard points out that by using the king the bourgeoisie attempted to bring about a certain balance between the people and the bourgeoisie without, however, intending to relinquish its actual power. Yet the people was not aware of its position of strength and assisted the bourgeoisie against the king (*ibid.*, p. 46). Karl Rotteck, a liberal, understood the significance of this situation for the political history of the following century: he bitterly accused the French monarchy of having forced the bourgeoisie, during the French Revolution, to appeal to the people (*Allgemeine Geschichte vom Anfang der historischen Kenntnis bis auf unsere Zeit* [Rottenburg am Neckar, 1834], IX, 83).

Originally, the *Rechtsstaat* was the timidly wielded weapon of the "propertied and educated" strata who were concerned to consolidate their exclusive financial domination [10] and to safeguard their private entrepreneurial activities from the hazards of arbitrary adjudication. But later it became the dividing line between two struggling groups neither of which is willing to regard it as the definitive law regulating the domestic distribution of power. The tacit agreement on the rules of the game, which is the existential basis of formal democracy, was bearable only for the fighting groups when the limits of governmental prerogative were circumscribed as narrowly as possible, when the government was given as little *de facto* decision-making power as possible and, instead, a mass of legally defined administrative functions. These administrative functions were mass-produced from scratch after liberalism's attempts to deprive the state entirely of the power to regulate economic affairs had proved to be neither successful nor desirable.[11] Yet, above every administrative function loomed the hierarchy of the courts, which would snatch any decision from the array of social forces at a given time in order to spirit it away into the sphere of the law. In all fields of endeavor things are turned into law (*Verrechtlichung*); all factual decisions involving actual power relations are avoided, whatever the issue: the dictatorial powers of the President of the Reich, or the settlement of labor disputes, or anything else. Everything is formalized juridically and thereby neutralized. And now begins the true epoch of the *Rechtsstaat*. For this kind of state consists exclusively in its laws. Decisions are felt to be bearable only because they appear colorless and nonauthoritative, and because they seem to emanate from independent judges [12] freely deciding on the basis of their conviction. Thus the paradox has arisen that the value of the decision lies in its character as a legal ruling handed down by a generally recognized legal authority, while on the other hand it embodies

10 In formally democratic regimes, the right to control the budget has completely lost its former importance since with alternating governments this permanent control has become very secondary in nature.

11 The idea of the administrative state is most clearly advocated in Heinrich Cunow's *Die Marxsche Geschichts–, Gesellschafts– und Staatstheorie* (Berlin, 1920–21) and in Karl Renner's *Marxismus, Krieg und Internationale* (Stuttgart, 1918), written during the war.

12 See Eugen Rosenstock, *Vom Industrierecht, Rechtssystematische Fragen* (Berlin, 1926), p. 167.

only a minimum of decisional content. The state lives off the law; yet it is no longer law (*Recht*), it is only a legal mechanism, so that those who think they are guiding the affairs of the state actually wield only a legal machinery which claims their attention in the same way a machinist is tied down by the apparatus he serves.[13] In this age of the equilibrium of class forces, the state is essentially characterized by the curious fact that things have been transferred from the realm of factual reality into that of legal mechanics. This is the new phase of the *Rechtsstaat* now that it has shed the traditions of authentic liberalism. What remains is nothing but a legal mechanism if, to be on the safe side, we except those areas which cannot be turned into law (*Verrechtlichung*), such as religion and military service.

We are now ready to investigate the problem of the Russian Revolution and the state. Here the question is whether the Soviet state, too, is the result of the destruction of such a legal machinery. Was the Russian state also a mere arena in which class antagonisms were fought out? Certainly not. The official Russian state was most intimately connected with the Russian Orthodox Church, whose head, the Czar, was simultaneously head of the state. This explains, *inter alia*, the lack of influence of the Western-oriented intelligentsia and the liberal bourgeoisie; it explains why their historical role was confined to participation in the general revolutionary movement and to the brief interlude between the Empire of the Czars and the Soviet Republic, whereas their counterparts in Western Europe have not lost their historical significance to this day. In 1867, in his *Russia and Europe*, the Bible of Panslavism, Danilevsky poignantly outlined the essence of the Russian prerevolutionary state. He contrasts Europe's cultural-political task with Russia's divine mission and therefore declares any revolution incompatible with the essential qualities of the Russian nation. Thus, the Russian state is a non-state; it is nothing but the terrestrial epiphany of a divinely inspired mission, a realm filled with spiritual

[13] Cunow's and Renner's administrative state (*Verwaltungsstaat*) resembles the concept of "service" in Anglo-American theories of public law. So Léon Duguit (*Traité de droit constitutionnel*, II, 52 ff.) who tends to consider all public law as servicing the social process. American legal theory is outstanding for abstracting from political group concepts; in so doing it changes the concept of "service" into an entirely liberal one of social classification. Julius Hirsch (*Das Amerikanische Wirtschaftswunder* [Berlin, 1926], p. 277) calls it "public service for His Majesty the customer."

treasures. And the closer the twentieth century approaches, the more irreconcilable becomes the contradiction between Russia's true mission and those who reject it. Finally, Berdyaev,[14] a present-day Russian counterrevolutionary thinker, raises these views to the grandiose vision of the Kingdom of God as the true, the holy Russian Empire, whereas the empire of the Antichrist is that of the Bolshevik, atheist Devil. What is most remarkable in Berdyaev is not his positing this radical contradiction between Good and Evil, his ethical evaluation to which he subjects all political processes in the Russian Empire: it is his budding insight that Bolshevism has thrown out all half-measures and neutrality, has broken with the humanist Empire of the Golden Mean, so that now the true, real, and final decision is upon us. Thus, the characteristic aspect of the Russian Empire was the moral and theological dialectic which dominated its political imagination. Its economically most pressing problem, as we know, was the question of land distribution.

Karl Marx was aware of the quite different structure of Russian conditions. In a letter to Vera Zasulich [15] he pointed out that it was only in non-Russian Europe that the capitalist process of development was historically necessary. And in the preface to the Russian edition of his *Communist Manifesto* he remarked that the overthrow of Russian absolutism might trigger a revolution in the whole of Europe. It is true that Russian Social Democracy under Plekhanov's leadership paralleled the course of the Western European labor parties until the parting of the ways came at the London Congress of 1903. The Russian Social Democrats, too, assumed that a gradual transition would take place, an "organic" development leading from absolutism via parliamentary democracy to the point when a workers' party would be the parliamentary majority of the democratic state. This attitude inevitably led to the view that the developmental process leading from absolutism to the perfect, the socialist democracy represented constant progress. Especially it was felt that freedom of the press and of assembly and similar institutions which necessarily go with a formal

[14] Nicholas Berdyaev, *Das neue Mittelalter: Betrachtungen über das Schicksal Russlands und Europas* (Darmstadt, 1927).

[15] This correspondence was first published in 1924 by the Marx-Engels Institute in Moscow (Vol. I, Part III, pp. 263–86). I owe this and much other information to Stählin's excellent *Russland und Europa* (Berlin, 1926).

democracy, with its social equilibrium, were permanent achievements. These were "fetishized," to use Marx's term.

All of Marx's disciples, who after him had a decisive impact on the workers' parties, have evolved a theory of twofold progress.[16] Progress in capitalist economic development is paralleled by progress in the development of humanity and its education toward humanitarianism, which is expressed in its methods of struggle during succeeding periods. The peace for which Jean Jaurès died in 1914, usually called "the peace of the Second International," was a component of this belief just as was the faith in a peaceful majority within the framework of formal democracy. According to Kautsky this democracy involves the struggle of organized, enlightened masses filled with steadiness and moderation. This theory of double progress, we must emphasize, stems from Marx's disciples, not from Marx himself. For Marx the political world was nothing but a reflex of economic development. The dawn of social revolution is not brought nearer by the maturing proletariat; instead, the development of capitalism will organize and discipline the proletariat. In the words of Georges Sorel,[17] Marx's thinking is dominated by "technological continuity."

Lenin, *the* theoretician of the Bolshevik party, never showed any interest in the theory of twofold progress. Yet the special Russian situation made him quickly aware that his cause could hardly triumph so long as it was assumed, with Marx, that the political maturation process of the proletariat was unconditionally dependent on the development of capitalist economy.

The specific content of Lenin's activity and doctrine was not tied to the development of capitalism, even though he maintained the theory of the inexorable necessity of capitalist economic evolution and of the progress of mankind to be achieved after the victory of socialism. And after he had conquered power he sought to bring about this progress in ways that were thoroughly rationalist, materialist, and oriented toward

[16] Schmitt has this in mind when he refers to the imagined identity of progressive-democratic thought and social-democratic organization (*Die geistesgeschichtliche Lage des heutigen Parlamentarismus*, 2d ed. [Munich, 1926], p. 32). See, among many others: Renner, *op. cit.*; Karl Kautsky, *Terrorismus und Kommunismus: Ein Beitrag zur Naturgeschichte der Revolution* (Berlin, 1919). Very instructive: Kautsky, *Georgien, eine sozialdemokratische Räterepublik, Eindrücke und Beobachtungen* (Vienna, 1921).

[17] Georges Sorel, *Réflexions sur la violence*, 6th ed. (Paris, 1921), p. 199.

the patterns of the twentieth century. In order to bring about the rule of the proletariat Lenin replaced the theory of twofold progress and of the increasing humanization of the methods of political struggle by a doctrine of unmitigated, all-embracing struggle. Rather than rely on the humanization of a progress embracing all classes, Lenin threw ethics itself into the battle, making it subservient to his cause instead of being its servant. It is this struggle that, according to him, brings about the true grouping of mankind into embattled formations. "According to us," he said, "morality must be entirely subordinated to the demands of the class struggle. Everything is moral that serves the annihilation of the old exploiting society and the seizure of power by the proletariat. Consequently, our morals consist exclusively in firm discipline and in the consciously fought battle against the class of exploiters. Far from believing in the 'eternally valid' catechisms of morality, we shall unmask that swindle. Communist morality amounts to the struggle for the confirmation of proletarian dictatorship."

In their extreme formulation these programmatical statements are, as it were, the counterpart of Berdyaev's thesis of the Christ versus the Antichrist, except for the transposition of all religious imagery into the political sphere: the political foe has taken the place of the infidel or Antichrist. As to content, they belong to the *Weltanschauung* of Sorel,[18] with whom Lenin has more in common than the hatred they share of the parliament-oriented socialists' superstitious faith in progress. Both Lenin and Sorel regard the faith in a peaceful achievement of majority rule in parliamentary democracy as utopian. Yet utopias are rational projections of human thought into the future which are never quite compatible with reality.

Pareto already distinguished between effective and ineffective utopias, referring as he did to liberalism as an ineffective utopia and to socialism as an effective one.[19] This, however, presents the true state of affairs under a false designation. Economic and political liberalism, the theory of free competition and the Rights of Man, Economic Man and the abstract Citizen—all these are, indeed, a connected series of utopian concepts. For they are rational thought constructions that project futuristic images by synthetizing the merely epochal with that

[18] *Ibid.*, especially ch. 4.
[19] W. Pareto, *Les systèmes socialistes*, II, 65.

which has been longed for since time out of mind. Nevertheless they lack a direct impact upon the present. This, however, is the essential difference between utopia and myth: the latter influences the present and transforms it creatively in its own image,[20] while utopia, which projects the distant future in its totality, remain powerless vis-à-vis the present. Myth has its being in the past and in the present, but it affects the future only in so far as the future is incarnated—through living experience—within a portion of the present or the past.

For Sorel, the myth of the present age, the myth of the proletariat, is embodied in the epic event of the General Strike. According to Sorel, Karl Marx neglected the organization of the struggling proletariat, engrossed as he was with his inquiry into the development of capitalism. Thus he kept within the bounds of a rationalist schema which landed him in the vicinity of utopia. Sorel's syndicalism, on the other hand, was to grasp and realize the true kernel of Marx's theory: the doctrine of the class struggle. But in this way Sorel cast doubt upon Marx's most characteristic contribution, the functional dependence of the proletarian movement on the process of capitalist development. Moreover, in taking this stance Sorel made the doctrine of the class struggle autonomous. He provided it with its own foundation and meaning, for Sorel's "la force" essentially coincides with Marx's concept of the capitalist process of development, that is, with rationally calculable relations of forces. This rationality, which presupposes only patience, insight, and cognition, Sorel confronts with a political category of an essentially different kind: "la violence," that is, the drive with which a resolute band marches on to victory. For this, Lenin used the Russian word for élan. What is meant is the last battle, "la bataille napoléonienne," which we discover here, too, as an important component of the myth. This unhinged the concept of a power struggle into which people had been forced by an unreal, intellectually motivated class consciousness and an equally unreal class struggle and by the inevitable guilt syndrome stemming from individualist ethics and

---

[20] It is typical of a myth that it attempts to influence man directly. Sorel: "Il faut juger des mythes comme des moyens d'agir sur le présent" (op. cit., p. 180). This concept of "agir sur le présent" represents a clearly prelogical consciousness and is thus found, in pure form, only in primitive ethnic groups. See Lévy-Bruhl, Mentalité primitive, especially p. 94, as to the emotional character of the primitive imagination.

utopian leanings. This somewhat unreal power struggle is replaced by an ethic of struggle which derives its legitimacy from the grandeur of the myth as well as from the individual's ability to participate in it. All this removes the general strike from its original, purely economic sphere. For the general strike is no longer resorted to by workers demanding their wages; it is now fought by the heroes of a new epic who are fated to usher in the dawn of a new historical epoch. The heroes of the myth, the striking workers, are the pure, the better ones, those who were chosen for the final victory. And therefore the proletariat, marching in serried ranks under the ensign of "creative violence," is sure to conquer "la force," the purely technical and economic strength of the bourgeoisie, just as the irrational devotees of myth who rely on faith are forever in the ascendancy over the rational adherents of utopia who merely calculate.

The political myth has the capacity to bring about an extremely decisive grouping according to political values. Being convinced of the inevitability and the grandeur of the final battle, the followers of the myth are genuinely afraid of having to do with an enemy who has ceased to be one. They hope that the no-exit situation of the bourgeoisie, its realization of the inevitability of the final decision, will induce the bourgeoisie to pull itself together and to fight the battle with a dignity commensurate with its significance. True to an age-old tradition, they see the bourgeoisie as the Arch Foe by definition.[21]

The theory of "action directe" amounts to an attempt to restore immediacy to politics by rejecting all intermediary layers such as those of neutral humanitarianism and progress, and by deriving strength and symbolism directly from life in the present. "Action directe" is not afraid of the close connection between economics and politics because the formative power of myth is strong enough to overcome all inertia. The myth has a preference for the theory of elites in order to guaran-

[21] Eduard Bernstein, the typical representative of the theory of twofold progress, was praising the moral integrity of the bourgeoisie already in the nineties, whereas Sorel and Pareto tried to see through the attempts at relativization undertaken by parliamentarism by pointing without illusions to the true battle fronts. Following Sorel, René Johannet in his *Éloge du bourgeois français* (Paris, 1924) attempted to counter the image of the proletariat by holding up the ideal of the bourgeoisie. All these men are in the tradition of Bakunin who wrote: "L'honnête homme, homme moral, c'est celui qui sait acquérir, conserver et augmenter la propriété" (*Oeuvres complets*, III, 172ff.). On the image of the bourgeois, see also Franz Werfel, *Der Tod des Kleinbürgers* (Berlin, 1927).

tee the efficacy of the political will to construct. Thereby it acknowledges an organizational principle of its own. Thus, the views upheld by
Sorel and the revolutionary syndicalists were harmonized with official
Leninism, according to which the Communist party is the guide and
leader of the proletariat and the latter's true and only representative in
the great struggle against the global rule of the bourgeoisie which, in
turn, is seen as representing the wrong, the evil, and the immoral cause
(by Lenin in *State and Revolution*).[22]

Of fundamental importance for every political theory is the position
it adopts toward the concept of dictatorship, to what extent it takes
account of, and admits into its texture, the principle of emergency. As
I see it, three concepts of dictatorship confront each other in socialist
literature. Marx's concept of dictatorship took shape at a time when
issues of economic power had their first impact on political beliefs,
openly, unmistakably, and in their own right. It has retained little
political content of its own. Lacking in political valuation, it merely
characterizes the moment in history when capitalist development has
arrived at the point where the seizure of power by the workers is
meaningful and has a purpose. Marx's successors, who advocated the
theory of twofold progress, attempted to dissolve the dictatorship concept into two parallel avenues of progress, the economic-technical and
the political-humanitarian. What they thought they had discovered as
the final principle of the political structure of the capitalist age was a
parliamentary democracy embracing both avenues of progress. In this
way they managed to transplant dictatorship from the realm of political reality into that of utopia, and having been fitted out with Marxian
"economic laws," utopia was fashioned into an "organic, transitional
phase." This medley of economic development and democracy, of
majority vote and humanitarianism, made it easy for the Bolsheviks to
counter the attacks that were leveled against their dictatorship concept
from among the adherents of the theory of twofold progress.

The sovereign contempt of the Bolsheviks for such third-class liberal
strategies is revealed by reactions like this: "Far from arguing with its
foes, the Revolution crushes them. So does the Counterrevolution. And
both are contemptuous of the reproach that they have paid no heed to

[22] For the present official party line, see Stalin, *Problems of Leninism*.

the procedural rules of the German Reichstag." [23] This shows that the political myth of the world revolution is a more effective catalyst for political array and a more effective formal principle than is the utopia of a potential majority within parliamentary democracy.

The Bolshevik concept of dictatorship is an authentic one because it serves to designate an emergency, an exceptional situation, whereas both of the other socialist concepts of what a dictatorship embodies are less authentic: one of them hardly comes under the definition of political dictatorship at all and the other refers to political progress at precisely the point at which no further progress is needed, which makes it a convenient utopia. We must keep in mind that the Bolshevik dictatorship is a sovereign dictatorship although, it is true, a type of provisional dictatorship (*Kommissarische Diktatur*) [24] has likewise emerged as a result of the transfer to the state of many sectors of the private economy; the latter, as Lenin said, is "dictatorship of individuals with purely executive functions with regard to certain economic processes." [25] Furthermore, the Bolshevik dictatorship does not embody an organic process of transition; its exceptional quality as an emergency situation consists in the fact that in order to establish the socialist state of social equality it must first create the prerequisite conditions. This leads to a number of political measures which reveal the characteristic trait of every dictatorship: in order to realize its cherished ideals it is forced to resort to measures that *ipso facto* contradict the ideal to be realized. When engaged in this course, the dictatorship uses what it calls "Soviet democracy." While this does not constitute the "most highly developed form" of democracy, it nevertheless amounts to a purposeful attempt to introduce into the consciousness of the agricultural masses a body of beliefs regarded as correct beyond dispute. In other words, the aim is to bring about participation in the affairs of the state. It was for this purpose that the thesis of the replacement "du gouvernement des hommes par l'administration des choses" was to be carried into effect, an effort which on the whole has been a failure.

[23] Thus K. Radek in the preface to Bukharin's *Programme*, p. 23.
[24] As to the fundamental difference between "kommissarische Diktatur" and "souveräne Diktatur," see Carl Schmitt, *Die Diktatur*.
[25] Lenin, *Die nächsten Aufgaben der Sowjetmacht* (Leipzig, 1920), p. 39.

However, embodying as it does the working reality of "Soviet democracy," and representing as it does the realization of the new formal principle already conceived by syndicalism, the entire system of soviets is intended to serve this purpose.[26]

In the USSR, the political significance of elections must in no way be sought in their results. In Germany, elections are at least mildly significant in that the crew servicing the state machinery changes according to their results. Soviet elections do not even have that function. For whenever those who represent and make the official value system encourage a debate of those values, this does not at all mean that their intrinsic worth is subjected to a majority vote. On the contrary, their correctness is assumed to be beyond discussion. Thus, the significance of Soviet elections, far from lying in their results, must be sought in the electoral process as such. The pivotal point is that the elections are public. The voter can say "yes," or nothing at all, or practically nothing by voting for a nonparty candidate. Yet those who vote "yes" are doing so openly and publicly, clearly setting themselves off from those who fail to vote. It is the "yes" vote with which the Soviet government is desperately concerned, for it is the symbol of integration, of the awareness of one's participation, and of one's desire to participate.[27] Hence the Soviet elections, while of no significance so far as actual decisions are concerned, have yet acquired a specific po-

[26] This is a new aspect of the Soviet system. Originally, the form in which revolutionary groups resort to spontaneous political action on the basis of class and professional groupings contributed to the establishment of Bolshevik power. (For the history of its theoretical development, see "The Role of the Agitator in Cromwell's Army," in E. Bernstein, *Sozialismus und Demokratie in der grossen englischen Revolution* [Stuttgart, 1908]. On the role of workers' councils during the first Russian Revolution, see Trotsky, *Neue Zeit,* 1907, p. 76.) In Russia, syndicalist theory is being developed consciously; the councils (soviets) elected directly by the enterprises are used as carriers of political functions such as administration and elections.

[27] The constitution does not deal with the question of public elections. However, the gubernatorial commissions which have the power to decide have spoken unanimously in favor of publicity. On election procedures during the official election assemblies, see Timashev, p. 83, who is anti-Soviet. The practical aspects of the last election are interestingly described by R. Maltsev in *Kommunistische Internationale,* No. 19, 1927. The difference between secret and public elections amounts, on the practical level, to a total break with the traditions of parliamentary, individualistic, and liberal concepts. It does away with the belief that the fate of the ruling group can in any way be decided by the election. Public elections amount to confirmation and affirmation, but in no way to decision.

litical value in that they have become a tool for the integration of the masses into the state.

Soviet law has a similar function as far as its significance for political life is concerned. All modern law, including Soviet law, is technical to a high degree. Moreover, we saw the specific character of our legal system in the inverse relationship between its lack of actual power to decide and the constant increase in the quantity of legal norms; we saw that its content in terms of fundamentals of public policy is decreasing while legal-technical formalities and precision are on the increase. In short, the state tends to disappear behind its own legal mechanism. Lenin,[28] on the other hand, visualized the task of law as follows: "Obviously, we have not yet finally liquidated the traditional view of the legal apparatus, inherited from the bourgeoisie, as something official and hostile. It is not yet sufficiently realized that the legal system, more than anything else, constitutes the connecting link between the poorer strata and the state apparatus. For the judiciary is the organ of the government of workers and peasants; it is an instrument for education and for imparting discipline."

This does away with the view of the judiciary as an independent third force, as an arbiter above the contending parties, the view of the liberals which made a virtue of a necessity. Instead, Lenin's point of view restores the image of the substantive character of law which in Europe, since the age of liberalism, has tended to disappear and has been totally dissolved into the legal mechanism of formal democracy. Wherever a state exists, be its form intrinsically democratic or dictatorial, legal judgments are rendered in the name of definite value concepts. Therefore it is entirely logical for the USSR to base the status of its judges not on their independence and nonremovability but on limited periods in office as a result of elections and on previously tested reliability in party service, not on the judge's subordination to the law but rather on his "revolutionary consciousness" with regard to applying the law. Typical of this attitude is the case of a Moscow judge who rejected a claim in spite of its legal merits because it violated the interests of a worker; in a nutshell, this case demonstrated what the Soviet government has in mind when, in accordance with the Soviet constitution, it allows appeals against judgments of the highest courts

[28] *Ibid.*, p. 30.

to the Chief Executive Committee, that is, to a political body.[29] Thus, we have here a substantive function of the law which from the point of view of the *Rechtsstaat* has been called, somewhat deprecatingly, a "valeur instrumentale." [30] It is so dependent on the government objectives at any given time that the suggestion was even made to limit the validity of the new Soviet Civil Code to only two years. This underscores the fact that Soviet law, far from being meant for eternity, is temporary law to the highest degree.[31] Soviet law does not stand in need of a *clausula rebus sic stantibus* since it *is* itself the law of the *clausula rebus sic stantibus*.[32] The awareness of this fact completely dominates Soviet thinking on international law. It is the irreconcilability of class antagonisms that has brought the Soviet state into being; to it the Soviet state owes allegiance, and by virtue of it the Bolsheviks hope eventually to hold sway over the whole earth. Consequently, international law in the traditional sense is for the Soviet state the most dubious of all legal constructions.

The USSR does not recognize common interests among states except on a purely technical level. It therefore does not respond to endeavors to bring about a closer international legal community or to support peace propaganda. It considers international law as the rules of truce, not of peace. It regards the sum total of all activities based on international law merely as an attempt to stabilize the customs and legal rules of a dying age and hence feels it cannot join in those activities. Consequently, in this transitional period (*époque transitoire*) it must find makeshift solutions through precisely worded individual agreements with the several powers. In the absence of any homogeneity of interests and views, however tenuous, that could become the prerequisite of a decision in the legal sense, the USSR is forced to reject not only the majority principle in international practice but also any internationally recognized court which would claim for itself the authority to render binding decisions.[33] Thus, the USSR was bound to

29 Cf. the Russian constitution of July 6, 1923, Part II, ch. 7.
30 Mirkine-Guetzévitch in *Revue nouvelle de droit international public*, 2d ser., VII (1925), 314.
31 On this point, see Eugen Rosenstock, *op. cit.*, p. 122.
32 See the interesting articles by Korovine and M.-Guetzévitch in the above-cited journal (n. 30).
33 See Carl Schmitt, *Kernfragen des Voelkerbundes*, Section 11 (Berlin, 1926).

develop hostility against the Geneva League of Nations as a matter of principle, not merely occasionally as did Germany.[34] As regards the attitude of the League of Nations toward the USSR, its sharp hostility has never flagged, beginning with Viviani's first address down to this day. This was predicated on the League's role of protector and advocate of formal-democratic principles of legitimacy, notwithstanding the fact that Wilson's first draft preamble, according to which it was the purpose of the League of Nations to be a regular government of the member states, was omitted. What the USSR thinks of the League emerges clearly in a speech by Rykov: [35] "The League of Nations is a merchant who deals in peoples, selling them to the so-called civilized states under the name of 'mandates.' " The Western powers in turn have used the formal-democratic principle of legitimacy as a pretext for imperialist intervention on USSR territory.

England attempted to justify her intervention in the Russo-Polish war by pointing to Article 11 of the League of Nations Covenant. This argument was rejected in Chicherin's thought-provoking memorandum of May, 1921, and the USSR has consistently held to the views expressed in that document. It refers to a "so-called League of Nations" the existence of which was "brought to the USSR's attention by news reports," and it stresses emphatically the incompatibility of Article 11 of the League of Nations Covenant with the sovereignty of the Russian working people.[36] Thus, at a time when Europe deemphasizes the concept of sovereignty [37] practically and theoretically, Bolshevism

[34] This explains the very ambiguous statement of Kunz (*Zeitschrift für Völkerrecht*, XIII, No. 4, 584) to the effect that Soviet international law is characterized by a remarkably reactionary tendency. The expression "reactionary" belongs to a different context and presupposes a particular political unit. It is meaningless with regard to the struggle between states and classes, where is must be replaced by more comprehensive concepts of political grouping.

[35] *Internationale Pressekorrespondenz* (published by the Third International), 1925, p. 2446.

[36] *Russische Korrespondenz*, Jahrg. I, Vol. II, p. 559.

[37] Most precisely formulated by Harold Laski in *Studies in the Problem of Sovereignty* (New Haven, 1917) and *Authority in the Modern State* (New Haven, 1919). Likewise in Kurt Wolzendorff, *Der reine Staat* (Tübingen, 1920). The problem of sovereignty is closely interdependent with that of the strength of the principle of political form. Wherever a strong principle of form is lacking, and where the state is a mere legal mechanism in the form of social classes taking turns in the government, there will always be theorists who try to eschew the ultimate consequence by eliminating the concept of sovereignty. In this way it is possible to proclaim, as a matter of law, the complete autonomy of the

strangely engages in ushering in new victories, *de facto,* for the very concept of sovereignty from which, theoretically, it withholds recognition. The Russian writer Korovine [38] argues that in falling back on the concept of sovereignty the USSR was attracted by the *intérêts réels* of the socialist body politic rather than by the beauty of a juristic theorem. This may be useful for the evaluation of legal theories in the USSR but it does not touch upon the essential question. That in Europe concepts connected with the nation-state are on the wane is brought out most tangibly by the following situation: the colonial and other annexations carried out after the peace of Versailles could not be morally defended by the traditional arguments having to do with the national unity of peoples; instead, in order to justify the desired result, one had to have recourse to the legal construct of the League of Nations as trustee. The need to use, at Versailles, makeshift constructions of this kind underscores the weakness in practical life of the concept of the sovereignty of the nation-state. Likewise, the theoretical impasse is brought out by the impossibility to find, in our age of formally democratic structures aiming at social equilibrium, a satisfactory answer to the question of who is the wielder of sovereignty, that is, who makes the actual decision in a conflict situation. The USSR has singled out a definite and well-known locus of sovereignty with a clarity that is sensational when held against the present-day tendencies of masking and concealment. In the history of political theory this in itself might at most have netted the Soviets some recognition for having made a sweeping restoration attempt; however, the really new element in the Bolshevik concept of sovereignty is contained in the intentional separation—performed for the first time—of the concepts of state and sovereignty.

Bolshevism has been instrumental in dissolving the traditional and now untenable conceptual tie between state and sovereignty by replac-

---

economy—this with the help of cooperative (*genossenschaftliche*) arguments, as Wolzendorff and Laski have done. Taking it from there, one can plausibly talk of a "pure state" (Wolzendorff) which is in reality nothing but the liberal legal construct which limits the state to police functions and arbitration. Similarly Laski's "cooperative sovereignty," which is mere camouflage. He is clearer when he says: "The real rulers of a society are undiscoverable, but with the real rulers must go sovereignty."

[38] E. Korovine in *Revue nouvelle de droit international public,* 2d ser., VII (1925), 299.

ing the sovereignty of the state with that of the class. Thus it has filled a gap that had opened up. This new sovereignty is not limited to any state frontiers; it tends to be universal. Hence the problem of intervention has been placed in a different perspective.

While intervention when practiced by imperialist national states came to a halt as soon as the thirst of their economy was slaked, the USSR's policy of intervention knows no limits; its thirst is unquenchable as a matter of principle. For potentially the rule of the working class applies to every member of the working population, and every member of the class can occasion its intervention, either to protect him or to use him to influence the fate of other countries. This, however, raises the question whether Soviet Russia is still a state. For whoever claims or practices an unlimited right of intervention foregoes the specific characteristic of the state, which is self-limitation at some point or line of this world. This is not to say that the USSR represents something less than a state. On the contrary, it has restored integrational character to law and elections, albeit in order to make them servicable to more comprehensive population segments than heretofore. By making use of them, and of the political myth of world revolution, the Soviets have regrouped the political forces. They have torn open the gap at the place where the state had stood until far into the nineteenth century. What still exists in the West is the mere shell of the state; the state has become something less than itself, a mere legal mechanism for which enthusiasm was just barely sufficient to give birth to the theory of twofold progress. Such a state—which no longer is one—can no longer have an enemy; for it lacks tangible forms of political expression. The Bolshevik prophets of the political myth of world revolution—who consider Russia merely as the launching pad— are the sworn, irreconcilable enemies of the powers that are lined up behind the façade of "the state," that is, on the one hand, the capitalist power groups with their imperialist policies and, on the other, the holders of the theory of twofold progress, the wardens of the legal mechanism, namely, Social Democracy and the petty bourgeoisie.

MARXISM, DICTATORSHIP, AND THE

ORGANIZATION OF THE PROLETARIAT

THESE DAYS, the espousal of Marxism is considered a symptom of national and human degeneracy. At the same time public discussion to a large extent now adopts a concept of dictatorship that was decisively molded by Marxist thought. In Marxist theory "dictatorship of the proletariat" points to a definite stage in the over-all evolution of economic relations. It merely represents the external reflection and final consummation of a process already completed beneath the cover of the hitherto existing conditions.[1] This formulation of Marx's dictatorship concept correctly moves the center of gravity away from a formalistic definition of terms to the identification of a particular phase of social evolution. The role of dictatorship in the structure of Marxian dialectics,[2] and the specific position it assigns to the working class, can be unmistakably gleaned from Marx's *The Civil War in France*. This work deals most concretely of all with the question of the dictatorship of the proletariat and it has caused widespread misunderstanding because its special purpose was not always sufficiently understood. *The Civil War in France* points out that the working class did not expect miracles from the Commune. It was resigned to living through long-

Translation of "Marxismus, Diktatur, und Organisationsformen des Proletariats"; originally published in *Die Gesellschaft*, X (1933), 230–39.
[1] See the discussion on the concept of dictatorship of the proletariat in Ernst Troeltsch, *Der Historismus und seine Probleme* (1922), p. 333.
[2] Gurland emphasizes in his polemic against Otto Bauer and Max Adler, *Marxismus und Diktatur* (Leipzig, 1930), pp. 66 ff., that Marx's concept of dictatorship must be understood legalistically (*formaljuristisch*).

lasting struggles and a whole series of historical processes for the sake of working out its own emancipation and with it that higher form of life toward which present society is striving irresistibly by virtue of its economic evolution. By these struggles and processes men as well as conditions, so it is believed, will be thoroughly transformed. The element peculiar to the concept lies, therefore, in the necessary linkage of proletarian action with a definite state of economic maturation; it is thus intimately connected with Marx's over-all theory. Futhermore, Marx's image of "dictatorship" resulted from the contemporary usage of the term which he had accepted in the *Communist Manifesto* and, especially, in his historical-political writings dealing with French conditions. There "dictatorship" means the purely *de facto* rule of a class or group over another, regardless of the legal forms through which such rule takes place. This meaning of "dictatorship" is well expressed in Paul Levi's introduction to Rosa Luxemburg's remarks on the Russian Revolution:

Now we can see what dictatorship of the proletariat is. It is nothing that takes place within the vast regions of social philosophy, nor is it a patented form of government carrying within it some secret force. It is, rather, the conquered state power when, and so long as, it is backed by the will, the strength, the enthusiasm, and the certainty of victory of the proletarian class.[3]

In the turmoil of interests and opinions within the world's workers' parties, Marx's concept of dictatorship has not received much attention. Much more was paid to the complex of questions concerning the relationship between democracy and dictatorship in the formal-political sense, to democracy as the possible juristic form within which the proletarian dictatorship may take place. In this connection reference has often been made to Engels' formula of democracy as the specific form of the dictatorship of the proletariat, though it was less frequently mentioned that Engels—at this place in his *Critique of the Erfurt Draft Program*—had primarily been concerned with the idea of democracy as antithesis to Germany's semifeudal military monarchy. Nowhere, however, does Marx or Engels claim that democracy with the institutions typical of it as a form of government constitutes the

[3] Rosa Luxemburg, *Die Russische Revolution*, ed. and introduced by Paul Levi (Berlin, 1922), p. 59.

necessary chrysalis leading to the dictatorship of the proletariat during the dialectical crisis. Ever since the publication of the *Manifesto* Marx had consistently taken the position that the rule of the proletariat must mean the rule of the vast majority in the interest of the vast majority. From this it follows that the best chance for the peaceful transformation of the bourgeois state into a proletarian state exists under conditions of political democracy, the more so because, as a matter of historical record, the battle for democracy was usually won with the decisive participation of the proletariat. This possibility of peaceful transformation varies from country to country, depending on the economic and political situation; accordingly, Marx and Engels have evaluated it differently at different times and with regard to different countries.

As far as Marx was concerned, the only certain thing is that nineteenth-century democracy is the typically last apparition of the state. In other words, it is that form of the state which, by virtue of the conditions in which it originates, represents a structure of bourgeois society within which the class struggle must be finally fought out.[4] This follows from the level of political organization achieved by the proletariat as well as from the economic maturity of society.

Even Marx and Engels could only offer hypotheses as to the possibility of effecting the transformation peacefully within an existing democracy. Engels' well-known introduction to Marx's *Class Struggles in France*—even if Engels' complete text is taken into consideration—contains only such anticipations of the possible future evolution as correspond to Engels' own experiences during his later years. This implies that the proletariat, representing as it does the interest in the development of society as a whole, desires a mode of transition in which conflicts are reduced to a minimum. As Marx once put it: "How nice it would be if one could buy out the landed gentry."

Not only must it be left to the concrete historical process how the transition from bourgeois-democratic republic to proletarian dictatorship will be effected. Phenomena of the kind loosely referred to as "fascism" make it even appear problematical to what extent—especially under more primitive conditions—the bourgeois parliamentary and democratic state can still be considered the political formation

[4] See Marx in *Critique of the Gotha Program*.

preceding the dictatorship of the proletariat. And it is likewise uncertain whether the transitional epoch from capitalism to socialism will contain the element of democracy as a constant factor.

Evaluations of the role played by the middle class and the *lumpenproletariat* in the revolutionary process are part and parcel of every Marxist analysis. Already in the *Communist Manifesto* Marx and Engels pointed out the choice that is available to the middle class in the political process. And with what amounts to prophetic insight, they realized that the *lumpenproletariat,* as the passive rot of the lowest strata of the old society, will be ready to be bribed into serving as a tool of reactionary machinations once it has been propelled into motion by the proletarian revolution.

In *Class Struggles in France* and in *The 18th Brumaire of Louis Napoleon Bonaparte* the social and political role played by the middle class and the *lumpenproletariat* is examined in detail and they are assigned their due place in the flow of political events. While Marx as historian makes allowance for their participation, he does not concede them an independent role in the totality of dialectical development. This is because at the historically decisive moment they will submit themselves to that class which alone is still capable of social initiative (that is, the big bourgeoisie), as Marx said of the Parisian petty bourgeoisie in *The Civil War in France.* It is also because Marx habitually sketches factors of actually realized history but casually and for the most part with polemic intent, as, for example, in the 1875 *Critique of the Gotha Program.* Involved here are questions as they were presented by reality from time to time, and Marx could and would only deal with them in terms of the concrete vantage points provided by his era. To go further he would have rejected as utopian phantasy; for, as we know, he did not consider it his task to discover the political forms of the future.

Nowadays, apart from an objective sharpening of class antagonisms, we also witness the emergence of independent armed political shock troops. They are not, primarily, forming as parties but as troops armed for battle; they join certain social groups exclusively in order to gain political power, that is, in order to use the help of these groups to seize governmental power and make it their exclusive possession. In so doing, leading strata of these private armies aim less and less at social change, for the assistance offered certain social groups has as its sole purpose the cementing of political domination and the exploitation of the governmental power apparatus.

This, however, destroys the mechanism of parliamentary democracy which depends on the balancing of social forces by taking into account changes resulting from successive election results. From then on, not only are political decisions arrived at outside parliament—on principle this would be feasible through free agreement among the social contestants with decisive cooperation from the bureaucracy—but political decisions no longer involve a balancing of the several social forces which nowadays do not seem to have any technical tool at their disposal except the parliament. For the forces now reaching for political supremacy are no longer able in terms of their own vital interests to grant the workers the freedom of action needed for organizing their forces, of which up to now even the workers' sharpest antagonist, the big bourgeoisie, could not, by its own efforts, deprive them. Fascism, on the other hand, has no choice in this matter. It is forced—from its own premises—to hold down the social forces by means of the most ruthless bureaucratic apparatus of repression. For countries exposed to fascist power drives this means that an open clash occurs between the incipient fascist political structure and the existing degree of economic maturity—that is, in those countries which, as in the case of Germany, have reached the stage of fully developed capitalism,[5] as distinguished from its embryonic stage.

Such developments reduce the chances of "twofold progress," that is, of political evolution keeping pace with economic development, as expressed in the notion of a transition from a democracy with bourgeois content to one dominated by proletarian forces. Wherever an armed force intervenes autonomously in the process of social development, using its power decisively for or against certain social strata, there very possibly the proletariat is blocked from taking the democratic road. In that case we are probably facing the situation expressly

[5] See Franz Borkenau's essay "Zur Soziologie des Faschismus" in *Archiv für Sozialwissenschaft und Sozialpolitik*, LXVIII, No. 5. It contains a detailed discussion of the relationship between the big bourgeoisie and fascism. It is assumed there that genuine fascism, like every kind of dictatorship, represents a way station on the road to the creation of industrial capitalism. On this basis Borkenau shows that German national socialism cannot be compared with the dictatorships of countries with still not fully developed capitalist systems.

foreseen as possible in the Linz Program of the Austrian Socialist party,[6] namely, that the working class can conquer executive political power only by a civil war which has thus been forced upon it.

Thereby, however, the center of gravity of the discussion moves once again from the question of a democratic transition, which monopolized the arguments of the last decade, to the problem of proletarian dictatorship. This amounts to a shift in the geographical location of the dialogue between West and Central European socialism and Russian Bolshevism. On the other hand, the discussion is bound to be even more vehement since Bolshevism is the carrier of an idea that has become historically effective, and with respect to which theoretical statements as well as practical experience must be taken into account. The theory of the dictatorship of the proletariat has found its theoretical expression in Lenin's *State and Revolution*. This book originated in the summer of 1917, during the brief but historically decisive period between Russia's bourgeois and communist revolutions. Consequently, it could not as yet embody the practical experiences of the Russian October revolution; it is of especial interest because it reflects Lenin's conception of the proletarian state independently of its realization under Russian conditions. Within Soviet literature, as elsewhere,[7] this work is considered the direct continuation of Marx's teachings on proletarian dictatorship. In Russia it has become the cornerstone of the official theory of government. Hence we are entitled to make it our point of departure.

The work is characterized by its vision, throughout, of an antithetical relationship between power and violence toward the outside world as against the absence of rule or domination in the internal social sphere. With particular pleasure and emphasis Lenin cites Engels' view of revolution as the most authoritarian thing there is; as an act by which a part of the population enforces its will on the other part, by means of rifles, bayonets, and cannon. He heaps scorn upon the parliamentary democratic ideology which then flourished in Western and

---

[6] 1926 ed.

[7] For the tendency to identify Marx with Lenin, see the remarkable description of the Marxist theory of the state by Sherman H. M. Chang, *The Marxian Theory of the State* (Philadelphia, 1931). Interestingly, John R. Commons—in the preface—as well as the author himself, underlines the very great importance, for the concrete Chinese conditions, of a correct interpretation of Marx's theory.

Central Europe and in the corresponding parties in Russia—the scorn of the politician to whom current history seems to have furnished conclusive proof that the opposite is true. In this role Lenin, in the best French revolutionary tradition, appears as a believer in centralism; leanings in the direction of a federal republic he describes as "petty bourgeois prejudice." However, he also believes that a special repressive force is no longer needed when the majority of the people suppresses its own oppressors. Referring constantly to Marx's description of the Paris Commune of 1871, he points out first the necessary changes in the structure of the bureaucracy to be brought about by making the officials elective and removable: further, the generally equal treatment of officials, employees, and workers; and, finally, the vast importance of abolishing the regular army. By these measures, which must be coordinated with the expropriation of the expropriators, Lenin believes it is possible to restore primitive democracy or, as he puts it with an eye on the interests of the peasants, "inexpensive government." Lenin considers this naïve democratism realizable by transforming capitalism into socialism. This "primitive democracy" (his own expression) is the only concept of the realization of proletarian democracy that characterizes Lenin's theoretical horizon. He expressly asks his critics: "In what other way can the people, the majority of the population, gradually take over the functions of government?" To him this primitivity of proletarian democracy within the framework of the dictatorship of the proletariat is not a transitional measure designed for the period of the proletarian seizure of power; he obviously believed that thereby, with one dialectical jump, that stage is reached where the government of men becomes the administration of things. For by the extinction of the characteristics of the bourgeois state, the functions of government shall be reduced to their technical components, accessible to everyone. The model of the post office is explicitly mentioned as an apparatus of the highest technical perfection, by means of which all workers will henceforth carry on administrative acts in accordance with their respective functions.

In the elaboration of the revolution's political objective, described as democratic, a contrasting note is struck by the preconceived structure of the subject of the revolution, the proletarian party, in that any thought of direct democracy is excluded in Lenin's theory of the party. Lenin's theory of the party is dominated by the familiar concept of the necessarily conspiratorial nature of a hierarchical group of professional revolutionaries, of the "Jacobins attached to the organization of class-conscious workers." This is the thesis of the need for a heteronomous discipline not based on existing mass consciousness, and this is the famous doctrine that led to the splitting of the Russian workers' movement with all its grave consequences now demonstrated by history.[8] Lenin derived it from the special exigencies under Russian absolutism.

Rosa Luxemburg already opposed Lenin's theory of the party in 1904, thereby adopting the standpoint of the West and Central European proletariat. She regarded the sharp marking off of an organized party nucleus from the surrounding revolutionary environment as an attempt to transfer Blanquist principles of organization into the social-democratic movement of the working masses.[9] According to her, social democracy is not only *connected* with the organization of the working class, it is the workers' *own* movement. Rosa Luxemburg sharply criticizes the mechanical transfer of principles of capitalist factory discipline to the autonomous discipline of the working class, a view of Lenin's emerging far more clearly after the revolution than in his theoretical credo of 1902.[10] Rosa Luxemburg emphasizes the supreme importance of spontaneity. The sole function of the party is to synthesize the will of the workers. The higher the degree of spontaneity the smaller the double danger of a lapse into sectarianism on the one hand and of degenerating into a bourgeois reform movement on the other. It is conceivable that in taking this position Rosa Luxemburg underrated the ever present need of a degree of autonomous hierarchical power. However that may be, the deep cleavage appearing in the dispute on organization comes up again in Rosa Luxemburg's evaluation of that part of the Russian Revolution which she still witnessed.

[8] See Lenin's essay "Was Tun?" ("What Is to Be Done?") which appeared in 1902 and was reprinted in his *Selected Works*.

[9] This discussion appeared in German in *Neue Zeit*, XXII (1904), Cf. Martov, *Geschichte der russischen Sozialdemokratie* (Berlin, 1926), pp. 74 ff.

[10] See Lenin's essays on the next tasks of the Soviet power, 1918, where he speaks of the unconditional submission of the masses under the unified will of those who direct the production process.

Russia's empirical reality has not confirmed the dialectical leap which Lenin had developed theoretically by pointing to the Paris Commune,[11] from the violent rule of proletarian dictatorship to the primitive purity of proletarian democracy. During the early post-revolutionary period, it is true, the actual Russian conditions corresponded to a certain degree to Lenin's teachings on primitive democracy, but with a characteristic and essential difference. Lenin saw in the transfer of all political functions to the mass of proletarians the beginning of, and the transition to, the building of proletarian democracy. Yet the Russian soviets in their heyday were only the organs for liquidating the existing conditions and for satisfying the most urgent needs of the day. The population strata which the soviets represented, that is, organized and unorganized workers as well as peasants, are—it is true—among the essential supporters of the Russian Revolution. Without their participation the November revolution in Petrograd would have been isolated and condemned to failure. But the soviets still did not become the seeds of a proletarian democracy. When the civil war with its dire need for the centralization of all energies was over, the structure of the state practically coincided with that of the party.

[11] Although Lenin refers often to the experiences of the Commune, as Marx described them approvingly in *The Civil War in France*, it must be pointed out that his interpretation differs from Marx's and also from his own earlier comments on the Commune. Arthur Rosenberg, *Geschichte des Bolschewismus* (Berlin, 1932), p. 25, has recently pointed out once again the essential differences between Marx's opinions and those of the Commune. After the defeat of the Commune, Marx sided in public unconditionally with the Commune (which of course did not preclude the criticism he expressed in his letters) and pointed out to the proletariat the deeds of the Commune as a glowing example for all time. This, however, reveals nothing as to his view of the effectiveness of the Commune's actions, nor whether he considered success possible at all under the existing conditions. *The Civil War in France* contains mainly a moral evaluation which acquires a political tinge by contrasting each single act with the bourgeois horizon of the nineteenth century, the world of Thiers and Bismarck. All Lenin's earlier comments on the Commune must be read in this light (see *Kleine Lenin-Bibliothek*, Vol. V, under the title "Lenin: On the Paris Commune"). In an essay written in 1911 Lenin explains why the Commune could not turn into a victorious social revolution (*ibid.*, p. 15). He points out that two conditions were lacking, the necessary stage of development of the productive forces and the related maturity of the proletariat. However, although we must not—today less than ever—underestimate the moral importance of this heroic historical model for the proletarian battle of emancipation, we should only use it in relation to the question of the structure of the proletarian state if we also point out, for each concrete instance of comparison, the structural differences and the enormous shift in the social foundations which have taken place since then. In *State and Revolution* Lenin hardly pays attention to this.

The soviets had become empty shells and Lenin's theory of the state with its dialectical contradiction between authoritarian revolution and primitive democracy had been definitively transformed to conform to his unequivocally authoritarian theory of the party. And the authoritarian party had found its linear continuation in the actual structure of the state.

Thus the decisive importance of the prerevolutionary form of organization for the establishment of the proletarian state becomes clear beyond any doubt. It is true that many different forces bore on the final shape of things in this area also. For the seizure of power, apart from the organization of the proletarian party, the nature of its connection with other social strata, as well as their organizational maturity, plays a decisive part. The weaker the organization of the other strata, the sooner, in keeping with the immanent tendency of a hierarchical party, they can be eliminated again; but the greater also is the possibility for a democratically organized party to enlarge the democratic basis of the proletarian state from the very beginning. The Russian example is classic for that narrowing of the governmental basis which most gravely jeopardizes the chances of a proletarian democracy, as Rosa Luxemburg, as well as Martov and Dan, showed again and again. This narrowing down is caused not only by foreign and military policy, that is, by inevitable trends, but also by the natural unfolding of the party structure and its imposition upon the structure of the state. Rosa Luxemburg rightly notes with regard to this point that proletarian dictatorship is defined by the way it applies democracy, not by the way it abolishes democracy; it consists of energetic, determined encroachments upon the duly vested rights and economic conditions of bourgeois society, without which the socialist revolution cannot materialize.[12]

The actual basis, however, of the supplantation of Lenin's theory of the state by his theory of the party resides not only in the strength of this autocratic party organization; the primitivity of Lenin's image of democracy, all too restricted as it was by the ideas of the Paris Commune, hardly takes into account the technical complexity of the governmental apparatus of the twentieth century. The Russian example

---

[12] See *op. cit.*, p. 116, and Martov's "Thesen über die soziale Weltrevolution und die Aufgaben der Sozialdemokratie," *Der Kampf*, XX, 237.

has shown that primitive democracy is soon displaced by an oligarchical bureaucracy that will dominate the state and the party. For this reason the question of the size of the bureaucracy and of its necessary limitation to technical functions, as well as its separation from political decision-making, coincides with the question whether a proletarian democracy is possible. Thus, the party organization not only fashions the shape of the revolutionary battle of the proletariat; it can become decisive—as the Russian example shows—for the structure of the proletarian state itself. The Central European workers' movement must not ignore these Russian organizational experiences. Lenin's party demonstrates to us the inestimable importance of a solid political organization, dominated by a central will, for especially difficult periods during the struggle of the working class. But it also shows that the lack of a democratic foundation constantly conjures up inner party conflicts; that wherever there is insufficient confidence, the broad proletarian strata will fail to be integrated; and that this failure of mass integration will be compensated by increasing emphasis on the repressive power of the state.

This, however, jeopardizes both proletarian democracy inside the party and the possibility of transition to democratic institutions on the state level for the great mass of the working people. The great historical task of the European working class will consist in finding the "middle road" securing the decisive role of a solid proletarian organization during the last stage of the power struggle, as well as the vitally needed confidence of the whole working population. For according to the rich experiences gained during the last decade, only the combination of these two factors will bring about the final victory of proletarian democracy through which the rule of the proletariat, as the rule of the vast majority in the interest of the vast majority, can come into being. This was the basic motivation of Marx's whole effort.

WEIMAR—AND WHAT THEN?

— — —

AN ANALYSIS OF A CONSTITUTION

Any extant constitutional legislation can only be the product of revolution. Where the revolution is a politically creative act in the history of classes, legislation marks merely slight changes in essentially vegetating societies. Legislative reform drives possess no dynamic independent of revolutions. In all historical periods they can be carried forward only as long as there remain after-effects from kicks and blows dealt out during the preceding convulsion, and only within the framework of that reform of society which that convulsion bequeathed to the world. That is the essential point of the problem.

ROSA LUXEMBURG, Sozialreform oder Revolution

THE ORIGINS OF THE REPUBLIC

IN BISMARCK'S REICH the people were ruled by allied dynasties together with allied bureaucracies. Prussia, represented through its Hohenzollern monarchy, exercised a predominant position constitutionally and politically. The rule of the Hohenzollern monarchy meant rule of the aristocracy and of the army which was so intimately intertwined with it. The traditional position which the army inherited from precapitalist times achieved a new significance and function as a consequence of the power-political tendencies within modern Germany, with its strong but politically powerless proletarian population.

This translation of "Weimar—und was dann?" is published by permission of Suhrkamp Verlag, Frankfurt/Main.

Besides these bases of German constitutional life, around the turn of the century various groups of industrialists came to exercise an influence which was quite uncontrolled by public opinion. Their influence grew increasingly stronger, but never achieved the continuity of that exercised by the aristocracy and the bureaucracy. After late August, 1916, the government had all but passed from the stage, and in its place had appeared the military dictatorship of General Ludendorff. He was opposed by the *Reichstag* majority, consisting of the Majority Social Democrats, the Center, the Progressive People's party of Naumann's coloration, and the left wing of the National Liberals. But they were at the same time his captives. For all these groups had been ready to sign a political truce with the ruling powers. In so doing, these elected representatives of the majority of the German people threw away the only possibility though which their wills might have decisively affected decision-making. The German Social Democratic party also joined this political truce. It thus forgot the lessons of the French Revolution, especially those of the year 1793, which had taught that periods of extreme danger can also be periods of political rejuvenation.

Whereas the workers in the Allied countries received for their war services on behalf of capitalist governments not only nominal wage increases but also nominal representation in their governments (e.g., Munitions Minister Thomas, today chairman of the International Labor Office in Geneva), in Germany they received only nominal wage increases. Dictator Ludendorff blocked the way which Bethmann-Hollweg had at least wanted to keep open. On July 6, 1917, when its intellectual leader, Deputy Erzberger, read out the peace resolution of the *Reichstag* majority, the political truce ceased being a two-sided pact and became the dictate of the dictator-general. The desire for a peace based on conciliation, which the *Reichstag* majority had espoused in accord with the will of the Social Democratic and Center voters, was crushed in the struggle between the *Reichstag* and the general from which the general emerged as victor. Ludendorff's rule was an intermezzo between the Hohenzollern monarchy and the parliamentary democracy. Although not constitutionally sanctioned, it was patiently acquiesced in by the bourgeoisie and the aristocracy. The monarchy, in terms of its older social and political significance, was not overthrown through a popular rising but was superseded by the seizure of power of General Ludendorff. Even if Ludendorff's gamble had come off, the reestablishment of the monarchy as it had existed until 1916 would have been blocked by the influence of heavy industry, which had given Ludendorff's rule its political imprint.[1]

As the dictatorship was defeated and the old political and military system of Central Europe broke down, the dictator himself selected his old opponent, the bourgeois–Social Democratic *Reichstag* majority, as his heir. Thus there developed the need so to alter Bismarck's constitution as to make it conform to the new situation of rule by the parliamentary majority. The parliamentary system was in principle established through the introduction of the rule which required that the chancellor maintain the confidence of the *Reichstag* for the conduct of his office. This constitutional amendment, which meant a change of the entire constitutional system, occurred in a legal manner with the approval of the monarch, who had been reduced to insignificance ever since 1916. A government on a parliamentary basis, the first coalition government, was formed with the participation of the Majority Social Democrats.[2] When, then, in November 1918, the revolution spread from Kiel throughout Germany, doing away with the constitution which had been amended in accord with the will of the *Reichstag* majority, it could be seen as possibly significant in one of two different ways. Either it was nothing more than a reaction of the masses, who believed that they must finally free themselves from the pressures which had been bearing down on them, but who had not yet realized that the abdication of the old system had been sanctioned through this constitutional amendment and that peace—in whatever form—was in the offing. In that case the reaction of the masses had to be directed primarily against those insignificant supernumeraries, the land princes, but beyond that it could have an effect at most in the sense of an elemental push for a unitary state. Or it could also be that the revolting masses were not satisfied with a democratization of the

---

[1] In this section the author is indebted for valuable insights to Arthur Rosenberg's book, *Die Entstehung der Deutschen Republik* (Berlin, 1928).

[2] It is indeed noteworthy that the present Reich Minister of Justice, Bredt, in a contribution to the *Preussische Jahrbücher*, has expressed the opinion that in view of the course of events of the last decade the revolution has not served any long-term historical function. In his view the constitutional reality of today is identical with the constitutional reality of October, 1918, based on the amended Bismarckian constitution.

constitution and that they strove for a direct realization of socialism. The pace of developments has shown that the masses, even many of those who were in the ranks of the Independent Social Democrats, sought to achieve through the revolution only the overthrow of the dynasties. For the rest their demands emphasized social issues strongly, but on the whole did not go beyond the framework of bourgeois democracy. Their goals were so diverse that the bureaucratic particularist influences, which continued undiminished after the overthrow of the dynasties, were able to make the revolutionary movement follow their lead. The demand for a unitary state, which would have been quite consistent with a bourgeois-capitalist rationalization attempt, was for these reasons doomed to failure.[3] In view of the lack of broad popular participation it is possible to bypass the question of whether an attempt to carry the German revolution forward, as Rosa Luxemburg and Karl Liebknecht advocated, might have had a chance of success under the given circumstances. On the other hand, it is certainly clear that the methods through which these revolutionary circles were repulsed gave the military, under the leadership of the imperial officers, an influence which was later often enough used to force back the entire working class, or which was at least played out against it.

Even before the final fate of the revolution was clearly decided, ties were forged elsewhere which had the greatest significance for the origins of the Weimar Constitution. In October, 1918, the employers and the unions initiated a series of conferences under the leadership of Hugo Stinnes and Karl Legien which resulted on November 15, 1918, in an agreement which was to be implemented through a central working association (*Arbeitsgemeinschaft*) founded at that time. It was significant for the relationship between economic and political power

[3] When Friedrich Meinecke in his book *Die Idee der Staatsräson* (Munich and Berlin, 1924) describes how tragicomical the effect of *raison d'état* was when Kurt Eisner crawled into the just then empty shell of Bavarian statehood, his statement does indeed not apply to Kurt Eisner. Eisner and his collaborator Gustav Landauer did not want to carry on the traditional trade of governing; their policy was an attempt to lead a new concept of federalism to victory, a concept which had nothing to do with the *raison d'état* of the old particularism. Meinecke's observations, however, may very well be justified if applied to the majority of Eisner's southwest and north German Socialist antagonists. The sentence which Remmele cites complacently in his book on the revolution in Baden: "The battalion takes its orders from the reservist Remmele," typifies that kind of revolution which in its effects, as well as in its ideological basis, was nothing more than a change of elites.

in the revolution of 1918 that the programmatic formalization of the future role of the trade unions, as laid down in the *Proclamation to the German People* of the Council of People's Representatives (*Rat der Volksbeauftragten*) of November 12, 1918, was really nothing more than the result of just that Stinnes-Legien Agreement. Thus the trade unions were assured of their future position in the economic process, and were guaranteed their new rights only in a very formal way through an act of the revolutionary powers. In reality these rights were granted through an agreement with the employers' association. Through this arrangement the trade unions proclaimed that they expected to be treated as fully equal and legitimate factors in economic life, and the entrepreneurs saw the need of agreeing to these demands. On the other hand, this agreement could have had a meaningful effect only under a political system in which capital and labor were granted equal rights, which would not have been possible in a socialist state. Thus the fate of the future constitution over which the politically influential structures, the Council of People's Representatives and the Workers' and Soldiers' Councils, had not yet achieved clarity was in effect preempted. It is not our task here to evaluate the historical justification for the decision of the unions. It can only be determined that they then chose the path of collaboration with the entrepreneurs in accordance with an evaluation of political and economic relationships which was also shared by the majority of the German population. Just as the building blocks of our contemporary constitutional structure date from this period, so too do the bitter struggles between the partners to this treaty. For whereas the entrepreneurs regarded this arrangement as marking the maximum of their concessions, the whittling down of which they then made the goal of their subsequent policy, the trade unions saw the new achievement as providing a peaceful and riskless point of departure for the further pursuit of their socialist goals.

The political path which was to be followed in the future was marked by the constitutional amendment of October, 1918. The Stinnes-Legien Agreement of November, 1918, proclaimed the will of those trade union circles which dominated the labor movement to follow the route charted by the constitutional amendment of October, 1918, despite the change in political circumstances. It was left to the Reich

Conference of Workers' and Soldiers' Councils, which met in Berlin from December 16 through December 19, to make the formal decision that the future fate of Germany would be entrusted to a national assembly which would emerge from general elections. This was followed by the elections to the National Assembly of January 19, 1919. As a matter of public law, the revolution found its formal ending in the National Assembly's law for the establishment of a provisional government of February 10, 1919, which also opened the way for the Weimar Constitution.

DEMOCRACY AND DICTATORSHIP

Germany, France, England, and the United States of America are, together with other more or less important states of the world, democratic according to their written or, in the case of England, unwritten constitutions. The more states profess to be democracies, and the more they get in the habit—as in the United States—of referring each of their political acts to democratic principles, the more democracy runs the risk of losing real meaning and of declining to a form under which hide the most contradictory political principles. The poor delimitation, and therefore the increasing lack of meaning, of the concept "democracy" is clearly revealed through the fact that in general the above-named states are considered democracies only because they grant voting privileges to the largest possible number of their citizens. (R. Thoma.) This interpretation of the concept of democracy appears dubious, not very functional, and historically incorrect. With reference to it Jean-Jacques Rousseau's view that democracy is so perfect an institution that it is fit only for gods but not for men would be incomprehensible. Universal franchise has been introduced in very many countries since 1919 without this having caused anybody to believe that such states had therefore reached anything like "perfection." And it would appear that democracy is granted a more just appreciation by Rousseau's skepticism as to its implementation potential than it is by those who believe that the mere abolition of franchise barriers will lead to the realization of democracy.

Since the nineteenth century the decisive problems of democracy

WEIMAR—AND WHAT THEN? 39

have been social in character. In the first decades of the century not only was the question of national unification and freedom indissolubly joined with democracy, but both paved the way for each other. In Germany and Italy, the two countries which were then not yet nationally unified, democracy really appeared on the scene in the name of national unity. But it soon developed that a democracy which contained no other principle than that of the national unity of a politically free people could not be the last and decisive stage of democracy. The proletarian strata, with whose sacrifices national unity and freedom had been won, soon noted that they had only changed their masters; they wanted to move beyond national democracy so as to achieve social democracy. The enemies of the workers soon perceived that the dialectic inherent in democracy would lead to that which the bourgeois fears most: to the disappearance of even the bare possibility of maintaining political equilibrium. For that can only reappear after the realization of the most basic idea of democracy, when each particle of potential influence has become converted into real power.

It is from this perspective that we can understand the complaint of Guizot, the typical representative of the French bourgeoisie of the 1840s, when he speaks fearfully of social democracy as an echo of the old social war cries which in his days rose and echoed within all sections of society. It was Karl Marx who revealed the real essence of the democratic state in the era of bourgeois rule in a formulation which had direct reference to the French constitution of October 23, 1848, but which applies equally to the Reich constitution of August 11, 1919.

The basic contradiction of this constitution consists in this: through the establishment of universal suffrage it places political power in the hands of just those classes, the proletariat, the peasants, and the petty bourgeoisie, whose social slavery it seeks to perpetuate. And it removes the guarantee of political power from that class, the bourgeoisie, whose old social power it sanctions. It makes its political rule conditional on certain democratic conditions which at any moment might help the hostile classes to victory and which might thus place in jeopardy the very basis of bourgeois society itself. From the one group the constitution demands that it not proceed beyond political emancipation to social emancipation, and from the other that it not regress beyond social restoration to political restoration.

The "comprehensive contradiction" of which Karl Marx speaks also more or less characterizes the constitutions which are in effect today. Some, like that of the United States and the nineteenth-century constitutions, do not recognize the problem of social democracy. Others recognize the tasks of social democracy, as do the German and Austrian constitutions of the postwar period, but do not enable the relevant principles to achieve enough of a breakthrough.

We are indebted to Max Adler's work *Die Staatsauffassung des Marxismus* (1922) for reasserting the distinction between political and social democracy which all the great political thinkers of the last century were aware of, and for making it pertinent in its full incisiveness for our contemporary political life. "Political democracy" is a typical tautology. Etymologically democracy means the political rule of the people (more specifically, the rule of the people in the *polis*, the ancient city-state). The coupling of the word "political" with the word "democracy" emphasizes that thereby reference is made only to the political rule of the people, and that nothing is said about those economic power relationships which in the twentieth century have become the determinant ones. The difference between social and political democracy is by no means arbitrary, as is suggested by those critics in the Social Democratic camp who claim that one can never decide where political democracy ends and where social democracy begins. German constitutional development in the recent period shows that this distinction is by no means idle theory, for it is only with reference to it that the contemporary type of constitutional system can be adequately recognized.

The principle of majority rule is comprehensible only with reference to that social homogeneity which incorporates the principle of a democratic value community in our time.[4] Only in a society with a Socialist social structure do majority decisions not imply doing violence to those who are outvoted; here majority decision means only the application of a tested technique for settling differences over which means are technically the best ones for achieving the principles which are adhered to by all. The less agreement there is about the preconditions and the social principles of the society, the more the

[4] Again we wish to refer the reader to Max Adler's *Politische und Soziale Demokratie* (Berlin, 1926), ch. 10.

ruthless application of the majority principle tends to transform it into a technique for oppression, with the general will becoming a phantom.

If within political democracies the majority principle is utilized to forestall the fulfillment of the social demands of the workers, as is today the case almost everywhere, then these democracies contain, despite all disguises, a considerable portion of bourgeois dictatorship. For the essence of bourgeois dictatorship consists in the maintenance of the economic predominance of the bourgeoisie by all available means. The crucial point on which proletarian dictatorship differs from the bourgeois variety is that, while the one serves the maintenance of an existing social order, the other serves to realize a new social order. This idea of the proletarian dictatorship has guided all thinkers of the proletariat, whether they viewed the proletarian dictatorship more from the technical-economic aspect, as did Karl Marx, or from the political aspect, as did Max Adler. They all agreed on the essentially revolutionary and uprooting character of the proletarian dictatorship. Fascist Italy offers a clear example of the difference between bourgeois and proletarian dictatorship. Fascism in its initial stages gave the appearance through its manifold syndicalist elements of belonging among the proletarian dictatorships. It appeared to want to bring about a thoroughgoing change in the total social and political conditions. But in the course of the years it has become increasingly clear that it constitutes an example of purely bourgeois dictatorship which aims at maintaining the existing social order.[5]

Article 48 of the Reich constitution is supposed to constitute an exception to the rules of democracy. The ruling classes in a socially heterogeneous democracy are often not in the position to bring about by democratic means decisions enjoying general support. Therefore they are forced from time to time to exclude the democratic representative body, so as to achieve by means of a dictatorship what the will of large segments of the people prevents them from achieving in a

[5] The fundamentally bourgeois character of the Italian dictatorship does not contradict the fact that fascism has successfully attempted to convince itself and others that it represents a fundamental rejuvenation of the entire political status of the Italian people. A system's political ideology must be clearly separated from its actual materialization. Every political system which intends to stay in power must perceive itself as a realization of a political innovation. That the official German republicanism cannot even do this proves the weakness of its position.

legal manner. Depending on the given situation, democracy may be fully transformed into a permanent dictatorship (sovereign dictatorship,[6] as in Italy), or democracy may be restored after the opposition has been knocked out (Saxony, Thuringia, 1923).[7] In the modern world it has occurred only once that the preconditions for democracy were at the same time the preconditions for dictatorship. The Paris Commune of 1871 is the example of a population shaped by nearly equal political and social preconditions which in an extraordinary case exercised dictatorial powers without at the same time departing from the basis of democracy. But apart from this case the relationship between democracy and dictatorship has so far not been consistent with the way in which bourgeois constitutional politicians like to portray it. Because democracies have always been only political democracies, the constitutional institution of emergency powers (temporary dictatorship) has usually only served the purpose of allowing force to be used to reintegrate the proletariat into the existing political order when it could not be silenced by traditional parliamentary means.

In this context it must be mentioned that the frequent use of Article 48 in the postwar years must in part be attributed to the inadequate parliamentary consciousness of the bourgeois parties, who still saw themselves all too readily as the irresponsible critics of the actions of a bureaucracy which was largely beyond their influence. It was only in the course of a slow republicanization process that the German bourgeoisie perceived that a decisive share of political power now lay within its grasp.

The point at which bourgeois political democracy is transformed into bourgeois dictatorship is not clearly definable. Since each bourgeois democracy necessarily carries within it an element of dictatorship, it is often only a question of expediency whether a regime masks itself externally as a democratic or dictatorial one. The rule of the economically powerful class has usually been imposed at least in regard

---

[6] For the theoretical basis of this concept, see Carl Schmitt, *Die Diktatur* (Munich and Leipzig, 1927). Max Adler in his *Staatsauffassung des Marxismus* (Vienna, 1922) has also utilized this terminology.

[7] Left-wing state governments with Communist participation in Saxony and Thuringia were forcibly removed from office by the Reich government acting on the basis of Art. 48, par. 1 of the constitution. (Ed. note.)

to the general guidelines of foreign, military, and economic policy in those countries in which the presence of a well-organized workers' movement sets certain limits to the bourgeois class rule within a democratic framework. This economic predominance of capitalism forms the common background of all bourgeois politics. Thus Mussolini had to appoint a leading banker as minister of finance. And although *Reichsbank* President Schacht already represented the interests of private business, the German coalition government named expert advisers from the Federation of German Industry to attend the Paris conference of 1929. These expert advisers in reality decided what burdens in large part had to be borne by the German proletariat. Since the bourgeois strata struggle everywhere to maintain the capitalist system, the fundamentals and essential problems of bourgeois rule are fairly uniform no matter through what political form it might be exercised. Large portions of the bourgeoisie quite rightly regard the difference between political democracy, temporary dictatorship according to Article 48 of the constitution, or permanent dictatorship with suspension of the constitution purely as a matter of expediency. The decision is mainly made from the point of view of what best serves the maintenance of the economic status quo.

By contrast, the socialist constitutional position must weigh all constitutional institutions, those of democracy as well as those of dictatorship, in regard to the concrete question of how these institutions will change the position of the working class. For state and governmental forms are in themselves never good or bad. Each class must decide on its own responsibility whether in a given instance the one or the other form is good or bad for it.

ELECTORAL LAWS

In Germany there is increasing sentiment of dissatisfaction with the present electoral system. Critics charge that it is inorganic and incapable of forming a true mirror-image of the will of the population. They believe they perceive in each successive election not a political decision of the German people but the monotonous countenances of near identical party machines. The personality of the deputy is supposed to have fallen victim to the modern mania for quantity, and the representation of interests is supposed to have displaced the representation of ideas. We concede to the critics of the present electoral law all of the facts on which their criticism is based, and nevertheless spring to its defense. We maintain that they completely misunderstand the meaning and significance of the electoral law. Not today, nor at any time in history, has it been the purpose of an electoral law to change social conditions and the political forms conditioned by them. It is not the technical weapon of the electoral system which changes the political or social order; the conditions of human society are changed by politically creative acts based upon social upheavals. None of the many possible electoral systems have ever been introduced by the respective powerholders in order to withdraw support from the existing social order; they have all been introduced with the conscious purpose of maintaining the existing social order.[8] When France, in 1791, introduced an electoral law which tied the franchise to a certain standard of wealth, this restrictive condition had a political purpose. It was to maintain in power the propertied bourgeois strata who had taken over the French government after the fall of the absolute monarchy, and to make political participation impossible for large parts of the poorer population, mainly in radical Paris. In 1793 just this Parisian population which had recently been denied the suffrage helped to power the men who then formed what has unjustly been called the "government of terror." These men had no higher priority than to abolish all property qualifications and to give all citizens the right to vote. After their overthrow property qualifications were once more introduced in order to guarantee power to the well-to-do and, from the standpoint of the bourgeoisie, more thoughtful and prudent strata. The *régime censitaire*,[9] so dear to the heart of the bourgeoisie of the first half of the nineteenth century, which

---

[8] In the Bismarckian Empire, however, it was the proletariat which profited from this "cunning of the Idea." Universal suffrage, introduced as a weapon of the conservative government against particularism and the propertied bourgeoisie, turned into a promotional platform of a proletariat which had become self-sufficient.

[9] Statutory property qualifications for the suffrage. (Ed. note.)

was enforced in Prussia until 1918 as the three-class electoral law, was a convenient means to prevent the working class from exercising that political influence which was its due. These examples make clear that each electoral system can only be evaluated according to the goal which one seeks to achieve by it. No electoral law is good or bad, correct or false, of itself; so long as social cleavages exist in the world, the suitability of an electoral law is determined only by the political purpose which one seeks to achieve with it.

It is only from this point of view that we can understand the electoral law of Soviet Russia. It excludes large strata of the Russian population from electoral participation, is based upon indirect election and, indeed, often lets voting occur publicly under the supervision of the state apparatus. This electoral mode can scarcely have the purpose of determining exactly what opinion the Russian population, and especially the peasant in the countryside, holds of Bolshevism. For this the system is unsuited. The same is true of the electoral system of Fascist Italy where, under the electoral law of May, 1928, the candidate lists are put together by the Grand Council of the Fascist party on the basis of the suggestions of the various fascist organizations. This leaves the voters no other choice than to vote for the candidates of the single official list, to vote "No," or to abstain from voting. In both countries the elections signify nothing more than signals of acclamation or warnings which do not commit the powerholders. It is only one of many means through which the rulers cultivate the favor of the masses. Quite apart from the conformist terror which is usually associated with it, public voting provides an opportunity for binding the broad popular masses to the ruling strata. Thus the electoral systems of Russia and Italy do not at all have the purpose of providing a basis for political decisions. Their specific political value consists purely in attaching the popular masses to the existing power system without having to grant them any compensating influence.

By contrast the electoral systems of the parliamentary democracies have another significance. In England, France, and the United States the election result itself determines which party groups shall take power. Of decisive importance, however, is the fact that the differences between the parties, up to the most recent past, were determined less by policy issues than by their partnership in the election game (*Ämterpatronage*). The Bismarckian electoral law [10] was liquidated as the liberal bourgeois era in Germany was superseded by the Weimar Constitution, and a proportional representation electoral law based on lists gave great power to the party leaders. This system expresses the fact that the idyllic era of the bourgeoisie has ended. The proletariat marches with equal rights into the arena of democracy. The list system electoral law, introduced at the same time, has effected a clear change in the inherent sense and purpose that electoral laws have had in parliamentary democratic states. German elections have certain similarities to those carried on under the Bolshevik and fascist electoral laws in so far as they too do not decisively affect the stream of political events. The experiences of the postwar period have thoroughly taught the German proletariat that even a very large number of parliamentary seats does not signify decisive political power. The old dream of the 51 per cent majority has been finally revealed as that which it has always been—a crude mechanistic game. On the other hand, the German electoral law shares with the French and Anglo-Saxon ones their freedom and universality. The system of proportional representation in force in Germany causes class boundaries to be mirrored with mathematical exactness, without allowing the political potential of each record-taking to be fully exploited. The impersonality of the electoral law, which is incorporated in the list system and in the large election districts, serves certain circles as the main target for their attacks. But it is only the result of the fact that in the contemporary state the election law is dominated by the carrying out of class antagonisms. The German professors' parliament of the nineteenth century, in which the educated discussed public issues which were decided by others, is gone and cannot be brought back again. It could not be resurrected even through the creation of smaller election districts or through granting the voter greater freedom in the selection of individual deputies. Parliaments are not places in which the educated of a nation discuss cultural matters; parliaments are arenas for the carrying out of the class

10 The *Reichstag* of the German Empire (1871–1918) was elected by universal suffrage in single-member districts, but not by a plurality of votes. In each district, if no candidate obtained an absolute majority in the initial poll, a run-off election was held with the voters' choice limited to the two top candidates. (Ed. note.)

struggle. And the parties,[11] which struggle against each other on the outside as representatives of the employers and workers, are the proper spokesmen of this struggle in parliament.

Reforms would only disguise these facts, not change them. It is more honest to let each voter know which class interests his deputy represents than if the various local notables whom an election reform might possibly bring into parliament were to be "captured" by various organized interests without the knowledge of their voters.[12]

We must be content to recognize that in a democratic state universal suffrage will not by and of itself bring about political decisions for which the way has not been paved by the will of the various groups. Even the freest electoral system can only support a preexisting political will, the intensity of which can be clearly discerned from the election results. Universal and equal suffrage is no substitute for the political will of the proletariat which must be presupposed if the former is to have any meaning for the working class.

THE PARLIAMENT

According to the traditional point of view prevailing in Western countries, it is the task of parliament to accomplish the realization of democracy and its translation into governmental practice. The Weimar Constitution has on the whole followed this tradition, and the National Assembly of 1919 rejected all those amendments of the Independent Socialists (USPD) which sought to build on the experiences of the Russian Revolution.

The power which the text of the constitution grants to parliament

[11] A special chapter on "Party and Deputy" had to be left out because of lack of space. The concept of party as consistently presented by the Social Liberal Radbruch is not acceptable to a Socialist for whom Marxism, while not a dogma, is still the best method for the analysis of social reality. In the reality of class parties there is no room for secret cooperation between adversaries. The "cunning of the Idea," which can modify institutions, has a place only in the realm of historical necessity.

[12] Changes in the electoral law are only necessary with respect to the Reich and *Land* lists. These should be abolished and the extra seats distributed among the individual districts. For by virtue of its existence, the Reich list constitutes a legal guarantee of the party bureaucracy. It protects not only that portion of the party bureaucracy which is necessary but all its existing components.

is great when measured by that accorded to the other state institutions which constitutionally exercise political influence. Apart from the Reich President, whose position must be examined separately, the constitution bestows certain permanent political influence in the first place on the *Reichsrat*.[13] But its character as a representative of the various *Land* interests lets it become a significant counterweight to the *Reichstag* only in those instances where it is a question of guaranteeing the specific financial and administrative concerns of the *Länder*. The *Reichsrat* has up to now made no difficulties for decisive political decisions of the *Reichstag* which do not lie in this area. And in view of the defensive role into which the *Länder* are being increasingly pushed, it is not likely to do so in the future.

Another constitutional element which can inhibit the decisions of the *Reichstag* or force them to take another direction is the People. The expression "People" is here used in the sense in which it is used in the sections of the Reich constitution dealing with popular referenda. These rules constitute a theoretical undermining of parliamentary power, and they were therefore envisioned in the strictly liberal constitutional draft of Hugo Preuss only in so far as they served to surmount differences of opinion between the highest Reich institutions. The rules which have now become part of the constitution give the people the possibility of going over the head of parliament in order to reject laws which the *Reichstag* has passed or to initiate and pass new laws. However, the people, which means all of the enfranchised population living in a state, can only answer "Yes" or "No" to previously formulated questions which are laid before it. Thus the people are dependent upon the formulation of a question which a public authority or interest group forces upon them. Then there is the fact that actual practice has pointed up significant sources of error in regard to the actual handling of this constitutional problem. According to the prevailing point of view the precondition for the success of a referendum is the participation of half the eligible voters. This practically makes the decision dependent upon the number of nonpartici-

[13] The upper house of the German parliament under the Weimar Constitution. The *Reichsrat* was a federal chamber composed of representatives of the executive governments of the German states. Its veto of bills passed by the *Reichstag* could be overridden by a two-thirds majority vote of the latter or by popular referendum. (Ed. note.)

pants. While this group remains uncounted in the case of elections, it usually tilts the balance against the initiating side in the case of referenda. In addition the government, with reference to the rules of the constitution which reserve to the President the power to initiate referenda on taxation and budget laws, can block the road for almost all popular initiatives. Thus a real constitutional instrument has become a propaganda technique which neither binds the one who utilizes it nor intimidates the one against whom it is directed.

The limited resistance which the parliament has encountered from the other decision-making factors legitimated by the written constitution apparently leaves a wide leeway for its activities. The great constitutional potential possessed by parliament has touched off discussions of its political leadership role, and of the reciprocal relationship between political leaders and parliament. A typical example of this from the socialist point of view is the work of Geyer on *Leader and Masses in Democracy*. Such discussions originate for the most part in a lack of knowledge of the change in significance which parliament has undergone since the beginning of the nineteenth century. At the beginning of the last century the "rule of parliament" was the slogan of the liberal bourgeoisie; under this slogan it fought against the semifeudal monarchy and achieved power. The German bourgeoisie has idealized this historical period which found its expression especially in that France of the 1840s which Karl Marx has so realistically portrayed in his *Class Struggles in France*. Of all this bourgeois glory there remained for Germany only the short dream of the 1848 period. The dreams and the hopes of the educated bourgeoisie in Germany related in reality to the intermediate stage which had developed in France and England after the power position of the feudal monarchy had in fact been broken and while the proletariat was still in the beginnings of its political rise. The dominance of the strata of "property and education" was exercised through parliament and was the basis of the leading role of parliament, the untouchability of which was guaranteed by an electoral system based upon property qualifications (*régime censitaire*). That dominance was exercised in part directly through the parliamentary parties, and in part through the English prime ministerial system which is still so much admired here today. The significance of parliament in the unified Reich of the Bismarckian and post-Bis-

marckian period was built on an essentially negative feeling of identification. Negative also was its most important *de facto* power, that of
approving budgets, which was the jealously guarded source of its political significance.[14] The unity of parliament meant in all cases the unity
of those who were dissatisfied with the ruling system. That unity
dissolved at the moment in which the semifeudal monarchy disappeared as the common enemy, to give way to the achievement after a
delay of at least half a century of just that parliamentary power which
had been so ardently desired. With the breaking apart of the unity of
parliament its power also disappeared. Following Max Weber, the late-
liberal interpretation leaves out of account the real basis of the parliamentary system of the nineteenth century and regards this system only
as a means for the selection of leaders. In so doing, it forgets that
leadership selection is a rather technical function which could only be
exercised by the parliament in that period because of the prevailing
class cohesion of the bourgeoisie. That parliamentarism of the nineteenth century has lost its existential basis in the dualistic class state of
the twentieth century. The technique of leadership selection is now
applied outside of parliament within the various class organizations,
and parliament is only the publicly more visible arena within which the
selected leaders appear. There they proclaim the demands of the various classes, which in the parliamentary debates can be asserted but not
examined as to their correctness. Formally the Weimar Constitution
has excluded the direct economic influence of various interest groups
on parliament. It has also foregone the attempt to lay down constitutionally the spheres of influence of capital and labor; in 1919 there
could only have been a question of settling the influence of the labor
side. The constitution has not been able to prevent the various economic forces from achieving political power positions according to
their respective strengths. Disguised in the form of political parties, the

14 Budgetary matters, which played a significant role in Parliament from 1870
until the outbreak of the war, no longer have any real significance, contrary
to many present-day pronouncements. The majority of the appropriating parties
and the government which is to be controlled belong to the same or allied
interest groups, and the opposition, as a minority, is not in a position to exercise
an effective check. The "self-confident Parliament" of which Hugo Heimann
speaks in his book *Der Reichshaushalt* (p. 27) also belongs to past history, and
day-to-day political practice, with its logrolling, has greatly debased budgetary
practices.

economic power blocs took possession of parliament and utilized its techniques as a simplified and relatively peaceful means of conducting the class struggle, provided this gave them advantages. But they were by no means ready to accept these techniques when in the form of majority decision they threatened to turn against them.

THE BASIC RIGHTS: THE STATE'S
SUBSTANTIVE JURISDICTION

There is a contrast between basic rights as they were transmitted from the eighteenth century and the constitutional principles of democracy, and no one has pointed this out better or more pointedly than Karl Marx. In one of his early writings, *The Holy Family*, especially in the chapter "Critical Blow Against the French Revolution," he emphasized the tension which existed between consciousness of the unitary democratic state and the liberal principle of civil and human rights. This tension was the more significant since it was precisely the French bourgeois revolution which wanted to make these human and basic rights the immanent principle shaping its new antimonarchical state. Marx says there:

Robespierre, Saint-Just, and their party failed because they confused the realist-democratic communal order of antiquity, which rested on the basis of real slavery, with the modern spiritual-democratic representative state which rests on the emancipated slavery of bourgeois society. What a colossal deception to have to recognize and sanction modern bourgeois society—the society of industry, of freewheeling competition, of anarchy and natural and spiritual self-alienation—in the Rights of Man, and then to repress these social manifestations in the individual and to seek to fashion that society's political head according to the ancient model.

With all their freedoms the transmitted basic rights were from the start guarantees of the bourgeois individual against his own state. However, the solemn proclamation of the rights to freedom, property, security, and the right of resistance did not become so significant because these principles in their basic content had long before belonged to the spiritual equipment of the declining eighteenth century.

Rather, the Rights of Man, which were taken over by all subsequent French revolutionary constitutions, contributed to endowing France in the eyes of the rest of the world with that moral greatness and propagandistic effect which to a very great extent constituted the success of revolutionary France. In the founding of the French bourgeois state the Rights of Man had a share which should not be underestimated. They lost much of this solidifying power in the nineteenth century; then the task became one of adjusting to the achievements of the bourgeois state and they proved unable to surmount the latter's basically antipolitical and asocial content. The gulf would have grown wider still if in the nineteenth century the bourgeoisie had not urgently required the protective function of the basic rights in order to strengthen its class position in the face of the numerous absolutist remnants.

When in 1919 the new German republic required a new constitution, the taking over of the basic rights in their transmitted form was out of the question. For in the face of the existing strength of socialist currents these basic rights were not an adequate constituent principle for the new state. Of all the participants in the constitutional deliberations, the parliamentarian Friedrich Naumann saw most clearly that the new basic rights could not follow in the dead-end Liberal track, lest they be reduced to meaninglessness. Naumann saw that a new state had evolved in Russia which was determined to achieve a breakthrough for socialist principles and which had expressed this will in a propagandistically highly effective manner in its basic rights, the "Rights of the Working and Exploited People." It was the idea of the social state with which Naumann confronted the individualism of the liberal basic rights on the one hand and the workers' commitment to socialism on the other. Naumann anticipated that the representatives of the capitalist economic order would show enough empathy and readiness for self-limitation to conform to the policies of a humane national state even if it substantially met the demands of the working class. Naumann's succinct headings, as well as the final draft of the basic rights, were developed with the intention of providing a directional guide and a binding program for the state's activity. They defined the jurisdiction of the state. After answering the question of how the state organs should be constituted, the constitution answers the question of where they should be effective. Unlike the Western liberal constitutions, it does not seek to answer this question with a list of prohibitions but rather through positive stipulations. The state thus draws culture as well as the economy into the realm of its regulatory activity.

But the problem arises of whether the areas about which the constitutional legislators wanted to draw up long-term rules were really at their disposition to the extent necessary. The extremely instructive originating process of the Weimar basic rights showed that this was by no means the case. It developed that in certain areas where the legislator wanted to lay down rules in the name of the whole people, others had already made themselves at home in the name of a part of the people. This held for the church in regard to schools, and for the civil servants in regard to the most basic domain of the state, the administration. Thus by the end of the constitutional deliberations, relatively little was left of the original comprehensive character of the basic rights for which the open-minded ideas of Naumann's social state had been extremely influential, even though its outward formulation had been rejected. For in the meantime the various interest groups had been seized by a fear of the insatiability of socialism. Following the example of the German *Länder* governments, they had demanded the anchoring of their vested rights, that is, their spheres of interest. All claims to a constitutional anchoring were given satisfaction, including those of the agricultural, business, and commercial middle classes (*Mittelstand*). And since all wanted to be anchored down, there was not much left to do for the force which supposedly dominated the constitution, socialism, but also to let itself be anchored down. The Weimar system of basic rights, which is often inexactly labeled a compromise, consisted in reality of this row of anchors. The designation "compromise" could open the door to errors.[15] Compromise is usually understood to mean a solution which is brought about by concessions from both sides and through which a particular problem area is regulated finally and unambiguously for a given time period. Such concessions were not part of the basic rights arrangement of the Weimar Constitution. What was

[15] This state of affairs can be designated as a "compromise on a dilatory formula," as Carl Schmitt has done in his *Verfassungslehre* (Munich, 1928); that is, an agreement of the negotiating parties on a formula which postpones the real substantive decision. For clarity's sake I would rather not associate the term "compromise" with such a state of affairs.

done there repeatedly, rather, was to take from Naumann's social-political thesaurus various ornamental preambles or introductory articles,
and to append to them clauses based on the most contradictory cultural
and social perspectives. Thus the Weimar basic rights are in their
essentials not a compromise but constitute rather a unique linking and
acknowledgment of the most varied value systems, which is without
prededent in constitutional history. The more significant of the manifold influences which participated in the creation of the basic rights
were the socialist, the liberal-capitalist, and the clerical influences reflecting political catholicism. Thus failed the plan to incorporate in the
basic rights an unambiguous social and cultural program which would
unify the nation and be realizable. The implementation or nonimplementation of the economic and cultural futuristic goals which were
laid down and offered in the basic rights depended upon the strength
the various interest groups were able to muster in carrying through
those of their programmatic points which had been inserted in the
basic rights.

The first section, entitled "The Individual," contains most of the
bourgeoisie's "old-liberal inheritance." This section deals mainly with
protecting the individual against encroachment by the government
administration. These bourgeois-*rechtsstaatliche* formulations are related to the earlier monarchical state within which the citizen as an
individual stood defenseless against the arbitrariness of an absolutist administrative apparatus. The bourgeois administrative apparatus, far
more rational than the absolutist one, admits of no special treatment of
individuals. Furthermore, the single threatened citizen needy of safeguard barely exists any more in the age of associations, so that these
rules have lost in significance to the degree that we have taken them
for granted. Only a few of these formulations have a significance beyond that of the protection of the individual. One such is the sentence
which opens this constitutional section: "All Germans are equal before
the law." Its significance is, however, more than problematical. Historically it developed out of the citizens' justified fear of unequal
application of the laws and administrative arbitrariness. But today
there is a lively argument as to whether it does not have the more
important role of serving as protection against discriminatory legislation and limiting the legislature itself. This interpretation of the prin-

ciple is to be found mainly in the judicial decisions of the United States. There the Supreme Court has long relied upon the principle of the equality of all men before the law to throttle a modest program of social legislation in so far as it ruled workmen's protection legislation unconstitutional as violating the freedom of contract. Both the old interpretation and the new one, which inflates the applicability of the equality principle beyond measure, constitute only incompletely developed way-stations which do not do justice to the true meaning of the sentence. Since, according to the more recent point of view, the acts of legislative organs may be examined as to their compatibility with the criteria of equality, this requires special watchmen, namely, the supposedly independent judiciary. These judges are already claiming the right to test laws as to their constitutionality. For the subjectivity of parliament there is thus substituted the subjectivity of a collegiate bench of judges, a body which is intellectually and socially much less comprehensive, and which is entrusted with a task that is in truth purely political. For there is no such thing as a juridically measurable abstract equality. It is not the task of judges to evaluate according to their own standards historically contingent concepts of the equality of others. Thus the principle of equality before the law, which was justified in the age of monarchy because it served as a defense against arbitrariness, will remain a fiction or something worse, an instrument of reactionary forces. It will do so as long as the formal, political equality of rights and opportunities has not developed into substantive, that is, economic, equality, and as long as economic equality has not transformed in a merely legal sense equal possibilities into concretely equal chances of their realization. Today this clause serves only as a guarantee of the existing order, and it enjoys an increasing popularity among all capitalist interest groups because it is used as a blocking device against all changes of the economic status quo. Under the guise of the equality principle the existing system of economic distribution is sanctioned in all its inequality. The adaptation of the old constitutional principle of equality before the law thus shows the ambiguity of such seemingly clear constitutional rules. The principle of equality before the law has in reality three different meanings for as many eras. In the early liberal era it served as a defense against administrative arbitrariness, in the advanced capitalist period it serves as a guarantee of the existing social order, and in the socialist era it will serve to establish a basis of economic equality. It is only through clarifying its function within any given social order that the real significance of the clause of equality before the law can be revealed.[16]

The problematical attempt at regulation of economic life is of decisive significance for the fate of the Weimar constitutional edifice as a whole. In regard to the main question, private property or collective economy, the Weimar Constitution remains true to the method described above. Apart from commonplaces, which bind no one and on which no one can base himself, it grants equal status to capitalism, which seeks to perpetuate private property, and to socialism, which presupposes communal property.

It tolerates private property but explicitly foresees the possibility of its transformation into communal property. In view of the fact that the alternative mention of the two economic systems envisions the possibility of transforming the one into the other, an opinion has developed which sees Article 153 [17] of the Reich constitution as no longer unequivocally guaranteeing the concept of property. This view makes much of the fact that the possibility of expropriation is even mentioned. But such a view can only be based upon an ignorance of the rules regarding private property which have been contained in all bourgeois constitutions since 1789. For especially in this regard the Weimar Constitution has closely followed the transmitted examples of earlier bourgeois constitutions. They all protect private property with more or less pathos, and yet foresee the possibility of expropriation

[16] A specific application of this principle can be found in Article 134: "All citizens without distinction contribute to all public burdens in proportion to their means, according to the provisions of the laws." This statement is found in the section on social relations, which has not been discussed in detail here. The scarcely community-oriented practice of German tax legislation indicates to what extent this provision has remained in accord with the late-capitalist "concept of equality."

[17] Article 153 reads: "Property is guaranteed by the Constitution. Its content and limits are defined by the laws. Expropriation can only take place for the public benefit and on a legal basis. Adequate compensation shall be granted, unless a Reich law orders otherwise. In the case of dispute concerning the amount of compensation, it shall be possible to submit the matter to the ordinary civil courts, unless Reich laws determine otherwise. Compensation must be paid if the Reich expropriates property belonging to the Lands, Communes, or public utility associations. Property carries obligations. Its use shall also serve the common good." (Ed. note.)

against adequate indemnification in exceptional cases when the public interest calls for the satisfaction of a specific concrete need. Thus the traditional expropriation procedure of Article 153 does not do away with private property. It can be contended that Clause 1 of Article 153—"Property is guaranteed by the Constitution. Its content and limits are defined by the laws"—allows the legislator a much freer hand in limiting private property than was the case in earlier centuries. For even though it maintains private property, the article allows the substance and limits of private property to be defined much more by laws than is the case in the other modern European constitutions. The bourgeois legal theoreticians have, however, not shared this thoroughly plausible point of view, which was surely favored by a part of the constituent assembly. On the contrary, they have successfully sought to narrow the area within which the state can take over property without indemnification even more than was the case under the legal conditions of the nineteenth century. The decisions of the *Reichsgericht* show how exclusively Article 153 has been utilized in constitutional and administrative practice for the purpose of protecting private property. They have widened the expropriation concept to such an extent that the state has been made liable to pay compensation for every interference with private property in the public interest. In conjunction with the previously mentioned clause of equality before the law, Article 153 has become a legal bulwark shielding the capitalist economic system.

Articles 155 and 156 [18] foresee the possibility of socialization and of

[18] Article 155 reads: "The distribution and utilization of the land shall be supervised by state authorities in a manner to prevent abuse and with the object of ensuring a healthy dwelling to every German and to all German families, especially those with numerous children, living and working quarters in accordance with their needs. War veterans shall be particularly considered in the enactment of homestead laws. Real estate, the acquisition of which is necessary for housing purposes, for the promotion of settlements and land cultivation or to improve agriculture, may be expropriated. All entails (*Fideikommisse*) shall be dissolved. The cultivation and utilization of the soil is a duty owed by a landowner to the community. An increase in the value of land which arises without the expenditure of work or capital on the property shall be utilized for the common benefit. All treasures of the soil and all natural forces of economic utility are under the supervision of the State. Private mining rights (*Regale*) shall be transferred to the State by legislation."
Article 156 reads: "The Reich may, without prejudice to the right of compensation, by law transfer to public ownership economic enterprises suitable for

forced amalgamations of enterprises. But the Reich constitution makes each socialization measure dependent upon the alternative economic system, capitalism based upon the private ownership of the means of production, in that the rules about expropriation are also applicable to socialization. Thus each socialization measure is treated as though it were an instance of expropriation, requiring adequate indemnification. The ever present weight of the status quo, in this case of private property, is strengthened by the fact that the constitution fails to settle the question of which is to be the dominant economic system, leaving as it does the possibility of socialization dependent upon subsequent implementation laws. This arrangement, in conjunction with the expropriation clause, has done something to favor the development of conditions under which there has been a total absence of socialization of individual enterprises. In the area of land and real property, homestead laws have been passed to implement the socialization provisions of Article 155. These laws, even if they had been implemented more intensively than has actually been the case, would still not have compensated for the decisive failure of the constitution to recognize the real enemy of every democratic system. From the days of Tiberius Gracchus through those of the Agrarian Law of the French Revolution to the present day, the question of land distribution has been essentially a question of setting a maximal size to large landholdings. Instead of dealing with it through immediate land redistribution on the basis of a constitutional provision, the Weimar Constitution ignores this question and provides merely for the possibility of individual expropriation measures for the benefit of small land- and homeowners. Thus it not only impedes the economic solution of the most important

---

socialization, applying thereby analogously the regulations relating to expropriation. The Reich may allot to itself, the Lands, or the Communes a share in the administration of economic enterprises and associations or secure to itself a controlling influence therein in some other way. The Reich may also, in case of urgent necessity for socioeconomic interests, by law effect a combination of economic enterprises and associations on the basis of self-administration with the object of securing the cooperation of all working elements of the population, of allowing employers and employees a share in the management, and of regulating the production, fabrication, distribution, utilization, price fixing, and the importation and exportation of economic goods according to the principles of national economy. The cooperative industrial and economic associations and their unions (*Erwerbs- und Wirtschaftsgenossenschaften*) shall at their request be incorporated in the socialized economic system, their constitution and peculiarities being thereby taken into consideration." (Ed. note.)

agrarian problems, but it also leaves the most dangerous enemy of any democratic constitution, the large landlord, undisturbed in his economic power position. This he will use as long as he can to keep the agricultural workers in a state of political and economic dependency. The development of the last ten years has brought about a clear and unambiguous decision in favor of private property of the means of production. And it has decided which of the economic forms possible under the Weimar Constitution shall be the *real* economic form of the contemporary era.

The complete maintenance of the capitalist economic system has also determined the role of the so-called works councils' article (*Räteartikel*) of the Weimar Constitution. It represents the constitutional implementation of the Stinnes-Legien Agreement of November 1918, and proclaims that "the workers and employees are entitled to participate in the regulation of wage and working conditions, as well as in the total economic development of the productive forces, in co-determination with the entrepreneurs" (Art. 165). Whereas in some immediately preceding articles of the constitution socialism and private property are posed as available alternatives, here an attempt is made to fuse the most contradictory principles. This can be viewed as an attempt to continue on a permanent basis the temporary collaboration of capital and labor which had been instituted in order to facilitate the joint surmounting of external difficulties, such as the liquidation of the consequences of the war. This would have been possible only if there had been agreement upon underlying social principles. The course of development has in fact determined that the councils' article and its most important implementation law, the works councils' law, have become what the situation foreordained: a system of protective measures for workers and employees which in reality serves only as a counterweight against the tremendously increased power which the increasing rate of concentration and rationalization has placed into the hands of the employers.[19] The more far-reaching significance which the works councils' law sought to achieve by getting the workers to share in the control of their enterprises was never achieved. The prevailing relationship between political form and economic power has also robbed the Reich Economic Council (*Reichswirtschaftsrat*) of much of its

[19] Cf. the article by Ernst Fraenkel in the February, 1930, issue of *Die Gesellschaft* on the occasion of the tenth anniversary of the works councils' law.

political significance. It was intended as a representative body, albeit very limited in its influence, of all economic interest groups. But since today's parliament serves as the political form for the waging of economic conflicts, it leaves little room for the ideally parallel, but legally much weaker, Reich Economic Council. These facts are fully acknowledged in the draft of the law which is intended to finalize the status of the Council. It would transfer the main activity of the Economic Council from the plenary sessions into the committees, and introduce a special kind of investigating committee. It also reorients the institution by reducing the number of permanent members and introducing the possibility of participation of nonmember experts. The Reich Economic Council, as well as the similarly structured council introduced in France in 1925, was assigned three fields of activity: to study, to seek solutions, and to pave the way for their implementation. Of these the creation of a comprehensive research apparatus equipped with inquisitorial powers may have been the most important. For both the identification of solutions and the recommendation of steps necessary to their implementation would today appear more appropriate for organs which the power of circumstances has equipped with greater authority.

Thus the basic rights of the German people have on the whole not achieved the functions which basic rights should fulfill. Their origins and contents determine that they could not become values in the name of which the German people could attain unity.[20] Rather they have, through their opalescent ambiguity, significantly intensified that serious lack of political decision-making capacity which marks the agony of our contemporary political life. They have not provided the democratic state with that clear programmatic support which it and its organs needed more than ever before.

THE GOVERNMENT

In regard to the formation and leadership of governments, the Weimar Constitution contains no conclusive and necessarily binding regulations. Following the interpretation of Carl Schmitt, one can identify

---

[20] Rudolf Smend, *Verfassung und Verfassungsrecht* (Munich, 1928).

four groups of regulations which, without being mutually exclusive, provide a constitutional basis for the formation and leadership of governments. First there is the influence of the parliamentary majority, whose confidence in more or less explicit form provides the basis for any government. The Reich constitution also allots influence to the Chancellor, in that it allows him to lay down the guidelines of policy and endows him with the chairmanship of, plus the tie-breaking vote within, the Council of Ministers. Parallel to this potential for the development of a prime ministerial system, the constitution contains direct and indirect suggestions of a cabinet system based on the political collegiality of the ministers.[21] Evidence of this is contained in the constitutional provisions for collegial decision-making in the cabinet, effectively supplemented by coalition agreements among the party groups which in reality determine in advance what guidelines of policy will be followed. Lastly, mention must be made of the President's constitutional sphere of influence, which will be more amply treated in the next section. In the realm of political practice, the many government formations of recent years can in essence be fitted to one of three basic types:

1. Government formation by appointment of a nonparliamentarian Chancellor, called an expert, who draws into the cabinet other so-called experts as well as individual party politicians who serve as contact men between the parties and such a "super-party" government (Cuno type, 1923).[22]

2. Government formation based on definite limited coalition agreements relating to specific problem areas (Marx-Keudell type, 1927–28).[23]

3. Government formation through the nomination to the chancel-

---

[21] This collegiate cabinet decision has been abandoned in one case. Paragraph 21, Sentence 3 of the Budget Statute (Reichshaushaltsordnung) enables the Finance Minister in cooperation with the Chancellor to prevent the cutoff of expenditures or changes in the budget plan even against the majority of the other ministers.

[22] A center-conservative coalition cabinet headed by Dr. Wilhelm Cuno, a conservative Catholic without party affiliation, during the crisis of the French occupation of the Ruhr. (Ed. note.)

[23] A conservatively oriented coalition government with Dr. Wilhelm Marx (Center party) as Chancellor and von Keudell (German National People's party) as Minister of the Interior. (Ed. note.)

lorship of a party leader who enjoys the greater or lesser support of party groups, but without specific agreements (Mueller type, 1928–30).[24]

This classification provides merely some basic clarification in regard to the practice of cabinet formations.[25] Basically all these cases are subject to one norm which usually is already apparent at the cabinet formation stage, but always in regard to the manner in which the government's power is exercised: that they essentially mirror the existing social relationships. In this respect all governments have for quite a long time shown a very great consistency. Just as the total political situation in the years 1918–20 was determined by the fact of the German defeat, so it is today determined largely by the fact that the capitalist economic system in Europe has for the time being repulsed all its opponents. While these opponents were numerous in 1917–19, they lacked the necessary mutual cohesion and they were limited in their effectiveness by the varying concrete national aftereffects of the outcome of the war. The capitalist system, through its internal concentration and through forcing a cutback in the economic activity of public bodies, has significantly enlarged its sphere of influence in the recent period. Amalgamation in the sphere of production, and the placing of control in the hands of a few economic leaders, now enables these leaders effectively to determine the direction of foreign, trade, and economic policies. Thus the United States is no longer the only place where it remains unclear—for instance, in the case of trade or tariff agreements—whether treaty partners are governments or private capitalist interest groups which usually represent special interests having little in common with the interests of the total population of their country. Furthermore, German political development caused the monopolistic instrument of physical power, the *Reichswehr*, to become a factor in the maintenance of the capitalist economic system to an extent that should not be underestimated. Since the formation of the

[24] A "Great Coalition" government of parties loyal to the Weimar Constitution, headed by Dr. Hermann Mueller of the Social Democratic party. It disintegrated in March, 1930, over disagreements between the coalition parties concerning ways to deal with social and economic problems of the depression (social insurance). (Ed. note.)

[25] Paul Levi, in one of his ingenious articles, "Wieder einmal eine Krise," *Der Klassenkampf*, No. 8 (1929), has pointed out that it would take a doctoral dissertation to explore the differences between these various types of government.

republic the *Reichswehr* Ministry has been a so-called expert ministry, and as such has been insulated from the effects of domestic political change. It was placed explicitly in the service of a bourgeois order whose existence was taken for granted and which was represented by experts who remained in office throughout successive cabinets.

Distinguished from these over-all political arrangements, fixed as they are for a lengthy period of social conditions, is the sphere which is left open to the free play of political forces. In contrast to the "sphere of management," which is subject to the laws of the existing capitalist order, it may be called the "sphere of distribution." It encompasses the claims on the national product of population groups dependent upon the capitalist economic system as they are expressed in wage agreements, determinations about social insurance, unemployment, housing, to name only the most important. Here are felt the effects of currently prevailing power relationships between workers and capital, which depend on numerous factors and for which the political elections often constitute only deceptive indicators. Whereas within the "sphere of management" the government has to adjust itself with greater or lesser willingness to the laws imposed by the capitalist economic order, within the "sphere of distribution" it has more and more assumed the character of a clearinghouse. This task is one of reconciling the contradictory demands of the economic organizations, as represented through their peak associations, with reference to the strength of the various groups and in such a way as to avoid jeopardizing the previously agreed-upon over-all political line.

The many recent long-drawn-out attempts at cabinet formation and reorganization led to much thoroughgoing criticism of the relationship between cabinet and parliament. The business of government formation has always been a much more difficult one in Germany than, say, in France. But the crisis which has now led many to consider the "shop" ready for bankruptcy has very real roots. The most recent elections have permitted the representatives of the workers to enter parliament in a strength which according to the laws of political mechanics should have allowed them a decisive influence on the formation of the government. But the results were not in accord with the economic power relationships between workers and capital, which have been tilted increasingly in favor of capital. All attempts to achieve a rejuvenation of German political life by eliminating the "pernicious" parliament with its rigid party principles really aim at nothing else than at removing the imbalance between political mechanics and economic power. Such attempts seek to insulate the "sphere of distribution" against the influence of political change, and to reanchor it within the framework of the bourgeois order. They have already achieved considerable success in practice. Thus the sphere which was previously subject to the play of domestic political forces has been considerably reduced by the power position of the *Reichsbank* president in the area of currency and credit policy. The cities, which have been especially active in the area of social policy, have recently come to feel the impact of the functional dependency of the "sphere of distribution" on the "sphere of management." The various attempts, moreover, at alleged neutralization of specific functional areas (*Reichsbahn, Reichsbank*) have had the effect of shielding these against the influence of the workers operating within the framework of the "sphere of distribution."

The curbing of parliament's freedom of decision-making, which mirrors all too clearly the opposition of large segments of the people, has in constitutional terms usually been expressed in attempts to make the government largely independent of parliament. This attempt to separate parliament and government found its most radical expression in the abortive constitutional amendment proposed by the German People's party which called for a two-thirds majority in the *Reichstag* on motions of no confidence, except in the case of the third reading of the budget. These constitutional reform attempts culminated in the proposals of the Federation of German Industry,[26] which have been taken up by the German People's party, concerning parliament's position in the area of finance policy. Appropriation bills are thus in future to be made dependent upon the approval of the government and the *Reichskommissar*. It is in this manner that they seek to do away with the imbalance whose cause Popitz once identified with remarkable frankness as due to the fact "that the representative bodies formed on the basis of universal suffrage are not infrequently so composed that it is not those in the higher income brackets who feel the impact of tax increases most, who exercise the preponderant influence, but largely

---

[26] *Aufstieg oder Niedergang? Deutsche Wirtschafts- und Finanzreform 1929: Denkschrift des Präsidiums des Reichsverbandes der Deutschen Industrie.*

those who represent the less well-to-do population groups." [27] These plans are thoroughly logical from the point of view of those who wish to resolve the tension between real economic power and outward political forms in favor of the former. But those who perceive behind these tensions the forces that oppose the present distribution of economic power will have to strive for the activation of such forces. For the continuation of these tensions into the indefinite future is impossible. No state can permanently sustain such disproportionalities.

RECHTSSTAAT AND CIVIL SERVICE

The balancing out of conflicting interests within the "sphere of distribution" is not solely the task of the government. This is so firstly because the government can of course deal only with the larger objects and must leave detailed work to subordinate organs, but also because it lacks the consistency and the interparty (as distinct from supraparty) qualities which this work requires. The traditional legal institutions constitute desirable forms for coping with this task. The idea of the Rule of Law (*Rechtsstaat*) [28] once played a role in the struggle between the liberal bourgeoisie and the monarchy, but after emerging from the intellectual horizon and political arsenal of the constitutional parties it was subjected to a deep-seated change of function. Originally it constituted a cautious weapon of the propertied and educated strata which aimed at creating all manner of specialized jurisdictions that would limit the expansion of the powers of the monarchical executive. Today the principle of legality constitutes the form through which a large part of the decisions relating to the "sphere of distribution" are carried out in a seemingly juridical manner, surrounded by piles of procedural regulations. Arbitration chambers, labor courts, and housing boards all rest on the principle of removing decisions from political to seemingly apolitical bodies bound by legal regulations. Usually these end up by proclaiming compulsory settlements. Thus the

---

[27] Article on "Finanzausgleich," *Handwörterbuch der Staatswissenschaften*, III, 1013.

[28] For a treatment of the problem of *Rechtsstaat*, see the interesting but problematic book of Hermann Heller, *Rechtsstaat oder Diktatur?* (Tübingen 1930).

legal forms through which the social struggles are transformed into legal processes become the demarcation line between hostile social groups who are far from ready to accept legal decisions as final. But they recognize that a compulsory arbitration proceeding in legal form, while not affecting the prevailing distribution of power, provides at least a guarantee of receiving a hearing. This explains why the workers welcome the introduction of legal procedures in those areas where they have hitherto been denied all influence. That is why their attempt to exert influence on the previously inaccessible organization of the capitalist economy culminates in the demand for an independent quasi-judicial cartel supervision office. In addition to these legal forms, which hide compromise settlements behind procedural rules, there is also the form of achieving settlements through an arbitrator. The arbitrator's value lies in his not being bound by the coincidences which all elaborate procedural rules may on occasion produce; he represents just the opposite of the quasi-objectivity of the law. The arbitrator may exercise his function because of his personal attributes or by virtue of his office. The specially created cabinet office to help arbitrate the Ruhr conflict constitutes an instance of the latter case. The purpose which the institution of the arbitrator seeks to fulfill is the same as the one which the legal forms seek to achieve. Both utilize legal, official, or personal resources to achieve settlements in the "sphere of distribution."

The functioning of the legal and arbitration organs does not have to be guaranteed through the granting of formal independence. The development of the last ten years has shown that in the areas touching upon the "sphere of distribution" the civil servants can only act by taking into consideration the given social conditions. In their behavior toward organizations of the workers and employees, the civil servants themselves have an interest in pursuing policies which give due regard to the various points of view. For their administrative success requires at least a well-disposed attitude on the part of these organizations which influence many people through the press and through their meetings. It is otherwise with the civil servants of the "sphere of management," although as military officers, diplomats, etc., they too are, for the most part, dependent officials. But they are not subject to the influence of the various social organizations. Rather, as a consequence of the real economic power relationships and despite all so-called republicanization attempts, they are exclusively within the sphere of influence of the bourgeoisie and its large economic organizations.

The concept of the independence of the judiciary shows how much the world of political economic facts can reduce to meaninglessness concepts which in an earlier century had perhaps a quite definite constitutional meaning. The independence of the judges [29] has not been able to prevent the activity of the German Supreme Court (*Reichsgericht*) from becoming, in questions relating to high treason (properly within the "sphere of management"), a mere reflex of the prevailing power relationships. And in so far as other areas of criminal law exercise guarantee functions for the prevailing economic system, the courts still fulfill their old task of preserving the established order of property, albeit in a slightly more humane and rationalized manner. In regard to the politically irrelevant question of the intracapitalist distribution of goods, the courts are nonpartisan not because they are independent but because the legal rules applicable to these questions have become formalized in the course of centuries and are not subject to changing politico-economical standards. Thus the example of the judiciary shows best of all how little the workings of the civil service are governed by constitutional principles, whether these relate to the independence of the judiciary or to the duty of protecting the constitutionally established republican state. It is solely the actual political and economic power relationships which determine the direction and form of administrative activity.

THE PRESIDENT

Following American practice on this point, the Weimar Constitution provides for the election of the president by the people. But he is not, as in the United States, an independent chief executive, for all his orders and directives require the countersignature of the chancellor or a minister, who thereby assume political responsibility vis-à-vis the

[29] On the problem of judicial independence, see the excellent book by Ernst Fraenkel, *Zur Soziologie der Klassenjustiz*. Detailed material on the theses presented is also provided by Franz Neumann, *Die politische und soziale Bedeutung der arbeitsgerichtlichen Rechtssprechung* (Berlin, 1929).

Reichstag. Nevertheless the president has a less dependent position vis-à-vis the government than the latter has toward the *Reichstag,* bound as it is to that body's votes of confidence. He is elected by the people, not by parliament; he nominates the chancellor and appoints the ministers; he has the power to dissolve the *Reichstag;* and because of his seven-year term of office he constitutes an element of stability in contrast to the changing parliaments and governments. These constitutional rules may have contributed toward the erroneous conception that the president is the only true representative of the entire nation because he is removed from party quarrels and is not responsible to parliament or to special interests. Radbruch's remarks, in an essay on the gold balance of the constitution, move in this direction in so far as he says of the conduct of office of the first president that it cannot be measured by the yardstick of partisan politics because he may represent only the *volonté générale,* the ideal will of the people, the true interests of the nation. Radbruch's point of view related to President Ebert's conduct of the office, but the same viewpoint is also occasionally expressed in regard to the way in which von Hindenburg has interpreted the presidency. The point of view here developed, taking off from the constitutional position of the presidency and from the personal qualities attributed to its incumbents, is that the position of the president is above and beyond class cleavages. This is a fiction, partly because the constitutional characteristics of the office do not have the significance which is often attributed to them. True, the president is elected by the people, but this election too is dominated by the parties which, because of their monopoly control over the process of political organization, alone have at their disposal the necessary electoral apparatus. They either put up their own candidate or agree with somewhat like-minded groups on a man who enjoys their confidence. Moreover, the president's power of affecting political developments by selecting a chancellor of his choice is considerably narrowed by the practical need to pay due regard to the outcome of recent elections or other political events. In any case, if the man he selects is to win the approval of the *Reichstag* majority the president must take care to appoint a man whose policy is approximately consonant with the existing power relationships among the classes. It is only within this limited framework that the president can exercise his political discretion and personal will by influencing policy through the power of nomination as well as through continuing influence on pending cabinet decisions. Indeed, the president can only exercise his office if he is in accord on all basic political questions with the government and thus with the concrete power relationships of which any government is the product. A specific example may clarify this. In 1923 Thuringia and Saxony were ruled by socialist governments which pursued a pure socialist policy without reference to the conditions prevailing in the Reich. In Bavaria at the same time an extreme right-wing government refused to permit the implementation of Reich laws. It persuaded the Bavarian troops to turn against the Reich government and sought with their help to force a political reorientation on the Reich level. In Thuringia and Saxony the governments were quickly deposed under Article 48, *Reichswehr* troops and *Reichkommissars* were ordered into these Länder, and with their help a new election was forced through in Thuringia whose outcome could not be in doubt.[30] In Bavaria the government was not deposed, no out-of-state *Reichswehr* troops set foot on Bavarian soil, and the Bavarian government was not troubled by the prospect of new elections. Rather, a gentleman's agreement was drawn up between the Reich and Bavarian governments which has been perpetuated in constitutional history under the name "Homburg Agreement." Its amicable character may be characterized by the sentence reading, "The preceding agreement does not prejudice further consideration of desires expressed in the Bavarian memorandum." Thus the president, as head of the executive, applied Article 48 in quite different ways in two situations which were at least legally very similar. The political reason for this is clear. The case of Central Germany concerned a deviation from the maxim of the bourgeois state, which by 1923 had been fully reestablished and become uncontested, whereas the Bavarian case involved no deviation from the bourgeois state but only two different conceptions about the manner of its implementation.[31] These could be reconciled through an agreement, which was not possible in relation to socialist princi-

---

[30] The case briefly mentioned here is described in detail in Walter Fabian, *Klassenkampf um Sachsen* (Löbau, 1930).

[31] The vacillating attitude of the bourgeois cabinet toward Nazi Minister Frick is characteristic. Since it is only a new variety of bourgeois policy that is involved, adjusted to current conditions, it is not to be blocked from the beginning.

ples.[32] The behavior of the president in these specific cases makes evident that the president's moderating activity, his "pouvoir neutre," is limited indeed. Such a balancing role can be exercised only within the given political power relationships of the bourgeois state. Beyond these, even the arbitrator becomes a partisan. Thus it was consonant with the logic of the then-prevailing political conditions that President Ebert acted as an intermediary between Bavaria and the Reich, but that he acted as head of the executive power in the struggle between Saxony and the Reich.

If the president can exercise political influence, be it as adviser, fiduciary, or arbitrator, only within the framework of the established power system, it is even more necessary that his representative functions be exercised within this sphere. The president must represent the Reich as a whole and proclaim its will in such a way as to provide guidance both for the entire people and for its partners in international law. But it is only possible to represent something that currently exists. Friedrich Ebert and Hindenburg might have wanted to tie to their representative function various different value concepts, but the character of the representation is shaped neither by the ideas of him who represents nor by those at whom the representation is directed, the people. Rather it is shaped by the concrete configuration of that which is really represented, the prevailing power relationships. In this unavoidable and constantly recurring process the representative figure is eclipsed by the make-up of that which he represents, regardless of whether the person involved is called Stalin, MacDonald, or Friedrich Ebert. When, as in a class society, an ideal general will is simply nonexistent, it cannot be created through the person and the conceptions of the representative figure. Each president may proclaim that he represents all the people, including those opposed to the existing power relationships, and this is the practice in all social systems based upon hierarchical class structures. But the related anti-Marxist concept of the president's position as above and beyond classes still remains a

---

[32] In spite of all the controversies between Reich and Länder concerning financial, administrative, and so-called sovereignty matters, this example clearly indicates that fundamentally all potential differences between Reich and Länder are rather unimportant as compared to the questions: Are Reich and Länder homogeneous in their political structure? Are they based on the same principles of social order?

fiction. So much for all the special value conceptions which one is accustomed to associate with the office of *Reichspräsident*.

THE CONSTITUTION WITHOUT DECISION

The great and famous French constitutions of the 1790s marked the beginning of a new order in human affairs. They proclaimed the victory of the new bourgeois age with a pathos that made sense in terms of the historical setting, and which still reverberated in the successful and unsuccessful constitutional attempts of the 1840s. At one of the high points of the bourgeois era, immediately following the bloody suppression of the Paris Commune, the first harbinger of a new historical period, both republican France and Bismarckian Germany gave themselves new constitutions. The authors of these constitutions did not bother to remember that the French bourgeoisie had once overthrown the feudal monarchy in the name of inalienable human rights, and that it had proclaimed itself their protector. For the France of this period the constitution was nothing more than it was for Bismarck, the organizational basis of the status quo.

The origin of the Weimar Constitution coincides with the second high point of the bourgeois era. The last remnants of a feudal or semifeudal system had succumbed in the face of a systematic permeation of the entire world by a self-organizing capitalism. The idea systems of a powerfully strengthened working class, which in Russia seemed to have overthrown the bourgeois state in the first storm, threatened the bourgeois state generally. All of these developments, which had in a relatively short time changed the cultural and economic profiles of peoples and countries, cast their projection onto the origin of the Weimar Constitution, which was nurtured by the particular destiny of the German bourgeoisie. Thus although Germany was already a bourgeois country in its intellectual structure in the 1840s, and in its economic structure by the late 1870s, the German bourgeoisie achieved a power position commensurate with its economic position only at a time when many already believed prematurely that the power of the bourgeoisie had come to an end. Nearby, the peoples in the Austrian and Russian successor states, who had achieved national freedom only recently, also sought democratic constitutions. Glancing respectfully to the West and timidly to the East, they copied the inherited constitutional forms of the nineteenth century without considering that the nineteenth-century nation-state, to which these constitutions were tailored, cannot help solve the problems of the twentieth-century class state. The consciousness of newly achieved statehood led these countries thoughtlessly to reformulate the European bourgeois constitutions, but they soon succumbed to anarchistic conditions. But the Germany of 1919, which was then still viewed as the strongest fortress of continental socialism, wanted to take a step forward in its basic rights. It sought through its basic rights to open the door for a new social order while yet taking over intact the bourgeois organizational apparatus, complete with its old civil service cadres. Germany was ready to place the state apparatus at the disposal of the old as well as the new social order and to provide the new order, whatever it might turn out to be, with the appearance of legality. Following Weber, who in this respect completely misunderstood the essence of a constitution, the Weimar Constitution opened the way for all conceivable manner of tasks to be assigned to the administration. But herein lies the basic and irreparable error of this constitution: it did not come to a decision; it fell prey to the misconception that the principles of democracy alone constitute the principles of a specific social or ideational order; it forgot that democracy cannot do more than articulate already existing conditions. What a democracy can do is to give external expression to an existing social order and to represent it meaningfully. Because of the confusion between the form of democracy and its content no one undertook to endow this constitution with a political program. Since 1919 the German bourgeoisie has undertaken with luck and dexterity to fill this all too pure form with particular bourgeois components.

It is the purpose of all constitutions, which seek to constitute a turning point in political development, to proclaim a specific program of action in whose name the organization of a new social order is to proceed. This action program will be the more realizable the more it is consonant with economic conditions, as was the case with the program of the French Revolutionary constitution. It will be the more difficult to implement the less it is adequate to the prevailing economic conditions, as is the fate of the constitution of the Russian Revolution. The fathers of the Weimar Constitution did not endow it with an action program, but contented themselves with presenting a choice among the most varied electoral systems. They thought that democratic constitutional institutions could be a substitute for a political program, whereas it would have been the task of democracy to create such a program. However, "its character was such that it stood for nothing and permitted everything." [33] Half a century earlier a liberal democratic constitution might still have been able to achieve greater efficacy as a national organizational principle in a country with a relatively significant number of politically interested—and not just patronage chasing—citizens, and a press relatively independent economically. At the end of the bourgeois era, when such venerable institutions as the *Rechtsstaat*, the bourgeois *Bildung*, the independence of the judiciary, and freedom of opinion had lost their inherent meaning by virtue of the specific survival rules of the capitalist economic system, democracy might have been revivified only through an unambiguous commitment to a substantive principle of social organization, that of socialism.

It was the tragic fate of the Weimar Constitution that at its birth the German proletariat could not muster the will power to accomplish the task of creating a real socialist democracy free from all radical phrasemongering and yet ready to do the historically necessary. Behind schedule by almost a century, the German bourgeoisie came into the possession of political power just as the spiritual and economic basis of its rule had already become extremely questionable. The semifeudal monarchy had been able to hold it back politically by accepting its economic demands. In the present situation no one can expect of the bourgeoisie the self-sacrifice—and this is the significant difference from the position of the bourgeoisie vis-à-vis the semifeudal monarchy in the last century—through which it might fulfill the economic demands of the proletariat in return for being allowed to continue to dominate the spheres of government and bureaucracy. The independent functioning of democratic constitutional institutions is called into question by the inseparability of the political from the economic sphere. Since there is no possibility of playing off polity and economy

[33] Lorenz von Stein on the French constitution of 1795 in his *Geschichte der sozialen Bewegung in Frankreich*, 1921 ed. I, 395.

in favor of a nonexistent third, the constitution is degraded to a formal rule of the game, which, lacking a higher level of appeal, the more powerful may annul at will. Only a socialist politics, based on a knowledge of the grave fact that the gulf between these positions is indeed unbridgeable, would not seek to evade the problem by providing the mere appearance of a solution. Only it can and will muster the courage for a substantive commitment. By contrast, this constitution of a bourgeois value system in the process of dissolution can be nothing more than the servant of whoever is momentarily the more powerful.

CONSTITUTIONAL REACTION IN 1932

PUBLIC OPINION is presently occupied with the question of constitutional reform. Since the organizations responsible for public opinion in today's Germany know how to distance themselves inconspicuously from their products, the outside observer can only have vague notions about the relative degree of spontaneity and of central planning behind such demands for constitutional change. Right now the general call for a reform of the constitution sounds so urgent that it seems as though the speed with which parliamentary democracy is reorganized were the precondition for a corresponding increase in the rate of employment. At least this is what one might assume if one did not know that for this government a "restoration of souls"—to use Seipel's [1] phrase—is just as important as the restoration of the economy. Or is it perhaps a matter of solidifying their power?

At any rate the time is approaching when the government will have to transform its political metaphysics into concrete measures. Until now all one knew was that this government was designed as a polemical instrument against the Weimar Constitution. But the institutional consequences of the government presently in power were already problematical if for no other reason than that they depend to a not inconsiderable degree on the person of the present President of the Reich. But even if our authoritarian government rejects on principle the "emptiness" of democracy, the "impossibility" of anonymous parliamentary majorities, of heterogeneous, interest-directed parties (for

Translation of "Verfassungsreaktion 1932"; originally published in *Die Gesellschaft*, XI (1932), 415–27.

[1] Ignaz Seipel, Catholic priest and antisocialist Chancellor of the Austrian Republic, 1922–24 and 1926–29. (Ed. note.)

that is how it views democracy), and even if it ties its legitimacy to the *hic et nunc* of the present President, already its claim "to stay in power for four years" must lead it to believe that perhaps a necessary, though not sufficient, condition of its existence is to provide the German people with the illusion that an enduring reform of its political order will take place—a reform to be carried out under the auspices of the strata and ideas which this government represents and yet one in correspondence with the people's needs. The underlying thought that permanence is an essential element of all constitutional planning is no doubt correct. Yet one seems oblivious to the absence of that societal basis which alone would make possible the legal establishment and functioning of such a constitution, at the moment of its creation as well as for the long run. After the Chancellor's speech in Munich[2] it has become doubtful whether the government even considers it important that a new constitution be introduced legally (every constitutional reform at the present moment has its counterrevolutionary logic). The fact that the *Reichstag* was elected and is "able to work," thanks to the existence of some governing majority, seems to have become insufficient to legitimate it in the eyes of the government, which demands that it submit to its will. The *quid pro quo* offered to this democratic institution does not even amount any more to the concession the Prussian aristocracy used to make to their prince: "Und der König absolut, wenn er uns den Willen tut."[3] Within the framework of the reform the annulment of legality becomes the condition of the legality of the annulment.

An attenuation of the ideological superstructure can be distinctly observed in the political sphere concerning us here. It can be considered one of the decisive structural characteristics of postwar Germany. It has also manifested itself from time to time—on the ideological level—in the workers' indifference to anything but day-to-day politics. There is a surprising disproportionality between the widespread fascist ideological surrogates and the small amount of independent intellectual

---

[2] Speech of Chancellor Franz von Papen on October 12, 1932, before the Bavarian Association of Manufacturers in which he announced a forthcoming government draft of a new constitution providing for a "powerful state above parties" with an authoritarian executive government independent of parliamentary majorities. (Ed. note.)

[3] "Let the King rule absolutely as long as he does what we want." (Ed. note.)

production. If one were to compare the great ideas which so decisively influenced the French period of constitution-making at the end of the eighteenth and in the beginning of the nineteenth century—which in their effect transcended by far the actual realm of bourgeois existence —with the amalgam of feudal-conservative-fashionable-fascist principles of today, one would be tempted here, too, to measure the objective importance of a historical process by the content of its ideological manifestations. The difference in levels just indicated clearly shows the almost *postum* character of the episode of which we are witnesses. When a later epoch takes inventory of the intellectual content of this one, Carl Schmitt's *Legalität und Legitimität* [4] will prove itself a work superior to others both because it bases itself on the foundations of political theory and because of the reserve of its conclusions. Carl Schmitt, like the majority of the constitutional reformers of 1932, revived the platform of 1925: More power to the President! From the viewpoint of democracy, however, one recognizes in the difference between the concrete objectives of then and now the regressive movement which has taken place in the interim, which corresponds to Herr von Hindenburg's first term of office. While the first call to Hindenburg amounted to a call for constitutional reform within the Weimar Constitution, the present one is for a constitutional revolution. While at that time two legal institutions were warring within controversial marginal areas, today's demand is to nullify parliamentary legality by presidential legitimacy. Nor should one ignore in this respect the fact that the direct political role of the people, which has a major place in Schmitt's concept of the constitution (of which, it is true, he only drew the contours in his above-mentioned work), is also a leading element in the constitution of the Reich. It is not only a matter of express differences in the content of the existing and the planned constitution. Today the dominant role of the parties in parliamentary elections is transferred to the plebiscite as well and stamps it, in form as well as in content, as party or class action. That our parties do not just organize the people intermittently for election campaigns as they do in the United States, where they are mere election platforms, is manifest, *inter alia*, from the conduct of popular initiatives. Either the parties themselves promote an initiative or, if it has been started in some other way, they give it

[4] Carl Schmitt, *Legalität und Legitimität* (Munich and Leipzig, 1932).

their support, thereby alone providing it with a chance of success. For Carl Schmitt, on the other hand, the democratic character of the plebiscite consists purely in an unorganized answer which the people, characterized as a mass, gives to a question which may be posed only by an authority whose existence is assumed. Structure and accountability of this authority are unknown; only its existence is a distinct point in the picture which otherwise is dominated by ideological criticism. The concept of the people is treated in exactly the opposite way. While in the first case it is assumed without bothering with an institutional guarantee that the government desires the Good, in the other case it is assumed that the people cannot will the Good, but can only acknowledge it. Defining the Good in an antagonistic class society is assumed to be no problem. The constitutional position of the people in this new constitutional construct is exactly tailored to fit its anthropological characteristics:

The people can only say yes or no, it cannot counsel, deliberate, or discuss. It cannot govern or administer, nor can it posit norms; it can only sanction by its "yes" the draft norms presented to it. Nor, above all, can it put a question, but only answer by "yes" or "no" a question put to it.[5]

In so far as this description of Schmitt's is meant for the Germany of the future, it seems to be suffering from a double anachronism. This people (*Volk*) would be the people of a postdemocratic constitution— but West European democracy only became possible through a transformation of the masses from merely passive objects of history into an active, organized force. This process was long and painful and ran parallel to the growing industrialization. Democracy changed the structural character of the masses decisively and with a speed that contradicts all theses about the unchangeability of human nature:

At least in European history up to the present, the vulgar had never believed itself to have "ideas" on things. It had beliefs, traditions, experiences, proverbs, mental habits, but it never imagined itself in possession of theoretical opinions on what things are or ought to be—for example, on politics or literature. What the politician planned or carried out seemed good or bad to it, it granted or withheld its support, but its action was limited to being an echo, positive or negative, of the creative activity of

[5] *Ibid.*, p. 93.

CONSTITUTIONAL REACTION IN 1932

others. It never occurred to it to oppose to the "ideas" of the politician others of its own, nor even to judge the politician's "ideas" from the tribunal of other "ideas" which it believed itself to possess. . . . The necessary consequence of this was that the vulgar never thought, even remotely, of making a decision on any one of the public activities. . . .

Today, on the other hand, the average man has the most mathematical "ideas" on all that happens or ought to happen in the universe. Hence he has lost the use of his hearing. Why should he listen if he has within him all that is necessary? There is no reason now for listening, but rather for judging, pronouncing, deciding. There is no question concerning public life, in which he does not intervene, blind and deaf as he is, imposing his "opinons." [6]

However one may evaluate this process Ortega y Gasset has called *The Revolt of the Masses*, it seems clear that the condition which is interpreted either as self-limitation or as submission of the masses, depending on one's ideological attitude, belongs to the past. This sociopsychological *habitus*, doubtless still an attribute of the beginning of mass democracy, has receded as a consequence of the watershed of the Great War and of the changes connected with it. The crisis of democracy which Schmitt uses as historical background for his theory has only accelerated this development. Nothing would be more erroneous than to overinterpret a momentary low tide in the political dynamism of the masses and thus to believe that the concentration of power of bourgoisie, military, and bureaucracy in the German state apparatus runs parallel to a diffusion of the political interest of the masses. It would seem, therefore, that the condition of its birth would be the worst defect of such a new constitution. The predemocratic basis of Schmitt's theory gets in the way of its intention to liquidate a developed democracy.

But even assuming the feasibility of this new distribution of power, planned for a long period of time, it seems that the problem of the constitutional dynamic, of the regulation of changes of power within the framework of the new constitutional order, has remained unsolved. Must the administration resign from office if defeated in a referendum, even though the plebiscitary question was properly posed? Or would

[6] Ortega y Gasset, *Der Aufstand der Massen* (1932), pp. 75-76. (This translation is taken from pp. 70-71 of the authorized translation from the Spanish by an anonymous translator, W. W. Norton & Co., 1932 and 1960. Ed. note.)

the gap in the constitutional theory not have to be filled even today by the ideology once characterized by Schmitt as "Jacobin logic?" [7] This ideology substitutes what the people objectively ought to think for what they do think subjectively. Despite its shortcomings, modern democracy is after all the sole form of government which constitutionally makes possible the cooperation or the alternation of different groups at a time of increasing social and national heterogeneity. By its system of universal, equal, and secret suffrage and by its guarantee of political freedom, it alone permits changes in the social structure to be reflected on the political level. But for a "postdemocratic" constitution this poses very great difficulties, which thus far none of the modern caesaristic versions of democracy have managed to solve. For in our traditionless age any and all conditions for an institutionalization of personal charisma are lacking. A lost battle, an aborted economic plan, or the death of an officeholder will bring a great upheaval, which will be the consequence not merely of the social dynamics at work but primarily of the changed political institutions. Given the enormous administrative apparatus of the twentieth century, this upheaval again will have not only political consequences but immeasurable social ones as well. But apart from these general reasons for the impossibility of institutionalizing changes of power within the framework of a caesaristic order of government,[8] there is a special circumstance which makes it impossible in present-day Germany to go beyond general antitheses. As the case of Mussolini has shown, an attempt to institutionalize personal charisma can be undertaken only after the charisma has visibly established itself as effective. As long as this has not come about, one can conjure up the image of authoritarian as well as plebiscitarian rule without being able to say anything concrete about the conditions of its existence.— At this time of transition to a postdemocratic era in Germany the controversy as to who shall be the bearer of the charisma has not yet been settled!—Legitimization can here be brought about by achievement only. Even an antidemocratic mass mood, assuming it existed, could not institutionalize a new power independent of the people and not substantiated by any historical

[7] Carl Schmitt, *Die geistesgeschichtliche Lage des heutigen Parlamentarismus,* 2d ed. (Munich, 1926).

[8] Cf. Rudolf Smend, *Verfassung und Verfassungsrecht,* par. 11, n. 3, on the *contradictio in adjecto* of a charismatic constitution.

event. For it is a matter not of the quality of impersonal institutions but, on the contrary, of the indomitable power of personal elements which would first have to come into existence in order then to be sanctioned. For only then could an attempt at institutionalization be risked whose chances of success would, however, remain completely unpredictable.

Eugen Schiffer [9] presents a program of thirty-eight points which he calls a proposal for a new constitution. This proposal does not remove the demonstrated impossibility of imagining under present circumstances a basically new antidemocratic constitution for Germany. For Schiffer's draft is essentially a codification of our present constitutional conditions. Its dominant figure is the president, who is not only chief of the executive and entitled to decree individual measures, but whose entire present-day practice of issuing statutory emergency decrees is legalized.[10] Thereby almost all power is placed in the president's hand and is thus at the disposal of antidemocratic arbitrariness. As to the only right left to the people, to elect a new president every four years, two possibilities emerge: Either the army jointly with the bureaucracy—the only independent institution in the author's scheme—corrupts even this election, thereby eliminating the last vestige of popular influence, or the people succeed in electing a president who is independent and outside the bureaucracy's sphere of influence. In the latter case the constitutional system must collapse in the struggle between bureaucracy, army, and holders of antiquated property titles, on the one hand, and the people represented only by the president, on the other. The lapidary "contrariwise" that Marx opposes to Hegel's sentence—"The government is not a party that confronts another one" [11]—would become real even for the illusionists of the authoritarian state, who do not want to see that the state is a societal institu-

---

[9] Eugen Schiffer, *Die Neue Verfassung des Deutschen Reichs* (Berlin, 1932).

[10] The German parliamentary election of September 14, 1930, polarized the composition of the *Reichstag* to such a degree (the number of National Socialist seats rose from 12 to 107, of Communist seats from 54 to 77) that it was no longer able to produce the majorities needed to support the Cabinet and to legislate in the regular way. From then on until the collapse of the Weimar Republic the successive cabinets legislated by means of presidential emergency decrees (*Notverordnungen*) based on Article 48, par. 2 of the Weimar Constitution. (Ed. note.)

[11] Karl Marx, "Kritik der Hegelschen Staatsphilosophie," in "Der historische Materialismus," *Frühschriften*, I, 105.

tion. Yet even presupposing all concerned acted fully within the law, the variability of this state's contents, hence its instability, would be greater than in the parliamentary constitutional state. For such a far-reaching unification of the will of the plebiscitary element in the person of the president would make policy undergo greater vacillations than it is undergoing as a result of the typical differences between the parliamentary parties.[12]

Schiffer's parliament has as little to do with the institution which was called parliament from the nineteenth century to our time as has the parliament of prerevolutionary France. The only exception is that in the post-Weimar Reich the "lit de justice" is transformed into a normal function by the right of the president to make laws independently. The continued use of the word must be explained by the same ideological tactic by which the postdemocratic constitutions present themselves as "true democracies." For whatever the composition of parliament may have been since the foundation of its independence in the Glorious Revolution and whatever social strata were privileged in or excluded from it, one of its qualities has hardly been disputed: its right to participate in the making of laws. If the new parliament is not only limited by the dictator-president's right to decree measures and by his autonomous law-making power, but is also deprived of the possibility to annul these presidential laws,[13] then its legislative function is done away with. This is brought about in this unique constitutional project by the personal union it establishes between the president and a neutral third power, so that the control of constitutionality and the application of the constitution are both in the president's hands.[14] Parliament's right to legislate can thus only be exercised in

---

12 The same fear is voiced by Meineke in his article "Ein Wort zur Verfassungsreform," *Vossische Zeitung*, October 12, 1932.

13 Article 14, par. 2: "He [the President] may proclaim a law even without a vote of the *Reichstag*, if it is urgent and the *Reichstag* is unable to vote it in time." Article 15, par. 2: "They [the laws and measures of the President] are to be annulled if the *Reichstag* so demands and declares at the same time that they lack justification. If the *Reichstag* so decides, it must then vote on whether the President, the Chancellor, and the responsible Ministers are to be indicted for culpable violation of the constitution. If the *Reichstag* fails so to decide, the contested measures remain in force unless the *Reichstag* by its vote replaces them by others serving the same purpose."

14 Article 7: "The President is the guardian of the constitution. He may reprimand any infringement of the constitution and take measures against behavior violating the constitution."

consequence of an act of presidential grace. The legally still existing competition between parliament and president is thereby made illusory. In addition, the parliament's right to vote a motion of no confidence in the government is so seriously curtailed that it is most unlikely to happen during the normal functioning of this constitution.[15] All of which contributes to the impression that this will be constitutionalism by appearance only, in the sense of the concept used by Max Weber for czarist Russia from 1905 to 1917. Thus, to use the latest sociological terminology, the nineteenth-century theory that the executive power is in the hands of the government and not of the parliament becomes Herr von Papen's theory that "the government, not the parliament, wields the power of the state." Yet in the concept of "state power" the legislative should be included, lest one wishes to pursue the fascist theory "l'atto procede la norma" (the act precedes the norm) to its ultimate consequence, that is, to the elimination of general norms altogether. The function—very dubious as regards its success—of such a parliament belonging to a phantom constitutionalism consists merely in preserving the faith in its function.

The existence of such a parliament without a function is graciously permitted. This category of the feudal gracious grant appearing here, by way of an inadequate denaturation of Kantian concepts, as a moral duty dominates not only the establishment of this parliament. It is a basic category not only of the political but also of the social structure of the new regime. Just as the welfare state is criticized not only because it gave too much to the working class but above all because it gave it the *right* to receive much, so also is democracy criticized not mainly because it gave too much to the people but for giving it rights and thus the possibility to make demands where—according to Schmitt's anthropology of the "mass"—only receiving or rejecting is to be permitted. In the light of the findings of the theory of ideology it would be surprising if such a substitution of customs for law were to occur without any essential change in the actual processes of giving and taking, be it in the economic or in the political sphere.

In trying to provide a rational justification for such an abdication of

[15] Article 30: "The *Reichstag* may demand the dismissal of the government by a joint request of both houses, which must give their reasons. If the President refuses to dismiss the government, the *Reichstag* may request the removal of the President by referendum. The resolution of the *Reichstag* requires a two-thirds majority of both houses."

the parliamentary lawgiver, Schmitt points out that in the present epoch individualism and lack of permanence are the only norms which correspond to the existing substructure and are required by it.[16] One might agree with this thesis but would have to point out that two different changes in the substructure are involved here: [17] on the one hand, the organization of society in its social and economic sphere, which cancels out the infinitesimally small importance of the individual, and, on the other, the special speed of social dynamics in certain, though not all, periods of this historical epoch of "organization," which includes Late Capitalism as well as Early Capitalism. In any case the "thou shalt not pass," by which parliament is kept back whenever it ventures beyond the limits of the concept of the generality of law, is inconclusive. At a certain period of capitalist development, for social reasons that were not directly political, the general character of the law became a structural concept of the parliamentary statute. Today one tries with great emphasis to make generality a necessary characteristic of every parliamentary law, concluding from the erosion of this corollary of parliamentary rule that parliament must give way to the dictatorship of the administrative state. Such an argumentation leads to ascribing the malfunctioning of parliament to the change of the social substructure itself, whereas it has entirely different causes (which are mainly accidental ones). In this way the prognosis for our *maladie parlementaire* is presented as hopeless. In reality, it is by no means proved that universality is a necessary attribute of the law or that the bureaucracy is in a better position to legislate in the present situation than is parliament. The bureaucracy, with its less cumbersome procedures, can regulate things faster, more kaleidoscopically, and without that minimum of protection for the affected parties which characterizes parliamentary rule. But this is probably no longer regarded as an advantage even by large strata of the bourgeoisie.

The curtailment of parliamentary rights is not only to be brought about by presidential power, an element sharply distinguishable from parliament, but parliament is to be redoubled, as it were, by the historically well-known institution of an upper house. The plebiscitary

---

[16] Schmitt, *Legalität und Legitimität, passim.*
[17] See the contributions to this subject by Ernst Fraenkel in *Die Gesellschaft,* October, 1931.

legitimacy of the president which has turned antidemocratic is joined by the always antidemocratic element of so-called functionalism.[18] It is a strange mixture of caesarism and corporate state, of expectation of a breakthrough of personal integration and the exact determination of a system of spheres of life and of those belonging to them. As to the question which of the two elements outlined roughly by Schiffer will be preferred by the German reactionaries of the future, the institutionalization of the status quo or a system of functional representation, the answer must be in favor of functional representation (*Ständeparlament*). For while the system of the presidential elections—given the social structure of the German people—does not guarantee that the most "deserving" is elected, corporatism offers a guarantee for reaching the true goals of this constitutional reform. (The corporate state is *eo ipso* a true political reflection of the existing social power conditions.) Sooner or later this new government will abandon the foundation of plebiscitary self-legitimation. At that time the second constitutional foundation, practically and theoretically, will have to be laid and according to this government's intentions it will be final. At that moment the bureaucracy, independent as it is of any popular election, will enlarge the specific weight of its contribution to the legitimation of the regime as well as increase its functional importance within the framework of the newly changed governmental system. The corporate state does not solve the problem of the unification of the political will; it only postpones it. It therefore needs as a correlate a *pouvoir neutre*, the bureaucracy, which becomes the *deus ex machina*.[19] Then the legal starting point of revolution, which could consist in the election of an independent president, is removed. The popular safety valve of elections, now lacking, is replaced by universal corruption. Carl Schmitt's "all is sinecure, nothing lives," which he applied to the parliamentary legislative state, applies more adequately to a political system in which all dynamism is suppressed in favor of an illusory

---

[18] Article 19: "The members of the House of States and Estates are designated by the governments of the states, the heads of the communities and community organizations, and by the organizations of economic, cultural, and social life."

[19] Thoma in his article "Staat" in *Handwörterbuch der Staatswissenschaften*, VI, 743, has correctly emphasized that a functional parliament requires constitutionalism with a self-governing bureaucracy: "One must want both or renounce both."

static condition. And the last chance of a continuity of the legal order vanishes when this static condition is based on the unchangeable nature of the constitution itself (except by a *pouvoir constituant* whose legal basis is not even hinted at).[20]

The critics, theorists as well as practitioners, nowadays consider themselves above the Weimar Constitution. They thereby prove nothing but the truth of Hegel's pronouncement: the only thing one can learn from history is that people learn nothing from it. The reason for Weimar's breakdown seemed at first glance to be its social heterogeneity, which was not sufficiently counteracted by a naturally democratic behavior and which reached dimensions hitherto unknown. Yet this breakdown does not prove that this heterogeneous body politic would be able, with the help of an authoritarian state, to absorb the second element of instability in the Weimar democracy, that is, the autonomous army and bureaucracy. To be sure, the chance of this taking place is very uncertain in a plebiscitary system. In a corporate society the disintegrating energies of the conflicting social forces are on the increase. For these social forces are cut off from any possibility of reforming the existing distribution of social power and no longer seek a compromise. Thus, this constitutional reform is not adequate even from the secondary viewpoint of pure stability, the simple reason being that one cannot solve the problem of political stability without solving the problem of social structure. If according to Papen's Munich speech the power of the state is to be stabilized like a *rocher de bronze* (of which the military, the bureaucracy, and their social connections have always dreamed), this cannot be done without the parties. For even the ideologists of the new regime ought to see that the contrasting of parties and people is nothing but a catchword of the presidential party (*Präsidialpartei*), not a sociological reality. If the government tries to reach and represent the people directly over the

[20] Schiffer cannot base himself on Schmitt when he provides in Article 38 of his draft that his constitution is to have no amending process and can be abolished or changed only by a new national assembly. For Schmitt in his above-mentioned book undertakes a conscious devaluation of all organizational forms and merely reaffirms the unchangeable material values of the second main part of the Weimar Constitution. Schiffer, on the other hand, consciously omits fundamental rights on the ground that everything is fluid and that it is more than risky to commit oneself now with regard to the future forms of marriage, family life, or the economy (p. 33).

heads of the parties, then, according to all historical experience, this "true union of government and people" (Papen in Munich) will become, in the eyes of the government, a permanent union of government and people. Yet the relationship of mass party and people is much closer, since it forces even the most recalcitrant party bureaucracy, for reasons of competition and on pain of extinction, to turn itself into a transformer of mass energies. A mass party's authority has to be reaffirmed by the people almost daily whereas a government ordinarily emphasizes its authoritarian character only when the voluntary recognition of its authority appears threatened. The substitution of self-legitimation for popular legitimation may have a liberating effect from the antidemocratic standpoint, but it has nothing to do with the goal of "solving the tasks assigned by reality through hard, positive work" (Papen in Munich). "To work in the best interests of Western culture"—our agreement with Herr von Papen is confined to this generality—means to us to accept democracy as the regulative principle of our actions in the political and social sphere. From this perspective the goal of stability, pursued by the government above all else, at least so far as its ideology is concerned, becomes a fetish. Furthermore, as social conservatism contrasts this goal with permanent social instability, political stability might well be merely a "bien de surcroît"—a by-product—of the socialist revolution. "Only in an order of things where classes and class contrasts have ceased to exist will social evolutions cease to be political revolutions." [21]

[21] Karl Marx, *The Poverty of Philosophy*.

THE LEGAL ORDER

OF NATIONAL SOCIALISM

IT IS ONE OF THE STRONGEST contentions of the National Socialist legal system that it has finally closed the gap which, under the liberal era, had separated the provinces of law and morality.[1] Henceforth, the legal and the moral order are one and the same. What is the reality against which we have to measure this contention? The National Socialist legal order substitutes racial homogeneity for equality, and therefore abandons the conception of human beings equipped with similar capacities and equally capable of bearing legal rights and duties. It was easy for the Nazis to make fun of this conception. Under the conditions of our advanced industrial society, it usually did not offer a profitable tool for the adjustment of differences which frequently represented claims of social groups and not of mere individuals. But our legal heaven does not consist exclusively of group claims and counterclaims. There exist also parallel relations among individuals and between the individual and the state. Indeed the subjection of individual and government alike to the same rules of the game is one of the happiest and not unintentional consequences of the liberal emphasis on general notions, with its quest for equality between the contending parties. Under the veil of the community ideology, the system of general legal conceptions equally applicable to all cases falls.[2] With it

Public lecture given in Columbia University in December, 1941. Reprinted, by permission, from *Studies in Philosophy and Social Science*, IX (1941), 456–75.

[1] H. Frank, *Rechtsgrundlagen des Nationalsozialistichen Führerstaates* (Munich, 1938), p. 11.
[2] Cf. G. A. Walz, *Artgleichheit gegen Gleichartigkeit* (Hamburg, 1938), p. 19.

falls the beneficial fiction of a government bound by law to the same rules as the individual contesting its commands. Now the individual is checked by two forces, the official social grouping and the government, whose commands are not subject to discussion and who are organized so that their jurisdictional disputes cannot be exploited by the individual. The individual is subjected to the law of his professional group as well as to the impetuous command of the state. For the run of his daily task the government relinquishes him to the paternal care of the group, but does not hesitate to make use of its own coercive machinery when the latter's persuasive and disciplinary means of professional, racial, and intellectual coordination and discrimination have been of no avail. The group's police power is in itself no creation of the National Socialist regime. But before, the power of the professional and trade associations was limited by the individual's chance to stand aloof from them and was further subjected to the rule of the civil law interpreted by the civil courts. With the access to power of National Socialism the common legal bond of a generally applicable civil law disappeared more and more, and at the same time the professional organizations lost their voluntary character. The labor organization, economic groups, the handicraft and peasant organizations became compulsory organizations. By the same token the National Socialist system dispensed with an outside body to whose authority a group member could appeal when faced with an inequitable group decision.[3]

The authority of the group bureaucracy in industry, trade, and the professions, representing the most powerful interests or combinations of interests, is steadily increasing with the number of executive tasks relinquished to them by the state bureaucracy.[4] For this reason the

---

[3] Even in cases involving the coercive power of an organization as much affected with public interest as that of the social insurance doctors, the civil courts have shown the utmost reluctance to examine the orders of the group leadership which deprive a member of his livelihood. Cf. German Supreme Court, April 26, 1940, *Entscheidungen des Reichsgerichts in Zivilsachen*, 164, pp. 15, 32; German Supreme Court, December 21, 1937, *Zeitschrift der Akademie für Deutsches Recht*, 1938, p. 131, with comment by E. R. Huber; L. Kattenstroh, "Rechtscharakter und Nachprüfbarkeit von Anordnungen der Wirtschaftsgruppen," *Deutsches Recht*, 1939, p. 676.

[4] The most recent shifts in the distribution of functions between state bureaucracy and group bureaucracy have been discussed by A. Dresbach, "Aemter und Kammern, Bemerkungen über die staatliche Wirtschaftsverwaltung," *Die Wirtschaftskurve*, 1941, No. 3, p. 193.

conventional notions of property and expropriations are in need of redefinition. What profit an individual is able to draw from his real property, trade, or ownership of means of production depends mainly on his status within his professional group and on the general economic policy of the government. It is the group that determines the quota of available raw material and with its authoritative advice guides the labor authorities in deciding the vital question as to the labor force to which an individual entrepreneur should be entitled.[5] Should his property lose its economic value in consequence of such decisions of the group bureaucracy, it is once more the organs of the group and not the courts that will decide whether and to what amount and in what form indemnity may be granted.[6] They also will decide whether his exclusion from the ranks of the producers shall be permanent or transitory, whether he should be allowed some trade privileges or should become a rentier fed on a more or less liberal allowance, to be paid by his more fortunate competitors, or whether, as in the handicraft organization, he should simply be thrown into the ranks of the working class.[7] The logic of economic concentration has never worked more smoothly than when the ideology of the community deprived the weaker group member of the right to appeal to an outside body which would be prepared to maintain the intragroup balance. In the same vein the separation of the legal title to property from the enterpreneurial function has been legally stabilized by the new joint-stock company legislation. The minority stockholder has lost the last vestiges of legally enforcible influence on the administration of industrial enterprise, regardless of whoever may actually be in control, the old majority interests or new managerial elements. If the newspapers and court

[5] Cf. "Auskämmungskommission," *Frankfurter Zeitung*, May 18, 1941, Nos. 250–251, p. 7. Interestingly enough in this commission where members of the military and the state bureaucracy, the bureaucracy of the groups, and the chambers of commerce are always present, representatives of the Labor Front are called upon only irregularly.

[6] Cf. F. Wieacker, "Die Enteignung," in *Deutsches Verwaltungsrecht* (Munich, 1937), p. 749. The practice of the estate courts in indemnity cases is discussed by L. Gebhard and H. Merkel, *Das Recht der landwirtschaftlichen Marktordnung* (Munich, 1937), and by P. Giesecke, "Entschädigungspflicht bei marktordnenden Massnahmen," in *Festschrift für Justus Hedemann* (Jena, 1938), p. 368.

[7] We do not have figures on the depletion of these groups as a result of the war combing-out measures. As regards the prewar figures cf. *Der Vierjahresplan*, 1939, p. 1029.

decisions report at length instances of legal skirmishes between minority stockholders and the controlling group of an enterprise, this may serve the welcome aim of humanizing the world of corporate giants, but the decisions on the scant amount of information to be thrown open to stockholders do not affect the security of tenure assured to the controlling group and the complete economic domination it may exercise.

In the realm of agriculture, the government has gone as far as to sanction the redefinition of property relations brought about by the activity of the official groupings, which are more tightly knit in this field than in any other.[8] In the hereditary farm legislation it has created a powerful tool for the preservation of an agricultural aristocracy and middle class throughout the whole country. The creation and the security of tenure of a class of well-to-do peasants and landowners was of such great concern to the government that it took pains to create a strict legal order of succession in favor of the oldest or, as the local custom may be, the youngest son of the family, pushing the other children into the ranks of the proletariat. The decisions of the special hereditary farm courts make it abundantly clear that undivided preservation of substantial agricultural units in the same family takes precedence over considerations of proven ability.[9] The legislation on the so-called dissolution of entailed property, which enables the Junkers to take cover under the status of hereditary farmers, follows exactly the same pattern. When the present occupant of the entailed estate is in good standing with the authorities and the undivided preservation of his property fits into the Food Estate's agricultural program, he will become a "peasant." [10]

This legislation was introduced without delay in the territories regained from Poland.[11] While the great landowners thus get preferential treatment, the inverse process may be observed with regard to the internal settlement and colonization policy.[12] Under the Third Reich

---

[8] Cf. the remarks of A. Dresbach, *op. cit.*, p. 196.

[9] Supreme Hereditary Farm Court, May 30, 1939, *Entscheidungen des Reichserbhofgerichts*, 6, p. 295; December 20, 1939, 7, p. 237, and January 30, 1940, 7, p. 256.

[10] Statute of July 6, 1938, Art. 31, 1, *Reichsgesetzblatt*, 1938, 1, p. 825, Decree of March 20, 1939, *Reichsgesetzblatt*, 1939, 1, p. 509.

[11] Decree of March 18, 1941, *Reichsgesetzblatt*, 1941, 1, p. 154.

[12] *Wirtschaft und Statistik*, 1941, p. 285.

the internal settlement policy, which theoretically at least would have corresponded so well to the blood and soil ideology, receded more and more into the background. Agriculture now takes on the color of a large-scale industry; small units vanish, mechanization advances, cheap labor is furnished by the government, products are standardized and their sale monopolized by the Food Estate bureaucracy that fixes the prices in a bargaining process with the other powers of the realm.

In the case of the hereditary farmer, the government has taken care to lay down binding legal rules of succession in the interest of conserving a reliable rural upper class and in order to produce a maximum amount of staple food. In all other cases the new statute on wills of July 31, 1938, left fairly intact the right of the individual to dispose of his worldly goods.[13] It only strengthened the position of the family of the testator and gave government and family the legal weapons to harass the churches in case they might be beneficiaries and to nullify all dispositions in which an absent-minded testator might have shown some affection for a Jew or other enemy of the community.[14] This freedom to testate would be a problematical one and would not hinder the breaking-up of big industrial and rural estates if the legal succession were subject to a heavy tax burden as is now the case in England and the United States. But the German inheritance tax as established in 1925 was already comparatively mild, and it was further modified in 1934 in the same direction by granting more generous exemptions to smaller fortunes and large families and total exemption for the succession into a hereditary farm. Inheritance tax rates for children do not exceed 15 per cent in the highest bracket. That the inheritance tax is meaningless in terms of the German tax system may be seen from the fact that out of 23 billion marks total revenue collected in 1939, only 104 millions—that is to say, not even one half of one per cent—was derived from inheritance taxes.[15] Thus, of the two pillars which characterize

---

[13] *Reichsgesetzblatt*, 1941, I, p. 973.

[14] Cf. A. Roth, "Zum Art. 48, 2 des Testamentgesetzes," *Deutsches Recht*, 1941, p. 166, and G. Boehmer, "Die guten Sitten im Zeichen nationalsozialistischer Familienpflicht," *Zeitschrift der Akademie für Deutsches Recht*, 1941, p. 73; German Supreme Court, September 17, 1940, and September 19, 1940, *ibid.*, pp. 84–85.

[15] *Wirtschaft und Statistik*, 1941, p. 235. It should be borne in mind that there is only a Reich Inheritance Tax in Germany.

the legal order of the liberal era, private property in the means of production and the freedom of contract, property, even if heavily mortgaged to the political machine, has managed to survive. But what about contracts? Is it still justifiable to say, as is officially done in Germany,[16] that the liberty of contract, together with private property, competition, and the continuance of free private trade associations, forms the irreplaceable fundamental of the racial community? This characteristic utterance itself gives a clue to the answer. The right to combine freely into trade associations is, under prevailing German conditions, synonymous with the existence of powerful cartels and combines, which exercise public power either directly or under the thin disguise of official chambers and groups. Liberty of contract and government-sponsored monopoly are incompatible. The effect of this state of affairs was to reduce to a minimum the sphere in which free contracts are still concluded. We witness an acceleration of the long-drawn-out process by which general norms and conditions are substituted for individual contracts. The conditions of business relations between producers in different stages of the process of production, or between producers and agents of distribution, are either covered in advance by a general agreement between partners of approximately equal economic strength or are forced by the more powerful party on its economically weaker partner. Only where this unilateral dictate threatened to become too disastrous in its possible consequences did the government take the supervision of these dictated norms into its own hands. Under the Third Reich the pseudo-contractual relations shaped by such unilateral dictates are steadily increasing. As cartels acquire official titles as authorities for distribution, their clients can do nothing but acquiesce in the general conditions laid down by them. Criticism and suggestions of academic writers notwithstanding, the general norms and conditions incessantly replace liberty of contract and make it meaningless.[17] But whereas the government took only an

16 C. H. Nipperdey, "Das System des bürgerlichen Rechts," in *Zur Erneurung des Bürgerlichen Rechts* (Munich, 1938), p. 99, and Hans Frank, *op. cit.*, p. 21.

17 The German literature in this field is increasing. We note only the scholarly discussion by L. Raiser, *Recht der Allgemeinen Geschäftsbedingungen* (Hamburg, 1935); the characteristically vague reform proposals by H. Brandt, "Die allgemeinen Geschäftsbedingungen und das sogenannte dispositive Recht," *Deutsche Rechtswissenschaft*, 5 (1940), p. 76; and the cocksure attitude of the representative of industry, C. van Erkelens, "Lieferbedingungen der Industrie im Kampf der

intermittent interest in the conditions under which so-called free contracts were concluded, it did not hesitate to interfere more and more with the stages of execution of individual contracts. At first it limited its interference by refusing the creditor its help in executing a judgment against a small debtor. Later it went further and extended to every reliable racial comrade the help of the judge in getting wholly or partially rid of the debts he had contracted during the "pseudo-prosperity" period or the previous depression.[18] The war decrees generously widened the frame of this legislation. Liquidation of most of the small creditor-debtor relations, whether they concern rents, mortgages, doctor's or furniture bills, was entrusted to the administrative skill of a judge, who was expected to alleviate the little man's burden wherever feasible.[19] Contract, therefore, is steadily disappearing from the legal horizon of Mr. Everyman. The workers, the small businessmen, and the small farmers, as well as the consumers in general, have no bargaining power, as they are prohibited from combining for such purposes. The local representatives of the Party, of the Labor Front, or of the National Socialist welfare organizations may find it convenient to recommend a change in a particular working, wage, distribution, or price arrangement. They may or may not be able to carry their point against the industry and industry's bureaucratic spokesmen. But these battles are fought and compromises are reached over the head of Mr. Everyman. For him contract has been replaced by the peculiar compound of private command and administrative order. This compound, which joins in the same individual undertaking the interest of private property and of the administration, the private advantage, and the public purpose, is one of the first characteristics of the new legal

---

Meinungen," *Zeitschrift der Akademie für Deutsches Recht*, 1940, p. 367. More interesting than the theoretical discussion is the attitude of the bureaucracy which favors more and more the policy to make standardized contracts universally binding and applicable. Cf. C. Ritter, "Legalisierung der allgemeinen deutschen Spediteurbedingungen," *Deutsches Recht*, 1940, p. 779, and especially K. Nehring, "Das neue deutsche Speditionsrecht," *Hanseatische Rechts- und Gerichtszeitung*, 1940, 23 (1940), Abt. A, pp. 75, 80.

[18] Statute of August 17, 1938, *Reichsgesetzblatt*, 1938, 1, p. 1033. Cf. H. Vogel, "Die Rechtsprechung zur Schuldenbereinigung," *Deutsches Recht*, 1940, p. 1343.

[19] Decree of September 3, 1940, *Reichsgesetzblatt*, 1940, 1, p. 1209. Cf. Breithaupt, "Die Neufassung des Gesetzes über eine Bereinigung alter Schulden," *Deutsches Recht*, 1940, p. 1602.

order. Taken in this sense, the National Socialist legal doctrine rightly claims to have overcome the traditional gulf between private and public law.[20] Free agreement and contract are restricted to the province of the mighty. Their contract, in turn, has lost its private character, since their working agreements are the basis of the new constitutional order.

We may venture to define the present conditions of property in Germany as follows: the ranks of the proprietary class, controlling the means of production, are steadily shrinking through such well-known devices as concentration, Aryanization, combing-out legislation, quota restrictions, and closing-down "on account of war emergency." [21] Those proprietary elements that belong to the rentier group suffer from the administration's control over investment conditions and rents. They suffer also from the general ability to gain a foothold in the process of production, which, with the administration's active furtherance, has been monopolized by a few powerful individuals and combines. New property titles are accumulating in the hands of the newcomers from the ranks of party, army, and bureaucracy. Yet, members of these groups do not always find it advisable to acquire formal titles to property but find it sufficient for their purpose to reap the fruit of administrative control. The freedom to transfer property titles and the lack of onerous inheritance taxes are intended to perpetuate the property structure as it is developing from this process of concentration.

The German lawyer has acquired the habit of separating rather sharply the rules which dominate family life from the realm of contractual property relations. In fact, it is one of the most frequent reproaches against the old civil code that its general rules placed business relations on the same footing as the order of the family; the National Socialist legislation takes pride in having radically separated the issues of blood and money.[22] It contends that in its new racial and family law it has prepared a basis for the development of the racial community. This new legislation excels in two characteristics: the

---

[20] E. R. Huber, "Neue Grundlagen des Hoheitlichen Rechts," *Grundfragen der neuen Rechtswissenschaft*, 1935, pp. 143, 151.

[21] Even the German legal literature has to recognize this process. Cf. J. W. Hedemann, *Deutsches Wirtschaftsrecht* (Berlin, 1939), p. 209: "The distribution of property becomes more critical or assumes at least other forms."

[22] F. Schlegelberger, *Abschied vom B. G. B.* (Munich, 1937), p. 9.

thoroughgoing extirpation of the Jews and, above all, its outspoken populationist traits. We do not have to dwell here upon the anti-Semitic legislation, as it constitutes the most widely known element of the German legislative and administrative endeavors. The populationist traits of the new family legislation are visible everywhere. They are evident in the social and welfare policy, with marriage loans, substantial tax reductions and exemptions, and special family allowances. They are evident in the manifold attempts to improve the position of illegitimate mothers and children. That such adjustment measures are due not to moral or humanitarian but to purely populationist motives, a recent edict shows very distinctly. This edict orders the school authorities to see to it that illegitimate children do not feel at a disadvantage psychologically, provided that racially and biologically they are not objectionable.[23] The exemption of parents from punishment under antiprocurement statutes in case they allow their children to have premarital sexual intercourse under their own roof has been forced on a recalcitrant higher judiciary, mainly by the propaganda of the influential weekly of the SS Blackshirts, *Das Schwarze Korps*.[24] In spite of earlier judicial utterances to the contrary, an employer is no longer allowed to dismiss female workers on grounds of pregnancy, regardless of whether the expectant mother is or is not married.[25] This relaxation of conventional moral conceptions, noticeable everywhere in Germany, was accompanied by open attacks on some of the most basic doctrines of the established churches, calculated to keep down to a minimum any ecclesiastical influence on the social life of the family. Since millions of Germans today live a barracks life rather than a family life, the state found it easy to encourage *ad hoc* sexual relations. Together with this encouragement went the official endeavors to minimize legal as well as social consequences of illegitimacy. Such moves could not fail to influence deeply the sex mores of the German population and especially of German youth, who would, of course, be

---

[23] Edict of the Ministry of Education of May 29, 1940, reprinted in *Deutsche Justiz*, 102 (1940), p. 1143.

[24] German Supreme Court, June 29, 1937, and the new line of thought in the decision of the Cottbus *Schöffengericht* of February 7, 1937, in *Juristische Wochenschrift*, 1937, pp. 2386–89.

[25] German Supreme Labor Court, August 21, 1937, *Juristische Wochenschrift*, 1937, p. 3057.

more immediately affected. This change in turn was bound to leave a heavy imprint on the institution of marriage, even if not a single word of the family law, as contained in the old civil code, had been changed. But, in fact, the government subjected the family law to complete revision in 1938.[26]

While this policy generally transforms every woman into an official agent of procreation, marriage in particular is regarded as a state institution to which the main responsibility for raising the birth rate had been transferred. Marriage becomes a business relationship, the success or failure of which is measured in terms of the production of soldiers and future mothers who live up to the physical and intellectual standards of the Third Reich. The Hereditary Health Courts are instituted to uphold such standards at the admission into marriage and during its continuance; divorce and annulment procedures perform the same tasks at its dissolution. Under the limited divorce facilities granted by the earlier German legislation, the parties who wanted to separate usually had to reach collusive agreement which then was registered by the court under one of the existing legal categories. The new statute of 1938 has opened a wide field for controversial divorce proceedings by abandoning the principle of guilt. It has introduced a number of situations in which circumstances outside the control of the partners are grounds for a divorce. Foremost is the sterility of either partner, but contagious diseases, mental defects, or a three-year separation are also sufficient grounds for issuance of a divorce decree.[27] Whatever progressive characteristics this statute may have had, they have been completely submerged in the course of its interpretation by the courts. Not in all cases may the decisions rendered be as crude and morally shocking as the following one handed down by the German Supreme Court. A woman had lost her fertility through an operation necessitated by an abdominal cavity pregnancy. The husband's request for a divorce was granted and a plea of duress was denied to the defendant mainly on the grounds that the state had an active interest in the plaintiff's getting children from a new marriage.[28] But such decisions set precedents, and it is no wonder that the chief reasoning in divorce

[26] Statute of July 6, 1938, *Reichsgesetzblatt*, 1938, 1, p. 807.
[27] *Ibid.*, Art. 50–55.
[28] German Supreme Court, September 5, 1940, *Deutsches Recht*, 1940, p. 2001.

cases gravitates more and more around the rights and duties deriving from the fulfillment, partial fulfillment, or impossibility of fulfillment of maternal functions.[29] On the one hand, egotistical or immoral motivations of a partner are encouraged when they happen to coincide with the government's desire to raise the birth rate.[30] But on the other hand, the same official considerations may lead to the maintenance of an entirely meaningless marriage as a reward for services a mother has rendered to the state by the production of a numerous progeny.[31] It is too early to surmise all the consequences of this policy. The rise in the rate of divorce and annulment proceedings, which began immediately after 1933, may have been partially caused during the first years by the desire of many to avail themselves of generous facilities for getting rid of Jewish partners.[32] Under the new law of 1938, the divorce rate, as was to be expected, jumped up. In 1939, out of every 10,000 marriages 38 were terminated by divorce as against 29 in 1932 and 32 in 1936.[33] That the institution of marriage does not stand to win much by its instrumentalization, which makes it the most convenient breeding agency, seems a fairly safe conclusion.

Before we enter into a discussion of the ways and methods peculiar to the coercive machinery of the Third Reich, let us have a moment's look at the personnel which runs this machine and at the principles according to which it is run. The personnel of the judicial bureaucracy, especially in the higher ranks, still consists overwhelmingly of the very persons who held office under, and to the detriment of, the Weimar Republic. As late as the beginning of 1941, a lifelong member of the bureaucracy of the Ministry of Justice, Dr. Schlegelberger, was appointed Acting Minister of Justice.

Yet, under the traditional conceptions, the judiciary is only a con-

[29] German Supreme Court, June 29, 1940, *ibid.*, p. 1567; July 8, 1940, *ibid.*, p. 1627.

[30] German Supreme Court, May 7, 1940, *ibid.*, p. 1362.

[31] German Supreme Court, March 6, 1940, *ibid.*, p. 1050; March 20, 1940, *ibid.*, p. 1049; May 22, 1940, *ibid.*, p. 1363.

[32] As late as 1939 an appeal court helped a writer to an annulment of his marriage, reasoning that only after the events of 1938 (vom Rath assassination and November pogroms) did the appellant get a clear perception of the Jewish question. Munich, Appeal Court, December 11, 1939, *ibid.*, p. 327.

[33] *Wirtschaft und Statistik*, 1941, p. 37, including some interesting comments showing how the rise of the birth rate has become the uppermost official consideration.

comitant to an established body of laws which it adapts to the special needs of the community. The procedural formulas which it develops provide a certain amount of predictability.[34] The contending individuals and groups, though they never are sure which of the many possible interpretations of their behavior will prevail in a given case, usually could confine their actions within such limits that these could not be said to contradict openly the wording of the law and the procedural requirements of the established courts and agencies. The business of individualization carried on by the courts contained a certain amount of rationality, in so far as their decisions tried to satisfy as many as possible of the so-called legitimate interests of society.

The rationality which we can observe in the courts and agencies of the Third Reich is of quite a different nature. Rationality here does not mean that there are universally applicable rules the consequences of which could be calculated by those whom they affect.[35] Rationality here means only that the whole apparatus of law and law-enforcing is made exclusively serviceable to those who rule. Since no general notions prevail which could be referred to by the ruling and the ruled alike and which thus might restrict the arbitrariness of the administrative practice, the rules are being used to serve the specific purposes of those ruling. The legal system that results is rational for them only. This, then, is a strictly Technical Rationality which has as its main and uppermost concern the question: How can a given command be executed so as to have the maximum effect in the shortest possible time? In a recent speech Reich Minister Hans Frank, President of the Academy of German Law and Governor General of Poland, quite correctly compared this kind of rationality to the working of a good machine. "A smoothly functioning and technically superior administration is to a chaotic despotism what precision machinery is to an unreliable makeshift instrument producing only chance results." [36] Frank wants the

[34] *Vide* K. Loewenstein, "Law in the Third Reich," *Yale Law Journal*, XLV (1936), 779, 782, 814.

[35] Cf. the opposite conclusions drawn by E. Fraenkel, *The Dual State* (New York, 1941), who holds that the existence of a rational law is necessary for the existence of a monopoly-capitalist society, overestimating, however, the importance of some isolated judicial decisions of the earlier epoch. *Vide* my review of this excellent book in *Political Science Quarterly*, LVI (1941), 434.

[36] H. Frank, "Technik des Staates," *Zeitschrift der Akademie für deutsches Recht*, 1941, pp. 2 f.

industrial methods of taylorism introduced into the realm of statecraft
in order to get the most precise answer to the question as to how the
will of the political leadership can be put into practical effect as speed-
ily as possible. Such an attitude is not the wishful dream of a particular,
if highly placed, individual. Technical rationality simply follows a pattern drawn by the organization of industry. There, it was not conceived as a method for production departments only. The now officially sponsored Dinta (Institute for Scientific Management and Rationalization of Work), when still owned by representatives of industry, was the first to introduce the same principle into the business of
human relations.[37] Technical rationality, as dominant over all governmental organization, precludes the existence of a general body of
law in which the rules do evolve but slowly. Under the new system, a
legal rule can have only a purely provisional character; it must be
possible to change a rule without notice, and, if necessary, retroac-
tively. The Third Reich, with an unlimited legislative and decree
power given the Führer and liberally delegated by him to his paladins,
amply provides for such facilities. With this legislative omnipotence
and latitude for delegations goes also an unlimited willingness to
abandon any pretense of logical coherence. Out of every individual
situation the maximum of advantage must be drawn, even if the second
step contradicts the premises under which the first was taken.[38] Moreover, technical rationality makes it necessary to search always for the
shortest ways of transmission from the top to the bottom. That too has
been taken care of. Once an agreement is reached by the mighty of the
realm and promulgated under the Führer's authority, there is no intermediary organ which could venture to arrest or delay its execution.
No court has the right to contest the constitutionality or legality of
any legislative enactment. Whereas the judge is given a certain amount
of leeway to examine the extent to which anterior legislation conforms
to the National Socialist principles,[39] he is emphatically discouraged

---

[37] As to the Dinta cf. F. L. Neumann, *Behemoth: The Structure and Practice of National Socialism* (New York, 1942), p. 429.

[38] Cf., for instance, the Decree of March 27, 1941, *Reichsgesetzblatt*, 1941, I, p. 177, which legalizes until December 31, 1942, the practice of Aryan successors to Jewish business concerns carrying on their premises the name of their Jewish predecessors side by side with their own.

[39] On National Socialist "equity" cf. K. Loewenstein, *op. cit.*, p. 804.

from making similar inquiries into any piece of Nazi legislation.[40] In short, the idea of technical rationality which underlies the new governmental organization actually finds its nearest approximation in a perfectly running, though complicated, piece of machinery. Nobody save the owners is entitled to question the meaningfulness of the services which the machine performs: the engineers who actually operate it have to content themselves with producing immediate reactions to the owners' changing commands. They may be ordered to proceed more rapidly or more slowly, they may be ordered to change some technical processes and to attain some variations in output. The purport of the results achieved lies beyond this kind of rationality, which is aimed only at the certainty that every order will produce an exactly calculable reaction.

In its judiciary the Third Reich has created an almost perfect tool for the realization of its orders. For reasons we have already explained before, the judiciary has lost much of its earlier importance as an agency for deciding differences between various groups and between individuals. The judicial statistics amply prove this thesis. With the above-mentioned exception of matrimonial cases, the number of legal procedures shows a startling decline. Thus, for instance, the roles of those courts which had jurisdiction over civil disputes involving 500 RM or more show a decline from 319,000 cases in the prosperity year of 1929 to 112,000 in 1937.[41] That does not necessarily mean that the courts are going out of business. But they have thoroughly changed their character. From independent agencies of society, able to throw their weight with any of the contending social groups, they have turned into executive agencies of the government. They are employed with preference where a certain amount of individualization is desired. As such they clear up the debtor-creditor or producer-consumer relation, and as such they decide many of the issues which come up in the course of the racial legislation.

As the law, decree, or edict on whose authority the judge bases his decision can be changed without delay, an inopportune decision of his has only the effect that the legal rule will be immediately changed. In

[40] German Supreme Court, June 17, 1940, *Zeitschrift der Akademie für Deutsches Recht*, 1940, p. 304.
[41] *Deutsche Justiz*, 100 (1938), p. 1140.

the realm of criminal law, the stake of the authority of the state is too important to allow an undesirable decision to go unchallenged. The war legislation has, therefore, introduced the possibility of changing every individual criminal judgment in the desired direction. A Special Section of the *Reichsgericht* is directed to take up the case again and revise the decision [42] in the direction desired by the Führer as indicated by the *Oberreichsanwalt*. The first case to be carried before the Special Section was as follows: A man known for a long time to be a homosexual had profited from the blackout to force a younger man to become the object of his desires. A Special Court had sentenced the offender to hard labor. There are no appeals by either the defendant or prosecutor from sentences imposed by the Special Courts. Nevertheless, under the new law, the case was reopened before the Special Section of the *Reichsgericht* at the request of the *Oberreichsanwalt* and terminated, as desired, in a death sentence.[43]

A decision which is disadvantageous to government interests, though rarely apt to be forthcoming, is frequently of neither legal nor social consequence for the establishment of a precedent for future cases arising in similar circumstances. In addition the judge, like any other administrative official, is accountable for the contents of his decision. Where the relentless pressure of the party through channels like the *Schwarze Korps* should prove of no avail, the new organizational statutes provide ample facilities for discharging or transferring a recalcitrant judge.[44] The judiciary is entitled to have and to express opinions of its own only in those cases where it does not act as a kind of

[42] Decree of September 16, 1939, *Reichsgesetzblatt*, 1939, 1, p. 1841. Cf. W. Tegtmeyer, "Der ausserordentliche Einspruch," *Juristische Wochenschrift*, 1939, p. 2060, and my article "Criminal Law in National Socialist Germany" *Studies in Philosophy and Social Science*, VIII, 444 ff.

[43] German Supreme Court (Special Section), December 6, 1939, *Zeitschrift der Akademie für deutsches Recht*, 1940, p. 48, with comment by Klee.

[44] Judges are subject to the provisions of the Civil Service Statute. *Vide* A. Brand, *Das Deutsche Beamtengesetz* (Berlin, 1937), p. 462. Regarding the possibilities of transferring judges to other jobs, cf. the Decree of September 1, 1939, *Reichsgesetzblatt*, 1939, 1, p. 1658, and especially Art. 4,3 of the "Decree on the Organization of a Supreme Administrative Court" of April 3, 1941, *ibid.*, 1941, 1, p. 201. For an interesting definition of the meaning of judicial independence under National Socialism, cf. Hans Frank, "Reichsverwaltungsgericht," *Deutsches Recht*, 1941, p. 1169.

LEGAL ORDER OF NATIONAL SOCIALISM

common executive organ to the combined ruling classes. There are some boundary spheres where the distribution of power between the mighty of the realm has not been finally settled. The judiciary, for instance, may trespass into the sphere of the party and try with varying success to apply the general rules of civil and criminal responsibility to acts of party officials.[45] The party, of course, does not stand by passively in such jurisdictional conflicts, and presses forward vigorous attacks of its own against the bureaucracy. Right now it uses the party-dominated police as a cover to wrest from the judicial bureaucracy the complete control of the criminal police and, therewith, the final direction of criminal prosecution.[46] Generally speaking, however, the industrialists and landowners, party and army, as well as the corresponding bureaucracies, jealously see to it that nobody trespasses into the provinces carved out for each by common agreement; the tendency is, therefore, toward departmentalization, toward disappearance of a unified system of law behind innumerable steadily increasing special competences. If technical rationality is nevertheless to be preserved, two conditions have to be fulfilled. First, every official agency must grant recognition to an official act of other public agencies. Second, each of these groups must be equipped with a penal power of its own in order to execute swift reprisals against malefactors in its own sphere. The party has established its own jurisdiction over its members and over its special subdivisions like the SS;[47] the army achieved the

[45] A. Lingg, *Die Verwaltung der NSDAP* (Berlin, 1940), p. 257. The right of the courts to pass on this question is upheld by S. Grundmann, "Die richterliche Nachprüfung von politischen Führungsakten," *Zeitschrift für die gesamten Staatswissenschaften*, C (1940), 511 ff., and by the German Supreme Court, February 17, 1939, *Deutsches Recht*, 1939, p. 1785.

[46] W. Best, *Die Deutsche Polizei* (Darmstadt, 1940), p. 28, against which E. R. Huber is polemizing in his review, in *Zeitschrift für die gesamten Staatswissenschaften*, CI (1941), 723, where he gives the legal and administrative arguments of the higher bureaucracy in its fight to restrict party influence.

[47] One of the first statutes of the Third Reich, dated April 28, 1933, *Reichsgesetzblatt*, 1933, I, p. 230, enables the Führer to institute special disciplinary and penal courts for the SA and SS. Cf. also the Decree of October 17, 1939, *ibid.*, 1939, I, p. 2107. That the party, even under actual war conditions, does not relinquish its grip upon its special formations becomes evident from the Decree of April 17, 1940, *ibid.*, 1940, I, p. 659, which takes the jurisdiction over members of SS formations in the armed forces away from the courts-martial and transfers it to the SS Court in Munich.

reestablishment of its own courts-martial as one of the first rewards of the new order; [48] the industrial groups and chambers as well as the official organizations of the Food Estate can levy fines of their own; the Ministries of Finance and of Economics and the Price Commissioner also have been equipped with extensive powers to fine.[49] The latest newcomer in this list is the compulsory Labor Service. By decree of November 17, 1940,[50] extensive penal powers, which for some time it had been exercising "illegally," [51] were confirmed to it. This list of exemptions and penal privileges is not given merely for curiosity's sake. With the one exception of the penal privileges granted to the bureaucracy of the Ministries of Finance and Economics which allow powerful individuals to buy off their penalties without adverse publicity and thus make the businessman prefer this kind of administrative jurisdiction to the general one of the criminal courts, this development appears as a death warrant to individual rights.

The separation of functions between the employer and the coercive machinery of the state was one of the main guarantees of individual liberty in a society where an ever diminishing number of people controlled the means of production. This separation is swept aside when the organizations—Party, Army, Food Estate, Labor Services—on whose attitude depends the social existence of the individual are able to bolster up their commands with a, so to speak, "company-owned" disciplinary and penal power. It is at this point that the inroads of the National Socialist machine into the daily life of the average citizen appear the most striking and that absence of an outside agency willing and able to sift the individual's grievances will bring the greatest moral and material hardship.

The repressive activities of this joint enterprise, officially called the Racial Community, are exercised by the already mentioned special agencies, by the so-called People's Court, the Special Courts, the regular criminal courts, and last, but by no means least, by the party-dominated police. The police has a special and comprehensive jurisdiction:

[48] Statute of May 12, 1933, *ibid.*, 1933, 1, p. 264.
[49] Cf. K. Siegert, *Wirtschaftsstrafrecht* (Berlin, 1939), and the Decree of April 6, 1940, *Reichsgesetzblatt*, 1940, 1, p. 610 regulating the procedure in regard to contraventions in the sphere of distribution.
[50] *Ibid.*, p. 1513.
[51] Cf. my article, *loc cit.*, p. 453, note 3.

it may kill or imprison for an indeterminate time persons whom it thinks to be inimical to the people's welfare, without taking the trouble of handing them over to other agencies [52] for examination of the merits of the case. It may likewise apply the same technique after the other agencies have relinquished an accused person, either after he has served his time or has been acquitted. The latter does not happen too frequently—the rate of acquittals in the regular criminal courts has gone down from 13 per cent in 1932 to 7 per cent in the second quarter of 1940.[53] The procedures followed by the agencies of repression correspond in the highest degree to the already formulated principles of technical rationality. To attain the results desired by the government with the maximum speed and with the greatest possible degree of accuracy, criminal procedure, that part of the law that was the most formalized hitherto, now had to become its most formless one.[54] Careful preparation was sacrificed to speed, all possibilities for effective defense were abolished,[55] the functions of the judge, traditionally the central figure in a German criminal trial, completely receded behind those of the prosecutor, and, finally, the opportunities for an appeal were severely curtailed and often completely abolished in capital cases. The same technical calculation dominates the methods applied to the different categories of offenders. The substantive penal law has been equipped with a network of conceptions which with every succeeding legislative enactment became broader and less definite.[56] Within a framework sufficiently broad to include easily every supposed wrongdoer, the government has unlimited latitude to be lenient or brutal. It has shown the utmost leniency against the small fry in general and against every criminal in its own ranks. A most generous

[52] W. Best, "Die politische Polizei des Dritten Reiches," in *Deutsches Verwaltungsrecht* (Munich, 1937), p. 417.

[53] *Wirtschaft und Statistik*, 1941, p. 247.

[54] Cf. the somewhat melancholic reflections of G. Dahm, "Richtermacht und Gerichtsverfassung," *Zeitschrift für die gesamten Staatswissenschaften*, CI (1941), 287.

[55] As regards the limitations set to the lawyer's representation of his client's interest, cf. the much publicized Groepke case, *Deutsches Recht*, 1941, p. 918.

[56] Cf. R. Freisler, "Rechtswahrer-Gedanken zum Kriegsjahr 1940," *Deutsche Justiz*, CIII (1941), 6, 17. Cf. also the Decree of September 7, 1939, *Reichsgesetzblatt*, 1939, 1, p. 1683, forbidding listening to foreign broadcasts, which penalizes the spreading of news which might weaken the power of resistance of the German people, with the comments in *Deutsches Recht*, CII (1940), 1415.

succession of general amnesties and general *nolle prosequi*, repeated fairly regularly every second year, was turned out to the benefit of the host of wrongdoers of little consequence, granting absolution of nearly every crime committed by overzealous party members.[57] Directed likewise by the desire to enroll as large as possible a number of racial comrades into the regular labor process, the government passed on November 17, 1939, and complemented in 1941, some enlightened rules which allow criminals, after a certain period, to pass as not previously convicted.[58] The same viewpoint has dominated for a long time the National Socialist attitude toward juvenile crime, where reformation long remained the official slogan. Still, in 1940, thanks to the combined efforts of the youth and the labor authorities, who were eager not to lose a single part of their most precious capital, labor power, fines and short-term imprisonment for juvenile criminals were replaced by a special light and short form of detention.[59]

However, long before the beginning of the war this policy was overshadowed by the increasing brutality which became the rule against all those regarded as criminal enemies of the people at large. The number of enemies who did not find mercy continued to increase. In the beginning these comprised mainly habitual and professional criminals who were taken into preventive custody, as well as traitors who were believed to have menaced or to threaten to menace the internal and external security of the Reich. Soon this category of enemies of the people was extended to cover the new crime of "race defilement" and was applied to the ever increasing body of sex offenders, which seems to have arisen from the general brutalization of sexual morality. Now, after two years of war, the list of enemies of the people's community who have to be extirpated to protect the home

[57] As regards the earlier amnesties cf. my article, *loc. cit.*, p. 457. A new amnesty has been granted at the beginning of the war by a decree of September 4, 1939, *Reichsgesetzblatt*, 1939, I, p. 1753. No figures have been published, however, as to the effects of this amnesty.

[58] *Reichsgesetzblatt*, 1939, I, p. 139, and the announcement in the *Frankfurter Zeitung*, September 12, 1941. Cf. also M. Wachinger, "Die Wirkungen der Tilgung eines Strafvermerks," *Deutsche Justiz*, CII (1940), 863.

[59] Decree of October 4, 1940, *Reichsgesetzblatt*, 1940, p. 1366. Cf. also Rietzsch, "Neuordnung des Jugendstrafrechts," *Deutsches Recht*, 1940, p. 698. Contrast the Decree of October 4, 1939, *Reichsgesetzblatt*, 1939, I, p. 2000, which tends to deprive juveniles in the more serious cases of the privileges granted in the special juvenile jurisdictions.

front comprises those perpetrating almost every type of criminal act if committed by means of violence [60] or as an exploitation of the state of war. It comprises, too, violations of the War Economy Decree of September 4, 1939.[61] In this connection the Führer claimed that in this war, for the first time in history, the principle by which the merchant made his gain, whereas the soldier died,[62] had lost its validity. As if to confirm this, the German newspapers are at present announcing the first death sentences for usury. But since Sec. 25,4 of the above-mentioned War Economy Decree exempts cartel prices, it is obvious that the main war profiteers are in no actual danger of punishment. But as a means of popular oppression and general deterrence rather than of monopoly control the death penalty has become fairly widespread during the last two years. There are no accurate figures available. The published statistics, even if accepted as accurate, cover only the number of offenders convicted through the channels of the special and regular law courts, which probably means that they embrace only a small percentage of criminals liable to the death penalty. For the sake of comparison, however, those figures are important in that they indicate a sharp increase in the use of the death penalty. In the following figures the number of convictions for murder is compared with that of death sentences in general. In 1937 the quarterly average of all convictions for murder, attempts at or participation in murder, was 45, as against a total of death sentences for all crimes, including murder, of 14; the quarterly average for 1939 begins to show an inverse ratio between murder convictions and death sentences, 34 murders as against 39 death sentences, and the known figures for the second quarter of 1940 show only 14 sentenced murderers, but 80 death sentences.[63] The death penalty thus covers a steadily widening range of so-called criminal behavior.

Relatively late German writers and officials have realized that the

---

[60] For an extensive interpretation of the term "weapon to cut and thrust" as including the use of the bare fist, cf. Stuttgart Special Court, February 1, 1940, *Deutsches Recht*, 1940, p. 441.

[61] *Reichsgesetzblatt*, 1939, I, p. 1609.

[62] Cf. "Bekanntmachungen über die Bekämpfung der Preistreiberei," Executive Decree of January 11, 1941, *Deutsche Justiz*, CIII (1941), 110, 112, which contains detailed instructions as to the procedure to be followed in the case of offenders of the War Economy Decrees.

[63] *Wirtschaft und Statistik*, 1939, p. 553; 1940, p. 557; and 1941, p. 257.

complete subjection of criminal law and procedure to the idea of technical rationality is bound to shatter completely the specific protective functions inherent in traditional law; and the hope is being expressed that it might be possible, after the war, to reconcile what we called Technical Rationality with somewhat enlarged protective devices and guarantees.[64] Yet, it stands to reason that a system of law which seeks to operate by technical rationality and which at the same time attempts partial retention of liberal guarantees—two mutually exclusive and incompatible objectives since they derive from different social systems —must soon exhaust itself. The social processes that have taken place under National Socialism provide the explanation of the changes which the legal system has undergone. The concentration of economic power which characterizes the social and political development of the Nazi regime crystallizes in the tendency toward preserving the institution of private property both in industrial and in agricultural production, whilst abolishing the correlative to private property, the freedom of contract. In the contract's place the administrative sanction now has become the *alter ego* of property itself. Equality of law and freedom of contract tended to secure protection to everyone who had acquired legal title to property. The new system of administrative property relations, while abolishing the general rules and uniform procedures, shifts the decision on what property titles may be validated to the monopoly-dominated group.

Within every power grouping, the position of those in control is enhanced through subordinating the individual member of the group to the omnipotence of the group hierarchy that acquires a relatively autonomous jurisdiction of its own. Thus, in the very structure of society the rights and privileges granted the individual in his own right are abolished. Intragroup conflicts in which the individual may fight for the preservation of his claims and legal titles become an arena of mere force collisions and the economically atomized individual becomes a mere object of domination by monopolistic group and estate machines. Simultaneously, legality, no longer serving as an armor to protect the individual, becomes null and void and dissolves into technical rationality which now is the foundation of the structure of legal

[64] G. Dahm, *op. cit.*, and Hans Frank, "Die Aufgaben der Strafrechtserneuerung," *Zeitschrift der Akademie für Deutsches Recht*, 1941, p. 25.

institutions, of the legal apparatus, and of the machine that applies them, the judiciary.

But then, no rights of the individual have to be preserved and maintained in spheres outside economic and political life either. Legal regulation of human relations, whether it be in the sphere of contractual relations, family life, or criminal infractions, becomes subject to demands of everyday necessities of the totalitarian regime without mediation or indirect transmission. Necessities of securing sufficient labor supply preside as directly over legislation on matrimony as they rule over criminal procedure and substantive criminal law. Where there is a labor shortage which must be overcome as soon as possible, no ethical considerations will influence the decision as to the status of marriage or divorce, and no stipulations of the criminal code will prevent the government from refraining to prosecute or from pardoning numerous offenders. At the same time, special categories of offenders will be outlawed and victimized to serve as mementos of the defenselessness of the atomized individual and of the omnipotence of the groups and machines that run the state with the assistance of a technicalized apparatus of law and law-enforcing.

The system of technical rationality as the foundation of law and legal practice has superseded any system for preservation of individual rights and thus has definitely made law and legal practice an instrument of ruthless domination and oppression in the interest of those who control the main economic and political levers of social power. Never has the process of alienation between law and morality gone so far as in the society which allegedly has perfected the integration of those very conceptions.

DECREE POWERS AND

CONSTITUTIONAL LAW IN FRANCE

UNDER THE THIRD REPUBLIC

In the World War period and after, the use of extraordinary powers by the executive for legislative purposes became so widespread in Europe that constitutional theorists began to find it convenient to give up the doctrine of legislative supremacy. The constitutional basis for these extraordinary powers has been found in one of two ways: either the parliament may authorize the government to exercise certain legislative functions by way of delegation, or certain provisions in the constitution may be interpreted as giving the executive the right under certain circumstances not only to take specific administrative steps but also to issue rules of a more general character.[1] In either case, the question invariably arises as to how far the delegation of power may go, or as to the degree to which alleged constitutional emergency provisions may be used to supersede parliamentary legislation.

In France, no constitutional emergency power is provided in the "organic" laws of 1875 which could give a starting point for independent rule-making activity. A law of April 3, 1878, defined very closely the conditions under which a state of siege may be declared and surrounded such a declaration with elaborate provisions for parliamentary

Reprinted, by permission, from *American Political Science Review*, XXXIV (1940), 1104–23.
[1] It is a merit of the interesting article by F. M. Watkins, "Constitutional Dictatorship," in Friedrich and Mason, eds., *Public Policy* (Cambridge, Mass., 1940), p. 355, to have sharply separated both issues, the original constitutional emergency powers and the parliamentary enabling acts.

supervision. It is apparent that this statute does not allow the government to decree rules of a general character.[2]

The possibility of an executive power lacking a parliamentary vote of confidence, the so-called *Präsidialregierung*, which German theorists in the pre-Hitler period tried so hard to establish, could therefore never find a legal basis in France. The history of French enabling acts begins, interestingly enough, with failures. In December, 1916, the Briand government requested power to issue all decrees necessary for the conduct of the war, but was forced to abandon the bill in the face of the manifest hostility of the Chamber.[3] The second attempt was made by Poincaré in 1924. In a discussion which dragged out for five weeks, Poincaré argued that, in the final analysis, it is in the interest of parliamentary government that the Chamber sometimes accept a temporary restriction of its constitutional rights. When economies must be made quickly, he contended, Parliament loses precious time because of conflicting interests and long debates.[4] Poincaré did, however, insist on

[2] The "state of necessity" theory which is also used sometimes to justify governmental activity in fields reserved to the legislature, gained some favor with the Conseil d'État in the immediate postwar period in order that it might uphold governmental war measures running counter to statutory limitations in the interest of the national well-being; see, e.g., the decision in the Heyriès case printed in M. Hauriou, *Jurisprudence Administrative* (Paris, 1929), I, 78. But the application remained restricted to cases arising from war emergencies. In Coudert and Arrighi, *Recueil Général de Jurisprudence*, S. 1937, III, 33, commented on by Mestre, the use of the state of necessity theory is disavowed in discussing the decree laws of 1934.

[3] The whole development until 1924 is very adequately treated in H. Tingsten, *Les Pleins Pouvoirs* (Paris, 1934), trans. from the Swedish. See also René Ladreil de Lacharrière, "Le système des décrets lois et le régime parlementaire," *Revue d'Histoire Politique et Constitutionelle*, III (1939), 122–50, which should be used with caution, however, because the author deals with the subject without any regard for the underlying social problems, and is chiefly interested in proving the feasibility and constitutionality of government by decree. A short history of decree legislation is to be found also in W. R. Sharp, *The Government of the French Republic* (New York, 1938), pp. 133–37. See also K. Loewenstein, "The Balance between Legislative and Executive Power," *University of Chicago Law Review* (1938), pp. 566–608, and S. B. Jacoby, "Delegation of Powers and Judicial Review," *Columbia Law Review* (1936), pp. 871–907. R. Bonnard, "Le droit public et la guerre," *Revue du Droit Public*, LVI (1939), 549–647, and LVII (1940), 90–125, gives a rather uncritical description of the constitutional developments since 1939. The article, however, is valuable on account of its wealth of documentation.

[4] Session Ordinaire, Chambre, 1924, p. 326. Similar arguments were later brought forward by Laval, Sess. Ord., Chambre, 1935, p. 1818.

limiting the subject matter upon which the government might issue decrees. Strong opposition came not only from the extreme left but also from such moderate statesmen as J. Paul-Boncour and E. Herriot, who insisted on the incompatibility between parliamentary government and the concession of such broad discretionary powers to the executive.[5] The bill was passed, although with reluctance. It allowed the government to issue decrees for administrative reorganization in the interest of economy, during a period of four months. Before the cabinet could issue any decree, however, elections were held bringing in a new government, which did not use the enabling powers.

After the failure of the Briand-Caillaux government to obtain an enabling act in June, 1926,[6] Poincaré returned to office and on August 3, 1926, received power, without time limit, to adjust all kinds of custom duties to the new value of the franc and, further, to reorganize the administration by December 1.[7] But decree powers first became a permanent feature of French government in 1934.[8] The Doumergue-Tardieu "national unity" government tried to pursue a deflationist policy. Since this was opposed by labor and the bulk of civil servants, and would have met serious resistance from Parliament, which had been elected in 1932, the cabinet requested *pleins pouvoirs*. This was granted by a vote of 338 of the right and center parties to 185 of the left, with 40 abstentions.[9] The enabling provision, Article 36 of the budget law, went into effect on February 28, 1934, and terminated on June 30. The language of the act is more vague than that of the Poincaré statute. The stated purpose is the "taking of all measures necessary to balance the budget." The Chamber's resistance to the deflationary policy which the Bank of France forced upon the subsequent Flandin and Buisson cabinets led the Chamber to the refusal of *pleins pouvoirs*.[10] From the struggle over deflation, the Bank of France

---

[5] Sess. Ord., Chambre, 1924, pp. 338 *et seq.*, 477 *et seq.*

[6] See Lacharrière, *op. cit.*, p. 130.

[7] The decree laws of Poincaré are discussed by Roger Bonnard in "Les décrets-lois du Ministère Poincaré," *Revue du Droit Public*, XLIV (1927), 248–88.

[8] The Daladier cabinet, 1933, inserted an enabling clause restricted to administrative reforms and economies in the minimum amount of 300 million Poincaré francs into Article 8 of the budget act of December 22, 1933, but resigned before taking any action.

[9] Sess. Ord., Chambre, 1934, p. 674.

[10] For the history of this crisis, see A. Dauphin-Meunier, *La Banque de France*, 6th ed. (Paris, 1936), and Paul Einzig, *World Finance, 1935–37* (New York, 1937), pp. 47 *et seq.*

emerged victorious in the end. On June 8, 1934, by 324 votes of the right and center parties against 160 votes from the left, and 106 abstentions,[11] the Laval government was authorized to "take until October 31, 1935, all dispositions in order to avoid the devaluation, to fight against speculation, and to defend the franc." The whole parliamentary battle over the decree power was fought in remarkable contrast to the tactics of the parliamentary opposition in the twenties. In 1934, there was no battle over principles or in defense of parliamentary rights. The question debated was not whether decree powers ought to be granted at all, but whether such powers should be granted to a specific government and to further specific aims. In fact, the use of decree powers was now taken for granted.

The Laval decrees were issued during the recess period. They not only introduced a complete deflationist program where the principle of the inviolability of private obligations was no deterrent, but went far beyond the limits of the economic policy prescribed by the enabling act itself. The decrees issued on the last day before the expiration of the *pleins pouvoirs*, October 30, 1935, covered the most varied subjects, and even a benevolent interpretation would find it often difficult to discover the link with the aims set forth in the enabling act.[12]

When the Blum government came upon the scene after the victory of the *Front Populaire* in June 1936, it refrained for a whole year from asking for *pleins pouvoirs*.[13] Thus, for its new social legislation, for its proposal to change the statutes of the Bank of France, for the introduction of the *Office du Blé* (Grain Board), it chose to use regular parliamentary procedure and to leave only the execution of details to administrative regulation. In June, 1937, the government finally asked the chambers for *pleins pouvoirs* so that it might cope with the new financial difficulties which had arisen. These *pleins pouvoirs* would be used to raise taxes, permit further devaluation of the franc,

[11] Sess. Ord., 1934, Chambre, p. 1829.

[12] The Laval decrees of October 30, 1935, and the reports to the President of the Republic explaining and motivating the decrees occupy 300 pages in the *Journal Officiel* of October 31, 1935. They range from salary cuts and forced rent decreases to improvements in child welfare service and a more vigorous prosecution of those aliens who, unable to obtain permission to enter other countries, forcedly remained in France.

[13] On the reasons for this abstention, see the remarks of Lindsay Rogers, in "Personal Power and Popular Government," *Southern Review*, III (1937), 232, and "M. Blum and the French Senate," *Political Science Quarterly*, LII (1937), 321-39.

and put the principle of exchange control into effect. The Chamber
granted these powers by a vote of 346 from the left (including Radical
Socialists) against 248 of the right and center and 11 abstentions.[14]
However, the Senate majority realized that, after the reorganization of
the Bank of France and the resultant decrease in the possibility of
overthrowing a government by the Bank's refusal to rediscount treasury bonds, the flight of capital and the strain on the gold reserves
would remain the deadliest weapon which the opposition could marshal against left governments. Therefore the Senate substituted its own
enabling bill giving the government practically no power at all (188
votes of the right Senate majority against 72 of the left and 40 abstentions).[15] The government preferred to resign.[16] On June 30, 1937, the
Chautemps cabinet obtained *pleins pouvoirs* until August 31 by 374 to
206 votes in the Chamber (28 abstentions) and 160 to 78 in the Senate
59 abstentions).[17] It was at once apparent that this enabling bill had a
feature totally different from its predecessors (and also from its successors). We give the full text: "The Government is authorized until
August 31, 1937, to take by decree adopted by the Council of Ministers all measures to assure the repression of attempts to undermine
public credit, to fight against speculation, to further economic recovery, price control, budget balancing, and *without control of exchange*
to defend the gold holdings of the Bank of France." The decrees must
be placed before Parliament for ratification within three months following the promulgation of the act, or, at any rate, at the first extraordinary session of 1937.[18] For the first time in the history of the
French enabling acts, we find a clause explicitly forbidding a certain
form of governmental action. In contrast to the usual practice of an
enabling act following the victory of one political group over the
policy and ideas of their opponents, this act rested on a compromise

14 Sess. Ord., Chambre, 1937, p. 2048.
15 Sess. Ord., Senate, 1937, p. 695.
16 As one of the arguments in favor of his enabling bill, Blum (Sess. Ord.,
Chambre, 1937, p. 1979) had promised that, unlike previous governments (Laval),
he would not attempt to issue decrees while the chambers were in recess. But it
is evident that the constitutional arguments played a distinctly secondary role.
See, e.g., Flandin, Sess. Ord., Chambre, 1937, p. 1969, and Reynaud, *ibid.*, p. 1972.
The proposed policy is the only issue of importance.
17 Sess. Ord., Chambre, 1937, p. 2104; Senate, 1937, p. 730.
18 *Journal Officiel* of July 1, 1937.

between different political groups. It was the expression of a delicate balance of power. The conservative elements were not yet strong enough to make a frontal attack on the social policy of the *Front Populaire* and to dislocate it, but they were strong enough to dictate some of the most important features of the general economic policy of the cabinet; though the presence of Socialists in the cabinet was a guarantee that the social reforms would be preserved for the time being. This compromise character can be seen in the written promise, embracing a six-point program, which the President of the Council, Chautemps, and his finance minister, Bonnet, were forced to give to the Senate before the latter granted the *pleins pouvoirs*.[19]

In March, 1938, Blum returned to power for a short period; but when he asked for an enabling act to continue the *Front Populaire* program, even though modified to meet the needs of national defense, he once again met the hostility of the Senate. By a vote of 214 to 47 and 37 abstentions, it defeated his enabling bill, which had obtained an affirmative Chamber vote (311 to 250, with 42 abstentions). During its initial stages, the next (Daladier) government followed the compromise lines of the previous year and justified its request for an enabling act, not by the necessity for structural changes in French economic or labor legislation, but by immediate budgetary and national defense needs. The compromise character is revealed by the virtually unanimous vote (Chamber: 514 to 8, with 76 Communist abstentions; Senate: 290 to 0, with 75 abstentions).[21] The enabling act was passed on April 12, 1938, giving the government power to take all measures necessary for national defense and the economic recovery of the nation. The powers were to be terminated at the end of the session, not later than July 31, 1938. The decrees which the Daladier government issued under this enabling act were in no way restricted to immediate

---

[19] The promise which the government made to the Senate was read and commented on in the Senate by Abel Gardey, who, with Caillaux, was the chief parliamentary leader of the senatorial opposition to the *Front Populaire*. Sess. Ord., Senate, 1937, p. 718. Material on analogous "compromise enabling acts" in the earlier years of the Weimar Republic may be found in Poetzsch-Heffter, *Jahrbuch des öffentlichen Rechts*, XII (1925), 212 et seq. See also F. M. Watkins, *The Failure of Political Emergency Powers under the German Republic* (Cambridge, Mass., 1939), p. 76.

[20] Sess. Ord., 1938, Chambre, p. 1183; Senate, p. 562.

[21] Sess. Ord., 1938, Chambre, p. 1183; Senate, p. 562.

aims. Although Parliament was in session until June 17, a comparison between the legislative work accomplished by it and the rules issued under the decree power shows that Parliament had lost almost all significance as a legislative body.[22]

The turn away from a policy of compromise, already evident in summer, became much sharper in October, 1938, when, after his return from Munich, Daladier asked for new decree powers. On October 1, these were granted by the Chamber until November 15, with a vote of 331 to 78 Communist votes and 203 (mostly Socialist) abstentions,[23] "in order to bring about an immediate recovery in the finan-

[22] Here is a brief indication of *some* of the matters on which the *Journal Officiel* of June 26 and 29, 1938, contains regulations issued in pursuance of the enabling act (though somewhat similar smaller groups of decrees had already been issued on June 15, 17, 18, and 19): public utility regulations, treatment of vagabonds, surveillance of private aid societies and welfare institutions, reorganization of the French Red Cross, regulation of broadcasting, reorganization of seamen's social security benefit, reorganization of state architectural services, institution of a medical service for students, reestablishment of criminal "relegation" to Guiana (abolished under Blum), reform of local finances, coordination of transportation system, gold production in colonies, repression of spies, organization and functioning of national and regional agricultural credit institutions, modification of custom duties, reorganization of the military hierarchy, amelioration of agricultural laborers' housing conditions, agricultural professional training, amelioration of fiscal efficiency, agreement with the Bank of France, and introduction of administrative surveillance of privately owned historical documents. Compared with this sampling of regulations issued in one batch in accordance with the enabling act on June 17, 1938, the *whole* legislative output of the French Parliament in June, 1938, amounted to the following: modification of one article of a statute in regard to military pensions (*J. O.*, June 14), a statute containing some budget modifications and a statute on the exercise of veterinary surgery (*J. O.*, June 22), a statute disjoining one rural community from canton X and transferring it to the jurisdiction of canton Y, a statute for avoiding double tax imposition on profits in Tunis and France (*J. O.*, July 25), two statutes ratifying earlier decrees, two statutes giving the War Ministry more Légion d'Honneur crosses for distribution (*J. O.*, June 27 and 28), a statute regulating the exercise of property rights over apartment houses belonging to several persons and a statute on obligatory antidiptheria vaccination (*J. O.*, June 30), extension of accident insurance regulations in Alsace-Lorraine to people working in hospitals and modifications of earlier accident insurance rules (*J. O.*, July 2), a statute creating two new administrative positions (*J. O.*, July 8), ratification of a commercial treaty with Germany, and ratification of two other decrees (*J. O.*, July 9 and 10).

[23] Sess. Extraord., 1938, Chambre, p. 1598; Senate, p. 736. No new constitutional arguments were brought forth in the discussion. The speech of Daladier, Sess. Extraord., Chambre, 1938, pp. 1553 *et seq.*, gives no constitutional justification for his demand. The Socialist speaker Philippe reminded the Chamber of the abuse of decree powers by Brüning and complained that Parliament is always dismissed

cial and economic situation of the country." The decrees issued in consequence of this enabling act attempted to reconcile the reestablishment of a greater liberty for employers and of the investing public in general with efficient war preparation. Both motives led to a virtual nullification of all the essential features of the Blum social reforms.[24] In the three-and-one-half-month interval between the lapse of the second Daladier enabling act and the German occupation of Prague, the government made use of a reorganization clause inserted in a decree law of November 13, and consolidated in Article 61 of the budget law of December 31, 1938, to carry on the uninterrupted stream of decree legislation. After the occupation of Prague, the cabinet, which had won a large following by its vigorous suppression of the general strike of November 30, asked for a third enabling act. By a vote of 321 from the right to 264 from the left, it received new emergency powers until November 30, 1939. It was authorized to "take all measures necessary for the defense of the country." In the debate, Daladier did not put forth a well-defined policy; instead, he argued for the necessity of the enabling act by stressing the advantages which authoritarian governments had against democratic government—independence, rapidity, and secrecy of action.[25] The decrees issued under this new enabling act accentuated the features of war preparedness and buried the last vestiges of the Blum social policy under the impact of the approaching war.

Daladier's fourth enabling act of December 8, 1939, dropped the last important limitation which had still been present in earlier acts, the closely defined time limit. The enabling clause was inserted into Article 36 of the statute of July 12, 1938, on the General Organization of the Nation in Time of War. This statute, as amended by Parliament

---

as soon as possible. *Ibid.*, p. 1547. Abel Gardey, Sess. Extraord., Senate, 1938, p. 730, particularly stressed the promise not to institute an exchange control, and he also quoted a promise by the government not to issue decrees on matters not directly connected with financial recovery. As for constitutional arguments, he appealed the republican conscience of his brethren by emphasizing the temporary character of the power.

24 See the report of Paul Reynaud, minister of finance, to the President of the Republic, which accompanied the publication of the decree laws of November 12, 1938, in *J. O.*, November 13, pp. 12855–61. An unofficial English translation may be found in the (London) *Economist* of November 19, 1938, pp. 363 *et seq.*

25 *Le Temps*, March 19, 1939.

on December 8, 1939, authorizes the government in urgent cases "to take by decree adopted by the Council of Ministers all measures imposed by the exigencies of national defense." [26] By voting this enabling act 309 to 189 (chiefly Socialists), with 56 abstentions and 47 Communists and Alsatian Separatists under arrest and therefore barred from voting, the Chamber (not without utterance of serious misgivings) for the first time in the history of the Third Republic conferred emergency powers on the government which it could invoke at any moment as long as hostilities were going on. This enabling act resembles rather closely the ill-fated emergency powers of Article 48 of the Weimar Constitution, in that the government was now at liberty not only to issue decrees without being specifically empowered to do so but also without the hindrance of the rather narrow time limits usual with enabling acts. In fact, from 1934 we can trace a gradual eclipse of parliamentary legislation which becomes increasingly marked as the years go on. In 1928, government decrees were still confined to narrowly limited fields, and even the Doumergue and Laval emergency powers were tied to concrete objectives in intent, although tending in fact toward all-embracing objectives. Daladier's regime marks the completion of this change. The objectives to be attained by decree procedure became a secondary consideration. Decree powers are required as the process of parliamentary legislation is declared incapable of withstanding the competition of fascism's unrestricted governmental action.[27]

Before entering upon a discussion of the constitutional features of the transition from parliamentary to executive legislation, we must consider the restraints placed on governmental legislative activity by judicial bodies. The doctrine accepted by all French courts that they have no right to examine the constitutionality of laws has not undergone any change since the recent practice of enabling acts and decree

---

[26] Cf. Bonnard, "Le droit. . . ," pp. 565–68.

[27] The Belgian developments, which we are unable to deal with here, are described in detail by Buttgenbach in "Pratique des pouvoirs spéciaux en Belgique," *Revue du Droit Public*, LVI (1939), 80–154. A concise treatment and an excellent evaluation of the Belgian decree practice may be found in R. Ruttens, "Législation extraparlementaire," *Revue de l'Administration et du Droit Administratif Belge*, LXXXVI (1939), 245–60.

laws came into effect.[28] In the case of Coudert and Arrighi,[29] concerning forced pensioning of officials in pursuance of decrees issued by virtue of the 1934 enabling act, the Conseil d'État closed all avenues to a determination of the constitutionality of enabling acts with the dictum: "In the present state of French public law, this argument cannot be raised before the Conseil d'État." The control of the judicial section of the Conseil d'État is restricted to determining whether or not the decree laws exceed the power given by the enabling act. But there is no judgment on the advisability or wisdom of the decrees.[30] The first question which the Conseil d'État examines is whether the time limit set by the enabling act has been observed. The decrees are valid only if (1) they are issued within the time limit specified by the

[28] The recent attempt made by Joseph Barthélemy in "Un tournant dans la conception française de la loi," *Revue d'Histoire Politique et Constitutionelle,* III (1939), 161–68, to interpret a decision of the Conseil d'État as implying a trend toward judicial control of legislative acts cannot be found convincing. The decision is printed in Dalloz, *Recueil périodique et critique de jurisprudence* (Paris, 1938), III, 41, "La Fleurette," with commentary by Professor Rolland. The commentary by Rolland clearly states that, according to the principles of French constitutional law, the principle of the equal sharing of public burdens on which the decision rests would have no validity in the face of the expressed will of the legislature.

[29] Quoted *supra,* note 2.

[30] The first Poincaré enabling act provided for the consultation of the administrative section of the Conseil d'État before the issuance of decree laws, but the second Poincaré enabling act left the Conseil d'État out. A decree of March 25, 1939, established the following machinery for the issuance of decree laws. At least three days before the Council of Ministers is to be convoked for discussion of proposed decrees, the decrees must be submitted to a committee made up of the director of the cabinet, the president of the council, the secretary-general of the ministries of war and finance, and one representative of the ministry specifically concerned with the decree in question. As the Council of Ministers will not give more than formal consideration to the decrees, the supervision remains largely in the hands of three officials who can check or confirm the actions of the various departments. (See *J. O.,* March 26–27, 1939.) An example of how the decrees are rushed through the Council of Ministers may be found in Lindsay Rogers, *op. cit.,* p. 239; se also C. J. Friedrich's interesting article, "Paul Reynaud," *Atlantic Monthly,* Oct., 1939, pp. 490–501. During the parliamentary debate on the April, 1938, enabling bill, Louis Marin brought forward an amendment which would have obliged the government to lay any proposed decree before a parliamentary committee at least three days before its issuance. This amendment might have eliminated the excesses of decree legislation through the publicity involved, but it was defeated by a vote of 429 to 97. Sess. Ord., Chambre, 1938, pp. 1159 et seq.)

enabling act, and (2) the requirements regarding *rapport*, ratification, or confirmation by Parliament within a specified time are observed. In a 1939 case, the Conseil d'État was faced with a situation in which the government had extended by decree its powers in a certain field beyond the time limit set by the enabling act.[31] The Conseil invalidated this section of the decree on the ground that at least the principles of the proposed reform must be defined within the legal time limit. The door was thus still left open for actual extension of time as long as done skillfully.

The requirement of *rapport*, ratification, or confirmation by Parliament does not mean much. A *rapport* merely requires the cabinet to report on its activities within a given time. The validity of the decree laws is not affected, however, by Parliament's reaction, no matter how negative. As for ratification or confirmation, the enabling acts merely require that the decree laws be placed before Parliament for ratification within a fixed time.[32] This does not mean that the decrees must be ratified, however, but merely that they must be submitted.[33] If Parliament formally ratifies a given decree, it becomes law from the time of the ratification and is no longer subject to judicial control. If, as is the usual practice in France, Parliament takes no action, the decrees remain in force and are still subject to control by the Conseil d'État. Only if Parliament refuses to ratify does the decree become void from

[31] *Amicale des anciens combattants,* S. 1939, III, 33 *et seq.*

[32] See, e.g., the wording of the Daladier enabling act of March 19, 1939. "The decrees must be submitted to the Chamber for ratification before December 1, 1939." (*J. O.* of March 20, 1939.)

[33] See M. Hauriou, *Précis de Droit Constitutionnel,* 2d ed. (1929), p. 453; G. Jéze, "Des règlements faits en vertu d'une compétence donnée au gouvernement par le législateur," *Revue du Droit Public,* LV (1938), 503. For Belgium, see Buttgenbach, *op cit.,* pp. 106 *et seq.* Similarly, see the decision of the Conseil d'État: Fédération des syndicats professionnels des cheminots, S. 1937, III, 102. Only if the enabling act (*e.g.,* the French customs act of July 9, 1937, Art. III) makes ratification a condition of validity would nonratification within the time limit provided by the statute affect the validity of the decree. During the parliamentary debate on the last French enabling act (December, 1939), the finance commission of the Chamber proposed that the decree laws should lose their validity if the parliamentary session following their issuance should conclude without ratifying them. Daladier opposed the amendment and it failed. See the report of the session in *Le Temps* of Dec. 2, 1939.

the time of the rejection. All actions taken under the decree up to that point, however, remain valid.[34]

We come now to the question of the extent to which the Conseil d'État may examine the contents of decree laws. Decrees must not exceed the material competence set by the enabling act. The act may define specific aims to be accomplished by the decrees, or it may limit the methods by which these aims can be attained (a frequent procedure in Belgium, but used only once in France). In actual practice, however, the Conseil d'État has been quite reluctant to invalidate decree laws which exceed the powers granted by the enabling act. The Conseil found the most varied governmental regulations, including salary and pension cuts and reorganization schemes, falling within the economy aims defined by the "deflationist" enabling acts of 1934–35.[35] All the new restrictions making serious inroads in the already not very extensive administrative power of the municipal governments were also approved as "economies." The Conseil d'État reasoned that in view of the close inter-relationship between municipal and state budgets any amelioration of the financial situation of the smaller governmental units has a favorable effect on the general financial situation.[36] Only in very rare and unimportant cases has the Conseil d'État occasionally voided individual paragraphs of decrees, and then because

---

[34] This last is largely an academic question and has evoked considerable discussion in legal literature. It is treated in full by L. Duguit, in "Des règlements faits en vertu d'une compétence donnée au gouvernement par les législateurs," *Revue du Droit Public*, XLI (1924), 313–49. See also Jèze, quoted *supra*.

[35] (1) Coudert and Arrighi, quoted *supra*. (2) Fédération des syndicats professionnels des cheminots, quoted *supra*. (3) Olphe-Gaillard, *Recueil des arrêts du Conseil d'État*, R. 1937, p. 304. The fact that the costs of the supervision of private insurance companies are eventually borne by the companies themselves did not lead the Conseil d'État to invalidate pensioning of state insurance inspectors as an economy measure merely because their salaries are formally paid out of general government funds. (4) Ramarony, R. 1938, 252. Rapid and simplified expropriation procedures introduced by decree under the Laval enabling act of June 8, 1935, reduce administrative costs and are therefore held to come under the aims of the enabling act. Additional cases may be found in the initialed commentary to S. 1937, III, 97.

[36] R. 1936, p. 817, Ville de Strasbourg, approving for these reasons the appointment of state officials to the Strasbourg Hospital and Welfare Commission. See also R. 1936, p. 509, Ville de Suresne, where the reform of the municipal accounting system was approved on the same argument.

not even the most sympathetic interpretation could fit them into the economy requirement.[37] All these cases, it must be remembered, refer to the 1934 and 1935 enabling acts, which limited decree action to measures for financial recovery and a balanced budget. With the enlargement of the aims to include national defense, the opportunities for discovering a connection between the decree and the aims of the enabling act become even greater. Control by the Conseil d'État thus ceases to be a real check on the exercise of the decree power, and as the legal phraseology of the enabling acts becomes more general, it becomes still more hopeless to try to attack the validity of a decree law.

Until very recently, constitutionality of enabling acts was frequently judged from what we may call a version of the "material conception of law." This material conception of law took shape in the early nineteenth-century struggle between the relatively independent army, bureaucracy, and landowning classes on the one hand and the parliamentary opposition on the other. In the course of this conflict, it was established that all rules pertaining to the spheres of property and personal liberty are excluded from the jurisdiction of the executive and may be regulated only by act of Parliament. These fields, some now argue, also mark the limits to every enabling act. It is a rather difficult theoretical venture to attack the decree laws from this angle,[38] and it

---

[37] Besides the case quoted above (*Amicale des anciens combattants*), there is the case *Union des véhicules industrielles*, S. 1937, III, 97. Here the government introduced extensive regulations on road traffic. One section contained detailed rules about the right of way for heavy trucks. While upholding the general features of this decree, the Conseil d'État was unable to find a connecting link between rules about right of way and the alleviation of the country's financial burden, and therefore voided that section. Only in one set of cases, where the admissibility of municipal enterprises was in question, the Conseil d'État refused to acknowledge the validity of government decrees issued in pursuance of enabling acts and sanctioning such enterprises; but even in this case, characteristically enough, this was done by interpreting, or rather misinterpreting, and not by invalidating, the decrees in question. Chambre syndicale de commerce en détail de Nevers, and Giaccardi, S. 1931, III, 73, with commentary by Alibert. Zénard, S. 1934, III, 105, Tesnière, S. 1935, III, 63, both with commentary by Mestre. Chouard, S. 1936, III, 17. See also Waline, *Manuel élémentaire de droit administratif* (Paris, 1936), pp. 243 et seq., and W. R. Sharp, in W. Anderson, ed., *Local Government in Europe* (New York, 1939), p. 167.

[38] The whole doctrine in both its German and French versions is fully analyzed and criticized in Carré de Malberg, *Contribution à la théorie générale de l'État* (Paris, 1920), I, 285 et seq. See also C. Schmitt, "L'évolution récente du problème

is particularly difficult to lay special stress on constitutional precedent,[39] since during World War I the government had already received broad powers infringing on all of these fields. Therefore, no
such constitutional custom exists today, and even if it did so, as Barthélemy points out, it would not act as a brake on parliamentary action.[40]

The decisive question, therefore is: What does the constitution itself
say? The constitutional laws of 1875 do not include a specific bill of
rights. All attempts to declare that the bill of rights nevertheless forms
a part of the constitutional system do not concern the constitutional
system proper, but concern questions of social legitimacy.[41] In but
two fields do the constitutional laws of 1875 seem explicitly to require
statutory action: the issuance of amnesties and certain kinds of international treaties (not the vital ones). Yet even in these spheres the
administration has paid little attention to such reservations and has
issued decree laws.[42] It seems, therefore, that neither the more or less
accidental use of the word "statute" in the constitutional laws nor the
nineteenth-century constitutional theory that infringement of so-called
fundamental rights requires a legislative act carries much weight in
arriving at a correct understanding of the limits upon executive action
in a parliamentary regime. The competence of Parliament is a general
one.[43] There is no field where the executive is free to compete with
the legislature. The French constitutional law of February 25, 1875,
states this point unequivocally when in Article 1 it assigns the legislative power to Chamber and Senate and in Article 3 defines the duties
of the president of the Republic as the supervisor and guarantor of the
execution of the law.

If the executive therefore has no original rule-making power under a

---

des délégations législatives," in *Introduction à l'étude du droit comparé* (Paris,
1938), III, 200-10 (translated from the German). Its application to the 1924
Poincaré enabling act is to be found in L. Rolland, "Le projet du 17.I. et la question des décrets-lois 1924," *Revue du Droit Public*, XLI (1924), 42-74.

[39] See, for example, Rolland, *op. cit.*, p. 61.

[40] Barthélemy-Duez, *Traité de droit constitutionnel* (Paris, 1933), p. 763.

[41] Hauriou, *op. cit.*, p. 239. See the discussion of this point in K. Loewenstein,
"The Demise of the French Constitution of 1875," *American Political Science Review*, XXXIV (1940), 892-93.

[42] Law of February 25, 1875, Art. 3, and July 18, 1875, Art. 8.

[43] On the constitutional development of legislative omnipotence in parliamentary
democracy, Rudolf Smend, *Die preussische Verfassungsurkunde im Vergleich mit
der belgischen* (Göttingen, 1904) is still of considerable value.

parliamentary regime, our question is narrowed to this: Within what limits may Parliament delegate its functions to the executive? The more one accepts the notion of a separation of functions, the narrower will one set the limits to delegation of powers. In order to emphasize the view that the power given to Parliament by the constitution may in itself not be transferred and that only certain well-defined and well-delimited tasks may be delegated, Hauriou, for example, is careful not to speak of delegation of *power*, but only of delegation of certain *fields* to another authority; and Duguit speaks of "attibution des compétences." [44] It is therefore evident that the practice of all-embracing delegation incorporated in the more recent French enabling acts was not compatible with the constitutional system in which a strict conception of separation of powers still prevailed. Carré de Malberg's treatment of the problem is the most interesting.[45] He rejects as incompatible with positive French constitutional law the material conception of the law both in its restricted nineteenth-century form of guaranties to liberty and property and in its eighteenth-century form (resuscitated in the twentieth century) which requires the general character of a rule. According to Carré's thesis, the authority of statute under the French constitution derives solely from the general will. It is the expression of the general will because the legislature is supposed to represent the general will, and therefore it receives its justification only in the assumed generality of its origin. Whatever contents the statute may have, nobody may question it, since it is presumed to express the general will.[46] One corollary of this doctrine is to give Parliament wider scope for delegation of power. If there is no material difference between the activities of Parliament and the activities of the executive, between parliamentary statute and administrative regulation, there is

[44] Duguit, *op. cit.*, p. 315. We give the full formula elaborated by Hauriou because it exemplifies the attempt to unite the need for delegation with the preservation of clear distinctions between the spheres of the executive and the legislative: "The delegation of the forms of power is impossible, but the delegation of fields of activity is permissible, with the proviso that the power to whom the activity is delegated rules under the forms appropriate to itself." Hauriou, *op. cit.*, p. 265.

[45] Carré de Malberg, quoted *supra*, and still better the very lucid exposition of his ideas in his later work, *La loi, expression de la volonté générale* (Paris, 1931).

[46] *La loi* . . . , pp. 17-18. That this general will in itself is a fiction, Carré has never denied. See "Considérations théoriques sur la combination du referendum avec le parlementarisme," *Revue du Droit Public* (1927), pp. 225-44, and La *loi* . . . , pp. 214-22.

no reason why Parliament cannot make use of "habilitations," as Carré calls the transfer of rule-making power to the executive. Yet even this theory must set limits to such "habilitation." Rejecting all material differences between legislative and executive action, Carré nevertheless comes to the same restrictions as do other theorists upon the transfer of power. In order that the relations between the enabling act and the ensuing regulations correspond to Article 3 of the constitutional law, Carré argues, the enabling act must have determined with sufficient precision the object and extent of the competences to be exercised by the executive. A statute authorizing the President for an unlimited time to take all necessary measures would transfer to the President the power which Article 1 of the constitutional law of 1875 reserves for the legislature.[47] With this argument, the theory which gives Parliament the widest latitude of action joins the main body of French constitutional theory. This shows that the development which began in 1934 and reached its climax in 1939 cannot be reconciled with the postulates that had dominated French constitutional law as elaborated in the revolutionary constitutions and stated in the constitutional laws of 1875.

One of the stereotyped arguments designed to prove that the enabling acts do not exceed the frame of parliamentary government is that the cabinet still requires the confidence of Parliament, and that Parliament retains the legal and political possibility of overthrowing the government, thus exercising an all-important check on its otherwise unrestricted activity. This argument has been considerably weakened since a decree of July 29, 1939, extended the life of the French Chamber by two years.[48] Article 2 of the July 29 decree stipulates that even by-elections may take place only in case of death or appointment to a public office which requires the resignation of a member. Therefore the ejection of the members of the Communist party does not require new by-elections. It is a fair question whether such a parliament can still claim a representative character, since its political composition has

[47] *La loi* . . . , p. 37.
[48] The report to the President accompanying the publication of this decree, J. O. of July 30, 1939, tries to justify the encroachment upon the rights of Parliament by arguing that the question of a possible extension by decree was discussed during the debate on the enabling act of March 19, and that in voting the enabling act the majority automatically acquiesced in this measure beforehand.

undergone considerable change through the ejection of a group of its members, and the electorate will not be allowed to pass judgment upon the activity of their representatives.

A related argument often heard in defense of the practice of enabling acts is that it represents the appropriate form of parliamentary government for our time.[49] The difference between traditional parliamentary procedure and the procedure inaugurated by the enabling bill, it is stated, is very slight and inconsequential. Whereas the old-fashioned parliamentary method insists on *a priori* approbation of governmental measures, now the approval is given *post facto*. This difference is supposed to reduce itself to a mere question of legal technique. In the political aspect, there is no difference at all, since the cabinet is invested with the confidence of Parliament. The enabling acts are therefore a perfect method adapted to the intricate problems of our society, while remaining fully in conformity with the principles of parliamentary rule.

Of course, the practice whereby Parliament establishes general rules and leaves the execution to the administration, preferably with the active participation of all interested groups, is accepted in France as in any other country. Even the practice of transferring special fields *in toto* to the executive—a practice sometimes followed in France as well as in Belgium—may still be regarded as within the constitutional framework, since specific fields are involved. But there is a considerable difference between the need for delegated legislation within the framework of parliamentary legislative supremacy, as set forth, for example, in the well-known English report of the Committee on Ministers' Powers, and the complete surrender to the executive of the right to determine the principles of public policy.[50] The contention that there is no vital distinction between ordinary parliamentary legislation and *post facto* approval—or, to put it more correctly in the light of

[49] B. Mirkine-Guetzévitch, "Pleins pouvoirs sous le régime parlementaire," *Annales de l'Institut de Droit Comparé* (Paris, 1938), III, 69-86, and the same in "Le régime parlementaire dans les constitutions européennes d'après guerre," *Annuaire de l'Institut International du Droit Public* (Paris, 1936), pp. 39-85. See also Lacharrière, *op. cit.*, p. 148.

[50] Cf. also the exhaustive treatment of English delegation practice in W. I. Jennings, *Parliament* (Cambridge, 1939), pp. 451-92.

recent experiences, no formal *post facto* disapproval—of delegated legislation is without foundation.[51] Normal parliamentary discussion of a bill provides for separate consideration of every article, giving the opposition the opportunity to propose amendments to every article.[52] How is it possible to reconcile the *en bloc* adoption of hundreds of decree laws as we know it from Belgian practice, or the mere recording of decrees (for that is what the French practice of presenting the decree laws to Parliament for ratification actually amounts to) with the normal detailed parliamentary procedure? The contention that Parliament can change the decree legislation after the expiration of the emergency powers does not face the real issue. When and if Parliament is called to try its hand after months or even years of rule by decree, it cannot profit much from the knowledge that, legally speaking, it may void all the decrees. The actions taken by the government in the meantime will have definite political and social effects and will have created a new situation which Parliament cannot neglect, and which the simple invalidation of the decrees cannot eliminate.[53]

Since most of these points are obvious, we must seek a more substantial reason for alleging the identity of parliamentary legislation and governmental rule-making by decree. It is explained to us as a kind of a logical consequence of the changed structure of the constitutional system itself.[54] In a society, it is argued, which no longer knows of an opposition between parliament and monarchy, army and bureaucracy,

[51] We shall not discuss Mr. Mirkine-Guetzévitch's argument in so far as it refers to the theories of the separation of powers, which he declares obsolete. The Panama Refining Co. and the Schechter Poultry Corp. cases (293 U.S. 388 and 295 U.S. 495) show that even an obsolete theory may sometimes celebrate a revival of some momentum. It is sufficient to emphasize once again that Carré de Malberg, the least separationist of all French theorists, arrives at substantially the same conclusion about the unconstitutionality of a general delegation of powers as the authors who follow more separationist lines (see his exposition in *Théorie Générale* . . . , II, 94 *et seq.*).

[52] These arguments are stressed in the Belgian literature. See Buttgenbach, *op. cit.*, p. 128, and H. Speyer, "Les dangers des pleins pouvoirs," in *Le Flambeau* (1934), pp. 641–49.

[53] Incidentally, even from a strictly legal point of view, Parliament could not undo the decree legislation, since obligations entered into and rights created under the decree laws would have to be upheld. On these very intricate questions, see Duguit, *op. cit.*, pp. 345 *et seq.*

[54] Mirkine-Guetzévitch, *Annuaire* . . . , pp. 73, 76.

parliament has only secondary importance; elections are contested, not in order to gain a majority which may limit the power of the ruling classes more and more, but merely in order to form a government. Since there is thus a substantial identity between the parliament and its cabinet, and since the parliament has only to sanction the program of the ministry, there is no difficulty in giving the ministry full rule-making power. This theory is not supported by the facts of postwar Europe. The importance of election results unquestionably arose in France and Germany alike as a result of the postwar democratization. However, the attempt to form homogeneous governments in accordance with the election returns was never successful. No matter how successful in the elections, whether in France or in Germany, the major parties were never able to obtain clear parliamentary majorities. England might seem to offer a better argument for the thesis of the essential homogeneity of modern cabinets and parliament, as we have only the two MacDonald minority cabinet exceptions of 1924 and 1929–31 on the record. But precisely because Bonar Law, Baldwin, and Chamberlain had a fairly homogeneous following in cabinet and Parliament, they never needed a peacetime enabling bill. The election returns may have been important in registering fashions in public opinion and in reflecting changes in social composition and age structure. The fundamental fact is not altered that the major social factors like employers' associations, agricultural interests, trade unions, churches, and so on, had to reach agreements on major objectives in the normal process of political life, even though their numerical representation in Parliament underwent fluctuations and their social weight shifted from time to time. The parliamentary groups were the actors in this give-and-take procedure. Legislation became legislation by compromise, a compromise determined by the actual status of the political parties as revealed in the most recent election, by the ups and downs in economic conditions, and by the power which the respective social forces were able to yield at any given moment. These parliamentary combinations also produced what we have earlier described as "compromise enabling acts"; that is to say, under certain circumstances, the major political groups agree to grant power to coalition governments for the purpose of carrying through necessary decisions by means of delegated legislation. But frequently the coalition government could not reach an agreement on the necessary course to be followed any more than the multiple party parliament whose structure it reflected. With the granting of enabling powers to cabinets which could command a more or less comfortable parliamentary majority (as in France), but which nevertheless represented only one section of the country's social structure, the whole picture undergoes a distinct and far-reaching change. The compromise structure formerly inherent in both the legislative and the political decisions disappears. The unequivocal policy followed by these recent governments forces the hand of all political groups; it carries with it a complete unification of political outlook, since the interests which usually avoid clear-cut engagements and change their allegiance from issue to issue according to the objective in question are forced to make a long-range choice between unconditional support of the government's political and social program and serious conflict with it. The parliamentary minority, or that part of the population in general which is not represented in the cabinet invested with decree power, finds its ability to fight the government's policy seriously weakened. Either Parliament is in recess when the decrees are issued, or, if it is in session, the government limits its activity to votes of confidence and enabling acts. Under such conditions, the temptation either to develop an antiparliamentarian attitude or to follow the enticement of the cabinet and its bureaucracy to give up the difficult struggle and to become part of the governing machinery with pay and pensions guaranteed, but without freedom of action, is obviously strong.

In sum, the theory that decree government represents "parliamentary government in our time" simply ignores the problem of the groups not represented in this government. In France in 1938–39 parliamentary action by opposition groups and popular control through election had been seriously curtailed. One might argue that government by compromise is no longer feasible in a country torn by dissension and menaced with destruction from without, and that therefore the shift to the semi-independent governmental and bureaucratic machinery, ruling by the legal device of recurrent enabling acts squeezed out of a frightened majority, was more or less unavoidable.

We cannot here enter into the eternal argument as to whether parliamentary democracy is still possible in a society in which the degree of political homogeneity is decreasing.[55]

One conclusion seems to stand out clearly. The degradation of Parliament to a mechanism recording votes of confidence and authorizing enabling bills only hastens the disintegrating process of parliamentary government as such. No apologetic theory can hide the fact that parliamentary government in the twentieth century has come to rest mainly on a double basis: the trust which the population as a whole puts in this institution as the embodiment of their wishes and wants, and the ability of the organized social forces to find a solution of social problems with the help of the rules and procedures established by this institution. When Parliament loses this position of trust and abdicates its function as guarantor of universally acceptable compromises, the time of parliamentary democracy will have passed.[56]

[55] The different points of view are brought forward clearly in H. J. Laski, *Parliamentary Government in England* (New York, 1938), on one side, and C. J. Friedrich, "Democracy and Dissent," *Political Quarterly*, X (1939), 571–82, on the other.

[56] As this article, written before the French debacle, goes to press, the Third Republic has succumbed under Hitler's war machine. Important as the constellations of foreign policy and the fortunes of war may have been, it seems safe to assume that internal developments had their full share in the downfall of France as a sovereign state. The evisceration of democracy which had taken place with increasing tempo since the end of the Popular Front intermezzo left the country with a considerably weakened political structure in the gravest moments of its history. Whatever may be the changes that the remaining democracies shall have to undergo in their struggle for survival, the French example, coming eight years after the German *Präsidialregierung* of Brüning and Papen, shows that the unlimited decree-rule of a constitutional government with a dubious popular or parliamentary basis serves only as an intermediate station on the road to complete authoritarianism.

CHANGES IN THE STRUCTURE

OF POLITICAL COMPROMISE

MODERN POLITICAL THEORY has established a close relationship between political compromise and government in a developed industrial society.[1] In this context, compromise means that the foremost political decisions are reached by agreement among individuals as well as among social groups. The following remarks will not evaluate this definition but will try to analyze the conditions and nature of compromises as far as they influenced the European political system under liberalism, mass democracy, and fascism. To the latter stages correspond three different types of agreement which have characterized European constitutional history: to liberalism corresponded the complex of working agreements among parliamentary representatives and between them and the government; to mass democracy, the agreements between voluntary associations; and to fascism, the pacts by which the heads of the compulsory estates distribute power and booty.

I. COMPROMISE UNDER THE REPRESENTATIVE
SYSTEM AND UNDER MASS DEMOCRACY

In his reflections on the French Revolution, Burke, with characteristic vehemence and pointedness, depicts the shift in the location of power

Reprinted, by permission, from *Studies in Philosophy and Social Science*, IX (1941), 264–89.

[1] See, for example, H. Kelsen, *Vom Wesen und Wert der Demokratie*, 2d ed. (Berlin, 1929), and, more recently, E. P. Herring, *The Politics of Democracy* (New York, 1940).

to the plutocratic oligarchies, a development which, according to him, had been initiated by the revolutionary policy of confiscation. The "volatilization of property," of which this representative of the English landed aristocracy accuses the revolutionary legislators, is responsible for the creation of a commonwealth founded on "gaming," in comparison with which, in Burke's opinion, the "known scandals of history amount to comparatively little." [2]

The all-embracing medium of money profoundly conditioned the political institutions of the era. Today we are accustomed to regard money more in its role as one technical means of domination among many. But this purely technical role of money is a phenomenon which did not appear until the monopolistic period. In any case the nineteenth century saw the incontestable application of the sociological thesis that the personal security derived from the possession of money was the most concrete form and expression of confidence in the public order.[3]

Possession of money was just as important for the political weight of an individual within the nation as the degree of credit-worthiness is for the nation's position in the international concert. Legal equality of citizens and equality of states before international law were the juristic premise for the working of the free exchange process.[4]

An integral part of the representative system was the conception of an agent who was no longer bound by the estates but who at the same time had not yet become a spokesman tied to definite group interests. The French constitution of 1791, Sect. III, Art. 7, by denying the admissibility of binding instructions given by the electorate to the representatives, marks the final transition from the *mandat impératif* of

---

[2] E. Burke, *Collected Works*, 5th ed. (Boston, 1877), III, 485 ff.

[3] Georg Simmel, *Philosophie des Geldes*, 5th ed. (Munich, 1930), p. 165.

[4] Bagehot, *Collected Works*, ed. Barrington, VI, 14. "Lombard Street, 1873": "It is sometimes said that any foreign country can borrow in Lombard Street *at a price*, some countries can borrow much cheaper than others; but all, it is said, can have some money if they choose to pay enough for it. Perhaps this is an exaggeration but confined as, of course, it was meant to be to the civilized nations, it is not much of an exaggeration." As regards the conceptions of civilized and commercial, which are used synonymously, see Kunz, "Zum Begriff der *Nation Civilisée*," *Zeitschrift für öffentliches Recht*, VII (1928), 86.

the estates to the representative system of the nineteenth century.[5] Theories of public law have taken the opportunity to stress the element of freedom contained in the condemnation of the *mandat impératif*, this condemnation being the very basis of the representative system.[6]

In its relatively pure form, the representative system did not prevail in Europe for a particularly long period. Even at the beginning it was alloyed by elements of absolutism and by elements of the still older estate system. Its period of fruition occurred in the second and third quarter of the nineteenth century when it combined with the doctrine of public opinion. Its territorial extension was confined to those states "where there is no honest poverty, where education is diffused and political intelligence common," [7] that is to say, to the sphere of developing capitalist economy. With the decline of the central position of money as a universal measuring rod and with the effacement of the correlative independence of representation by the monopolizing society, the remnants of the representative system were becoming rapidly submerged. This process characterized the period of mass democracy.

The political system of mass democracy had, as one of its decisive characteristics, the antagonism between public control of government and private control of central banks. The latter had most important public functions. When the central bank legislation of the nineteenth century took shape, there was no doubt as to the political significance of the administration of this type of joint-stock company, "on whose wisdom it depends whether a country shall be solvent or insolvent." [8]

Robert Peel, when he introduced the Bank Charter Act of 1844, described the sphere of influence which the domination of the credit apparatus brings with it, and his words show a tendency to reification typical of the period: "There is no contract, public or private, no engagement internal or individual which is unaffected by it [the bill].

[5] See the excellent exposition of this point in K. Loewenstein, *Volk und Parlament nach der Staatstheorie der französischen Nationalversammlung* (Munich, 1922), pp. 191 ff., especially p. 200.

[6] For the best account of this see G. Leibholz, *Das Wesen der Repräsentation* (Berlin, 1929).

[7] Bagehot, *op. cit.*, I, 345.

[8] *Ibid.*, VI, 32.

The enterprises of commerce, the profits of trade, the arrangement made in all the domestic arrangements of society, the wages of labor, pecuniary transactions of the highest amount and of the lowest, the payment of the national debt, the provision for the national expenditure, the command which the coin of the smallest denomination has over the necessities of life are all affected by the decision to which we may come." [9] This administration of the central bank, by far the most important office in Great Britain of those "outside the gift of the Crown," [10] is carried on by officials elected from among the ranks of the banking community. If Brooks Adams appears to have been too pointed in his opinion that the Bank Act of 1844, by yielding the control of the currency to bankers, marked a definite transfer of sovereignty to Lombard Street, [11] it is only because in the nineteenth century there was no serious conflict between Whitehall and Lombard Street. Since throughout the nineteenth century the restricted parliamentary franchise did not permit of any disharmony between the interests of the financial community and those of parliamentary government, the relation between the central bank and the government was equally unproblematic, whether the central bank had statutory independence or whether it was to some extent subject to governmental regulation. This state of affairs was only rarely interrupted; symptomatically, interruption occurred in 1870 when the defeatist interests of the upper middle class, anxious for the rapid termination of the Franco-Prussian war, found themselves faced by the credit requirements of a government presided over by Gambetta and having a policy of resistance à l'outrance. But even in this period the respect for the reputation of the *Banque de France*, which was supposed to represent public credit, was very high, as may be seen from the humble restraint of the Paris Commune's delegate to the bank. [12] Even the change in the governorship, effected by Gambetta when he returned to power in 1882, had no real significance. [13]

In the postwar period of mass democracy, it becomes generally rec-

[9] Hansard, LXXIV, 720.
[10] *The Economist*, March 29, 1941, p. 399.
[11] Brooks Adams, *The Law of Civilization and Decay* (New York, 1895), p. 283.
[12] Charles Beslay, *Mes Souvenirs* (Paris, 1873), Chapter "Ma délégation à la Banque."
[13] A. Dauphin-Meunier, *La Banque de France* (Paris, 1936), pp. 220–27.

ognized that the complete independence of the central bank as a transmission belt for the financial community can be profitably used to hold the government and parliament in check. One of the earliest resolutions of the Council of the League of Nations insists on the independence of central banks from governmental interference.[14] The more the respective countries were dependent on outside loans, the more stringent were the requirements for the noninterference of governments in the central banks, which in their turn were subjected to a system of mixed control exercised by private national and international financial interests. Thus the degree of independence of a small country was basically conditional upon whether it had to deal with a unified creditor pool—as Austria had to do with its creditors, pooled under the auspices of the League of Nations—or whether political competition between prospective creditor nations left the governments with a greater amount of liberty of movement in their foreign policy—as in the case of the Balkan nations. The desires and demands of the home banking community were reinforced by the backing of international banking organizations which, in the persons of financial commissioners and representatives, resided in the respective capitals themselves, and this was one of the decisive factors favoring or obstructing changes in the political balance in those countries.[15] In Germany the Bank Law of 1924 took most of the powers which the government formerly had exercised and transferred them to the Board of Directors of the *Reichsbank*—and to a much lesser degree to the internationalized "*Generalrat*" and the stockholders.[16] In this new fortified position the presidency of the *Reichsbank* very soon became the cohesive organism about which gathered the big financial and industrial interests. It acted as a channel of communication for them and as their accredited representative in their dealings with the government.

---

[14] The resolution is quoted in Kisch-Elkan, *Central Banks* (London, 1932), p. 17.
[15] Cf. the lucid exposition of the tie-up between international loans and retrogressive tendencies of governmental policies in postwar Austria and Hungary, in P. Szende, "Der Staatshaushalt und das Finanzsystem Oesterreichs und Ungarns," in *Handbuch für Finanzwissenschaft* (Tübingen, 1929), III, 206–9, 220.
[16] See H. Neisser, "Die alte und die neue Reichsbank", in *Strukturwandlungen der deutschen Volkswirtschaft*, II (Berlin, 1929), 293, and *Deutschland unter dem Dawesplan*, Bericht des Generalagenten (December 22, 1928) (Berlin, 1929), p. 116.

In this function, for instance, *Reichsbank* president Schacht was instrumental in barring the cities from further access to the foreign loan market in order to prevent the extension of their successful competition with the privately owned public utilities.[17]

This intervention was also felt in the case of the so-called Hilferding Loans, and it was of primary importance in the German crisis of 1929 which led to the downfall of the last parliamentary government. When MacDonald replaced the second Labour Cabinet with his National Government, it was likewise the administration of the Bank of England that was instrumental in provoking this change by asking for budget cuts known to be unacceptable to most of the labor leaders.[18] The strategic position of the Bank was enhanced by the very fact that, had its demands been refused, the necessary loans would not have been forthcoming.

In many aspects, postwar France represents a special case. In Germany or England the strategic position of the central banks was only made use of as a last resort. In contrast to this restraint, the *Banque de France* and the parliamentary government represent the two opposite poles around which the whole social and political life of the nation revolved in the twenties. Several factors worked together to create this situation. The extraordinarily large public debt, which was carried over from the war and which was not wiped out by such a thorough inflation as in Germany, was an adverse condition to start with. It was aggravated by the inability to obtain sufficient tax revenue from the defective system of income taxes, which, in itself a symbol of middle-class selfishness, was effectively supplemented by what was probably the lowest level of tax morality known in modern history. These conditions reduced the government to a state of perpetual dependency upon the bankers, whether for bridging a temporary shortage of cash for some weeks or months, or in order to place new loans. Under these

---

17 See, e.g., Otto Braun, *Von Weimar zu Hitler*, 2d ed. (New York, 1940), p. 217, whose testimony is valuable on account of his position at the time as head of the Prussian government.

18 See, e.g., Philip Snowden, *An Autobiography* (London, 1934), II, 945–47, who quite naturally, given his role at the time, tries to play down the influence of the Bank of England and of the Federal Reserve Bank, without, however, being able to deny that they asked for cuts in the social services. See also L. McWeir, *The Tragedy of Ramsay MacDonald* (London, 1938), pp. 349–57.

conditions the help of the *Banque de France* was indispensable either for rediscounting the treasury bonds taken over by private banking institutions, for conducting a generous nation-wide campaign in favor of new loans through its system of branches, or for procuring a foreign loan. The strategic advantage which the chronic difficulties of the government gave to the private regents of the bank, whose attitude was shared by the government-appointed governor, was invariably used whenever an undesirable government had to be outmaneuvered.

The story repeats itself over and over again in 1924, 1928, 1932, and 1936. The electorate shows tendencies to the left and puts into power some government combination shaped according to this image. But scarcely has the government begun to develop a timid program of social reform when the *crise de confiance,* with all the well-known features of the fall in the value of government bonds and the export of gold and foreign exchange, gets into full swing. The government finds it difficult to obtain even short-term credits, and with the depreciation of its long-term credit, the *deus ex machina,* the new long-term loan or, what is the desire of each successive minister of finance, the conversion of interest rates is out of the question. With a little help from the governor and regents of the bank, who chastise the wrong set and are prepared to oblige the right set of politicians, the untrustworthy government disappears, *la rente* goes up, and all reforms are forgotten.[19] In the twenties this system worked fairly smoothly—apart from the fact that in 1928 the *Banque de France* forced on its own hero, Poincaré,[20] a much too low stabilization level for the franc, and that

---

[19] The best insight into this process is given by the memoirs of Governor Moreau: "Le relèvement financier et monétaire de la France," *Revue des deux Mondes,* March 1, March 15, April 1, and April 15, 1937. See here especially his characterization of the Herriot ministry, pp. 55 ff.: when he wants to get rid of a cabinet, he decides "de crever l'abcès" (p. 58), in the opposite case he speaks of "les intrigues de certains parlementaires" (p. 30) against the government he wants to stay in office.

See also the already cited Dauphin-Meunier and Bopp, "Government and the Bank of France," in *Public Policy,* II (1941), 3 ff.

For a general judgment by a politician who experienced some rather rough handling by these institutions, see Caillaux in *Sénat.* Session Ordinaire, July 23, 1936, p. 814: "It was always in the atmosphere of this institution to consider the notes of the Banque de France as independent of government credit and to believe that the Banque de France was not created to come to terms with the government."

[20] Cf. Moreau, quoted *supra,* pp. 825–27.

this later proved a distinct disadvantage. In the thirties, however, this process of "correcting" the popular will ran into difficulties. The *Banque de France* then tried to force its deflationary policy *à outrance* on successive political combinations. It succeeded only at the third attempt with the accession of Laval to the premiership. From this time on, the revision of the statute of the bank and the synchronization of its administration with the political leadership became the catchword of the formative period of the *Front Populaire*. But significantly enough, when the victorious *Front Populaire* abolished the overlordship of the *Banque de France* and tried, according to the popular slogan, to transform it into the *Banque de la France*, it did not have enough power to stop the flight of the franc. When the French republic was already drawing its last breath, the financial community reserved its *liberum veto* against the government decree-powers by prohibiting close scrutiny of the "éternels mobilisés de l'armée Condé," [21] i.e., by refusing to put the principle of exchange control into effect. Paradoxically enough, the Enabling Act, given by Parliament to the Chautemps cabinet on June 30, 1937,[22] marks precisely the point at which the private manipulators of the financial apparatus retained their leadership while destroying the political fabric as a whole. This act enables the ministry to take all necessary measures but refuses it the most essential means for their execution. It orders the ministry "to assure the suppression of attempts to undermine public credit, to fight against speculation, to further economic recovery, price control, budget balancing, and, *without control of exchange*, to defend the gold holdings of the Bank of France." France is an extreme case. In no other country was the conflict between political democracy and private command over the sources of credit allowed to develop so far as to lead to the complete breakdown of the whole social organism.

Successive devaluation in different countries, the control of foreign commerce and exchange, and the abandonment of the cherished doctrine of budget equilibrium in favor of deficit spending have done

[21] Vincent Auriol in *Chambre*, Session Ordinaire, 1937, pp. 1964 f. He compares the manipulators of capital flight, always eager to stab their government in the back, with the French *émigré* nobility who, under the leadership of Prince Louis-Joseph Condé, tried at every turn of the French Revolution to stage a comeback.

[22] See *Journal Officiel*, July 1, 1937, and especially the deliberation of the Senate on June 30, 1937, in *Sénat*, Session Ordinaire, 1937, p. 718.

away with the dependence of the government upon the whim of private bankers. To a certain extent the so-called investors' strike in the privately owned section of the economy—that is to say, the increasing difficulties in the profitable employment of capital—has contributed to this turn of events by establishing exceedingly low interest rates for government loans, especially in the United States. At any rate, the political importance of this change is evident. The government which has developed into the largest customer of industry, often buying more than 50 per cent of the national output, is today in a strategically much more advantageous position than any other competitor for power. The possibility which always hung in suspense over the heads of previous governments in the pre-crisis period, that the financial interests might exercise their veto to throw the currency system out of gear, now seems remote and perhaps even nonexistent.[23]

But at the same time there is apparently a fairly widespread belief that the new system of government spending and the more or less complete abandonment of the doctrine "that natural forces may produce recovery" is intended to uphold the system of "production of wealth by private activity and enterprise." [24] In other words, the abandonment of the supremacy of money as an automatic regulator of social relationships is not supposed to cause a serious break in the scale of social evaluations prevalent in our society. But to what degree the desires which accompany the changes in the relationship between the government and the financial and industrial community may be fulfilled, modified, or entirely thwarted depends upon the relationship between the various social forces and the form they assume under the changed conditions. The relationship that persisted between the financial community and the government up to the last crisis may illuminate the degree to which political power was exercised in the form of indirect power. The symbols of politics appealed and appeared to us

[23] See the remarks of Berle, *New Directions in the New World* (New York, 1940), p. 121.

[24] See, e.g., the interesting discussion between governor Eccles, Federal Reserve Bank, the representative of the school of government spending as a means of upholding the existing private property relationships, which he in turn regards as the surest safeguard of democracy, and Senator Byrd of Virginia, representative of an old-fashioned "balance-the-budget" school, in the New York *Times*, December 20 and 27, 1938.

with the entire emotional apparatus which we were accustomed to find on the front page of newspapers. Yet, for the realities of political power, their evaluation and appreciation, we had to turn to the financial page. We were certain that the deterioration we could see there would rapidly spread to the front page until a change in symbols would reestablish a balance between both.

In our day, the balance is definitely shifting in favor of government, marking a world-wide tendency that has been consummated in the authoritarian countries. Fascist authors have been quick to conclude that in these countries all indirect power has been replaced by direct power. If this transition from indirect to direct power has a more than merely technical meaning, it implies that the antagonism between state and society, and with it the compromise structure of the state, has permanently disappeared in civil affairs, and that there is no longer any contradiction between the social content and the political form of a society. In reality, however, the contradictions continued to prevail unabated, and what changed was only the form and structure of the compromise. The general tendency of this change leads away from the liberalistic form of compromise, which was essentially a delimitation of spheres between the individual and the government, to a compromise among conflicting power groups. This tendency may be illustrated by the shifting emphasis in the ideology of compromise.

In the liberalistic period, it was Herbert Spencer who gave an evolutionary superstructure to the doctrine of political compromise.[25] Political compromise was the vital condition of a society which marched toward ever higher forms. John Morley's[26] distinction between legitimate and illegitimate compromise furnished the specifically liberalistic element. The legitimacy of the compromise, he wrote, consists in the right of the outvoted individual or minority to uphold and advocate publicly the principles which the majority has rejected. The essence of the compromise thus lies in the guarantee of dissent which is regarded as the guarantee of a liberal system of government. This characteristically individualistic argument, however, recedes in John Stuart Mill's famous *Considerations on Representative Government*.[27] Here,

[25] H. Spencer, *The Study of Sociology*, 1st ed. (New York, 1874), p. 396.
[26] J. Morley, *On Compromise*, 2d ed. (London, 1877), p. 209.
[27] London, 1876. See especially Chapter VI: "Of the Infirmities and Dangers to which Representative Government is Liable."

the compromise becomes a group compromise. Mill declares that the very existence of representative government requires it to maintain a balance between capital and labor and their respective satellites. His idea of compromise betrays a desire to avoid the possibility of one social group gaining predominance over the others. In general, the justification of the idea of compromise varies with the social and political affiliations of its advocates. One of the last forms of the doctrine is to be found in the Austro-Marxian theory of the provisional equilibrium between the social classes.[28]

What was the reality which corresponded to the changing ideology of compromise? In a strictly technical sense the sphere of compromise expanded with the transition from competitive to monopoly capitalism. The growth of huge social units which accompanied the modern industrial process had a dual impact upon organizational developments. While destroying the older personalized form of association, it prepared the way for an intricate framework of working agreements among the monopolies which emerged victorious from the liberal era. The day-to-day compromise which the politically independent representative in liberalistic society concluded with the government and with his colleagues has given way to the compromise between large social and political organizations in the "pluralistic" state. What seems most interesting from a constitutional point of view is the transformation of the liberal rights of the individual—John Morley's guaranteed right of the individual to dissent as premise of the working of the compromise itself—into a set of guarantees for the existence of the accredited social groups, the partners in compromise. This process of absorption of individual rights by monopolistic groups, although noticeable throughout the whole world, was especially apparent under the Weimar Constitution, where the mixture of traditional liberties and status quo guarantees under the misleading title of fundamental rights offered an excellent legal starting point for such developments.[29] Property rights became a protective screen for the process of monopolization, freedom of religion was used to strengthen the existing religious corporations, and freedom of speech and association had

[28] Otto Bauer, *Die Österreichische Revolution* (Vienna, 1923), p. 196. Cf. Gurland's critique in *Marxismus und Diktatur* (Leipzig, 1930), pp. 95 ff.
[29] Schmitt, *Freiheitsrechte und institutionelle Garantien der Reichsverfassung* (Berlin, 1931), and Huber, "Bedeutungswandel der Grundrechte," *Archiv für öffentliches Recht*, XXIII (1932), 1–98.

to be supplemented by strong protecting organizations in order to obtain recognition. It was the social group, as far as it was recognized by other groups, that got protection, not the individual. A member of a group found the authorities willing to protect him as against his group only in extreme cases or if the degree of social legitimacy of the group was rather problematic. And if one of the traditional rights of the individual was challenged, it could prevail only in the form of a group guarantee.[30] The individual was thus forced into the group, and this fact, in turn, consolidated the status of the group. The functioning of political compromise became increasingly dependent upon the workability of pacts among the predominant associations of capital and labor as well as among the organizations within each of these categories.

II. COMPROMISE UNDER NATIONAL SOCIALISM

With the disappearance of the old compromise structure and its accompanying internal checks in Europe, a new type of government is emerging of which, at first glance, greater independence and power seem the outstanding characteristics. The new type is found in various more or less transitional forms. The automatic integration of the political structure by money in the nineteenth century and the systematic use of the credit apparatus to this end in the period of mass democracy has given way to forms of domination by institutionalized monopolies. These changes have occurred in their most pointed form in Germany.

The German economic system consists of various monopolies in which the competitive elements have only an "oasis" character.[31] The monopolies are of three kinds: the government's labor monopoly, the private monopolies in industry, and the Food Estate. The character of these monopolies must be defined in terms of their relationship to the public authorities and in terms of their inner structure. Whereas the

[30] N.L.R.B. v. *Chicago Apparatus Co.* (C. C. A. 7, Dec. 1940) 116 F. 2 d. 753. See also Charles Killingsworth, "Employer Freedom and the N.L.R.B.," *Wisconsin Law Review*, March, 1941, pp. 211-38.

[31] W. Neuling, "Wettbewerb, Monopol und Befehl in der heutigen Wirtschaft," *Zeitschrift für die gesamten Staatswissenschaften*, XCIX (1939), 316, speaks of scanty "oases" of competition in the realm of the Food Estate.

monopoly for industrial and agricultural labor is a public monopoly under joint state and party control, allowing few opportunities for self-expression to individuals, the industrial monopolies and those in the Food Estate are administered by private interests which have been given a public character.[32] As such they form the backbone of a new system of guarantees which has taken over the role of the checks and balances inherent in the social structure under the older compromise system.

The first of these guarantees applies to the privileged groups in general. The abolition of institutional fluctuations produced by the democratic process of elections and the replacement of this process by a "strong government" has dispensed with the need to rely on the pressure potentialities of credit control. Greater security is calculated not only to outweigh the restrictions in the possible choice of investments, especially the inability to diminish risks by investing abroad, but also to counterbalance the diminished degree of personal freedom. There is an increased economic security for the propertied and professional classes as a whole to replace the smaller degree of individual liberty and the arbitrariness which the individual finds in the totalitarian state. For various reasons the democratic government of the Weimar Republic distributed unsystematic favors and, although not having promised to do so, was forced to take over the bulk of losses in the realm of banking and heavy industry. The economic policies of the Fascist government, however, have not only reduced these risks almost to nil, but have enabled big industry to make investments which are required by conditions of modern technology, but to which, because of the risks involved, it was formerly unable or unwilling to commit itself. A further guarantee lies in the active encouragement of the process of monopolization and cartelization and the transformation of a private power position that was only tolerated by law into a monopoly that remains private, yet is vested with public power.

This monopolization takes two forms: first, cartelization is extended through the establishment of a complete network of market regulating

[32] According to the estimates of the Institut für Konjunkturforschung, *Weekly Reports*, IX (1936), 198, at the end of 1936 all internally produced raw materials and semifinished goods, and assuredly half of the industrial finished goods, were bound by agreements. This figure does not define the kind of agreement, whether direct monopolies or only regulatory procedures.

bodies in every sphere, and second, the number of independent units in a given field is progressively reduced. Both processes are intimately interrelated. The cartel policy of National Socialism shows three stages of development. At the beginning, in 1933, we find a policy of active help granted to private market organizations in two ways, first, by considerably restricting the jurisdiction of the Cartel Tribunal, and second, by making cartelization compulsory and compelling outsiders to attach themselves to existing cartels. Even at this stage we can see a process which is significant for the new relationship between industry and the public authorities. Every increase in organizational power granted to the private industrial and trade associations is accompanied by an increase in the supervisory power of the corresponding government agencies. Whereas "state sovereignty" is used to "give the cartel power it could not obtain on a voluntary basis," [33] the government builds up its own apparatus which acts as an organ to harmonize the group interests of business with the interests of other recognized social groups. The second stage occurs when the official organization of industrial self-administration, which has replaced the earlier *Reichsverband der deutschen Industrie* and its branches, emerges as an active agent in the process of cartelization. In theory, the system of industrial groups and chambers now formed is specifically excluded from any tasks pertaining to market regulation, although its jurisdiction embraces almost all other fields of industrial policy and organization. But in practice it is inevitable that the cartels, the supervision of which is one of the main tasks of this new organization, soon begin to dominate these official organizations. In the years 1936 and 1937, when attacks were being launched against the price level produced by this thoroughgoing cartelization, and when the office of the Price Commissioner was created, there was a kind of sham battle against this growing identity between the official groups and the private organizations which regulated the market. But in this battle no use was ever made of the coercive machinery of the government, and the Reich Ministry of Economic Affairs contented itself with issuing orders asking for reports and justifications of this identity of personnel and with promul-

[33] C. Russell, "Die Praxis des Zwangskartellgesetzes," *Zeitschrift für die gesamten Staatswissenschaften*, XCVII (1937), 500.

gating general lines of direction.[34] Even this sham battle soon subsided, and in 1939 we reach the third stage in which the cartels, in their role as executive organs of the Reich Boards, are officially recognized as "all-embracing organs of market regulation." [35] As mandatories of the Reich Boards, which, in their turn, are independent legal personalities though subordinate to the Ministry of Economic Affairs, they now to an increasing degree regulate the distribution of both raw material and finished products.[36] Thus the process of cartelization has reached its logical conclusion in the final merger of private power and public organization.[37]

The process of concentration which accompanied thoroughgoing cartelization was accelerated for many reasons. The necessity for maximizing the speed of all deliveries pertaining to armaments required the use of labor-saving devices which, in their turn, depended on substantial investments—a need which became more and more evident with the increasing scarcity of labor. The shortage of raw materials worked against the small firms which had few import and bureaucratic connections of their own, and the expropriation of the Jews led in the same direction. In commerce, and especially in retail trade and handi-

[34] An acknowledgment of the thoroughgoing identity of personnel in both organizations is given by Neuling, quoted *supra*, p. 304, n. 1. For the organization in industry in general see Kuehn, "Der vorläufige Aufbau der gewerblichen Wirtschaft," *Archiv des öffentlichen Rechts.* XXVII (1936), 334–63, and the official commentary by the official of the Ministry of Economics, E. Barth, *Wesen und Aufgaben der Organisation der gewerblichen Wirtschaft* (Hamburg, 1939). As regards the relationship between cartel and official organizations see Kley, *Aufbau und Rechtscharakter der Neuorganisation der gewerblichen Wirtschaft und ihr Verhältnis zu den Kartellen*, Kölner Dissertation, 1938.

[35] "Kartell im Staatsdienst," *Deutscher Volkswirt*, January 12, 1940, p. 447, and "Entlastung der Reichsstellen," *Deutscher Volkswirt*, July 12, 1940, p. 1452. For a rationalization of the impossibility of separating the functions of official groups and cartels, see Merkel, "Wirtschaftslenkung und Kartellrecht," *Kartell-Rundschau*, 1939, p. 307, and H. Drost, "Der Krieg und die Organisation der gewerblichen Wirtschaft," *Zeitschrift der Akademie für Deutsches Recht*, 1940, pp. 25–26.

[36] That the persons who function as mandatories of the Reich Boards are often identical with the personnel of the cartels may be seen from the regulations for paper and wrapping material in Posse-Landfried-Syrup-Backe-Alpers, *Die Reichsverteidigungsgesetzgebung*, Vol. 2, IV, Papier, pp. 83–88.

[37] An isolated but vigorous protest against this development may be found in F. Boehm, *Die Ordnung der Wirtschaft als geschichtliche Aufgabe und rechtsschöpferische Leistung* (Stuttgart a. Berlin, 1937), whose main arguments closely parallel those of the American antitrust movement.

craft, firms with the largest turnover increased their competitive advantages as they were able to obtain a greater supply of goods for distribution. They were also able better to withstand the reduction of the profit margin, necessitated by the rather rigid control of prices for consumers' goods.

The economic pressure leading to concentration is accompanied by direct legal pressure. This has been used most vigorously against the owners of small shops and workshops. Pressure by powerful competitors who want to increase their sales in order to balance other unfavorable developments in cost factors has been aided and abetted by the government's desire to force marginal shop-owners into the factories. At first there was a process of indirect strangulation by governmentally approved exclusion from discounts, if the small shops did not reach a certain sales figure, and pressure was exercised in the same direction through a closer supervision of smaller plants by the social honor courts. This was soon followed by legislation aimed at a whole-sale combing-out.[38] The slow disappearance of the small businessman is speeding up; shops are closed if they are deemed unnecessary for the national economy, the debts, as far as is thought advisable, are paid by official organizations, and the former shopkeepers and businessmen are sent off to the factory.

For industry as such, the direct legal measures furthering concentration are of a double nature. In the first place, the process of compulsory standardization of types carried on from 1938 deprives many producers of their independent status and thrusts them down to the level of specialized departments of larger units by restricting them to the production of parts of the finished product. This was especially the case in the automobile industry. The war has given new force to this development by causing the compulsory closure of the technologically more backward factories. Some of the owners of these have been entirely removed from the field and have become mere rentiers; others

[38] Somewhat neglected so far, this role of the social honor courts, the supervision of small and medium-sized shops, is frankly acknowledged in *Soziale Praxis*, 1940, p. 1459. For the approval of those restrictions see the decision of the Cartel Tribunal of April 26, 1939, in *Kartell-Rundschau*, 1939, p. 420, which, already employing the terminology of the combing-out legislation, stipulates that a business which cannot, without endangering its existence, withstand a decrease of RM 50 in its annual profit cannot enjoy legal protection.

have been temporarily degraded to the level of wholesalers in their respective fields, receiving a special "colleague discount" which had to be given to them by the more fortunate members of the industry.[39] Whatever the manifold individual variations in the various industries, it is clear that, in spite of a somewhat contradictory ideology, the mergers that have thus been brought about tend to become permanent and tend permanently to eliminate the units which were closed provisionally.[40]

The stronger the organizations, the greater the degree of liberty they have in administering the regulations that apply to their members. At the bottom, in handicraft, where the head of the organization lives more from his proved devotion to the National Socialist cause than because of the weight of his economically and financially weak organization, the administration's direct interference is comprehensive. The head of the organization simply acts as an executive organ of the state bureaucracy in combing out the weaker members.[41] In the sphere of large-scale business the transformation of positions of private power into public organs of economic "self-administration," though accompanied by the transfer of legal omnipotence to the supervisory ministries and special boards, has increased rather than decreased the power of those who dominate the organizations. Behind the legal screen of the leader principle which requires that the group leaders be appointed by the public authorities, the absolutistic principles governing monopolized business groups continue unabated, especially since the complete demise of the stockholders as a supervisory organ. Even the legal prescriptions have to take this reality into account, and the group leader is required to submit to annual votes of confidence by his advisory boards. A negative vote would not legally be followed by his dismissal but, as the official commentator says, would only necessitate inquiries by higher bodies.[42] But, of course, the social function of this

[39] See, e.g., the regulations for the soap industry given by Posse-Landfried, quoted *supra*, Vol. 2, IV, Seife, Introductory Remarks.

[40] As regards the ideology, see the wording of the decree on Gemeinschaftshilfe der Wirtschaft, February 19, 1940, *R.G.Bl.*, I, 395, which starts with the supposition that the shutdown is only of a temporary character.

[41] Before the great combing-out of April 1, 1939, there were still 1,471,000 handicraft units employing less than 6 employees as compared with 1,734,000 in 1933.

[42] Barth, quoted *supra*, p. 67.

vote of confidence cannot be obscured by placing it in the context of the new constitutional phraseology. It expresses the state of affairs which prevails throughout the organizational setup of German industry. The advisory board is constituted as an oligarchical body dominating through the same persons both private cartels and official trade organizations. Under the officially sanctioned leadership of one of the industrial lords, who is *primus inter pares* so far as the monopolists are concerned and who is leader so far as the plebeian rest is concerned, the professional bureaucratic personnel administers the law for the whole group. Consequently, this personnel has the task of adjusting the various interests within the group, either as the agency of last resort, or, as is increasingly the case, as a kind of preliminary sifting organ whose reports provide the raw material for the official decisions of the Reich Ministry of Economic Affairs. It represents, so to speak, the group interest as against the interest of the individual concern. Although this function served to strengthen the independence of the group bureaucracy as against individual concerns, this process did not go very far. The constitutional framework governing the organization of the group makes the group administration partial to the big interests within its jurisdiction no less than did its forerunner under the Weimar Republic. Every big concern has its own specialists who zealously and competently watch the work of the representative of the group. Significantly enough, the democratic element, a remnant of earlier estate ideas,[43] which would have required a vote of confidence from all members, not only from the advisory board, was already removed from the statute book by executive order in 1935,[44] and the relations between leadership and small and medium-sized producer have been adapted to the German reality. The status of the smaller producers has been changed from that of active participants into that of objects of propaganda. The war has not altered any part of this organizational structure. On the contrary, the building up of District Economic Boards has only established these characteristics the more firmly. At the same time, when the provincial and regional state bureaucracy was given supervisory power over the distribution of consumers' goods for

[43] T. Cole, "Corporative Organization of the Third Reich," *Review of Politics*, II (1940), 438–62.
[44] Barth, quoted *supra*, p. 68.

the whole population, the presidents of the regional organizations of trade and industry, of the Chambers of Industry and Commerce, saw themselves raised to the rank of Reich commissioners with the duty of seeing to it that the tasks of production were carried through.[45] And when the most recent legislation tried to reduce war profits, it likewise to a large extent placed the power to determine what is to be considered appropriate profit in the hands of the groups whose members were the very ones to make the profit.

To a large measure the governing ranks of the Chambers of Industry and of the Economic Groups are the ones that, either directly or by the weight of the advice which their experts set before the state bureaucracy, decide on the chances of making profits from any given means of production. This method of determining the use to which a given means of production will be put has become the rule rather than the exception. Many owners have been totally or partially deprived of the possibility of making use of their machinery. The measures by which these expropriations have been carried through have a dual aspect. In most of the cases covered by the government's authority, quota restrictions and other measures have been actually carried through by the career group officials who have been vested with public authority, the profit of such operations accruing to certain members of the group. In the case of Jewish expropriation the question of indemnity for the damaged person does not arise.[46] In the other cases interference with private property invariably raises the question of indemnity. Under the Weimar Republic the courts that had jurisdiction over expropriation claims gave a very extensive interpretation to the concept of expropriation by public authorities. It was to be expected under fascism that such an interpretation, as well as the insistence on full compensation, would be upheld by the courts in all cases where

---

[45] Decrees on "Wirtschaftsverwaltung," August 27, 1939, November 28, 1939, R.G.Bl., I, 1495 and 2315, with regulations of September 20, 1939, R.G.Bl., I, 1872.

[46] We can see the curious spectacle of the government running behind the private experts in Aryanization and trying belatedly to snatch a share of the loot, thus squeezing out the small businessman who had acquired Jewish property but did not have sufficient capital to run it, or, especially in the field of real estate, to preserve part of it for the warriors when they return from the victorious war. See the decree on the reexamination of Aryanization acts of June 10, 1940, R.G.Bl., I, 891, where, in case of inappropriate gains through Aryanization, compensation has to be paid to the Reich.

the physical property was left intact but where its profitable use was excluded in consequence of a governmental authorization or decree. The government therefore decided to throw the traditional procedures overboard. The differences arising from the transformation of the apparatus of production were to be treated as a pure intragroup concern and there was to be no appeal to an outside authority.

So we can see that the tendency already mentioned as characteristic of mass democracy, the absorption of individual rights in group rights, reaches its extreme form. This tendency was already visible in the cartel legislation of 1933, which prevented the Cartel Tribunal from interfering in disputes arising between members and the cartel. The principle of refusing to grant access to regular courts was also soon employed in numerous decrees, especially in those concerning the Food Estate (agriculture). These ruled that the parties have to content themselves with the decision of an intragroup arbitration court or, as far as questions of quotas are concerned, with committees of complaint provided for by their respective organizations.[47] The same state of affairs has prevailed in regard to the compensation granted in the case of compulsory shutdown of plants for the duration of the war. Here, too, the economic groups have sole jurisdiction in deciding whether and what indemnity should be given, and appeal is possible only to the Reich Economic Chamber, the coordinating body of these organizations. The remarkable feature of this legislation is, first, the abandonment of the principle, accepted throughout the liberal era and still acknowledged by the regular courts in Germany, that the individual should not suffer any loss through the acts of expropriation, that he should receive either a full or at least an "appropriate" indemnity.[48] If an indemnity is granted, it is granted by equity and not by law, and to

---

[47] Cf. L. Gebhard and H. Merkel, *Das Recht der landwirtschaftlichen Marktordnung* (1937), who present an elaborate commentary on the organization of arbitration courts as far as agricultural market regulations are concerned (statute of February 26, 1935, *R.G.Bl.*, I, 1293). They remark (III, 25) that appeals against the decisions of the committee of complaint to the arbitration court would have a chance of success only in very exceptional cases. See also W. Weber and F. Wieacker, *Eigentum und Enteignung* (Hamburg, 1935), pp. 26–33, for a list of the expropriation features in the various decrees. As regards the elimination of ordinary courts in general, see the remark of Wieacker in *Deutsches Verwaltungsrecht*, 1937, p. 466.

[48] See, e.g., the decision of the Prussian Supreme Administrative Tribunal of March 29, 1935, C, 329.

say, as does the official language, that the "vital necessities of the whole region have to be considered before the interests of the individual" is only another way of justifying the redistribution of property.[49] But even more important than the degree of indemnification granted on account of the loss of professional and economic status is the fact that these rules deny access to the courts and, by so doing, close the iron ring which the new economic constitution of the monopolistic society places around the less favored members of a business or trade group. They are prevented from combining with other social groups or airing before a public forum their grievances against the monopolist dominating the group. The increasing factual subservience to the command of a monopoly-dominated group has now become a legalized subservience.

Industry and agriculture are not the only realms in which the dominant forces of the group have seized the right of decision in intragroup controversies—even where these controversies only thinly veil the life struggle of marginal firms against monopolies. The same process is to be found elsewhere in the German political structure. One might almost determine the status of the different groups in Germany by the degree to which they have attained the *privilegium de non appellando*, to adopt a well-known concept from German constitutional history. That is to say, one might determine their status by the extent to which they have succeeded in depriving the individual member of the group of the possibility of appealing to external bodies against group decisions. This *privilegium de non appellando* exists in its most concentrated form in the army. The army command is made absolute master over every individual in its service by virtue of denying any separation between the personal and the professional status of its members. Business does not need to strive for such a position; it is satisfied to control the social and economic functions of its members. As regards members of the state bureaucracy and of the party and its affiliated organizations, we have to differentiate between the direction of public affairs and the task of controlling the population. In so far as this first function is concerned, no judicial interference is allowed. The

---

[49] The practice of the arbitration courts of the Food Estate has been discussed in P. Giesecke, "Entschädigungspflicht bei marktordnenden Massnahmen," in *Festgabe für Hedemann* (1938), pp. 368–81.

ever expanding lists of activities which, by legislative order, are excluded from any judicial examination make the discussion of whether the judiciary may itself decide which acts are to be included in the category of political acts, and therefore to be exempted from examination, a mere theoretical squabble.[50] The judiciary has thus been degraded from the rank of an arbiter of intergroup conflicts to that of an "assistant"[51] of the administration. The judiciary competes with the various administrative services[52] as an organ to enforce discipline in the lower ranks of the bureaucracy, in the party, and among the population at large. The "taylorized" methods adopted especially in the administration of criminal law largely through granting the public prosecutor a dominant position over the procedure, and allowing a quick and "satisfying" disposal of a maximum of cases unhampered by procedural quirks,[53] have torn away the sanctity of the judiciary[54]

---

[50] For the status of the controversy see G. Ipsen, *Politik und Justiz* (Hamburg, 1937), and S. Grundmann, "Die richterliche Nachprüfung von politischen Führungsakten," *Zeitschrift für die gesamten Staatswissenschaften*, C (1940), 512–44.

[51] Cf. Under Secretary of the Treasury Reinhardt in *Deutsche Steuerzeitung*, 1935, p. 485; see also G. Schmoelders, "Die Weiterbildung des Wirtschaftsrechts," *Zeitschrift für die gesamten Staatswissenschaften*, CI (1941), 78. The organization of a Supreme Administrative Court for the whole Reich carries the new status of the judiciary to its logical conclusion when it prescribes that the judges can be removed from the Court at the end of the fiscal year. See *Frankfurter Zeitung*, April 22, 1941. As regards the small part played by the labor courts in determining the relationship between employers and employees, see Cole, "National Socialism and German Labor Courts," *Journal of Politics*, III (1941), 196.

[52] As regards the civil liability of the party for offenses committed by party functionaries, see the party point of view in A. Lingg, *Die Verwaltung der NSDAP* (Munich, 1940), pp. 257 ff. The right of the courts to pass on this question is upheld by S. Grundmann, quoted *supra*, pp. 541 ff., and the decision of the *Reichsgericht* of February 17, 1939, in *Deutsches Recht*, 1939, p. 1785. The lower courts, however, more exposed to party pressure, do not seem to follow the Supreme Court. The criminal liability of party members for embezzlement is at times enforced in the courts—provided that one of the numerous amnesties does not intervene. But the secrecy of the procedure and the absolute prohibition of reports on such trials deprive them of any function of control. See E. Roper and C. Leiser, *Skeleton of Justice* (New York, 1941).

[53] See O. Kirchheimer, "Criminal Law in National Socialist Germany," *Studies in Philosophy and Social Science*, VIII (1940), 444–63.

[54] Reich Minister Frank speaks of "taylorism" in criminal procedure in his somewhat melancholy reflections on the fate of German criminal law under present conditions in "Die Aufgaben der Strafrechtserneuerung," *Zeitschrift der Akademie für Deutsches Recht*, 1941, p. 25. See also G. Dahm, "Richtermacht und Gerichtsverfassung im Strafrecht," *Zeitschrift für die gesamten Staatswissenschaften*, CI (1941), 287–308.

and have deprived the government of the moral and propagandistic value inherent in the services of the judiciary. It becomes less important as a problem whether the regular judiciary or a service bureaucracy is chosen to carry out these functions, and the field is left open for minor rivalries. However, even here the observed tendency to acquire as far as possible the *privilegium de non appellando* is always noticeable throughout the administrative services of party and state bureaucracy.

Within the constitutional framework of the Weimar Republic, it became the function of the bureaucracy continually to keep under scrutiny the relationship between big business and labor, but also to preserve the status quo of agriculture and small-scale business. The cohesive element which united the bureaucracy was the preservation of its social status against encroachments from the outside and, whenever feasible, the desire to extend its activities. The ideological emphasis on its impartial service to the nation as a whole hid the fact that, as far as the object of its policies was concerned, the unity was more apparent than real. The controversies between the social groups reappeared in somewhat mitigated form, free of propagandistic tinge, in the relationship between the various divisions of the public services. When we try to assess the impact of the changes in the political power structure on the bureaucracy and on its relationship to the National Socialist party, we realize that the unity of the bureaucracy was shaken still more. In part it lost its identity through its steady permeation by, and association with, the party machine, and in part its general negative attitude to outside control lost its *raison d'être* in the new and much less controlled setup.[55] Thus we are confronted with the strange picture of an intense centralization within each administrative unit going hand in hand with certain tendencies to departmentalization. Each of the highest subleaders jealously guards against a loss of status by being subjected to anybody's command but the Führer's. As in

---

[55] The remaining control organ over the bureaucracy, the Rechnungshof (Court of Accounts Control), never very effective in the observations which it issues on expenditure incurred years before, has under the Third Reich become a repository for high officials from the Weimar period who prove their right to the salary they have drawn in their former positions by checking accounts "as soldiers *in Zivil* imbued by the spirit of the leader." (H. Mueller, "Die Stellung des Rechnungshofs im 3. Reich," *Finanzarchiv*, VII [1940], 193, 205.)

older systems, what counts is the individual's proximity to the supposed fountain of the charisma itself, not the fact of belonging to the rational council of government. In consequence, "the position of Ministers of the Reich has undergone a fundamental change. They do not form a collegium, an organizational unit." [56] The number of administrative organizations under the direct command of the Führer and exempt from any other supervision is steadily increasing. And the interpenetration of party and bureaucracy leads to jurisdictional regulations compared with which the most difficult intricacies of federal problematics are relatively easy to follow. Thus, for example, we have such a figure as the Reichsführer SS who, as head of the police, is administratively incorporated in the Reich Ministry of the Interior without, however, being subject in his decisions to the approval of the Reich Minister.[57]

The official constitutional theory likes to regard the relationship between state and party as one between a technical apparatus and a political movement, the former following the directions of the latter, which is supposed to be the immediate expression of national life and will. The official ideology, therefore, sees the party as an indissoluble unit. In reality the structure of the National Socialist party and its place in the political power structure of modern Germany can only be understood in terms of its dual function. First, the National Socialist party arose as a mass party and as such is the heir to the other mass parties which existed during the era of mass democracy. Second, the party and the state bureaucracy together constitute an organ of mass domination. It is a competitor of, and later an heir to, the left-wing mass parties. It not only tries to cater to the economic desires of its followers but also incorporates in its structure some vision of a new

---

[56] U. Scheuner, "Deutsche Staatsführung im Krieg," *Deutsche Rechtswissenschaft*, V (1940), 26. For earlier formulations in the same direction see R. Höhn, *Wandlungen im staatsrechtlichen Denken* (Berlin, 1934), p. 39.

[57] The same exempt position within the foreign and labor ministries is held by the Reich leader of the Germans abroad and by the Work Service leader of the Reich. As regards the structure of the Youth Organization, see H. Dietze, "Die verfassungsrechtliche Stellung der Hitler-Jugend," *Zeitschrift für die gesamten Staatswissenschaften*, C (1940), 113–56, who comes (p. 154) to the conclusion that the youth movement is an institution which does not belong exclusively to the party or to the government, cannot be measured by conceptions of party law or constitutional law, and thus is subject only to those of the Reich law.

political order. The fact that its following is a heterogeneous one makes necessary a constant shift in the ideology, a greater emphasis on the purely political elements of the new order as against the economic basis, and heavier emphasis on propaganda—lest its following dissolve into its separate social components. When the trade unions and left-wing political parties were destroyed, the new mass organizations of the National Socialist party took over at least some of the social functions of the defunct groups. The numerous individuals who, both before 1933 and to a certain extent afterwards, transferred their loyalty to the National Socialist organization helped to establish this continuity.[58] In the conditions of party pluralism under the Weimar Republic, in order to balance the heterogeneity of its membership, the National Socialist party had not only to adopt a special vehemence in the competition for political power but also to establish the principle of an unquestionable faith in its leadership. Having achieved predominance in the state, but being without a clearly defined social program, the party followed the line of least resistance. It confirmed the titles of business and the army but at the same time hastened to build up a competitive apparatus of its own, gradually reinforcing it with the services of the technically efficient state bureaucracy.

This process changed the structure of the party itself and brought the party's ever present bureaucratic element sharply to the fore. The party proved no support for the independent middle classes in their struggle for survival but, instead, actually hastened their final decline more than any other single factor in modern German history. On the other hand, the capture of the state machinery by the party, the vast extension of this machinery, and its duplication in many cases by a corresponding party bureaucracy, though depriving many of the middle-class elements of their position in the process of production, gave them in compensation economic security and social standing.[59]

[58] The inherited elements in the National Socialist party are naturally effaced if the party is contrasted with the somewhat literary and artificial political styles of nineteenth-century representation instead of with the mass parties of mass democracy. Cf. Ipsen, "Vom Begriff der Partei," *Zeitschrift für die gesamten Staatswissenschaften*, C (1940), 406.

[59] There are no figures available for the period since 1935, but even up to then, with the process of aggrandizement going on, the proportion of officials in the total membership of the National Socialist party increased from 6.7 per cent in 1933 to 13 in 1935. Cf. Gerth, "The Nazi Party, Its Leadership and Composition,"

The fact that, although many of the new functionaries have come from the independent middle classes, this same middle class was crushed as never before with the active help of the new bureaucracy shows how far and fast this new social group has already traveled in its alienation from its earlier basis. Besides demonstrating that the new group was becoming separated from its earlier social interests, this also testifies to its adaptation to the various (often far-flung) new tasks with which it has been entrusted, jointly with, or in addition to, the state bureaucracy. Whereas the party official rises to a position of equality with the government official and even in some cases succeeds in entering the ranks of the business group, the lower party member only holds honorary and onerous office and becomes almost indistinguishable from the ordinary nonparty citizen as a zealously watched object rather than a subject of political power.

The new legislation concerning administrative leadership in the *Landkreise*,[60] which has been given much attention in Germany,[61] must be understood as a rear-guard action which, for propagandistic aims, attempts to revive the theoretical conception of the unified party as an independent entity in its relationship to the state bureaucracy. It starts from the principle that leadership over persons (*Menschenführung*) is exclusively the task of the party. The competent party official is responsible to his party superior for the conduct and attitude of the population. The township president or the mayor, however, is responsible for the orderly execution of all administrative tasks in the framework of legal jurisdiction. Both organs are forbidden to meddle in each other's business. The psychological usefulness of such a regulation is undeniable. It protects the party official against requests from the rank and file of the membership by emphasizing a separation which for

---

American Journal of Sociology, XLV (1940), 527. Some of this increase, however, may only be apparent, as, e.g., in the case where the party acknowledges the right of a wife to transfer her low party membership number to her husband though he himself refrained from openly joining the party while he was an official. See Lingg, quoted *supra*, pp. 172–73.

60 In spite of its misleading title, which only refers to the *Landkreise* (rural districts), the statute of December 28, 1939, R.G.Bl., I (1940), 45, is designed to provide general control over the relationship between the middle ranks of the bureaucracy and the corresponding party officials.

61 O. Redelberger, "Partei und Staat im Landkreis," *Reichsverwaltungsblatt*, LXI (1940), 47.

all practical purposes does not exist, and after laying down these principles the statute itself has thus to define the different degrees of cooperation between both hierarchies. Though the relation between party and bureaucracy may give rise to ostentatious jurisdictional disputes, it is not in these that we find the deeper-lying conflicts, but within the structure of the party itself. So long as the party has not exclusively become a huge apparatus for mass domination, so long as the desires, fears, and wishes of the atomized masses still filter through the numerous channels of party organizations, like the Labor Front and the National Socialist Welfare Agency, which exercise *Betreuungsfunktionen*, duties of a "guardian of the masses," there are still some deteriorated remnants of the earlier form, the mass party. Even in their bureaucratic form, those elements of the party which are entrusted with the care of the masses represent, in some degree, the unrepresented sections of the community who have no independent voice in the balance of power.

By carefully restricting itself exclusively to the military sphere, the army, from the very beginning, was able to uphold the independence it had reestablished under the Weimar Democracy. Business, trade, and the independent ranks of agriculture became a closed monopoly. Government and party not only accepted its inner power distribution as they found it but actively helped to drive it still more pointedly in the direction of an oligarchic combine. The relationship of these groups to the army and the party hierarchy is in flux; especially the respective weight of the party bureaucracy and the army is subject to sudden shifts, owing to the impact of the war changes, the transitional or permanent character of which is not yet discernible. But one permanent pattern stands out. While sections of the new party and state bureaucracy act as transmission belts for those groups sufficiently vocal in their own right, other parts of the state and party bureaucracy which exercise the *Betreuungsfunktion* represent the unrepresented.[62] The compromise between the more articulate groups and these "guardians of the masses" more often than not resembles the arbitration award of Marshal Balbo who, while permitting a salary reduction asked for by the employers, awarded to the workers of Ferrara the *epitheton*

[62] As regards the modified compromise, see the comment of F. Morstein Marx, "Bureaucracy and Dictatorship," *Review of Politics*, III (1941), 101.

ornans "valiant." [63] One of the chief compromises, if not *the* chief compromise, they concluded in the name of the unrepresented, the "Leipzig Agreement of 1935," was as farcical as the Balbo award. By this agreement the "Self-Administration of German Economy" became formally affiliated with the Labor Front. No practical consequences, however, were ever drawn from this "liaison." [64] But there is compromise, nevertheless, as in every other society which has a high degree of social stratification.

In the compromise structure of National Socialism as it arose after the disappearance of all independent representation of the masses, the old question is brought to the fore: how can the interest of the various partners to the compromise, the monopolies, army, industry, and agriculture as well as the diversified layers of party bureaucracy, be brought to a common denominator? It is apparent that the Führer, or, as we should more appropriately say, the group of persons identified with the Führer, has established an authority which acts as an ultimate arbiter in all cases where the respective monopoly groups are not able to reach a decision by themselves. The leadership is able to decide intergroup differences with relative ease, and these decisions are carried through with a minimum of resistance only because the unfolding program of expansion has given the various groups the possibility of extending their activities (though on a different plane) and of satisfying their desires without too much need of getting in each other's way. [65] The ultimate decision of the Führer group is therefore the more easily accepted the more it takes the form and function of a permanent guarantee of the imperialist order. [66] It is this interdepend-

---

[63] This story is related in Rosenstock-Franck, *Les étapes de l'économie fasciste italienne*, (Paris, 1939), p. 233.

[64] Its wording in W. Mueller, *Das soziale Leben im neuen Deutschland* (Berlin, 1938), pp. 136–37.

[65] See for the whole problem the semiofficial commentary in G. Neesse, *Führergewalt* (Tübingen, 1940).

[66] Characteristic of the intimate connection between the establishment of the authority placed in the German leadership and the execution of its imperialist program is a sharp refutation of the conservative writer Triepel who attempted to uphold the view that a state may be called sovereign even if it has no external independence, provided that it controls its own subjects. See H. Triepel, *Die Hegemonie* (Stuttgart, 1938), p. 143, rejected by E. Huber in his review in *Zeitschrift für die gesamten Staatswissenschaften*, C (1940), 179. In fact, the form of domination which the large-space *(Grossraum)* imperialism of Germany

ence between the unquestionable authority of the ruling group and the program of expansion which offers the characteristic phenomenon of the compromise structure of the Fascist order, directs its further course, and decides upon its ultimate fate.

To summarize our remarks, we can describe the changes in political compromise as follows. During the liberal period of modern society, political compromise operated among parliamentarians and between them and the government. Every representative acted on his own, promoting certain financial, business, and agricultural interests and changing allegiance from one to another of them according to his own interests and judgment. Thus, through individual agreements the functioning of parliament was constantly kept in harmony with the prevailing economic structure. With the beginnings of "mass democracy" (about 1910-11), the task of keeping political compromise in harmony with the economic structure devolved to a considerable extent upon the central banks. At the same time, the agreements tended to evolve from individual ones into voluntary compacts between the main groups of capital and labor and their subdivisions.

Fascism characterizes the stage at which the individual has completely lost his independence and the ruling groups have become recognized by the state as the sole legal parties to political compromise. Since money, a rather adequate expression of social power during the liberal period, ceased to mediate between economic and political life, another coordinator of public life was sorely needed. There remained only the institution of leadership to arbitrate between the groups. Its power rests on its ability to compensate every group sacrifice with advantages which, however, can ultimately be got only in the international field, that is to say, through imperialist policy.

-----

creates is not very amenable to the fiction of a sovereign restricted to the domestic realm. "The developing large-space order might, contrary to earlier imperialism, constitute a system of direct and open domination"—says E. Huber, "Position und Begriffe," *Zeitschrift für die gesamten Staatswissenschaften*, C (1940), 143.

IN QUEST OF SOVEREIGNTY

FASHION in political theory seems to change quickly in our days. Hardly more than ten to fifteen years have elapsed since the state was declared moribund in pluralistic theories. With their peculiar mixture of shrewd analysis and ethical utopias, these theories seem to be the legitimate successors of nineteenth-century liberal theories. Liberal theories, though at times still professed, look like apologetic rear-guard actions.[1] Theory cannot but take cognizance of the fact that what was called "free institutions" in the language of the nineteenth century suffocates under the impact of all the changes in the social structure which industrial society has engendered. Their remnants rapidly turn into propaganda tools to be indifferently used by friend and foe alike. Ever increasing discrepancies between the power of the subject and the impotence of the object of domination give birth to a crop of diverse interpretations. They have been used for building up the totalitarian theory of the state. But the same set of facts has also supported the doubts often expressed in our days in opposite political camps as to whether the term "state" may still be considered an appropriate starting point for an inquiry into the power relationship of social forces in present-day society. Since statements concerning the concept traditionally called the state, or the absence of such concept, refer to the form and contents of mutual relations between individual social

Reprinted, by permission, from *Journal of Politics*, VI (1944), 139–76.

[1] The manner in which liberal constitutional doctrine which takes its task seriously has to turn thoroughly interventionist in order to attain an effective equilibrium of social forces is impressively demonstrated by David Riesman, "Civil Liberties in a Period of Transition," in *Public Policy* (Cambridge, Mass., 1942), III, 33–96.

bodies, it seems convenient first to investigate the present stage of such relations.

SOCIAL, POLITICAL, ECONOMIC GROUPS

The importance of groups in political life is somewhat obscured by the liberality with which the pluralists of the immediate past bestowed political capacity onto each and every social grouping. Pluralist doctrine never tired of describing "the vast complex of gathered nations" [2] to which men are entitled to give their allegiance. If human personality shall find its fulfillment, men must be free to participate in the widest range of social and cultural experiences, and they may accordingly divide their loyalties among different organizations. No societal rule, pluralists insisted, can make loyalty to the political organization prevail automatically in the event of a conflict between group loyalty and loyalty to the state. Loyalty to the particular organization of our free choice might well prove to be the stronger one, as shown by the example of historical conflicts between the state and religious bodies.[3] Whether situations of conflict do or do not arise depends upon our arbitrary decision to grant or withhold support.

In the pluralists' zealous endeavors to destroy the image of the centralized state and to install the free reign of the voluntary groups on its ruins with a kind of vast "super clearing-house" [4] as a coordinating agency, social reality of group life in industrial society was invariably romanticized. It is one thing to harmonize relations between different clubs which may be indiscriminately and simultaneously joined by the same individuals; it is an entirely different matter to harmonize the life of mutually exclusive groups. Human beings as a rule do no more choose their social affiliations than they do the place where they live or the quality of the consumer goods they prefer. Even in the case of the church, the showpiece of a well-functioning pluralist society, social status is often a formative influence in the

[2] John N. Figgis, *Churches in the Modern State* (London, 1914), p. 70.
[3] Harold J. Laski, "De Maistre and Bismarck," in *Problems of Sovereignty* (London, 1917), p. 211.
[4] G. D. H. Cole, *Social Theory* (London, 1920), p. 134.

choice of religious preferences. Mere multiplication of organizational affiliations is without any significance when the organizations in question have only the character of satellites working in the same social zone as the main organization.

It is true that modern society has produced a host of voluntary social organizations which unite members of the most different social strata on a religious, national, or racial basis. It is an accepted technique of such associations to operate on a basis of strict equality. Yet such equality is a precondition to the smooth coordination of heterogeneous social elements which are made to fit into the accepted pattern of society, and coordinating them often forms the main purpse of such organizations. The authors of one of the most formidable enterprises yet undertaken in the field of statistical analysis of group structure say that "within the associational membership per se there is equality, but class attitudes still operate to differentiate the people who belong to the different positions within this structure." [5]

The primary political function of such organizations is the advancement of general patterns of life deemed desirable by the groups that dominate them. In consequence, their political activity exhausts itself in the task of integration. They envisage direct and concerted group action only when the specific objectives of the organization are under discussion, for example, subsidies for denominational schools, pensions for war veterans. This does not exclude the possibility that a prominent member of such an "integration" organization will take an advanced stand on some vital question. Although such an attitude may carry heavy weight, as shown by the recent case of the Archbishop of Canterbury, it must not reflect upon, or commit, the organization as a whole. The organization will be the less affected, the better it has succeeded in keeping its main dogmas out of the area of immediate social conflict. Such organizations as the Catholic Church have through long experience developed a well-functioning system of "intraorgani-

[5] W. Lloyd Warner and Paul S. Lunt, *The Status System of a Modern Community* (New Haven, 1942), p. 20. The authors split the class structure of modern society into six groups. As transitions in a system of advanced group differentiation are bound to be very numerous, their first conclusion that "constant interpenetration takes part between neighboring classes" is self-evident. Their second conclusion, "that the classes at the two ends are much less related than the others" (p. 23), is more interesting although it does not necessarily follow from their working premises.

zational equilibrium." It purposely allows prominent members to serve as contact men to the most different social groups, and often "satellite" groups with radically opposite social goals are encouraged. The net political effect is invariably the aggrandizement of the main group. At the same time, such measures destined to preserve the "intraorganizational equilibrium" tend to enhance leanings toward political "neutrality." [6]

Such organizations form the subterranean channels which give stability to the dominating pattern of society. They support a structure which allows for acceptance of changes only over fairly long periods. The structure and composition of such organizations preclude their more direct initiative in shaping social and economic policies. General formulas and popular phrases cover the area of social disagreement.

Transitory social alignments may express themselves in the sudden appearance of new social groupings. The impoverishment of the independent middle class may create special pension groups. The disenchantment of the world may produce new religious groups which will concentrate their endeavors on some especially objectionable features of a radically mechanized world. But their action, for the most part, does not reach the political level; it disappears in the vast sea of formless discontent reserved till the day of final reckoning. Consumer organizations, for example, always remain groupings of secondary social importance, although they seem predestined to cover a wide area where substantially identical interests prevail.[7] Indeed, of all configurations around which the organization of society could center, "consumer sovereignty" seems the one which remains at maximum distance from the realities of present-day society. The failure of such organizations to develop beyond a somewhat insubstantial influence in the field of consumer protection stems from the fact that the status of a community member is regulated by his position within the process of

[6] This division of functions within the church had earlier attracted the attention of Georges Sorel, *Réflexions sur la Violence*, 6th ed. (Paris, 1925), p. 430; as regards the distinction between the political beliefs of individual church members (in which they may indulge at their own risk) and the mere integrating function of the church ("création d'un esprit essentiellement chrétien"), see Jacques Maritain, *Humanisme et Intégral* (Paris, 1936), p. 287.

[7] See, e.g., a well-founded judgment in Temporary National Economic Committee, *Reports*, Vol. XXI, *Competition and Monopoly in American Industry* (Washington, D.C., 1941), p. 11.

production. A consumers' victory may impose some price cuts; it may standardize or improve some lines of consumer goods; it may within certain well-defined limits help to work out a more satisfactory family budget, but it will not change the social status of an individual or of a family. Changes in the individual's status as a producer, however, must inevitably affect his general social status. If the change is far-reaching and of an enduring nature, it will involve either surrender or the capture of positions within the social group; it will mean social degradation or social advancement. The more society is mechanized and depersonalized, the more societal standards are calculated according to the quantities of easily measurable goods at the disposal of the individuals. This comparability of consumption standards stops only at the top strata of society. The handful of those who dispose of the means of production, emulated in more recent times by the "practitioners of violence," show their exalted rank by entering into a competition for maximum individualization of consumption standards. But this competition for "conspicuous waste" takes place, on account of its expensiveness, on a rather restricted scale. Even for those holding rank immediately below the top strata, individualization means standardization of consumption habits, though on a comparatively high level. Personality is in the end merely one side of the equation; the other side is possession of certain goods.

Prebourgeois society attempted to freeze societal positions at a given level and invented artificial devices for deferring and penalizing changes in social status. Such static policies and delaying tactics are alien to the acquisitive society. It knows of few, if any, royal *Schatullen* for impoverished members of erstwhile mighty clans, and its social registers mirror truthfully the ups and downs of individual fortunes. In fact, aquisitive society relies on the tonic effects of immediate debasement or loss of social position caused by changes in status in the process of production to enforce "voluntary obedience" to its usages.[8] Acquisitive society may not have found a remedy for the changes which modern fascism or socialism seeks to introduce into its structure. But the all-pervading mechanism of calculable success which has molded its

[8] "The singular effectiveness" of this arrangement is markedly emphasized by Joseph A. Schumpeter, *Capitalism, Socialism and Democracy* (New York, 1942), p. 73.

human material forestalls any chance of social foundations being broken up by any kind of passive resistance to prevailing social patterns that might originate from present-day followers of St. Francis of Assisi.

Social struggle consists primarily in a strife for possessions within the process of production, the spheres of distribution keeping second place when they are not—as seems to happen in an increasing measure —dominated by the forces of production themselves. Political parties are only incomplete instruments for recording individual stages of this process. Sometimes they may be patterned according to group functions in the process of production, but often such a simplifying denominator is missing, and in such circumstances political groups fail to mirror the social landscape. Then the already mentioned integrating function overshadows the function of indicating and measuring social power relations. Further inquiry must thus be focused on those forces which take part in the process of production proper.

ORGANIZATION OF ECONOMIC INTERESTS

There seems to be no doubt in our minds that the different national economies have taken "an associational character" [9] by now. Fascists build their spurious charters on that assumption, and lawyers in liberal countries take pains to reconcile this fact with the individualistic principles of the respective constitutions. But it is a long way from the image created by any kind of *Genossenschaftstheorie* to the reality of groups as they have emerged from the vagaries of industrial society. The concept of communal life as independent of the narrow interest of the individual member fails to take cognizance of the character of the bonds which tie the individual to the group.

Organization means the most rational and effective form to realize a maximum of profit for the individual member. A true image of such organization may be seen in the American type of management organizations. Here no cooperative body whatsoever comes into existence. Several members of the same trade hand over those activities in which

[9] James J. Robbins, "The Power of Groups to Govern," *United States Law Review*, LXXIII (1939), 380.

concerted action seems mutually advantageous to a business concern which specializes in the field of organizational management.[10] Management organizations are frequent in small-scale industries, where emphasis is laid mainly on the gathering and exchange of information and every member may use the information in a way he deems most suitable for his purpose. Management corporations may be able to coordinate the activities of trade members of similar strength. But the protective value of this system rests on nothing else than the individual producer's willingness to take advantage of an exact knowledge of the marketing conditions of his product.

Yet, reliance on the insight of the individual producer is a haphazard procedure, especially when conditions are bound to turn rapidly; any action of an individual producer, however legitimate it may be from the point of view of self-defense, may upset a precarious equilibrium. A higher degree of centralization, a more permanent collaboration is deemed necessary to that effect. Names and labels do not mean much and are subject to all changes which individual laws of different countries may make necessary. Some association may only be the signboard for a single corporation; behind the front of another association a whole hierarchy of dependency relationships may hide; still another one may unite producers of fairly equal bargaining power. In each individual case the degree of voluntariness or, conversely, of the permanence of the individual's subjection will reflect in the coherence, strength, or weakness of organized group action.

Within the wide range of possible group action, the "constitutional" goal of the producers' group will always be the same, though the degree of the success or failure may depend on many, partly unpredictable factors. Strategical elements determining the growth of production will be secured and consolidated with all possible devices of legal procedure and marketing technique. To attain this aim the group must try to achieve such strength that rupture from within shall seem as unprofitable as competitive attack from without. The danger coming from substitute products must be appropriately met either by removing them from the market permanently or by strengthening the

10 Temporary National Economic Committee, *Reports*, Vol. XVIII, *Trade Association Survey* (Washington, D.C., 1940), p. 38.

competitive position of the group's own product through changes in the price structure or through improving its quality.

Consolidation of group positions was facilitated by the advance of specialization. Organization of production and technical equipment were specialized without, however, requiring higher skills for the majority of the operating personnel. The advance of specialization, accompanied by the fact that only a few have knowledge of the entire process of production, facilitates the exclusion of would-be intruders. For these exclusive practices individual ownership brings welcome support.

Private property connotes more than the juxtaposition of private and state enterprise.[11] It also contains the justification for excluding all others from the use of privately appropriated resources, processes, and services. Stretching out this private title as far as conceivable has provided major weapons in the fight for domination over production processes. In order to prevent premature depreciation of expensive investments, exclusion of others from the use of improved or substitute processes has become the primary object of well-coordinated industrial policy. Would-be competitors, inventors, and researchers are taken on the payroll; patents are hoarded regardless of whether their exploitation is planned or not.

The aim of such a policy of domination would be completely reached when no independent technician, corporation, or agency is left within the specialized field of production; the objective is not only in the exclusion of any conceivable danger of competition but also in forestalling any indirect pressure which could arise if the public or the government had the opportunity to form opinions of their own by using such independent channels. Exclusion is at the same time one of the potent weapons with which to mold the inner structure of the group to the image of the ruling few. Cartel democracy thus may become only a convenient mask. Even the disparity of shares will not always indicate the full extent to which the association is but an association on sufferance and small units are satellites.

The existence of a comparatively small number of production units

[11] W. H. Hutt, "The Sanction for Privacy under Private Enterprise," *Economica*, IX (1942), 237.

with ample financial resources which may be staked for a well-planned long-term policy seems to enhance changes of effective monopolization. The existence of a great number of small units seems more likely to prevent the rise of autonomous associations. In many distribution and service trades, capital requirements are small, access to business is wide open, and specialization is no more than a function of individual skill. To gain a monopolistic position may prove an almost impossible task for an individual or a corporation even on a strictly local basis. But manifold pressure exercised by producers, by vertical combines extending into the retail field, and by financially better equipped, mechanized distribution giants causes a general stampede in favor of protective measures of restraint for the sake of the trade as a whole. Where a combination of producers and large-scale distributors has taken over the task of organizing the trade and dictates the laws, the small-scale retailer will sink to the position of a risk-bearing employee who has to be content with the discount granted to him.[12]

However, in the absence of clear-cut relations of dependence to serve as levers for an effective group consolidation, organization was sought by other means. Sometimes physical violence was resorted to either by members of the trade themselves or by professional groups of "practitioners of violence," thus performing functions of a management corporation in a rather uncivilized way. But combinations kept together by the display of physical force have usually proved to be much weaker than creations of more respectable brethren. First, their very methods lay them open to attacks from the official bearers of the monopoly of physical force. The latter, though unconcerned about the legitimacy of the aims pursued by the groups, resent their intrusion into a theoretically uncontested reserved sphere. Second, the very scope of retail and service trades and their peculiar propensity to rapid expansion and contraction have increased the cost of private policing to the point of unprofitableness. If the method of violence has proved only partially successful in the fight for coordination of small units, it has been singularly ineffective in checking the rise of large-scale retail and service operators. Only service organizations like the American

---

[12] Hermann Levy, in *Retail Trade Association: A New Form of Monopolist Organization in Great Britain* (London, 1942), reports that such is the present situation in a number of retail trades in England.

Medical Association, which disposes of an arsenal of "legitimate" weapons, such as the exclusion of nonmembers from hospitals, have been able to maintain monopolistic practices over a considerable period.[13]

GROUPS AND GOVERNMENT

If physical violence and similar means of coercion fall short of enduring success, the support of the legitimate purveyors of coercive power may give the "small fry" a better chance to attain the desired goal with a higher expectancy of success. Trades which, because of the number of units present or of any other circumstances, are unable to exercise effective measures of control often attain some success with the active help of public authorities. The degree of governmental assistance varies from reserving administrative favors to association members to an outright system of compulsory licensing and banning of new businesses.[14]

Compulsory organizations as well as voluntary agreements usually base the intraorganizational distribution of power on existing production capacities or sales volumes of individual concerns. They are neither intended nor framed to rectify the prevailing distribution of power within a trade so as to favor the "small fry." If the consent of the holders of public power can be obtained, existing power positions will get the additional benefit of legitimacy; and resources which otherwise would have to be spent in court fights, advertisement cam-

[13] It is unfortunate that the interesting book by Oliver Garceau, *The Political Life of the American Medical Association* (Cambridge, Mass., 1941), confines itself mainly to the description of practices through which the inner ring of the association perpetuates itself in power. It remains yet to be shown what makes the association as a whole succeed in enforcing a remarkable degree of conformity to its practices in spite of the fact that its monopoly position is far from being complete.

[14] For the United States the process has been recently described by J. A. C. Grant, "The Gild Returns to America," *Journal of Politics*, IV (1942), 302 ff. A detailed account of the practice and organization of small business on a compulsory basis may be found in the monograph by Arkadius R. L. Gurland, Otto Kirchheimer, and Franz L. Neumann, *The Fate of Small Business in Nazi Germany*, printed for the use of the U.S. Senate Special Committee on Small Business, 1943, 78th Cong., 1st Sess.

paigns, and political horse-trades may be put to better use. Even when the government's interest in advancing genuine community aims seems to be paramount, as, for example, in the land use program of the United States Department of Agriculture, the barriers drawn by existing property arrangements subsist in their entirety.[15]

The "small fry's" claim to compulsory organization is often—especially under nontotalitarian conditions—heeded by various national administrations only hesitantly or in a perfunctory way; they shun such a manifest surrender of the last vestiges of freedom of commerce. But in the field of mass production a high degree of organization responds quite often to the needs of government as well as of labor and meets in different countries with spontaneous official sanction and encouragement. Under prevailing war conditions this process, which has been going on for a considerable time, leads to a wholesome transfer of public authority to the principal agencies of private self-administration. In Germany, where the private trade groups relatively early embraced almost the whole sphere of production, the Nazi government transferred to the self-administration of the groups all the manifold tasks which occurred at successive stages of the policy of rearmament, autarchy, and world conquest. Gestures outwardly aiming at separating the private functions of cartels from the public functions of self-administration were never meant to be taken seriously. By no means can they be compared with the American Anti-Trust enforcement policy that attained some symbolic victories in the interval between the end of the NRA and the beginning of the war-preparedness policy and even now has the validity of an officially avowed ideology.

The *Reichsvereinigungen* which stand at the end of the long and varied German experience have accentuated the tendency toward transferring public authority to existing trade organs, the degree of the transfer depending solely upon the importance of the trade in question. Complete control of the sources of raw materials, as well as the conclusion of binding agreements with satellites and foreign countries, has been entrusted to the *Vereinigungen*, which are enabled by their very

[15] That the local committees only reflect the viewpoint of the landowners rather than that of tenant elements is shown by John D. Lewis, "Democratic Planning in Agriculture," *American Political Science Review*, XXXV (1941), 232.

composition to make an effective use of such privileges. The "Führer principle" has been judiciously tuned down to secure the preponderance of those personalities and oligarchies in every individual instance which hold predominant positions in their respective trades.[16] The English controller, whose office is mostly financed by the respective trade itself and who works under the supervision of a ministry, seems to differ from the American one-dollar-a-year-man inasmuch as the latter becomes an integral part of the administrative machinery. However, the semi-independency of the English controller must not lead to the conclusion that the original imperium of British trade associations is more extensive than that of similar American organizations. It is only that the coordination of governmental and trade association policies is in a more advanced stage in England than it is in the United States.[17] Here the *en masse* occupation of the directive nerve centers of the administrative machine by representatives of the business community has not succeeded in producing more than partial obedience of business to the roll call of the united machines of business and government.

Every individual businessman or trade association official who has been entrusted with the task of administering restrictions, quotas, compensations, etc., is, of course, tempted to look out for the advantage of his own business or group, to which he expects to return after the war. This is so, whether he serves the government "without compensation," as "dollar-a-year-man," or as salaried employee, and whether or not he receives from his own company the difference between his federal and his former private salary. This holds true even if he voluntarily severs, or is compelled [18] to sever, his business connections, or even if he goes so far as to sell his securities. Yet, criticism of recent developments is based less on this set of facts than on the unconsciously biased interpretation of public interest which such administrators are bound to follow

[16] Hans Kluge, "Reichsvereinigung," *Die Deutsche Volkswirtschaft*, 1942, p. 567; Hans W. Singer, "The German War Economy VI," *Economic Journal*, LII (1943), 186.

[17] The English development, especially the institution of "*ex parte* controllers," has often been presented in critical terms in *The Economist*: "The Cartelization of England," CXXXIV (1939), 551; "The Economic Front," CXXXVII (1939), 362; "The Controllers," CXLVI (1942), 417; see also N. E. H. Davenport, *Vested Interests or Common Pool?* (London, 1942).

[18] See the order of the Department of Agriculture (New York *Times* of January 17, 1943, p. 1).

in most instances.[19] Criticism of this kind fails to perceive that there rarely is another alternative for modern governments—either constitutional or fascist—if only they want to uphold the prevailing property structure of present-day society and to adapt, at the same time, industrial policies to the day-to-day functioning of the administration. We may here for once use the problematical analogy [20] to feudal society: the act by which the king confirms the powerful seigneur in the possessions which the latter has grabbed for himself through a colonizing expedition effects no change in the actual power relation between the two. The king assents to confirm the title, and the seigneur desires such confirmation, because both expect it to exercise a favorable influence on the future development of their relations.

There is another point which critics tend to neglect. Independent experts belong to the past, and available knowledge in specialized fields has been monopolized by the industrial groups themselves. The government thus faces the alternative either of relying on *ex parte* advice of the group, or of building up independent administrative counterparts of its own. But this last feature, which has come to the fore in the United States, does not indicate a process of substitution. Though it may involve a threat to the future,[21] at present it only foreshadows the possibility of a new equilibrium wherein the controlling or regulat-

---

[19] Besides the already mentioned article of *The Economist*, see my paper on "The Historical and Comparative Background of the Hatch Act," in *Public Policy* (Cambridge, Mass., 1941), pp. 341–73; the report of the "Committee of Public Accounts" of the House of Commons, 1941, H.C. 105, p. 24, and the "Additional Report of the Special Committee Investigating the National Defense Program," 77th Congress, 2d Session, Senate Report No. 480, Part 5, 1942, pp. 8–9, which is couched in almost the same phrases as the English report. The attempt of the Department of Agriculture to eliminate, by its order mentioned in note 18, the much discussed "divided allegiance" serves to focus public attention on the fact that, in the boundaries of present-day industrial organization, the problem appears to be well-nigh insoluble. After all, would it not be superhuman to expect a $50,000-a-year corporation executive to be induced by an $8000-a-year federal salary to forego in his "public" decisions all thoughts of whether or not he is jeopardizing his chances of returning to a $50,000-a-year job in his field after the war?

[20] The analogy is questionable since the so-called new feudalism is singularly free from the penumbra of personalized duties which form the very core of any feudal tenure.

[21] On the policy of duplication and its possible consequences, see Robert A. Brady, "Policies of Manufacturing Spitzenverbände III," *Political Science Quarterly*, LVI (1941), 515, 527.

ing government agency may fulfill some of the functions which the market mechanism was supposed to exercise in an earlier period.

MONOPOLY SITUATION OF TRADE UNIONS

If trade unions could succeed in eliminating the competition between the workers which takes place in the labor market, their position would be much more dominating than that of industrial monopolies. They would be to a much lesser degree subject to the threat emanating from the existence of substitutes. A certain minimum of human labor will always be needed even when entrepreneurs rationalize production and manpower is replaced by labor-saving machinery to a hitherto unknown degree. Suppose a water-tight monopoly could be ensured covering all available labor supply. Relations between employers and employees then may take forms that so far have been known to occur only in exceptional cases, as, for instance, in the case of theatrical entrepreneurs on New York's "Broadway," whom the American Federation of Musicians compels to hire a whole orchestra even if they need only a pianist. Enterprises would then be under the compulsion to hire several union members in order to secure the services of a few whose work cannot be replaced. The only limitation of the monopoly of labor would be in the threat of the entrepreneur to retire from such field of production and to invest his capital in fields less exposed to labor trouble. But even this limitation is less valid today than it was thirty years ago,[22] as the proportion of fixed capital has considerably increased and the possibilities of shifting capital to another field have become more restricted. Should an individual entrepreneur collapse or a whole line of business have to be abandoned for some reason or other, a labor organization that monopolizes the labor market would still be able to protect its members and enforce "socialization of losses" in imposing the burden upon the rest of the entrepreneurs and the public. Why, then, in the presence of these possibilities, is any relative monopoly of labor infinitely weaker in fact than that of the other participants in the process of production?

At the outset, efforts to create an effective labor monopoly are sub-

[22] Rudolf Hilferding, *Das Finanzkapital* (Berlin, 1910), p. 483.

stantially hampered by such difficulties as arise from a huge number of small operators, as discussed above. In the sphere of labor the "unit" is the individual worker or, to state it more correctly, every individual who at a given moment may be under the compulsion to sell his labor power in the market. It is difficult enough, as a rule, to organize even actual workers. When to acquire the skill required for operating a machine becomes a matter of hours, everybody can become a worker at a minute's notice, and the organizing hazards tend to multiply. A partial solution to difficulties is the sporadic use of violence as a means to enforce monopoly—a situation similar to the one we found in the sphere of distribution. But violence is a scant guarantee of success in an actual labor dispute. Internal conflicts arise from the use of violence and from general difficulties of keeping in check such vast human agglomerations. Thus unions often are denied that degree of inner coherence which would make them relatively immune from outside interference.

If the union takes the aspect of a rational business organization, the individual member is inclined to look at his affiliation with the same "business" eyes. He then dissociates his own prospects from those of the union whenever this seems advantageous to him. As he usually is less exposed to retaliation from the union than the entrepreneur is to retaliation from his group, the individual feels more easily inclined to bolt the orders of the union or even to have recourse to an outside agency, such as a court of justice, to air his grievances. Thus additional possibilities for outside interference are opened. Furthermore, as government to an ever increasing degree intercedes in the regulation of wages and labor conditions, the temptation increases for the individual worker and the union alike to become passive beneficiaries of government-sponsored collective agreements which automatically become a part of individual labor contracts.[23] Of course, government enforcement of such clauses presupposes the abandonment of, or at least far-reaching restrictions on, the use of the very weapon on which unions have to rely as an *ultima ratio*, the strike. Deprived of their main arm of combat, unions develop a tendency toward losing their character as

[23] As regards the American situation see the recent material in the article of William G. Rice, Jr., "The Law of the National War Labor Board," *Law and Contemporary Problems*, IX (1942), 470.

independent institutions within the relationship of the agents of production. They tend to become administrative dependencies of other and more powerful social groups. Implications of this development will be discussed below.

Making the monopoly of labor supply effective on a nation-wide scale would presuppose a well-knit system of close collaboration between local as well as functional labor units. Personal rivalries, jurisdictional disputes, difference of political tendencies, all sorts of subterfuges a union may use to profit from a neighboring labor dispute in order to advance its own social position—all this would have to be put aside if the full weight of organized labor were to be placed behind every important individual dispute. There have been instances where all these conditions were maximally fulfilled, for example, in recent decades during the general strike in England in support of the striking miners in 1926. Why were such attempts to make use of the monopoly of labor supply totally unsuccessful? The answer lies in the apparent impossibility to restrict a generalized labor conflict to the contending parties.

A comparison between the operations of industrial and labor monopolies will explain this thesis. The advance of industrial monopoly has nothing of the spectacular; it proceeds by leaps and bounds. The public is neither invited nor in a position to take a stand prior to the consummation of each individual act which affirms and builds up the monopoly position. The individual cartel agreement, the use or the abuse of a patent, the planning or restriction of production facilities will affect our habit of life, our employment chances, the measure of consumer goods of which we will be able to dispose—they may even, as recent experience has shown, ultimately determine a nation's ability to resist the onslaught of an external enemy. But action of this kind originates from private decisions. Decisions are taken over our heads, and nobody has the mission to inform us unless we regard as information the advertisement campaigns which build on our absence of knowledge. If any knowledge of such decisions reaches us at all, this only occurs *post festum* and by chance. We may snatch a piece of information during a patent suit, a parliamentary investigation, or through an antitrust suit. Exact data rarely will be at our disposal. The participants will spare no pains or money to prevent us from obtaining information and piecing together, from the mosaic of individual impressions, an adequate picture of the industrial landscape which surrounds us. As a directive, industrial monopoly builders seem to use the successful pattern of Borden's World's Fair Elsie: show the customer enough details of how milk is produced, and he will forget to ask about essentials. The avalanche of technical information freely and liberally forwarded to everybody is likely to bury any doubts as to the difference between the 5 cents received by the farmer and the 12 cents paid by the ultimate consumer.

No such protective devices surround the rise of the labor monopoly. Every individual stage from the first unsuccessful attempt to organize a union until the final test, the organization of a strike, is visible to the whole community. Meetings in the public square, clashes at the factory gate, the grocery store's waning sales, and the empty pots in the worker's kitchen are integral parts of its stage. Every step has its public and publicized aspect which transcends the comfortable privacy of the conference room and of the private contract. The tenets of the dispute are relatively simple. Officially they concern only wages and working conditions. But most members of the community will instantaneously feel its repercussions without having to take recourse to more involved logical operations and interpretations. Strive as the union may to keep the struggle within the boundaries of a private conflict, the other party and the public will have none of it. The public authority, even if formally neutral, is permanently on the alert and has a thousand ways to throw its weight into the balance in behalf of the one or the other party. Of the many elements which oppose the rise of a trade union monopoly in the labor market, none seems more insurmountable than the rapidity with which the battle for wages and hours turns into a question of public policy.

What is true of a limited strike action is true a thousand times of a general strike. Whether it be a success or a failure, the very fact of a general strike not only changes the given equilibrium of the social and constitutional order but also works a profound change in those who carry on the movement. No one was better aware of the implications of a general strike than Georges Sorel. He not only insisted on drawing and sharpening the line which separates the parliamentary practitioner from the realm of syndicalist action, he also emphasized that "la grève générale, tout comme les guerres de la liberté, est la manifestation la plus éclatante de la force individualiste dans les masses soulevées." [24] In the spontaneous action for a common goal which in width and scope transcends all individual concern, the worker breaks through the frame set to his action by the rules of industrial society. This obviously is the ultimate reason why the builders of industrial monopolies, carefully remaining within the confines of private law, were so much more successful than their trade union antagonists. The latter were terrified by the very magnitude and possibilities of the weapons at their disposal.

The foregoing discussion is based on the assumption that the trade union movement is bent upon coming as near to a total monopoly in the labor market as possible. But perhaps insisting on such an assumption would mean unduly to neglect the process of transformation which labor organizations have undergone during the last decades. Many a union today resembles a business organization conforming strictly to standard patterns. Union energies often are exclusively directed at seizing well-defined strategic positions in the process of production—a mode of behavior which has been furthered by the advancing process of specialization. It is true that "die absolute Disponibilität des Menschen für wechselnde Arbeitserfordernisse," [25] which runs parallel to this process of specialization and simultaneously counteracts it, must to some extent facilitate reinforced emphasis on the common goals of all individual sections of organized labor. Very often, however, labor prefers to utilize specialization as an easy means for establishing narrow reservations. Far from striving for common action, it often concentrates on, and is satisfied with, restricting the supply of labor within the narrow confines of one or another particular field.

The tangible success which the organizations achieve seemingly justifies such policies. But in submitting to, and furthering, this practice of "fencing in" special fields, labor itself seems to have become a captive of pseudo-objective requirements of technological rationality.[26]

Foremen appear as experts, supervisors as industrial engineers, workers as technical collaborators in a process in which the differences

[24] Sorel, *op. cit.*, p. 376.
[25] Friedrich Engels, "Anti-Dühring," in *Marx-Engels-Gesamtausgabe*, VI, 518.
[26] See Herbert Marcuse, unpublished manuscript, "Operationalism in Action."

between those at the top and all others take the appearance of technological distinctions. The objects of domination seem to have shifted.
Specialized organizations of labor and producers work in combined
consolidation;[27] labor even serves as a kind of police against restive
outsiders who disturb the peace of the producer organization; and a
mutually beneficial policy of restraints "passes the buck" to the consumer. Of course, these restricting practices do nothing to alleviate the
problems of those who remain outside of the sheltered zones. Labor
organizations seem to relapse into provincialism—perhaps to a higher
degree still than organizations of producers, since the latter at least
have learned to think in world-wide terms and develop a certain
amount of flexibility under the constant pressure of demands for new
fields of profitable reinvestments. Campaigns for organizing new fields
of industrial activity may cause some disruptions. But once the task is
fulfilled, the quota reached, the organizations settle down to the routine [28] of government-sponsored agreements, collusive restraints, and
jurisdictional disputes. They thrive through specialization but they also
suffocate in it.

RACKET AND SOCIETY

In the lawyers' language, always more restrictive than explanatory,
monopolistic practices which are carried through by physical force,
violence in trade disputes, or similar objectionable means have been
given the name of "rackets." Restricted application of a term may have
an important function when seen from the viewpoint of a sound technique of domination. Singling out particularly objectionable methods
serves as a convenient tool for bringing the guilty to account and
depriving them of the sympathies of the community at large.[29] For it

[27] See Davenport, *op. cit.*, pp. 45, 60, 88. On prospects of such "consolidation"
in the postwar world, cf. Joan Robinson, "The Industry and the State," *Political
Quarterly*, XIII (1942), 400, 406, and "Future of Politics," *The Economist*, CXLII
(1942), 456.
[28] On the relation between routine and *esprit corporatif* see Sorel, *op. cit.*, p.
369.
[29] This certainly does not mean that those elements and the apparatus of
physical violence they have created will not be kept alive at times, as "socii"
against other groups.

is obvious, of course, that most of those whose position in the process of production or distribution has become unstable will have to resort to such desperate weapons. But if there is a difference in methods as between "haves" and "have-nots," firstcomers and latecomers, "decent citizens" and "racketeers," there is no difference in their aims, which are essentially the same: establishment of domination over a segment of the process of production or distribution. Common usage of the language has, therefore, justifiably generalized the use of the word *racket*.[30] In popular usage the term carries a related connotation of apparent significance. If somebody asks another, "What is your racket?," he may intend merely to inquire about the other's professional status, but the very form of the question refers to a societal configuration which constitutes the proper basis for any individual answer. It expresses the idea that within the organizational framework of our society attainment of a given position is out of proportion to abilities and efforts which have gone into that endeavor. It infers that a person's status in society is conditional upon the presence or absence of a combination of luck, chance, and good connections,[31] a combination systematically exploited and fortified with all available expedients inherent in the notion of private property.

Rackets seem to correspond to a stage of society where success depends on organization and on access to appropriate technical equipment rather than on special skills.[32] As the number of positions in which organizational or other specialized intellectual skills are required becomes rather restricted, most aspirants have merely to adapt themselves to easily understandable technical processes. Privileges that depend on distinctions in individual ability become increasingly rare. In acquiring and maintaining social positions it is not so much special skill that matters; what matters is that one gets the chance to find access to,

[30] The justification of the generalization has been acknowledged, and the importance of the difference between the "means" and the "ends" type of racket refuted in one of the monographs of the Temporary National Economic Committee, *Reports*, Vol. XXI, *Competition and Monopoly in American Industry* (Washington, D.C., 1941), p. 298.

[31] Cf. Max Horkheimer, "The End of Reason," *Studies in Philosophy and Social Science*, IX (1942), 377: "If the individual wants to preserve himself, he must work as a part of a team."

[32] This point has been stressed by George C. Allen, *British Industries and Their Organization* (London, 1933), p. 303.

and be accepted by, one of the organizations that dispose of the technical apparatus to which the individual has scant possibility of access.

The term *racket* is a polemical one. It reflects on a society in which social position has increasingly come to depend on a relation of participation, on the primordial effect of whether an individual succeeded or failed to "arrive." [33] *Racket* connotes a society in which individuals have lost the belief that compensation for their individual efforts will result from the mere functioning of impersonal market agencies. But it keeps in equal distance from, and does not incorporate, the idea of a society wherein the antagonism between men and inanimate elements of production has been dissolved in the image of a free association for the common use of productive forces. It is the experience of an associational practice which implies that neither the individual's choice of an association nor the aims that the latter pursues are the result of conscious acts belonging to the realm of human freedom.

DECREPITUDE OF TRADITIONAL INSTITUTIONS

No general cartel dominates our society. Beyond the level of trade associations and cartels, giant corporations working in different industries may be bound together to varying degrees of solidarity through interlocking directorates, services of identical financial institutions, and intercorporate stockholding. The existence of such connecting links may in many instances ensure the working of certain directives, according to which differences between various producer groups will be settled without any outside interference. Common interests with respect to labor policy and similar political issues work also in favor of intergroup harmony. In these fields momentary success which might result from separate action would be outweighed by the permanent damage done by such procedure to the position of industry as a whole. Manufacturing *Spitzenverbände* have done much to establish a common phalanx and to concentrate divergent interests on common objectives. But all these phenomena taken together fall short of the estab-

---

[33] This seems to be generally admitted so far as the upper strata are concerned. See e.g., Brady, *op. cit.*, p. 524. But it is of equal importance for non-executive jobs.

lishment of a general cartel, of "an agency which determines the amount of production in all spheres." [34] There is no all-embracing super group incorporating all divergent interests in the economic sphere. There is, instead, a multitude of groups which occupy and defend their strongly entrenched respective positions, and each of these groups operates under special conditions of its own.

The common meeting ground where different groups of producers face each other as well as all other social groups is the state. Before organized groups rose to a position of predominance, i.e., in the epoch which came to an end at the latest at the outbreak of World War I, parliament was both meeting ground and decision-forming organ for the national community as a whole. It was the center which forged the general rules to prevail in the competitive game, out of the multitude of divergent individual interests. Parliament also granted assistance to, and put under its protection, the manifold private interests which the more undertaking citizens acquired in colonial and semicolonial countries. The antinomy between state and society, as it appeared to the German social thinkers of the first half of the nineteenth century, was no longer valid. "The self-contradictory abstract political state," as the young Marx had called it, was only artificially kept alive to be used as a convenient theoretical construction, as an addressee of the claims which the individual was entitled to lodge against society. Every new procedure which was opened to the individual in his struggles with society was enthusiastically saluted as a milestone on the way to the liberal millennium. [35]

Parliament proved an excellent institution as long as the individual entrepreneur could forge ahead singlehanded, in need only of the general advantages of legal security, a permanently available police force, an adequate army, and that minimum of educational and social institutions which the lower classes had to have if they were to fulfill their tasks in industrial society. The emergence of solid economic blocs broke the political power of parliament as a unified and unifying insti-

---

[34] Hilferding, op. cit., p. 314; for recent criticism of the concept of General-kartell, see Paul M. Sweezy, The Theory of Capitalist Development (New York, 1942), p. 340.

[35] Léon Duguit, Transformations du Droit Public (Paris, 1913), is most characteristic in this respect.

tution. In the now emerging system the economic groups more and more assume the functions of selective organs which choose the candidates whom the general public is invited to endorse. Consequently, parliament is no longer the exclusive club where good people of equal social standing discuss and determine public affairs. Its usefulness is restricted to that of a meeting ground where diverse social groups find convenient gratuitous facilities for propaganda activities. New devices and institutions must take the place of parliament.

In the advanced stage of universal infiltration into parliament, the appeal from parliament to the electorate is precluded, too. The electorate has been relegated to a role similar to that of the consumer in a system of imperfect competition. A few giant corporations conduct a restricted battle for their relative share in the market. The consumers' incidence on this competition is symbolized by advertising campaigns confined to a general and irrelevant praise of some product or other—so that choice of advertising slogans is all that is left of the "consumer's choice." Much in the same fashion the body politic gets presented a selected personnel, out of which favorites may be chosen. The presenting groups acting on tacit understanding utilize all the available devices of social and legal pressure to prevent the people from transferring their loyalty to outsiders. Their common interest in maintaining the established groups as going concerns checks at every moment the motions of competition they have to go through so as to fix their respective shares in the market. An electorate whose habits have been formed by the mental and social climate of industrial society can no more be styled sovereign on the political than the consumer on the economic level. Individual preferences affect the quota of profit or the number of votes cast for different competitors, but they do no longer determine either the quality or the price of services offered to the public. Voters are called upon to air opinions which may furnish pertinent data for group decisions, but their utterances lack the elements of precision, understanding, and resolution which alone would enable them to become volitional determinants of the final choice.[36]

Among the traditional organs which conceivably might serve as a

[36] "Under existing democratic institutions the will of the unorganized majority is impotent to assert itself against the domination of organized economic power." Edward Hallett Carr, *Conditions of Peace* (London, 1942), p. 27.

body of final arbitration to grant or deny legitimacy to actions of the groups, none was more predestined to success than the courts. Exempt from the sphere of influence of the groups, removed from the temptations surrounding the popular politician, vested with the aura of disinterestedness, they were trusted to pronounce sentences carrying such finality and authority as the popular verdict cannot lay claim to. Yet, they failed conspicuously and uniformly wherever they tried to occupy the vacant seats of authority. To live up to that task they would have had to exercise constant vigilance and quickly to render orders sufficiently generalized to cover comprehensive areas of dispute, instead of narrowly constructed specific rules squeezed out of long-drawn-out procedures and followed up by antiquated modes of securing performance.

Authority is best adapted to its task when its very existence causes the parties to mold their behavior according to the rules the issuance of which is anticipated. If the decision to be expected carries less weight with the would-be litigant than the time and cost element involved in a law suit, courts are bound to lose all vestiges of regulatory influence.[37] The extent to which court decisions may penetrate and loosen up group structures depends on the degree of coherence of the groups themselves. Apparently the ratio of success is inverse to the degree of formalization of group structures. In certain circumstances a labor racketeer may get entangled with the formalized statutory and procedural structure which such organizations usually possess. But the rules of evidence are of no avail against those who are sure enough of their power to dispense with the formalities of written instruments.[38]

If legal battles actually do occur, even a clear-cut victory won in court by one of the contending parties will have no lasting impact on the existing institutional framework if there is no adequate machinery

[37] See instructive details on the impact of procedural rules on the relation of small and big industrial units in 77th Congress, 2d Session, *Hearing of the Senate Committee on Patents*, Part 4, p. 1924 (1942).

[38] "The stronger a cartel is, the less necessary it finds it to apply a formal boycott against a corporation, and it is hardly possible to provide legal proofs that boycott has been in progress. The smaller cartel has to place greater reliance than does a closely knit syndicate upon the visible application of organized discipline within the organization and of the boycott as a measure against outsiders." *Ausschuss zur Untersuchung der Erzeugungs—und Absatzbedingungen der deutschen Wirtschaft*, I, III, 4, p. 69 (1930).

to enforce and police conformity.[39] The antitrust policy of the United States government, for example, is comparable to an occasional wanderer in a forest,[40] who might cut down cobwebs which a spider was careless enough to build across the path. But the spider waits patiently until the wanderer disappears and hurries to spin another web to catch up with the rest of his gang.

COMPETING BUREAUCRACIES

"The experience of generations makes the Cafoni think that the state is only a better organized Camorra." [41] If the traditional regulatory and supervisory organs seem out of breath, one turns to the manifold new crystallizations of state power which have grown up in recent times. Whether we fully agree with Silone's value judgment or not, he is surely right in emphasizing the identical features of governmental bodies and the great private bureaucracies. The roots of the state bureaucracy are manifold. A sizable part of it, the welfare, labor, and social security bureaucracies, are direct offsprings of modern industrial society and of the dismemberment of the social fabric which is cut up into different unrelated segments. As they replaced the church and the local community, they had to take all risks shunned by other groups. They had to take care of all those who were ejected from their positions in the process of production and distribution and of those who

[39] Temporary National Economic Committee, *Reports*, Vol. XVI, *Enforcement of Anti-Trust Laws* (Washington, D.C., 1940), pp. 77, 78.

[40] Corwin D. Edwards, in his article, "Thurman Arnold and the Anti-Trust Law," *Political Science Quarterly*, LVIII (1943), 338–55, shows that it was not before Thurman Arnold took charge of the Antitrust Division that a policy of antitrust enforcement began to be worked out as against the handling of isolated cases practiced previously. But Edwards has to admit that "circumstances robbed his [Arnold's] most important programs of their expected effect" (p. 354). The wholesale suspension of antitrust prosecutions during the war forced upon the Department of Justice by way of "administrative agreement," coupled with the new impetus associational practices take under the war economy, will most probably have a greater imprint on future developments than the five years of "the new antitrust policy."

[41] I. Silone, "The Things I Stand For," *New Republic*, November 2, 1942, p. 582. Similarities between private and public forms of coercion have been discussed by Robert L. Hale, "Force and the State: A Comparison of 'Political' and 'Economic' Coercion," *Columbia Law Review*, XXXV (1935), 149.

never had been accepted by one of the established groups. To cope efficiently with their millions of clients, these bureaucracies had to forsake individualization and take over industrial methods.

A similar kind of technical efficiency is present to the highest degree when large-scale cutthroat competition is dominant. As competition for power has been going on between the states on an ever enlarged scale since the beginning of the century, military establishments, the oldest part of the government machine, by necessity developed more features of large-scale mass production than other parts of the machine. Modern industry and the military machine have much the same characteristics.[42] They not only condition each other in their material existence, measured by the rate of creative destruction, but they also rely heavily on each other in the formation of the proper mental attitude.

Until recently, private industries lived under the regime of formal responsibility to stockholders. Yet, they may have been subject to the "overriding power of the state" as well.[43] In fact, supremacy of government over private industry modeled on the pattern of spurious stockholders' sovereignty may serve as a protective screen at a time when private titles seem to be losing in public esteem. It makes no difference whether a section of social activity is styled private or public as long as its inherent structure, its attitudes, and its roots of authority are so similar as those of private and public bureaucracies.

In the lower ranks of both sections the money incentive of acquisitive society has been brought into harmony with, but has not been replaced by, the category of hierarchical advancement. Hierarchical structure presupposes the existence of rigid rules of conduct which make the lower depths of the administration easily controllable from above. In both sections again security of tenure becomes an appendage of the stability of the prevailing social structure; legal norms guaranteeing the individual members' rights become unnecessary and, in the event of a major social conflict, inefficacious. Executive office, whose holders often change between both spheres, has successfully resisted all

[42] Temporary National Economic Committee, *Reports*, Vol. XXII, *Technology in Our Economy* (Washington, D.C., 1940), p. 21.
[43] See the proposals of Samuel Courtauld, "Future Relations of Government and Industry," *Economic Journal*, LII (1942), 1–17.

attempts at legal formalization, regardless of whether such attempts have been made by special legislation or by the courts. Absence of formalization in the high ranks of private and public bureaucracy is paralleled by a rigid conventionalism and disciplinarianism in the lower grades. Skillful use of that well-disciplined force which is the low-rank bureaucracy enlarges the scope of action open to the group of executives. Action moves in accord with the institutional traditions of the organization within material limits of disposable means, and in accord with the degree of respect and inviolability which other groups may be able to claim for their own protected areas.

Whether individual groups attempt to trespass upon one another's province or not,[44] repercussions of group actions are bound to be far-reaching. The treaty-making power of private groups on an international scale is a perfect example of this kind of unilateral change of data essential to the community's existence. International organizations of labor always remained propaganda centers whose appeals may be heeded, or more often not, by these national groups. Contrariwise, industrial groups began to enter international agreements providing for effective sanctions in case of nonperformance as early as the period preceding World War I. Treaty-making as it became universal in the period between the two world wars was more often than not entrusted either to various national cartels united in an international cartel, or to individual companies, in the event that the latter happened exclusively to dominate the market. A simple distribution of markets among the different partners to the treaty would take place, or the participants would combine their efforts, beginning with the pooling of patents, and ending with a common organization of production centers.

Within the scope of such activities, action of individual governments is looked upon as an inevitable source of disturbances which should be localized for the benefit of all participants.[45] As cartelization of indus-

---

[44] "The fine art of executive behavior consists in not deciding questions which are not pertinent, in not deciding prematurely and not making decisions that cannot be made effective, and not making decisions others should make." Chester J. Barnard, *The Function of the Executive* (Cambridge, Mass., 1938), p. 194. Barnard's is an understatement, but it adequately describes one side—and not the least important one—of executive activities.

[45] Cf. the classical text of the Standard Oil–I. G. Farbenindustrie agreement of November, 1929. It provided that "in the event the performance of these agreements should be hereafter restrained or prevented by the operation of any exist-

try proceeds on an international scale, the industrial policy of the state loses, furthermore, the weapon of the tariff policy. Price and sales conventions of private cartels which supersede tariffs do not reflect any considerations for nonparticipating parts of the respective national economies. Moreover, they tend to minimize the efficacy of governmental price or tax policy, as has been amply shown by the experience of the last decades.[46]

IN QUEST OF SOVEREIGNTY

Of course, the unilateral action of the great estates has its unavoidable repercussions on the body politic as a whole. So our previous question has to be taken up again: Is there no supreme body which may take the place of parliaments, courts, and people as the final authority of last

---

ing or future law, or the beneficiary interest of either party be alienated to a substantial degree by operation of law or government authority, the parties should enter new negotiations in the spirit of the present agreement and endeavor to adapt their relations to the changed conditions which have so arisen." 77th Congress, 2d Session, *Hearings of the Senate Committee on Patents*, Part 4, p. 1786 (1942). The 1940 negotiations between Standard Oil and I. G. Farbenindustrie, as well as the special agreements made by Dupont and I. G. Farbenindustrie in the same year, may be regarded as special instances of this policy of restricting to a minimum the disturbances in the relations between the partners owing to war conditions. These and similar cases are discussed by Corwin D. Edwards in *Economic and Political Aspects of International Cartels*, Sen. Doc. No. 1, 78th Congress, 2d Session, 1940, pp. 68-69.

[46] Those writers who start with the assertion that international cartelization furthers international cooperation have taken a favorable attitude toward international activities of industrial groups. See e.g., Alfred Weber, *Europas Weltindustriezentrum und die Idee der Zollunion* (Berlin, 1926), p. 130, or the memorandum submitted to the League of Nations by the French government in May, 1931, quoted by Alfred Plummer, *International Combines in Modern Industry* (London, 1934), p. 127. On the other hand, writers anticipating that such agreements might be profitably used by specifically imperialistic countries have rejected what they call "the tendency to a world planning by a central body;" cf. Albert Prinzing, *Der politische Gehalt internationaler Kartelle* (Berlin, 1938). Both assertions seem equally unfounded. In the measure that international cartels contribute toward disturbing the economic equilibrium of individual countries, social tension results which intensifies nationalist attitudes and largely offsets all tendencies toward international cooperation on a larger basis. There is no world planning, either. Cartels and combinations are restricted to limited fields and do not any more constitute a *Generalkartell* on an international plan than they do on a national plan. Cf. also the cautious statements of Herbert von Beckerath, *Modern Industrial Organization* (New York, 1933), p. 233.

resort? Has no procedure developed to alleviate and control the constant pressure and counterpressure exercised by the different organizations, public and private alike, to anticipate the repercussions of each individual action and thus to balance them? Does the present organization, as Silone contends, really differ from private organization only by a higher degree of efficiency?

The relation between the state and the economic group as the prime agency of societal activity has often been retraced. One of these discussions, which dates back to the end of World War I, stands out by its incisiveness and originality. Rejecting the idea of the state as a big coercive machine with exchangeable machinists, Wolzendorff tried to draw the border line between the functions of the state and those of other social organizations. Social organisms develop their own customs and usages and form their own rules. The specific province of the state is the political order and nothing but the political order. To make clear the difference between the all-embracing social state, which he rejects, and the state as mere guarantor of the existence of various free group activities, Wolzendorff calls his conception "der reine Staat." [47] The state's law-making activity with respect to individual spheres could certainly not be dispensed with in its entirety, but it should be restricted to a minimum required for the maintenance of state power. The state should in the first place represent "a responsible and lastly decisive guarantee" of the law developed by the groups themselves. On the other hand, Wolzendorff adds, "the state can only administer law which is compatible with its existence and its will." [48] His formulas seem not to be too distant from those of a modern theory of state sovereignty as developed, for example, by Dickinson. Sovereignty, according to Dickinson, consists not so much of exercising a "creative influence" as of effecting the "final choice." [49]

Both discussions emphasize the form element, the necessity of decisions transcending group relations. Implicitly, both "the last decisive guarantee" of Wolzendorff and the "final choice" of Dickinson presuppose the existence of group-transcending organs able and will-

[47] Kurt Wolzendorff, *Der reine Staat* (Tübingen, 1920).
[48] *Ibid.*, p. 24.
[49] John Dickinson, "A Working Theory of Sovereignty," *Political Science Quarterly*, XLIII (1928), 32, 47.

ing to grant benefits of delegated powers or withhold them from recalcitrant groups, to decide on their interrelationships, and—which is still more important—to enforce decisions against particular groups if need be.

Permanent coordination presupposes the compatibility of diverse group aims or the suppression of "undesirable" groups or both. But whether it is agreement on coordination or agreement on suppression, in both cases the holders of supreme political power—be they a court, a parliament, or an oligarchic group of politicians and practitioners of violence—must have enough residual power to make the necessary common arrangements and to create the general conditions for group-approved purposes. Once the general agreement is in existence and the private and public agencies are imbued with the spirit of the common purposes—whatever ideological make-up be used to create that spirit—decentralization and delegation of power may prove eminently useful devices for upholding the authority of the holders of supreme political power. If, however, delegation takes place without agreement on fundamental issues, it only involves an additional reinforcement of divergent group structures. It then "strengthens a system strong in the parts, weak in the center." [50]

The history of the NRA is an example. The NRA was conceived by the first Roosevelt administration as a general move to restore prosperity by improving industrial relations and trade practices. The National Recovery Act itself shows that fundamental agreement on purposes was conspicuously absent at its inception. Administrators taken from the ranks of interested producers' groups were entrusted with the elaboration of codes designed to attain the self-contradictory aim of stamping out unfair trade practices without permitting monopolistic devices. Practically, the task was thus transferred en bloc to organs of industrial self-administration, with the only reservation being executive correction of the proposed codes. The way for any revision of existing intergroup relations was barred from the outset.

Individual codes were shaped with exactly as much labor participation as was warranted by the actual strength of the interested labor organizations. The consumer representatives with no bargaining power at all were left stranded in the same social vacuum in which they find

[50] See "The Controller," The Economist, CXLI (1942), 417.

themselves under the present wartime economy. Differences between industries applying for codes and other industries fearing competitive disadvantages were ironed out without any regard for community interests "by inter-industrial diplomacy and even informal coercion." [51] There were no administrative agencies disposing of adequate enforcement devices. Criminal prosecution of code violators was restricted to a few selected cases and had a purely symbolic character. In consequence, the effectiveness of the codes depended on the strength of the trade associations in the respective fields. The degree of compliance was smallest in small-scale industries and economically backward regions,[52] that is, those very sections where public interest in compliance was greatest. Group conflicts had been accentuated, and the pursuit of public ends, the sovereignty of the community over its particular divisions, had been thwarted by the government's inability to prevent specific community objects from being submerged in the struggle for position by the individual groups,[53] when finally the Supreme Court ended the impasse which the administration of the codes had created and struck the NRA from the statute book.

This is but a particular instance of individual group interests superseding the (real or alleged) sovereignty of the community. Now, some modern theories on sovereignty have given characteristic expression to the absence of bodies or persons able to concretize the political will of territorial communities. Pluralistic theories, for example, have tried to make a virtue out of the fact that the real rulers of society are undiscoverable; they discovered, instead, a multitude of various organizations which they credit with the gift of having their conflicts "cleared" in a kind of cooperative superassociation.[54] Everything is all right as long as the divergent interests do the "clearing" themselves, or are so homogeneous as to make arbitration by the "super-clearing-house" a mere technicality. But what if the group conflicts are much too great and intense to be "cleared away" without a basic agreement between the contending parties? And if there is fundamental diver-

[51] See the interesting commentary, *The National Recovery Administration: An Analysis and Appraisal*, published by the Brookings Institution (Washington, D.C., 1935), p. 120.
[52] *Ibid.*, p. 260.
[53] See the concluding observations of the Brookings publication, *ibid.*, pp. 881–85.
[54] See the discussion on p. 161 above.

gence of interests, what makes the groups enter into such agreements which then insure the execution of the state's "final choice"?

Carl Schmitt's "decisionism," too, as early as 1922 had given up the hope of finding a permanent subject of sovereignty that would be intent on, and capable of, balancing the interests and volitions of different groups and factions.[55] He then proceeded to attribute sovereignty to those persons or groups that would prove able to exercise political domination under extraordinary circumstances. But Schmitt himself pointed out that his concept of sovereignty was structurally akin to the theological concept of miracle—which makes his subject of sovereignty a rather problematical one. Emergencies, like miracles, may take place in infinite number. In order to be recognized as such they have to be authenticated. "Il y a des miracles qui sont des preuves certaines de vérité. Il faut une marque pour les preuves certaines de vérité. Il faut une marque pour les connaître; autrement ils seraient inutiles." [56] Emergencies as well as miracles are exceptions to rules that prevail in "normal" situations. Their contours are determined by these rules of "normalcy" which they "confirm" through being exceptions. In the absence of an authentic rule, emergency in permanence becomes the genuine symbol of the very absence of that system of coordination to which history traditionally affixes the attribute of sovereignty.

"Emergency" theories merely indicate that society has reached a stage where the equilibrium of group forces is utterly unstable; there is no automatism of coordination which may insure the operation of the "final choice" on the basis of the equilibrium system. But when the mechanism of coordination does not function any longer so as to guarantee fundamental agreements between the groups that contend for the power to make final decisions, the most powerful ones among them are compelled to resort to building a machine of violence that would enable them to suppress "undesirable" groups and restrict competition among the "desirable" ones. Agreement among a few groups is then reached through the medium of a paramount common interest in suppressing or restraining many others. Enforcement of the agreement is of necessity entrusted to the newly built machine whose operators,

---

[55] *Die Diktatur* (Munich, 1921); *Politische Theologie* (Munich, 1922).
[56] Blaise Pascal, *Pensées*, Seconde partie, article XVI, ii.

"practitioners of violence," form new groups themselves, groups linked with each other through clusters of rackets. Old groups must share power with new groups. Initial agreements which originally insured coordination must be revised and a new compromise looked for. Intergroup relationships are in flux once more, and unstable equilibrium is preserved only through common interest in the suppression of undesirable groups.

Of the forces which have been at work to produce changes in the relations of the group empires, fascism is the most characteristic one. It thoroughly destroyed the organizations of all "undesirable" groups, labor being the first. It then set out to extend the sphere of control exercised by organizations recognized as "legitimate" ones. The authority of the state was tremendously widened and enlarged to be vested in these very groups on the basis of compulsory inclusion of nonmembers. The last vestiges of societal freedom precariously preserved through coexistence of rival organizations with a wide margin of intergroup friction were definitely annihilated. In addition, coordination of the legitimate groups for the common imperialist enterprise brought large areas of former group conflicts to provisional disappearance. As in the frame of this substantial agreement controversies that arise have but secondary importance for the time being, avenues for informal compromise, or if need be even for formalized adjustment of group differences by the charismatic fountain of authority, were not difficult to design.

Within the large-scale competition that is going on in the realm of interstate relations the policy of coordination of major group aims, as operating in Germany, was bound to secure a differential rent to the country that was the first to effect it. Incidentally, this was the case in the province of international trade relations. The policy of imperialist coordination has made the fascist government a silent partner to private international business agreements and enabled it to insert clauses into private contracts which were seriously to weaken the war potential of the country to which the other party to the contract belonged.[57] Yet, under the impact of the war the policy of central co-

---

[57] Cf., e.g., the destruction of the Jasco acetylene plant in Baton Rouge at the request of the I. G. Farbenindustrie in 1939 (77th Congress, 2d Session, *Hearings of the Senate Committee on Patents*, Part 3, 1942, p. 1363). Here the German

ordination of group aims spreads all over the world. As matters stand now, the differential rent which ruling groups in Germany were able to secure through being the firstcomers in the field is bound to disappear. The foundations of the agreement between the group empires, enforced by the "practitioners of violence," again become unstable. They are no longer held together but by the common interest of the legitimate groups in suppressing the illegitimate or "undesirable" ones, and it is rather doubtful whether suppression can be maintained when the system that insured it has been substantially shaken. It also remains to be seen whether the differential rent accruing to victorious countries will be sufficient to insure a group compromise, as unstable as it may be, without further recurrence to eliminating and suppressing those major group interests which might endanger the functioning of co-ordination.

---

government had no difficulty in pursuing its strategic and military aims through private claims of a private concern. In democratic countries the coordination of government and industrial interests so far has functioned on a much lower level, if it has functioned at all. When there was already war in Europe, embassies of the United States still carried mail for representatives of American business corporations negotiating with Germany and presented them with certificates of patriotic behavior without even making any attempts at getting information on, or supervising such negotiations between, their nationals and representatives of enemy countries (*ibid.*, Part 6, 1942, p. 2608). A typical example of differences in the behavior of business groups in a forcibly coordinated and in a noncoordinated system is offered in the history of the "private business relations" between the German I. G. Farbenindustrie and the American Sterling Products, Inc., as related by Walton Hale Hamilton, "The Strange Case of Sterling Products," *Harper's Magazine*, CLXXXVI (1943), 123-32. Says Hamilton: "A corporation [meaning Sterling Products], beset on all sides by hazards, sets out to exploit and to secure its estate. To hedge in its markets and guard its frontiers, it commits itself to an international treaty. It acts without regard to the interest of the nation to which it belongs; it accepts no duty to report its acts to its own government. It binds itself to an ally overseas which is subject to the will of a hostile and revolutionary state. The Nazi party commands and its orders are imposed upon the American ally through the obligations of contract" (p. 130). The obvious conclusion is: "Concerns like Sterling are led by the desire for gain into situations where they are powerless to help themselves; only resolute and drastic surgery by the government can break the shackles of their bondage" (p. 132). But "resolute and drastic surgery by the government" presupposes a different mechanism of coordination of group empires.

PART TWO

THE TRANSFORMATION
OF DEMOCRATIC POLITICS

NOTES ON THE POLITICAL SCENE

IN WESTERN GERMANY

WE ARE LOOKING for an explanation of the German miracle. Only yesterday an outcast among the nations, eternal troublemaker, never to be trusted, Germany is today the eagerly sought ally to the Western world, next to Great Britain apparently the most stable of the European states. How has this transformation occurred?

The obvious can serve as a starting point. The origins of the new state cannot be separated from Western policies and initiatives. If its creation reflected the desires of an overwhelming majority of Germans, it was also guided by a Western aim to prevent the decay of the European heartland, so that it would not fall prey to Eastern aggression. In spite of surface commotion among German political groups just awakening to a sense of their own importance in the European scheme of things, there was little real opposition, not to mention any practical alternatives, to the joint policy pursued by Germany and the West. For better or worse, Germany was tied to the chariot of the West—fed, protected, and encouraged to become a full-fledged member of the Western political and social system.

In short, the endless debate between German rearmament and various forms of German neutrality as a means to reunification was largely rhetorical. While some German politicians and publicists lustily demanded nothing short of full sovereignty and equality, there was much nostalgia beneath the surface for a less ambitious pursuit of economic reconstruction under the umbrella of American military might. Such sentiments may well have outweighed the ardor for becoming a major

Reprinted, by permission, from *World Politics*, VI (1953–54), 306–21.

European power, with the wider responsibilities that it would entail. But the word "nostalgia" connotes the inevitability of the course set by Adenauer's administration toward full participation in European political, economic, and military responsibilities. The Germany of 1953 could not continue as a ward of the West, nor could it accept the role of buffer between East and West.

Numerous fertile minds have developed ingenious schemes calling for German reunification at the price of neutrality between the power blocs. There is not a shred of evidence that the Russians would be such deplorably bad social and economic analysts as to risk a venture of this type unless all the odds were on their side. Their daily contacts with the German people are sufficient to show them where the East German choice would lie; the model of Western-style reconstruction has provided the basis for a sort of everyday plebiscite in which the preference of the East Germans is a foregone conclusion. The West Germans have already made theirs and are on the way to becoming one of the major partners in the Western system. The USSR knows this well; its reiterated proposals for German unity invariably contain enough jokers to permit it to keep control over the East Germans.

In the face of this situation, German policy cannot be separated from the policies of the other Western European nations, and it appears somewhat unrealistic to assume that the individual states can freely follow their own predilections. Western Europe as a whole may adopt a strong or a weak policy, develop forceful tactics or an ostrich strategy. Depending on their relative influence, their understanding of the issues, and the strength of their political and military fabric, the various Western states may contribute solidly to the development of common policies, or act as a drag upon them. Such divergencies are possible and even probable, but it is scarcely likely that they will reach proportions amounting to a pro-Eastern policy.

This absence of any real foreign policy alternative is an important factor in Germany's internal stability. While the official opposition, the Social Democrats, always had reservations concerning the government's foreign policies, their objections were not of the treason-shouting variety, but rather in the nature of a loyal opposition.[1] Such op-

[1] Even Carlo Schmid's polemic antithesis between the "true Europe," embracing the whole of Europe, and "little Europe" contains the affirmation of "Europe as

position more often than not is valuable to the government, which may then raise the price of agreements with foreign states by pointing out the difficulty of securing acceptance in the face of domestic criticism. There is no doubt that Adenauer's government has on occasion drawn substantial profit from this pressure.[2] If such loyal opposition helped the government, it did not advance its own cause. In the eyes of the German voter, the foreign policy recommended by the opposition during the election campaign appeared only a minor variation from the government's course.

It has often been taken for granted that the German election results primarily expressed a verdict on the foreign policy of the Adenauer government. This is at best debatable. Looking back at the election propaganda, it appears that the government preferred to rest its case on broader grounds. In the personal letter signed by the Chancellor which his organization distributed during the campaign, foreign policy was not unduly emphasized. The rearmament issue was carefully avoided, and instead it was stressed that, thanks to the cooperative effort of people and government, things in Germany were once more in good shape, and that if cooperation continued, the situation would continue to improve all around. Naturally, this letter also contained the standard assurances in regard to the goal of German reunification, but its appeal was focused predominantly, and apparently with great success, on the theme of reconstruction.[3]

---

the Fatherland of us all" ("Die Aussenpolitik der Machtlosen," *Aussenpolitik*, No. 2 [1952], p. 17). To the same effect, cf. the remarks of Kurt Schumacher which he prepared for delivery at the 1950 SPD party convention; reprinted in *Turmwächter der Demokratie: Ein Lebensbild von Kurt Schumacher* (Berlin, 1953), II, 224.

[2] Gerhart Lütkens makes a claim for the generally beneficial effect of the foreign policy influence of the opposition under the Bonn regime ("Parliamentarische Opposition in der Aussenpolitik," *Aussenpolitik*, No. 2 [1952], pp. 403-4).

[3] It may be pertinent to give the wording of its foreign policy passages, which comprise one out of a total of seven paragraphs. They show skillful and well-calculated restraint: "You know which important program faces us now—the reunification of our two still separated Eastern and Western territories. For achieving this goal we need friends in foreign lands who support us. None of us wants war. Therefore, our whole policy aims at solving problems which concern us by peaceful negotiations. All our plans and actions, however, promise success only if there is a government which pursues a straightforward policy. Just look around and you will see how the absence of a firm, lasting government weakens a country. If I was often successful in my negotiations, this was largely due to

There is very little likelihood that the majority of those who supported the government paid much heed to the complexities of Allied-
Soviet negotiations on the question of German unification, or—to take
a heretical view—that their decision was influenced to any significant
extent by the government's promises to work with utmost energy
toward the achievement of unity. At most, the voter reacted to the
foreign policy question with some pride and satisfaction in Germany's
rapid rise, after the most disastrous war in its history, to the status of a
coveted partner of the Western world and, moreover, one safely
ranged on the side of the greatest and most modern power on the
world scene today.

Presumably, the mass of voters who supported Adenauer included
some who acted from widely different motives than those stated above.
If the majority gave him a vote of confidence as harbinger and
guarantor of economic prosperity, a minority may have seen in him
and in his policy the means of restoring Germany to its former preeminence. These motives may even have been present together in the
minds of some voters. However this may be, more than 16 million of
the total 27 million who voted accepted the Chancellor's program substantially or in full, with his own party taking the lion's share, or 12.5
million.[4] It is significant that this 12.5 million included at least three
million who had come of age since the last election or who had simply

---

the comforting feeling of security which is caused by the knowledge of being
backed by our healthy and peaceful people."

[4] COMPARATIVE VOTING STRENGTH, 1949 AND 1953

Party *	1949 Vote	Valid Votes (%)	Seats	1953 Vote **	Valid Votes (%)	Seats
CDU-CSU	7,359,084	31.0	139	12,444,549	45.2	244
SPD	6,934,975	29.2	131	7,944,252	28.8	151
FDP	2,829,920	11.9	52	2,629,473	9.5	48
KPD	1,361,706	5.7	15	607,634	2.2	
BP	986,478	4.2	17	465,552	1.7	
DP	939,934	4.0	17	896,944	3.3	15
BHE				1,616,123	5.9	27
WAV	681,888	2.9	12			
Z	727,505	3.1	10	217,078	.8	2
Ind. and others	1,910,908	8.0	9	729,707	2.6	

* CDU-CSU—Christian Democratic Union–Christian Social Union; SPD—Social
Democratic party; FPD—Free Democratic party; KPD—Communist party; BP—
Bavarian party; DP—German party; BHE—All-German Bloc; WAV—Reconstruc-
tion party; Z—Center party.

** Figures for the 1953 vote are taken from the second ballot.

not bothered to vote before.[5] The refugee party, which had hoped to assume the role of a balance wheel, was supported by only one in three of the refugee population. This indicates not merely the successful integration of the refugees into West German life but the increasing improbability of parliamentary representation for the refugee party in the future. Of the opposition parties, only the Social Democrats remain of major significance. Although this party managed to gain one million votes above its 1949 total—more than half of these were direct transfers from the dwindling ranks of the Communist supporters—it failed to make a dent in the middle-class vote, whose support it had so eagerly sought during the campaign. The parliamentary representation of the Social Democrats was ten seats short of the number necessary to block constitutional amendments.

Before making prognostications as to the future of the German establishment, a broader explanation of the apparent stability and moderation of the German political system may be offered. To any observer of the German scene in recent years, one feature stands out. In the midst of the tumult of group claims on the government and on the community at large, the majority of claimants have proceeded in almost an Anglo-Saxon fashion—that is, in highly pragmatic style. Refugees and bombed-out persons, denazified civil servants, other officials expelled by Russian or Polish or Czech governments, or victims of Nazism claiming similar restitution rights—none of these followed what one might consider a characteristically German procedure, namely, to build a whole political system on the basis of their particular grievances. Instead, they were content to pursue their claims

[5] In addition to three million new voters, coming in part from the ranks of those first eligible to vote in 1953 and to a larger extent from those who had previously abstained from voting, the CDU most likely drew over three-quarters of a million votes from smaller Catholic parties, which were all but eliminated, and almost a million from former rightist voters. The SPD in all likelihood contributed not more than 250,000 to swell the CDU ranks. The SPD, for its part, suffered from the large ballot, which increased from 78.5 to 86.2 per cent of the eligible voters (it did much better in the subsequent Hamburg election, where participation decreased considerably), from its inability to make any dent in the following of the center and right-of-center parties, and from the continued preference of women's and old-age (above sixty) groups for the CDU. See *Statistische Rundschau für das Land Nordrhein-Westfalen*, Nos. 10–11 (October-November, 1953), *Staat und Wirtschaft in Hessen, Statistische Mitteilungen*, Vol. V, No. 1 (October, 1953).

through the normal channels of lobby and pressure-group activities, as well as through the delegation of their representations to the parliamentary factions. The reason for this un-Germanic approach is probably to be found in the surprising ability of the state to satisfy very quickly at least a part of the claimants' desires. The significant rise in production and tax receipts enabled the state to satisfy many claimant groups without jeopardizing the claims of their rivals.[6] Thus each group could concentrate on fullfillment of its claims on the government rather than waste its energies competing outright for power with other groups. Equally important from the point of view of the individual citizen seeking redress or restitution, or primarily interested, as Chancellor Adenauer put it, in getting his own backyard into shape again, is the fact that the state provided him with the procedures necessary to give voice to all these variegated claims. One could have argued—and a leftist regime might conceivably have done so—that the terrible convulsions which Germany had experienced in the past two decades could not be rectified by admitting a mass of complicated claims and counterclaims, none of which could ever be completely satisfied. Instead, the argument would run, the historical process should be brought to its logical conclusion—a complete economic and social revolution which would dwarf all previous injustices and transformations. But the reaction of the East German population to a solution of this type shows conclusively that nothing was further from their minds than the idea that one set of injustices could be submerged in a sea of bigger and better injustices.

The alternative solution was contained in West German legislation which, after German solvency was reestablished, created during 1951 and 1952, with infinite passion for detail, a universe of legally enforceable or at least legally arguable claims.[7] Coming after a decade of

[6] Expenditures for social services alone rose from 4.6 billion DM in 1949 to 9.3 billion DM in 1953, or from 15.9 per cent to 18.4 per cent of the total net social product (figures taken from *Deutschland Jahrbuch 1953* [Essen, 1953], p. 197).

[7] Today constitutional lawyers are apt to consider as a basic liability to the new state the hypertrophy of legal procedures which were encouraged and to some degree made necessary by the Basic Law. It may be conceded that danger might conceivably develop in this direction from the too far-reaching judicialization of the political process via the Federal Constitutional Court. German literature on this point is already abundant; for a concise discussion, see Karl Loewen-

intensive lawlessness, this "universe of claims" and the promise it held for the individual became one of the greatest assets of the new state. Moreover, the pressing of claims demanded a new army of officials, and the apathetic attitude of the population in the first years of occupation experienced a sudden change when it became clear that the new authorities had something positive to offer. Thus, together with the establishment of the "universe of claims" came the revival of the traditional concept of the German civil service, shielded by the setting-up of a governmental authority which was made almost constitutionally foolproof for at least four years.

Of equal significance in the stabilizing process has been what I should like to call, for want of a better term, the "conversion of the militant." It is easy to recall the eternal soldier of the years following World War I, who rather than convert to civilian pursuits remained available to participate in the half-military, half-political adventures of those turbulent years, and thus formed one of the greatest hazards to the development of orderly constitutional government. Unlike the period after 1918, the post-1945 Germany had no Baltic provinces, no Upper Silesia to keep or to reconquer; there were no East Elbian estates on which unemployed professional soldiers could hibernate; there was no need for paramilitary organizations to keep the left wing in check. Public order, both in regard to domestic affairs and in regard to relations with the outside world, was distinctly the province of the occupying powers. The ex-soldier, professional or conscript, simply joined the millions engaged in the effort to convert to civilian life as rapidly and successfully as possible. After the most atrocious of modern regimes and of modern wars, the reestablishment of an ordered society was a goal highly desired by the mass of the population, despite the many elements of disorder latent within the postwar structure of Germany. And, strangely enough, the very impotence of the German population to prevent the mutilation and partition of its territory served to accelerate the return to normality and order. To be sure,

---

stein, in *Governing Postwar Germany*, ed. E. H. Litchfield (Ithaca, N.Y., 1953), pp. 260–61. Yet there is a tendency to overlook the fact that, from the viewpoint of the citizen at large, the grandstand proceedings before the Constitutional Court in Karlsruhe are infinitely less interesting than is his individual case, pending, as may be, before any of the multiplicity of social, economic, finance, labor, or administrative courts which have come into existence since 1950.

every German wanted the refugees and expellees to go back to their East German or Silesian or Sudeten homes, once those homes were liberated from the Soviets and their satellites. But what could a band of volunteers do to free East Germany? Who would gain anything from such an action? Surely not the East German population. Only as the social and government system of West Germany grew more coherent and self-reliant could Germans hope once more to play a role in deciding the fate of Central and Eastern Germany. National reconstruction was not merely the precondition for a new lease on life for the individual but the basis of any effective claim to national unity.

The militant left has virtually disappeared from the German political scene and it will probably not revive. Three reasons may be given for this, the first of which is obvious. The Communist experiment in East Germany and the experiences of the German soldier in Russia have deterred any development of sympathy for Communism. After the riots of June 17, 1953, it became evident that the East German worker may have to live for some time to come in a state of silent submission, but he will hardly in our lifetime move to join hands with his oppressors.

The second reason is not derived from anything new, but rather represents the culmination of a long-developing trend. As early as the 1920s, the majority of the German working class—despite the efforts of a powerful and energetic minority—had indicated that they found the prevailing political and social system on the whole acceptable, even though in need of overhauling and revision. The consequences of the war have only accentuated this tendency. In the present German social structure, the majority of the working class occupies the middle levels, only a minority falling within the lower categories. It is the over six million pensioners, war widows, and women who must support themselves and their families who occupy the lower brackets.[8]

---

[8] Ilse Elsner and Rüdiger Proske ("Der Fünfte Stand: Untersuchungen über die Armut in Westdeutschland," *Frankfurter Hefte* [February, 1953], pp. 108 ff.) include among the poverty groups two million old people, 1,800,000 women and 750,000 men without access to the labor market, 500,000 structurally unemployed, and 1,700,000 women over twenty-four years of age who are unmarried or no longer married. To these they add 1,900,000 men without adequate income. While the last category may seem problematic and possibly dwindling, it should be noted that another estimate, starting with 5,700,000 pensioners and publicly supported persons, and adding 2,600,000 dependents, ends up with figures of roughly the same magnitude.

Thirdly, we arrive at one of the decisive characteristics of German postwar life, a phenomenon recognizable among the working classes and the rest of the population. This is the trend toward privatization, a turning inward of interests and a concentration upon private affairs.[9] No element of the German population wishes to become deeply involved or identified with public concerns; the contemporary social-political process is too complicated, the chances of individual injury from political changes too great—to keep one's distance appears the better part of wisdom. Though noticeable to some extent almost everywhere in the world today, this feeling is more obvious in a country like Germany, where since the early 1930s the fear of sudden change and the desire to provide effective individual safeguards have been at a maximum. This tendency does not, of course, exclude membership in the trade union federation, nor does it stand in the way of high voter participation in elections. But the intensity of such organizational and political participation is not what it was; the approach has become rational and pragmatic, and there is little of the direct sense of personal involvement or mission. Advantages and disadvantages of a given political position are coolly weighed. But in the scale of preoccupations, political interest, especially among young people, ranks well behind sports, dancing, and in fact the sum total of private and personal considerations. In such an atmosphere, militant attitudes do not readily flourish. The official representatives of the German working class have had to set their sights low, or run the risk of losing their following. In this connection, it is significant that the only institutional advance which the trade unions have succeeded in securing beyond their established position under the Weimar Republic, the so-called codetermination rights in the steel and coal industries, fell into their lap through the intervention of the British Labour government, which enacted these reforms by virtue of its occupation powers in 1947. The unions were barely able to translate their advance into indigenous legislation,

[9] Privatization is probably the most important single social phenomenon of the postwar German scene. The most fruitful hypotheses on both the reasons for privatization and its impact on the social and political structure may be found in the basic study by Helmuth Schelsky, *Wandlungen in der Deutschen Familie der Gegenwart*, 2d ed. (Stuttgart, 1953). Yet the concomitance of increasingly uniform social standards with unchanged ideologies raises many still uncharted problems; see *ibid.*, pp. 237 ff. There also exists a highly impressionistic account of the phenomenon of privatization as evidenced among young Viennese workers by Karl Bednarik, *Der Junge Arbeiter von heute—ein neuer Typ* (Stuttgart, 1953).

and they had to be satisfied with what in balance at best amounts to the Weimar status quo in other fields.[10]

Thus in West Germany today there exists neither a militant right nor a militant left as a serious political force. The foreign occupation, preoccupations of the individual, and the coincidence of a desire for respite and enjoyment of one's private life with a world-wide economic upswing have thrust politics into the background and discouraged schemes for institutional innovations.

Ironically enough, this resistance to innovation not only has excluded any radical social reform but has also negatively affected the much less ambitious reform proposals of the Allies, primarily those of the Americans. The three D's—decartelization, denazification, and decentralization—were gradually modified or abandoned, along with plans for educational or civil service reform, even when these fitted to a limited degree into the postwar German scene.[11] This tendency

[10] Not enough time has elapsed since the Plant Constitution Law of October 14, 1952 (*Bundesgesetzblatt*, 1952, p. 652) came into effect to permit an adequate judgment of its operation. The material so far published relates mostly to the effects of codetermination in the steel and coal industries as enacted by the statute of January 27, 1951. However, the parliamentary report of the Bundestag Committee for Labor (*Anlage 3 zum stenographischen Bericht*, 223d Session, July 16, 1952, pp. 1010–27), as well as the speeches made during the discussion (223d Session, pp. 9946–53; 225th Session, July 17, 1952, pp. 10058–94), amply shows how little the actual terms of the legislation corresponded to the objectives of the SPD and the DGB. The satisfaction of employers' organizations is expressed in "Wirtschaftsbürger ohne Gängelband," *Der Arbeitgeber* (August 1, 1952), p. 576. The weakness of the legal position of labor representatives on boards of directors under the Plant Constitution Law becomes apparent from the discussion in D. Spethmann and S. Schnorr, "Die Beteiligung der Arbeitnehmer in Aufsichtsräten nach dem Betriebsverfassungsgesetz," *Recht der Arbeit*, No. 6 (1953), p. 448; see especially the conclusion 5b on page 456, which seems to re-open the door to the time-honored Weimar practice of excluding labor members from important committees of boards of directors. Lack of interest in and understanding of union and works council objectives among workers as a major difficulty in implementing union policies becomes apparent from A. Mausolff's detailed study, *Gewerkschaft und Betriebsrat im Urteil der Arbeitnehmer* (Darmstadt, 1952).

[11] The last scaffoldings of the occupation regime are still in the process of being taken down; no full account, therefore, of its achievements and failures in terms of its impact on German institutions exists as yet. However, material may be found in many of the individual chapters of Litchfield, ed., *op. cit.*; the unavoidably distorted focus of responsibility may be considered as a paradoxical feature of any democratic occupation regime. Such a regime remains unaccountable to those whom it administers; to the extent to which its home authorities care enough to enforce the responsibility of its occupation officials, they inevitably

crystallized as it grew obvious that American interests were becoming primarily concerned with foreign policy objectives, rather than with the specific institutional forms to be adopted by the German people. Yet when all is said, and despite the failure of the reform plans as such, the Allied operation in Germany was still a success. It provided West Germany with a strong authority in its formative period. Whatever steps had to be embarked upon, whatever Gordian knots cut, the responsibility could always be laid at the door of the Allies rather than at that of the new German government, which had yet to earn full domestic recognition. The successful operation of the Berlin airlift demonstrated to the world for the first time that German-Allied relations could achieve a voluntary and fruitful cooperation. And then, exactly at the right time—one year after the currency reform had provided the cornerstone for Germany's rapid economic recovery—the new Bonn regime was launched.

Now, it may well be argued that this regime was installed and placed in operation only by means of Allied interference, so that the Socialist opposition had less opportunity to present itself as a more vigorous and socially conscious alternative to the present government. It might be pointed out, and not without some justice, that the peculiar form in which the currency reform was installed in 1948 under American guidance gave a substantial advantage to those elements who, by accident or design, had managed to hang on to their property or stocks of goods.[12] But it is also true that the mere availability of a large number of people possessing nothing more than willingness to work was a major incentive in bringing about the miracle of German recovery. Moreover, a portion of the injustices of the currency reform were at least partly remedied within a few years, when the legislature of the

start from premises and use yardsticks which are not necessarily meaningful to the occupied.—In a humorous vein. Federal President Heuss recently spoke of the "education" of the lower grades of the fly-by-night school (*Klippschule*) which the members of the German national community were made to attend (*Stuttgarter Zeitung*, January 27, 1954).

[12] For a detailed account of the inequities created by the currency reform, cf. the Bundestag deliberations in connection with the passage of the *Lastenausgleichsgesetz* (Equalization of Burdens Law) in 1952. In particular, the arguments adduced by members of the SPD are revealing. See *Deutscher Bundestag Stenographische Berichte*, 207th Session, May 6, 1952, pp. 8980–82; 208th Session, May 7, 1952, pp. 9055, 9063 ff.; 209th Session, May 8, 1952, pp. 9130–31; 211th Session, May 14, 1952, pp. 9263–68.

Federal Republic established what has been referred to here as the "universe of claims."

In sum, even a regime under Social Democratic leadership and somewhat differently constituted would hardly have adopted policies too much at variance with those of the Adenauer government. Alternatives were certainly limited in view of the restricted possibilities of action in the field of foreign policy and the widespread popular distrust of anything that might smack of a directed economy. Even if a somewhat more equitable distribution of consumer goods had been aimed at, or—what is more likely—a policy reflecting Schumacher's principle of austerity by concentrating on reequipment of basic industries rather than consumer goods production, these would have been merely modifications of, rather than basic changes in, the structure of the postwar regime. Of course, such modifications might have led to a more active integration of the workers into the postwar administrative set up.

Under such circumstances, the early development of a two-party system, made up of labor versus a conservative mass party, might have taken place. Instead, by reason of voter preference for a conservative catch-all party, there now exists a one and one-half party system. On one side, there is the predominant CDU, with its minor middle-class and refugee party satellites, which are not necessary for the formation of a majority, and on the other, a labor party which is not strong enough even to prevent constitutional changes, let alone to influence decisively the legislative process in the face of the massive parliamentary majority of the present administration.

What chance is there that this lopsided situation may be modified? Can a conventional two-party system emerge—that is, will the SPD develop into a catch-all mass party rather than a democratic working-class party, and thus retain the possibility of leading an alternative government? If not, how long can the present imbalance between the two major parties be expected to continue? And is a return to a multi-party system possible? The answers to these questions presuppose some specific hypothesis concerning West German development over the next decade. Adenauer's success is the result of several factors, some unique and temporary, others perhaps more permanent. The temporary, nonrepetitive factors may easily be discerned: the favorable start of the government under Western protection, plus some economic factors, like the long-deferred demand for consumer goods and over-all reconstruction, and Germany's favorable export position at a time when her historical competitors were preoccupied with rearmament. But what of the conversion of the militant to civil pursuits, the decline of political interest, and what of the effects of privatization on the political scene? Are they, too, specific aspects of postwar phenomena, or are they harbingers of a more significant psychological transforma-tion? What of the impact of the indefinite partition of Germany and the raising of an armed establishment?

Obviously, we are in the realm of guesswork. But some guesses appear less risky than others. Political and social strife, which have been almost absent from postwar Germany, are likely to increase, if for no other reason than that economic progress is bound to be less rapid in the future.[13] The opportunities for any social group to ad-vance its interests merely by claiming its share of a greatly increased national product, rather than improving itself at the expense of another social group, are likely to be smaller. Consequently, there will be greater need for group compromises, both as between the CDU and the only social group of importance outside its ranks—namely, labor—and within the CDU, among the variegated social groups which com-pose this conservative mass party.[14] On the other hand, even a recession

[13] Rate of increase of gross national product (in constant prices) since the second half of 1948 (after currency reform):

Year (July 1-June 30)

1949/50–1948/49	15.5%
1950/51–1949/50	20.4%
1951/52–1950/51	8.2%
1952/53–1951/52	5.5%

Source: *Wirtschaft und Statistik* (September, 1953), p. 393.

[14] German research on the interrelationship of pressure groups and political organizations is still scant; cf. some interesting remarks in *Deutschland Jahrbuch 1953*, p. 90. Among the CDU-CSU faction, the degree of representation of the most important social and economic groups in the 1953 Bundestag is as follows: refugees and war-damaged, 3.7 per cent; proprietors and managers of financial and industrial enterprises, 12.7 per cent; officers of industrial associations, 3.3 per cent; proprietors of agricultural enterprises and officers of the corresponding as-sociations, 17.2 per cent; artisans and retail proprietors and officers of correspond-ing associations, 10.7 per cent; trade union, consumer cooperatives, and related organizations, 5.3 per cent; white-collar employees, technicians, and officers of related organizations, 1.2 per cent. For comparative figures for the first Bundestag and a description of the criteria used, cf. Otto Kirchheimer, "The Composition

would shake the regime to its foundations only if the population had the feeling that the government was either unable or unwilling to take effective countermeasures. The need to prove to the world that Western democracy is a viable alternative for Germany to the dehumanization of the East places a high premium on the willingness of all participants to prevent any such crisis from getting out of hand.

In so far as Germany's economic position turns upon the problem of the balance of payments, the United States holds the key to the situation. But to the extent that it is a problem of adapting economic devices and institutions, the maintenance of economic stability is up to the German administration. At present there exists a marked predilection for a liberal type of economy, which its adherents prefer to call, with an eye to the propaganda value of the phrase, a social market economy, meaning that a liberal economy results in the greatest benefits for the society as a whole.[15] But this economy is not literally a liberal one; just as in most nontotalitarian systems, Germany's liberal economy is a blend of competition, state controls and regulations, efforts at private concentration or cooperation, and—for possibly rather temporary reasons—a fervent interest in the speedy establishment of free and unfettered international exchange. Nor is there very much doubt that, if the necessity arises, Germans will be quite undogmatic about their present propaganda emphasis on the social market economy, and will make whatever adjustments are necessary to support living standards and employment opportunities.

---

of the German Bundestag, 1950," *Western Political Quarterly*, III (December, 1950), 597.

[15] German neo-liberalism remains closely connected with the literary endeavors of the school of which Wilhelm Röpke is the most indefatigable member; see, e.g., *Civitas Humana*, 2d ed. (Erlenbach-Zurich, 1946), and, more recently, *Wirtschaft und Soziale Ordnung als Aufgabe der Freien Welt* (Dortmund, 1952). However, as Röpke and his friends recognize the necessity of what they call "Marktkonforme Intervention," the gap between neo-liberals and their foes narrows down considerably; cf. Friedrich Wilhelm Dörge, "Der Neuliberale Interventionismus im Wandel Zweier Jahrzehnte," *Gewerkschaftliche Monatshefte*, IV (December, 1953), 725 ff. While the head of the Ministry of Economics, Ludwig Erhard, has for a long time been an adherent of Röpke, Berg, the president of the German Federation of Industrialists, in a speech before the Chamber of Commerce in Hagen on December 4, 1953, rejected the neo-liberal credo and demanded that any forthcoming cartel legislation only be promulgated with what he called a "positive regulation of fair competition." A recent official statement deferring cartel legislation altogether until after the passage of tax reform measures represents a full-fledged victory for the foes of neo-liberalism.

In sum, German conservatism or, as some critics are wont to say, the German restorative tendency is not so much an espousal of specific political or economic doctrines; it is, rather, a general and widespread state of mind. After the unhappy experiences of the recent past, it is understandably suspicious of innovation for innovation's sake; it places a high value upon preserving for the individual a small niche of his own, free from the pressures and intrusions of society at large. If compulsion is necessary, it prefers roundabout, subtle methods rather than the use of the sledge hammer. This mellow conservatism may even color attitudes and expectancies in regard to the most important of the many unknown factors on Germany's political horizon: the future armed establishment. After so many unhappy experiences with incompetent leadership and weak control over army affairs, both the politicians and the cadres of the future officer corps themselves regard the European Army not merely as a necessary technical device for effective European cooperation but also as a release from responsibility which they do not want to assume singlehanded. To this extent, the case of the cynics who think of EDC as a simple pretext to reestablish German military power pure and unadulterated may not be as strong as it would appear at first glance. Obviously, this is not to say that there are not elements among the population at large as well as among the future army components who visualize German armed forces primarily as a means of augmenting Germany's power and scope of action. Yet have these elements caught the true mood of the German population? If the many signs are not misleading, there will be fewer German surprises in the 1950s and 1960s than there were in the 1930s and 1940s. Germany may not figure too large in future headlines, yet achievements are likely to be built on a firmer foundation, and the goals which the Germans set themselves may be more universally acceptable than they were during the turbulent decades behind us.

FRANCE FROM THE FOURTH TO

THE FIFTH REPUBLIC

In 1958 as in 1799 Frenchmen were asking: What is in the constitution that we have been asked to approve in the plebiscite? The patent analogy of the answer—Bonaparte and de Gaulle—is as deceptive as it is clear.

Bonaparte established his ascendancy after a decade of revolution had worn out both friends and foes. Thermidor had been followed by Germinal and Prairial, the abortive revolts of the left, and by Vendé-miaire, the abortive uprising of the right. With neither able to make any headway the new social order cast about for a more permanent political formula; hence Brumaire. Bonaparte tried his own brand of stabilization: accepting the revolution's social consequences he at the same time modified its effects in a chain of foreign wars, at first inherited, but increasingly self-initiated.

De Gaulle's assumption of power indicates neither revolutionary convulsions of the body politic nor a definite stabilization of new social relations long in the making. Neither is he cast in the role of a Robespierre, revamping the polity and its symbols to redouble its effectiveness, nor does he perform a Napoleonic act of consolidation of acquired positions. France's transition to a full-fledged industrial society, long retarded, is still going on incessantly, with only its tempo and not its direction subject to modification. The change in the fortunes and functions of various social groups and—equally important—in their consciousness of this change, progressing at a quite uneven rate, is still

Reprinted, by permission, from *Social Research*, XXV (1958), 379–414.

in full swing. The emerging patterns of domination and accommodation are at present subject to too many momentary deformations to be capable of permanent stabilization. Also, the complexity of French institutions reflects in a large measure the presence of currents and political situations transcending the French scene, and is consequently incapable of isolated solution at the national level.

I

If we understand political revolution as an organized onslaught of vital population groups on the constituted order, France of the twentieth century, though it may have undergone bad cases of fright, has had no revolution. Whenever a break in the political continuity has occurred —1940 and 1958—it has been the consequence of a surrender of the traditional political elite, acquiesced in by the population and taking place as the result of events that the elite had no means or no resolve to master. Civil war, major domestic upheavals of German, Italian, or Spanish dimensions, have been noticeably absent from the French scene since the days of the Paris Commune.

Seen in this perspective the May 13, 1958, pronunciamento of the colons and colonels, in spite of attempts to evoke wider revolutionary symbols, was a limited affair: it was the response of the Algerian French leadership, of related army formations, and of an inchoate group of mainland sympathizers to the government's unwillingness to subscribe to the colonialist program of action that they had resolved to apply to the Algerian imbroglio. Metropolitan irresoluteness in the face of the clash between colonialism and Algerian nationalism became the handmaiden of the regime's downfall. If the regime was left with few resolute adherents, if its police and the metropolitan army cadres had become unreliable—the one grumbling over increased professional burdens and risks rather than concerned with the political kaleidoscope, the other concerned with having to shoulder the responsibility for dubious and ineffectual rearguard actions in France's erstwhile colonial possessions—this should not be evaluated as ingredients of a revolutionary situation, with only the Algerian match needed to start a general conflagration.

France of the middle 1950s was by and large a prosperous country;

full employment and rapid industrial progress, connoted by increasing levels of consumption, were undeniable facts, half-heartedly admitted even by the foes of the regime. In the light of this situation the chronic ills of the French body politic—still widespread restrictive practices in economic life, the effect of continuing inflation on income distribution, the lack of an orderly process of urbanization (with dwelling units needed for 14 million inadequately housed people), the slow pace of adaptation of many middle-sized and small agricultural production units and, especially, of the retail sector to more rational processes of production and distribution—marked major disproportions in the process of social transformation, not insuperable roadblocks to further economic and social change, requiring revolutionary action. But even if these shortcomings did not arrest the social and economic advance of the country, their repercussions certainly helped to increase existing political fissures, which were accentuated by the deepening malaise caused by the Algerian war.

The gap continued to widen between the realities of power distribution and the precepts of the constitution of 1946, which concentrated political power in the hands of the popularly elected assembly and the ministry installed by its confidence. As usual it is not too profitable to trace what is cause and what is effect in an intertwined chain of action and reaction. Did the majority of the French working class and an appreciable number of rural smallholders give their vote to the Communist party as a protest against prevailing conditions and because long before the days of Mollet and Lacoste they could find no other suitable channel of articulation for their grievances? Or did they to some extent merely act out the playful tradition of always voting for the most advanced party, without connecting any far-reaching consequences with their political action? Was it out of sheer necessity or as a facile device for getting rid of disagreeable political competitors that the traditional parliamentary formations used their opportunity to quarantine the opposition of principle, depriving it of any influence on the political business at hand—an opposition that included one quarter of the voters, augmented by another 13 per cent after 1956, with the emergence of intransigent rightists? At any rate, what matters is that through the combined processes of exclusion and self-exclusion of the opposition of principle, the group of interests entitled to consideration in the formation of political decisions was artificially narrowed down, thus vitiating the balance of political forces.

In reducing the frame of reference for political decisions to the purely tactical game of factional and personal politics, the Fourth Republic returned to the habits of the Third, habits possibly appropriate to the political climate of an incipient industrial society but already outmoded in the twenties and thirties. Politics as a game of avoiding responsibility and fighting delaying actions—played more for its effect on role distribution among the participants of the game than for the social consequences connected with it—did not provide the necessary procedures appropriate to the needs of the administrative state. Consequently authority went on migrating to the professional echelons elsewhere. Major interest groups, which unlike the Communist-led CGT did not swim against the current and were not averse to playing along with quite heterogenous political équipes;[1] the higher ranks of the various service bureaucracies, whether intertwined with or battling against interest combinations; given the continued recourse to colonial warfare, the commanding ranks of the armed forces—they all entered the policymaking game.

The public reaction to this process of migration of political substance was political apathy; the conversion of the participant citizens into bewildered, bemused, or embittered spectators, as the case might be, pulling back from the political game and withdrawing into private existence, became widespread. To some extent this reversion of the citizen to the status of a private individual, minding his own business and regarding the apparatus of public power as an alien phenomenon with which he has intercourse only through the agents of interest-group ambassadors, is part and parcel of a more generalized process in industrial society. But the additional stultifying effect of conscious depolitization, carried on by modern mass media, hit home much harder in a country that had previously prided itself on its citizens' independent judgment than it does in countries where political literacy has never been more than a privilege of a select few.

---

[1] Systematic inquiry into the mutual relations of political formations and interest groups has only recently been undertaken. See Henry Ehrmann, *Organized Business in France* (Princeton, 1957), and Jan Meynaud, *Les groupes de pression en France* (Paris, 1958), especially pp. 187 ff.

Thus over two million weekly copies of *Paris Match* and one and a half million daily copies of *France Soir* are a yardstick of deterioration, whereas two to three million daily copies of the German *Bildzeitung* only pinpoint a long-established phenomenon. The majority of the French media had learned to follow the trade winds, and they became "noncontroversial" long before scattered outposts of independent judgment were closed in on by the 1956–58 policy of seizing whole newspaper editions, and by Information Minister Soustelle's effort to endow the media under his control with a political mission.[2] Increasing feelings of anomy in the face of towering private and public bureaucratic structures led to a new height of cynicism in regard to the possibilities of meaningful political participation by the citizen at large.

Even in the France of the Third Republic the relation between political-action patterns and verbalization in political programs was very tenuous. But expectations do not necessarily remain stationary. There is some difference between the amused and benign attitude with which the citizen of yesteryear watched the histrionics of the professional politician, expecting from him not much beyond entertainment and some personal services, and the uneasiness of the new generation, accustomed to less haphazard standards of performance and correspondingly disgusted with the unrelatedness between felt need and political performance. In addition there is the return of almost compulsive forms of nationalism. The war, too easily lost; the ascendancy of the United States, both needed and resented; the voluntary acceptance of antinational symbols by a sizable part of the working-class community, for all practical purposes contracting out of the political community; the melancholy business of the Indo-Chinese retreat—all this culminated in the Algerian affair. Here the immediate interests of too many Frenchmen were involved to allow for a consistent adoption of rational patterns of thinking—their interests as fathers of mobilized soldiers, as friends or relatives of the Algerian French, or as potential sufferers from a reflux into France from Algeria (the tale of the posi-

[2] When Gayman, the Director of Information of the French State Broadcasting System, complained about his dismissal, he made the special point that he had always scrupulously avoided any criticism of incumbent governments; see *Le Monde*, June 24, 1958.

tive effect produced on West Germany's economy by the influx of German refugees has not yet reached the average Frenchman).

It is in such an atmosphere that the Pflimlin government brought an end to the institutions that had endured twelve years, through making its choice between surrender to de Gaulle, as acceptable trustee of both the political elite and the Algiers factions, and an attempt, never seriously considered, to resist the importunities of the Algiers crowd by accepting the mortgage of Communist support. The popular reaction to the uprising and to the last parliamentary government's demise manifested less the degree of estrangement between the population and the tumbling regime of the Fourth Republic than the much wider and more decisive degree of total alienation of the population at large from the small band of political, associational, and military professionals engaged in one way or another in the political game. There were childish pranks by the Paris *jeunesse dorée* and a few instances of protest strikes and protest meetings (with only the teachers showing themselves willing and able to engage in cohesive and disciplined action), but during the decisive May days the great majority of the population went on with its business and leisure as usual, waiting for the power-holders in Paris and Algiers to make up their minds. The Communists indulged in verbal vacuities, extolling the collaboration of the left, but carefully refraining from any test of strength against the government. The gross disproportion between Communist verbal efforts and Communist inaction might be rationalized as indicating nebulous Communist expectations regarding the new government's changing alignments on the international scene. But in essence the party's behavior was an act of self-preservation, mirroring its correct anticipation that its adherents would probably fail to heed any call to major political action.

In this situation the majority of the parliament abdicated into the hands of the General, not only entrusting him with the power to guide France's steps in the present crisis of authority, but entrusting his government with the power to draw up France's future governmental patterns. Constituted and constituent power were merged in the same transitional government, symbolized in the person of General de Gaulle.

II

Michel Debré, high official by formation and political polemicist by vocation, was installed by de Gaulle as his Minister of Justice and as kingpin of the new constitution-making enterprise. Casting about for appropriate forms that would stabilize the fruits of surrender—the surrender of the reigning though scarcely governing parliamentary elite to the new but not necessarily always unified triad of military rank, bureaucratic efficiency, and nationalist emotions—Debré ostensibly went back to the arsenal of nineteenth-century constitutionalism. He borrowed pieces here and there, with shades of Napoleon's *senatus consultum* of 1804, the charters of 1814 and 1830, and the organic laws of 1875 becoming visible in the new document's twenty-five titles and ninety-two paragraphs.

What is the meaning of these trappings? To some extent they are an accident of the concrete historical situation out of which the new regime arose. The combination of Algiers colons and colonels could find a substitute for the Fourth Republic only with the help of de Gaulle, representative of authoritarian technocracy rather than of plebeian totalitarianism. But to the extent to which any twentieth century authoritarian government has to try to find a formula combining the seemingly independent exercise of executive authority with some degree of popular sanction, however limited, the option of the constitution has a more fundamental significance.

Debré's draft, revised by a mixed group of bureaucrats and four major politicians, participants in the new Gaullist enterprise, was adopted by the cabinet on July 26. It was then submitted to a constitutional committee, of which two thirds were "friendly" parliamentarians and the remainder officials, and thereafter to the Conseil d'État. The government conceded some points of distinctly minor significance; but in essence it maintained its resolve not to brook any interference with the constitutional program. In its final form the document was adopted by the government on September 3; on the following day it was presented to the public in a maladroitly handled public ceremony on the Place de la République, marking clearly the distinction between an authoritarian and a totalitarian decor; and it was formally adopted by thumping popular majorities on September 28.

The new constitution rests on a double foundation: on a widely entertained but somewhat exaggerated assumption as to the roots of the evil affecting French polity; and on a thoroughly realistic appraisal of the mechanisms governing the *de facto* exercise of political authority in France, that is, widely shared practices transmuted to the rank of recognized institutions. The exaggerated but popular theory concerns the primordial contribution made to the misfortunes of the realm by an omnipotent group of politicians, Debré's *princes qui nous gouvernent* (the phrase was used by him as the title of a book published in Paris in 1957). According to this image the politicians intentionally prolonged their own nefarious rule, interrupting their ideological squabbles, Byzantine verbosity, and proverbial irresoluteness only long enough to intone their periodical "no" to any attempt to take initiatives consonant with the national aspirations. A less dramatic picture, but probably a bit closer to reality, would perhaps emphasize more the loss of authority that the standard-bearers of and competitors for governmental authority increasingly suffered in the last decade.

During that period the transfer of decisive power to the higher echelons of army and bureaucracy was accelerated, but without entailing a corresponding shift in ultimate political responsibility, which continued to be carried by ephemeral governments and their parliamentary backers. De Gaulle's 1944 national-unity formula for a provisional government had already shown a distinct predilection for government by technically qualified specialists, protected by a *dosage* of professional politicians. This formula, however, operated under commonly accepted programs and agreed-upon priorities. Here belongs also the Commissariat Général du Plan, entrusted with the elaboration of programs for the economic reconstruction, a field taken out of party competition by common consent in 1947. The events of the late forties pushed incessantly toward a much more decisive cumulative shift in the location of political power. The tripartite government formula of 1945–47, while establishing outward government stability, threatened to dissolve the government into semi-independent satrapies of the participant parties.

After the ejection of the Communists from government in the spring of 1947, there was a return to the weak and unstable *combinaziones* of the Third Republic, half interparty arrangements, half personal clientele relationships. Lack of stable parliamentary majorities left the successive governments neither time and authority for developing long-range policies nor leeway for dealing with concrete incidents on their own terms. This situation was aggravated by the resumption of large-scale colonial warfare. In Indo-China and then in North Africa colonial warfare was conducted by the military elite under only nominal political supervision. Faced with an uninterrupted chain of *faits accomplis,* the government played a role conforming more to the pattern of a *bouc émissaire* than to that of a responsible director of operations. In each instance—whether it was General d'Argenlieu interpreting the Fontainebleau accords of the government with Ho Chi Minh, or the military leaders in Algiers kidnaping the FLN leaders, devising a system of counterterror, ordering the bombardment of Sakhiet—the parliamentary and government leadership was relegated to the task of post-factum sanctioning of policies elaborated and carried out without its knowledge and often against its own volition.

The new constitution draws the logical conclusions from this change in the structure of public authority. By concentrating authority in the hands of the same bureaucratic elite that had previously exercised a good portion of it *sub rosa,* it regularizes this change. In order to stabilize the authority given the bureaucratic elite, the constitution reverses the traditional scheme of concentrating political authority in the hands of a government selected by a national assembly, the body that hitherto formed the apex of the political command structure.

There is no attempt to clothe the document in the language of separation of powers as a seeming justification for the *capitis diminutio* suffered by parliamentary authority. On the contrary, everything is done to create the impression that parliamentary sovereignty has been completely superseded by executive leadership, concentrated in the hands of an almighty president. Even the rank order in which the public powers appear in the document is set forth in a way to impress this change on the public. The president is immediately introduced after the traditional, though drastically curtailed, preamble—which is a reference to and incantation of the nationally accepted tradition and image of a community of free states associated in a common enterprise—and the regime's own adaptation of the theory of national sovereignty.

The president functions as guarantor of the whole national establishment. He is cast in the role of the *deus ex machina*, the demiurge, removed from the daily strife of factions, who by some intermittent but well-aimed strokes puts the world in order. He alone decides on timeliness and on the extent of emergency measures needed to face both external and internal threats. Likewise he alone has the power to dissolve the National Assembly. At the same time he also functions as the regular chief of the executive body. He installs a prime minister with his cabinet.

The cabinet's position seems to mark a strange halfway house between the practices of early and late nineteenth-century constitutionalism. On the one hand the ministry is psychologically removed from pressure by the assembly, through enforcement of strict rules of incompatibility, preventing the ministers from holding on to membership in parliament—one of the most controversial but hotly defended cornerstones of the new constitutional edifice. The prime minister appears as the servant of the president, who selects and appoints him and supports him, if he so chooses, by exercising his right to dissolve the popularly elected National Assembly. Thus, at first glance, the ministry seems to live completely in the shadow of the president. But on the other hand the constitution, here following the traditions of the Third and the Fourth Republic, accepts the idea of ministerial responsibility toward the National Assembly, thus creating for the ministry some political quality of its own midway between the president and the assembly.

Nevertheless, the National Assembly's means of enforcing ministerial responsibility are narrowly circumscribed, reflecting the aura of mistrust of that body. The assembly is not asked to vote its confidence in a cabinet newly installed by the president. Its confidence is presumed until a motion of censure proposed by one tenth of the assembly is adopted by an absolute majority. (Conversely, the government may link its existence to any legislative text, which then is assumed to have been adopted by the assembly even without having been explicitly voted on, unless the assembly musters enough votes for a motion of censure, leading to the resignation of the government.)

Moreover, in thus returning to practices of early constitutionalism —already in evidence in a milder form in the December 9, 1954, constitutional amendments—parliamentary sessions are of strictly limited duration. There is one of a month and a half in October, and one of three months in the spring. Even if the parliament musters a majority for calling an extraordinary session, the decree of adjournment will be read after a maximum of twelve days. The number of parliamentary standing committees is limited to six, and the order of priorities of parliamentary business is determined by the government. What with the president's power to dissolve the assembly once every year, and to take it by surprise with the use of his all-embracing emergency powers —frequently contested through the public debate in the summer of 1958, but firmly upheld and scarcely circumscribed in the final document [3]—the assembly looks indeed like a poor relative of the mighty master, the executive.

But though the document's confidence in the president's wise exercise of his completely discretionary powers is as marked as its all-pervasive antiparliamentary bias, there is little evidence that the presidency has been intentionally construed to serve as a springboard for the assumption of Caesarean-Napoleonic or modern totalitarian dictatorship. If de Gaulle had shown the slightest desire to pave the way for such contingencies he would have taken care to install a popularly elected president. In this way the constitution might have been possessed of two popularly elected organs of equal legitimacy, with the president easily able to affirm his ascendancy.

De Gaulle's own estimate of his role as providential restorer of French national grandeur, joined with his tendency to look at the people at any given moment of history as a coincidental vessel of eternal national destiny, led him to a skeptical view of popular participation in the historical process. Even though democracy is necessary as fountainhead of political legitimacy and parliaments have to be preserved as functional institutions, democratic devices should not be emphasized to the point of no return.[4] Since the holder of executive

[3] The relevant emergency provision (Art. 16, 1) reads: When the institutions of the Republic, the independence of the nation, the integrity of its territory, or the fulfillment of its international commitments are threatened in a grave and immediate manner and the regular functioning of the constitutional public powers is interrupted, the President of the Republic shall take the measures required by these circumstances, after official consultation with the Premier and the Presidents of the Assemblies, as well as with the Constitutional Council.

[4] In keeping with the tenets of the document, recourse to direct democracy is infrequent. One of the exceptions is to be found in Article 11, which allows either

power can never be so effectively checkmated as an assembly, it seemed much better to refrain from adding to his temptation or his backers' expectations by giving him the sanction of popular will. Hence the curious, almost intentionally anachronistic modus of selection of the omnipotent president. The elevation to that office is tied (December, 1958) to a body of 81,508 *grands électeurs,* of whom 38,959 represent communities with fewer than 2,000 inhabitants. This makes the president appear as symbol of rye and chestnut tree, the traditional small peasant economy, rather than as a representative of wheat and sugar-beet producers, the big wheels of French agriculture.[5]

Although the election of the first president was a foregone conclusion and the role of the rural notables in de Gaulle's elevation is of more symbolic than political import, the reestablishment of the senate—on a somewhat similar basis of indirect elections—as a continuous stronghold of these same local notables assumes immediate political importance. This is particularly true since the senate has the status of a full-fledged political assembly,[6] with corporativism—in the form of the Economic and Social Council—again relegated to purely advisory functions. The senate, here again in conformance with the 1954 constitutional revision, is restored to nearly even rank with the assembly in the legislative process.[7] And the senate is not only construed as a device to checkmate the will of the assembly, from the inside of the legislative fortress, as it were; it is also cast as a last-ditch guarantor of the present constitutional establishment. Attempts at constitutional amendment need an initial concurrent vote of the majorities of both houses.

---

the president (on proposal of the cabinet) or the assembly to initiate a referendum on "community agreements" (as defined in title 12) and on those international treaties likely to affect the "functioning of the institutions." The second device may have been chosen to enlarge the French government's freedom of maneuvering when negotiating with foreign partners; the community provision may visualize the North African situation, where the government may one day want to appeal from a badly informed parliament to a possibly better informed voter.

[5] See Georges Vedel in *Le Monde,* June 20 and 21, 1958.

[6] The present senate will remain in office until April 26, 1959, when 301 new senators, among them 253 metropolitan senators, will be elected.

[7] The prime minister, while not able to ask for a formal vote of confidence before the senate, may ask for "a general approval of a policy declaration" (Art. 49), thus acquiring the possibility of playing one house against the other. A deadlock between the senate and the assembly in the legislative process can be solved only if the government is willing to interfere; on government decision, but only on government decision, the National Assembly will have the final say as to the formulation of a disputed provision (Art. 45).

But the events of 1940 and 1958 give little indication that the local notables are more willing to withstand the pressures of the moment than their colleagues nearer the political battle front. Neither in 1940 nor in 1958 were the procedures followed that were designated by the then operative constitutions for constitutional change. In both cases constituent powers were conferred on the government of the period, Pétain in the first and de Gaulle in the second instance. While it is true that in the second case there were provisions for popular acceptance, and thus a bow toward democratic constitutionalism—which was manifestly not the case with Pétain—both instances show the strictly limited significance of amendment barriers when circumstances generate pressure for swift constitutional change.[8]

For this reason the amending process may also be initiated by the president; acting at the government's request, he may convoke both houses for a joint meeting, in which case a three-fifths majority would suffice for amendment. The referendum that would be necessary after separate majority decisions of both houses would then be omitted. Thus in practical terms the executive is expected to take the leadership and to generate the necessary pressure for quick constitutional change. This fits into the now established pattern that a new executive mirrors newly established power relationships and can therefore command a hara-kiri performance by a legislature that runs behind the times. The new amendment procedures thus reveal that conservatism constitutes less a balancing element than another embellishment of executive predominance.

III

In the new order aiming at a domesticated legislature, the central core is the scheme of jurisdiction over legislative fields. It is in this realm, rather than in the much more spectacular reassessment of the position of the president, that the constitution reveals the working scheme of

---

[8] Of course, from a legal viewpoint one may construe a difference between the delegation of constituent powers and the modification of procedures for revision, the first inadmissible because a prohibited delegation of powers, the second well in the province of the assemblies. Moreover, from a purely positivist viewpoint one might argue that whoever exercises constituent power may utilize it as he sees fit.

the new order and also contains some formulas that may still radiate influence on developments in public law long after the present document has met the fate of its numerous predecessors.

Even in the twenties, and especially in the thirties, the theoretically omnipotent parliament had increasingly abdicated its legislative function by resorting to the practice of enabling acts, thus clothing the government and its permanent staff with the authority to legislate by decree. In a sharp reaction against this divestment of function the 1946 constitution reasserted legislative supremacy, inserting somewhat less than watertight prohibitions against the divesting of legislative powers and their transfer to other agencies. Nevertheless, the cleavage between constitutional theory and government practice persisted. In 1948, covered by formulas emanating from the Conseil d'État and referring to the parliament's sovereign right to determine the scope of its legislative action, French parliaments returned to the system of wide delegation of legislative power to the executive.[9]

While in theory the new constitution marks a radical break with previous constitutional law, in practice it only draws the logical conclusion from the continued shift of legislative power to the executive. Dispensing with the notion of legislative omnipotence, it restricts the legislative effort of parliament to a number of enumerated fields, handing over the remainder to the executive for rulemaking in its own right. The legislative grant to parliament is limited in scope and ambiguous in its terms. There are a number of fields where parliament retains full legislative power,[10] but in others it retains only the right to establish broad principles. And the new functional division of parliamentary and executive regulatory competence by no means excludes recourse

[9] See Jacques Soubeyrol, *Les décrets-lois sous la quatrième république* (Paris, 1955).

[10] The absolute grant refers to civil rights and other fundamental guarantees of public liberties; personal-property restrictions in the interest of the national defense; citizenship, status, and legal capacity of persons; marriage and divorce; inheritance and donations; criminal law and procedure; amnesty; institution of new courts and the status of judges; the basis, rate, and method of tax collection; issuance of currency; election laws, except for the current elections; rules for the establishment of public enterprises; the fundamental guarantees for civil servants and the military personnel; rules governing nationalization and denationalization (Art. 34); the authorization to declare war (Art. 35); the treaty power according to specifications (Art. 53).

to the older procedures of enabling acts. The government, with a view to carrying out its program, may demand full legislative power for a limited period in fields otherwise left in the parliamentary domain.

If one adds that the parliamentary right to amend bills has been severely restricted, that parliamentary motions are out of order if they reduce taxes or increase expenditures, but that the government has a right to promulgate budgetary provisions not voted on by the two houses within seventy days, it becomes evident that the notion of legislative sovereignty has been radically eliminated. It has been replaced by a system of limited participation of parliament in the carrying through of governmental programs. Such programs are presented by a government that—because of its new relationship to the president and the strict incompatibility rules—will tend even more frequently than before to act as mouthpiece and shield of its higher bureaucracy.

This officialdom, which elaborates and increasingly also promulgates new rules and administers the realm, consists of a congeries of professional elite groups; they are recruited by an unmerciful process of competitive selection, but as a result of the working of France's educational system they heavily reflect a background in the upper and upper-middle classes. Although assured of tenure, influence, and prestige in government service, they are subject to considerable salary disadvantages, which encourage a system of *pantouflage*, a changeover to more rewarding private or semipublic positions.[11] Far more stringent rules have now been imposed, subjecting a former officeholder to temporary incapacities in representing private interests in their dealings with state agencies, and making it more difficult to exploit for private gain the knowledge and relations consequent on public office. Whether such rules will sufficiently protect the independence and concept of duty of these *grands commis* is a problem made especially cogent by the present increment of power in their hands.

With the president constituted as an arbiter outside and above the strife of parliament, government, and the civil service, but functioning

[11] This subject, covering a vast, vital, and not well explored field, has been evoked by Jean Meynaud, "Les groupes d'intérêt et l'administration en France," *Revue Française de Science Politique*, VII (1957), 573–93. Intrabureaucratic tensions and working methods of the higher bureaucracy are explored by Alfred Diamant, "A Case Study of Administrative Autonomy: Controls and Tensions in French Administration," *Political Studies*, VI (1958), 147–66.

also as the effective semipermanent (seven-year tenure) head of the whole executive establishment, a second-line interorganizational arbiter had to be established. This is the Constitutional Council, composed of former presidents of the republic as life members—thus rewarding the cooperative attitude of Vincent Auriol and especially of President René Coty during the period preceding the demise of the republic— and of nine appointees, one third to be renewed every three years, nominated in equal numbers by the president and the presidents of the assembly and the senate.

Of the plethora of functions devolving on the Council, the settling of controversies between parliament and the executive over the scope of parliamentary powers in the legislative process is easily the most important.[12] On questions of parliamentary intrusion into the executive field the Council is presumed to deliver its universally binding interpretation within a month, and in case of urgency within a week. But there is no equally swift control over executive action in the legislative field.[13] One might have expected that the sense of symmetry between parliament and the executive would suggest a wider grant of power to the Council. It might have been allowed to check not only parliamentary intrusion into the executive sphere of action but also, on the petition of parliament, any asserted executive infringement of the legislative jurisdiction of parliament, thus opening the way to establishing full-fledged determination of the constitutional correctness of all participants in the political process. As it is, the gap between the two powers is rather symptomatic.

Thus the new constitution marks the high-water mark for the

---

[12] Among its other functions: decision of election contests (Arts. 58, 59); examination of the constitutionality of organic laws made in execution of constitutional provisions (Art. 61), to the extent that the government, during the four-month transitional period in which it keeps practically unlimited legislative power (Arts. 91, 92), leaves some work for the parliament rather than itself adopting the implementing laws; decision on the constitutionality of international agreements (Art. 54); and tendering advice to the president on the use of his emergency powers (Art. 16).

[13] The Conseil d'État, to the extent that it is competent to judge the validity of this type of ordinance, would interfere through its *judicial sections* only within the framework of regular administrative-law proceedings—in most cases a number of years after the ordinance in question has become effective. Its *administrative sections* only tender advice *in camera* before the government issues the rules in question.

ascendancy of the administrative personnel over the political professional. It is imbued with the fear that the political professional could
interfere with the decisions of the executive. Consequently the safeguards have all been constructed in a lopsided way. If one excepts the
heavy and traditionally little-used ammunition of impeachment before
a parliamentary high court, establishing an exclusively criminal responsibility of president and ministers, the document spends its greatest
effort in assuring a chastised and domesticated National Assembly. The
idea—probably much more pertinent under the new scheme of things
—of establishing guarantees that the higher bureaucracy and army
leadership and their semipolitical superiors, the president and the
council of ministers, will not stray from the path of constitutional
rectitude seems not to have occupied the attention of the constitutional
draftsmen. They are content to leave guarantees of the personal liberties of the citizens—now more and more deformed by a growing body
of loosely worded emergency legislation [14]—in the hands of a judiciary
ill equipped for such tasks.

In conformity with the spirit of the document any trace of parliamentary participation in judicial appointments has vanished. Appointment, and through it influence on professional discipline, rests on a
mixture of professional cooptation and selection by the president, for
that purpose styled guarantor of judicial independence. He also becomes final dispenser of pardons, not an unimportant function in circumstances where there is an increasing shift to military tribunals,
inroads into the immovability of Algerian judges, and a rash of police
brutality, not to speak of the independent repressive function that the
military are now exercising as a matter of course in Algeria, commissions of inquiry notwithstanding.

IV

The framers of the constitution were fully aware that an administrative system holding the reins of government—even if it was temporarily shored up by the authority of a recognized national hero, who

[14] The most recent example is a decree of October 8, 1958, allowing administrative internment of any person who has given direct or indirect material aid to
the Algerian rebels. The duration of the internment, if ordered by the Minister
of the Interior, is unlimited, subject only to verification through written proceedings by a mixed administrative and judicial commission.

was more than a synthetic product of the opinion factories but an intellectual and moral power in his own right—would furnish at best a stopgap device. Political currents, even though "purified," should be allowed and encouraged to circulate, and not be sacrificed to the motions and countermotions of administrative and interest blocs. This consideration entailed not only the institution of a chastised National Assembly, but as a logical consequence—and probably more important —the continuation of the troublesome, confused process from which the assembly would draw its legitimacy: the parties and their participation in the electoral process.

The constitution's section on sovereignty recognizes this necessity by stipulating the free formation and activity of parties. Yet at the same time some possibility of administrative tutelage is discreetly referred to, in the part self-evident, part Pandora-box-like formula that "parties must respect principles of national sovereignty and democracy." The final formula was a battleground of conflicting expectations, projections, and fears in the constitutional committee, which inserted the phrase in the original draft, and the Conseil d'État, which took umbrage at its indefiniteness. Inserted without a mandate to implement it by organic law (as provided in the constitutional committee's version), it leaves the door wide open to a variety of governmental policies. For the moment the government's intentions as to its most noisy adversaries, the Communist opposition of principle, are clear: to decimate it, through the time-honored method of electoral reform rather than through an open ban.

The government did not see fit to follow the demands of the constitutional committee to include arrangements for the immediately forthcoming elections in the pattern of confirmation by popular consultation. Electoral ordinances passed in the beginning of October rested on specific governmental powers to that effect inserted in Article 91 of the constitution. At the same time, de Gaulle withheld his endorsement from any of the new groups, whether transmuted or newly formed—like the UNR (Union pour la Nouvelle République) —that were eager not only to demonstrate their loyalty to the General but to obtain a semiofficial approval as their most valuable election capital. Thus the General, reinforcing the policy already followed in the choice of the *modus* of presidential election, gave another pledge that so far as it was in his power he would avoid the first steps toward a transformation into a totalitarian system through the agency of a semi-official mass party.

In France, as anywhere else, election systems have been adopted with little regard for theoreticians' calculations concerning their likely contribution to the most efficient functioning of the polity or, conversely, their correspondence to the ideal of attaining photographic faithfulness to diversified opinions. They have been and continue to be determined by practical calculations of expected benefits or loss for those who have been given the opportunity to frame them.[15] In 1945 the General opted for a modified form of proportional representation, likely to produce, in the situation at that time, a small number of well-organized and disciplined parties but also avoiding the threat inherent in the application of a plurality system—that slight margins for one party, possibly the Communist party, would bring it in sight of the absolute majority. In 1958 he opted for 465 metropolitan single-member constituencies, with a runoff ballot decided by plurality if none of the competitors received a straight majority on the first ballot.

An alternative proposal, propounded in the cabinet discussions, would have equally jettisoned proportional schemes but would have provided for larger districts, with a possibility that in the run-off election the parties could combine lists and, with majorities thus assured, snap up all the seats. Either system would do irreparable damage to the Communists, but adoption of the alternative proposal would assuredly have given a decisive advantage to the right; the latter is much better equipped to enter into election combinations than the left, which is inveterately split into its isolated Communist and its moderately left components. At the least the alternative proposal would from the out-

15 The French have even been so unorthodox as to adopt, as a matter of pure electoral advantage, different election procedures not only in overseas districts, where wide differences in conditions might be a justification, but also in the various metropolitan districts themselves. From 1951 a system of proportional representation, resting on the highest average, was generally used on the departmental level, but the largest-remainder principle, more favorable to small groups, was introduced for the Paris region as an anti-Communist device. For the April, 1959, senate elections different election systems for the average district and for the urban agglomerations have been generally introduced, a patent violation of the principle of equality before the law, but looked upon in France as a normal incident of the political game. French election systems are discussed in detail in Peter Campbell, *French Electoral Systems and Elections, 1789–1957* (London, 1958).

set have brought the new groupings, claiming a Gaullist ancestry or linkage, into too intimate a relationship to the classical right, narrowing down their all-important freedom of maneuvering in the new assembly. To save the "constitutional" left from extinction and to avoid a replica of Louis XVIII's *chambre introuvable* or a 1919-type *chambre "bleu horizon"*—which would narrow down the government's freedom of action, especially in the controversial field of Algerian policies—an integral return to the last election system of the Third Republic seemed indicated.[16]

Population shifts since 1936, the last time elections were held under a system comparable to the present one, and the reduction of metropolitan membership in the assembly from 544 to 465 made complete reapportionment necessary. Some phases of the redistricting may have been due to a desire to mitigate the effect of unavoidable losses in representation for predominantly rural departments; some very few actions may conceivably be explained as an act of reverence to one or another outstanding political figure; but in the main the gerrymandering was clearly directed toward minimizing the electoral power of the potential Communist clientele. While the average electoral district was supposed to be calculated on a basis of 93,000 inhabitants, quite a number were created that held 10,000 to 20,000 people, more or less, and were carved out in such a way that the disadvantage from the viewpoint of electoral weight would lie mostly in heavily populated working-class districts. Moreover, the often necessary cutting up of large urban agglomerations into several electoral districts was more often than not handled in such a way as to join their separated halves or thirds to suburban or rural areas, in order to dilute the effect of a potential Communist electoral clientele on the outcome of the contest.

The constitution's provision in regard to the overseas areas marks in one respect a definite new departure. The possibility for a member state to leave the "community," as the form of association of France

---

[16] Deviations from the pattern of the Third Republic concern mainly a requirement that each candidate choose a substitute to appear with him on the ballot, thus avoiding the necessity of a by-election if the elected member dies or is elevated to ministerial rank (though not in the case of resignation); a prohibition of the nomination of new candidates between the first and the second ballot; and introduction of a deposit of 100,000 francs for each candidate, to be forfeited if the candidate does not reach 5 per cent of the total.

with the overseas areas is called, is definitely envisaged and—as the case of Guinea shows—is accepted as one way of regulating France's relations with these areas. Every territory is more or less supposed to avail itself of the new possibility of transforming into an autonomous state. For those willing to remain in the community, and for which France will continue to foot part of the bill, the constitutionally acknowledged autonomy remains inevitably restricted—in spite of the French practice of hiding continuing French hegemony behind a plethora of community organs—to certain areas of self-administration: schools, police, and the like, with major defense, economic, and foreign-policy decisions resting with the community, that is, until further notice, under metropolitan jurisdiction.

The question, fundamental for the development of the regions south of the Sahara, whether territories will be allowed to form federations of their own—thus acquiring a chance to deal with the metropolitan administration on some more realistic basis of equality, rather than being submitted to the continuation of the divide-and-rule policy of the past—is at best very vaguely alluded to (Art. 82, 2). The document is understandably silent on Algiers, though according to its inherent logic the permissive provision for secession—on the basis of a regional legislative decision confirmed by regional referendum—would apply equally in this case. Article 88 alludes to association agreements that any state may enter into with the community in order to develop its own institutions—a conveniently vague formula that may one day cover whatever agreements France will be able to reach with the whole Maghrib political complex.

With the region south of the Sahara tied to France only in a much looser form, and with the fate of Algiers still to be decided on the actual battlefields of North Africa and the political battlefields of metropolitan France, the October election ordinances had to determine the participation of these regions in the metropolitan parliament. When conversion of the territories south of the Sahara to autonomous states is achieved, their participation in the metropolitan assemblies will terminate. This event will deprive the government of some 30 to 40 votes usually available to any government.[17] But it will also deprive

[17] For the influence of native politicians on the early parliaments of the Fourth Republic, see Otto Kirchheimer, *A Constitution for the Fourth Republic* (Washington, D.C., 1947), p. 70.

the native African politicians of their most effective means of wringing concessions from the French government for their respective areas.

Unfortunately—from the viewpoint of the democratic composition and likely career of the new assembly—the Algerian contingent has been increased from 30 to 67 deputies, plus 4 from the Sahara.[18] Of these 67 seats, 46 were reserved for indigenous deputies, under the assumption that bona fide Algerians would come forward, independent of the French administration and possibly even acceptable to the Algerian nationalists; 21 seats, based on a disproportionately favorable ratio of 48,000 inhabitants to one deputy, were reserved for the French population. Since no independent Algerian candidates were forthcoming, the various rightist sections among the French—having effectively shut out the voice of the dissident French element in Algeria—will not only fill the disproportionately large number of their own seats but also dispose of the votes of their 46 *béni-oui-oui* retainers.

V

In the propaganda battle concerning the popular ratification of the constitution, the contents and merits of the document soon became obliterated by more immediate and more pressing issues. The vote had a different meaning for the population of metropolitan France from its implication for the overseas voters. For the African elite south of the Sahara, guiding the votes of their largely illiterate brethren, the question reduced itself to judging the advantages of a continued stay in the new community, including as it did the guaranteed right of secession. For the French population of Algeria the question boiled down to how best to minimize the concessions that had to be made to keep the General, and with him metropolitan France, to the policy of continued French predominance in Algeria. For the population of metropolitan France acclamation of the constitution or the entering of a dissenting vote embraced a range of contradictory evaluations: were the General and his constitution to be upheld as liquidating the whole system of traditional democratic institutions, or as stabilizing and guaranteeing them;

---

[18] The representation of those overseas areas that continue their status as French *départements*, mainly the West Indies, has not been changed, continuing at the 1946 figure of 10.

as the rallying point of the French national mission in Africa, or as harbinger of early negotiation and peace with the Algerian nationalists?
Moreover, what was the character of the vote that the Frenchman
was asked to cast? Was it a plebiscite, as so many insisted? Or did it
have the character of a referendum, as officially maintained? The distinguishing marks between the two seem to concern less the subject
matter than the area of choice. A referendum, taking place within an
established constitutional order, proposes some modification of existing
patterns.[19] A plebiscite usually wraps two propositions into one package; whatever the trappings of its official wording, it asks for confirmation of already executed changes, even though these changes may form
the necessary precondition for future blueprints equally referred to in
the plebiscite. The referendum, if rejected, puts no obstacles in the
way of a continuation of the old order; at worst, if the subject is
pressing, the rejection may engender a new referendum, most likely on
the basis of a somewhat readjusted formula. A plebiscite, taking its
point of departure from an already effected change, excludes a return
to a status quo ante; the voter, whatever his intentions, cannot recap-
ture what has ceased to exist. The Fourth Republic had died when the
major parliamentary organizations yielded their power to de Gaulle
without more than minor public stirring, and under a high degree of
public apathy mingled with almost universal relief over the solution,
albeit temporary, that his assumption of power provided for number-
less difficulties.

In these circumstances the acceptance of the September, 1958, constitutional plebiscite was a foregone conclusion. If the foes of the new
constitution spoke of a constitutional convention in case the plebiscite
failed, they did so with tongue in cheek, in order to beat the argument
that refusal of the General's constitution would be tantamount to invit-
ing chaos. What mattered was only the likely size of the majority.
Most of the commentators knowledgeable in French political ways
were convinced that in any case the constitution, in the form it had
been drawn up, would not survive for too long, containing as it does
too many glaring shortcomings and too many provisions cut so obviously to the measure of one man. Hence recommendations to approve

[19] For a different interpretation of the concept see Karl Löwenstein, *Political
Power and the Governmental Process* (Chicago, 1957), p. 267; but see Carl
Schmitt, *Verfassungslehre* (Munich, 1928), p. 86.

or disapprove rested less on the evaluation of the document itself than on its usefulness for ending the existent impasse without prejudice to the future of constitutional government.

What would better serve the latter purpose: a massive vote of confidence for de Gaulle's constitution, confirming the General as a completely unfettered spokesman of the nation as a whole; or a sizable block of opposing votes, holding the General strictly to his mission as umpire and preventing him from being annexed by some right-wing faction? Under the guise of voting for or against the General's constitution the next battle was being prepared, the battle over the composition of the parliament and over the personnel invited to form the members of the new *équipe*. While the majority factions in all major political parties—Communists excepted—recommended adoption, the unions either remained mute or, like the CGT, were openly hostile. On the other hand, the Catholic bishops, though they still disliked the traditional evocation of the lay character of the Republic in the preamble, were fully mollified by the preamble's *petite phrase assurante* that "the Republic shall respect all beliefs," and acted vigorously to implant their favorable disposition on their flocks.

	September 28, 1958	*October 13, 1946*
Affirmative votes, in number	17,666,828	9,002,287
Affirmative votes, in % of total valid votes	79.2%	53.6%
Negative votes, in number	4,624,475	7,790,856
Negative votes, in % of total valid votes	20.7%	46.4%
Abstentions, in number	4,011,245	7,775,893
Abstentions, in % of eligible voters	15.1%	31.2%

The voting results (for metropolitan France, and not including invalid votes) are shown in the accompanying figures, along with the results of the October, 1946, constitutional referendum.[20] To explain

[20] The overseas figures are here omitted because they reflect quite different conditions. Those for the area south of the Sahara do not relate to the same objectives. And the huge affirmative Arab vote in Algeria attests to the administrative efficiency of the French army, an important consideration in many respects but not exactly germane to the issue of voting as commonly understood in the Western world. As regards the voting on October 13, 1946, it should be mentioned that this was a referendum and not a plebiscite. The voting took place in the framework of an operating, commonly agreed-upon provisional constitutional organization, some points of which had been settled on October 21, 1945, by an

the size of the metropolitan majority by the degree of official pressure would be deceptive. To be sure, the transfer of Soustelle to the Ministry of Information gave the signal for a massive policy of official propaganda, with the five-minute broadcasting time granted to every political organization that took part in the campaign constituting nothing but sheer window-dressing. Moreover, it is more than likely that the climate produced by the Algerian terrorist acts in metropolitan France, and their exploitation by Soustelle for the purpose of gratuitously linking the Communist party—main organized mainstay of the antiplebiscite campaign—with the Algerian terrorists, may have had something to do with the size of the majority. But official pressure is only a very partial explanation, which misses the many broader and partly contradictory motivations that produced the result.

The plebiscite took place at the moment new political ground had just been broken, yet before the effect of recently initiated policies and future plans could be projected with any degree of probability. Its backers profited from the general willingness to accept the *fait accompli*, to the extent that it was not clearly in conflict with established interests—and the General and his entourage had striven manfully and successfully to avoid any such impression. On the one hand, acceptance corresponded to the rule of minimum engagement, whereas vigorous dissent would have created new and unforeseeable complications. On the other hand, assent gave every Frenchman, at a trying period in national affairs, an opportunity eagerly coveted by so many who had turned with disgust from the political scene: to perform an act of faith and identify themselves with the plans drawn up in the name of the national leader.

VI

While the constitution's adoption by a massive majority indicated a relieved or possibly reluctant acceptance of a *fait accompli*, the figures on participation in the election of a new National Assembly, held two

---

overwhelmingly affirmative referendum (96.4 per cent as against 3.6 per cent negative votes, with 20.2 per cent abstentions). The constitution voted on in October, 1946, represented a modification of a text that had been rejected by a majority of over 1 million voters in a referendum of May 5, 1946. In the October referendum of that year, General de Gaulle was the leader of a sizable and vocal opposition to the constitutional project.

months later, show a somewhat smaller degree of willingness to convert an act of passive consent into an active expression of political preference. The voting figures for the first ballot, on November 23, 1958, are presented in the accompanying tabulation, along with the seat allocation as determined by the November 30 runoff ballot and the comparable figures for 1956 and 1951. The 22.9 abstention percentage on November 23, representing over 6.7 million eligible voters, marks a new high in postwar parliamentary elections. Did these citizens who preferred to stay at home think that the adoption of the new setup had made a further civic effort unnecessary?

NATIONAL ASSEMBLY ELECTIONS AND SEAT ALLOCATION, 1958, 1956, 1951 [a]

	1958			1956			1951		
	elig. voters 27.2			elig. voters 26.8			elig. voters 24.5		
	votes cast 20.5			votes cast 21.5			votes cast 19.1		
	abstentions 22.9%			abstentions 17.3%			abstentions 19.8%		
	11/23		11/30						
	votes cast		*seats*	*votes cast*		*seats*	*votes cast*		*seats*
Parties	*no.*	*%*	*won*	*no.*	*%*	*won*	*no.*	*%*	*won*
Communists	3.9	18.9	10	5.5	25.7	145	5.1	25.4	97
Socialists	3.2	15.5	40	3.2	14.8	88	2.7	14.3	94
Misc. left-wing groups	.3	1.4	2	.4	2.0	4	.04	.2	
Rad. Soc. & center groups	2.3	11.5	35	2.9	13.3	71	1.9	9.8	77
Gaullists (UNR 1958)	3.6	17.6	188	.9	4.4	16	4.1	21.5	107
MRP	2.4	11.6	57	2.4	11.0	71	2.4	12.3	82
Conservatives	4.1	19.9	132	3.1	14.3	94	2.7	13.5	87
Extreme right (incl. Poujadists)	.7	3.3	1	2.8	13.1	55			
Miscellaneous				.05	.2		.09	.5	

[a] The figures pertain only to metropolitan France, and those for voters and votes cast are expressed in millions. Data on 1958 votes are from *Le Monde*, November 24, 1958. For 1956 and 1951 votes the component items do not include invalid votes, and hence the percentages add to slightly less than 100. The number of eligible voters on November 23, 1958, was 633,027 higher than it was for the plebiscite on September 28. It is likely that a good part of this discrepancy can be explained as reflecting a transfer of the votes of military personnel serving in Algiers to the voters' metropolitan domiciles, as provided for in the October electoral ordinances. From the viewpoint of the military authorities these votes could be more "useful" on the home front than in Algiers, where the electoral situation was anyhow well under control.

It is clear that the Communist party experienced a sharp drop in strength. This was the first time since the liberation that a sizable block of voters cut loose from Communist electoral allegiance—doubtless because of the cumulative effect of the Hungarian revolt, Communist impotence in face of the scuttling of the Fourth Republic, and the revival of strong nationalism.

In November, 1958, the convergence of reviving nationalism and the active reappearance of de Gaulle on the political scene proved to be again—as it was in 1951—a quasi-automatic electoral rallying point, even without the benefit of the General's endorsement. The 3.6 million voters of the Union pour la Nouvelle République came from many directions. Almost a million Gaullist holdouts from the 1951 enterprise were joined by probably half a million voters from the left center and by probably around three quarters of a million of 1956 Communist adherents who had voted affirmatively in the plebiscite. (It is likely that another three quarters of a million Communist voters assented to the constitution but abstained on November 23, preferring not to go any farther in their contact with the national political establishment.)

The rest of the story reflects the regrouping of right-wing voters. Four fifths of Poujade's clientele dispersed as quickly as it had gathered in 1956. Probably half of it went to the UNR, with another million returning to traditional Conservative politics, giving Conservative politicians, who more often than not were running under a variety of purely local labels, their biggest postwar electoral triumph. On November 23 the strength of two electoral groupings—the Socialists and the MRP—was scarcely affected by the new trends. A week later, however, these were to pay their tribute to the new rightist trend in a different, though not less effective, form: through the decimation they suffered at the November 30 ballot, and in the state of mind of a goodly number of their representatives.

What made this motley crowd of voters, coming from the most variegated social strata and, as in 1951, counting among their numbers many workers and white-collar people, move under this hastily put up electoral roof, which was scarcely adequately scaffolded when the voting began? What made them favor an organization created to give an attractive political coat of arms to old-line local and national politicians, intent on refurbishing their shingles, to new hopefuls, and to some of the officers who had recently developed an active interest in politics? The vote expressed a mood, a receptive reaction to the recent constellation of forces. It gave vent to the joy of being able, at long last, to join the winning side, rather than remaining on the protest van, as in previous sojourns in the Communist and Poujadist outer confines of the political spectrum. Many voters, having recently been successfully mobilized for the plebiscite campaign, acquired, as it were, a vested interest in the personages of the campaign, and—more persevering and perhaps more sanguine in regard to things to come than those who dropped out after the plebiscite—decided to see the business through. Many availed themselves of the possibility, opened up by the new election law, of penalizing those old-time "notables" who had had the temerity to campaign against the plebiscite.

The second ballot, of November 30, 1958, which was needed for a runoff decision in 426 out of 465 constituencies, made a shambles out of the attempt to create an election system that would have the effect of decimating Communist representation and at the same time giving the constitutional left a chance to continue as an effective political force. The classical right and Soustelle's forces were able to exploit to the hilt the tactical advantage of a hopelessly split left. The Socialists, under the leadership of Guy Mollet, the main architect of the Fourth Republic's defeat, were let in on a few deals here and there, especially if it helped to beat a Communist, but they went down to almost as stunning a defeat as the isolated troops of the Communist party.[21]

It would be erroneous to assume, however, that the election as a whole revealed an overwhelming change of sentiment among the people who bothered to take part in the two ballots. The political lineup was changed by a small percentage of the voters, helped along by the scrapping of the previous election system. The change was much too decisive either for the good of the country or for the working of the new constitution, resting as it does on the now forlorn assumption that the president's authority can effect an arbitrage between political

---

[21] Communist withdrawals from the second ballot occurred in only 30-odd electoral districts. In most cases they took place in order to favor candidates—dissident Socialists and Mendès-type radicals—who had openly come out against the plebiscite. More often than not they failed to swing the balance to the candidate in whose favor the Communist had withdrawn.

groups that, if not equally balanced, are at least not so far out of balance that a knockout is a foregone conclusion.

In 1936, the last time elections were held under the system now adopted, a 3.1 per cent shift from the right to the left (as compared with 1932), accompanied by a rash of electoral alliances in which the Communist party participated, produced a shift of 6.5 per cent in favor of the victorious *Front Populaire*. Between 1956 and 1958 an 8.5 per cent shift toward the right and a change of the electoral system produced a 40.7 per cent increase in right-wing representation.[22] The brunt of the losses was borne by the Communists, who in the second ballot were scarcely able to register any withdrawals of candidates in their favor. Hitherto the most unfavorable ratio between the original intention of Communist voters and the final result reached in a second ballot, prevailing in 1928, had shown 11.4 per cent Communist votes cast as against 2.4 per cent of the seats obtained. The 1958 Communist ratio was 18.9 per cent of the votes as against 2.2 per cent of the seats.

Of course an election system able to produce such disproportion between the final outcome and the original intentions of a large section of the voters is bound to raise a serious question. The single-member district system, whether practiced on the basis of a single ballot, or, in a more pronounced form, on the basis of a second ballot if no majority is reached on the first, has different meanings according to the individual circumstances of the society in which it occurs. It may adequately serve a homogeneous society, to whose members an election is not only an opportunity to indicate a preference for one viewpoint over another but also, and emphatically, a chance to confirm their partnership in a universally upheld consensus. The system puts a premium on the competitors' narrowing down their range of differences in order to be in a better position to compete effectively for the allegiance of broad voter strata. Conversely, the voter whose preferred candidate has lost out will not be unnecessarily disturbed, knowing that the victorious candidate will try, for the sake of his own reelection, to stay as closely as circumstances will allow to the middle range of opinions and preferences. But if existing conflict situations in a given society are both so

22 For the purposes of this calculation the MRP has been counted with the right, but since the votes cast for this group have remained very stable the point is of minor consequence. Of its 57 members in the new assembly, 14 who ran on a "Démocratie chrétienne" ticket should definitely be counted with the right.

strong and so persistent over a considerable period of time that vicarious representation of every voter by the finally elected representative becomes a fiction, representation will scarcely exercise an integrative function, and will, instead, become a more or less naked form of political domination of one group over another.

Thus the fact that the presently adopted French election system pulverizes the effect of Communist votes, rather than treating a sizable Communist representation after the fashion of the Fourth Republic by the method of political quarantine, is in itself of little probative value one way or another. Manipulation of election systems does not eliminate major cleavages in the body politic. What matters is whether France's new political management will be able to use its present political respite to absorb enough Communist voters and recent abstentionists into the national community to be able and willing to face the voters' verdict again with equanimity, thus continuing the voters' interest in the democratic electoral process; or whether it will use the advantage gained by some slight shift in popular attitudes, and the much larger advantage gained by the artifice of a voting system, to switch to elections that connote the abolition of any political risk.

The apparent incoherence of the new political nucleus—consisting of 188 metropolitan UNR deputies operating within the framework of a drastically changed assembly, only about one third of which is old-timers—defies any prognosis. It is only just to remark that the inconspicuous record of its 1951 predecessor, the Gaullist Rassemblement du Peuple Français, has little bearing on the destiny of the present party, operating, as it does, in a quite different set of circumstances. Power solidifies ranks and may even produce some meaningful idea about what to do with it, beyond the self-evident job of hanging on to it. Yet, the juxtaposition of a ravaged parliament with an executive power in the hands of a technocratic leadership leaves the course of the party open to many uncertainties. Will it become a conservative, people's party type of electioneering organization, resting on a nice balance of apathy and consent, so evident in the happy fortunes of Mr. Adenauer's party; or will the task of reintegrating the straying sheep and propping up the present leadership cadres produce a more militant type of political organization, potentially as dangerous to those who might create it as to those who are bound to be its immediate victims?

VII

How does the new constitutional formula face up to the problems and practical necessities of French politics? The constitutional model visualizes executive power heavily determined by the highest administrative echelons, in some fashion absorbing into their ranks selected political leaders able to transmit to the administration the impulses emanating from the electorate and protecting the establishment in its skirmishes with a tamed assembly. As a going concern the model leans on the chief executive's ability to arbitrate among discordant administrative and interest groups, as well as on his skill in dealing with the partly devastated but by no means replaced political substructure. Inasmuch as the armed forces raise a far-reaching claim to possessing an independent appreciation of the national interest, their acceptance of the president's arbitrage has so far been only conditional. At least as long as the Algiers conflict lasts, it may well be that the much vituperated former system of parliamentary sovereignty—if compared with the nuances of approval now governing the actual relations between the armed-forces cadres and the rest of the executive establishment, including its presumed arbiter, the president—will come to look like a rather simple and clear-cut arrangement.[23]

The constitutional model is construed from the viewpoint of administrative efficiency rather than from a careful consideration of the supporting political structure. Amounting to a sort of running polemics against its predecessor, it puts a premium on the untrammeled course and the largest possible field of action for the administrative cadres. But in doing so it shows little comprehension of the need to construct

---

[23] In his recent rather highly stylized utterances, General Ely, chief of staff of the armed forces, approaches this burning problem by indirection. He insists that the present enlarged role of the armed forces intermeshes with necessities derived from world-wide developments. According to his opinion, the country at large has been able to conform with the tides of the time only on the economic front, but the armed forces, serving France in the four corners of the world, have kept in step with the rhythm of our time. Such considerations both justify and set the tone for somewhat conditional loyalty relations beween the cadres of the armed forces and the civil government. In an attitude of profound respect for "véritable légalité"—whatever that may mean—loyalty goes to "a strong government that knows how to command." Ely does not elaborate on the criteria of the conditional loyalty presumably granted by the army cadres on the basis of their exalted spiritual vocation and their superior knowledge of world conditions. See Paul Ely, "L'armée et la nation," *Revue Militaire d'Information*, September, 1958.

an adequate frame for the relations between the administration and the necessary supporting cast, the political substructure. In spending part of its energy on keeping the National Assembly in a subordinate role, it largely fights against windmills, because in France, as everywhere else, the legislature—constitutional provisions notwithstanding—has ceased to be a decisive factor in political life, having yielded many of its functions to the administration and the political parties. Yet, it still has the job of serving as a conduit between the administration and the political process. The new constitution, unable to establish a clear-cut relationship between the administration and the political process, confuses the role of the first and leaves the second empty-handed.

Neither the role of the president nor that of the prime minister is so construed as to fulfill the requirement that political leadership relate the political process to the administration. The president is conceived as a hybrid, both supreme arbitrator and administrative chief; he is bound to lose on both levels, for no man can maintain both the universal confidence needed for the first task and the driving energy demanded by the second. The prime minister is left in limbo. Half servant of the president, half go-between for president and parliament, he is artificially severed from the task of political leadership, which is to form majorities and keep them in being. Thus the constitution ends up by entrusting neither of them with the job of political leadership: the one is kept from it by the definition of his role, the power he holds in reserve for the maintenance of national unity; the other by his lack of independent political status.

It may well happen that a prime minister will emerge who enjoys the confidence of a working majority, even if it is, as at present, unrepresentative. But if he tries to exercise decisive authority he will sooner or later come up against the necessity of making mincemeat of the president's powers, reducing him to the size of a Fallières or a Lebrun. Or the president—trustee of the nation as a whole—in order to save the original constitutional establishment from an unrepresentative majority, might brandish the weapons the constitution has forged for him: presidential emergency measures and dissolution of the assembly after one year's existence.

Whatever the immediate consequences of either possibility, little would remain of the present edifice. A prime minister victorious over the president would find it necessary, if he wanted to stay within the democratic framework, to build a political party strong enough to supervise the administration, a job for which the parliamentary establishment as now set up gives at best a very imperfect starting point. A victorious president, a somewhat less likely hypothesis, would have to not only regularize his position by scrapping the anachronistic presidential electoral system but also cast about for more permanent popular support in order to build up his own political machine. Either way the constitutional job would have to be thoroughly redone. Would there be time?

PARTY STRUCTURE AND

MASS DEMOCRACY IN EUROPE

I

In Germany the intensive study of political parties was blighted for a long time by the romantic approach. Parties were considered disturbing factors interfering in the relations of mutual trust between government and people. Even Heinrich Triepel, who in 1928 made the study of political parties a respectable enterprise, was not free from this prejudice. While recognizing them as components of contemporary public life, he nevertheless unabashedly anticipated a future when their activities would be replaced by more organic structures.[1] This changed only during the period after World War II, when a more rational point of view replaced the romantic approach. The tendency to confront the state with the parties as one among many kinds of pluralistic structures, thereby assigning to them a low rank in the order of legitimacy,[2] gave way to the recognition that their special task of political structuring sets them apart sharply from the variety of other social organizations.[3] At the same time the difference was worked out

Translation of "Parteienstruktur und Massendemokratie," printed with permission of J. C. Mohr (Paul Siebeck), Tübingen; originally published in *Archiv des öffentlichen Rechts*, LXXIX (1954), 301–25.

[1] Cf. the conclusions in Triepel, *Die Staatsverfassung und die politischen Parteien* (Berlin, 1928), p. 36.

[2] Werner Weber, *Spannungen und Kräfte im westdeutschen Verfassungssystem* (Stuttgart, 1951), pp. 39 ff.

[3] Otto von der Gablentz, *Politische Parteien als Ausdruck gesellschaftlicher Kräfte* (Berlin, 1952), p. 25; Grewe, "Zum Begriff der politischen Partei," in *Festschrift für E. Kaufmann* (1950), pp. 69, 80.

between the old-fashioned liberal parliamentary party [4] and the modern democratic mass parties that tend to bypass parliament. Leibholz especially emphasized this distinction.[5]

Undoubtedly, the face of the modern parties is shaped more and more by universal suffrage and the related necessity to reach as many voters as possible by means of the latest technological developments—in the United States television plays an important role in political persuasion. The resulting forms of competition dominate the structure and the organizational principles of the parties. They compel them to resort to simplifications and to the identification of programs with typifying personalities suitable for public exposure. But the far-reaching uniformity of behavior on the part of the parties does not relieve us of the duty to examine and differentiate the several types of parties. In spite of transitions, overlappings, and many special cases, we will be able to get along with a somewhat schematic tripartite typology of modern parties.

Paradoxically, the first category does not belong to the democratic type of party; but its existence is nevertheless a characteristic feature of our present party structure. It is the totalitarian party and movement as it developed under National Socialism, Fascism, and Communism.[6] Its appearance has greatly influenced present-day party life in democratic systems. Many features of our present party activities—the increasingly emotional rather than rational appeal, the formation of a leadership apparatus not necessarily interwoven with the institution of parliament, and the emphasis on party indoctrination rather than on intraparty discussion—might have existed before embryonically. But

[4] The word "cadre-party," which has been used in this context (Maurice Duverger, *Les Partis politiques* [Paris, 1951], p. 84), has since acquired a quite different meaning in Communist practice: instead of loosely cooperating political elites it there designates subordinates trained for the pursuit of current party goals.

[5] Gerhard Leibholz, *Der Strukturwandel der modernen Demokratie* (Karlsruhe, 1952).

[6] For the purposes of this study the differences between National Socialism and Communism do not matter. They certainly do not amount to a qualitative difference with regard to the totalitarian element. In both cases the beneficial effect of elements taken over from former systems—as, e.g., the affirmation of individual welfare as the final goal in Communism or the conscious preservation of traditional economic institutions by National Socialism—is lost to a large extent, as a result of systematic political terror. Cf. the remarks of J. L. Talmon in *The Origins of Totalitarian Democracy* (London, 1952).

the modern totalitarian movements brought about a breakthrough of these features. Moveover, their influence is more than indirect; the totalitarian party exists illegally, semilegally, or legally in many countries. It deeply influences the party structure of those countries, either by its mere existence or by virtue of its quantitative impact.

Such intrusion of antagonistic political forces opposed to the existing constitutional order is not as extraordinary as it may seem at first glance. Already in the era of liberal parliamentarianism, more or less fundamental opponents of the existing regime frequently sat in parliament. The great question in such situations is always whether they can be absorbed; and the answer often sounds more skeptical today than it did before World War I. The same is true, *mutatis mutandis*, of the rupture of the national framework caused by the existence of such organizations. International cross-connections already existed during the period of the First International. Relations of particular groups and politicians with foreign powers were the perennial problem of the ancient Greek democracies. But changing foreign connections of local politicians and occasional exchanges of experiences as well as international programmatic announcements are one thing; the total administrative and political steering of a party from a policy center situated outside its national framework is another. As long as, e.g., Mosley's Fascist party in England or the Communist party in England, Switzerland, or Scandinavia remains relatively unimportant, it influences the political scene as a whole psychologically more than institutionally, in spite of the party's low rate of assimilability. Matters are different where such parties influence entire segments of the population politically and socially. This is the case in France and Italy where the possibility of absorbing the Communist party hardly exists and where the absorption of the Rassemblement Français and the Movimento Sociale Italiano is as yet a matter of doubt. The result is the well-known attempt by one side to undertake the conquest of political power positions with the help of the democratic process but without the corresponding readiness to abide by the rules of the democratic game. The other side reacts by attempting to eliminate such disturbing elements to the maximum extent possible within the limits imposed by the constitution. It is characteristic of democracy, however, that the elimination of a group's political influence goes hand in hand with a decreased concern for the social interests of the population strata represented by it. Hence grave functional disturbances and distortions, going far beyond the actual political orbit, result from the massive presence of totalitarian groups within the democratic system.

The *mass* democratic party in its various forms is probably nowadays the most widespread type. It tries to appeal to a maximum of voters in order with their help to take over the administration and sometimes, though not necessarily,[7] to carry into effect a definite program.[8] It proclaims its unconditional readiness to accept the judgment of the voters; the democratic mass party refuses to conclude alliances with those basically opposed to the democratic system for the sake of momentary advantages. Its chances for success seem to be the greater the larger the strata of the population to which it can appeal and—this is often overlooked—the less fear there is among the people that a change of government might topple the country's political and social institutions.[9] A maximally functioning democratic mass-party system therefore either presupposes a considerable and readily accepted homogeneity of the population thanks to modern industrial civilization (as in the United States), or depends on the readiness of the victor of the moment to respect, as an integral part of the national system, the

---

[7] The lack of binding programs of action is an often-criticized aspect of public life in the United States (cf., e.g., the report of the Committee on Political Parties of the American Political Science Association, "Toward a More Responsible Two-Party System," Supplement, *American Political Science Review*, September, 1950, p. 16). But in spite of all criticism it is still one of the basic aspects of American public life.

[8] M. Einaudi, in "Social Realities and the Studies of Political Parties" (lecture given at the meeting of the *Political Science Association*, in Washington, September 12, 1953), timidly attempts to characterize the mass party by the discipline demanded of its parliamentary representatives. Yet this would only be a criterion of the efficiency of such an organization. The author consequently returns toward the end of his lecture to the watershed of the beginning of the twentieth century as the essential mark of distinction beween old-fashioned parliamentary parties and the democratic mass party.

[9] Cf. the characteristic remarks of Carl Becker, *New Liberties for Old* (New Haven, 1941), pp. 106–107: "The party system works best when rival programs involve superficial aspects rather than fundamentals and majority rule works best when the minority can meet defeat at the polls in good temper because they need not regard the decision as a permanent or fatal surrender of their vital interests." For some differing views on this theme, see P. R. Nixon, "Freedom or Unity: A Problem in the Theory of Civil Liberty," *Political Quarterly*, LXVIII (1953), 70–88.

changes previously made by the defeated party.[10] In England the conservatives are presently denationalizing the steel and transport industries. The Labour party, however, declares that these acts will be reversed when it returns to power. The behavior of these two groups
merely demonstrates that they have quietly acknowledged the secondary role of nationalization; it has become a more or less harmless
football in the political game.[11] The less homogeneity there is and the
more traditional and social differentiations remain, the smaller the
chance of achieving a majority, and the stronger will be the leaning
toward particular interests. The latter, although they may not help to
achieve a majority, will help to gain a solid political power position and
will thereby curtail the elbowroom available to competing groups.
This is true of the relation between the moderate Socialist parties on
the one hand and the Christian parties on the other, in France, Belgium, the German Federal Republic, and Austria.

The relics of *older parliamentary parties* as well as of regionally or
socially *closely restricted* groups with varying degrees of importance
still exist on the periphery of this system of totalitarian and democratic
mass parties. And finally, in a few countries we find parties in a state of
transition between totalitarian and democratic systems—a threshold
that is hard to define at present. Their organizational basis and potential membership are too small to give them a chance to develop into
mass parties. Examples are, to a certain degree, the British Liberals of
the twenties and thirties and the resurrected French Radical Socialist
party, but also a party like the All-German Bloc with its limited program of particular interests. Two facts are worth mentioning in this
context. The chances of survival of such groups differ greatly, depending on the social structure of the country in question. This is true even
when a specific parliamentary situation places them in a key position
temporarily. Something else, however, is even more important: parliamentary groupings not affiliated with larger social organizations, as
well as parochial-interest groups entering politics directly, incur the
obvious danger of becoming the prey of totalitarian organizations. The

[10] Cf. R. Basset, "British Parliamentary Government Today," *Political Quarterly*,
1952, pp. 380, 387.

[11] Cf. the contributions of R. H. S. Crossman, C. A. R. Crosland, and R. Jenkins
in *New Fabian Essays* (New York, 1952) for changed attitudes with regard to
socialization priorities in the face of the dangers of a "managerial society."

latter promise them the satisfaction of their sectional interests not as an isolated operation depending on parliamentary chance but as an integral part of the over-all totalitarian ideology.

The fact that a party can be characterized as totalitarian or as a democratic mass party implies nothing as to the degree of its internal cohesion. There are some very badly integrated totalitarian groups, as is demonstrated at present by the Rassemblement,[12] and there are, on the other hand, very coherent mass parties, as, e.g., the Austrian Social Democrats, and vice versa. If we disregard American conditions,[13] under which the parties to a certain degree even today are primarily organisms dedicated to the purpose of winning the next election, the democratic mass party as well as the totalitarian one—in so far as it must work under democratic conditions—will combine two goals: on the one hand, they must strive to surround their paid functionaries as well as their more or less spontaneous active members with a sufficient number of passive sympathizers in order to organize a maximum of potential voters.[14] At the same time, they must guard against an unlimited expansion which might jeopardize their internal cohesion and political freedom of action.

The problem is most acute for the democratic mass party. Here two types of organization confront each other. On the one hand we have organizations—like most of the European Socialist parties[15]—whose

[12] It is questionable, to be sure, to what extent the Rassemblement du Peuple Français can be considered a totalitarian party and to what extent it has had Bonapartist-Boulangist traits since its inception. In this respect S. Hughes, "Gaullism," in *Modern France*, ed. Edward M. Earle (Princeton, 1951), p. 260, may have to be revised.

[13] According to the most recent interpretation of American party conditions— an interesting one—the dynamism of the U.S. party system is based upon dissensions within the majority party. Since both parties consist of agglomerations of the most variegated interests, the current majority party can only be defeated when it is no longer able to neutralize split-offs by winning the adherence of new groups (Samuel Lubell, *The Future of American Politics* [New York, 1952]). But one is tempted to talk about discontinuous continuity, because the new energies will again be balanced out in the never-ending game of group combinations.

[14] In a well-disciplined totalitarian mass party like the French Communist party, for every six active members there are four merely paying members. Cf. Alain Brayance, *Anatomie du Parti Communiste Français* (Paris, 1952), p. 207. The number of inactive members is still far greater in the democratic mass parties.

[15] With the exception of the French Socialist party. The transformation of the SFIO has often been described with regard to its spiritual attitude as well as

members are unified to a degree by the similarity of their dependent social position and by shared notions regarding future developments they intend to promote. It is true—and to this extent Carlo Schmid [16] is right—that one can hardly speak of a community of faith and *Weltanschauung*. This is not due to a changeover from a determinist view of history to an indeterminist one, as Schmid suggests; it is simply the result of the general devaluation of parties, which in postwar Europe has spread from the totalitarian parties to all others. Today the outsider as well as the party supporter considers the party as a functionally rational instrument for the realization of current group interests. But has the party organization been affected by its diminished status when it comes to intensity of human hopes and expectations?[17] At least as far as the Socialist mass party is concerned, such tendencies of dissolution have so far remained within rather narrow bounds.

The internal compromises that have to be made between, e.g., civil servants, employees, and workers within the Socialist parties cover a rather limited area of conflicting interests. This is the reason why most of the Socialist parties are still relatively homogeneous, even today. On the other hand, the typical Conservative or Christian party that is in need of mass membership is exposed to much greater tensions.[18] In the

---

to the strata represented by the party. The road from Marxism to democratic "humanism" is typically expressed in the personality and writings of Léon Blum who himself stood at the center of this transformation (cf. *A l'échelle humaine* [Paris, 1945]). For the best description of the social-political situation, see H. W. Ehrmann, "The Decline of the Socialist Party," in *Modern France*, pp. 181 ff. For the psychological-political function of the party within the French political order, cf. J. Fauvet, *Les Forces Politiques en France* (1951), pp. 66 ff.

[16] Carlo Schmid, "Die Sozialdemokratische Partei Deutschlands vor der geistigen Situation dieser Zeit" (lecture given at the Hamburg Party Meeting, 1950). This stimulating speech faithfully mirrors the present party situation in that it attempts to place party structure and party goals on a completely rational foundation. The observations of Karl Bednarik in *Der junge Arbeiter von heute—ein neuer Typ* (Stuttgart, 1953), p. 61, emphasize the predominance of purely rational elements in the party choice of the worker.

[17] For the devaluation of the parties, cf. R. E. Chartier, "Les Contradictions Internes des Groupements," *Revue Française des Sciences Politiques*, October-December, 1951, pp. 465, 474.

[18] This is especially the case where—as in Italy—the absorption of wide strata of the population by a revolutionary party transforms a Christian-Conservative mass party almost automatically into the principal organization able to handle economic and ideological conflicts democratically. See the pertinent remarks on this in the unpublished Cornell Univ. Ph.D. thesis by E. Tananbaum, "Christian Democracy in Italy" (1952), p. 150.

extreme case—for which we still cite Austria, in spite of sufficient parallels in other countries [19]—such a party consists of three socially as well as territorially differentiated parts. A numerically insignificant, yet socially important, industrial and commercial wing faces a numerically strong agricultural and relatively weaker workers' section.[20, 21] The Austrian case is especially expressive. On account of power conditions, more than by virtue of the role of individuals, compensatory prestige factors do not count as much in Austria as they do in Great Britain or Germany where leading conservative politicians [22] are dominant, especially in the field of foreign policy. This makes for greater need to reach a balanced compromise within the party than

[19] The conservative Belgian mass party of the twenties and thirties, the Union Catholique Belge, was composed of the "en bloc" membership of large peasant and middle-class groups. The Parti Social Chrétien, its successor, tried for a while to abandon this principle and to adopt that of individual membership. But this seems to have been an interim solution. The appeal to establish a middle-class Christian "Volksbund' (Handelsblad, Antwerp, June 6, 1953) announces as an inexorable necessity the return to the group organization within the party.

[20] Duverger, op. cit., pp. 22 ff., blurs the various social groups' significance for the organization of the conservative mass parties by defining the latter as parties with indirect party structure analogous to the Anglo-Saxon type of Labour party. There may be differences in political philosophy between individual members of the Labour party and the affiliated groups; yet the differences among the component groups of a conservative mass party (agrarian-industrial-crafts) are based on social and economic conflicts of interest. Cf. Georges E. Lavau, Partis Politiques et Réalités Sociales (Paris, 1953).

[21] The official doctrine of the Democrazia Cristiana, based on Article 91 of the party rules of 1949 ("organized party factions and wings within the party are prohibited"), differentiates sharply between admissible ideological shadings and tendencies with regard to specific problems and the inadmissible formation of corporative and professional groups. Cf. the remarks of Party Secretary Taviani, "Il Partito, compiti, struttura e funzionalita" (Relazione all' Assemblea nazionale organizzativa della Democrazia Christiana 6-9 Jennaio 1949); the same attitude in the official party reports of the 4th party congress of 1952 (Relazione della Direzione Centrale 1949-52, Atti e Documenti, pp. 68, 104). Thus the official rejection of intraparty proportionality for the filling of party positions; but the practice of job distributions absolutely recognizes the existence of different tendencies. In contrast to Austria, the various tendencies within the party are not fully identified with concrete interests, and personnel questions as well as differing interpretations of Christian social doctrine occupy a certain space at least in the voluminous periodical and pamphlet literature.

[22] For Italy, the identification of the party with the government led by the party leader and the use by the Prime Minister of the threat to resign as a means to consolidate his position with his own party is discussed by Tananbaum, op. cit., p. 165. J. M. Williams, "Storia e struttura del partito laborista" (in Occidente, Revista Bimestrale di Studi Politici 8, 1952, pp. 404, 415), has treated the same patterns for the British Labour party of the 1940s.

would be the case under conditions where the prestige of a statesman can at times overcome such difficulties. The totalitarian party avoids the necessity of intraparty compromise by rejecting or excluding political responsibility as well as by erecting ideological structures which are supposed to neutralize conflicting interests within its membership by holding out the hope for institutional changes. Moreover, the application of the hierarchical principle, the conscious emphasis on the charismatic character of the leadership—once it has been agreed upon —and the psychological experience of being the persecuted and the elect also help to produce the needed degree of internal cohesion.

What results for the functioning of parliament from the existence of such different types of parties?

On the one hand, we have the party type of the United States. The secondary role of the party organizations facilitates the continued existence of Congress as the organ of political decision, where decisions are made from case to case, often with changing majorities crossing party lines. Together with the system of the separation of powers, this leads to the well-known difficulties confronting the executive in trying to achieve a unified political leadership. If this system functions more or less in spite of the resulting inconveniences it is because of the above mentioned politico-social homogeneity of the country which protects those defeated in a particular election. They need not be afraid that the victors will crush them.

On the other side of the scale are Great Britain and the dominions following her system. Clear-cut election results between two democratic mass parties always in a position to form a responsible government push Parliament into a side role.[23] Since the voters make basic political decisions in a quasi-plebiscitary way the Parliament mainly serves two important yet secondary purposes. It operates as the medium through which continuous contact is maintained between the majority and the minority, which in Britain may be numerically stronger than the victorious party. Through Parliament the minority constantly participates in the legislative and political process, via the contact and information available to its top functionaries. The other purpose the system serves—and today this is of growing importance—

[23] On the decline of the political sovereignty of Parliament, see Lord Campion in *Parliament: A Survey* (New York, 1952), p. 24.

is to secure intraparty democracy and thereby the possibility of intra-party development within the framework of the democratic mass party. The more activity is required of the individual M.P.'s or groups within the parliamentary opposition, or—even more pronouncedly—within the government party, the more their position gains in impor-tance. The individual member is thus able to use the mere existence of the parliamentary forum and the opportunity to take a stand against the official party line in order to promote intraparty discussion [24] and to participate in the fight for the leading party positions. In this guar-antee of intraparty democracy lies the decisive significance today of the continued recognition by most democratic constitutions of the independence of the individual parliamentarian.

A different situation presents itself when the role of the parliament is limited by the weakness of a democratic mass party system as con-trasted with its optimal functioning in Great Britain. In France and Italy the democratic mass parties and certain others find themselves locked in a struggle for existence against the totalitarian parties. For this struggle they have armed themselves with electoral systems espe-cially devised for the situation. This may, on the one hand, help to avoid the return of the German situation of 1932, that is, the existence of a majority composed of totalitarian parties of the Right and Left paralyzing the country's political institutions. On the other hand, such emergency measures diminish the specific weight of parliament by damaging its representative character. They also allow very little com-petition between the existing nontotalitarian parties. Regardless of the official government and opposition labels, they give these parties the character of mandatory cartels. A loosening up of such a cartel would then only be possible to the degree to which the totalitarian parties are weakened and transformed, as is the case with the Rassemblement (RPF) in France.[25]

[24] Bevan's resignation from the British cabinet in the spring of 1951 and the controversies between the party leadership under Attlee and the "Bevanites" which continued through 1952 sharply illuminate the strategic role of the party minority within democratic mass parties; on an earlier case of breach of party discipline (1943) by Bevan and on the reasons why he was not expelled ("but to expel him would involve the 15 other MP's who had voted with him"), see Vincent Brome, *Aneurin Bevan* (London, 1953), pp. 153, 154.

[25] For the process of the transformation of Gaullism, see François Goguel-Nyegaard, *France under the Fourth Republic* (Ithaca, N.Y., 1952), p. 178.

There remain the countries with democratic mass parties none of which is strong enough to gain a clear majority. The German Federal Republic—until the summer of 1953—Austria, and Belgium belong in this category. It differs from the American party type by its relatively strong organizational cohesion; from the British as well as from the American type by the already mentioned multiplicity of parties and by the lack of mutual confidence between them which would be the basis for a successful party system. These countries do not suffer, however, from the additional complication which results in Italy and France from the competition and lack of elbowroom caused by totalitarian mass parties. On a theoretical level one might therefore argue that the coexistence of social democratic mass parties with less cohesive conservative parties would make possible alternating parliamentary majorities and would thus give a decisive role to parliament. In reality all parties concerned have done their utmost to eliminate such elements of insecurity by forming strong coalitions. (In some cases they were fortified, as in the Federal Republic until 1953, by the impregnable constitutional position of the head of government for the entire parliamentary term.) Such a coalition may amount to an almost mathematical ratio between the Socialists and the Conservatives, as in Austria, or to a coalition between a conservative mass party and the other bourgeois parties, as in the Federal Republic.

The extent to which such firm coalitions have become the rule is shown best by the borderline cases. During the coalition negotiations in Austria in 1953, both parties involved, the People's party and the Socialists, reserved the right to leave certain subject matters on which interparty agreement could not be reached to free parliamentary decision. Such decisions would have to be arrived at with the cooperation of the Independent party, that is, the third party of the country. These decisions, needless to say, could only concern problems which neither of the two parties considered truly important. The victory of a coalition partner on a decisive question in an open parliamentary contest would necessarily mean the end of the entire coalition.[26] On the whole

[26] Party agreements are probably the most important secondary source of present-day Austrian constitutional law. While leaving untouched the validity of the constitutional norms, they transform, *praeter legem*, the interplay of the constitutional organs, outside of as well as inside parliament. Since neither of the partners has published the agreements of 1949 or 1953, they have become

we may say that the smaller the basis of interparty confidence and the larger, within a conservative mass party, the circle of groups whose interests have to be balanced out, the less inclination there will be to leave important political decisions to parliamentary chance.

After the war there continued the shift of the center of gravity away from parliament—with the exception of the United States, whose case we do not analyze here. While during the twenties and thirties attention was focused mainly on the shift of power from the legislature to the executive, today we are concerned at least as much with the party aspects of this process. The chain of command between the political parties and the executive has become more direct. This is most clearly apparent in a two-party system with good party discipline. Yet the same tendencies can be observed in countries with coalitions of several mass parties as, e.g., in present-day Austria, frequently in Belgium and the Scandinavian countries, and especially in France during the tripartism of 1945–47.

The reasons for this shift of the center of gravity from parliament to the parties are complex: the narrowing of the parliamentary elbow-room by the continued existence of totalitarian parties; the fact that conservative mass parties mostly consist of heterogeneous elements and therefore cannot do without the unifying force of party discipline; and, finally, the fact that the Socialist parties are relatively closed associations of interests despite the attenuation of their doctrine. As another reason we may add the well-known phenomenon referred to as the transition from the legislative state to the administrative state. If under the conditions of the modern industrial state the parties intend to preserve their dominant influence on public affairs, they must, in addition to their share in the legislative process, keep the government

---

known only in so far as the parties themselves have referred to them in their discussions. The agreement of 1953 differs apparently from that of 1949 in that it does not include municipalities and provinces in the coalition scheme (*Neues Wiener Tageblatt*, March 4, 1953), and further by setting up the already mentioned "coalition-free area," i.e., the area of untrammeled parliamentary voting, albeit after prior agreement in each case between the coalition partners. Semi-official party communiqués confirm this interpretation. "The cooperation of the two coalition parties continues on the basis of an agreement, similar to the coalition agreement which has hitherto regulated their common enterprise. It contains the specification that the 'coalition-free areas' of parliamentary activity can only be designated by agreement between both parties" (*Arbeiterzeitung*, February 4, 1953, p. 1).

and the administration under tight control. This does not exclude important secondary functions for parliament. For Great Britain we have already described this process. In a country combining totalitarian and democratic elements, parliament may become one of the starting points for the relatively smooth transformation of a totalitarian into a conservative party. But this does not change the fact that in the public consciousness the party, on the one hand, and the government, on the other, have become the decisive institutions. Undoubtedly there exist countertendencies resulting from reactions to the overemphasis on the party in the totalitarian systems. The diminished prestige of all parties has possibly created a vacuum which, however, has not restored parliament to its former position. But the essence of democracy lies hardly in the changing relationship between executive and parliament, but rather in the continuing chance for the population to choose its government and, with the same measure of freedom, to replace it by a more suitable one. This, by the way, is the most decisive factor which for all the differences in the relationship of legislature to executive constitutes the unifying element between English and American institutions.

II

In the following pages we will try to sketch the consequences resulting from the structure of the present-day party system for three important problem areas: the question of the subjection of the deputy to the discipline of his parliamentary group; the relation between the parliamentary group and its national party; and, finally, the present system of party finance.

a. As far as the totalitarian parties are concerned, the effects of the new state of affairs on the representative's subjection to party discipline present no problems at all. From Maslov and Ruth Fischer to Karl Müller and Marty the choice was always between obedience or exclusion; the change in the last twenty-five years consisted only in the increasing crudeness of the pressures that were applied. In a mass democracy, the parliamentary party is the individual representative's primary vehicle for exercising his political influence. It enables him not only to voice his opinion publicly, loudly, and clearly, assuming he has something significant to say—the modern state has more and better opportunities for that—but also to make his opinion politically effective. At the same time the constitutional norms enable the representative to vote contrary to the decisions of his parliamentary party. Cases of this kind are not too frequent because such behavior diminishes the representative's influence within his party group and practically precludes his reelection; in many cases it even destroys his ability to make a living.[27] But the mere ability to protest openly against the party line and to form a minority group makes, as we saw, for a strengthening of

[27] On the relationship of Art. 21 to Art. 38, § 1 of the Basic Law, see among many others Leibholz, *op. cit.*, p. 28; on the diminished status of the representative as a consequence of party discipline, cf. the remarks of Lord Campion and I. Thomas in *Parliament: A Survey*, pp. 25, 197 ff. Still more articulate complaints can be found in Peter de Mendelsohn's "Letter from London," *Der Monat*, May, 1953. The picture is distorted, however, as it hardly takes account of the power shift from plenary session of parliament to party caucus. And the position of the individual representative becomes even stronger if he also holds a party or interest group position in addition to his parliamentary mandate; only the politician without any office is seriously hampered by party discipline, especially if he also lacks connections with the press. On the whole, parliamentary activity has been somewhat rationalized as a result of the transfer of actual decision-making from the parliament itself to the big parliamentary parties. The individual deputy's chance to carry his point within his party group is, under conditions of mass democracy, hardly smaller than that of the free lancer in parliament; for similar points of view see Klemens Kremer, *Der Abgeordnete* (Munich, 1953), p. 51. On the compromise within the parliamentary party as the normal prerequisite for disciplined party voting in parliament, see Reif, *Verhandlungen des 38. deutschen Juristentags* (Frankfurt, 1950), p. C 35.—G. W. Keeton, *The Passing of Parliament* (New York, 1952), p. 61, also blurs this fact by saying that the deputy only counts at party meetings or congresses. The degree of parliamentary party discipline varies from country to country, by the way. Léon Blum (*op. cit.*, p. 46) has almost raised the breach of party discipline for reasons of conscience to the level of a moral principle. The standing orders of the Parliamentary Labour party, while declaring caucus resolutions as binding, at the same time acknowledge the member's right to abstain from voting out of deeply felt convictions. Even in parties like the Democrazia Cristiana, which continuously emphasizes party discipline, deputies of the left as well as the right wing have broken party discipline with impunity.

Dissenting members of the party executive or of the party's parliamentary leadership are often bound by a stronger discipline than ordinary members of parliament. Outside the party or in other party bodies they are not allowed to take positions rejected by the majority of the party executive or its parliamentary leaders. For the Executive of the English Labour party, see Kingsley Martin, *Harold J. Laski* (New York, 1953), ch. 9. Erler in *Protokolle des Parteitags der SPD* (Hamburg, May 21–25, 1950, p. 56) argues against the same practice of the SPD Bundestag leaders. But as soon as it becomes a matter of more or less cohesive groups or ideological circles and not merely of individual cases, the effect of such prohibitions becomes negligible.

intraparty democracy. A parliamentary party may, it is true, override its minority and, if party discipline is firmly enough rooted, make it vote against its convictions. In the case of the famous vote of war credits by the Social Democratic party in 1914, the self-abnegation of the minority went so far that one of its leaders, in his capacity of floor leader in the *Reichstag*, publicly justified the stand taken by the party as a whole. Yet one and a half years later the same minority under this very same Hugo Haase separated itself from the majority on this same question of the attitude toward the war. This shows that a well-advised parliamentary group will weigh votes rather than count them.

b. The second question concerns the *relationship between parliamentary group and party*. The traditional parliamentary party, incarnated most completely by the French Radical Socialists, is characterized by its absolute primacy over the party organization. The loosely organized parliamentarians are the mainstay of the party. The party's rules as well as usage secure the absolute primacy of the parliamentarians.[28] The totalitarian mass party's position is the opposite extreme. The more totalitarian its character, the more its members of parliament are assigned the role of messengers and postmen who merely make known the decisions of the central headquarters.

With regard to democratic mass parties the situation is more complicated. Here three factors are involved: party membership, party bureaucracy, and parliamentary party. In recent times parliamentary group and party organization have been interwoven to such an extent, personnelwise, that their contradictions no longer have any decisive weight. This diminishes the chances of party congresses to make effective their theoretical primacy in political leadership.[29] To retain a

[28] Cf. Duverger, *op. cit.*, pp. 212 ff.

[29] Most of the mass democratic workers' parties have tried again and again to safeguard the decision-making power of the party organs vis-à-vis the influence of the parliamentary group. Regarding Australian attempts to establish incompatibilities between membership in the party executive and membership in parliament, cf. Louise Overacker, *The Australian Party System* (New Haven, 1952), p. 96. Within the SPD discussion repeatedly flared up on the question of limiting at the Party Congress the number of votes assigned to the parliamentary group and the party apparatus. This problem was again the subject of discussion at the recent Hamburg SPD Party Congress. (*Protokolle*, pp. 54, 61.) In this context attempts were made to prevent artificial majorities which would hamper genuine formation of opinions by creating partial incompatibilities. See, e.g., § 10 of the SPD Party Rules which allows the representatives of the Bundestag's SPD mem-

maximum of political freedom of action is thus made relatively easy
for the parliamentary party so long as it can count on having its rear
covered by the central party bureaucracy. By and large one may say
that, the greater the discrepancy between the social and the political
position of the active party members and that of the strata supporting
the party by their votes, the more the influence of the party's deputies
is felt. The often much more radical party membership has the less
influence on the parliamentary party the more the deputies realize that
their reelection depends on their conservative voters. This is why discrepancies between the party line and the political orientation of the
voters promote a high degree of independence of the parliamentary
party from the party apparatus. The histories of the Socialist party of
France,[30] and recently of the MRP,[31] are full of examples in this
regard. Wherever there exists a substantial identity between the politi-

---

bership at the Party Congress only an advisory vote as to questions concerning
parliamentary matters. The material covering the Romance countries is discussed
by Duverger, *op. cit.*, pp. 212 ff. The German discussion is by G. Rabus, "Die
innere Ordnung der politischen Parteien im gegenwaertigen deutschen Staats-
recht," *Archiv des öffentlichen Rechts*, LXXVIII (1952), 163 ff.

[30] Conflicts between the parliamentary group and the Comité-Directeur of the
Socialist party occur so frequently in France that new procedures for their rec-
onciliation have to be created all the time. When the devices described by J.
Fauvet (*op. cit.*, p. 84) proved unsuccessful, the 1952 Party Congress instituted
joint consultations of the parliamentary group and the Comité-Directeur for all
decisive questions. Decisions made by a 60 per cent majority are considered binding. If such a majority decision cannot be reached, the Comité-Directeur decides
by simple majority; the parliamentary group may then appeal to the Conseil
National against such a decision. See the report in *Franc Tireur*, May 23, 1952. It
would be interesting to try to find out how far the changes in the French
electoral law—the transition from single member districts with runoff to proportional representation on a departmental basis—have affected the position of
the party bureaucracy and, to a degree, that of the party activists vis-à-vis the
deputies.

[31] In Mario Einaudi and François Goguel-Nyegaard, *Christian Democracy in
Italy and France* (Notre Dame, Ind., 1952), pp. 155 ff., Goguel emphasizes with
regard to the MRP the extent to which the MRP statutes reenforce the position
of the parliamentary and cabinet representatives in the most important party
organ vis-à-vis the local activists, with the result that a conflict between party
executive and parliamentary group is virtually excluded. This, of course, does not
exclude significant disagreements between activists, parliamentarians, and ministers
even if the latter win in the final vote. Cf. the report by R. Barillon on the MRP
Congress of May, 1953, in *Le Monde*, May 26, 1953: "After discussions lasting
for hours a majority agrees to conclusions amounting to the opposite of what
appears as the logical consequence of the majority of speeches at the party
Congress."

cal orientation of the membership on the one hand, and the party's general electorate on the other, as in many European democratic workers' parties, such tensions are relatively insignificant.[32] More radical tendencies among the party members are mostly aborted by the party apparatus, and the relationship between party organization and parliamentary party is consequently much less tense.

Recently a proposal was made to free the parliamentary group from the tutelage of the party by creating legal incompatibilities between parliamentary mandate and the holding of party office.[33] But what sense would this make? Such a proposal, meant to protect the representatives who are responsible to the voters from the pressure of the party apparatus, proceeds from the mistaken idea that it is the parliamentary group, not the party, which is called upon to make policy. This is hardly true for the democratic mass party. With regard to propaganda, the planning of programs, and the methods of fighting opposing groups—all very important for democratic mass parties—the party apparatus has nearly exclusive primacy. The parliamentary members are concerned with such current affairs as legislation, formation of governments, etc. Besides, no party leader who wants to preserve his authority can afford to fail to maintain his control over the command posts of the party apparatus as well as of the parliamentary leadership, and to ensure their harmony. In a democratic mass party discrepancies of a deeper social and political nature between the party and its voter-oriented deputies always seem to be at the bottom of any antagonism between parliamentary group and party bureaucracy going beyond normal personal and institutional tensions. Such discrepancies are normally overcome by splits and the founding of new parties, not by legislation.

---

[32] In Great Britain the specific weight of the individual party members is diminished by the "en bloc" membership of the labor unions, which thereby prevents individual members from acquiring a majority of the seats on the National Executive of the party. The party statutes also prescribe a two-thirds majority for changes in the party program. Despite all these precautions, at the Party Congress of 1952 Herbert Morrison deemed it necessary again sharply to emphasize the two-sided responsibility of the parliamentary party to the party executive, on the one hand, and the voters, on the other. Cf. the *Report of the 51st Annual Conference of the Labour Party* (Morecambe, 1952), pp. 90, 110, 111.

[33] Ernst Forsthoff, *Die politischen Parteien im Verfassungsrecht* (1950), p. 23.

c. The financing of democratic mass parties of the socialist type is based upon direct collection of membership dues from very large membership strata or the en bloc membership of trade unions. The process is different for conservative mass parties, for fringe parties, and sometimes also for totalitarian parties. The relatively narrow membership basis and its inconstancy often preclude the accumulation of sufficient means, if not for the conduct of ordinary party business, at least for election campaigns. As a rule this leads to the following consequences: The big industrial firms—for the smaller firms and agricultural enterprises this would be too difficult because of their large number as well as their habits—contribute a certain amount for political purposes which is determined according to some ratio per ton of their product or per worker employed. Either the employer organizations directly or organizations created for this purpose distribute the amount thus collected to the political parties in question. It can happen that such election funds are given to parties competing with each other, or often even to such different types of parties as conservative mass parties, fringe parties, and totalitarian parties.[34] Neither the unions nor the employers' organizations finance the parties they are connected with exclusively in order to obtain direct advantages for their particular group interest. Quantity and recipients of such bestowals are detemined mostly by general political considerations.[35]

[34] A. Heinrichsbauer, *Schwerindustrie und Politik* (privately printed, Essen-Kettwig, 1948), pp. 44, 54, 55, in spite of its apologetic features, provides a good insight into industry's methods of financing, especially as far as the financing of differentiated party types is concerned.

[35] General judgments on the practical effects of political financing are difficult, if only for the reason that hardly any party has a starting position completely comparable to that of others. The research of I. F. C. Ross, "The Incidence of Election Expenses," *Political Quarterly*, XXIII (1952), 175 ff., does not lead to definitive results. It only shows that the expenses of the successful candidates of the two large parties in the 1950 British election were slightly higher than those of the defeated candidates. The average expenses, however, of the successful as well as of the defeated conservative candidates were 15–20 per cent higher than those of the Labour candidates. But of 609 conservative candidates only 289 were elected, whereas of 612 Labour candidates, 315 were elected. The results may be inconclusive also because the research covers the expenditures of the individual candidates only, and not the institutional propaganda of the groups close to the candidates. For scattered remarks concerning the interesting hypothesis that excessive amounts of money influence the election results negatively, see Lubell, *op. cit.*, p. 194.

The financing of parties by organizations is supplemented by gifts of individuals or individual firms, made for the most varied reasons. A gift may be used to smooth the way into politics for a family member, as in the United States. For there, much more often than in Europe, people enter politics by way of substantial investments of money instead of making it a career like any other. Entering politics by way of large commitments of money implies nothing concerning the political allegiance one is going to adopt. One may settle down on one or the other side of the political spectrum, depending on one's taste, inclination, and general circumstances. Political contributions may also serve to promote the policy preferences of the contributor. Thus the representative of an interest group may distribute the amounts coming to him from the members in a very conservative way. The individual industrialist may, of course, give special subsidies to certain groups within a group; he can also make life easier for groups that aspire to but have not yet attained respectability. This action may be the result of political passion or political calculation, including the felt need to protect one's rear, given the anxieties that are so prevalent nowadays. Finally, it is possible that a specific group, like the chemical industry, the metal industry, or the mining or textile unions, may send a deputy to parliament as their permanent spokesman. But I should like to stress the element of continuous representation of important interests by permanent parliamentary representatives. Individual grants of money in the expectation or against the promise of definite one-time advantages for industrial firms are more characteristic of the regional or local sphere than of the national one, apart from the fact that such agreements by their very nature can only be made with individual politicians, hardly with larger groups. The *député d'affaires* who represents diverse interests in return for special grants has become more an exception than the rule.[36] More characteristic of mass democracy is the financing of the

[36] The events of the last ten years have not led me to change my conclusions expressed in "The Historical and Comparative Background of the Hatch Act," in *Public Policy*, ed. Friedrich and Mason, II (Cambridge, Mass., 1941), 351. For the same differentiation between the illegitimate representation of individual interests and the justified representation of group interests, see Leo Hamon, "Gouvernement et intérêts particuliers," *Esprit*, June 21, 1953, pp. 839, 840. If American practices continue to fluctuate, this is due to the different party structure, the weakness of the central party organs, and the mainly local and regional orientation of the representative.

organizateion as a whole by membership dues or by subsidies of interest groups close to the party.

Sporadic attempts to subject parties to stricter legal rules accompany the growing importance of the mass parties. The danger to democratic institutions posed by totalitarian organizations, on the one hand, and legal or *de facto* privileges enjoyed by political parties on the basis of the constitution or legislation, on the other, has stimulated attempts to ensure the democratic character of these parties by legislative means. The necessary and yet problematical attempts to blockade totalitarian mass parties without abandoning the principles of constitutionalism cannot be considered here. However, we want at least to mention the matter of legislative regulation of the internal affairs of democratic mass parties.[37] The discussion of the relationship between parliamentary group and party has already demonstrated that one should be skeptical with regard to legislative intervention in dynamic political situations. This applies also to the problem of legislative control of party finances.

In the first place: Gifts of money to individual politicians in return for special advantages belong rather to the sphere of criminal law than to a law governing parties. Of course, one could think of allowing a minimum of officially sanctioned propaganda (posters, official ballots, radio time), in order to guarantee an equal chance to all parties. Maximal expense ceilings as they exist in Great Britain, and in hardly effective form in the United States, are much more problematical, because nowadays one has to consider the compensatory effect of institutional propaganda. "Institutional advertising" developed fully in the commercial field during the war. At that time various mass consumer items

---

[37] G. Rabus's (*op. cit.*, p. 172) careful description of German conditions stresses the point that encroachments on the legal autonomy of the party may eventually benefit it; for since all Germans congenitally respect everything "official," this could help to overcome their dislike of parties. The question how such a "Verbiedermeierung" of the parties will affect their political effectiveness is not asked. In agreement with the majority of the speakers at the 38th German Lawyers' Congress ("Verfassungsrechtliche Stellung und innere Ordnung der Parteien," in *Verhandlungen des 38. Deutschen Juristentages*, Staatsrechtliche Abteilung, 1951, siehe Empfehlung 9), Rabus fully recognizes that the control of party expulsions by the judiciary can only apply to the observance of formal norms—approximately analogous to what Anglo-Saxon practice usually categorizes under the concept of "rules of natural justice" (*op. cit.*, p. 185). Cf. *Russell* v. *Duke of Norfolk* (1949) 1 All E.R. 109.

for private consumption were taken out of production. The car or motorcycle manufacturers, fully occupied with the production of war matériel, did everything to keep the articles not momentarily on the consumer market in the public eye by massive advertising. Today such institutional advertising plays an increasingly important role in politics. One praises a product in general terms, without necessarily letting the potential buyer know where it is found for sale. Nonpolitical institutions like chambers of commerce, industrial associations, or labor unions may theoretically advertise in this way the benefits of private enterprise or of old age benefits and social security. They do not openly descend into the political arena, and they refrain, at least directly, from advertising a particular party. This does not make their contribution any less effective in favor of particular parties or party groups. But in a constitutional system it would be difficult to include such advertising expenses in the legally admissible maximum amount for party propaganda.

But objections of principle to legislative control of internal party affairs are more important than these technical difficulties, at least in so far as such regulation would go beyond the necessary prevention of attempts at totalitarian take-over. Owing to the special conditions of our time, the democratic mass parties have already drawn all too close to the state. They have lost much of their mobility and political dynamism. By this relationship we mean mainly all the necessary verbal arrangements and controls linking party and state apparatus which have become unavoidable for protecting the party from totalitarian infiltration or Trojan horse tactics. The various institutional links between democratic mass parties, regardless of whether they happen to be in opposition or in the government, and the decisive economic and social institutions belong in this same category. All this interrelatedness is necessary and it is only through it that democratic institutions become fully effective. But on the other hand it seriously limits the parties' initiative, their political vitality, and their willingness to innovate. The involvement of party and state is one of the main roots of the disgust with parties briefly mentioned before. This weariness toward parties, which at first amounted to a rejection of totalitarian parties only, has turned into skepticism toward the democratic mass party as well. It not only restricts the government party's freedom to maneuver, but also casts a shadow on the policy of the democratic mass party in opposition. Critical observers therefore already attack the state and the democratic mass party as one and the same machinery of oppression playing merely a game with divided roles.[38] Yet it is precisely if one does not want to draw such basically anarchistic consequences that one arrives at the following crucial question: How do we ensure for these mass parties the freedom of decision-making with respect to essential political problems? This freedom of decision-making they must retain if they are to be able adequately to fulfill their task of presenting the electorate with an alternative to what the government proposes, instead of merely putting forward the demands of the social groups close to them—a necessary function of political parties, but certainly not their only one. By exposing internal party matters to a greater or lesser degree of government intervention one risks restricting the already limited autonomy of the party decisively without gaining much—except arguments, strife, and trouble.

Democratic mass parties are very unstable structures and require an enormous expenditure of energy, intelligence, and organizational genius to preserve their capacity to function. At times providence or chance provides such parties with charismatic leaders. By virtue of their political magnetism they give inner cohesion to their own group or, in the most favorable circumstances, to the whole nation, the sort of cohesion which the state apparatus can, after all, not bring about. But generally speaking a party cannot and should not count on such strokes of luck. Persons who have to rely on the authority of their positions and on the granting of privileges take the place of those with personal charisma who can get along, with a minimum of actual coercion, merely by personal affinity or withdrawal of friendship. But it is equally frequent that such bureaucratic bodies handle tasks of leadership with diligence and loyalty even though they have to confront frictions without end. No party legislation of any kind will be able to cramp the style of the charismatic leader, and so far as the others are concerned, it should not aggravate their task, which is difficult enough. Safeguards against abuses on the part of democratic mass parties are provided essentially by their need to submit themselves to the judg-

---

[38] Cf. P. v. Oertzen's symptomatic discussion on "Strukturwandel der Demokratie," *Deutsche Universitätszeitung*, April 20, 1953, p. 11.

ment of the electorate. Safeguards also consist in a maximum disclosure of party finances,[39] which should be supported by legislation while deriving its primary force from public opinion. Those personally involved usually take care of publicizing internal arguments between the wings of a party.

We must also note that every democratic mass party shows a desire of its own, quite independent of present-day circumstances, maximally to identify itself with the state. It aspires to monopolize for itself the traditional symbols of the state. It seeks to create the impression, among its members as well as among outsiders, that precisely this party incarnates the state adequately and meaningfully for the present era. Especially if the objective is to give a visible share of public power to new and hitherto not fully integrated groups of the population, such identifications are completely legitimate, especially as they can at any time be repudiated by the sovereign electorate. Yet by enriching and consolidating the state through the realization of new social and political horizons the democratic mass party must take part in a decisive way in the continuous process in which the state renews and refashions itself. Premature identifications are equally pernicious for the party and state alike.[40] They amount to democratic mass parties existing under the protection of the state's symbols, while yet lacking the strength and the will to fashion this same state according to their own image.

The democratic mass party is neither a comfortable nor a very secure political instrument. But in the light of the old parliamentary party's obvious inability to integrate broad population strata politically, and in view of the abyss opened up by the totalitarian party, the choice facing the electorate is limited. The democratic mass party has at least two advantages. It is subject to the principle of free political

[39] Government financing of election campaigns according to a ratio based on the most recent election results, as Rabus (*op. cit.*, p. 192) suggests, would do more psychological harm to the constitution-conscious old parties than it would benefit them financially. Presumably they would be the only parties involved. They would thereby be earmarked as official organizations, not to mention the danger that a powerful interest group might hit on the idea of placing its propaganda facilities at the disposal of a new, non-earmarked party.

[40] The history of the German Social Democracy of the Weimar period consists of a sequence of such premature identifications. The memoirs of Keil, Noske, Severing, and Stampfer are full of material demonstrating this point.

TRANSFORMATION OF DEMOCRATIC POLITICS

competition which reduces the risks inherent in it. And it further appears to be the only organization making available to wide strata of the population not merely an occasional share—dangerous by virtue of its erratic character—but a permanent share in the business of government. The inevitable skepticism we all feel toward the party system may thus be partly beneficial. As Rousseau put it: "If there were a nation of gods, it would govern itself democratically." [41] On the basis of our experience we may transform this saying: Precisely because we know that we are less than perfect, democracy appears to our generation as the most suitable form of government.

[41] *Contrat Social*, III, 4.

MAJORITIES AND MINORITIES IN

WESTERN EUROPEAN GOVERNMENTS

I PROPOSE to confine myself to political parties as they operate as majorities and minorities within the framework of political regimes typical
of Western Europe. Democratic regimes know only one permanent
majority-minority relation: the one between the majority power,
which is the popular sovereign, and the minority powers par excel-
lence, that is to say, those which act through the constituted organs of
the state, parliament and executive. Contrasted with the popular sovereign, the groups that operate the executive branch and those that
dominate parliament are themselves in a minority position. The control
of the permanent minority, which is the executive, by the popular
majority makes such a situation tolerable. The political party, agent of
liaison between the constituted organs of the state and the popular
sovereign, tones down some of the inevitable consequences of the permanent majority-minority relationship, that between those who rule
and those who are ruled. It can do so effectively, because in contrast to
the unchangeable and permanent majority-minority relations between
the sovereign people and all the constituted organs, the concept of a
majority party or a minority party implies reversibility of majority
and minority positions. As the agent that connects the popular sovereign with the sphere of governmental action the political party undergoes a change in this very process; it will never lose sight for very long
of its birthright, its claim to conquest of full power, or at least partici-

Reprinted from *Western Political Quarterly*, XII (1959), 492–510, by permission
of the University of Utah, copyright owners.

pation in effective exercise of power. In the modern party, the democratic system has found the elixir, which—concededly at high cost—dissolves enmity and obstruction and generates and engineers maximum consent and satisfaction. But this elixir is made of the eternal hope, sanctioned by constitutional law and enforced by the climate of opinion, that today's party minority will be the majority tomorrow and establish itself at the seat of government.

The degree to which such a system proves workable depends largely on the nature of the political parties which are operating under it. The most important type, dominant by now in many countries, is the democratic mass party. It rests on a nucleus of professional political personnel and on a party membership of great variety in size and intensity of loyalty feelings. At the same time it entertains amicable relations with and finds support among a variety of interest groups. Both form and intensity of relations with the latter groups, whether they are religious, middle-class, or entrepreneurial organizations, who are among the traditional backers of Christian type catch-all people's parties, or trade unions, as in the case of labor or socialist mass parties, are governed by limiting considerations. The parties need to appeal to as large as possible numbers of voters and the interest groups similarly need to avoid irreversible commitments antagonizing too deeply other and possibly momentarily more weighty political forces. Hence the marked watering down of purely ideological commitments. The stress now lies on the complex interplay of a multitude of groups which, as the 1957 draft program of the SPOe, the Austrian Socialist party, has it, may combine in a great variety of ways.[1] The style and *modus operandi* of the parties thus adapt to the new social economic and intellectual landscape of our period.

Social status and position in the production process may still be the most important single determinants around which the public's party preference is built,[2] but democratic mass parties need to aggregate as

[1] *Das Neue Programm der SPOe* (Vienna, 1957), p. 11.

[2] Cf. Hirsch-Weber/Schütz, *Wähler und Gewählte* (Berlin, 1957), Table 52, p. 249, and conclusions, p. 403. According to the remarkable analysis of voters' preferences during the January, 1956, National Assembly election in the first sector of the Seine department, 7 out of 10 participating workers voted Communist: Jean Stoetzel and Pierre Hassner, "Resultats d'un sondage dans le premier secteur de la Seine," in *Les Elections du 2 Janvier 1956*, ed. Duverger, Goguel, Touchard (Paris, 1957), pp. 272, 274. The quite different distribution of the

many interests as possible in their fight for majority status. Both the consequent need for as broad a social basis as possible and some regard by both adherents and voters for proclaimed party goals and featured personalities have their effect on party patterns, outlook, and clientele. They look the less "chemically pure" the more they are geared toward immediate political action rather than toward common recitation of belief systems.[3] Modern industrial society has contributed to breaking down barriers among various elements of the new employed middle class, the skilled workers, the middle ranks of the white collar, and the civil service ranks. Similarities of situation and expectations outweigh existing traditional distinctions, even though we are far from the unified middle-class society stressed by some authors.[4] "Celebration of individual character and effort," says an industrial sociologist, "has in some measure been superseded by a belief in individual adaptation, just as the struggle for survival and the pursuit of self-interest has been superseded by the image of co-operative teamwork."[5] Essential goals for which the individual had been fighting in earlier times are now wrapped up in his standardized "existence package"; this includes softening of hardships from loss of employment, sickness, and old age.

At the same time that the condition of the new middle class becomes materially more comfortable, secure, and perhaps, correspondingly, more boring, the cleavage that separates this new middle class from the more successful elements of the older independent middle classes—the artisans and peasants of medium-sized holdings, both with enough capital equipment to profit from technological progress—is diminishing.

---

peasant vote with 56.75 per cent calculated to have gone to the right in 1956 is discussed in Joseph Klatzmann, "Geographie électorale de l'agriculture française" in J. Fauvet and H. Mendras, eds., *Les Paysans et la Politique dans la France Contemporaine* (Paris, 1958), pp. 39, 48. The same volume also contains excellent monographs tracing, among other factors, the influence of both variations in property structure and degree of industrialization on the political attitude of the peasantry. *Ibid.*, pp. 389–461.

[3] G. E. Lavau, "Définition d'un parti politique," *Esprit*, January, 1958, p. 427; the point is made in some detail in Jeanne Hersch, *Idéologies et Réalitiés* (Paris, 1956).

[4] S. Landshut, "Die Auflösung der Klassengesellschaft," in *Gewerkschaftliche Monatshefte*, VII (1956), 451; the same point is made in H. Schelsky's speech, "Haben wir heute noch eine Klassengesellschaft?" reprinted in *Das Parlament*, February 29, 1956.

[5] Reinhard Bendix, *Work and Authority in Industry* (New York, 1956), p. 339.

The technological revolution is changing the outlook of these tradition-bound and conservative groups at the same time that it reduces their size. Increasingly enmeshed in the fortunes of the national economy, they now raise claims, identical with those of the new middle class, for guaranteed real-income levels and participation in social-insurance schemes. To this extent the struggle between the independent old middle class and the employed new middle class is more a struggle for larger shares of similar social welfare provisions than a clash of incompatible programs. The impact of this changed social structure permeates all political parties, whatever their official label.

The lower degree of social polarization is to be seen in other groups as well as among the middle classes. At the same time the parties often feel greater community of interest in resisting the invasion of alien political systems. The consequences are more rational party structures, less bound by ideology. This fact eases interparty relations and increases the parties' potential to develop—below a thin veneer of ideology—many features of an interest market.

A look at the composition of the parliamentary groups of major mass democratic parties might exemplify the system of party–interest group interrelation and show how the parties are integrating a great variety of groups with at times parallel, at times contradictory claims on the state, and how they equip themselves for the job of both representing and in this process mediating between group interests. Most available tabulations of occupational background and status data for parliamentarians are not conclusive, for they focus mostly on the past, which is an element—but only one element—in the analysis of the legislator's specific role after he enters parliament. It would be more practical to break down parliamentary personnel into three categories, with allowances for changing roles or cumulation of different roles even through one legislative term. The three categories I visualize would be:

1. A small group of leading party men, a group identical in part with what the French call *ministrables* and in part with the parties' principal officeholders, who initiate and, after proper consultation with competent party bodies and parliamentary groups, negotiate the outline of agreements on major issues of foreign policy and nonspecialized areas of domestic affairs.

2. The much larger supporting cast of political professionals who act as transmitting agents—i.e., party executives, propaganda experts,

organizers, party men in public administration, etc.—in brief, the large army of party officials or appointees on the national or, more often, the regional or local level in charge of a two-way communication system that puts the people in contact with political decisions.

3. The large body of direct representatives of specific interests. A legislator in this group may have arrived there in any one of many different ways. He may have been active in both interest group and party organization, functioning as a natural liaison man; he may have come up from party ranks and then taken charge, as a local government executive, of a specific sector of public enterprise; or he may be a farmer, an industrialist, an artisan, or a self-employed professional and have been propelled, on the strength of business reputation or professional standing, into a leading position with his farm, trade, or professional association, acting on its behalf within the associated party and representing it in governmental councils or parliamentary bodies. Or else he may be a technician (economist, lawyer, chemist, engineer, public relations counsel, etc.) on the staff of an interest group holding a parliamentary seat as part of his staff assignment. At least in the latter two cases more often that not affiliation with the interest group is the decisive element. Often the interest group will have made a special contribution to the campaign fund of the party in question for "the acquisition" of the parliamentary seat.

Quantitative proportions do not really matter. Group influences are weighed, not counted.[6] Generally, a key committee assignment for one liaison man in parliament is more important to an interest group than votes cast on the floor by a whole bunch of backbenchers. And if there should be danger that the parliamentary process produce results detrimental to the interest group, it will rely on its normal access to key men of the administrative machine, or, if need be, party and government bosses, to have the right proportions restored. Often direct access to administrative personnel assigned to legislative groundwork will promise more substantial returns than proper proportional representation among parliament members.[7]

[6] Failure to differentiate between major politically relevant pressure groups and their party connections on the one hand, and a great variety of minor groups and "causes" on the other, mars, e.g., the study by G. D. Stewart, *British Pressure Groups* (New York, 1958).

[7] This point is brought out very well in Henry Ehrmann, *Organized Business in France* (Princeton, 1957), p. 258.

As for relative numerical weight among the legislators of career politicians as against representatives of specific group interests, the proportions will vary from party to party and from country to country, influenced by tradition, party mechanics, degree and character of interest organization, and the vagaries of the election law. Men of specific group interests will be less numerous among parliamentarians representing a traditional party of organized labor with its solid but relatively homogeneous group connections and proven advantages of recruiting legislative personnel from the ranks of salaried or honorific party officeholders and union leaders, than among middle-class parties of the "people's" party type. Among them recruitment from the top strata of voluntary organizations, professional and community groups outside the area of career politics has been part of the cultural tradition. Participation of interest group representatives will be heavy in a country like Western Germany where the party system is stable with few, rather well-disciplined parties, and organized interests through well-nigh a century have developed a closely knit network of political connections.[8] The proportion will be much smaller in France,[9] where the great number of parties, the organizational weakness of most parties, and their ideological orientation allow both parties and individual members to be put more easily under interest pressure emanating from outside parliament.

No matter through what channels the interest representative got into parliament, he usually is concerned with arrangements desirable to his group as a whole rather than with promoting individual business propositions. It is worth noting here that, although not yet down to zero, the share of lawyers, who used to fill the ranks of parliament in former times, has been well on the decrease.[10] The lawyer still may

[8] See the forthcoming study of Arkadius L. Gurland on the "Pattern of Interest Representation in German Postwar Parliaments."

[9] Ehrmann, *op cit.*, pp. 242–56.

[10] In the century between 1848 and 1949 the number of practicing lawyers went down from 11.5 per cent sitting in the Paulskirche to 6.3 per cent in the first Bonn Bundestag, calculated after Karl Demeter, "Die soziale Schichtung des deutschen Parlamentes seit 1848 im Spiegelbild des Strukturwandels des Volkes" in *Vierteljahresschrift für Sozial- und Wirtschaftsgeschichte*, III (1952), 1–29, and Otto Kirchheimer, "The Composition of the German Bundestag," *Western Political Quarterly*, III (1950), 590–601. In order to understand these figures correctly it might be worth mentioning that in the 1848 assembly judges comprised 31.6 per

perform his traditional part as a mediator of group interests—especially in middle-class parties—but if he were out to use his office to perform services for individual clients, which he is used to doing professionally, he would be jeopardizing rather than helping his career in European politics.[11]

In a way, the declining importance of the practicing lawyer in parliamentary life points to the changing role of the party, whose influence has come to rest on the interpenetration of political machines and group interests. If corruption be taken to mean conduct designed to influence public agencies in a sense deemed undesirable by the community, this certainly would include, and stigmatize, any use of political office for the furtherance of individual as against group interests. [12] To be sure, there remains quite a sizable marginal area. Influence-

---

cent while the total number of professional civil servants excluding political officeholders in the first Bonn Bundestag was 3.6 per cent. The total number of *hommes de loi* comprising lawyers and a much smaller number of magistrates and notaries in the French second chamber went down from 26.5 per cent in 1910 to 12.7 per cent in 1956: cf. Mattei Dogan, "Les candidates et les élus," in Duverger, *op. cit.*, p. 456, and the same author's "L'origine sociale du personnel parlementaire français," in *Partis Politiques et Classes Sociales en France*, ed. Duverger (Paris, 1955), p. 309.

[11] In March, 1958, the lawyer chairman of the Bundestag committee for restitution resigned from the committee chairmanship when it became known that he held power of attorney from the lawyers of a sizable bloc of restitution claimants residing in foreign countries. 1958 legislation of the bureaucratic semi-authoritarian de Gaulle regime has established a system of severe incompatibilities for various kinds of officeholders: among others, the parliamentary lawyer's right to represent clients in negotiation and controversies with public bodies has been severely curtailed; he is equally barred from most criminal trials regardless of whether they have a financial or a political background. The latter point does not so much involve the government's zeal to avoid conflict-of-interest situations, but rather mirrors its general tendency to keep possibilities of parliamentary interference with and supervision of the administration at an irreducible minimum. However, a recent decree (*Journal Officiel* of February 7, 1959) has relented somewhat, making allowance for a partial comeback of the *avocat parlementaire*.

[12] The British material tracing the recognized demarcation line between legitimate representation of group interests within the framework of the parliamentary group and illicit exploitation of political office for the private gain of the parliamentary representative has been collected in Madeline R. Robinson, "Parliamentary Privilege and Political Morality in Britain, 1939–1957," *Political Science Quarterly*, LXXIII (1958), 179–205; see especially p. 197, the interesting remark by Churchill, who recognizes representation of particular groups of nonpolitical character within the parliamentary parties as a "condition of our varied life"; in the same sense, Earl Attlee in "The Attitudes of M.P.'s and Active Peers," *Political Quarterly*, XXX (1958), 29, 31.

peddling as a gainful pursuit of the individual politician is becoming less frequent; what is more important are the efforts by zealous party officials to wangle private funds for depleted party treasures.[13]

The point is illustrated by a recent political skirmish in Austria. Since the war Austria has been ruled by a coalition of the Austrian People's party and the Socialists (on which I shall comment later), sharing office and spoils but continuing to compete with each other in electoral terms. Recently the Vienna district chairman of the Austrian People's party had made a deal, sealed in a formal contract [14] with Transfines, a private import-export firm, wherein he undertook to furnish for cash his party's business contacts; the size of his fee—with which to pay off the debts of the party office—was to depend on the success of transactions made possible through his efforts. The attitude the party took when the story broke was a bit ambiguous. A party honor court and the party's headquarters expressed disapproval but the influence-peddling party dignitary was not disqualified from holding party office, and the slate of candidates he headed obtained a thumping 95 per cent of the delegates' votes at the next district convention of the party organization; two officeholders who had been directly responsible for the deal were given other assignments. Party authorities were aware, and so stated officially,[15] of the general public's sour reaction to the deal. But regularizing the flow of income for a party unable to live on membership fees remains problematical. Presently the party chairman, Federal Chancellor Raab, endeavors to mobilize his prestige in order to put party finances on a broader and more stable basis. Following the example of the well-heeled German sister organization, the

---

13 This statement is not intended to convey a judgment as to the political effect of increasingly strict normative limitation on the pursuit of self-interest; it may well be argued that transformation of an individual into a conscious group representative and bearer of a group mission diminishes chances of accommodation; perfect integration of the individual into the group may be reached at the expense of wider integration of the individual into the community. The point has been widely discussed in American and German sociological literature: cf., e.g., Lewis Coser, *The Functions of Social Conflict* (Glencoe, 1956), pp. 115 *et seq.*
14 Published verbatim in Socialist *Arbeiter Zeitung* (Vienna), January 12, 1958, p. 1.
15 According to *Die Presse*, January 11, 1958, p. 3, the party's national chairman, Weinberger, Deputy Mayor of Vienna, stated, after some discussion of the party's financial plight as the affair's background, that the Vienna chairman's conduct was neither "popular nor likeable."

CDU,[16] he tries to convince the party's potential sponsors that they should remain satisfied with having supported a program generally in line with their broader social and economic orientation rather than continue to press for consideration of their particular claims in exchange for financial support of the party.

The line separating acceptable political representation of group interests from illicit pressuring for individual claims is hardening. The party performs a legitimate and approved-of function when it brings major interest groups into harmony with the political community at large, and when it filters the groups' claims, checking and weighing them against others.[17] Before chaperoning this or that interest grouping for a rendezvous with public powers the party-commissioned duennas may see to it that the grouping's claims be aligned with more general policy requirements attributable to the common weal.[18]

If all individuals were well integrated into either parties or party-connected interest groups and if general standards of values were commonly accepted, the government formula would become a purely technical matter, a kind of applied statistics securing satisfactory consideration of all the group claims, with majorities and minorities changing places according to their ability and perspicacity in foreseeing, correlating, and servicing the wants of their respective clienteles. But this, of course, is a far cry from reality. The individual is not always well integrated to his social or professional group—his membership may be nominal or he may be in permanent revolt against his group's leadership—or he may be a member of a variety of groups with conflicting party affinities.

[16] See Arnold J. Heidenheimer, "German Party Finance: The CDU," *American Political Science Review*, LI (1957), 369–85.

[17] One of the most "perfect" examples of a party integrating interest groups is the Belgian Catholic PSC (Parti Social Chrétien). This is the successor to the Catholic party which was officially a *Standespartei*, a federation of Catholic farmer, labor, and middle-class organizations, plus the aristocratic and bourgeois Catholic political clubs. The PSC now is a "unitary" party of individual membership in form, but in practice it still functions by intraparty deals at national and local levels among its constituent social groups. A. Simon, *Le Parti Catholic Belge* (Brussels, 1958); R. H. Hojer, *Le Régime Parliamentaire Belge, 1918–1940* (Uppsala and Stockholm, 1946).

[18] On the largely uncharted subject of party autonomy in relation to supporting interest groups see the interesting remarks of Jean Meynaud, *Les Groupes de Pression en France* (Paris, 1958), pp. 180, 181.

The same process that has created a new middle class and lessened the distance between the old and new elements has everywhere up-rooted diverse other social strata, and has so far failed to assign them a satisfactory position within the new society. The main victims of this process of transformation have been older people whose income has not kept pace with inflation, small peasant holders, small artisans and retailers without the capital to modernize their shops, and those white-collar elements economically outflanked by many groups of manual workers and unable to acquire a new feeling of "belonging" to com-pensate for the meagerness of their occupational existence.

These people may either remain isolated or belong to marginal, often fly-by-night protest groups which do not find a place in the universe of the accredited major interest groups. But all the same, whether remaining isolated individuals or becoming members of protest groups these people are entitled to vote. It may well be that the ubiquitous process of privatization, people's preoccupation with their own con-cerns and their lack of interest or ability to connect their own fate with that of the community at large, is somewhat further advanced among such non-group-integrated voters than among other members of the community. Still, a look at the election participation in many a Eu-ropean country bears evidence that most such citizens must exercise their voting privileges, even though they may not meaningfully con-nect this form of civic exercise with the affairs of the polity at large.[19] They emulate Beckett's Estragon with activity becoming another form of passivity.[20] Yet, whatever the meaning of this vote, it counts: par-ties will make efforts to play up to it, even if the difficulties in estab-lishing relations with the isolated individual are much more formidable than the job of coordinating group interests.

[19] From the already quoted opinion poll taken after the 1956 French elections in a cross-section of Paris voting districts (14) it may be seen, e.g., that about one half of the respondents did not relate their voting decisions to a current political controversy, or the concrete program offered by whatever party they chose. While party preferences appear interchangeable, the stated inclination of the choice indicated a vague expectation that the party or candidate selected would do a better job than those discarded in removing the cause of unspecified dissatisfaction. From what is known about the state of mind of the German voter it may be concluded that the major difference is in the psychological back-ground of equally vague and undifferentiated motives oriented toward a model of stability rather than change. Stoetzel and Hassner, op. cit., pp. 233–35.

[20] An interesting comparison of the voters' situation with the situation of the individual in our society may be drawn from Gunther Anders, Die Antiquiertheit des Menschen (Munich, 1956), p. 218.

The political parties' potentialities for integrating—even if only at a very superficial level—into the political community those numerous elements which are neither absorbed nor absorbable by party or interest group connections must therefore derive from the basic features of democratic government: every party shall have the chance to be associated with government operations as the responsible majority or a minority called upon to watch and criticize and in this process impress the population at large with its capacity to act as the spokesman for the community rather than as a skillful exponent of specific group agenda.

Measured by the classic standard of parliamentary rule, Western Europe's government formulas developed in the postwar period do not invariably show the simple contours of the traditional British government-opposition, majority-minority relationship. Frequent failure of general elections to return a clear-cut majority—not always determined by mere technicalities of the election system—certainly contributes to the deviation from the classical model; but it is not the only contributing factor. At closer view, parliamentary systems of the British type appear predicated on a combination of indispensable conditions, which have not always been met in continental experience. These requirements may be described as follows:

1. Wide area of agreement on basic features of domestic policy, or, at least, a considerable degree of mutual tolerance for policy changes, implying an understanding of the limits of permissible changes, which is the essence of the "modern Elizabethan compromise."

2. Reliance on the majority's willingness to keep the opposition—or its titular leader—informed of major foreign policy plans and take dissenting opinion under advisement.

3. Unquestioning acceptance of policies and orders emanating from the parliamentary government by the bureaucratic hierarchy and the military, acceptance precluding political plots of the personnel of government agencies against the exponents of parliamentary rule, whatever their political complexion.

4. General recognition of basic rules of conduct, under which the majority may be trusted not to use its hold on the governmental machinery unfairly so as to stay in power forever, and the minority may be expected not to turn its opposition into obstruction and sabotage.

In a parliamentary system most drastically deviating from the British model, no reciprocal loyalty will be taken for granted nor will one party give the other credit for sticking to the rules; distribution of power positions as between majority and minority will be negotiated in minute detail by advance agreement, and the utmost care will be taken to anticipate all possible change and build safeguards to prevent disruption of the negotiated balance. In its purest form this technique may be observed in Austria, where all cabinets since 1945 have originated in the continuing association of the two major parties, the Austrian People's party, with presently (before the May, 1959, elections) 46 per cent, and the Socialists with 43 per cent of the popular vote.

Located at opposite poles of the parliamentary government scale, the British and the Austrian systems display one common characteristic. Under both, maximum consideration is given to points of view and interests represented by the party with the smaller share in parliament seats, with the result that government policy is incessantly modified and adjusted to minimize operational frictions. This does not make the operation smooth, and a great deal of energy and labor goes into adjustment. But the machinery operates without major upset. The foundation in the British case is the self-enforceable usage, ensured by the governing majority's self-interest, which makes it look beyond the legislative terms and adapt policy-planning to such changes of political climate as may be inferred from content and vigor of minority criticism. By contrast, in the Austrian case nothing is entrusted to usage or precedent; nothing is left to chance; nor is any reliance placed in the rival's presumed self-interest or sense of fair play. From age-old mutual distrust, memories of an unhappy association in the 1920s, participation on opposite sides in the civil war of 1934, and enforced cooperation under the 1945-55 occupation regime, Austria's feuding parties have evolved a contractual system of combined management, which rigidly restricts their freedom of action; no piece of major legislation may be introduced, no major administrative decision or appointment made by one partner without consent of the other.[21]

Whatever the difference in techniques, the relationship between the

[21] Replying to criticism on the floor by two minor parties represented in Austria's parliament, the Socialist *Arbeiterzeitung*, December 8, 1957, p. 2, cogently observed that the two government parties, in permanent opposition to one another, were under reciprocal control as coalition partners. "With and against one another, cooperation and opposition—such is the Austrian government formula," the Socialist daily added.

leading party in the elections and its chief rival has specific implications, not too dissimilar for both Britain and Austria. In countries in which general elections produce parliamentary one-party majorities—as in Britain—the majority party forms the cabinet and has the initiative in determining the share to be conceded to the minority's concepts and demands. In Austria, where—barring electoral changes of landslide dimensions unknown in the history of either the first or the second Republic—neither party has a majority in parliament, the outcome of the election does not deliver the government machinery to either the Austrian People's party or the Socialists. But in giving the one party a plurality edge over the other, it determines their respective shares in governmental power. In proportion to the percentages of votes cast for either, governmental arrangements are immediately readjusted.

In the Austrian system, the minority's hope to acquire majority status has not been extinguished, but it has lost importance. Miniscule changes in electoral preferences instantly turn into gains or losses of individual positions and patronage. For the expectation of sudden and incisive change as a result of minor shifts in voting percentages (which indicated an odd trust in the miraculous mechanics of numbers) has been substituted the certainty that government action will be based on a weighted index of votes. The very terms, majority and minority, acquire a different meaning under the circumstances; here they merely denote quantitative positions under a cooperative program wherein elements of restricted and controlled competition have been assigned specific places.[22]

The classic majority-minority formula and the semipermanent joint management of government affairs by strong partners jointly control-

[22] The implications of the functioning of the Austrian system for the development of parliamentary institutions have been discussed by Otto Kirchheimer, "The Waning of Opposition in Parliamentary Regimes," *Social Research*, XXIV (1957), 127, 136; the effects of the Austrian system on socioeconomic institutions have been studied by Herbert P. Secher, "Coalition Government: The Case of the Second Austrian Republic," *American Political Science Review*, LII (1958), 791–807; some partly deviating interpretations in Charles A. Gulick, "Austria's Socialists in the Trend toward a Two-Party System: An Interpretation of Postwar Elections," *Western Political Quarterly*, XI (September, 1958), 539–68. The various types of "all parties governments" including the extension of the concept to the government formula of the Austrian provinces have been brought together in Axel Vulpius, *Die Allparteienregierung* (Frankfurt, Berlin, 1957).

ling an overwhelming majority in parliament show the wide range of variations in government formulas characteristic of different periods in individual countries. There is no need to dwell on transitional and anomalous subspecies such as minority cabinets tolerated by shifting heterogeneous majorities, caretaker cabinets made up of nonparty officials, all-party coalitions in national emergencies, etc., all essentially stopgap arrangements, which have no bearing on the problem under discussion. There is no need either to scrutinize in detail the Swiss pattern; not a parliamentary government in the exact meaning of the term, Switzerland's multiparty Federal Council comes as close to the Austrian model as frequent intercessions of referenda will permit.

When these atypical combinations are eliminated, four major types of continental European government patterns become discernible. They are:

1. The more or less classical majority-minority system, which has been operating with longer or shorter interruptions in Norway, Sweden, and Ireland.

2. Domination of the cabinet by one preponderant party, controlling over 40 per cent of the popular vote with the assistance of minor groups which provide the wanting parliamentary votes or important regional strongholds. This system has been in operation in the Federal Republic of Germany from 1949 to the middle of the fifties and occasionally in Sweden, Belgium, and Ireland.

3. Multiparty coalitions of groups of unequal and varying strength, as in Holland, Finland, or—a marginal case—Denmark.

4. A special type of types 2 and 3 dominated by the persistence and strength of an opposition of principle, or several opposition parties of that nature. In Italy (a special case of type 2) and in France during the Fourth Republic (a special case of type 3), there is close cooperation of parties committed to parliamentary rule and, though not necessarily participating in the cabinet, determined to keep out of the government rival groups of questionable constitutional loyalty. I add that different forms have occurred in the same country at different periods. And the first three categories are based on purely formal parliamentary and coalition mechanics without regard to the content of party politics, while the fourth category derives from this cleavage in fundamental political attitudes.

In terms of majority-minority relationships the system which is based on unequivocal electoral majorities brings about special frustrations when it perpetuates through decades, as it has in Norway and Sweden, the rule of one party again and again returned to office by the voters. Is the situation likely to be reversed? Controversial issues which may favor the opposition certainly have not vanished from the earth; the recent Swedish pension dispute raised such hopes among the opposition parties. When no such issues arise, there is not much minority parties can do outside of hoping for an all-party coalition or relying on the majority's sense of fair play and the general leveling off of party differences in areas not calling for radical political decisions.

A multiparty coalition resulting from considerable proliferation of independent political groups has been a somewhat cumbersome but workable government device, if the participants, as in Denmark, Finland, and the Low Countries, consist of interest and issue-oriented groups, partners in a broad national consensus. It has not worked well in major countries, e.g., Weimar Germany and France of the Fourth Republic. In both cases its partners were hemmed in by a sizable opposition of principle, sometimes on both ends of the political spectrum, with which the moderate groups had to compete in electoral terms while bureaucracy and army increasingly preempted the governmental functions. Moreover, interparty relations became the province of the political specialist, but were a hopeless jungle for the average citizen. As he had not the remotest idea of the parties' capacity for solving concrete problems, the alienation of the noncommitted voter increased to the breaking point.

Whatever the formula, there is common recognition of the legitimacy of any constitutional party's driving for access to governmental power. Even when interparty relations rest on a maximum of mutual trust, which certainly is not the general rule, as the considerable cleavage in Germany shows in contradistinction to Scandinavian harmony, no party enjoys being kept out of office for a lengthy period of time. A party which takes part in a major capacity in the exercise of power benefits by widening the scope of effective action and elevating its traditional program and the men who handle it to the level of national importance. When outside the government, performing brokerage services for its group clientele, the party is in the position of a broker with but little margin to offer to competing clients. Once in power, it has a chance to arbitrate. This not only enhances its prestige with the interest clientele but also provides an opportunity for autonomous action beyond the rival pressures of interest groups. A party in power may even have enough vision to make a success of its farthest-reaching program, and embark upon the road toward the promised land of independent self-initiated policy which gives the erstwhile interest agency the appearance of a spiritual force shaping national destiny. It will impress many an uncommitted voter with the image of the party as a projection of widely approved national interests and national symbols. Such a party and its chief become—as indeed happened in contemporary Germany with Adenauer and his party—a household word in daily use; it is not in need of laborious identification as it partakes of this pseudo-familiarity which in mass society has come to substitute for the irretrievable loss of personal contact.

At least in the cases of clear majority-minority relation, the minority's hope of a reversal of roles keeps its meaning even if in a somewhat reduced form. It not only signifies the acceptance of the reshuffling of old and the coming into operation of new interest combinations. It also represents the traditions, hopes, vistas, and projects of a number of loyal adherents and of a nucleus of political cadres. But whatever its degree of devotion and loyalty, the minority's chance to dispossess the present majority, or—as the case may be—the present senior partner of the majority, lies in the weakening and disintegration of the majority. Strategy directed toward this goal is as much an integral part of the patterns of minority behavior as the previously discussed forms of political cooperation with the majority. If the hoped-for split in majority ranks results from deep cleavages rather than from personal rivalries and incompatibilities, it might substantially affect the political situation. Every party in and out of government will concentrate its efforts at all times on causing dissensions and splits in the ranks of powerful rival groups. These splits may coincide and merge with directed strategy for taking away from the latter specific groups of voters. Thus, the Social Democratic party in Germany in the last half-decade has tried in vain to entice the Catholic manual workers away from the reigning Christian Democratic party. The Socialist party of Belgium has long hoped to wean Catholic workers, chiefly Flemish, away from the Catholic party. But its chances have recently been set back enormously because its school policy, seeking a long-run majority by a change in the balance of the Catholic school–public school population, offended Catholic workers along with other sections of the Catholic population. Dissension within the ranks of the majority party and its general discredit with the voters at large, rather than the switch of loyalties of a specific social group, is the goal when the minority throws some divisive issue into the debate to prevent the majority from carrying through a controversial program; witness the present German debate on atomic armament. Usually party planning in and out of government pursues preservation of cohesion in the ranks (sometimes extending beyond a single party's confines to a coalition) and disruption in the enemy camp. Success of such policies, which depends as much on extraneous factors as on the intelligence, inventiveness, and zeal of the majority, means the disappearance of old and the emergence of new majorities. It is disintegration of majorities rather than simple electoral defeats which alters the parliamentary and governmental landscape; the electoral results confirm the underlying process.

A radical, decisive change has been introduced into the majority-minority mechanism with the emergence of strong political groups not committed to the operational rules of parliamentary government. I am thinking of revolutionary movements and organizations which aim at a social and political order different from the established one but will not forego the use of the latter's institutions for the advancement of their cause. One aspect of the new phenomenon which puts the democratic government in a dilemma is the revolutionary groups' willingness to use both legal and illegal means to undermine the foundations of the democratic order. To the revolutionists the issue is spurious. Revolutionary movements at all times are inclined to think of themselves as the custodians of true, genuine, superior legality threatened or violated by established authority, whose wielders they accuse of ruthlessly manhandling law and justice to stay in power. To have to judge the validity of this claim in a concrete situation is just one among many equivocations with which democratic governments are confronted when revolutionary groups begin to attract great numbers of voters in free elections.

Everybody knows how often the problem has come up in recent decades. It is perhaps less well remembered that a similar problem used to vex constitutional governments in Europe long before the rise of modern totalitarian movements. What to do about a strong revolutionary minority had become a pertinent issue by the end of the nineteenth century with the rapidly swelling tide of organized labor socialism. Not integrated with the established political system, the growing socialist parties insisted on the freedom to operate within its framework. In an essential point, however, things were different in those days as compared to more recent experience with Communist activity. True, socialists prior to World War I took a dim view of assuming governmental responsibilites along with parties of capitalist complexion and kept outside the governmental process. Yet most of them consistently rejected the use of revolutionary means for attaining majority status, as they firmly believed that the ballot—unless interfered with—would get them where they wanted to go. A political movement partly disinclined to cooperate and partly prevented from cooperation in the governmental process by those in power, but unshakably convinced that in the long run the very system of legality and free elections would make for its triumph, is certainly something basically different from present-day Communist parties, to whom it is purely a matter of tactical expediency whether and when to use or not to use illegal means. Relying on the automatism of social and economic development in industrially advanced countries to turn the overwhelming majority of the voters into supporters of the socialist cause, the socialist parties of the pre-1918 era considered exclusion from governmental power a merely transitory stage; eventually they would be voted in by universal suffrage, and power would be theirs to use within a strictly democratic framework.

For the European Communist leadership of our day, however, seizure of power is only tangentially related to the prospect of a majority at the polls. What they primarily count on is a radical shift in the international power setup that would create a situation "objectively" insuring the resumption of the Communist march to power in Western Europe. That is to say, whether or not they stop being semipermanently in the opposition of principle hinges on a complex of factors of which the domestic situation is only one aspect, even though for tactical reasons the Communist party may constantly reiterate its willingness to share in a normal majority government. So far the communists have not envisaged giving up the isolated status of opposition of principle, to the point of participating in a constitutional government in any other manner than as a first step toward doing away with the established political system in its entirety.

Absence of "objective" inpulses for assuming an advance finds its reflection in the general condition inside Western Europe's Communist camp. Regardless of differences in organizational structure, ideology, and objectives as between the Communist organizations and other parties, the postwar vogue of depoliticalization and privatization has not spared the Communist rank-and-file. We might take Louis Aragon's verses as a base of comparison for the metamorphosis taking place in human beings as part of an all-embracing political experience.

> Mon parti m'a rendu mes yeux et ma mémoire,
> Mon parti m'a donné le sens de l'époque,
> Mon parti, mon parti, merci pour tes leçons,
> Et depuis ce temps là, tout me vient en chanson,
> Le colère, l'amour, la joie et la souffrance.

The political reality of the fifties bears little similarity to this image.

The party is hard put to call on sympathizers for political demonstrations, even of minor import; whenever the party machine is out to enlarge its range of influence in an indirect way, it has to be extremely careful to select limited economic objectives susceptible of mass appeal; and it never gets to a point where non-Communist groups could be drawn toward a more permanent partnership. The party's semipermanent minority position is determined not only by its reduced outside appeal but also, and more so, by the passivity of its voters, which sets narrow limits to political action. The "Communist apparatus" may be assured of the following's support at election time, and to a lesser degree for some other narrowly circumscribed campaigns, but the mass of the followers will not, at the present juncture, respond to a more drastic call for action. This may not disturb the party's leaders; they may even find the condition satisfactory, since it practically eliminates the great risk of spontaneous mass action. Spontaneous explosions certainly would not be welcome at a time when

Western Europe's communism is reduced to the standby job of a supporting cast, not unlike the chorus of Greek antiquity, called upon to induce in the public a state of receptivity, but not meant to take part in the performance. This about sums up the dynamics and potentialities inherent in the Communist party's status as a semipermanent minority.

The Communists' chances of using their position within the limits of the parliamentary process as a substitute for, or, perhaps, in support of mass action will depend on whether or not the other parties will be prepared to accept them as legitimate participants in the majority-minority interplay. This the latter so far have refused to do, even though they have not withheld from Communist legislators privileges guaranteed by the constitution. In France, this refusal on the one hand contributed toward freezing the Communists in the isolated position of a semipermanent minority, an opposition of principle; on the other hand it created the necessary minimum of cohesion to keep together or periodically to renew otherwise quite heterogeneous French governmental majorities.

Such has been, between 1947 and 1958, the development in France, and with certain modifications (due to the status of the Nenni Socialists and the commanding position of the Christian Democratic party) in Italy. Parliamentary quarantining of Communist representatives was achieved by means of procedural devices. One of these procedural devices of special savor was that of not counting favorable Communist votes as part of a majority needed for government formation—although a recent premier found it advisable to count the pro-Communist Progressives while virtuously excluding the Communist party votes. Such devices on the parliamentary and electoral level were supplemented—particularly in Italy—by administrative devices of varying legal validity and political effectiveness, such as a nonimplementation of constitutional rules for the formation of regional governments, discrimination in administrative appointments and assignments, etc.[23]

[23] For a criticism of these practices, cf. Piero Calamandrei, *La Constituzione e le leggi per attuarla in Dieci Anni Dopo*, 1945–1955 (Editori Laterza Bari, 1955), pp. 214–316, and Marino Bon Valsassina, "Profilo dell opposizione anticostituzionale nello stato contemporaneo," *Rivista Trimestale di diritto publico*, VII (1947), 531–623, esp. 578 ff. A good example of French Fourth Republic administrative technique of discrimination against "infiltrated" interest groups may be found in Jean Meynaud and Alain Lecelot, "Groupes de pression et politique de logement," *Revue Française des Sciences Politiques*, VIII (1958), 821–60.

On the whole, Communists are granted the freedom of the market place. There is agreement between them and the government to the effect that exercise in the market place may be refreshing so long as the exit is guarded by carabinieri; disagreement is minor—it merely refers to whose carabinieri should watch whom.

It might be interesting to speculate on why the Nazis' threat to the Weimar Republic, which was as deadly, if not more so, failed to produce a realignment of political forces and techniques similar to the one observed in recent years in France and Italy. Postwar lessening of social antagonisms, the presence of the external threat of the USSR, and the German lesson on what political disarray in the face of a common enemy can do to democratic institutions may have contributed toward keeping the political machine in operation in defiance of a powerful opposition of principle.

The semipermanent minority status of the opposition of principle has grown out of a specific historical situation. It took shape at a time in 1947–48 when the repercussions from the National Socialist and Fascist systems were still vividly felt, barring not only the alternative of a right-wing totalitarian mass movement as response to communism, but equally putting temporary obstacles of psychological, legal, and international nature into the way of any form of authoritarian government. The formula of mass democracy operating with a constitutionally admitted but administratively restricted opposition of principle seemed to offer some operative device. However, it does not make for the most beneficent functioning of the democratic system. In distorting the distribution of proportional weight, it blunts the edge of the system. It sins, to save the system itself, against the system's cardinal rule, that the claims of all major groups shall be respected, either by way of the group's inclusion in the government or by means of giving the most careful consideration to demands and interests of groups not so included, which assume the natural function of opposition.

It is possible that substitute channels will open up, contributing toward redressing the faulty balance. For competitive or prestige reasons groups other than the Communists may take it upon themselves to act as the vicarious representatives of social interests previously represented by the opposition of principle.

Generally speaking, vicarious representation is a haphazard device. Reduction in the relative weight of the one group subjected to political quarantine automatically increases that of other groups; this falsifies the standards by which public power arbitrates party claims. Distortion of power proportion not only affects issues of mixed social and political nature, in regard to which the urge to compete for votes may mitigate effects of the vitiated balance. The preweighted scale will prove much more lopsided in issues of greater political importance. There is, e.g., little doubt that curtailment of the party pool from which French government majorities may be chosen delayed workable agreement on disengagement in North Africa, thus creating emergencies which brought down the whole system.

This is neither the time nor the place for predictions as to whether and under what conditions in countries like Italy and France the opposition of principle will ever change into collaboration on the terms of the parliamentary system. It must, however, be said that the Communist parties and, more so, the labor unions under their control are under pressure to take care of the day-to-day needs of their clientele; they are exposed in their own ranks to growing insistence on modes of action more consistent with the pattern of traditional labor parties. Therefore, outside the field of well-publicized propaganda, some mutual accommodation might take place between parliamentary parties and the opposition of principle, be it in parliamentary commissions exercising as they do in Italy some measure of legislative prerogatives or be it on the local level.[24] This mitigates but does not extinguish the consequences of the fact that, for the time being, self-isolation preferred by the opposition of principle and the quarantine imposed on it by adverse political forces work hand-in-glove. Permanent exclusion from the government lets the revolutionary party stay virginal and avoids subjecting its doctrine to the challenge of political reality. But it poorly disguises the fact that the Communist machines' frantic efforts to arrest disaffection and win new recruits neither serve immediate revolutionary action nor secure favorable government response to their followers' demands. Beyond possibly salvaging the parties' prestige, such efforts merely husband potential strength against the unforeseeable day for redeployment behind the shield of a propitious "objective situation."

This brings up once more a consideration of farther-reaching impor-

24 Valsassina, *op. cit.*, p. 595.

tance. I have pointed out the transitory relationship between majority and minority parties; in a mass democracy, which must satisfy a number of conflicting and a great many parallel claims, only a slender dividing line separates the majority from the minority. But this does not in any way imply that mass democracy is doomed blindly to align itself with the lowest denominator and abandon the inseparably interlaced principles of majority rule and minority protection.

Europe's lopsided political compromise of recent experience essentially was forged by two factors, viz., the leveling impact of technological revolution and the shock of, first, the fascist, and later, in a more enduring form, the communist annihilation of democratic political life. But there are broad areas where neither factor has been able to transfigure large sections of the people and where status and class differentiations not only continue as the determining experiences but also have merged with new loyalties transcending national boundaries. There the majority principle in its unadulterated form has remained and must be upheld as the ultimate provider of democratic legitimacy; its enforcement alone can keep revolutionary minorities within the boundary of the legal order.

It is true that under such circumstances the majority principle is as arid in operation as it is unassailable in the realm of theory. It makes it possible to carry out a necessary holding operation which, however, becomes the more ambiguous the more it is met, if not paralyzed, by a kind of holding operation in reverse emanating, as in France and Italy, from an opposition of principle. Of all varieties of modern mass democracy the one operating under the handicap of a sizable opposition of principle is therefore the least safely anchored. It is deprived of democracy's major advantages, the close and constant interweaving between its basis of legality, the formal working of the majority system and its basis of legitimacy, the broad consensus of the citizenry. This type of mass democracy forms therefore—witness Germany in the thirties and present-day France—the point of departure for political venture in quite different directions.

THE WANING OF OPPOSITION IN

PARLIAMENTARY REGIMES

POLITICAL OPPOSITION is an eternal paradox. It postulates the principle that impediments to political action may be wholesome and are therefore to be protected. But what is the chance of institutionalizing such limitations? The parliamentary regime, and the favorable climate it created for the rise of the political party as a vehicle for the exercise of both governmental and opposition functions, has been one of the more felicitous inventions in the limited field of political institutions. But contemporary parliamentary institutions, working as they do in the framework of mass democracy, obey different laws and pressures from those governing their predecessors half a century or a century ago.

Reinvestigation of the meaning of opposition under the conditions of the present age may be in order. For the sake of preciseness these remarks will be restricted to European parliamentary regimes, omitting the role of opposition under presidential regimes, which obey somewhat different political and, as the case may be, social considerations.

I should like to put up three models, two of which pertain to the forms of political opposition. First is the "classical opposition" under the parliamentary form of government, developed from the practices of eighteenth-century England. Second is what might be styled "opposition of principle," bent not only on wrenching power from the government of today but on ending once and for all the system on which that government rests. The third is a counterconcept to the other two;

Reprinted, by permission, from *Social Research*, XXIV (1957), 127–56.

it relates to government under various forms of cartel arrangements among political organizations operating within the framework of parliamentary institutions.

I

If we look only at definitions we might regard Messrs. Eden in 1946 and Gaitskell in 1956 as the linear descendants of Edmund Burke and Charles Fox. Burke's 1770 formula,[1] describing a party as a body of men united for promoting the national interest, by their joint endeavors, on the basis of some particular principle on which we all agree, seems quite acceptable as a definition for the minimum of coherence needed to carry through an effective opposition. But we should not claim more for Burke or for Bolingbroke, his predecessor in the field of manufacturing political ideologies, than is due to them. For both of them, the Archimedean point of party was still "connexion, affection, and friendship" in the face of possible political adversity.[2] It needed the injection of a less savory character, John Wilkes, into the placid waters of eighteenth-century aristocratic politics to start the enlarging of faction to party and the assertion of more than evanescent group interest. But it is important to recall that this transition from the aristocratic parliament of the eighteenth century via the alternation of conservative-liberal governments of the nineteenth century, with their restricted basis of urban middle-class and landowning strata, to the present-day mass-democracy dichotomy of conservatives and labor has taken place in the framework of parliamentary institutions and their game of government and opposition.

What are the bases for this game of alternation? John Morley, the Victorian, considered the right of the defeated group to publicly maintain its principles after they were rejected by the majority to be the foundation of the opposition's functioning.[3] By the end of the 1850s, however, Walter Bagehot had already shown that this continuous right of vindicating solutions rejected by the electorate presupposes that the

---

[1] Edmund Burke, "Thoughts on the Causes of the Present Discontents," in *Works*, World's Classics ed., II, 82.

[2] To cite but one out of many, see H. Butterfield, *George III, Lord North and the People* (London, 1949).

[3] See John Morley, *On Compromise*, 2d ed. (London, 1877), p. 209.

participants in the political game consist of moderate elements. "An ultra-democratic parliament" could not preserve such a state of affairs. There each class would speak its own language, unintelligible to the others, and an "immoderate ministry" and "violent laws" would be the consequence.[4] John Stuart Mill applied similar considerations specifically to the conditions of a society resting on well-organized groups. Competition must be a competition of ideas as well as of interests, because without a competition of ideas and the duty to listen to them the victory of the momentarily more powerful group would always be a foregone conclusion.[5]

To this day the British system and the practices of most of the Dominions of English stock are well within the range of these considerations. On the social and economic level there is continued agreement either on major objectives or, at least, on the mutually permissible range of change. If this agreement no longer existed, it would be rather doubtful whether parliamentary government could be maintained along traditional lines. This would raise questions to which, as a contemporary Australian author puts it, "the current focus of politics hardly suggests an answer." [6] But the experience of the last decades seems not to have confirmed Harold Laski's well-known notions on "the unbridgeable abyss" between Conservatives and Labour, on which he laid so much stress in his analysis of the British parliamentary system in the 1930s.[7]

In an age when foreign policy may determine the very existence of a nation, parliamentary government also presupposes a high amount of opposition confidence in the government's sense of direction in reacting to situations that have to be handled without prior parliamentary discussion; at a minimum it presupposes a complete and unfaltering belief in the majority's sincerity, if it decides to make grave (but in its own mind unavoidable) changes. The Conservative attitude toward the Labour party's abandonment of India may in this connection be compared with the sea of hatred and mutual recrimination recently pro-

---

[4] Walter Bagehot, *Works and Life*, V, 269.
[5] John Stuart Mill, *Representative Government*, ch. 5; see also G. Burdeau, *Traité de science politique*, III (Paris, 1950), 327.
[6] L. F. Crisp, *The Parliamentary Government of the Commonwealth of Australia*, 2d ed. (London, 1952), p. 121.
[7] Harold Laski, *Parliamentary Government in England* (New York, 1938).

duced in comparable circumstances in France. The government-opposition game further presupposes conditions in the army and the civil service which make for firm control and responsiveness to the civilian government. Both army and civil service must leave behind them the idea of forming social-political blocs of their own, warring and coalescing at will with other forces, thus upsetting and falsifying the delicate balance of forces between opposition and government.

If all these conditions are met the respective roles of government and opposition become both clearly defined and constitutionally sacrosanct. As a ceaseless critic, the opposition will try both to wring concessions from the government and to force changes of policies. As the alternative government, it will try to focus public opinion on the possibility and desirability of a speedy change via the electoral process. On the other hand, it is the government's duty to give the opposition full opportunity to carry through its function. To exercise their correlative rights and duties, both majority and opposition are therefore equipped with prerogatives, weapons, and sanctions. The official and salaried position of the leader of the opposition, the practice of informing and conferring with him,[8] the opposition's right to debate topics chosen by itself, the differentiation between the normal function of opposition and obstruction, and the majority's right to use cloture and guillotine to break such obstruction mark the different phases in the institutionalization of opposition.[9]

The government-opposition duel, moreover, does not interrupt the government's relations with the social and professional groups that by tradition and inclination belong to what one may call the clientele of the opposition party. Acceptance of the claims of the opposition's clientele may be limited both by policy considerations and by prior

[8] There may be, however, self-imposed limits to the right of information. The leader of the opposition may find it inconvenient to burden his freedom of action by access to special-privileged knowledge. See *New Statesman and Nation*, LII (September 1, 1956), 234.

[9] In the individual instance it may become difficult to draw the dividing line between opposition and obstruction. Herbert Morrison, the parliamentary veteran of the Labour party, has even doubted whether the opposition has the right to suggest the absence of a quorum; see his *Government and Parliament* (London, 1954), p. 157. On the guillotine resolution to close the debate by compartments and allot a certain amount of time to the discussion of specific sections of a bill—and its democratic indispensability—see Lord Campion, ed., *Parliament: A Survey* (London, 1952), chs. 1 and 7, and I. Jennings, *Parliament* (London, 1939), p. 240.

incompatible obligations toward groups closer to the heart of the government. Within these limits, however, the test of the political skill of a new cabinet may often be found in its dexterity in dealing with and acquiring the confidence of the social strata belonging traditionally to the other flock. This is of the utmost importance as each party competes for the support of voters among the strata that are to a large extent among the opposition's traditional clientele.

The more skillful (or simply lucky) the government, the greater the opposition's quandary in developing what would amount to a policy alternative, and the more intensively must the opposition rely on purely tactical attitudes, taking its cues from the frequent boners that any far-flung administration is bound to commit at one time or another. Like its predecessors of former centuries, it will often pursue opposition for opposition's sake, but its scope of action is now many times enlarged, commensurate with the infinitely larger and more complex administration on which it can focus and pounce for criticism. But though the opposition's writ now extends further, its rewards may be as subject to caprice as those of its predecessors. No longer does caprice take the form of a king's whims and the accompanying reshuffling of party connections, which within the lifetime of a single parliament could bring victory to the opposition. Now, more often than not, the opposition has to wait for the decision of the sovereign electorate, possibly some years distant, to get another chance at power. Even then, the electorate may simply react to momentary situations or persevere in following long-standing social images, neither necessarily connected with the labors of the opposition, real or inconsequential as they may have been. This strong factor of chance, the difficulty in foreseeing which element in a given situation will determine the voters' choice, is inherent in the game of political competition and strengthens the camaraderie of all those participating actively in the political lottery.

While the players are the parliamentary leaders, the game is no longer played for the parliamentary theater alone, but for the quite different audience of mass democracy—the wholesale consumer, or the interest groups, and the retail public, the individual voter. The stage acting is essential only to get the show before the mass audience, the voter. In such circumstances resoluteness and energy are needed to prevent opposition from degenerating into mere routine, and to relate

it to the lives and expectations of a political clientele. The energetic
inclinations of the opposition leader are the weaker the more he has
come by habit, or just occupational disease, to react as part of the over-
all governmental machine. He may fall easy prey to the comfortable
belief that his political chances increase by minimizing rather than by
magnifying the policy differences between opposition and government.

If this should happen, the opposition that exists within every opposition is what becomes the moving force of the country's political machinery. The irregulars rather than the official leadership will strive to
inquire into the deeper reasons for the party's last defeat, clamor for
the overdue great inquest, shout for reformulations of principles and
goals, and redraw the battle lines between government and opposition.
The local party worker may be uninformed, the voter inarticulate; yet
such gadflies may force on the recalcitrant party leadership a sharper
differentiation between official opposition and governmental policies.
They may, at times, run ahead of both leaders and voters, or sometimes
even run amok. Their attitudes may lead the whole organization into
the political wilderness, but that danger may be no greater than the
disorganization threatening from total surrender to the government.[10]
For every Stafford Cripps there is always an aspirant for the position
of the 1931 Ramsay MacDonald. If the opposition may be called the
auxiliary motor of the government, the irregulars—whether in the
ranks of the opposition or of the government party—may well appear
to future generations as the conscience of the public enterprise.

The government-opposition relation as it has unfolded since Dis-
raeli's times presupposes that the government designated by the popularly decided interparty contest remains the final arbiter of the political
fate of the nation. This primacy has not gone unchallenged. British
history at the turn of the century presents a series of challenges of this
supremacy. Charles Parnell and Tom Mann, Sir Edward Carson and the
warlords of World War I, all opposed this leadership claim, and each
was in turn defeated by the political leadership of the nation.

Why did not the government-opposition pattern of parliamentary
government implant itself more firmly into the mores of the major continental countries of Europe? One decisive reason is that the monopoly

[10] This quintessence of a long political career is drawn by L. S. Amery, *My
Political Life*, I (London, 1953), 416.

of final political decision so long remained beyond the grasp of political parties. Until the middle of the nineteenth century, and often much longer, opposition remained "institutional opposition." To some extent parliament as a corporate entity formed the opposition to the government. In such circumstances parliament had to fight for recognition of strictly limited influence against the representatives of more traditional powers, arrayed against it under the cloak of the crown.[11] And even after this system ended—in France in 1869, in Italy in 1871, and in Germany in 1917—political decisions often remained subject to what one may call an *avis préalable*, or a veto exercised, as the case might be, by the army, the upper bureaucracy, or central-bank institutions.[12] With parliament bereft of decisive power and unable to concentrate political decisions in its own hands, strata of the people which had little chance to make their voices heard through other channels turned toward groups that promised remedial action by supplanting the political system as a whole. Hence arose what I should like to call the "opposition of principle."

II

Speaking of the opposition of principle, one thinks mostly of the last decades' totalitarian parties, and is inclined to forget that European socialism of the 1880s, 1890s, and the 1900s posed similar, though less insoluble, problems. The opposition of principle assumes that realization of its program requires full political power—or at least its intentionally or unintentionally ambiguous statements may be interpreted

---

[11] See F. Guizot, *Du gouvernement représentatif et de l'état actuel de la France* (Paris, 1816), pp. 25 ff. Nearly a century and a half later we read in a post-humously published article by one of the martyrs of the Weimar Republic, "In Imperial Germany the government is in the hands of the top of the bureaucracy; the bureaucracy is not dominated by politics; on the contrary, to a large degree it determines policy. On the other hand, in Western Europe the bureaucracy has much less independence of the political hierarchy, the really and immediately governing parliament": Rudolf Hilferding, "Das historische Problem," *Die Zukunft*, March, 1956, p. 83. See also Thomas Ellwein, *Das Erbe der deutschen Monarchie in der Staatskrise* (Munich, 1954); Ellwein (p. 126) characterizes popular representation as "only a limiting element in public life."

[12] On the role of the Bank of France under the Third Republic see Otto Kirchheimer, "Political Compromise," *Studies in Philosophy and Social Science*, Vol. IX, No. 1 (1941).

by its more moderate competitors in this fashion. At times the opposition of principle may be insignificant, and it may never have the chance to seize political power except with the help and as an instrument of foreign backers. At other times it may loom large enough to deflect competition partially or completely from the rules of the parliamentary game, and may force the parliamentary parties into a kind of compulsory cartel and even abdication of their powers into the hands of other institutions—the army, the police, the bureaucracy. In a sense, therefore, the opposition of principle makes its own analysis and prophecy come true. By postulating the uselessness of the whole parliamentary game it may, by its very existence, threaten the parliamentary parties enough to force them into abandoning many of the rules of the parliamentary game.

In these circumstances the meaning of both government and opposition deviates markedly from the classical model. Parliamentary opposition in its classical sense presupposes both the possibility and the preparedness to form an alternative government willing and able to grant its presumptive successor in the opposition the same privileges it enjoyed itself. The very character and goals of an opposition of principle limit its parliamentary chances. It threatens the existence of the other parties, and forces its competitors into preventive and defensive measures. New and discriminatory differentiations between loyal and disloyal opposition are introduced into the parliamentary game. There may be discriminatory constitutional changes, but even outside the sphere of explicit derogation from constitutional rules, new differentiations may be introduced.[13] The votes of the opposition of principle, though counted correctly according to constitutional rules, may be weighed differently in counting votes of confidence or no-confidence. Special rules and usages may be adopted to exclude the members of such an opposition from partaking in parliamentary functions and administrative positions.

Whatever the justifications for these precautions, they inevitably distort political reality by denying adequate representation to those who, for better or worse, insist on giving these parties their confi-

[13] See Georges Berlia, "La révision constitutionelle," *Revue du droit public*, LXI (1955), 164, and Roy Macridis, "A Note on the Revision of the Constitution of the Fourth Republic," *American Political Science Review*, L (1956), 1011–22.

dence. Parliament may continue to provide the basis for the exercise of governmental functions, and not be paralyzed into inaction as in the classic case of pre-Hitler Germany. But its representative function and its possibility of giving expression to the various currents of opinion are bound to suffer.

Thus one test of a democratic political system is the degree to which such opposition of principle, if it has reached some magnitude, may eventually be integrated into the existing political order without forcibly dissolving it or liquidating it or substantially weakening the pursuit of the legitimate interests it represents. Such integration is the more difficult the more elections and parliament are visualized from a purely instrumental viewpoint as a possible, but by no means exclusive, field of political maneuver. European experience in the first half of this century contains numerous examples of both alternatives. Each case of failure or half failure has left the parliamentary system of the country weaker and less able to form the basis for the exercise of political leadership.

III

We come now to the third model: the elimination of major political opposition through government by party cartel. What I have in mind here are not the national or national-unity governments of war and crisis vintage.[14] By their very definition they are exceptional occurrences. Moreover, two of them, the MacDonald government of 1931 and Doumergue's attempt in 1934, were nothing but transparent endeavors to hide an attempt at political realignment and to cash in on the possible good will of the national-unity label. Rather, I have in mind the more than temporary abandonment of the government-opposition relation in contemporary Austria.

Between the end of World War I and the 1934 civil war Austria had a record of bitter and incessant struggle between two major parties, both resting on an amalgamation of social class, political creed, and religious conviction, with a third party too small and inconsequential to play a balancing role. After a relatively short period of coalition between the two major parties immediately subsequent to World War

14 See Dolf Sternberger, *Lebendige Verfassung* (Gleisenheim, 1956), p. 107.

I, the Christian Social party entrenched itself firmly in the saddle of national government. For over a decade its socialist competitor hovered uneasily between the position of a parliamentary opposition and that of an opposition of principle. After World War II approximately the same party constellation emerged, with the two major parties dividing more than 80 per cent of the total vote almost evenly between themselves. In view of the difficult situation of Austria, occupied by both Eastern and Western powers, and the republic's historical record of political frustration and abiding suspicion, the parties decided on a carefully prearranged system of collaboration.[15]

Renewed after the 1956 election, this system has outlasted the occupation. Neither party has been willing to leave the conduct of public affairs in the hands of its competitor or of a civil service working exclusively under its competitor's direction.[16] The two parties proceeded with a detailed parceling out, among their adherents, of all cabinet posts and the majority of the significant administrative positions. This involved explicit understandings on many issues, on appointments, on the filling of regional, local, and semigovernmental jobs, and on the elaboration of legislative programs.[17]

[15] See Bruno Pittermann, "Oesterreichs Innenpolitik nach dem Staatsvertrag," *Die Zukunft*, July, 1955, p. 88.

[16] To quote Pitterman (*ibid.*): "The party that governs alone dominates not only the state apparatus but practically a great part of the economy. In such circumstances not only the employees of the administration of the federal enterprise come under its knuckle, but directly or indirectly also hundreds of thousands of independents and wage earners in the economy. To leave the government is tantamount to losing influence on both political and economic administrative hierarchies."

[17] After the wording of the 1949 and 1953 coalition pacts had become known piecemeal from parliamentary and newspaper discussions and polemics, the participants decided to publish the June, 1956, agreement in its entirety, together with the special agreements on the new delimitation of administrative jurisdictions. The main agreement, as translated from *Arbeiterzeitung* of June 27, 1956, is as follows: "1) The Austrian People's party and the Socialist party of Austria form a government to the exclusion of third parties; they obligate themselves to take over together the responsibility for governmental policy. 2) The relation of strength between the two parties is in principle determined by the results obtained in the elections of May 13, 1956. This proportion is to be applied to proposals for the top positions of the socialized enterprises. The same proportion applies for positions on the boards of directors and in the management of the state-managed banks. The federal government decides appointments as well as changes of the statutes and rules for the banks. 3) The collaboration of the two parties extends over the duration of the parliamentary period. Before the end of

This procedure has led to significant changes in the function of parliamentary institutions in Austria. The inconsequential right-wing and left-wing opposition parties have kept their freedom of parliamentary action. But the members of the two big parties can exercise their normal parliamentary prerogatives—what is now called "acting within the coalition-free area"—only with the permission of the partner party. It would jeopardize the functioning of the cartel agreement to allow party caucuses or individual backbenchers to oppose bills proposed by the government or to introduce motions themselves without previous clearance with the cartel. The area free of the binding rule of the coalition government is predetermined neither by general criteria nor by preestablished subject matter. In each case the parties' possibility of taking back their freedom of action rests on a particular agreement between the coalition partners.[18] Major parliamentary criticism is thus relegated to the status of opposition by joint license.

What have been the consequences of this cartel arrangement? Curiously enough, the restricted exercise of parliamentary opposition has not dried up the competition between the two major parties for the votes of the new voters, of potential switchers from each, and of the

its term new elections can be ordered only through the agreement of both parties. The next elections will be carried through by the cabinet as formed by both parties. 4) A coalition committee, consisting of five representatives from each party, is formed in order to guarantee smooth collaboration. It should convene regularly, and in any case in the event that differences arise between the parties. The federal Chancellor will preside; his deputy is the Vice Chancellor. The two chairmen of the parliamentary clubs are members of the coalition committee. 5) If the two parties represented in the government have unanimously agreed on government bills, as to both substance and form, the bills become binding for the two coalition partners in the national council. Amendments of principle need the consent of the coalition committee. If the government in presenting a bill decides to give the parties a free hand for its legislative stage, the parties regain their freedom of action in the national council. 6) In regard to all other bills and postulates both parties will decide on the modus of voting and, if the case should arise, on reestablishing the freedom of voting for their members. 7) As before, currency problems will be a common responsibility of the two parties. For this reason public statements on currency measures, above all by members of the government, may be made only with the agreement of the Chancellor and the Vice Chancellor."

18 This interpretation, based on the earlier coalition agreement, is confirmed by Bruno Pittermann, the speaker of the socialist faction and more recently Vice-Chancellor, though he expresses some regrets as to the emasculation of parliamentary functions which is thereby implied. See his "Aschenbrödel Parlament," *Die Zukunft*, February, 1955, p. 33.

declining reservoir of third-party voters.[19] In effecting this competition in face of the stringent rules of the cartel agreement, both partners have been quite ingenious in discovering and profiting from any opportunity for competition. A minister may utilize the key position assigned to him under the coalition pact in order to carry through some controversial policy by administrative fiat, thus trying to create a *fait accompli* in favor of his own party. On the other hand, if a party has to agree to a compromise particularly distasteful to its clientele, it will be allowed to make enough parliamentary and extraparliamentary noises to convince its clientele of the intensity of its reluctance. This then leads to a new kind of built-in opposition which the Austrians themselves have baptized *Bereichsopposition*, meaning opposition to what is happening under the agreed-upon jurisdiction of the other party.[20] The Socialists may fight verbal battles against a monetary policy of the Ministry of Finance, controlled by the Christian People's party. The latter may pay back in vehement extraparliamentary and measured parliamentary criticism of the conduct of the Socialist ministry responsible for transport, electricity, and—until the jurisdictional changes of last summer—nationalized enterprises.

Although Austria has come close to being a two-party state, the

[19] The relevant election results—taken from Hans Müller, "Die Wahlen im Spiegel der Statistik," *Die Zukunft*, May-June, 1956, p. 136—are as follows:

	1945	1949	1953	1956
Registered voters	3,449,000	4,391,000	4,586,000	4,614,000
Election participation in % of reg. voters	95%	96.8%	95.8%	95.9%
Percent of valid vote received by:				
Christian People's party (OVP)	49.8	44.4	41.26	45.96
Socialist party (SPO)	44.6	38.7	42.1	43.04
Independents (Freedom party 1956)		11.68	10.59	6.52
Communist party (KPO)	5.41	5.08	5.28	4.44

[20] In the words of Friedrich Scheu, "Die Kritik der Demokratie," *Die Zukunft*, February, 1956, p. 36, "Austria succeeded in inventing a political system in which two parties are permanently in coalition with each other and nevertheless continue to compete uninterruptedly between themselves. Each of them is simultaneously government party and opposition party, because each of them is opposition within the governmental jurisdiction of the other party." The same viewpoint is expressed by the spokesman of the Austrian People's party; see Alfred Maletta, "Wahlausgang, Regierungsbildung und künftiges Programm," *Oesterreichische Monatshefte*, May, 1953, p. 258. Representatives of the rightist opposition, excluded by these agreements from political influence, characterize the situation disparagingly as *Reserveopposition;* see Kraus in Nationalrat, 3d Session, 63d Meeting, March 1, 1955, *Stenographische Berichte*, p. 2937.

election does not decide which party will form the government and which will be relegated to the opposition. Nevertheless, as the 1956 election has convincingly shown, the electoral process retains a clear-cut meaning. The shift of votes decides the conditions of collaboration. Administrative and legislative determination of the issues that are controversial between the parties is heavily influenced by the verdict of the voters. But it takes place by agreement and compromise worked out on the basis of election results rather than by majority fiat.

What about the compatibility of the different social-economic orientations of the partners of a coalition government? How are the views of the proponents of extensive state intervention and of an important planned sector made compatible with the endeavors of those who want a so-called free-market economy? The problem looks more formidable in theory than it is in practice. All governments operate within the limits and necessities of their period, which rarely allow either a consistent interventionist or a consistent free-market pattern. The most arduous adherents of a free-market economy have steadfastly followed a policy of protection and interventionism in the agricultural sector, with the Austrian government assuredly no exception to this rule. Everything is therefore a matter of degree and compromise; and these compromises have to be carried out irrespective of whether they are forced on a classic one-party alternation government, by the needs of multifarious political clienteles, or on a coalition government, where the various currents are represented by distinct parties.[21] Changes rarely spring Minerva-like from Zeus's head at the prompting of program builders who got the ear of the public at election time. More often than not it is the imperative requirement of a new societal situation which makes such programs sprout and be adopted by all those who want either to stay or to get a fresh start in the political business. What at first looks like a clear-cut dichotomy is mostly in point of fact a continuum.

A more fundamental objection to the Austrian-type cartel agreement, and one that has been voiced against similar tendencies of some present-day German state governments, rests on the resulting absence

----

[21] See, however, Henri Bartoli, "Rôle et exigences d'une planification socialiste," *Esprit*, May, 1956, pp. 749, 755, who denies that a mixed economy could be feasible for any length of time.

of the opposition's control function. Each party may have an interest in covering up the inefficiency, waste, and corruption of its partner. Hence arise all the problems of institutionalized reinsurance practices. Neither public opinion, to the extent that such an animal exists independently of interest groups closely tied in with the major parties, nor the small opposition of principle represented in parliament has enough breadth of action, inside knowledge of the administration, or authority with the public at large to compensate for the absence of a major parliamentary opposition group.[22] Control is mutual control in the matrix of a government acting within the confines of the coalition agreement; the party and parliamentary discussion sets the frame for the compromise effected inside the government. And the contours of this discussion are doubtless more skimpy than those indicated by the classical distinction between opposition and obstruction. In any case the voters, by increasingly concentrating their votes on the two major parties, have decided that from their viewpoint the two parties' right to participate jointly in government and administration is of greater social and political consequence than the traditional opposition function, and has preference over it.[23]

[22] The post-mortem discussion concerning the U.S.-controlled radio broadcasting station Red White Red, with its popular Watschenmann broadcasts, illustrates the difficulties of independent criticism under a coalition-party government. Scheu (cited above, note 20), p. 38, remarks about this station: "It was a creation of the American occupation powers, and as such responsible to nobody in Austria. Aside from U.S. propaganda, it needed to consider nobody and to pursue nobody's interests. But its existence was a paradox, and this paradox terminated necessarily with the occupation. An Austrian office cannot be so irresponsible, it cannot risk besmirching citizens by assertions which might turn out to be wrong." Scheu goes on to emphasize how desirable it would be if certain broadcasts could be made within the "party-free area," though he hastens to admit how difficult it would be to create independent organs for criticism. The usual difficulties with media run by public authorities are compounded in this case by the fact that the authority is bipartite and that extreme care has to be taken lest the media create the slightest disturbance in the delicate interparty equilibrium.

[23] The East German bloc system, which forces artificially created parties into collaboration with the State party, has little similarity with the voluntary cartel described here, or, for that matter, with any of the other forms of coalition government. In order to protect the State party and the other admitted political organizations from unfair competition, the DDR prevents the rise of any nonparticipating organization. Its government thus becomes a full-fledged compulsory cartel, dominated by one of its members, the State party, with the latter allocating tidbits of power to the other participants, strictly according to its own devices. Moreover, any element of competition among the cartel participants themselves

One might argue that the Austrian case constitutes an extreme procedure responding to the particularities of a very difficult local situation in a weak nation. But while the Austrian arrangement may differ considerably from other European coalition governments, they all to a greater or lesser extent depart from the principle of concentrated responsiblity and alternative government inherent in the classical formula. The deviation may be small when the main governmental coalition partner, as at present in Sweden [24] or in the Federal Republic of Germany,[25] or the major opposition party, as in Belgium, is so strong that the system in some respects, though by no means in all, operates as if there were a clear-cut government-opposition dichotomy. The deviation is bound to become much more accentuated in France—at least until the disappearance of a unified Gaullist party—and in Italy, where the existence of a substantial opposition of principle forces the traditional parliamentary parties into a kind of compulsory cartel, irrespective of whether they form part of the government. If the regime is assailed by a substantial bloc of noncooperators on both the right and the left flanks, or if cooperation can be bought only on unacceptable terms, opposition and opposition of principle may become almost identical.

---

is excluded by the device of common electoral lists, with prearranged quotas of seats allocated to each participant. Steiniger, the theoretician of the system, referred to it—before he was forced into abandoning his somewhat too cynical exegesis—as "the maximum of artificial homogeneity which may be obtained by political technique," but he hastened to add that even this degree of homogeneity, in what he considered still a heterogeneous society, presupposes for its functioning some changes in the social order. See Alfons Steiniger, *Das Blocksystem* (Berlin, 1949), pp. 20, 21.

[24] The permanent hegemony of the Social Democratic party in Sweden, and the consequent permanent opposition in which the conservative and liberal parties find themselves, has led to a demand for a national coalition of all "constitutional parties"; see D. A. Rustow, *The Politics of Compromise* (Princeton, 1956), pp. 219 ff. Such proposals seem to have little chance, in spite of the favorable echoes they have found. Nobody seems to press them too hard, as there exists a high amount of mutual confidence among all parties and the actual administration is separated well enough from purely administrative positions to minimize the disadvantages of those who are not represented in the government.

[25] For an exhaustive discussion of the character of the federal government in Germany see Sternberger (cited above, note 14), p. 128. His acute observations and interesting formulations suffer, however, from a tendency to shove off sociological party analysis as unproductive for his constructs and then proceed on a somewhat problematic basis to proclaim the classic government-opposition relation both as norm and as desirable goal; see especially p. 147.

In France, despite the presence of a substantial opposition of principle, either the working of the election system—especially tailored for that purpose in 1951—or, in the present assembly, the availability of blocs of overseas deputies for a variety of governmental combinations has left a certain margin within which individual political figures may whip varying party combinations into line. But from the viewpoint of the public at large the major difference between parliamentary groups and extraparliamentary mass movements operating within parliament as an opposition of principle tends to blot out more subtle distinctions. The French elections of January, 1956, gave evidence that in the voter's mind the major decision lies between the traditional parliamentary groups and the opposition of principle. Transfer of votes to and from the opposition of principle is of greater importance than the internal transfer of votes among the various parliamentary groups. Acting in this fashion, however, the voter largely abdicates the role assigned to him under the classical government-opposition scheme, namely, to participate in the arbitration of conflicting leadership claims among parties operating within the framework of the regime. Thus the vote determines at best the margin that the groups loyal to the regime retain to form and reform their ephemeral alliances, and influences to a lesser degree the process of cabinet forming.[26] This insensitivity of government formation toward popular currents allows the opposition of principle to contest the moral title of the government to represent the country, thus confronting the *pays légal* with the *pays réel*.

There may be neither abiding suspicion, leading to a watertight voluntary cartel, nor crisis of the regime, leading to a compulsory or near-compulsory cartel arrangement: coalition government may be simply a consequence of a well-established multiparty system, as in present-day Holland, Weimar Germany, or interwar Czechoslovakia. But whatever the reason for the coalition arrangements, their establishment and practices are all bound to lead to deviations from the classical norm. The major government party may be concerned mainly with dislodging one partner or switching coalition partners. The opposition parties too may fight on various fronts; without the possibility of

[26] Some of these problems are discussed in R. A. Aron, "Electeurs, partis et élus," *Revue française des sciences politiques*, April-June, 1955, p. 304, and in Philip Williams, *Politics in Post War France* (London, 1954), especially p. 358.

308 TRANSFORMATION OF DEMOCRATIC POLITICS

setting up a government of their own, they may concentrate energy on improving tactical chances of government participation.[27] This purpose may involve subtle modulations of policy in regard to various governmental or other opposition parties. The possible variations and combinations are of great variety. Neither of the constellations is conducive to a sharp differentiation between government and opposition policies. The tortuous ways of the multiparty government and of multiopposition tactics are the province of the political professional. The public at large looks at the results, while the more loyal party public may judge also by intentions.

Nevertheless, a multiparty coalition government need not be congenitally weak, nor need a divided opposition be impotent. Everything depends on the character of the various participants and their leadership, and on the temper of national political discourse and action. The maxim "where all govern, nobody governs" does not correctly describe all relevant factual situations.[28] Prewar Czech and postwar Dutch governments, though they were difficult to assemble, show a reasonable record of stability and efficiency.[29] On the other hand, multiparty government in the larger countries has more often than not been weak. The difficulty in bringing together various factions, the limited minimum program to which the coalition partners are willing to subscribe, and the concomitant attempts to restrict the mandate given to the parties' representatives in the cabinets inevitably provoke sharp counterthrusts. Each cabinet minister will try to assert his maximum independence of his group, emphasize the dignity and independence of his office, and make the most of his assertion that he is His Majesty's or the nation's representative. He will therefore fall in most eagerly with the higher ranks of the bureaucracy who might liberate him from the embraces and demands of his party.

27 On this point see S. Landshut, "Formen und Funktionen der parlamentarischen Opposition," in *Wirtschafts und Kultursystem*, Festgabe für A. Rüstow (Winterthur, 1945), p. 223.

28 See M. F., "Vom Fug und Unfug der Koalitionen," *Gegenwart*, May 19, 1956, pp. 303, 305, underlining the statement by Sternberger (cited above, note 14) that the rise and acknowledgment of opposition is one of the most significant deeds in the history of democracy. While the historical truth of this statement is uncontestable, it has to be read in the light of all the modifications that have marked the fate of opposition in the last decades.

29 On the Dutch experience see H. Daalder, "Parties and Politics in the Netherlands," *Political Studies*, III, No. 1 (1955), 1.

Such "liberation tendencies" are not restricted to representatives of multiparty coalition governments. But the fact of having been carried to power by a strong party, whether within the frame of the classic two-party system or as participant of a strong and stable coalition, enhances the chance that a minster will be willing and able to implant his party's value scale and program. Ministers of a weak coalition government are more predisposed to become instruments in the hands of their official advisers. It is in such cases that the always latent nineteenth-century antinomy, with parliament opposing the administration as an intrinsically inimical institution—so well known from the practice of presidential regimes—has a tendency to become universal. But unless the parties want to be relegated to the role of political prayer mills, this can be only a transitional and, from the viewpoint of the parliamentary regime, uncomfortable solution.

Political opposition as a continuing function presupposes the existence of a yardstick for governmental performance. The opposition of principle need not bother to unearth such a yardstick, as the very existence of the government is sufficient proof of its wickedness. In contrast, opposition within the confines of the parliamentary system presupposes some semblance of coherence if at least some vestige of a rational alternative to the government's policy is to be preserved.

This coherence may have its roots in program, ideology, and tradition. To be sure, coherence is always threatened, if for no other reason than the fact that in our day and age both government and opposition are always faced with unforeseen and unforeseeable situations requiring immediate action without their catechism offering satisfactory or, indeed, any answers. Gone are the days when a man could make up a program at the outset of his career to last all his life.[30] But coherence is more likely with a party that has a tradition and some hold over its clientele, and therefore can afford the luxury of convictions, than with a marginal group whose survival, depending on the outcome of the next election, requires that it makes its decisions on exclusively tactical grounds. The freedom of movement of the first is principally determined by the objective requirements of the situation it encounters when it comes to power; the latter is subjected to all the additional impediments stemming from its uneasy and always imperiled relations

[30] See the instructive remarks of D. Ostrogorsky in *Democracy and Political Parties*, I (New York, 1902), 22.

with its more comfortable competitors. To the extent that coalition government and multifarious opposition rest on quickly shifting and purely tactical alignments, they provide only an indistinct focus for the exercise of governmental responsibility and the complementary function of parliamentary opposition.

IV

The question arises whether this desiccation of the opposition that has here been followed through a number of variations can be attributed to more or less technical factors, and hence could be reversed by technical changes in election procedures or parliamentary rules. Can it be maintained, for example, that the voluntary cartel system of Austria, the erosion of the opposition function under the semicompulsory cartels of France and Italy, the abuses of some multiparty coalition governments—all detrimental to the exercise of the classic opposition function—could be changed by the introduction of more suitable electoral systems or by different practices governing rules of no-confidence, dissolution, and the setting up of new governments? It seems unlikely. There is no meaningful connection between the form of the electoral system, the practices and malpractices of government formation, and the crisis of the concept of political opposition. It may be more rewarding to look into the incongruities between continental party systems and the social realities of the twentieth century.

Continental European parties are the remnants of intellectual and social movements of the nineteenth century. They have remained glued to the spots where the ebbing energy of such movements deposited them some decades ago. The more violent twentieth-century eruptions, fascism and communism, have surged much further, but in flowing back have petrified rather than envigorated the existing system. Postwar attempts at rationalization have produced some new variations, but have not eliminated the basic heritage of the parties. They were built around combinations of nineteenth-century class, occupational, and religious, or, as the case might be, antireligious interests. How does this heritage relate to the most important stages of twentieth-century transformation?

From the viewpoint of political dynamics, the most important change is probably the emergence of a substantial new middle class of skilled workers, the middle ranks of white-collar people, and civil servants. All their work is done under instruction from superiors. Similarities of situation, thought processes, and expectations outweigh still existing traditional distinctions. Their consumption expectations, resting on the concept of increasing prosperity, as well as the demands they address to the community at large for sufficient protection against institutional and personal hazards of life, are identical. The cleavage that separates them from the more successful elements of the older independent middle classes—the artisans and peasants of medium-size holdings, both with enough capital equipment to profit from technological progress—is diminishing. The technological revolution is changing the outlook of these tradition-bound and conservative groups at the same time that it reduces their size. Increasingly enmeshed in the fortunes of the national economy, they now raise claims, identical with those of the new middle class, for guaranteed real-income levels and participation in social-insurance schemes. To this extent the struggle between the independent old middle class and the employed new middle class is more a struggle for similar goals than a clash of incompatible programs.

To the extent that all major parliamentary parties are permeated by the opinions and attitudes of these groups, strategic on account of both their size and the compactness of their professional organizations, one may justifiably say that diminished social polarization and diminished political polarization are going hand in hand. As Beatrice Webb expressed this particular phenomenon forty-odd years ago, "the landslide in England towards Social Democracy proceeds steadily, but it is the whole nation which is sliding, not the one class of manual workers." [31] We are faced with a somewhat languishing system of interparty competition which in many cases is even overshadowed by intraparty competition, the attempt of the various interest groups represented in one party to have an official party stand adopted that is maximally favorable to them. [32] The parliamentary party has thus become in a double

[31] Beatrice Webb, *Diaries, 1912–1924* (London, 1952), p. 18.
[32] These trends appeared earliest and in the most succinct form in Sweden. See Herbert Tingsten, "Stability and Vitality in Swedish Democracy," *Political*

sense a harmonizing agency. It harmonizes first the conflicting claims within its ranks, and on this basis participates in interparty adjustments on the governmental level.[33]

The same harmonizing tendencies are potently reenforced by the contemporary opinion-forming process. The rise of the nineteenth-century party was inseparably linked with the growth of newspapers as vehicles for the creation and expression of public opinion. The newspapers, being politically oriented, and helping aspirants for political power to obtain recognition and spread their doctrine, were the handmaidens of emerging parliamentary government.[34] Twentieth-century media of communication are not primarily politically oriented. They are business enterprises bent on maximizing profits from huge investments by catering to the inclinations and aspirations of a presumed near totality of readers and listeners, rather than appealing to an educated elite. They interlace the consumption expectations of their readers and listeners with the interests of their backers and advertisers. In order to fulfill this dual mission they preserve a maximum of neutrality, not only between the possibly conflicting interests of the various advertisers, but also between the prejudices of the various strata of their readers and listeners. Resting on a presupposed harmony of interests among advertisers, financial backers, readers, and listeners, they are using the Hays-office technique of neutralizing and playing down divisive elements or transferring elements of conflict from the domestic to the international scene.[35] The rise of consumer-oriented public-opin-

---

Quarterly, XXVI (1955), 140–51: "As the general standard of values is so commonly accepted, the function of the state becomes so technical as to make politics appear as a kind of applied statistics." See also his statements (p. 148) on the nature of political parties.

[33] Compare the formula utilized by Fritz Erler, a leading contemporary German politician, in "Die Sozialdemokratische Partei—Eine Partei unter Vielen," *Neue Gesellschaft* (1956), pp. 200, 203: "The SPD even in its own concepts needs to harmonize the various group interests, in order to obtain in this fashion the total interest of a libertarian-democratic society."

[34] "A political party needs a newspaper for its propagandistic purposes. In order to keep the newspaper going one needs a literary section (*feuilleton*); therefore the author of a serial story must press the ideas of his party chief and his newspaper": A. Thiers, as quoted by A. Vagts, "Heinrich Börnstein, Ex and Repatriate," in Missouri Historical Society, *Bulletin* (January, 1956), p. 112.

[35] For a partial analysis see Jacques Kayser, *Mort d'une liberté* (Paris, 1955). S. Diamond, *The Reputation of the American Businessman* (Cambridge, Mass., 1955), brings out very well the importance of mass communication for the maintenance of consensus in the functioning of society.

ion formation has been one of the most powerful elements in the reduction of the political element to the semientertainment level.[36]

Thus objective factors of social development and conscious efforts join in breaking down barriers between some strata of society and in creating what has been rather prematurely styled a unified middle-class society. This theme of a unified middle-class society has been pressed most consistently in postwar Germany; one author has recently gone so far as to approximate present-day conditions with the classless society, alluding in this context to the well-known slogan of the transformation of the state into an organ for day-to-day administrative concerns.[37] It is open to question to what extent such utterances both overstress and generalize from some particular aspect of German postwar experiences. At any rate, analogous, if not always so pronounced, social and economic changes in other continental European countries have not been followed to the same degree by tendencies toward privatization which allow, as it were, for the transformation of political problems into administrative and technical routine; the persistence of a large opposition of principle in France and Italy is inevitably leading to an emphasis on the repressive function of the state.

Moreover, the same process that has created a new middle class and lessened the distance between the old and new elements has everywhere uprooted divers other social strata, and has so far failed to assign them a satisfactory position within the new society. The main victims of this process of transformation have been older people whose income has not kept pace with inflation, small peasant holders, small artisans and retailers without the capital to modernize their shops, and white-collar elements economically outflanked by many groups of manual workers and unable to acquire a new feeling of "belonging" to compensate for the meagerness of their occupational existence. These changes, too, have indelibly marked the present party system. These strata form a steady source, even in present favorable economic circumstances, for a predominantly but not exclusively right-wing oppo-

[36] The role of the "lowest common denominator" in the news presentations of the movie industry is forcefully analyzed in H. M. Enzensberger, "Die Anatomie einer Wochenschau," *Frankfurter Hefte*, XII (1957), 265–78.

[37] The extreme formulation is that of S. Landshut, "Die Auflösung der Klassengesellschaft," *Gewerkschaftliche Monatshefte*, VII (1956), 451; in the same direction is H. Schelsky's speech, "Haben wir heute noch eine Klassengesellschaft?" reprinted in *Das Parlament*, February 29, 1956.

sition of principle. By the same token, they are an element in the petrification of the traditional parliamentary parties.

To compete with the opposition of principle for this substantial vote, the parliamentary parties find it useful to fall back on their nineteenth-century heritage. This heritage may vary widely: with the socialists it may mean an occasional harking back to the class basis of political structure and its promise of a classless society; with the vaguely Christian catch-all parties, in vogue after the war, it may mean the concept of spiritual brotherhood or a specific religious appeal, transcending the cleavages of the day; and with the liberal or radical socialist parties it may refer to the autonomy claim of the noncollectivized individual, raised against both church and state. What we are here concerned with, however, is not the content of the often interchangeable doctrines but their survival as an element in keeping together or bringing again together the various elements of formerly unified groups, now torn asunder in the process of social transformation, employing here the unity of the working classes or there the image of a self-reliant independent middle class.

To be sure, not all—or even most—members of status-threatened disadvantaged and dissatisfied groups join the ranks of the opposition of principle. But this is probably less significant as indicating the continuing attraction of the parliamentary party than as emphasizing the fact that the primarily consumption-oriented thought process of their more fortunate brethren has become for them a natural habit. They momentarily accept the parliamentary party not because it struggles to uphold a lien on their grandfathers' social vision but because they grant some advance credit to its promise to give a high priority to their material claims.[38] Mistrustful of the more remote if all-embracing solutions of the opposition of principle, they accept the parliamentary party's arbitration regarding the extent to which their claims can at present be honored without conflicting with other weighty claims. But

---

[38] Thorough postelectoral inquiries into voters' motivations and preferences, recently carried through in the first electoral district of Paris, contain much material reinforcing this thesis as to voters' motivations in preferring parliamentary parties; see Jean Stoetzel and Pierre Hassner, "Résultats d'un sondage dans le premier secteur de la Seine," in *Les élections du 2 janvier 1956*, Cahiers de la Fondation Nationale des Sciences Politiques, LXXXII (Paris, 1957), 199-248, especially 228-30.

some claims have to be honored here and now if their loyalty to the parliamentary part is to last.

In the final analysis it is this urgency of group claims which militates against the parliamentary party's breathing for any length of time outside the precincts of government. It has greatly weakened the party's desire to don the robes of parliamentary opposition, as this would lessen its effectiveness in the adjudication of group claims, which in our time has become its *raison d'être*. If a party chooses voluntarily to go into opposition—which happens under conditions of a multiparty state—it does so for purely tactical reasons, in order to fasten the burden of unpopular policies on some political competitor, or in order to be free to outbid the opposition of principle by espousing some manifestly inflated group claims.

The rise of the consumption-oriented individual of mass society thus sets the stage for the shrinking of the ideologically oriented nineteenth-century party. After the unlimited extension of the party concept, first in the traditional *Weltanschauungs* party and more recently in the totalitarian movement, its recent reduction to a rationally conceived vehicle of interest representation becomes noticeable.[39] By and large, European parliamentary parties are reducing their special ideological and material offerings.[40] Instead, they substitute a demand for a wide variety of ever expanding community services, open on a basis of equality to whole categories of citizens. Unlike the totalitarian movements they are not equipped to overrun the state machine; at best they aspire to participate in the rewards and premiums it offers. In reminiscence of tradition,[41] or more likely as a planned investment in a public

[39] Of course, there are exceptions. Israel, with its odd mixture of avant-garde and arrière-garde elements, responds to a conscious transfer of traditional European institutional patterns and the pressing material needs of the moment. Its parties are conceived of both as ideological entities and as vehicles for special party-connected customer services. An intensive party life results. See Benjamin Akzin, "The Role of Parties in Israeli Democracy," *Journal of Politics*, XVII (1955), 507; but note especially his remark on page 519, visualizing the possibility of a receding of direct intervention of parties into social matters in the foreseeable future.

[40] Carlo Schmid's speech, "Die Sozialdemokratische Partei Deutschlands vor der geistigen Situation dieser Zeit," before the 1950 SPD convention in Hamburg, is characteristic of this tendency toward a sharp reduction of party functions.

[41] Heinz Meyer, "Struktur der deutschen Sozialdemokratie," *Zeitschrift für Politik* (1955), pp. 348, 354, reveals that only one of nineteen functionaries on whom the inquiry centered did not have a background of "family party tradition."

career, individuals may still become party workers. But the tendency for the party to exercise a brokerage function for specific interest groups is present, and is likely to become more accentuated as time goes on. Thus the nonprofessional in politics is destined to be relegated to a back seat. The interest group, however, as distinct from the individual party member, manifests a loyalty that is limited and contingent. Not only may this loyalty be transferred to more useful political groups, but support may be given simultaneously to groups competing in the political arena.

The modern party is thus forced to think more and more in terms of profit and loss. To it, opposition scarcely relates to the sum total of style, philosophy, and conduct of government, but concentrates on some concrete measure where the government decision may reflect a balance of forces disadvantageous to the interests the party represents. This does not mean that in other instances the balance may not be more favorable, or, even more important, that participation in administrative implementation could not redress the balance in its favor. In such circumstances government participation becomes a matter of necessity; the party would consider it an unmitigated evil if it were excluded for any length of time. But it is also worth while to look at the other side of the coin. While government participation furthers the claims of the party's backers, it also allows the party to assert its own authority over them. The radiation of state authority involved in the party's moving from the brokerage stage to the position of an arbitrator removes the party from many suffocating embraces and carries it beyond the confines of its interest configurations.

The party's alertness in first pursuing and then arbitrating the claims of its clientele is not necessarily related to an equally clear-cut vision of the processes of history at large. The modern party man knows where he has to take his stand if the roll call concerns a question of taxation of consumer cooperatives or an increase in maternity benefits. There are few guideposts to enlighten him as to the best course on EDC or the recognition of Communist China. A roll call of contemporary politicians of many countries and parties would show only a tiny minority who could meaningfully relate the broad canvas of international politics to their domestic objectives.[42] In addition, the more

42 Gerhard Lütkens, "Die parlamentarische Aussenpolitik in der Opposition," *Aussenpolitik*, II (1951), 398, makes a somewhat tormented attempt to vindicate

freedom of decision in the realm of foreign policy has narrowed down in the last decade, as a consequence of international developments, the more difficult becomes the offering of foreign-policy alternatives. No parliamentary opposition in Great Britain, France, Italy, or Germany can, without evoking the specter of incalculable and frightening consequences, propagandize a reversing of alliances as a goal and consequence of its coming to power. This lack of realistic alternative solutions leads to a certain sterility and artificiality in the foreign-policy arguments of parliamentary opposition parties, which for better or worse are tied to the geographic location, to the prevailing social system, and consequently also to the international engagements of their countries.

Differences within the precincts of parliamentary politics thus narrow down to squabbles over the most advantageous arrangements and courses of action within the concert of Western powers. Such differences, as the French battle over the ratification of EDC showed, do not necessarily set one parliamentary party against another, but may cut across party lines. Only the opposition of principle, which does not have to face the likelihood of its coming to power in the near future, may envisage and even risk its very existence on a revolutionary foreign-policy program, its opposition becoming the more irreconcilable the more its policy outlook as a whole is determined by its foreign-policy affinities. The present international situation need not last. The imminent loss of the major powers' monopoly of atomic weapons, and the consequent likelihood of a loosening up of the bipolar international system, may create new areas of foreign-policy choice. But as long as the present bipolarity lasts, it contributes both to widening the gulf between parliamentary parties and the opposition of principle and to shrinking the sphere of the truly parliamentary opposition.

This transition from the ideologically oriented continental party of earlier times to the more limited congeries of interest-oriented groups is one of the elements behind the erosion of the classic opposition. But the demise of the opposition is not tantamount to the complete dismantling of the European party, relegating it to some form of pro-

---

this dualism as more than technical in character. A more realistic German appraisal may be found in Wilhelm Hennis, "Parlamentarische Opposition und Industriegesellschaft," *Gesellschaft-Staat-Erziehung* (1957), pp. 205–22.

cedural device to be used for every comer to fight particular and eternally changing issues, as the stereotype of the political party in the United States would have it.[43] Other factors still favor some measure of party cohesion. One is the existence of an opposition of principle, threatening the continuation of present political patterns. Another is the fact that there are fairly constant elements—slurred and overlapping through they may be—determining which type of interest a party may pick up.[44]

Thus the parliamentary party may continue as a relatively stable entity. But the unifying and leveling element of the mass media and a certain lessening of social polarization mark a definite stage in the decline of this delicate part of our political heritage, the classic parliamentary opposition. It is in this sense that the Austrian practice of coalition pacts with built-in opposition devices commands interest. It presents a limited survival and revival of the opposition concept at a time when opposition ideologies either have come to serve as handmaidens of total and revolutionary social and political change or are becoming downgraded to the role of relatively meaningless etiquettes and advertisement slogans within the framework of interest representation.

[43] Interesting material for comparisons between reality and stereotype can be found in L. D. Epstein, "British Mass Parties in Comparison with American Parties," *Political Science Quarterly*, LXXI (1956), 97.
[44] Problems of "interest coloration" of political parties are discussed by R. Breitling, *Die Verbände in der Bundesrepublik* (Meisenheim, 1955), and by M. L. Lange in the postscript to *Parteien in der Bundesrepublik* (Stuttgart and Düsseldorf, 1955), pp. 507 ff. On the predominance of the interest motive in what is officially dubbed a *Weltanschauungspartei* see the interesting discussion by G. Schulz, "Die CDU," *ibid.*, pp. 3, 146.

GERMANY:

THE VANISHING OPPOSITION

IN THE PARTICULAR CONTEXT of the German experience, the terms with which we are concerned may be defined as follows:

1. We shall refer to "political competition" if political jobs are filled by selection from candidates whose number is in excess of the places to be filled.

2. We shall speak of "loyal opposition" if the political competition involves some form of goal differentiation between available candidates in harmony with the constitutional requirements of a given system.

3. We shall speak of "opposition of principle" if the competitor's behavior indicates the desire for a degree of goal displacement incompatible with the constitutional requirements of a given system.

Any form of political opposition necessarily involves some kind of competition. The reverse does not hold true: political competition does not necessarily involve opposition.

Our problem, in German terms, is about 100 years old. The Bismarck constitution functioned in a society split into two major camps. On the one hand was the military-bureaucratic complex which dominated Prussia, monarchic in principle; on the other, the up-and-coming bourgeoisie. While the monarchy represented the state, officially identified with the moral order, the bourgeoisie stood for the sum total of what the Germans would call *die bürgerliche Gesellschaft*. Executive power remained concentrated with and at the disposal of those in

Reprinted, by permission of Yale University Press, from *Political Oppositions in Western Democracies*, ed. Robert A. Dahl (New Haven, 1966), pp. 237-59.

control of the state, while legislative power had become a joint enterprise of those controlling the state and the forces of the *bürgerliche
Gesellschaft*. Since Bismarck's grant of federal universal suffrage in
1868, the urban proletariat had been brought to political notice as an
independent and rapidly swelling section of Germany's *bürgerliche
Gesellschaft*. Bismarck had not meant to integrate the working class
into the official order as both the Liberal and Conservative parties had
done in England. Rather he thought to keep the liberal bourgeoisie at
bay in its own bailiwick, the parliamentary assembly, by utilizing the
working-class franchise. But, as with so many of his domestic political
schemes, he was unsuccessful. Through Bismarck's grant of federal
universal franchise, the long-standing cleavage between the official
state power and the *bürgerliche Gesellschaft* acquired more disturbing
dimensions as Social Democratic party (SPD) opposition of principle
increased.

This opposition of principle grew by leaps and bounds during the
halcyon days before World War I. It was both a political party and a
chapel. Some of its leaders were intent on nudging out the incumbents
gently from the seats of both social and political power. Yet these
tacticians, who were concerned with the parliamentary impact of tomorrow's elections, had to contend with fervent adherents certain of
an impending millennium and scornful of any compromise that might
obtain only a bit of daily progress. Yet, kept at arms' length and
intermittently harassed by an official state organization which rejected
the SPD as unpatriotic, the SPD's executive body could comfortably
straddle the issue of tomorrow's policies by dilatory formulas.

THE WEIMAR PERIOD

The Weimar settlement presumably eliminated the cleavage between
the state and the *bürgerliche Gesellschaft*, between the executive and
parliament. Can we then, for the lifetime of the Weimar regime, speak
of political competition beginning to develop along lines in any way
familiar in America or England? Could the Weimar system be understood as a political game played by alternating leadership groups with
the tolerance, acquiescence, and electoral consent of the population at

large? Such a description would cover only a segment, and not the most important one, of the Weimar political reality.

There was rather a threefold system of political competition in this severely transfigured heritage of the previous constitutional period. There was the struggle between those parties which, half by inclination, half by political necessity, had become upholders of the constitutional order (most important of them, at least in numbers, the SPD), and the parties of opposition of principle, divided into Communist and nationalist components (including the Nazis), digging in for a siege of the establishment from two directions.

Opposition of principle had undergone mutations of thought and action as a consequence of and reaction to several developments. The left revolution which had failed at home had succeeded abroad to the East. There were drastic changes in conditions of existence among proletariat and bourgeoisie. Opposition of principle was no longer characterized by a state of mind patiently waiting to take over society's accumulated store of resources in the fullness of time but by the spirit of conquest here and now. The parties of opposition of principle were now very different from the half-political, half-chapel opposition of the benign pre-World War I days. They considered elections a ready-made battleground, where they might integrate and exploit their gains and then proceed to more far-reaching political action.

Between the parties operating within (or at least not clearly outside) the parliamentary system, there was a certain amount of political competition, genuine though slack and sporadic. These competitors were more intent on picking up pieces of disintegrating parties than on competing for each other's more or less well-established clientele. This intrasystem competition did not lead to clear-cut positions of majority versus minority, government versus loyal opposition.

The SPD had from the outset contributed to the frustration of such solutions by opting for proportional representation in January, 1919. Whether a majority election system would have led to a much different outcome is unclear, because the heritage of the Empire had left strong traditional and religious cleavages superimposed on social class differentiations in German society. The SPD option for proportional representation was probably only partly due to loyalty to an outdated party program, only partly inspired by the battles of yesteryear's lopsided imperial election districts. A more important motive was probably the SPD leaders' fear of facing undivided governmental responsibility and their incapacity for making any attempt at implementing the central core of their party program.

At any rate the results were clear enough. There was never a chance to establish a government–loyal opposition relationship during the decade in which, in constitutional theory at least, a sort of parliamentary government existed. The difficulties of a multiparty regime, the job interests of each party's members, the socioeconomic interests of each party's clientele, and above all each party's urge for self-preservation as a political unit in the face of the precarious existence of the whole republican state machine almost forced the major parties, loyal to the system, to try to hang on to some pieces of the central state apparatus, or at least to some strategic administrative positions in the strongest political component, Prussia.

Yet if elections were also a means to determine to what pieces of the executive and the administrative machine a loyal party could manage to hang on, the total amount of and the structure of executive and administrative power accessible to the parties were scarcely determined by shifting election results. This power depended (memories of the previous regime) on the relative strength of the military and civilian bureaucracy and the political apparatus proper. And here we face a certain level of highly significant political relations involving little competition: the interrelation between all military and certain bureaucratic powerholders and those officeholders emanating from and legitimized by the confidence of Parliament. Certainly the military considered itself an independent establishment willing to negotiate contracts with rival sovereignties but otherwise serving the political establishment only on its own terms.

Therefore, from the very outset, opposition of principle against the existing constitutional system and the power of the bureaucratic and especially the military officeholders narrowed down the significance of electoral competition as a political basis for the determination of policy. There was little room left for the development of a concept of loyal opposition resting on alternative policy choices propounded by parties working within the constitutional framework.

Toward the end of the regime a continuing process led to the rapid disappearance of both political competition and loyal opposition. First, any attempt of the parliamentary establishment to contest the military-bureaucratic power of decision ceased to exist. Then the parliamentary establishment was ignored during the bureaucratic and military rear-guard action against the growing forces of the opposition of principle of the Right. Finally, after Hindenburg's death in 1934, any idea of the military establishment's continuation as an independent factor in possible opposition to the National Socialist power was eliminated.

NAZISM AND THE OCCUPATION

The Third Reich permitted shared sovereignties as well as some sort of intrasystem competition. In the economic realm competition went on surreptitiously by quality differentiation or battle for administrative preference. In the political realm the system used an amount of intensive subleadership competition for the favor of the supreme leader. This intrasystem leadership competition might sometimes be artfully exploited to enlarge the interstitial space for opposition. Yet, and this is decisive: there was otherwise no bridge or easy communication between both competition and opposition. Opposition had to shed the purely competitive garb, and it became the banned and hunted opposition of principle, the only form of opposition meaningful or possible under the conditions of that regime.

The immediate afterwar and occupation period, 1945–49, brought an interesting separation of the functions of competition and opposition. There was a certain amount of competition among the various groups admitted to the classes for political reeducation put up by the Western Allied authorities, which included trial-run elections. The programs of these parties did not have much relation either to government decisions of the day, which were monopolized by the occupiers, or to the parties' own policies two or three years later, determined as they were by the swiftly changing political realities. Yet these programs served as posters for reassembling the various prewar party general staffs, reestablishing communication lines with old clienteles, and giving prospective recruits for political jobs a chance to look around. In addition they opened up to the public at large devices for getting reacclimatized to a sort of competitive politics, allowing them to show some innocuous preference for one or the other duly licensed competitor.

To the extent that there did exist an element of opposition it had nothing to do with the incipient German party or governmental structure but was opposition without any element of competition. This was an abnormality to be explained by the distorted focus of responsibility in occupation government; General Clay's customers were the Germans, but his responsibility and responsiveness ran to Washington. Opposition consisted of the open or subterranean resistance which indigenous leaders, most effectively those without jobs in the occupation-installed governments, such as Kurt Schumacher, put up to some of the policies of the occupation authorities. This opposition rested on different vistas of Germany's future role and organization, all related to the divergent national interests that separated foreign occupiers and incipient German political operators. The opposition became more effective as more discord between Western and Eastern occupiers necessitated close attention to German susceptibilities.

SOCIAL DEMOCRATIC OPPOSITION

The end of the Western occupation regime shades over into the beginning of the Bonn establishment. The new regime was put into the saddle by the Western occupation powers after the American authorities in early summer 1948 had taken the decision that was to determine much of the future course of German politics: to carry through a drastic currency reform without tying it in any way to a change in the distribution of property or in the ownership of the means of production. The new political regime, whose political viability was vouched for by the continued presence of the occupiers (now turning protectors and allies), rested on the acceptance of periodic elections carried on by competing parties. The whole apparatus was in the traditional Western style. It was tied up with and constitutionally answerable to a Parliament whose activities, in the long run, became at least as problematic as those of similar European institutions. The 1949 elections had given no party anything approaching a majority. But the future perennial chancellor, Konrad Adenauer, the leader of the catch-all

Christian Democratic Union, managed to squeeze into office with a one-vote majority.

Both the narrowness of the government coalition's original parliamentary basis, the contrasting personalities of the two leaders involved (Konrad Adenauer and Kurt Schumacher), and the initially sharply drawn issues made it appear that Germany now for the first time had a parliamentary opposition, performing in the classic parliamentary tradition. Kurt Schumacher characterized his party's role in this sense when he opened the debate after the first government declaration by Chancellor Adenauer on September 20, 1949: "The essence of opposition is a permanent attempt to force the government and its parties by concrete proposals tuned to concrete situations to pursue the political line outlined by the opposition." [1] Such opposition seemed grounded on both domestic and foreign policy issues.

On the domestic front the SPD had already lost the first round in 1948 before the establishment of the Bonn government. After the currency reform, Ludwig Erhard, the economic delegate in the bizonal governmental structure who became the indefatigable propagandist of the so-called social market economy, had his policy of doing away altogether with economic restrictions and rationing adopted, over the protest of the Social Democratic party, which was representative of the urban consumer at large. Under the new establishment, Schumacher would come back to the same charges with increased vigor, becoming the sharpest critic of what he called the authoritarian state defending the interests of the property owners.

In foreign policy Schumacher tried to fight a two-front war. As a participant witness of Weimar history he wanted above all to avoid having his party again labeled defeatist and unpatriotic. First and foremost, therefore, he was firmly set against the slightest attempt to compromise with the regime in the Eastern zone. But at the same time he initiated the fight, persevered in by his party for only a short while after his death in 1952, against making Western Germany a partner of the various initial European integration endeavors. He described them not as praiseworthy efforts at a union of all democratic European peoples, but as the suspicious and undesirable enterprise of the momentarily ruling capitalist and Roman Catholic forces of little Europe. To

---

[1] *Bundestag Stenographische Berichte*, 1 (1949), 32.

his mind European integration was a conspiracy not only against the revival of the German nation but also against the people of the largely socialist-oriented nations of northern Europe. Instead, his policy stood for a conscious effort to reunite Germany at the earliest conceivable moment as an independent national community outside the framework of Eastern domination or Western mortgages.

Both by the choice of its leaders and the orderly, not to say conservative, background of its party members, this Schumacher policy of opposition was, however, to be exercised only within the strict limits of parliamentary procedure as prescribed by the Basic Law which the Social Democratic party had prominently helped to shape. Opposing the present administration the SPD would steadfastly stand by the Bonn setup as established under the Basic Law. From the outset it might have looked as if the chance of unfolding such a type of loyal opposition was to be enhanced not only by the tenuous parliamentary hold of the government but also by the insignificance of any element of opposition of principle.

Under the harsh climate of economic deprivation prevailing in 1949, both the left- and right-wing oppositions of principle had managed to return to the first Bundestag a small band of followers, in spite of the recent experience with National Socialism and the current unfolding of the Communist regime in East Germany. But, totaling in the first Bundestag only about 6 per cent of the membership, these groups at no time had any appreciable influence on the work of assembly or government. Even at that early time, there was at no point a need for the parties loyal to the Basic Law to suspend their government-opposition battle in order to repulse the onslaught of destructive forces. Later, after the first apparent success of the Erhard economic policy, which was materially helped by the Korean boom, the opposition of principle disappeared completely from the Bundestag. It dwindled to a trickle among the public at large, even before the government read it completely out of the circuit of official party competition by courtesy of two Constitutional Court decisions.

But the disappearance of the Communist and rightist opposition of principle, which might have enlarged the scope for a loyal SPD opposition within the democratic framework, had no such invigorating effect. We might rather be tempted to say that disappearance was one element among others in the steady erosion of the potentialities of loyal opposition. Schumacher's initial attempt to force the will of the opposition on the government revealed itself through the years as a complete fiasco on all fronts. Two successive electoral defeats were instrumental in the SPD's ardent desire long before the start of the 1961 election campaign to disentangle itself clearly from any notion of opposing major governmental policies. The SPD consciously strove to eliminate parliamentary opposition as a desirable pattern for the conduct of political business.[2]

Let us first look at the stages of this breakdown of parliamentary opposition before trying to assess its reason and its impact on the larger political scene. In 1947 suspicion was general against the German entrepreneurial class—a consequence of its support of the rising Hitler regime and its close association with it during the war. Even the Christian Democratic Union (CDU) had to make some genuflection, in its Ahlen program exercise of 1947, to public ownership. Scarcely more than six years later the tables had turned. The seeming success of the Erhard brand of economic liberalism, proudly acclaimed at the 1953 Hamburg pre-election congress of the CDU, served to rehabilitate the image of the German entrepreneur.

The SPD, after its first election defeat in 1953, started the long road of retreat on all fronts. Immediately the SPD relegated the socialization of the means of production to an inconspicuous place. By 1959, when redrafting its program in Godesberg, its social and economic clauses had become a collection of vistas and projections for an expanding society designed, à l'Américaine, to play up to nearly all segments of society by the proper insertion of strategically chosen, yet vague enough recognitions of group positions. If somewhat greater concern was given to the party's traditional labor clientele, great ingenuity was exercised to refrain from recommending any definite form of societal organization. Explicit condemnation hit only those systems restricting the free development of the human personality. Attitudes regarding the government of the day became a matter of purely tactical concern.

---

[2] I am intentionally dealing here mainly with the SPD because it stood, at least for some time, for alternative policy goals. The smaller parties, including the still fully operative third party, the Free Democratic party, never had anything but a tactical motivation to enhance its competitive position, at no time making the slightest discernible attempt to sponsor alternative policies.

In such a tactical exercise, interparty competition still has an important role. On the domestic front, for example, the party continues to make a special effort to gain the ear of groups whose sympathies may be in relatively easy reach, such as Protestants in general and Catholic workers in particular. Both are supposed to be attracted by the unconditional shelving of the last vestige of the traditional "religion is a private affair of the individual." In the 1959 program, collaboration with the churches comes before a short reference to freedom of thought. Yet the 1959 program still took the view that children should be educated in common rather than in separate denominational state schools; three years later, in the light of modified tactical needs, such a clear-cut position had already again become outdated.[3] Catholic workers, for whom the party competes with the CDU, are also to be attracted by the heavy emphasis on the regressive character of government fiscal policy. The demand for extension of existing social welfare and pension schemes is also an ever recurrent theme.

All this then remains on the purely competitive level. The same social policy themes and suggestions will recur in the propaganda of the CDU's labor wing. The economic and social organization (in the form it has taken since the early fifties) is no longer challenged in principle. The present interplay between economic liberalism and oligopolistic power of individual firms, and between various economic and social groups, may not work out satisfactorily. In that event, the SPD, along with other parties, might be glad to accept changes suggested by experts to meet the new conditions. Yet the SPD's present

[3] See the instructive discussion at the Cologne SPD Parteitag (Protokoll, Bonn, 1962, pp. 391–92, 405–12), and the recent pamphlet, "Katholik und Godesberger Programm: Zur Situation nach *Mater und Magistra*," published by the SPD party executive in March, 1962; the pamphlet tries to show the similarities of approach between the Papal encyclical and the Godesberg program of the SPD. However, in the guise of interpretation, it offers the Catholic Church compromises on the school question which would not be smaller than those promised by other parties (pp. 47–51, esp. p. 51). The first postwar *Konkordat* concluded in February, 1965, between the Vatican and the SPD-led Lower Saxony state government kept this promise. It is, as a matter of fact, more favorable to the church in regard to educational policies than the provisions so far applying in areas under CDU-led state governments. What is relevant from our viewpoint is the intent. It matters little that an element of self-deception is involved in such tactics of accommodating the churches at any price. At any rate, the *Konkordat* aroused a certain amount of resentment, especially among teachers. It also led to the withdrawal of the FDP from the Land government and the substitution of the CDU.

program is an attractive sales prospectus for desirable group futures, and is designed to provide neither concrete answers for special contingencies nor, in contrast to the discarded old formulas, a total scheme for societal development.

The SPD not only shuns any frontal attack on the economic system but through the mouth of its 1964 convention keynote speaker on economic affairs paid special tribute to "the dynamics of market economy as an inalienable part of a libertarian economic order." [4] At the same time, however, in good catch-all party platform style the acceptance of the market economy is counterbalanced by an affirmative nod toward all those dirigiste policies required by modern industrial society. With an eye on the competitive advantages to be obtained it will press with a more lusty voice the claims of an actual and potential clientele. It has urged the continuation of a publicly sponsored housing program in spite of an overheated economic situation, and upheld, to a certain degree at least, the job interests of miners threatened by cheaper fuel resources.

In matters of economic policy, then, the SPD simply yielded to the overwhelming success of the German economy of the fifties. But the foreign policy picture is by no means as clear-cut. In spite of the SPD's initial resistance, a measure of Western economic integration came off as planned. Rearmament too has been carried through within the framework of the Western alliance. This policy paid off in economic terms and has enhanced German status within the Western community. Yet the policy has brought Germany no nearer the goal proclaimed by the SPD and echoed by the government: reunification in freedom. Nevertheless, the SPD's policy of opposition has caved in on this front more unconditionally than on any other. Until the middle fifties the SPD fought a rear-guard action to delay Western integration. Under Schumacher's initial impetus it opposed the Schuman Plan and the setting up of the Council of Europe. With the full support of its adherents and other large groups it fought in Parliament and in the Constitutional Court against the incipient rearmament effort. Its line

[4] See, e.g., Dr. Karl Schiller in SPD Parteitag, 1962 Protokoll, pp. 256–58, and his statements on the need for "cautious accommodation of the coal industry to the changed consumption structure" in the 1964 Karlsruhe party convention, quoted in SPD Parteitag Arbeitsgemeinschaft B, November 24, 1964 (uncorrected Protokoll, pp. 12–13).

faltered in the mid-fifties when it started to uphold the need for national defense and fully collaborated in implementing defense policies. In 1957 and 1958, however, it used the general abhorrence of atomic war for a vigorous parliamentary action. In 1959 it sponsored a socalled German Plan of foreign policy. To the need for accommodation with the Soviet Union to obtain a Western-style unity of Germany it tied a form of acceptance of a demilitarized zone in Europe. Yet by mid-1960 it had dropped the attempt at developing an independent foreign policy line. It solemnly abjured any thought of forcing the will of the opposition on the government; it now became its task "to find a common understanding to see what can be done, both in concrete situations and as a long-term proposition." [5] It condemned the idea of a third way between freedom and Communism which was still inherent in the "German Plan." To show their prospective political partners the seriousness of their intentions, the SPD leadership, dragging along the reluctant party chairman, Erich Ollenhauer, rammed a resolution through the 1960 Hannover party convention which whittled down the blunt rejection of German production, stationing, or use of atomic weapons contained in the otherwise tame enough Godesberg program of the previous year.[6]

By 1964 there were too few clear-cut foreign policy lines and initiatives left to allow one to speak of "the SPD foreign policy." A few distinctive emphases are still discernible—some continued opposition to the unnecessary dependence on nuclear weapons for European defense and vigorous resistance to the further spread of strategic nuclear weapons (in line with American strategy concepts) and special concern for both the needs and the propaganda possibilities inherent in the party's predominant position in Berlin. Yet none of these emphases is far from the tactical line of a broadly based interparty foreign policy, and none offers either basic criticism or alternative positions.[7]

The concept of opposition as a framework for presenting policy al-

[5] Herbert Wehner as official speaker in the foreign policy debate on June 30, 1960, *Bundestag Stenographische Berichte,* XLVI, 7055.

[6] The Hannover debate was a tactical exercise. Two years later the same leaders were to emphasize a maximum of restraint concerning independent Western European atomic weapons.

[7] See, e.g., Fritz Erler in the foreign policy debate of October 12, 1962, in *Bundestag Stenographische Berichte,* LI, 1773–80.

ternatives was officially abandoned in the speech given by the SPD's candidate-designate for the chancellorship, Willy Brandt, with the 1961 elections in mind: "In a sound and developing democracy it is the norm rather than the exception that the parties put forward similar, even identical demands in a number of fields. The question of priorities, of the rank order of tasks to be solved, and of methods and accents thus becomes ever so much more the content of opinion formation." [8] This statement sees the reduction of opposition to its purely competitive elements as both necessary and desirable.

The basic factors in this change of political style, which have operated in most advanced industrial societies, have in recent years been discussed extensively.[9] They may be summarized as follows: the modern welfare state can now provide solutions to problems of many social groups without in this process worsening the situation of competing social groups. This weakens the old clashes of immediate interests and converts them into mere conflicts of priority in the time sequence satisfactions. This has freed political parties of the necessity of concentrating their electioneering efforts on specific groups while antagonizing others. It allows them now to compete simultaneously for the electoral allegiance of a great variety of social strata. This situation allows their policies to be determined by tactical requirements of the moment, relegating ideologically determined long-range goals to a remote corner.

Foreign policy considerations work in the same direction. An opposition party may tactically exploit unpopular government decisions, especially those whose full meaning is slow to unfold. But first, such tactical advantage is balanced by the authority and prestige which the conduct of foreign policy bestows on the responsible statesman. Sec-

---

[8] Willy Brandt, *Plaidoyer für die Zukunft* (Frankfurt, 1961), p. 17.

[9] See, for an early succinct statement, Herbert Tingsten, "Stability and Vitality in Swedish Democracy," *Political Quarterly*, XXVI (1955), 140–51; for my own views, see "The Waning of Opposition in Parliamentary Regimes," *Social Research* (Summer, 1957), pp. 128–56, reprinted in John W. Wahlke and Heinz E. Eulau, *Legislative Behavior* (Glencoe, 1960). Most recently the point has been taken up in considerable detail in Manfred Friedrich, *Opposition ohne Alternative* (Cologne, 1962), and with an added request for a revision of political style in "Politik ohne Alternative? Zur Profilneurose der Parteien," *Neue Zuercher Zeitung*, April 21, 1963, p. 7. See also the articles by Karl Dietrich Bracher and Seymour Martin Lipset in "A New Europe?" *Daedalus*, Vol. XCIII, No. 1 (Winter, 1964).

ondly, the interstitial changes which an opposition party operating within a framework of national consensus may propose are either too technical and complex or too vague and general to have an appreciable impact on the voter's attitude. By the same token, the revolutionary social implications of technological progress—the threat of mass unemployment—are cushioned by major power competition with the corresponding armament efforts of the big and medium-sized powers. Such "prophylactic" expenditures prevent the pressures on major parties both from the outside and from within their own ranks for new and radical solutions of major foreign and domestic problems. They allow them to avoid raising the more important problems of our time (threat of universal atomic destruction, disproportion between the living standards and the expectations of advanced and former colonial countries, impact of technological change on social and economic structure of advanced nations), or, to the extent they cannot be disregarded, to handle them in vague, carefully modulated, and, above all, noncontroversial ways, thus barring them from the field of national party competition. Major interparty differences lose their *raison d'être* when overriding technological, international, and military problems are not debated among the parties.

In modern industrial societies, the parties loyal to the regime in addition carry on a certain amount of competition with each other. The wider and more diversified the appeal they try to make, the greater their competition; the more they restrict their appeals to specific social groups, the less their competition. If the potential clientele is as broad as the electorate, there will be a more concerted effort than if it is known in advance that the structure and goals of the organization militate against reaching more than a regional, religious, or occupational segment. But as long as comparative electoral standing in the population is by common consent a yardstick for allocating spheres of political influence, some competition has to go on. The verdict may not actually be related to the performance of the competitors, as the electoral outcome is likely to depend mainly on the voters' reactions to events outside the control of the political actors. But political convention has sanctioned this yardstick in preference to more complicated and less clear-cut ones.

Now in a figurative sense this competition involves some element of opposition, if for no other reason than that the party representatives take their places on opposite sides of the moderator in their TV contests. To what degree their competition involves an actual element of opposition in the sense of our definition—sponsoring differential goals in one or the other major field of political contention—is a different question. Different historical backgrounds, traditions, and ideologies and varying objectives of their leaders and their clienteles may lead to variations in emphasis in the vague proposals on how to face tomorrow's still undecipherable reality. At any rate, opposition and competition timetables do not necessarily jibe. The more closely the dates of elections correspond to a prearranged constitutional schedule, the less the likelihood that interparty competitive pressures will coincide with situations crying out for alternative political solutions. The candidates' fights may be more in the nature of a collision between people obliged to squeeze through the same narrow thoroughfare to punch the clock before 8:45.

Competition and opposition are related techniques for obtaining political power. Competition performs a sort of selection among those eager to arrive, unless the candidates take their precautions. They may come near to distributing the prizes beforehand by a combined operation, depriving the public of the essence, though not the fun, of its role of selection. An element of opposition makes a collusive agreement less likely. Goal differentiation may transcend the mere accumulation of personal, organizational, or social-status defense positions.

In democratic politics competition and opposition easily intertwine. Political practitioners may shuffle back and forth between competing and coalescing, refurbishing traditional goals to look like new ones and putting up new signposts while trying to minimize the shock of goal displacement. To these general reasons for the waning of opposition in advanced industrial societies should be added at least one German phenomenon unknown to any other European nation—the imposed division of the country into two parts. There is the all-pervasive fact that what used to be the Communist opposition of principle has now become a hostile state organization, which is master of a considerable part of Germany's former territory. From the German Democratic Republic's offices flows an uninterrupted stream of criticism—always prejudiced, often inane, and on rare occasions revealing—of West German institutions, policies, and personalities. This criticism is coupled with attempts to exploit every false step of the West German antagonists both in Germany and the world at large, but especially to set the West German population against its political establishment. The reaction in West Germany has been to play down divisive elements and internal criticism and to look with suspicion on any type of criticism which is parallel with, even if organizationally independent of, that coming from East Germany. The mere fact of the existence of two mutually exclusive regimes transforms any opposition into opposition between the two regimes, emptying strictly domestic conflict of much of its substance and meaning.

This overriding conflict has had an abiding effect on the internal structure of the SPD. Both Communist foes and domestic competitors of the SPD, each for their own propaganda reasons, like to point out the common root of Communism and Social Democracy in nineteenth-century Marxism. Naturally, then, the SPD seeks in thought and action to make clear its radical departure from these suspect origins, even if this leads to the opposite result of making it look nearly indistinguishable from its main domestic competitor, the CDU. The SPD endeavors to eliminate the picture of the political party as a community of true believers.[10] It substitutes the image of an association of people who have banded together for the pursuit of goals lying exclusively in the political field and left themselves complete freedom in all other fields. This development, officially emphasized at all times, is in line with the disappearance of intraparty debate. As long as alternatives to official policy persisted, internal party discussion and the democratic party structure played a significant role in policy elaboration. This party democracy was safeguarded not only by tradition but by the realities of the political process. Under Weimar, many voters shifted back and forth between an extreme party, such as the Communists, and a party which worked within the constitutional framework, such as the SPD,

---

[10] The Cologne 1962 SPD party convention was presented with a motion (55–56) asking it to abandon the habitual form of greeting, "Comrade" (*Genosse*), and substitute "party-friend" (Protokoll, pp. 466, 648). This motion might have arisen from the acute embarrassment caused the party when the late Chairman Erich Ollenhauer was not firm enough in his response to Khrushchev, who, upon meeting Ollenhauer, said, "We call each other 'comrade,' don't we?" While the motion was tabled without discussion, it seems symptomatic that the issue was raised.

each of which promised satisfaction of partly identical claims. (The same situation prevailed between the German Nationalist party and the National Socialist party.) The very possibility of such a switch gave the internal party opposition some leverage in combating the official party line. The demise of the Radical Left has thus become one element in the change of the internal style of the SPD. There are scarcely any remnants of such internal opposition left.[11]

Another element is the nature of present discontent and ensuing internal party discussion. Discontent now does not lie principally within the socioeconomic sphere; no crying needs of important segments of the population clamor for immediate action. Discontent revolves around more abstract problems of foreign policy and German unity. These generate a flood of professional and subprofessional comment, but neither heat nor popular pressure for immediate solution. This situation allows the party executive to ride roughshod over deviationists—mostly violators of resolutions which declare participation in other organizational activities, such as anti-atomic bomb marches or support of left-wing student organizations, incompatible with party membership—and to carry out swift policy shifts with a minimum of intraparty fuss and friction.

The reduction of the opposition to its competitive element does not determine whether such competition will emphasize electoral or bargaining elements. Electoral and bargaining tactics are not mutually exclusive but the two opposite poles of a continuum. Bargaining strength will, to a degree varying with the democratic propensities of a given polity, be underpinned by electoral success; on the other hand, electoral tactics may be modulated by interest in striking political bargains.

The SPD, exactly like its Austrian sister party, only so far less successfully, has laid more stress on bargaining than on electoral tactics. This may be due simply to a lack of self-confidence evidenced by its still holding on to a slightly modified system of proportional represen-

---

[11] Some of these problems have been perspicaciously treated by a meanwhile ejected academic representative of the intra-SPD party minority, Wolfgang Abendroth: *Aufstieg und Krise der deutschen Sozialdemokratie* (Frankfurt, 1964), pp. 50 ff., and "Innerparteiliche und Innerverbandliche Demokratie als Voraussetzung der politischen Demokratie," *Politische Viertel-Jahresschrift*, V, No. 3 (1964), 307–38.

tation. While PR makes it more difficult for the party to hope ever to obtain a clear-cut majority, it does serve as a guarantee against electoral reverses taking a catastrophic turn. However, its conversion into a catch-all popular party organization has produced some second thoughts in SPD ranks on this point. During the December, 1962, coalition negotiations the SPD turned down tentative advances by the CDU in the direction of adopting a straight majority electoral system. Yet the feeling of having successfully engineered the transition to a multiclass organization is making the SPD slightly more hospitable to the idea of a majority system as perhaps an additional, though by no means exclusive, approach toward gaining governmental positions.

The importance of the election system as a factor influencing the preference for electoral versus bargaining tactics should not be over-rated. The political style of a country's elite may be equally if not more significant. Unlike the British situation, the fate of a German politician is influenced only mildly by his party's ability to obtain a majority or a plurality at election time. Owing to the ways of access to politics in Germany, neither his livelihood nor his social standing will depend on the outcome of the electoral battle. Some major and middle-level politicians, irrespective of whether they want to escape the frustration of the intraparty politics of the CDU or the dampening of their ambitions through the SPD's prolonged failure to gain federal office, have a good chance to find berths with financial and status rewards in the top echelons of the state governments. The switch will allow them still to share some of the political limelight and perhaps make a come-back on the federal level. More important, political personnel on the intermediate level more often than not have entered Parliament as major officeholders of semiautonomous public or private organizations (cities, counties, employer or trade union groups, agricultural associations, etc.); in other instances they may have status as civil servants or judges. In a handful of cases their party's hold on the reins of the federal government may give such men a chance at federal office. Neither their professional standing nor their financial security depends upon such preferment. In view of the relatively limited number of top political officeholders on the federal level (about 20) and the slow turnover in Cabinet jobs, such careers would anyhow be rare. Major federal political office is at the same time only a mildly attractive prize in a country which provides for its professional, intellectual, and civic elite many comfortable berths requiring less exertion and furnishing sufficient pay and security. Hankering for the spoils of government by impatient politicians is not a major element in political party life, nor does it force what one may call an electoral style on political competition.

A major element in the prevalence of bargaining-type politics is the country's federal structure. From the outset no single party has ever been able to dominate all state governments. Consequently the federal and state administrations must be prepared to work with each other on a close and continuous basis in all matters pertaining to finance, legislation, and administration irrespective of the particular administration's political complexion. Even if the effect of election victories—never spectacular under proportional systems—were not diffused by the staggering of the dates of the federal and state elections, the permanency of different interest constellations as between the states and the federal government deprives the party label of much of its meaning. Any federal government must periodically try cajoling the states into abandoning part of their constitutionally sanctioned hold over income and corporation taxes. Conversely, any state wants to keep maximum administrative and financial powers against the expanding claims of both the federal intruder and the formally subordinate cities and counties. This situation puts a constant premium on bargaining tactics.

Such conflicts are in most cases handled through purely bureaucratic channels. While the professional skill and experience of one or the other politician or administrator-politician may be decisive for the outcome of such a bargain, such activity has low political visibility and little value for electoral debates. The parties function as one element, and not necessarily the most important one, in an interbureaucratic equilibrium in which central, state, and local bureaucracies all play their roles.[12] As a rule state politics and even state-federal relations are crowded out of voters' minds at the time of state elections by issues or sentiments of a more general nature. This makes it easy for all participants in the political game to keep many subjects exclusively within

[12] Related viewpoints might be found in Edward L. Pinney, *Federalism, Bureaucracy and Party Politics in Western Germany: The Role of the Bundesrat* (Chapel Hill, 1963).

bureaucratic channels. In cases of patent inability to reach an agreement, the terms of the federal-state bargain may be redefined [13] by a *deus ex machina* decision of the Constitutional Court. Electoral expectations or results figure only at infrequent intervals as determinants of action in this wide area of financial and administrative policy.

Another, and final, point on the decline of the opposition concerns the popular understanding of the concepts of party and state. The Bonn establishment was designed as an antidote to an adventurous and disorderly one-party government. In this establishment Adenauer himself—and this is part of his success story—embodied both the pragmatic virtues of an interest-compromise-oriented party politician and the traditional type of state authority, functioning above and beyond the day-to-day struggles and firmly directed toward national goals.

Thus there have been two political images operative in German minds. The one perceives the turning of the German political parties from ideologically oriented gatherings of loyal adherents into bureaucratic machines soliciting individual votes and the assistance or benevolent neutrality of interest congeries. The party here is a machine for receiving and sorting out claims on the state; it is thus one more instance, belated but significant, of the turn of Germany into a Western-style business society. The party that performs these functions of processing claims most efficiently is then rewarded with office by a perspicacious electorate.

The competing image of the state as an objective value structure above and beyond all interest organizations and all parties has not disappeared, however. It is vivid not only as a somewhat idealized description of their own social functions among bureaucrats and members of the academic profession, but among the population at large. The near-general acceptance of the welfare state—in spite of the official German trappings of the so-called social market economy—involves a community obligation to take care of the citizens' minimum needs. This mental climate reinforces already existing inclinations to stress administrative continuity behind the gyrations of the players on the political scene. It is more likely that the expectation of orderly and

---

[13] As happened in the 1962 television controversy, when a number of Land governments successfully sued the federal government for its attempt to put up a federal television station with privately financed programs. See *Entscheidungen des Bundesverfassungsgerichts*, XII (1962), 205.

continuous government performance was held against the Adenauer regime, once the prolonged uncertainties and incessant rivalries of the succession crisis had become public knowledge.

The parties themselves are by no means averse to looking on their own role in administrative-bureaucratic terms rather than in competitive-electoral terms.[14] To some extent this tendency rests on apparent or real necessities of relations between the Federal Republic and East Germany, which, e.g., has led Federal Republic jurisprudence to assimilate party documents and papers to state secrets. This tendency also appears in the patterns of party financing, which recently has been shifting from exclusive reliance on membership fees (mainly in the SPD) and business contributions (mainly in the CDU and Free Democratic party, or FDP) to federal treasury financing. At present the federal government distributes 38 million DM a year to the parties mainly according to the electoral strength of the federal party organizations.[15]

[14] Here is an example of bureaucratic-type state authority in the practices of what, in federal terms, is still the "opposition" party. The Socialist majority of the Diet of the city-state of Bremen in December, 1957, passed a bill referring differences between a legally instituted personnel representation and the state government over personnel policies, including appointments and dismissals of less than top-ranking state officials, to an arbitration board. The board was to be manned by representatives of both state employees and the state government, and the decisive vote would lie with the chairman, the Social Democratic President of the City Assembly. The state government, also headed by a perennial Social Democratic Lord Mayor, unwilling to tolerate such diminution of state authority, first took its grievance to the state Constitutional Court. After having narrowly lost the case in the Bremen jurisdiction, it resorted to the federal Constitutional Court, which promptly vindicated its position and voided the law. (*Entscheidungen des Bundesverfassungsgerichts*, IX [1959], 268.)

Nobody will be astonished that a German Constitutional Court manned by people with judicial, bureaucratic, and university professors' backgrounds would look with jaundiced eyes at an attempt to treat the state as an employer exactly on the same level as any other party to a collective contract. The court would see in such a law only the possibility of diminishing state authority beyond the critical point rather than visualizing the potentiality that a compromise effected by a strategic person with a position midway between the interest groups and the formal state authority could maintain the uninterrupted functioning of public services. What is revealing, however, is that a socialist-led state administration felt an irresistible urge to go to such pains to teach its own majority the sanctity of the principle that state authority transcends group claims.

[15] As the law stands now 20 per cent of the total sum is distributed in equal shares to the CDU, Christian Social Union (CSU), FDP, and SPD; the other 80 per cent is allocated to the various parties according to the number of seats they hold in the Bundestag, which presently nets the SPD slightly over 13 million

It is only logical that under such circumstances the SPD visualizes the goal of interparty competition more as that of universalizing bargaining practices than removing the stronger competitor from office.[16] That goal is in accord with popular ideas. An early 1963 poll indicated that a majority of those expressing an opinion considered a coalition of the two major parties, CDU and SPD, "a favorable solution in the

---

DM. The total election outlay for the 1961 Bundestag election may have come to 70 to 80 million DM. See Ulrich Dübber, *Parteifinanzierung in Deutschland 1962* (Cologne, 1962), and Ulrich Dübber and Gerard Braunthal, "West Germany," in *Comparative Political Finance*, ed. R. Rose and A. J. Heidenheimer (*Journal of Politics*, 1963). However, under a three-party agreement concluded in January, 1965, *central* expenditures for the 1965 elections will be both supervised and kept to a prearranged maximum level of 16.5 million DM for the CDU-CSU and 15 million DM for each of the other two parties. The SPD has protested the increasing reliance on state financing for political organizations—more favorable to the CDU and FDP with low membership receipts than to the SPD which in 1963 received 14 million DM in membership fees. It has therefore been able to spend part of the federal bonanza, which is augmented by various similar outlays in the individual states, for educational rather than for straight political purposes. The whole institution of official party finance underlines the degree to which German parties turn increasingly into quasi-official machines.

[16] Recently Wolfgang Kralewski and Karlheinz Neunreither (in *Oppositionelles Verhalten im ersten Deutschen Bundestag, 1949-1953* [Cologne-Opladen, 1963]) have studied in detail SPD participation in federal legislation during the first legislative period. We reprint part of an instructive tabulation which shows how many bills, at the time of the final vote, were passed against SPD opposition. The percentage relates to the number of total statutes passed in the respective fields during the first legislature (page 92):

Budget—78.9%   Internal affairs, police, culture, etc.—14.8%
Foreign affairs—55%   Labor, social legislation—11.8%
Agriculture—19.4%   Economics—7.4%
Finance—15.4%

In evaluating these percentages it has to be taken into consideration that SPD rejection of the budgets of most individual ministries is a pure matter of form, indicating the official opposition status of the party. The rather substantial number of rejections in the foreign policy field is, as explained in our text, a matter of the past. The removal of foreign policy from the field of party politics, so much desired by the authors ((pp. 93, 99), has long since taken place. On the other end of the scale we find the field of economics indicating that most reconstruction legislation, even at the height of SPD opposition under the Schumacher regime, was noncontroversial from the outset or mutually satisfactory compromises had been obtained before the final vote. Interestingly enough the book, which contains among other things exhaustive studies of the legislative process in regard to three particular subject matters (boundary police bill, bill protecting youth against obscene literature, and the Constitution Court bill), comes to the conclusion that the effectiveness of the opposition in the legislative process has depended mainly on the varying quality of the opposition experts in the respective committees (p. 213). The substance of the policy differences seems to have played a much smaller role.

interest of the Federal Republic." [17] What does this approval mean? As the poll did not ask how many people would have preferred clear-cut majority party rule, its meaning is open to doubt. But in conjunction with other inquiries it may signify some popular knowledge of the declining level of interparty controversy as well as some popular groping for orderly and steady government performance under conditions of maximal popular consent. A broad interparty compact may fulfill the same psychological function as the objective and independent state power for which people still hanker. Thus the enlarging of case-to-case, interstitial, and administrative bargains to the level of permanent political bargaining in the form of a major party coalition government might seem just a question of time.[18] Before it happens, however, the CDU, which still has a national plurality, has to be convinced that such a coalition would be both desirable and profitable for it.

The circle is nearly complete: the SPD now shuns the very idea of an opposition role, and multiplies both demands and offers of unconditional participation. All the government can do to protect itself from this impetuous urging is curtly to recall that no way exists to force the government to accept the SPD as a partner.[19] Such rebuffs only make the SPD strategists redouble their efforts to minimize their differences with the government and follow what is now commonly referred to as the "embracement" strategy. SPD energies are all bent to enhancing the chances for a permanent cut-in on the governmental organization.[20]

---

[17] *Emmidinformationen*, No. 13 (1963) of March 25, 1963, p. 2, lists 36 per cent favoring an SPD-CDU coalition, 23 per cent favoring a CDU-FDP coalition, 9 per cent an CPD-FDP coalition, with 32 per cent uttering no clear-cut preference.

[18] The details of the German variants of the demise of political opposition have recently been described, though with some ideological somersaults, in Waldemar Besson, "Regierung und Opposition in der deutschen Politik," *Politische Vierteljahresschrift*, III (September, 1962), 224–41.

[19] See the explanation of the CDU speaker, Von Brentano, in the debate on the government declaration of December 6, 1961, *Bundestag Stenographische Berichte*, L (1961), 65–73. The argument proffered by the same speaker that if the SPD were to join the government no controller would exist seems a bit tortured. The SPD had already on its own volition abandoned any thought of exercising a control function.

[20] All arguments for cooperative government by all parties may be found in endless variation in W. Brandt's keynote speech at the Cologne 1962 party convention. Protokoll, pp. 56–86; see also the characteristic discussion "Es hätte auch schlimmer werden können" between party boss H. Wehner and some *Spiegel* editors in *Der Spiegel*, September 25, 1963.

Competition with the goal of participation in the competitor's enterprise can make only marginal allowance for criticism. Conduct in Parliament must be modulated to express identity of thought patterns in all major affairs, but allow enough for small-scale needling to keep the advisability of joining forces steadily before the competitor. It may not be easy to keep about 200 M.P.'s always in line with the tactical requirements of the hour. Yet following both the listless general debates and the mass of trivia which the backbenchers pour out during oral questioning time impresses one with the lack of controversial issues or their studied avoidance. At question time there is universal eagerness to plead local and special interest group causes dear to the individual member or, at times, to prove one's loyalty and patriotic eagerness, to publicize German concerns and grievances throughout the world. The oral question remains by and large in the realm of the backbencher's title to recognition; it becomes an auxiliary weapon for political criticism only on special occasions.

One such rare flareup happened in 1962 when the question period was utilized for ventilating the *Spiegel* affair.[21] But one must immediately note the self-imposed tactical restrictions. Neither at that time nor in its written interrogatories submitted to the federal government did the SPD venture to raise the problem of freedom of critical opinion versus treason legislation which has aroused public concern. Instead it sought, successfully, to trip Minister of Defense Franz Josef Strauss on his inconsistent and incomplete statements and his unwarranted assumption of powers outside his own jurisdiction. The CDU's tactical retort—publicizing SPD members' irregularities in handling army committee material—was apparently sufficient to restrain the SPD from taking major parliamentary initiatives. Thus the SPD tacitly agreed to have the whole problem settled in the political no-man's-land where the judicial branch tries to figure out how to handle pernicious political dissent. It remains to be seen to what extent the quite recently introduced "current events hour," during which members may speak extemporaneously on recent events for five minutes up to a total of

---

[21] Bundestag session of November 7, 8, and 9, 1962. *Bundestag Stenographische Berichte*, pp. 1949–2091; see also Otto Kirchheimer and Constantine Menges, "The Spiegel Case," in *Politics in Europe*, ed. G. M. Carter and E. F. Weston (New York, 1965).

one hour, will relieve the boredom pervading the entire institution.[22]

This, then, is a society which started out to practice party government and at first attempted to make it work within the grooves of the government-opposition system. The trappings of party government are there. They may be used to establish government formulas ranging from government by the strongest party alone, via interstitial stages of coalition between a major party and satellite parties, to the so far unrealized aim of the SPD—an Austrian-type combined operation of the two great parties. Whatever the particular form of party government, both those forces operating everywhere in advanced industrial societies and those forces arising out of the specific contemporary German situation have led to the steady erosion of goal-oriented opposition. What remains is a certain level of interparty competition, whose edges are blunted by all-pervasive bargaining carried through on a bureaucratic rather than a political level. Permanent institutionalization of such a bargaining style on the political level would mean an interesting attempt to stabilize political relations. In the last analysis such an endeavor at a watertight political cartel can be successful only if every outside or potential competitor is eliminated.

This raises the question: To what extent does the German political system allow for legal opposition outside parliamentary and party channels? The question coincides with the problem of constitutional limitations on extraparliamentary opposition. The Bonn Basic Law has privileged the parties as organizations that take part in the creation of the political will. It has penalized parties that want to impede the working of the free democratic order or endanger the existence of the Federal Republic. It allows the Constitutional Court (Art. 21, par. 2) to ban them altogether. The same rule holds for any other organization whose activity is in contradiction with "the Basic Law, the constitutional order or the idea of peaceful understanding between nations" (Art. 9, par. 2). With this exception, so far applied to the Socialist Reich party and the Communist party, and that of the impractical rule of Article 18, allowing an individual to be divested under the same conditions of some specifically mentioned basic rights, extraparliamentary

---

[22] The first current events discussion of February 10, 1965, is reported in *Das Parlament*, February 17, 1965, together with the introductory remarks of Bundestag Vice-President Carlo Schmid.

opposition is legal. It is fully protected by the freedom of conscience, freedom of opinion-forming, and freedom of association provisions (Art. 4, par. 1, Art. 5, par. 1, and Art. 8) of the Basic Law. If the Basic Law narrows freedom of opinion by adducing the limitations of the general laws,[28] "those which protect youth and personal honor" (Art. 5, par. 2), this does not create any government prerogative for supervising questions of political style.[24]

Boundary-line cases may, as they do in the United States, involve weighing priorities between freedom of opinion and protection of the interests of either the individual or of state security. This task devolves in the main on a federal Constitutional Court, inclining in a number of situations toward preferred freedom doctrines. Beyond such areas of possible conflict and choice there exists a guaranteed area for legal, yet extraparliamentary, opposition. The boundary-line cases, however, demonstrate that there may exist a considerable gap between constitutionally sanctioned legal extraparliamentary opposition and widespread public assumptions as to the legitimacy of such extraparliamentary opposition. Owing to the increasing desiccation of parliamentary opposition, this question of the boundary lines of legitimate opposition has increased in importance. There is no doubt that uninvited suggestions, memoranda, and public discussion policy statements, emanating from academic or loosely church-connected groupings, on atomic policy, foreign affairs, inter-German policy, or social policy problems are considered appropriate even though they may often be considered unwelcome and inopportune in official circles. More and more general policy debates are taking place these days within the framework of such extraparliamentary groups rather than within political party organizations. Beyond this arena there is a gray zone of doubt.

[23] According to the interpretation of the Constitutional Court, these "general laws" have to be interpreted from the "value-creating impact of the free democratic order and therefore themselves be restricted again in their effectiveness as limits on the basic right" (of free opinion formation). *Entscheidungen des Bundesverfassungsgerichts*, VII (1957), 198, 208, and Professor H. Ehmke in his arguments in support of the constitutional complaint of the Spiegel Publishing Company filed with the federal Constitutional Court on May 1, 1963, pp. 66–79 (Verfassungsbeschwerde 1 BvR586/62, privately printed, Hamburg, 1963).

[24] See A. Hamann, "Das Recht auf Opposition und seine Geltung im ausserparlamentarischen Bereich," *Politische Vierteljahresschrift*, III (September, 1962), 241, 255.

There exists some tendency to look at systematic deviationism from official policies, especially in the field of East-West or inter-German relations, as illegitimate. This does not always involve condemnation of an advanced or deviant viewpoint, but simply a not uncommon conviction that such difficult problems should be handled by experts officially selected for the purpose. Consequently a television producer or a deviant press organ, like *Der Spiegel*, which does not observe these invisible boundaries may run into hostility. To what extent such hostility can be translated into action depends both on the legal situation and on community support for the attacked person or institution. The deviant producer's show may be put off the air by the public broadcasting corporation, as recently happened in the Panorama case. Putting legal impediments in the way of *Der Spiegel*, as the authorities found out too late, is much more involved and difficult. On the other hand, if it can be alleged with some degree of plausibility that the person or group involved not only wants to exercise unhealthy influence on the general opinion-forming process but also strays into the field of political organization proper, both the established competitors—the parliamentary parties and the administrative organs of the state—will scan the records of the newcomers with magnifying glasses to discover improper motivations and unconstitutional connections. While deviant opinion is to some degree tolerated, legitimacy is not easily granted to movements and parties moving outside recognized channels in a country where the devastating memories of the twenties and thirties are still vividly in the minds of the older generation and where present conditions do anything but invite radical reorientation. Legality and legitimacy are not altogether identical in the German order of things. But prevalent legitimacy notions have a tendency to narrow down the radius of action left for legal, but extraparliamentary, opposition.[25]

[25] The best introduction to this vast theme may be found in *Bestandsaufnahme: Eine Deutsche Bilanz*, ed. H. W. Richter (Munich, 1961). For the most typical recent case see R. Schmid, "Auf dem Weg zum Überwachungsstaat," *Die Zeit*, March 19, 1965, p. 3.

THE TRANSFORMATION OF THE

WESTERN EUROPEAN PARTY SYSTEM

I. LOAD CONCEPT AND PARTY FAILURES

I HAVE BEEN intrigued enough by the LaPalombara-Weiner concept of
the load to use it as a point of departure for inquiring into the successes
and failures of major European political parties as transmission belts
between the population at large and the governmental structure.

The British case has a pristine beauty: national unity brought about
in the sixteenth-century consolidation of the establishment, followed
by a seventeenth-century constitutional and social settlement allowing
for the osmosis between aristocracy and bourgeoisie. The settlement
happened early enough to weather the horrors and concomitant political assaults of early nineteenth-century industrialism. The fairly
smooth and gradual integration of the working classes was completed
late enough so that the unnerving cleavage between the political promise and the social effectiveness of democracy (LaPalombara and
Weiner's "distribution crisis") lasted only a couple of MacDonald-
Baldwin decades. Thus once we omit the 1910–14 interlude, Great
Britain offers a case where problems could be handled as single loads.
The time factor thus merges into and coincides with the load factor.
The impact of constitutionalism slowly unfolds in the eighteenth century, then follows the acceleration of middle-class and the beginning
of working-class integration during the nineteenth century, and the
tempestuous combination of the consequences of full political democ-

Reprinted, by permission of Princeton University Press, from *Political Parties and
Political Development*, ed. Joseph LaPalombara and Myron Wiener (Princeton,
1966), pp. 177–200.

ratization with the demands of a distributionist society after World War I.

Where do we get if we apply the single-load concept to the French case? If there was a French problem of national identity, it was almost oversettled by 1793, with the revolution only intensifying results in principle reached by 1590. Universal suffrage, that is, political democracy as the constitutional basis of the French state, has been almost continuously on the program since 1848 and was definitely achieved in the early 1870s. Whatever the subsequent upheavals in executive-legislative relations, the popular basis of the French regime has not been contested except for the short-lived Pétainist period. But why did political integration, the business of transforming the state apparatus of the bourgeois society into a cooperative enterprise of all social classes, stop so short of success? Why is it that this goal has been reached only now, to some extent at least, as a simple by-product of increased material well-being and ensuing lessening of social antagonism in the French species of industrial society? How is it that the political parties contributed so little to the end result?

There are reasons why French society in spite of, or because of, the early introduction of universal suffrage could force its working class to accept a position of stepchildren. They were a minority in a society not particularly favoring disruption of the existing social equilibrium by accentuated industrialization. Yet without such industrialization there was little chance of creating a unified party system. Instead there was a dichotomy between parties of individual representation (with their double basis in the local parish pump and the operations of the parliamentary faction) and the incipient mass party of the working class, the Socialist party of the first decade of the century. Most bourgeois parties remained restricted electioneering organizations with loose connections to still looser parliamentary factions having little radius of action beyond the parliamentary scene (Duverger-LaPalombara-Weiner's internally created parties).[1]

---

[1] The internal-external creation dichotomy has to be viewed in the light of presence or absence of a supporting framework of religious or class-motivated parallel organizations. The local committee of the internally created bourgeois party and its financial backers can never serve as such a foolproof prop of electoral success as can the network of parallel organizations typical of external parties.

Through the courtesy of Alain [2] these parties were equipped with an ultra-democratic theory of eternal vigilance to be exercised by the proverbial small man over his intermediaries in party and parliament. But the reality was far different. Behind the façade of democratic vigilance political fragmentation excluded the party from advancing from the stage of *ad hoc* parliamentary combinations to permanently organized transmission belts between population and government. Party organizations and party conventions were oversized *Café de Commerce* confabulations of *raisonneurs* without effective mandate.[3] Thus the bourgeois parties and the parliamentary government they carried saw themselves at every turn of events disowned as mere bubbles blown up by the *pays légal* to be confronted with the *pays réel* discovered from the confluence of thousands of discordant voices. Yet neither the *raisonneurs* nor the more or less benevolent intermediaries of the *Comité Mascuraud* watching over the parliamentary performance of rival political clans in the interest of the commercial and industrial community could substitute for the people at large.[4]

As these parties had to face less of a challenge from class-based integration parties than did their German neighbors, they could afford to become inoperative in semi-crisis periods. In such periods they were, as office-holding combinations, bailed out in the 1920s and early 1930s by proconsul saviors, Poincaré and his cheap imitator Doumergue. Yet as opinion-transmitting conveyor belts they had more and more to contend with the welter of antidemocratic organizations.

The last democratically legitimized attempt of the Third Republic to integrate the working class into the political system was Léon Blum's *Front Populaire*. Its failure was in part a failure of the parties, in part a consequence of international events. With its failure the Third Republic, with its juxtaposition of bourgeois parliamentary clans and class-based integration parties, was near its end.

---

[2] Alain, *Élements d'une doctrine radicale* (Paris, 1925).

[3] For a study of the working of the most characteristic of these parties see Daniel Bardonnet, *Évolution de la Structure du Parti Radical* (Paris, 1960).

[4] *Ibid.* Pages 251–56 contain details about the *Comité Mascuraud* (named after a Senator of the Seine Department), officially called the *Comité Républicain de Commerce et de l'Industrie*, the major agency for distributing commercial and industrial funds to bourgeois parties. For the *Comité Mascuraud* and other channels, more important later, see also Henry W. Ehrmann, *Organized Business in France* (Princeton, 1957), pp. 219 ff.

How did it happen that the Fourth Republic failed to integrate the Communist party into its political system and allowed both the SFIO (French Section of Workers' International or Social Democratic party) and the MRP (Popular Republican Movement, or Christian Democratic party) to slip into the habits of the bourgeois parties of the previous periods? Should we single out two load factors: the supervening, mutually exclusive international policy commitments of the majority of the French political parties and the Communists, and the crisis of decolonization? Yet the end of tripartism in 1947 need not have arrested the transformation of French parties into organizations able to integrate major social groups into the political system and able to work in coalition—collaboration or in alternative shifts. There is no reason why the challenge of *personalismo* in the form of Gaullism and the challenge of the Communist working class opposition of principle had to lead to an atavistic return to the party system of the 1920s. Decolonization was a challenge which the parties might have faced with clear-cut policy propositions. Working-class integration and decolonization, the former on the agenda for virtually half a century, the latter a limited problem, were burdens which an operative party system could have mastered.

Yet the majority of the French political parties had never progressed beyond the stage of local-interest messengers and parliamentary clubs with or without ideological overtones. They were equally unable to make commitments in the name of their voters or to obtain legitimacy through transforming the voters' opinions and attitudes into impulses converted into governmental action. They therefore had little to do with the continuity of the state, which remained the business of the bureaucracy. Major sociopolitical options were avoided, or, if and when they had to be faced, they became the work of individual politicians temporarily supported by strong elements in the community. It is doubtful whether even such a combination as that of Caillaux and Jaurès, which appeared likely in the spring of 1914, would have been able to establish the party as an effective transmission belt between population and government and a basis for policymaking. It might have failed because of the bourgeois distaste for devices which would transmit and thereby increase popular pressure on political action. In the single-load job of integrating the *couches populaires* into the French polity tthe performance of the political party remained unimpressive.

The rise of Italian and German political organizations in the middle of the nineteenth century cannot be separated from the history of belated unification. Unification was a competitive effort between the political endeavors of Cavour and Garibaldi and his adherents in Italy and between Bismarck and the Liberals in Germany. The respective statesmen's timing and actions cannot be understood without the urgency of these competitive pressures. But did the more nimble hand of Cavour provide the party system greater chances than the staccato fist of Bismarck? [5] What did Cavour's and Bismarck's styles of unification mean in terms of party loads and chances?

Could the Italian Left, the Partito d'Azione, have tried to find contact with the southern peasant masses? [6] Could it by such contact have established a basis for national loyalty transcending class and region? Or was it inevitable that it had to become part witness, part victim, of a *trasformismo* which remained an essentially commercial operation rather than an instrument of national integration? The possibilities may have been slight, but at any rate the attempt was never even made. In Germany, on the other hand, even the lateness and the Little Germany formula involved in the founding of Bismarck's Reich did not prevent that creation from soon becoming a socially and economically viable unit. All political forces, whether friendly or hostile to the Founding Father, accepted his Reich as a basis of operation. But in terms of the chances of the political parties the outcome was not much different. Italy had found a fictitious solution of its national identity problems, workable in constitutional but not in sociopolitical terms. Bismarck's heirs, the combined forces of bureaucracy, army, industrialists, and agrarians, upheld for about the same time both in Prussia and in the Empire a constitutional setup which prevented any approach to effective working-class participation in the government. In both Italy and Germany the mismanagement of the crises of national identity and of participation increased the problem load which

[5] A German author has recently put the case as follows: "Bismarck's policy to the Liberals was unfair in that he achieved what the Liberals wanted to have achieved, but he gave them neither the chance nor the means to do it on their own." E. Pikart, "Die Rolle der Deutschen Parteien im Deutschen Konstitutionellen System," *Zeitschrift für Politik,* 1962, pp. 12–15.

[6] The point is discussed in some detail in Antonio Gramsci, *Il Risorgimento, Opere di Antonio Gramsci,* IV (1949), 100–104.

the nation had to face at the end of World War I. However, it would be difficult to evaluate the differential impact of these load factors as compared, for example, with France. Here, without any crisis of national identity and without constitutional barriers to working-class participation, the long-smoldering participation crisis came fully into the open in the mid-thirties. I would argue that the extent of the 1940 breakdown is clearly related to this crisis of participation.

Is the load concept helpful, then, in analyzing the failure of the continental parties to assume their appropriate roles in the 1920s? May we, for example, argue that the belatedness in accepting a constitutional regime which would have allowed political democracy to become fully effective militated against successful political intergration of the working classes into the German political system in the 1920s? The acceptance of this argument hinges on some further differentiation. By "political integration" we mean here the capacity of a political system to make groups and their members previously outside the official political fold full-fledged participants in the political process. Many a mass party, however, was neither capable of nor interested in integrating its members into the existing political community. The party might even want rather to integrate its followers into its own ranks *against* the official state apparatus.

II. THE ANTEBELLUM MASS INTEGRATION PARTY

Socialist parties around the turn of the century exercised an important socializing function in regard to their members. They facilitated the transition from agrarian to industrial society in many ways. They subjected a considerable number of people hitherto living only as isolated individuals to voluntarily accepted discipline operating in close connection with expectations of a future total transformation of society. But this discipline had its roots in the alienation of these parties from the pre-World War I political system whose demise they wanted to guarantee and speed up by impressing the population as a whole with their exemplary attitudes.[7]

[7] The German end of this story and Bebel's emergence as commander-in-chief of a well-disciplined counter-army have often been commented upon. It has

During and soon after World War I the other participants in the political game showed that they were not yet willing to honor the claims of the working-class mass parties—claims based on the formal rules of democracy. This discovery was one of the primary reasons why the social integration into the industrial system through the working-class organizations did not advance to the state of a comparable political integration. Participation in the war, the long quarrels over the financial incidence of war burdens, the ravages of inflation, the rise of Bolshevist parties and a Soviet system actively competing for mass loyalty with the existing political mass organizations in most European countries, and finally the effect of the depression setting in at the end of the decade—all these were much more effective agents in the politicization of the masses than their participation in occasional elections, their fight for the extension of suffrage (Belgium, Britain, Germany), or even their *encadrement* in political parties and trade union organizations. But politicization is not tantamount to political integration; integration presupposes a general willingness by a society to offer and accept full-fledged political partnership of all citizens without reservations. The consequences of integration into the class-mass party depended on the responses of other forces in the existing political system; in some cases those responses were so negative as to lead to delayed integration into the political system or to make for its disintegration.

Now we come to the other side of this failure to progress from integration into the proletarian mass party and industrial society at large [8] to integration into the political system proper. This is the failure

---

recently been discussed in Guenther Roth, *The Social Democrats in Imperial Germany* (Ottawa, 1963). Similar observations on the social integration function of socialism are equally valid for Italy. As essentially hostile an observer as Benedetto Croce notes these factors in his *History of Italy, 1870–1915* (New York, 1963); Robert Michels in his *Sozialismus in Italien* (Karlsruhe, 1925), pp. 270 et seq,. provides ample documentary proof.

[8] Integration into industrial society: while the worker has accepted some aspects, such as urbanization and the need for regularity and the corresponding advantages of a mass consumer society, powerlessness as an individual and the eternal dependence on directives by superiors make for strong escapist attitudes. The problems are discussed in detail in André Andrieux and Jean Lignon, *L'Ouvrier d'aujourd'hui* (Paris, 1960). The ambiguous consequences to be drawn from these facts and their largely negative impact on the political image of the workers are studied in detail in H. Popitz *et al.*, *Das Gesellschaftsbild des Arbeiters* (Tübingen, 1957).

of bourgeois parties to advance from parties of individual representation to parties of integration, a failure already noted in France. The two tendencies, the failure of the integration of proletarian mass parties into the official political system and the failure of the bourgeois parties to advance to the stage of integration parties, condition each other. An exception, if only a partial one, is that of denominational parties such as the German Center or Don Sturzo's Partito Popolare.[9] These parties to a certain extent fulfilled both functions: social integration into industrial society and political integration within the existing political system. Yet their denominational nature gave such parties a fortress-type character seriously restricting their growth potential.[10]

With these partial exceptions, bourgeois parties showed no capacity to change from clubs for parliamentary representation into agencies for mass politics able to bargain with the integration-type mass parties according to the laws of the political market. There was only a limited incentive for intensive bourgeois party organization. Access to the favors of the state, even after formal democratization, remained reserved via educational and other class privileges. What the bourgeoisie lacked in numbers it could make good by strategic relations with the army and the bureaucracy.

Gustav Stresemann is the politician who stood at the crossroads of this era, operating with a threefold and incompatible set of parties: the class and the denominational democratic mass integration parties; the opposition-of-principle parties integrating masses into their own fold against the existing order; and the older parties of individual representation. Forever on the lookout for viable compromises among democratic mass parties, old-style bourgeois parties of individual representation, and the powerholders outside the formal political party structure, Stresemann failed. For the party of individual representa-

[9] For the typology of the denominational party, see Hans Maier, *Revolution und Kirche* (Freiburg, 1959).

[10] Another exception was that of parties such as the German Nationalist party of the 1920s, whose conservative predecessor in the days before World War I had already profited from the ability of the agrarian interest representation (*Landbund*) to funnel enough steady support to its companion organization in the political market. See in general: Thomas Nipperdey, *Die Organisation der deutschen Parteien vor 1918* (Dusseldorf, 1961), Vols. V and VI.

tion from which he came could not give him a broad enough basis for his policies.[11]

Not all bourgeois groups accepted the need for transformation to integration parties. As long as such groups had other means of access to the state apparatus they might find it convenient to delay setting up counterparts to existing mass parties while still using the state apparatus for keeping mass integration parties from becoming fully effective in the political market. Yet after World War II the acceptance of the law of the political market became inevitable in the major Western European countries. This change in turn found its echo in the changing structure of political parties.

III. THE POSTWAR CATCH-ALL PARTY

Following World War II, the old-style bourgeois party of individual representation became the exception. While some of the species continue to survive, they do not determine the nature of the party system any longer. By the same token, the mass integration party, product of an age with harder class lines and more sharply protruding denominational structures, is transforming itself into a catch-all "people's" party. Abandoning attempts at the intellectual and moral *encadrement* of the masses, it is turning more fully to the electoral scene, trying to exchange effectiveness in depth for a wider audience and more immediate electoral success. The narrower political task and the immediate electoral goal differ sharply from the former all-embracing concerns; today the latter are seen as counterproductive since they deter segments of a potential nation-wide clientele.

For the class-mass parties we may roughly distinguish three stages in this process of transformation. There is first the period of gathering strength lasting to the beginning of World War I; then comes their first governmental experience in the 1920s and 1930s (MacDonald, Weimar Republic, *Front Populaire*), unsatisfactory if measured both against the expectations of the class-mass party followers or leaders and

[11] See the conclusions of Wolfgang Hartenstein, *Die Anfänge der Deutschen Volkspartei* (Dusseldorf, 1962), and H. A. Turner, *Stresemann and the Politics of the Weimar Republic* (Princeton, 1963).

suggesting the need for a broader basis of consensus in the political system. This period is followed by the present more or less advanced stages in the catch-all grouping, with some of the parties still trying to hold their special working-class clientele and at the same time embracing a variety of other clienteles.

Can we find some rules according to which this transformation is taking place, singling out factors which advance or delay or arrest it? We might think of the current rate of economic development as the most important determinant; but it it were so important, France would certainly be ahead of Great Britain and, for that matter, also of the United States, still the classical example of an all-pervasive catch-all party system. What about the impact of the continuity or discontinuity of the political system? If this were so important, Germany and Great Britain would appear at opposite ends of the spectrum rather than showing a similar speed of transformation. We must then be satisfied to make some comments on the general trend and to note special limiting factors.

In some instances the catch-all performance meets definite limits in the traditional framework of society. The all-pervasive denominational background of the Italian Democrazia Cristiana means from the outset that the party cannot successfully appeal to the anticlerical elements of the population. Otherwise nothing prevents the party from phrasing its appeals so as to maximize its chances of catching more of those numerous elements which are not disturbed by the party's clerical ties. The solidary element of its doctrinal core has long been successfully employed to attract a socially diversified clientele.

Or take the case of two other major European parties, the German SPD (Social Democratic party) and the British Labour party. It is unlikely that either of them is able to make any concession to the specific desires of real estate interests or independent operators of agricultural properties while at the same time maintaining credibility with the masses of the urban population. Fortunately, however, there is enough community of interest between wage-and-salary earning urban or suburban white- and blue-collar workers and civil servants to designate them all as strategic objects of simultaneous appeals. Thus tradition and the pattern of social and professional stratification may set limits and offer potential audiences to the party's appeal.

If the party cannot hope to catch all categories of voters, it may have a reasonable expectation of catching more voters in all those categories whose interests do not adamantly conflict. Minor differences between group claims, such as between white-collar and manual labor groups, might be smoothed over by vigorous emphasis on programs which benefit both sections alike, for example, some cushioning against the shocks of automation.

Even more important is the heavy concentration on issues which are scarcely liable to meet resistance in the community. National societal goals transcending group interests offer the best sales prospect for a party intent on establishing or enlarging an appeal previously limited to specific sections of the population. The party which propagates most aggressively, for example, enlarged educational facilities may hear faint rumblings over the excessive cost or the danger to the quality of education from elites previously enjoying educational privileges. Yet the party's stock with any other family may be influenced only by how much more quickly and aggressively it took up the new national priority than its major competitor and how well its propaganda linked the individual family's future with the enlarged educational structures. To that extent its potential clientele is almost limitless. The catch-all of a given category performance turns virtually into an unlimited catch-all performance.

The last remark already transcends the group-interest confines. On the one hand, in such developed societies as I am dealing with, thanks to general levels of economic well-being and security and to existing welfare schemes universalized by the state or enshrined in collective bargaining, many individuals no longer need such protection as they once sought from the state. On the other hand, many have become aware of the number and complexity of the general factors on which their future well-being depends. This change of priorities and preoccupation may lead them to examine political offerings less under the aspect of their own particular claims than under that of the political leader's ability to meet general future contingencies. Among the major present-day parties, it is the French UNR (Union for the New Republic), a latecomer, that speculates most clearly on the possibility of its channeling such less specialized needs to which its patron saint de Gaulle constantly appeals into its own version of the catch-all party.

Its assumed asset would rest in a doctrine of national purpose and unity vague and flexible enough to allow the most variegated interpretation and yet—at least as long as the General continues to function—attractive enough to serve as a convenient rallying point for many groups and isolated individuals.[12]

While the UNR thus manipulates ideology for maximum general appeal, we have noted that ideology in the case of the Democrazia Cristiana is a slightly limiting factor. The UNR ideology in principle excludes no one. The Christian Democratic ideology by definition excludes the nonbeliever, or at least the seriously nonbelieving voter. It pays for the ties of religious solidarity and the advantages of supporting organizations by repelling some millions of voters. The catch-all parties in Europe appear at a time of de-ideologization which has substantially contributed to their rise and spread. De-ideologization in the political field involves the transfer of ideology from partnership in a clearly visible political goal structure into one of many sufficient but by no means necessary motivational forces operative in the voters' choice. The German and Austrian Social Democratic parties in the last two decades most clearly exhibit the politics of de-ideologization. The example of the German Christian Democratic Union (CDU) is less clear only because there was less to de-ideologize. In the CDU, ideology was from the outset only a general background atmosphere, both all-embracing and conveniently vague enough to allow recruiting among Catholic and Protestant denominations.

As a rule, only major parties can become successful catch-all parties. Neither a small, strictly regional party such as the South Tyrolian Peoples' party nor a party built around the espousal of harsh and limited ideological claims, like the Dutch Calvinists; or transitory group claims, such as the German Refugees; or a specific professional category's claims, such as the Swedish Agrarians; or a limited-action program, such as the Danish single-tax Justice party can aspire to a catch-all performance. Its *raison d'être* is the defense of a specific

---

[12] The difficulties of a party in which the dynamics of personalization substitute completely for agreed-upon goals as well as the style of operations fitting the personal loyalty variant of the catch-all party become readily apparent from the description of the Third UNR Party Congress by Jean Charlot, "Les Troisièmes Assises Nationales de l'U.N.R.–U.D.T.," *Revue Française de Science Politique,* XIV (February, 1964), 86–94.

clientele or the lobbying for a limited reform clearly delineated to allow for a restricted appeal, perhaps intense, but excluding a wider impact or—once the original job is terminated—excluding a life-saving transformation.

Nor is the catch-all performance in vogue or even sought among the majority of the larger parties in small democracies. Securely entrenched, often enjoying majority status for decades—as the Norwegian and Swedish Social Democratic parties—and accustomed to a large amount of interparty cooperation,[13] such parties have no incentive to change their form of recruitment or their appeal to well-defined social groups. With fewer factors intervening and therefore more clearly foreseeable results of political actions and decisions, it seems easier to stabilize political relations on the basis of strictly circumscribed competition (Switzerland, for instance) than to change over to the more aleatory form of catch-all competition.

Conversion to catch-all parties constitutes a competitive phenomenon. A party is apt to accommodate to its competitor's successful style because of hope of benefits or fear of losses on election day. Conversely, the more a party convinces itself that a competitor's favorable results were due only to some nonrepetitive circumstances, and that the competitor's capacity of overcoming internal dissension is a temporary phenomenon, the smaller the over-all conversion chance and the greater the inclination to hold fast to a loyal—though limited—clientele.

To evaluate the impact of these changes I have found it useful to list the functions which European parties exercised during earlier decades (late in the nineteenth and early in the twentieth century) and to compare them with the present situation. Parties have functioned as channels for integrating individuals and groups into the existing political order, or as instruments for modifying or altogether replacing that order (integration-disintegration). Parties have attempted to determine

---

[13] Ulf Torgersen, "The Trend Towards Political Consensus: The Case of Norway," in Stein Rokkan, ed., *Approaches to the Study of Political Participation* (Bergen, 1962); and Stein Rokkan and Henry Valen, "Regional Contrasts in Norwegian Politics" (1963, mimeographed), esp. p. 29. For both weighty historical and contemporary reasons the Austrian Social Democratic party forms a partial exception to the rule of less clear-cut transformation tendencies among major class-mass parties in smaller countries. It is becoming an eager and rather successful member of the catch-all club. For the most adequate treatment see K. L. Shell, *The Transformation of Austrian Socialism* (New York, 1962).

political-action preferences and influence other participants in the political process into accepting them. Parties have nominated public officeholders and presented them to the public at large for confirmation.

The so-called expressive function [14] of the party, if not belonging to
a category by itself, nevertheless warrants a special word. Its high tide
belongs to the era of nineteenth-century constitutionalism when a
more clear-cut separation existed between opinion formation-and-
expression and the business of government. At that time the internally
created parliamentary parties expressed opinions and criticism widely
shared among the educated minority of the population. They pressed
these opinions on their governments. But as the governments largely
rested on an independent social and constitutional basis, they could if
necessary hold out against promptings of parliamentary factions and
clubs. Full democratization merged the opinion-expressing and the
governmental business in the same political parties and put them in the
seat either of government or an alternative government. But it has left
the expressive function of the party in a more ambiguous state. For
electoral reasons, the democratic catch-all party, intent on spreading as
wide as possible a net over a potential clientele, must continue to express widely felt popular concerns. Yet, bent on continuing in power
or moving into governmental power, it performs this expressive function subject to manifold restrictions and changing tactical considerations. The party would atrophy if it were no longer able to function as
a relay between the population and governmental structure, taking up
grievances, ideas, and problems developed in a more searching and
systematic fashion elsewhere in the body politic. Yet the caution it
must give its present or prospective governmental role requires modu-
lation and restraint. The very nature of today's catch-all party forbids
an option between these two performances. It requires a constant shift
between the party's critical role and its role as establishment support, a
shift hard to perform but still harder to avoid.

In order to leave a maximum imprint on the polity a party has to
exercise all of the first three functions. Without the ability to integrate
people into the community the party could not compel other power-

---

[14] Cf. Sartori's paper, "European Political Parties: The Case of Polarized Plural-
ism," in *Political Parties and Political Development*, ed. Joseph LaPalombara and
Myron Wiener (Princeton, 1966). Cf. Sartori, *Parties and Party Systems*, New
York, Harper and Row, forthcoming.

holders to listen to its clarions. The party influences other power centers to the extent that people are willing to follow its leadership. Conversely, people are willing to listen to the party because the party is the carrier of messages—here called action preferences—that are at least partially in accord with the images, desires, hopes, and fears of the electorate. Nominations for public office serve to tie together all these purposes; they may further the realization of action preferences if they elicit positive response from voters or from other powerholders. The nominations concretize the party's image with the public at large, on whose confidence the party's effective functioning depends.

Now we can discuss the presence or absence of these three functions in Western society today. Under present conditions of spreading secular and mass consumer-goods orientation, with shifting and less obtrusive class lines, the former class-mass parties and denominational mass parties are both under pressure to become catch-all peoples' parties. The same applies to those few remnants of former bourgeois parties of individual representation which aspire to a secure future as political organizations independent of the vagaries of electoral laws and the tactical moves of their mass-party competitors.[15] This change involves: (a) Drastic reduction of the party's ideological baggage. In France's SFIO, for example, ideological remnants serve at best as scant cover for what has become known as *"Molletisme,"* the absolute reign of short-term tactical considerations. (b) Further strengthening of top leadership groups, whose actions and omissions are now judged from the viewpoint of their contribution to the efficiency of the entire social system rather than identification with the goals of their particular organization. (c) Downgrading of the role of the individual party member, a role considered a historical relic which may obscure the newly built-up catch-all party image.[16] (d) Deemphasis of the *classe*

---

[15] Liberal parties without sharply profiled program or clientele may, however, make such conversion attempts. Val Lorwin draws my attention to the excellent example of a former bourgeois party, the Belgian Liberal party, which became in 1961 the "Party of Liberty and Progress," deemphasizing anticlericalism and appealing to the right wing of the Social Christian party, worried about this party's governmental alliance with the Socialists.

[16] Ample material to points b) and c) may be found in the interesting study by a practicing German politician: Ulrich Lohmar, *Innerparteiliche Demokratie* (Stuttgart, 1963), esp. pp. 35–47 and 117–24. See also A. Pizzorno, "The Individualistic Mobilization of Europe," *Daedalus* (Winter, 1964), pp. 199, 217.

gardée, specific social-class or denominational clientele, in favor of recruiting voters among the population at large. (e) Securing access to a variety of interest groups. The financial reasons are obvious, but they are not the most important where official financing is available, as in Germany, or where access to the most important media of communication is fairly open, as in England and Germany. The chief reason is to secure electoral support via interest-group intercession.

From this fairly universal development the sometimes considerable remnants of two old class-mass parties, the French and the Italian Communist parties, are excluding themselves. These parties are in part ossified, in part solidified by a combination of official rejection and legitimate sectional grievances. In this situation the ceremonial invocation of the rapidly fading background of a remote and inapplicable revolutionary experience has not yet been completely abandoned as a part of political strategy. What is the position of such opposition parties of the older class-mass type, which still jealously try to hold an exclusive loyalty of their members, while not admitted nor fully ready to share in the hostile state power? Such parties face the same difficulties in recruiting and holding intensity of membership interest as other political organizations. Yet, in contrast to their competitors working within the confines of the existing political order, they cannot make a virtue out of necessity and adapt themselves fully to the new style of catch-all people's party.[17] This conservatism does not cost them the confidence of their regular corps of voters. On the other hand, the continued renewal of confidence on election day does not involve an intimate enough bond to utilize as a basis for major political operations.

The attitudes of regular voters—in contrast to those of members and activists—attest to the extent of incongruency between full-fledged participation in the social processes of a consumer-goods oriented society and the old political style which rested on the primordial need for sweeping political change. The latter option has gone out of fashion in Western countries and has been carefully eliminated from the expecta-

---

[17] However, even in France—not to speak of Italy—Communist policies are under pressure to accommodate to the new style. For a concrete recent example see W. G. Andrews, "Evreux 1962: Referendum and Elections in a Norman Constituency," *Political Studies*, XI (October, 1963), 308–26. Most recently, Maurice Duverger, "L'Eternel Marais: Essai sur le Centrisme Français," *Revue Française de Science Politique*, XIV (February, 1964), 33, 49.

tions, calculations, and symbols of the catch-all mass party. The incongruency may rest on the total absence of any connection between general social-cultural behavior and political style.[18] In this sense electoral choice may rest on family tradition or empathy with the political underdog without thereby becoming part of a coherent personality structure. Or the choice may be made in the expectation that it will have no influence on the course of political development; it is then an act of either adjusting to or, as the case may be, signing out of the existing political system rather than a manifestation of signing up somewhere else.

IV. THE CATCH-ALL PARTY, THE INTEREST GROUP, AND THE VOTER: LIMITED INTEGRATION

The integration potential of the catch-all mass party rests on a combination of factors whose visible end result is attraction of the maximum number of voters on election day. For that result the catch-all party must have entered into millions of minds as a familiar object fulfilling in politics a role analogous to that of a major brand in the marketing of a universally needed and highly standardized article of mass consumption. Whatever the particularities of the line to which a party leader owes his intraparty success, he must, once he is selected for leadership, rapidly suit his behavior to standard requirements. There is need for enough brand differentiation to make the article plainly recognizable, but the degree of differentiation must never be so great as to make the potential customer fear he will be out on a limb.

Like the brand whose name has become a household word, the catch-all mass party that has presided over the fortunes of a country for some time, and whose leaders the voter has therefore come to know on his television set and in his newspaper columns, enjoys a great advantage. But only up to a certain point. Through circumstances

---

18 This hypothesis is discussed in more detail in Georges Lavau, "Les aspects socio-culturels de la dépolitisation," in Georges Vedel, ed., *La Dépolitisation: Mythe ou Réalité?* (Paris, 1962), esp. p. 198. For some other explanations see Seymour Martin Lipset, "The Changing Class Structure and Contemporary European Politics," *Daedalus* (Winter, 1964), pp. 271–303.

possibly outside the control of the party or even of the opposition—a scandal in the ranks of government, an economic slump—officeholding may suddenly turn into a negative symbol encouraging the voter to switch to another party as a consumer switches to a competitive brand.

The rules deciding the outcome of catch-all mass party competition are extremely complex and extremely aleatory. When a party has or seeks an almost nation-wide potential constituency, its majority composed of individuals whose relation to politics is both tangential and discontinuous, the factors which may decide the eventual electoral outcome are almost infinite in number and often quite unrelated to the party's performance. The style and looks of the leader, the impact of a recent event entirely dictated from without, vacation schedules, the weather as it affects crops—factors such as these all enter into the results.

The very catch-all character of the party makes membership loyalty far more difficult to expect and at best never sufficient to swing results. The outcome of a television contest is dubious, or the contest itself may constitute too fleeting an exposure to make an impression that will last into the election. Thus the catch-all mass party too is driven back to look out for a more permanent clientele. Only the interest group, whether ideological or economic in nature or a combination of the two, can provide mass reservoirs of readily accessible voters. It has a more constant line of communication and higher acceptance for its messages than the catch-all party, which is removed from direct contact with the public except for the comparatively small number intensively concerned about the brand of politics a party has to offer these days—or about their own careers in or through the party.

All the same, the climate of relations between catch-all party and interest groups has definitely changed since the heyday of the class-mass or denominational integration party. Both party and interest group have gained a greater independence from each other. Whether they are still joined in the same organization (like British Labour and the TUC [Trades Union Congress]) or formally enjoy complete independence from each other (like the German SPD and the DGB [Workers' Federation]), what matters most is the change of roles.[19]

[19] See the conclusions of Martin Harrison, *Trade Unions and the Labour Party Since 1945* (London, 1960).

Instead of a joint strategy toward a common goal there appears an appreciation of limited if still mutually helpful services to be rendered.

The party bent on attracting a maximum of voters must modulate its interest-group relations in such a way so as not to discourage potential voters who identify themselves with other interests. The interest group, in its turn, must never put all its eggs in one basket. That might offend the sensibilities of some members with different political connections. More important, the interest group would not want to stifle feelings of hope in another catch-all party that some moves in its direction might bring electoral rewards. Both party and interest group modulate their behavior, acting as if the possible contingency had already arrived, namely, that the party has captured the government—or an important share in it—and has moved from the position of friend or counselor to that of umpire or arbitrator. Suddenly entrusted with the confidence of the community as a whole, the government-party arbitrator does best when able to redefine the whole problem and discover solutions which would work, at least in the long run, in the favor of all interest claimants concerned.

Here there emerges a crucial question: What then is the proper role of the catch-all party in the arbitration of interest conflicts? Does not every government try to achieve the best tactical position for exercising an effective arbitration between contending group claims? Is the catch-all party even needed in this connection? Or—from the interest viewpoint—can a society dispense with parties' services, as France now does?

A party is more than a collector of interest-group claims. It functions at the same time as advocate, protector, or at least as addressee of the demands of all those who are not able to make their voices felt as effectively as those represented by well-organized interest groups: those who do not yet have positions in the process of production or those who no longer hold such positions, the too young and the too old, and those whose family status aligns them with consumer rather than producer interests.

Can we explain this phenomenon simply as another facet of the party's aggregative function? But functionalist phraseology restates rather than explains. The unorganized and often unorganizable make their appearance only on election day or in suddenly sprouting pre-election committees and party activities arranged for their benefit. Will the party be able and willing to take their interests into its own hands? Will it be able, playing on their availability in electoral terms, not only to check the more extreme demands of organized groups but also to transcend the present level of intergroup relations and by political reforms redefine the whole political situation? No easy formula will tell us what leader's skill, what amount of pressure from objective situations has to intervene to produce such a change in the political configuration.

In this job of transcending group interests and creating general confidence the catch-all party enjoys advantages, but by the same token it suffers from an infirmity. Steering clear of sectarianism enhances its recruiting chances in electoral terms but inevitably limits the intensity of commitment it may expect. The party's transformation from an organization combining the defense of social position, the quality of spiritual shelter, and the vision of things to come into that of a vehicle for short-range and interstitial political choice exposes the party to the hazards of all purveyors of nondurable consumer goods: competition with a more attractively packaged brand of a nearly identical merchandise.

V. LIMITED PARTICIPATION IN ACTION PREFERENCE

This brings us to the determination of action preferences and their chances of realization. In Anthony Downs's well-known model action preference simply results from the party's interest in the proximate goal, the winning of the next election. In consequence the party will arrange its policies in such a way that the benefits accruing to the individual members of the community are greater than the losses resulting from its policy.[20] Downs's illustrations are frequently, though not exclusively, taken from fields such as taxation where the cash equation of political action is feasible. Yet Downs himself has occasionally noted that psychological satisfactions or dissatisfactions, fears or hopes,

[20] "It always organizes its action so as to focus on a single quantity: its vote margin over the opposition in the test at the end of the current election period." In A. Downs, *An Economic Theory of Democracy* (New York, 1957), p. 174.

are elements in voters' decisions as frequently as calculations of immediate short-term benefits or deprivations. Were it different, the long-lasting loyalty of huge blocks of voters to class-mass integration parties in the absence of any immediate benefits from such affiliation could scarcely be explained. But can it be said that such short-term calculations correspond much more closely to the attitudes connected with the present-day catch-all mass party with its widely ranging clientele? Can the short-term benefit approach, for example, be utilitized in military or foreign-policy issues?

In some countries in the last decade it has become the rule for catch-all parties out of office simply to lay the most recent shortcomings or apparent deterioration of the country's military or international position at the doorstep of the incumbent government, especially during election campaigns: thus in the United States the Republican party in 1952 with regard to the long-lasting indecisive Korean War, or in Germany more recently the Social Democrats with regard to Adenauer's apparent passivity in the face of the Berlin Wall. In other instances, however, the opposition plays down foreign or military issues or treats them in generalities vague enough to evoke the image of itself as a competitor who will be able to handle them as well as the incumbent government.

To the extent that the party system still includes "unreformed" or—as in the case of the Italian Socialist party—only "half-reformed" class-mass type integration parties, foreign or military issues enter election campaigns as policy differences. Yet even here the major interest has shifted away from areas where the electorate could exercise only an illusory choice. The electorate senses that in the concrete situation, based in considerable part on geography and history, the international bloc affiliation of the country rather than any policy preference will form the basis of decision. It senses too that such decisions rest only partially, or at times nominally, with the political leadership. Even if the impact of the political leader on the decision may have been decisive, more often than not election timetables in democracies are such that the decision, once carried out, is no longer contested or even relevant to voter choices. As likely as not, new events crowd it out of the focus of voters' attention. Few voters still thought of Mendès-France's 1954 "abandonment" of Indo-China when Edgar Faure suddenly dissolved the Assembly in December, 1955. While a party may benefit from its adversary's unpopular decisions, such benefits are more often an accidental by-product than the outcome of a government-opposition duel with clearly distributed roles and decisions.

A party may put up reasonably coherent, even if vague, foreign or military policies for election purposes. It may criticize the inept handling of such problems by the government of the day, and more and more intensively as it gets closer to election day. But in neither case is there a guarantee of the party's ability to act as a coherent body in parliament when specific action preferences are to be determined. Illustrative of this dilemma are the history of EDC in the French Parliament and the more recent battles within the British parties in regard to entrance into the Common Market (although the latter case remains inconclusive because of de Gaulle's settling the issue in his own way, for the time being). Fortuitous election timetables and the hopes, fears, and expectations of the public do not intermesh sufficiently with the parliamentary representatives' disjointed action on concrete issues before them to add up to the elaboration of clear-cut party action preference.

The catch-all party contributes general programs in the elaboration of domestic action preferences. These programs may be of a prognostic variety, informing the public about likely specific developments and general trends. Yet prognostics and desirability blur into each other in this type of futurology, in which rosy glasses offer previews of happy days for all and sundry among the party's prospective customers. These programs may lead to or be joined with action proposals in various stages of concretization. Concrete proposals, however, always risk implying promises which may be too specific. Concretizations must remain general enough so that they cannot be turned from electoral weapons to engines of assault against the party which first mounted them.

This indeterminacy allows the catch-all party to function as a meeting ground for the elaboration of concrete action for a multiplicity of interest groups. All the party may require from those who obtain its services is that they make a maximal attempt to arrive at compromises within the framework of the party and that they avoid coalescing with forces hostile to the party. The compromises thus elaborated must be acceptable to major interest groups even if these groups, for historical or traditional reasons, happen not to be represented in the governing party. Marginal differences may be submitted to the voter at elections or, as older class-mass parties do on occasion, via referenda (Switzerland and Sweden). But expected policy mutations are in the nature of increments rather than major changes in intergroup relations.

It is here that the difference between the catch-all and the older form of integration party becomes most clearly visible. The catch-all party will do its utmost to establish consensus to avoid party realignment. The integration party may count on majority political mechanisms to implement its programs only to find that hostile interests frustrate the majority decision by the economic and social mechanisms at their disposal. They may call strikes (by labor or farmers or storekeepers or investors), they may withdraw capital to safe havens outside the country, they may undermine that often hypocritically invoked but real factor known as the "confidence of the business community."

VI. INTEGRATION THROUGH PARTICIPATION IN LEADERSHIP SELECTION—THE FUTURE OF THE POLITICAL PARTY

What then remains the real share of the catch-all party in the elaboration of action preferences? Its foremost contribution lies in the mobilization of the voters for whatever concrete action preferences leaders are able to establish rather than *a priori* selections of their own. It is for this reason that the catch-all party prefers to visualize action in the light of the contingencies, threats, and promises of concrete historical situations rather than of general social goals. It is the hoped-for or already established role in the dynamics of action, in which the voters' vicarious participation is invited, that is most in evidence. Therefore the attention of both party and public at large focuses most clearly on problems of leadership selection.

Nomination means the prospect of political office. Political office involves a chance to make an impact via official action. The competition between those striving to influence official action puts into evidence the political advantage of those in a position to act before their political adversaries can do so. The privilege of first action is all the more precious in a new and nonrepetitive situation where the political actor can avoid getting enmeshed in directives deriving from party action preferences. Much as the actor welcomes party support on the basis of revered (but elastic) principles, he shuns specific direction and supervision. In this respect the catch-all party furnishes an ideal background for political action. Where obtaining office becomes an almost exclusive preoccupation of a party, issues of personnel are reduced to a search for the simplest effective means to put up winning combinations. The search is especially effective wherever the party becomes a channel by which representatives of hitherto excluded or neglected minorities may join the existing political elite.

The nomination of candidates for popular legitimation as officeholders thus emerges as the most important function of the present-day catch-all party. Concentration on the selection of candidates for office is in line with an increasing role differentiation in industrial society. Once certain levels of education and material welfare are reached, both intellectual and material needs are taken care of by specialized purveyors of communications and economic products. Likewise the party, which in less advanced societies or in those intent on rapid change directly interferes with the performance of societal jobs, remains in Western industrial society twice removed—through government and bureaucracy—from the field of direct action. To this state of affairs correspond now prevailing popular images and expectations in regard to the reduced role of the party.[21] Expectations previously set on the performance of a political organization are now flowing into different channels.[22]

At the same time, the role of the political party as a factor in the continued integration of the individual into the national life now has to be visualized in a different light. Compared to his connection with interest organizations and voluntary associations of a nonpolitical na-

[21] See the discussion of political attitudes in Habermas et al., Student und Politik (Neuwied, 1961), and the German preference scale quoted in R. Mayntz, "Loisirs, participation sociale et activité politique," Revue Internationale des Sciences Sociales (1960), pp. 608–22.

[22] See the contribution of S. Mallet, "L'Audience politique des syndicats," in Léo Hamon, ed., Les nouveaux comportements politiques de la classe ouvrière (Paris, 1962), esp. pp. 241–44.

ture and to his frequent encounters with the state bureaucracy, the citizen's relations with the political party are becoming more intermittent and of more limited scope.

To the older party of integration the citizen, if he so desired, could be closer. Then it was a less differentiated organization, part channel of protest, part source of protection, part purveyor of visions of the future. Now, in its linear descendant in a transfigured world, the catch-all party, the citizen finds a relatively remote, at times quasi-official and alien structure. Democratic society assumes that the citizen is finally an integral and conscious participant in the affairs of both the polity and the economy; it further assumes that as such he will work through the party as one of the many interrelated structures by which he achieves a rational participation in his surrounding world.

Should he ever live up to these assumptions, the individual and society may indeed find the catch-all party—nonutopian, nonoppressive, and ever so flexible—an ingenious and useful political instrument.

What about the attitude toward the modern catch-all party of functional powerholders in army, bureaucracy, industry, and labor? Released from their previous unnecessary fears as to the ideological propensities and future intentions of the class-mass party, functional powerholders have come to recognize the catch-all party's role as consensus purveyor. In exchange for its ability to provide a clear-cut basis of legitimacy, functional powerholders are, up to a point, willing to recognize the political leadership claims of the party. They expect it to exercise certain arbitration functions in intergroup relations and to initiate limited political innovations. The less clear-cut the electoral basis of the party's leadership claim and the closer the next election date, the smaller the credit which functional powerholders will extend to unsolicited and nonroutine activities of the political powerholders impinging on their own positions. This lack of credit then sets the stage for conflicts between functional and political leadership groups. How does the catch-all party in governmental positions treat such conflicts? Will it be satisfied to exercise pressure via the mass media, or will it try to re-create a militant mass basis beyond the evanescent electoral and publicity levels? But the very structure of the catch-all party, the looseness of its clientele, may from the outset exclude such more far-reaching action. To that extent the political party's role in

Western industrial society today is more limited than would appear from its position of formal preeminence. Via its governmental role it functions as coordinator of and arbitrator between functional power groups. Via its electoral role it produces that limited amount of popular participation and integration required from the popular masses for the functioning of official political institutions.

Will this limited participation which the catch-all party offers the population at large, this call to rational and dispassionate participation in the political process via officially sanctioned channels, work?

The instrument, the catch-all party, cannot be much more rational than its nominal master, the individual voter. No longer subject to the discipline of the party of integration—or, as in the United States, never subject to this discipline—the voters may, by their shifting moods and their apathy, transform the sensitive instrument of the catch-all party into something too blunt to serve as a link with the functional power-holders of society.[23] Then we may yet come to regret the passing—even if it was inevitable—of the class-mass party and the denominational party, as we already regret the passing of other features in yesterday's stage of Western civilization.

[23] For some recent strictures on slavish party dependence on the results of polls, see Ulrich Lohmar, *op. cit.*, pp. 106–8.

EXPERTISE AND POLITICS IN
THE ADMINISTRATION

AT DARTMOUTH COLLEGE the Mexican painter Orozco has presented his conception of the future relations of man and machine: a complicated machine runs automatically while the worker sits next to it with a book in his hand, acting merely as a kind of control mechanism guaranteeing smooth performance according to program. To what extent can the relationship between politics and administration attain a comparable form? The prognosis is not absolutely unfavorable. States like Sweden have made remarkable steps in this direction, and even in countries with complicated social and political conditions we find areas where already today the processes of control can be made largely automatic. Yet this can hardly be considered the rule in the major countries. The leap from the domination over men to the administration of things, Engels' utopia of yore, has still to be made. Its cruel parody in Russia, an ironic paraphrase of Lenin's *State and Revolution*, nevertheless was not able altogether to arrest its progress in the West. What are its immanent limits? How far will we be able to advance in this direction, provided the shadow of general barbarism which threatens us daily does not envelop us and put to rest forever the realization of this dream of mankind?

The following purports to be merely a sober report on the situation in its lower ranges. It will, I believe, be of interest to the German reader if I start out from certain phenomena in the United States.

Translation, by permission, of "Sachverstand und Politik im Bereich der Verwaltung"; originally published in *Gewerkschaftliche Monatshefte*, XI (1962), 670–76.

I

Presidents come and go, the civil service remains. Is this true under American conditions? Probably a little less than it is for Europe. A new presidency does shape the general direction of the state apparatus to a certain extent. The change of presidential portraits in the offices is not a mere formality. It expresses a readiness to identify with new vistas, impulses, and guidelines. At least it means an advance credit accorded by the civil service to the new master. This credit may be increased by strategically important appointments. The President is entitled to appoint Undersecretaries of State, the heads of the important regulatory commissions, and (if he is lucky and their terms of office are running out) also their members; in addition he can fill positions especially exempted from the civil service, quite apart from the postmasterships from the head of the giant New York Post Office down to the smallest, not particularly lucrative, ones. The juiciest jobs, the regional tax collectorships, have been incorporated into the civil service since the beginning of the fifties; this, however, does not prevent the central tax authorities in Washington from granting politically motivated favors to influential tax delinquents. The filling of the symbolically most conspicuous—if not the most important—offices, those of the nine Justices of the Supreme Court, naturally depends on the fortuities of death or medical advice. They are especially important today because so many decisions involving the Bill of Rights are reached by a 5:4 vote. This year the President receives an extraordinary political gift: he can appoint at one stroke one hundred federal district and circuit judges (partly newly created ones, partly judgeships long vacant because of difficulties between President Eisenhower and the Democratic Senate majority). Given the total of less than 500 federal judges, this number is very considerable, and we can anticipate that the way these appointments are handled during the coming months will substantially affect the domestic political climate of the United States.

In contrast to the Eisenhower administration, the Kennedy administration had an auspicious beginning, at least in so far as domestic politics are concerned. Because of the 6 million unemployed no one is thinking of a new "RIF" (reduction in force), that is, of a more

ologically than practically relevant dismissal of civil servants for
ons of economy. Lifetime tenure for civil servants is unknown, at
t formally, in the United States and would probably still be regarded as an illegitimate attempt to create property rights. Nor is it
likely that the McCarthy witch hunt will continue for the moment; it
is harmful psychologically to civil service morale and yet it was never
opposed by Eisenhower and even less by his Secretary of State, Dulles.
But the problem is still with us, I am afraid.

The psychological instability of the American population, the consciousness of lost security, and the sudden realization that the traditional political and economic solutions have become inadequate in the
international arena create new convulsions, as the mushrooming of the
Birch Society bears out. It is still an open question to what extent the
new political team, which is tactically very agile, will react to this
challenge. The majority of Kennedy's appointments are absolutely on
the plus side, however.

Here several factors have combined to bring about a turn for the
better. One of them is the intellectual energy of a President who,
unlike Eisenhower, sees himself less in the role of a chairman of a
board of directors, concerned only with the smooth functioning of the
business, than as one who intends to run things himself with the help
of carefully selected personal advisers. Another factor is—an historical
irony—the utilization of personal fortune against the survival of plutocratic holdouts in American society. What does this mean? Usually the
President is bound by certain obligations when appointing people to
office. The campaign managers have made promises in his name, sometimes without his knowledge, in order to obtain sufficient funds—in
the United States the reform of party finance and its plutocratic traits
is just as difficult an undertaking as it is in Germany. In this respect
President Kennedy enjoyed opportunities not experienced for a long
time, which are reflected in many of his diplomatic appointments
(Kennan, Galbraith) and possibly even more importantly in his appointments to federal commissions.

The fact that on account of his family fortune the President had far
fewer campaign obligations to repay—his heaviest obligation was of a
purely political nature—played a role here as did the awareness that
the immense tasks awaiting the President require an intellectual team

different from that of the former President, who was merely concerned to keep things on an even keel.

In addition to this, new impetus was given to a faster integration of the Negro population into the federal government apparatus by the analysis of the 1960 presidential election. For the Negro population had voted largely for Kennedy. A Negro for the first time attained cabinet rank by being appointed head of the Federal Housing Authority, and the Negroes' further progress in federal government careers appears limited only by the number of them possessing the necessary qualifications.

One must certainly not overlook the problematical aspects. The powerful chief of the FBI, J. Edgar Hoover, was again confirmed in his office. This precludes an investigation of the activities and status of the secret police, which is overdue in many countries. Its shadow is a cancer plaguing almost all governments of our era, enveloping, since its unhappy beginning in Russia, all social systems and largely contributing to, if not even creating, their conformist zeal. In the United States, England, and the Federal Republic (thanks partly to the most worthwhile German postwar institution, the Federal Constitutional Court), constitutional safeguards protect the individual from the worst threats to life and limb, without, however, being effective enough to overcome all syndromes of paralysis.

II

Thus we arrive at the fateful question concerning the administration of all modern countries: Who governs, who guides, who controls the giant administrative machines which have nowadays become the hallmark of all industrial societies? "Parkinson's law" has drawn attention to some of the most grotesque, though not necessarily most important, aspects of the question. As a former long-time member of one of the biggest bureaucracies of our Western world, I shall not deny that the desire to obtain promotion and the corresponding need to prove the urgency of new tasks and "slots" constitute a frequent reason for the inflation of bureaucracies.

But I believe that one has to make allowance for differences. In the first place there are the administrative services geared directly to the customer, such as post offices, traffic control, medical insurance, where the positive or negative results are more or less proportionate to the labor invested. Calculable events and the customers' insistence on smooth and quick performance make possible a correct relationship between input and output while taking advantage of processes of rationalization. For tax collectors and antitrust officials things are similar, even though their problems are somewhat more complicated. Yet it is clear that the personnel question in these fields constitutes a political problem. In the United States we have seen often enough that Congress, not being particularly interested in the effective carrying out of such tasks, has failed to assign sufficient personnel to these agencies. Personnel policy thus becomes an expression of sociopolitical decisions.

But how are we to evaluate the costs of modern military, paramilitary, diplomatic, and intelligence agencies, where it is questionable whether conclusions can be drawn as to the relation between input and output? One might answer that the fact that no enemy invasion was attempted or that no subversion has destroyed the political order is sufficient justification for the expenditures incurred. But this answer remains necessarily unsatisfactory. There is no proof that this or that form of political propaganda or of military preparation has brought the desired success, that is, the preservation of a peace however precarious and threatened. For the success may have been due, on the contrary, to the nature of the adversaries' power constellation. And it is exactly in those areas where the relationship between input and output cannot be reliably determined that new projects abound and bureaucratic proliferation flourishes.

III

What about the control of administrative action in the modern state?

We have more than enough mechanisms of control. Parliamentary, party, governmental, interdepartmental, and interest group controls compete with each other, but their effectiveness is very uneven.

The most questionable of them is parliamentary control. This applies not only to France, where constitutional changes have extremely restricted the role of parliament, but also to Austria, where the coalition committee has effectively taken the place of parliament, and to Germany and Britain, where parliament has receded behind the governing party, which, in turn, is guided by a majority government. Even under the conditions prevailing in the United States, where the political structure is quite different, the Congress only retains intermittent control functions. It may investigate a special problem using for this purpose one of its investigating committees, which are not always and not necessarily pure organs of propaganda. This is a function lacking completely in the Federal Republic. But apart from this parliament has become an outsider; it may follow up complaints (which do not always concern the most important problems of the administrative agency in question), but it will rarely possess the necessary expertise or the documents which would make its efforts lasting and effective.

The political party is somewhat better situated. It is able to exercise certain influences and controls via personnel policy. The result depends on the character of the party itself. If it is a mere patronage organization without any ideological or traditional inhibitions or a socio-demoscopic party—I have been told that some German parties are nowadays very much exposed to this danger—the personnel policy is scarcely worth the effort, either from the point of view of the party or from that of the government. Both are cheated in the same way. The person so injected into the administration will at once adapt to his new surroundings. Such an opportunist does not increase the influence of his party; and the administration, instead of obtaining a lively new element with fresh vistas, gets yet another conformist who only desires to make his colleagues forget that he did not obtain his position in the regular bureaucratic way.

This may possibly be different—in the Western world probably in countries like Belgium or Austria—where parties still represent certain sociopolitical ideals or concrete social interest organizations. In spite of occasionally grotesque aspects, this practice may nevertheless lead to the introduction of new social strata into the state machinery and thus to a better interpenetration of administrative apparatus and social structure which is apparently rather productive for both.

The relationship between the political executive and the permanent administration is important. According to the prevailing theory it is the government which gives general directives to the administration, funnels new impulses into it, and coordinates its activities politically. It would be interesting to determine which of the governments of the fifties, in the moderate political climate in which we live, still acts in accordance with this theory. Reactions to direct political situations, whether provoked by outside or inside forces, dominate the arena— how much time did the French military cost the governments of the Fourth and Fifth Republics? Whatever new stimuli are produced come from the regular research organizations which play a big, though not always definable, role, at least in the United States, whether they are official, semiofficial, or quarter-official in nature. These research bureaucracies may

1. be simply incorporated in the administrative apparatus or grafted onto it;

2. they may, like the RAND Corporation or O.R.O. for the Army, be nourished and provided with tasks by their sponsoring organizations, but otherwise lead an independent existence adapted maximally to independent research; or

3. they may have remained completely within the framework of the university so that the relations between government and university are limited to the conclusion of research contracts.

I need hardly emphasize that such a loose relationship to the organs of government, the fact that one does not have to take into account all their vacillations and reactions, is advantageous to scholarly efforts. But another question is how much this expertise is listened to when it comes to making the great decisions. If this expertise is part of the government apparatus, then there is—despite the enormous disadvantages involved—at least a bureaucratic channel ensuring that studies and suggestions are noted and possibly even reacted to. In the case of the semi- or fully detached research organizations, the question always arises (of course, more with respect to their work in the social than in the natural sciences) what chances they really have to be heard by the officials and to influence their deliberations. This varies from case to case and often depends on the intelligence and perception of the people in the higher government positions. As is well known, the willingness and the capacity to face problems from new angles do not necessarily increase as one ascends the echelons of the official hierarchy. Some of the highest offices in the federal government are said to have had official regulations during certain periods according to which all memoranda for the very highest officials were to be limited to one wide-spaced page. There naturally exists a second danger as well: that the larger public is informed of these scientific studies in a strangely distorted way and reacts accordingly.

This problem of the efficacy of purely intellectual authority is, of course, reduced, though not entirely removed, when the President surrounds himself with a personal staff of intellectual advisers, as under Roosevelt and now again under Kennedy. But their achievement lies hardly in establishing systems or guiding ideas. It consists rather in their having learned to think problems through to their final consequences. And it consists further in their being able to avoid (contrary to the politician and the conventional bureaucrat) what one calls "practicism" farther East, that is, thinking in compromises and half and quarter solutions and in terms of being covered on all sides. How many of the stimuli coming from the President's *adlati* find their way automatically into administrative practice by way of intellectual osmosis and how many are, on the other hand, translated into practice by way of the personal authority of the head of the government or one of its members, this is another question. During, or under the immediate threat of, a war, and limited to innovations necessary for the conduct of military operations, this sort of thing is possible—one need only remember Tizard's or Lindemann's position in England during the late thirties and forties.

Let us remember one thing: To make the right choice among the technical, military, and administrative authorities concerned, to protect them by exercise of his authority, to have the confidence that his intuition or his personal affinities have not led him astray while being courageous enough to admit grave mistakes and to repair them before they become irreparable—all this, in terms of personnel policy, is the most important contribution the head of the government and the administration and his ministers can make.

IV

This, however, means that interdepartmental and interest group controls become *nolens volens* the cornerstone of a regular rather than (as in the case of courts and political quarters) merely an incidental check upon administrative action. Both are controls by experts who have mastered their subject, each from his own perspective or interest orientation, something that can generally not be said of politicians and never of individual petitioners or complainants.

Departmental control itself has two aspects. First of all, it is the ex-officio control of financial behavior to which the Treasury, the Bureau of the Budget, and the Rue de Rivoli subject the projects of their colleagues. Their points of view may not always and not necessarily show the desired understanding for the respective line officials—the Keynesian influence has apparently always been greater in the British Treasury than in the Rue de Rivoli—but in any case the executive budget has by necessity become almost everywhere the central reference and control point of the state apparatus.

Second, departmental control consists in the competition among the several subject matter departments and their clienteles. What to the outsider often seems a ludicrous squabble over jurisdictions—whether within a department or between departments—is really at the same time a struggle over principles of social action.

From the American experience we may cite the struggle between the Treasury and the Federal Reserve Board centering on credit policy; the struggle between the Commerce and State Departments regarding tariffs; that between Agriculture and State as to policy on cotton and grain; between Labor and Agriculture about the admission of low-wage Mexican workers; between the armed forces and the Justice Department concerning the merits of restraints on competition; and the never-ending struggle among the several branches of the armed services over priorities of weapons systems and the related strategic concepts.

For this struggle each side mobilizes its auxiliary troops in parliamentary committees, editorial offices, and among the President's entourage. This is the real essence of present-day administrative politics. One could probably find dozens of parallels in Germany; the echo of such happenings as regards the relations between the Economic and Foreign Ministries is said to have penetrated as far as the courtroom of *Landgerichtsdirektor* Quirini.

In this new system of interdepartmental checks and balances, where priorities and decisions of substance are contested, the interest groups have their place as well. They are by no means mere auxiliary troops drawn into the vortex of their interbureaucratic struggles by the respective bureaucracies; nor are they—as the pious legend sometimes has it—always the driving forces. For it very often happens that a bureaucracy has not one clientele, but that rather from the very beginning several interests belong to its jurisdiction, which naturally increases the independence of the bureaucracy vis-à-vis its clientele. However that may be, the interest groups share the expertise with the bureaucracy, but differ from it in so far as their attention is primarily focused on the interests of their members and not on the essential business of the bureaucracy, that is, compromise with other bureaucracies or with differently structured clienteles.

In the relationship between bureaucracy and interest groups originates the often discussed problem of corruption. In the Federal Republic this problem is mostly discussed in terms of criminal law; thus we think, for instance, of the carpets of the mayor or the automobile loaned to the *Regierungsrat* or *Ministerialrat*. With some cynicism one might comment that he who receives gifts from everyone is subservient to no one and that he who must borrow a car can hardly be influential enough to do much damage. The real problem lies deeper and can hardly be grasped by dissertations on the limits of the concept of passive bribery, just as the efforts of prosecutor and judge must be regarded as a merely marginal contribution to the control of administrative action. It is not the peripheral phenomenon of private enrichment by drawing illegitimate pecuniary advantages from official acts, but rather the two-way traffic between the public sphere and that of private interests which gives rise to problems that none of our industrial societies have yet fully mastered.

Two problems are involved:

1. The enlisting of industrial leaders with organizational experience for higher federal offices; in the United States the position of the Secretary of the Armed Forces, the greatest organizational job, has been entrusted for many years to investment bankers or industrialists.

2. Something the French have so adroitly called *pantouflage*, the movement of higher civil servants into positions in private industry. The osmosis between private and government employment is in harmony with the nature of an era in which private and public organiza-

tions are often hopelessly intertwined and in which maximal success can often result only from their coordination. Nevertheless, as far as personnel matters are concerned, such a situation often provokes ill feelings. The public interest can be greatly injured when it is consciously or unconsciously pushed aside where interests collide. This creates additional competitional distortions even in a private economy which is largely monopolistic or oligopolistic.

Above all, and far beyond the intrinsic disadvantages of such practices, public morale is damaged. The little man develops a feeling of helplessness. Rightly or wrongly he considers himself stupid and abused, a feeling which can be dampened by higher wages but which can hardly ever be eliminated.

Is there anything that can be done? As experience has shown, conflict-of-interest laws are of little help, indeed probably do more harm than good by making unnecessarily difficult, through special stipulations which can always be evaded, the traffic between talents in various fields of endeavor. Salvation does not lie in the usual "stop the thief" kind of policy of penalizing interests. Such a policy is hopeless if only because we are all somehow accomplices in a primary kind of theft in so far as we equate our private interests with the public welfare.

At this point the expertise of the leading group of politicians should be put to work. This group has become more rather than less important since parliament has ceased to be an opponent of equal rank and since it is nominated by the parties and legitimized by the people at regular intervals. By virtue of his expertise the politician is able fully to assess the strength of the conflicting interests and to act upon his preferences correspondingly, and this in cases of conflict which the normal cycle of competition and compromise between departments and interest groups could not resolve. It is this political expertise which in the final analysis holds the key to the lasting success of a democracy.

PART THREE

MAN, VICTIM AND MAKER

OF SOCIETY

CONFINING CONDITIONS AND

REVOLUTIONARY BREAKTHROUGHS

I WANT TO TRY to connect the course of several regimes with what, for want of a better name, I shall call "confining conditions"—the particular social and intellectual conditions present at the births of these regimes. Do I prejudice the case by calling the sum total of the prerevolutionary situation confining conditions rather than calling them more neutrally, as Val Lorwin suggested to me, simply antecedent conditions? Yet every situation which a new regime finds at its inception is an antecedent one. I am concerned specifically—and only—with the conditions that have to be overcome if the new regime is to continue. How the new regime may accomplish this, or may fail to, is the subject of this paper. Therefore I consider the nature of the confining conditions, chiefly those of social structure; the nature of the new regime; and the nature of the methods available to it, as well as those it adopts to overcome the confining conditions.

In discussing political action, we often ask the question: did the man or the group have to act the way he, or they, did? What other options were open, e.g., to Stalin in the late 1920s? Not being satisfied with the answer that, given the character of Stalin, the eventual course of action was really to be expected all along, we might profitably shift the question to a different level. To what extent do the circumstances attendant upon the rise of a new regime determine its subsequent

Reprinted, by permission, from *American Political Science Review*, LIX (1965), 964–74.

actions? The late Franz Neumann raised such questions in regard to the course of the National Socialist regime. His *Behemoth* was an impressive attempt to show how the confining conditions under which the regime worked—especially the fact that it came to power with the help of leaders of German heavy industry—not only switched the track for the National Socialists, but explained many of their patterns of actions long after their regime was firmly established.

Yet Neumann's account of the German state organization and its supersession by the movement-type party already foreshadows the problems which increasingly preoccupied his thoughts (although only in fragmentary publications) in his later years. To what extent can a revolutionary power structure move away from the specific constellation of forces which presided over its origin, and move off in a different direction of its own?

I

Neumann had little difficulty with the negative test. Whoever fails to put his hands on the switch—either because of a lack of the social prerequisites (France in 1848) or because of a lack of will power (Germany in 1918)—cannot deflect the current into new circuits. Neither the leaders of the incipient French labor and socialist movement of 1848, nor the leaders of the numerically strong but unimaginative organizations of the German Socialists in 1918, ever tried to put their hands on the switches. Crowded from the center of power, they soon could not even hold to the position of initiating incremental changes. Even the modest role of setting into motion long-range changes, with all due anticipatory consideration of other powerholders' reactions, escapes the group which fails to make a political breakthrough. Such a group becomes an object, rather than a subject, of the political process.

The capacity to compress thoroughgoing or revolutionary change—as distinct from incremental change—into a minimum of time, according to the new powerholders' own timetable, is the test of revolutionary victory. What are the possible dimensions, and what are the limits of such capacity for change? In his later publications, and on the basis of Soviet experience, Neumann held that political power could make itself supreme and thereby make itself the font of economic power.[1]

II

But what does this supremacy amount to? Let us first look at Hitler's Germany and Stalin's Russia. By the 1930s Germany had become a highly industrialized country. Yet its style of intergroup relations, in spite of formal constitutional change, still reflected the mood and conditions of a bygone era. Perhaps scaling down the politically and economically expensive position of Eastern agrarian elements might have eliminated enough of the anachronism to allow the restructuring of class relations on a more modern, cooperative basis.

Instead of opting for that sort of program, Germany started a course of imperialist conquests in the heart of Europe, with the new political elite lording it over both the domestic scene and the subject countries. This course entailed extraordinary risks, which only a revolutionary group, able to ride roughshod over all opposition, would take.

To put it another way, the industrialists were a specialized functional elite falling in with the deliberate option of a revolutionary political group. Whatever the apparent short-term risks and the factors of long-range instability in this choice, the conquest of Europe, Western and Eastern, represented one way of producing an entirely new realignment of internal forces, superseding the need to rearrange internal group relations in a manner more common in Western Europe.

Intergroup relations had changed as a consequence of the economic crisis and were certainly overripe for restructuring. The degree of their restructuring was an open question, but not its direction. That restructuring had to take into account the loss of power suffered by the labor groups as a consequence of the economic crisis and of their own continuing fratricidal cleavages.

The brutal imperialism on a neo-populist basis, with its efficient mixture of revolutionary political organization and industrial-society ele-

---

[1] See esp. ch. 1, "Approaches to the Study of Political Power," and ch. 10, "Economics and Politics in the 20th Century," in Franz Neumann, *The Democratic and the Authoritarian State* (Glencoe, 1957).

ments, had its roots in the ideological and material conditions of German society. But this imperialism was at most the contingent, not the necessary, outcome. Within the context of an advanced industrial society, an authoritarian-bureaucratic regime that might have tried to overcome the political disequilibrium with the support or incorporation of some sections of a crisis-inflated mass movement was as much a possibility as the total seizure of power by a revolutionary mass movement itself. In fact, when the Nazis took over power, they operated for some months in a manner intended to leave the population in the dark as to whether their practices would correspond to or amalgamate with the bureaucratic-authoritarian solution. This tactic facilitated the undisturbed take-over of power by the mass movement.[2] Between the conditioning factors of its inception and the reality of the Third Reich were the intervening visions, the organizing genius, and the perseverance of the revolutionary political group.

Let us turn to the case of the Soviet Union. In order to obtain a measure of initial acceptance, the leaders of the Petrograd Revolution had to put their stamp of approval on the seizure of the gentry's land by the peasantry. However, this policy aggravated the age-old difficulties which had beset the Russian polity and which Stolypin's dissolution of the *Obshina* had only started to tackle: the need of accelerating transformation to an industrial society by simultaneously shifting population to the cities and modernizing agricultural methods. Stalin's forced collectivization was an answer to the difficulties caused by the lower rate of industrial growth and reagrarianization of the country in the 1920s, which coincided with the considerable rural exodus to the cities.[3] Having at his disposal a strong enough administrative apparatus to reverse the process of Kulakization under the NEP and to collectivize agriculture, Stalin had a range of choices in regard to the methods of collectivization. If he wanted to industrialize rapidly, however, he probably had little choice about the principle of collectivization. Left alone, the peasants would have dictated both the

---

[2] The various expectations during the transition period in 1933 can now be followed in Bracher-Sauer-Schulz, *Die Nationalsozialistische Machtergreifung* (Cologne-Opladen, 1960).

[3] Alexander Gerschenkron, *Economic Backwardness in Historical Perspective* (Cambridge, Mass., 1962), pp. 119–51.

pace and the direction of industrialization by consuming more and delivering less food to the rest of the country.

What matters in this context is the interrelation between socioeconomic conditioning and the discretionary element left to the decision of the regime. The setting up of larger agricultural units and the shifting of agricultural surplus population to industrial life were bound to take place under almost any regime. The revolutionary approval of land seizure by the peasantry, plus the conditions of the NEP period, had aggravated the regime's difficulties by creating an important new proprietary interest at a time when the regime was unable to offer enough industrial goods to entice the peasants to part voluntarily with their produce. Yet, at the same time, a coercive apparatus was at hand to collectivize the land and collect food surpluses. The general problem of the relations between the agricultural sector and the industrial sectors of a modernizing society was given, irrespective of whether the country was to be governed by an autocracy, a bourgeois democracy, or the Communist party. What the supremacy of a revolutionary group entailed was a much wider choice of means and strategies to carry out the transformation. The "whole-hog Stalin" [4] was not necessary, and Stalin's methods were counterproductive, if measured by the yardstick of what more gradual, part-cooperative collectivization could have obtained in both good will and direct production results. Yet given the need for accelerating the transformation as a condition for survival of

[4] Alec Nove, *Economic Rationality in Soviet Politics* (New York, 1964), p. 32. Cf. A. Erlich, *The Soviet Industrialization Debate, 1924–1928* (Cambridge, Mass., 1960): "A policy of moderate tempos would strengthen the position of the upper strata of the villages and would make the adroit balancing between them and the unruly radicals of the cities a necessity which could be adopted only as a temporary expedient. Had such a course been pursued over a long period of time the regime would have stood to lose not only from its possible failures but also from its successes. The alternative to such retreats and maneuvers leading to the gradual erosion of the dictatorial system was clearly a massive counterattack which would have broken once and for all the peasants' power over the basic decisions of economic policy. A high speed industrialisation with a strong emphasis on the capital goods sector which Stalin now favored provided the logical line for such a counterattack" (p. 174).

"The overhang of agricultural excess population permitted the manning of equipment which was physically usable with the surplus peasants of yesterday, which could be removed from the countryside without a notable detriment to agricultural output and be employed at a real wage barely exceeding their wretchedly lower consumption levels of the earlier status" (p. 184).

the revolutionary group, the internal leadership struggle resulted in the decision that the gain in time would out-weigh the costs of forced collectivization. Zigzagging in the course of the great industrialization debate, Stalin used changes in his own position to eliminate actual and potential rivals, and then used his ensuing supremacy over the dominant political group to enforce the most ruthless of the available options. But the need for industrialization created fundamental claims on the regime, as it had even on the Czarist regime.

The social and economic frame of the particular society, then, lays down a conditioning perimeter within which the original choice has to be made and solutions have to be sought. Hitler, for example, could not—as some of his loyal adherents had dreamt—do for the German retailers and craftsmen what he could afford to do for the German peasant: he could not convert small shops into hereditary entailed estates, protected against hopeless competitive odds.[5] The very progress of accelerated rearmament and the preparations for foreign conquest necessitated the most efficient industrial production units, leaving the small independent with the option of becoming a dependent factory hand. In realigning his norms and expectations with those of the new powerholders, the doomed independent could at least adopt as his own the choice of the regime, perilous and adventurous though it might be. In this way the very exercise of the regime's option might change the social preconditions of his existence, releasing new psychic energies before the regime's long-term options bore visible results. Thus the socioeconomic perimeter itself might seem expandable. Was it?

What we might call "expansion of the perimeter" is the alteration of the social structure or economic basis of society or—more slowly, but still visibly, by the processes of modern communications and education—the alteration of intellectual habits by the new masters of the polity. For the new rulers by then have arrived at a stage, which may come very quickly after a revolution, when they are working out the details of their options. They have arrested the acceleration of chaos,

<hr />

[5] Gurland, Kirchheimer, Neumann, *The Fate of Small Business in Nazi Germany*, 78th Cong., 1st Sess., Hearings, Sen. Special Committee to Study Problems of American Small Business, Comm. Print No. 14 (1943), p. 152.

The story and some figures can be found in Arthur Schweitzer, *Big Business in the Third Reich* (Bloomington, Ind., 1964), chs. 4 and 5.

as in Soviet Russia, or mastered their new tasks of propaganda and control, as in Nazi Germany. In these cases the rulers were not crushed by what might be called "societal due dates."

Among these societal "due dates," one repeats itself so often as to become a major confining condition: foreign intervention in national revolutions. Usually we would think of confining conditions as factors embedded in the social structure out of which revolutions originate. But the shrinking of the world, both physically and intellectually, the attendant and anticipated impact of revolutionary upheaval on other countries, and the power increments expected from successful intervention, or the power losses feared from the emergence of a new recruit to revolutionary causes—all these have caused a succession of foreign interventions.

Even with the present-day technique of fighting or forestalling revolution by stage-managing counterinsurgency, foreign intervention often carries its own antidote. It encourages the revolutionary forces to telescope changes into shorter periods and facilitates proper acceptance of those changes; it makes for a degree of unification and acceptance of a new national symbolism otherwise hard to obtain. But the possibility of overcoming this confining condition is aleatory; success or failure may depend on policy shifts in the intervening country, over which the influence of the revolutionary elite is far more limited than it is on domestic conditions.

In the face of all these difficulties, the political group may lose its momentum, return to the incremental pattern, or even cave in completely. Too many checks may have been drawn at the same time against the new regime's limited bank account, and the regime's very weakness may have accelerated the simultaneous presentation of demands. Yet, on the other hand, its interdependent supply of physical force and capital of community confidence may just allow it to scrape through, keeping some commanding positions fairly intact. In this latter case, we want to analyze what happens to the initial conditioning perimeter: have the original confining conditions been changed by a decisive breakthrough? Has the new political system really become supreme and able to develop systematic patterns of its own? If so, we then measure revolutionary change by the new system's ability to extricate itself from the confining conditions of the previous period.

The old data may still be present, though absorbed in a new context and thereby deprived of their confining nature.

The leaders of the USSR have achieved such a breakthrough, transforming Russia into a major industrial system. While they still experience difficulties with agrarian organization, and these in turn delay the fulfillment of urgent consumer expectations, such problems can scarcely endanger the subsistence level. Most of the confining conditions have been removed, at whatever cost to those who lived through —or died during—the long decades it took to accomplish that feat.

The German National Socialist experience remained abortive, but no conclusions as to the impossibility of overcoming the initial confining conditions can be drawn from the collapse due to external defeat in a two-front war. Certainly the wholesale program of conquest of Eastern Europe would have allowed a more drastic restructuring of internal group relations in Germany than would a more limited program of hegemony over Western Europe. The existence of a large industrial working class with a tradition of self-organization (even if momentarily without any organization), and of a bureaucratic and officer group only superficially and conditionally loyal to the regime, made the program of maximal conquest of Eastern Europe more attractive to the new rulers than the more restricted take-over of Western Europe. For such a conquest might have led to the pulverizing of existing German social relations for the benefit of the Nazi rulers. A vast imperial apparatus with Germans from all walks of life lording it over the indigenous Eastern Europeans, while German industry expanded into vast new territories, might have accomplished an efficient restructuring of German society. Such an apparatus would have constituted a major guarantee against renewed efforts of surviving splinters of former social and political elites to make comeback attempts— which actually were made at every new turn in the fortunes of the regime as long as its conquests were not consolidated.

In both the Russian case and the German case, the experiment was part of a unique conjunction of circumstances: the disorganization and breakdown of an economic and political system in Russia, and the incapacity and disorganization, although not quite the breakdown, in Germany, and the simultaneous activity and availability for power of a revolutionary group. In Germany the revolutionary group actively promoted the breakdown; in Russia it exploited a preexistent one. The breakdown thus had the effect of releasing revolutionary energies; it was in a certain sense a counterconfiguration of the confining conditions, and made action possible toward overcoming them. In the one case the group was more opportunistic; in the other more doctrinaire; but, at any rate, both were acting outside the frame of the traditional conceptual apparatus of politicians. They made only short-range compromises, which they revoked as soon as the slightest margin of safety allowed them to do so. In both cases we might ask how the action of the revolutionary group related to the sum-total of confining conditions.

Owing to the intervening external conditions, the German case does not carry much probative value either way. As to the USSR, the argument that the major outcome—conversion into an industrial society—would have taken place in any event does not upset our conclusion. The fact is that a "premature" industrial revolution, compressing various stages of social development into an extremely limited time span determined by its political elite—moreover, with primitive accumulation by the state and not private owners, and with national sovereignty exalted in the process—did take place. This is highly relevant to our original question: here a revolutionary regime did move beyond the confining conditions under which it arose.

III

To illuminate another facet of the problem, I want to discuss the conditions of collaboration of various political forces under a revolutionary regime. Where lies the wellspring of common action? To what extent does the variation in composition and orientation of such forces determine the confines of their actions from the very outset?

I have in mind here the well-known episode of the relations between Robespierre and the Committee of Public Safety toward the Paris *sans-culottes* from autumn 1793 to early summer 1794. One might describe the situation after the autumn days of 1793 as an uneasy coalition between the Committee and the Paris *sans-culottes*, ideologically represented and sometimes led by Hébert and Chaumette.[6] Neither group could have acted effectively without the other. Their presence served as a means for Robespierre to keep his hold over the Convention, as much as the Committee served as a means for the *sans-culottes* to push their political and economic demands. The common ground which provided both their dynamics and their larger justification was the unconditional pursuit of the revolutionary war. There was at best a partial meeting of minds and never a complete convergence on social and economic goals. In order to carry on the war and to avoid spiraling inflation, price and wage controls were indicated. Yet—apart from military procurement—farmers and merchants were frequently able to circumvent price controls. The Paris city administration, on the other hand, was lukewarm in enforcing wage controls. Such contradictions were partly solved by the trial and guillotining of Hébert and Chaumette. Although their execution was followed in *jeu de bascule* fashion within two weeks by the execution of Danton and Desmoulins, the victory of Fleurus in June, 1794, lifted, to some extent, the radical mortgage on Robespierre and allowed the dismantling of price controls. The result was to do away with the often uncontrollable district clubs, and to restrict the more egalitarian policies, in an attempt at securing a steady flow of bread at the official price to the urban population. The pay-off came on the 9th of Thermidor when the National Guard did not come out for Robespierre, but went home; and when the district assemblies meeting that evening were split wide open between loyalty to the Convention or to the more radical politics of the *sans-culottes*.

[6] For literature on the episode see the general discussion in Georges Lefebvre, *La Révolution française*, 3d ed. (Paris, 1963), pp. 354–430, and most interesting in this context his remarks on pp. 407–9; two more specialized works by Daniel Guérin, *La Lutte de Classes sous la Première République, Bourgeois et "bras nus"* (*1793–1797*), 2 vols. (Paris, 1946), and Albert Soboul, *Les Sans-culottes Parisiens en l'an II, Mouvement Populaire et Gouvernement Révolutionnaire, 2 Juin, 1793–9 Thermidor an II* (Paris, 1958), esp. pp. 427–33, 503–4, 1025–35. Guérin draws explicit conclusions as to the class content of the struggle between Robespierre and the *sans-culottes*. Soboul analyzes a wealth of hitherto unknown documents, among them papers of district assemblies and district clubs. His conclusions from the assembled material, though more shaded, are in line with those of Guérin as to the *sans-culottes*–Revolutionary Government relation. For the social composition of the *sans-culottes* see also G. Rudé, *The Crowd in the French Revolution* (London, 1959), pp. 178–84.

But is this the only, or a sufficient, reason for the turn of events? First, a seemingly more accidental fact: on the decisive afternoon, when the National Guard was assembled on the Place de Grève with all its equipment, there was no leader resolute enough to make them march against the Convention. What about the less obvious links in the chain of causation? There was the matter of sheer physical fatigue of the Paris *militants*, who had been in the thick of the political struggle for the previous five years; and the fact that many of the younger ones had departed for the war fronts. There was the phenomenon which we now call the circulation of elites: the most vigorous and the most intelligent of them had meanwhile taken government jobs in the central administration and war machine, and had formed new and different bonds of allegiance. This brings us nearer to another, more Protean constellation: *sans-culottes* are a political, not a social, category. Their major ties were common political sympathies: hatred of the aristocracy and support of the new regime and the military program. This motley crew of unemployed, journeymen, artisans, shopkeepers, lawyers, teachers, government employees, and even a sprinkling of merchants, could scarcely have a unified *social* outlook. Some of them being independent producers and middlemen, and others being wage earners, they would scarcely see eye-to-eye on economic issues. They remained parcels of various occupational groups. They could join the revolutionary battle all the more easily because their social and occupational distinctions had not always jelled into class consciousness. They remained accessible to a variety of sometimes contradictory appeals, guiding their behavior in speech and action.

Suppose that Robespierre had saved his neck on the 9th of Thermidor owing to a fresh intervention of the National Guard. Could this coalition of the national revolutionary government and its advanced urban clientele have lasted? While trying to find its way through a bedlam of conflicting interests, the Committee of Public Safety was ideologically committed to uphold the sanctity of private property—with exceptions necessitated by the conduct of the war. Moreover, its policy toward the disposal of the agricultural properties of the *émigré* nobles and the church bears little evidence of a sustained interest in the cause of the small peasant and the landless farmhand. How would it have related itself in the long run to the interests not only of the merchants but of the upper echelons of the peasants? Even if we disregard the discordant interests among the *sans-culottes*—bound to come out more sharply after the most urgent war pressures had receded—could the Robespierre—*sans-culotte* combination have long outlasted the immediate danger period of the war?

Seventeen hundred ninety-three marks the definitive entry of the urban masses upon the French political scene. But, given the forces present at that particular historical juncture, the 1793–94 episode is a great precursor of problems yet to come. Whenever they were in a position to make their own political contribution in the decades ahead, the peasants would make short shrift of "prematurely" radical political ideas.

If we except exceedingly short periods in 1848 and 1871, and abortive movements remaining below the most provisional governmental level, the people at large did not move into the center of political decision. It is for this reason that the coalition of the Committee of Public Safety and the *sans-culottes* of 1793–94 still retains such a paradigmatic interest. For here we must raise the question to what extent the possibility existed—which became so important in the Chinese and Russian revolutions of the twentieth century—of jumping stages of societal development and compressing two revolutions into one. To what extent could the 1793–94 combination have possessed the organizational cohesion, the unity of purpose, and the technical means to overcome its confining conditions—i.e., its being surrounded by a sea of peasantry and torn by the discordances between two constituent elements, the bourgeois-governmental wing and the popular Paris-street wing? The attitude of the governmental wing toward economic and social policy issues shows how alien the conscious reshaping of society by governmental fiat remained to them. They tried to keep the backdoor through which such measures entered—wartime necessity and the pressure of their Paris allies—as well guarded as they could under the circumstances of the day. The breakup of the combination and Robespierre's subsequent defeat without serious intervention by his erstwhile radical associates highlight the lack of cohesive social consciousness needed to take the revolution beyond its pristine bourgeois phase.

The heterogeneous nature of the short-lived coalition of the 1793–94 period of the Revolution was in itself the chief confining condition of that Revolution. The Paris *avant-garde*, with all its revolutionary fervor, was anything but unified and anything but uniformly proletarian (however we define "proletarian" in pre-industrial Paris). The National government, temporary coalition partner of the revolutionary Paris Commune, was riven by personal quarrels and conflicts among the various organs of government. Beyond that, and even more fundamental, the revolutionary government was unwilling to injure the interests of merchants and agricultural property owners beyond what the conduct of the war in its most desperate phase seemed to make necessary. Organizational centralization, the "maximum" for food prices, and the unfulfilled promise of the famous "Ventôse decrees": these were adopted to win the war, not to establish a social millennium or create the cadres to maintain the revolutionary regime.

IV

So far my attention has been directed toward the capacity of revolutionary groups to transcend the confining conditions which surrounded their coming to power. I now want to move on to a discussion of some facets of what Charles Beard called the "Second American Revolution," the Civil War. Must I first justify inclusion of the Civil War in this survey of relations of revolutionary outcomes to preexistent social structures? The Civil War, one might assert, was not started by a revolutionary group intent on changing the social structure of society; it only settled a limited argument over permissible forms of national property relations. And yet, the way the conflict was settled indicates an obvious connection between the structure of southern ante-bellum society and the final outcome of the conflict. Should we say that the solution—which gave the Negro only the outward trappings of freedom—indicated the absence of such a revolutionary group, and let it go at that? The case is not improved if we amend this statement to read that no revolutionary group was in undisputed control of the state machinery, not even during the reconstruction period. For saying this much is enough to make us realize that, even in the nineteenth century, revolution and civil war, if not cohabiting in permanent fashion as they do in the twentieth, kept close enough quarters to justify simultaneous discussion. What I am looking for here is a key to the peculiar mixture between recessive elements—the reprise of parcels of the ante-bellum structure—and supervening changes in southern society which marked the history of the conflict, of reunion and reaction.

Let me at the outset lay down some theses, mostly borrowed—with his kind permission—from an as-yet-unpublished manuscript of Barrington Moore concerning those features of the original conflict which might have had some bearing on the post-bellum development.[7]

1. The two distinct forms of social organization—emergent eastern business society and southern slaveholding agrarian society—contained certain, elements favoring coexistence.

2. The political marriage of convenience between eastern iron and western grain, between higher tariffs and more land for the present and future farmers of the West, spared the eastern industrialists the need to search for accommodation with the southern planters.

3. The outbreak of the war was facilitated by the absence of strong ties between the two sections, East and South, rather than by a head-on collision on economic issues.

4. The weakness of the federal enforcement apparatus, tied to the uncertainty of the eventual orientation of the territories, loomed large in the causal chain leading to the war.

By the 1850s, the East had become a manufacturing center, with both East and West becoming less dependent on the South and more complementary to each other. All the same, until the 1860s cotton had remained second in eastern manufacturing and the East continued to provide financial, transportation, and marketing services for the South. Eastern business and western farmers showed little animosity toward the "peculiar institution" of their southern trading partners. Eastern factory hands, fearing the competition of freed slaves, were lukewarm on the slave issue. While the South experienced some shortage in available new slave labor, its production system had not become unworkable from the viewpoint of either discipline or profit.[8] Points of con-

---

[7] It goes without saying that the conclusions I draw from Moore's analysis are entirely my own. [This work has since been published as *Social Origins of Dictatorship and Democracy: Lord and Peasant in the Making of the Modern World* (Boston, 1966). See esp. Ch. III, pp. 111–49. Ed. note.]

[8] Conrad and Meyer, "The Economics of Slavery in the Ante Bellum South," in *The Economics of Slavery and Other Econometric Studies* (Chicago, 1964). What is argued in such accounts is the question of profitability of slavery then

flict between the South and East seemed negotiable, with eastern tariff demands possibly to be compromised against southern wishes for consideration in the settlement of virgin western lands. Such considerations, however, have to be seen against some barriers hard to overcome. In the days before the gigantic public expenditures possible under endlessly expandable defense labels, the East could do little for the South except to buy its cotton, and such trade could not be expanded at will. The resumption of the slave trade remained a nonnegotiable proposition; to that extent a moral issue was of direct political importance. England remained the most important customer of the South, a fact which nourished the expectation of a viable independent South. In the East, labor trouble which would make the industrial community run for aid to the southern planter was not yet on the horizon, leaving the moderates only narrow scope in their search for viable compromises.

In the presence of such weak links between the regions, strictly political factors, the impact of the battle over enforcement procedures for legislative compromises, loomed large. In a society with a simple authority structure, official powers rest largely on the willingness of the respective political clienteles to abide by the terms of the agreements their political representatives reached. The clienteles' unwillingness to do so, coupled with great weakness and irresoluteness of the central authority, spelt uncertainty of expectations and diminished the individual's reliance on official procedures to a vanishing point. In such a situation, legislative compromises predicated on semi-automatic enforceability—the Fugitive Slave Act—or, like the Kansas-Nebraska Act, needing the services of an impartial state power able and willing to see things through, must falter in implementation. But somehow the notion of the state power ordering the relations of its citizens by active intervention was something rather alien to the thinking of the West in the nineteenth century. (We shall come back to this point a little later.) It certainly found little room in the minds of the pre-Civil War generation looking on the respective presidents, judges, and governors with their marshals and troops either as useful auxiliaries or as foes.[9]

---

and there, rather than long-term development prospects, which form the basis of Eugene D. Genovese's *The Political Economy of Slavery* (New York, 1965). See esp. p. 204.

[9] Allan Nevins, *Ordeal of the Nation*, Vol. II (New York, 1941), ch. 2.

The war thus appears as the product of uncertainty as to how to delineate authoritatively the various claims—especially over the status of slavery in the territories—of two societies resting on different social orders: an emergent democratic business society and an agricultural economy grounded on slave labor. The postwar peace could have had one of two meanings: it could have meant a change in the sum total of southern property relations, destroying the planter aristocracy by the use of northern military power and handing over agricultural property titles to the former slaves. Yet, "Lincoln's war" had not been conducted for that purpose.[10] Nor did eastern business society, balanced on the one hand by labor's capacity to move West and on the other by the inexhaustible replenishment of its labor force from Europe, have such wide-ranging intentions, which would have endangered the basis of all private property relations. Consequently, after the 1866–68 intermezzo, orchestrated by the radical congressional reconstructionists, the narrower peace goals gained ascendancy: only the property titles in slaves and in southern war bonds remained cancelled. The "Thermidor" of 1877 was the inevitable conclusion from the carpetbaggers' and the Negroes' inability to keep themselves going without the aid of the federal government, and from that government's unwillingness to go on supporting them. But it brought out in full all those recessive traits which had their origin in the ante-bellum southern society. It transformed the southern Negro from a sheltered slave into a formally free but unprotected sharecropper. In the same breath it deprived him of the possibility of exercising his political rights as an entrance wedge for full participation in the American society. "Henceforth," as Vann Woodward says, "the nation as a nation will have nothing to do with him." [11]

If the Negro's transfer from his slave to his sharecropper status—including his right to exchange his existence as a southern bondsman for that of an eastern or western unskilled factory hand or a migratory

[10] J. G. Randall and D. Donald, *The Civil War and Reconstruction*, 2d ed. (Boston, 1961), ch. 22. Kenneth M. Stampp, *The Era of Reconstruction* (New York, 1965), p. 44: "Indeed it may be said that if it was Lincoln's destiny to go down in history as the Great Emancipator, rarely has a man embraced his destiny with greater reluctance than he."

[11] C. Vann Woodward, *Reunion and Reaction*, 2d ed. (New York, Anchor, 1956), p. 232.

worker—had been the only difference in the social structure as a consequence of the war, we might well conclude that in this particular instance the recessive traits, mirroring the conditioning perimeter, the existence of a slaveholding aristocracy, did indeed prevail. But this is only part of the story.

The fact is that the second American Revolution did take place, and many of its effects did penetrate into the South. To what extent the second revolution as a whole was causally linked to the Civil War, to what extent the war even accelerated the progress of industrial society, is problematic; [12] assertions of causal relation have a *post-hoc-ergo-propter-hoc* sound. And the system of enlarged corporate property protection, which came into constitutional interpretation by courtesy of the Fourteenth Amendment, would no doubt have found its way into court practice by some other route. The same may be true of the southern impact on congressional voting patterns, which would probably have established themselves anyhow whenever sufficiently important interests needed an alliance with the South. But the opening up of the South to the influx of eastern industry, accompanied as it was by an enlargement and shift of the social basis of the predominant group through the impoverishment of the planters and the rise of a mercantile southern middle class, is a feature directly resulting from the outcome of the Civil War. Opening the South bridged the separation between the two formerly distinct types of society and so worked toward establishing in the South a modified subtype of American business society. In this subtype, narrowed down since the Civil War to a limited district with no chance of enlargement, the Negro remains a disadvantaged subspecies of the least fortunate segment of the population.

The American case is most intriguing because here we have the juxtaposition of recessive conditions going back to the ante-bellum social structure and the general pattern of change taking place within American society in the second half of the nineteenth century. While the victory of the business society was a universal phenomenon, its particular democratic garb found an inhospitable territory in the South. Surviving in the transfigured form necessitated by the advance

[12] Thomas C. Cochran, "Did the Civil War Retard Industrialization?" in *The Inner Revolution* (Harper Torchbooks, 1964), pp. 39–54.

402   MAN, VICTIM AND MAKER OF SOCIETY

of the business society, the confining conditions, from which the war had arisen, left their imprint on southern society. The writ of the federal government and, much more firmly, the writ of business society ran across the whole country. But in the South, these writs were always modified by the survivals of the old caste structure; the political form of southern society remained ambiguously predemocratic.

V

What separates the "Second Revolution" of mid-nineteenth century America from the pronouncedly political revolutions of the twentieth century is the subsidiary part that state power played in the transformation of nineteenth century society. In this respect there is a certain concordance between theory and practice. Nineteenth-century ideologists did not think of state power as something to be mobilized at will for the purpose of changing societal relations. Whatever the differences among Hegel's disciples, to this extent his panlogistic state concept had been drastically revised. His conservative disciple, Lorenz von Stein, built his doctrine on the juxtaposition of state and society. The fight for liberty and equality and the determination of the individual's position were to take place within society, with the state coming in only as a regulatory afterthought.[13] Stein's state amounted to a mixture of the *Rechtsstaat* principle—in itself a guarantee of regularity of proceedings rather than of active intervention—and his dreams of a social monarchy which would both assure the integrity of society and even out the inequalities emerging from society's struggle.[14]

Marx was more interested in discovering the laws governing the development of society. The reciprocal relations between state and society, which had fascinated his contemporary Stein, had few mysteries for him. He had little doubt about the place of law, state, and intellectual structures and assigned them their roots firmly in the material conditions of society. Interference with the modalities of the social process was rather in the nature of becoming conscious of its inexo-

[13] Lorenz von Stein, *Geschichte der Socialen Bewegung in Frankreich von 1789 bis auf unsere Tage,* Vol. I, *Der Begriff der Gesellschaft,* ed. Dr. Gottfried Salomon (Munich, 1921).
[14] Lorenz von Stein, *Verwaltungslehre,* 2d ed. (1869), I, 82 *et seq.*

rable course, at best with a proletarian advance guard as a midwife, but at any rate with no need for an independent directing force.

Against the background of his French experience, Tocqueville took to analyzing the partly chaotic, partly creative political scene of the United States in the early 1830s. Could the political authorities attempt to direct the societal process—that is to say, would individuals acting singly or jointly accept such decisions? He left little doubt that, given the state of mind of the American community, the banding together of freely acting individuals for self-appointed tasks—whatever the degree of administrative efficiency of such a procedure—was the only politically feasible way to make meaningful decisions.[15]

The acceptance of a number of amendments, civil rights, and enforcement statutes was one of the ways to mark the official victory of the Civil War. But once the battle over enactment was won the documents turned into a series of political propositions; they had to be absorbed and in this process were modified and even turned around by the various authoritative interpreters active in the constitutional system. Nineteenth-century America felt no need for a central organ in charge of transforming a battlefield victory into a system of political legitimacy of universal validity.

VI

Let us now look at the much more traditional Western and Central European society of the mid-nineteenth century, the era of the Chartists and the repeal of the Corn Laws, Prussian pseudo-constitutionalism, and the administrative system of Napoleon III. With all due consideration for differences in upbringing and societal outlook of their respective political elites—including for the European a somewhat greater distance between governing classes and the business community—the European ways of approaching political problems remained as circumscribed as those of their American counterparts. English conservatives might have a somewhat greater sense of urgency about what might be done for the submerged classes than their liberal brethren; the latter might be more confident in their ability to uphold what we

---

[15] De la Démocratie en Amérique, 14th ed. (Paris, 1864), I, 149.

now call civil liberties in the face of threatening lower-class agitation. Bismarck could make a show of demonstrating how a polity might be run, even if the bourgeoisie refrained from giving it budgetary support. But his was a conservative machine running it, scarcely given to innovation beyond the field of military techniques and bounties for promising businessmen. The differences appear to us today as nuances rather than qualitative distinctions. Neither was bent on pushing sudden social or political change, or remodeling the minds of men and the institutions of the country. Even the men of the Paris Commune, the most radical of the century's children ever to have acceded to government office, made few and cautious moves in the field of social policy.

The problem of diverse expectations based on the operation of free societal forces and the limited trust in the workings of the state machinery brings us nearer an explanation of why the Second American Revolution was accompanied by two seemingly discordant results. This revolution was carried out by independent social components of the polity, supported by, but not dependent on, the political machinery of the day. It succeeded well in transforming most of America; yet it allowed the political transformation of the South via the emancipation of the Negro to fizzle out for nearly a century. It is one thing to watch the destruction of property titles as an inevitable consequence of defeat in a rebellion. It is something entirely different to destroy them as part of a concerted plan to reorganize society by state fiat. Such a measure, though proposed, went beyond the horizon of the radical political leaders who thought in terms of advantageous political combinations rather than consciously engineered social revolutions.[16]

With World War I as a watershed, we are able to see the decisive differences between nineteenth and twentieth century revolutions. Masses had been brought together in the nineteenth century by political organizations on a semipermanent basis; their minds had been exercised by expectations of economic benefit, social innovation, or patriotic or religious exaltation. But only World War I showed how the public authorities, first with the joyous and later on the increasingly reluctant cooperation of the population, could mobilize huge masses of

---

[16] Stampp, op. cit., p. 130: "In addition confiscation was an attack on property rights—so much so that it is really more surprising that some of the middle class radicals favored it, than that most did not."

men and technical forces of hitherto unknown destructiveness and link them in huge organizations for official national goals.

While the official apparatus was everywhere quickly dismantled after the war, the experience was not lost on a new crop of political organizers. If such great results could be reached for the traditional goal of acting on the power structure of other societies, why not use similar methods on the domestic structure? The official state apparatus with its limited vistas, its simultaneous mixture of tradition-bound procedure and immersion in the particular interests of one group or another, with its hesitant and uneasy role of arbitration, was neither intellectually nor technically equipped for such a task. It is the merger of political movement and official state organization, the simultaneous unfolding of the mechanisms of change and the purveying of new loyalties, which mark the differences between the revolutionary dynamics of the twentieth and the largely uncontrolled social and economic revolution of the nineteenth century. The nineteenth-century government concentrated the energies of its much more slender and haphazard apparatus on emergency periods.

The revolution of the twentieth century obliterates the distinction between emergency and normalcy. Movement plus state can organize the masses because: (a) the technical and intellectual equipment is now at hand to direct them toward major societal programs rather than simply liberating their energies from the bonds of tradition; (b) they have the means at hand to control people's livelihood by means of job assignments and graduated rewards unavailable under the largely agricultural and artisanal structure of the 1790s and still unavailable to the small enterprise and commission-merchant-type economy of the 1850s and 1860s; (c) they have fallen heir to endlessly and technically refined propaganda devices substituting for the uncertain leader-mass relations of the previous periods; and (d) they faced state organizations shaken up by war dislocation and economic crisis. Under these conditions Soviet Russia could carry through simultaneously the job of an economic and a political, a bourgeois and a post-bourgeois revolution in spite of the exceedingly narrow basis of its political elite. On the other hand, the premature revolutionary combination of 1793–94 not only dissolved quickly but left its most advanced sector, the *sans-culottes*, with only the melancholy choice between desperate rioting—

Germinal 1795—or falling back into a preorganized stage of utter helplessness and agony.

Do I suggest that confining conditions had their place only in nineteenth century society, where people looked for autonomous development tendencies in society and when the state was restricted to merely secondary functions? Does that mean that the political and technical innovations of the twentieth century have created a capacity for unlimited political change?

The antithesis between state and society is itself not as meaningful as it appeared to theorists of the nineteenth century.[17] If we substitute government for state, as we do as a matter of course in an Anglo-American climate, we perceive that we are looking into the same mirror, only from different angles. The technical equipment at the disposal of the present generation introduces social change as a normal expectation with only the composition of the group in charge of the change a matter of controversy. Yet the government's new equipment may only allow it to catch up with the pressing problems raised by the sheer multiplication of numbers. In this context we recall Marx's famous dictum that society does not raise more problems than it can solve at any given moment.

There is also the fact that those who are making major political decisions are not working from a *tabula rasa*, merely projecting the most technically feasible solutions. The starting point for their projections, more likely than not, is their own personal experience in their own society, whether in conformism or revolt. Without pushing confining conditions into the area of psychoanalytical interpretations in vogue a decade ago,[18] let us nevertheless look for a moment at the life experiences of the top leaders of the German National Socialist party, the difficulties these leaders had in finding places in or accommodation with the German society of the 1920s. These difficulties help explain the twofold direction of their thrust. The leaders had to smash the leadership of the preexisting mass organizations to take power. But they also had a deep-seated desire—beyond rational considerations for

---

[17] The dubiousness of the state-society dichotomy is illuminated in Horst Ehmke, " 'Staat' und 'Gesellschaft' als Verfassungstheoretisches Problem," in *Staatsverfassung und Kirchenordnung*, Festgabe für Rudolf Smend (Tübingen, 1962).

[18] Nathan Leites, *A Study of Bolshevism* (Glencoe, 1953).

the safeguarding of their future—to eradicate the very elements of the independent leadership cadres in the upper strata with which they had had to find accommodation during their initial period. These earlier leaders had committed the unforgiveable sin: they had been the ruling elite whilst their successors were still wandering in the dark.

In making this remark, however, do I enlarge the concept of confining conditions much too much? Do I elevate the shadow of the previous regime to the dignity of a confining condition, rather than restricting this concept, as in the case of the USSR, to those specific conditions whose elimination proved to be a *conditio sine qua non* for the survival of the revolutionary regime?

The wall between shadow and substance may, however, be thin, as the German case has amply shown. And shadows become substance when they affect people's minds. Thus shadows also belong to those preexistent, given, and traditional circumstances from which human beings, according to the immortal introductory section of the *18th Brumaire*, produce their own history. In this sense every revolution is both phenomenon and epiphenomenon; it is both concentrated reaction to yesterday's reality and a mere construct to live by until history turns another page and delivers us from the necessity of breathing yesterday's air, that air both fragrant and pestilential.

POLITICS AND JUSTICE

L'équilibre seul anéantit la force. Si on sait par où la société est desé-
quilibrée, il faut faire ce qu'on peut pour ajouter du poids dans le plateau
trop léger. Quoique le poids soit le mal, en le maniant dans cette intention,
peut-être ne se souille-t-on pas. Mais il faut avoir conçu l'équilibre et
être toujours prêt à changer de côté comme la justice "ce fugitive du camp
des vainqueurs."

SIMONE WEIL, La pesanteur et la grâce

POLITICAL JUSTICE is the utilization of judicial proceedings for political
ends. The political end, thus pursued, may be revolutionary or conservative, necessary from the community viewpoint or frivolous. It is
not its legitimacy or illegitimacy with which we deal here, but only
that it is pursued via the judicial process.

I

There is an intrinsic contradiction between the judicial means and the
political goal. Political action is directed toward changing or confirming power relations; the apparatus of justice serves to resolve limited
conflicts between individuals and the community, or between individuals, according to preordained community rules. Whatever attempts
are made at settling power relationships, the very nature of power
defies limitation, calculability, and permanent obedience. Justice, in its
business of individualizing community values, is intended to create and
reenforce an attitude of obedience toward them. These are basic cleavages to be kept in mind.

Reprinted, by permission, from *Social Research*, XXII (1955), 377-98.

To be sure, there are several legitimate links between politics and justice. The first of these lies in the power of the policy-maker to change the established rules of the community, and thus by redefining the nature of substantive law—also to revise the goals of justice. Yet, whether such a change be undertaken via the long and arduous processes of orderly constitutional and legislative change, or pursued via the familiar expedients of emergency legislation operating in constitutional twilight zones, or instituted by outright communist or fascist methods, the objective goals of justice may to some extent be protected by the procedural safeguards. The momentum of a political credo may be half the story of its success; but the opportunity of justice to realize its aims in the face of impetuous demands for change clothed in the forms of law hinges largely on strict observance of the traditional rules of procedure.

A second link between the political authority and the legal apparatus lies in the fact that the judiciary does not initiate its own procedures; they are set in motion through the action of private individuals or through organs of the state—under the direct authority of the holders of political power, or at least in continuous association with them. Thus the decision to initiate action or to refrain from doing so, in short the responsibility for the selection of cases, rests largely with the political authority.

Finally, justice is linked to politics by the circumstance that magistrates are chosen through the machinery of political authority, whether directly by the people, by their legislative or governmental representatives, or by some compromise between the principles of co-optation and political appointment. Yet the judiciary, once chosen, is reasonably shielded in most moderate political climates against demands and temptations originating with the political authority— shielded by the rules of the fraternity, *esprit de corps*, the provisions of judicial establishment, and a modicum of economic security. None of these delicate mechanisms of protection is foolproof per se, and each undergoes its own stresses; but unless the social and political configuration as a whole undergoes swift change, the totality of these safeguards it not likely to be undermined or perverted.

In view of these considerations it might be alleged that the concept of political justice is a misnomer, that it should be rejected not only because it lacks terminological compatibility but also because the cumulative safeguards against political perversion of justice work strongly against the proposition, even as a working hypothesis, that political justice is a phenomenon worthy of particular study. The term would thus be reserved for the characterization of practices of extremist regimes, or for limited revolutionary and emergency periods of constitutional regimes. But although restriction of the term political justice to the practices of totalitarian regimes may well be justified for propagandistic purposes, it begs more questions than it is able to answer.

It is true that the difference between political justice under constitutional and totalitarian regimes may be indicated by the degree of effectiveness of the safeguards already mentioned. This fact, however, is not sufficient proof that no problem of political justice exists under nontotalitarian regimes. On the contrary, since World War I political justice has almost everywhere been utilized to an increasing extent. It is all-pervasive in the history and practice of Communism, and takes a large place in the annals of National Socialism. It was a constant element in the history of the Weimar Republic, and forms an integral part of French political experience. It has come to play an increasing role in shaping political reality in the United States. Of the major powers, only Great Britain has kept its role at a minimum.

The distinction between the totalitarian and the nontotalitarian practice of political justice is not exclusively a matter of frequency and severity. It also lies in the fact that it is impossible for a democratic government to calculate in advance the outcome of a criminal prosecution. Such a government cannot prevent the defendant from introducing evidence, nor does it control or manipulate the judge or the jury in order to obtain desirable results. But if the exercise of political justice under nontotalitarian conditions is subject to greater risks, it also may bring more glittering rewards to its practitioners. Under totalitarian conditions there are many alternatives, equally efficient, for combating political deviations and implanting desirable ideologies; a constitutional regime's alternatives for obtaining such results are more restricted, and the decision of an independent court ranks high as an effective means for disposing of political adversaries and for instilling desirable political credos.

This dual purpose of political justice must be kept in mind. It aims not only at eliminating political adversaries from the political arena.

The psychological effect of the proceedings on the population is also a large consideration. A picture of political reality is created in which the defendent incarnates socially undesirable tendencies. Under totalitarian conditions the machinery for these purposes remains exclusively in the hands of the official powerholders. Only the government of the day can use charges of treason, sedition, incitement to disobedience, for the purpose of eliminating enemies and impressing the population. Under democratic conditions, however, the adversaries of the present government may try, though in a somewhat more limited way, to work via the judicial apparatus. By provoking libel suits and starting the spadework for perjury charges they may try to change popular concepts of political reality as a condition precedent for dislodging the present powerholders.

Thus we cannot escape the reality of political justice. But neither can we, like former generations, salve our conscience by neatly separating legal duty from moral judgment. In the halcyon days of receding absolutism, of constitutional monarchies and liberal democratic regimes, this end was served by according a certain measure of privilege to the political offender. There was then an inclination to admit the sincerity of the political offender's motives while upholding the necessity of protecting society from his attempts at subversion. Much thought was given to the problem of how the necessity of defending the established order could be harmonized with recognition of its historical relativity and respect for the defendant's ill-guided but well-intentioned claims.

In purely criminological terms this special consideration shown to a political offender could be justified by pointing out that after all he fitted into none of the customary cubbyholes. Retribution, improvement, and deterrence were equally inapplicable to his case when the only ultimate aim was the protection of society without destruction of the offender's moral integrity. As we have learned from Hegel (*Philosophy of Law*, #100), the average criminal in his very act of breaking the laws of society implicitly recognizes their validity. But the political offender opposes his own order and its system of moral values, to which he has sworn allegiance, to the one that is officially recognized.

The image of the political offender as an individual standing in resolute opposition to the existing society, and entitled to a certain consideration, spread most effectively when knowledge of possible alternative regimes, a concept of the community of the future, was still in the discussion stage. Thus before the turn of the twentieth century Lombroso could characterize the political offender by his inclination to push political progress too rapidly and tempestuously, thereby offending natural tendencies toward inertia.[1] But Russian, Italian, and German experience during the twenties and thirties and forties seems to indicate that alternative political regimes are in our age characterized less by a dispute over the rate of speed of social and political progress than by a different concept of the dignity of the individual. The voluntary groupings of early socialist and anarchist days have given way to human robots in the service of a highly centralized political machine, carrying through bureaucratic orders as part of their political and, as may be, terroristic employment relation.

It is doubtful to what extent the older concept of political offender remains practicable under such conditions. Moreover, a number of special factors have put the operative value of the concept in doubt. We have seen that when a country was in a situation of acute political conflict its judiciary could not be relied upon to accord the privileges of the political offender indiscriminately to all enemies of the existing order, but only to those with whose motives it felt some sympathy. Moreover, what had started as a means of enforcing the law while making desirable moral differentiations became an instrument of pressure in groups hostile to the public order; they utilized the very possibility of special consideration for political offenders as a further means of massive pressure against the state apparatus.

All this restricted from the outset the privileges accorded to a political offender under the conditions of unstable societies. And more homogeneous societies, like the United States, became unwilling to recognize the inherent premise of the relativity of their political order. Their judicial personnel, as well as their average citizens, including members of parole boards, could not help viewing the political offender as something worse than the average criminal; the concept of the heretic does not take softer contours by becoming thoroughly secularized.

Thus the attempts of a more liberal age to protect the existing order

---

[1] Lombroso and Laschi, *Il delitto politico e le rivoluzioni* (Turin, 1890), p. 428.

without necessarily casting moral aspersions upon its enemies have been superseded in another climate of opinion and action. These attempts, however we evaluate them—as magnanimous, utopian, foolish, or socially harmful—are becoming an echo of bygone days. Limitation of the area of political justice must be sought by other methods. And to find these methods we should consider more closely the nature of political justice itself.

II

There are four levels on which political justice may operate.

On the first level it is inextricably mingled with elements of ordinary criminal cases, and only the personality or the motive of the offender suggests a political element. Murder remains murder, even when committed by a member of an impotent minority bent on taking revenge and calling attention to oppression. Stealing atomic secrets in order to transmit them to the authorities of another country remains a crime, even if the perpetrator thinks that the ensuing military strengthening of the preferred country offers better guarantees for the welfare of mankind than the continuing atomic monopoly of his own country.

Faced with such issues the prosecuting authorities will try to minimize the political elements of the case, whereas the defendant and his sympathizers will make the most of them. If the defendant admits the facts as charged, he will attempt, at least under nontotalitarian conditions, to publicize his own political motivations. The defendant will be most successful, at least propagandawise, if he can show that his government has displayed a singular zeal in singling out for prosecution persons who think as he does, or belong to a group he represents—as for instance Catholic circles have done in regard to both Nazi and Communist attempts to implicate members of their clergy in violations of currency regulations. Where the prosecution of criminal cases in this category is indeed politically selective, the moral validity of the proceedings is obviously impaired.

The second level on which political justice may operate is found when the defendant has tried to undertake a direct attack on the established constitutional order. Treason and sedition may occur without reference to forces outside the national state. But from Alcibiades' day to our own, revolutionary onslaughts and foreign attempts to subvert the constitutional order have often gone hand in hand. In a world that is daily becoming more closely integrated, treason, political relations with the enemy, and high treason—never legally separated in Anglo-Saxon thinking—are becoming well-nigh synonymous. Needless to say, this is only a description of an abstract situation. In each individual instance it is all-important to determine whether the defendant acted on foreign orders, and as part of a foreign organization, or whether there was only an effort to bolster independent political action by evoking parallel foreign intervention.

The interstitial zone that separates treason and sedition from opposition within the constitutional framework provides abundant examples of the third level of political justice, which therefore is best discussed in connection with treason and sedition. This level embraces the whole gamut of what we might call omnibus political prosecutions. Appearing under a variety of forms, they have in common a lack of definite action which would turn dangerous ideas, propaganda, discussions, incipient organizational forms, common elaboration of doctrinal platforms, and consequent indoctrination into something akin to concrete moves directed toward the overthrow of the constitutional order.

From the viewpoint of a full-fledged constitutional order of the traditional liberal type, the difference between the second and the third level is, at least theoretically, plain. On the second level the prosecution can follow definitely ascertainable patterns of political action, but on the third—the twilight zone between prevention of future revolutionary action and violation of free-speech-and-assembly guarantees—there is an effort to advance the defense line of the established order. In doing so every act of prosecution is faced with an intricate set of appraisals: given the defendant's antecedents, his doctrinal background and assertions, the tendencies and loyalties of the group of which he is a part, what, the prosecution asks, would he do in a situation that might give him an opportunity to develop a large amount of initiative unhampered by any effective deterrents? In other words, the prosecution, before making any legal moves, attempts to determine the defendant's actions in a hypothetical set of circumstances.

We know, of course, from the experience of recent years that an established constitutional regime may altogether exclude some group from operating in its midst. Logically it then dispenses with concrete proof of potential harm, substituting an en bloc legislative judgment as to the dangerous character of the group, with the intention of binding all administrative and judicial agencies to that judgement, as if it were a judicially established fact. Whether such legislative creation of something akin to the crime of *lèse majesté* involves a drastic curtailment of political freedom depends more on the social and political atmosphere of the given society than on the harshness of such exclusionary statutes. But in any event this approach toward cases of the third-level type still constitutes the exception rather than the rule under constitutional regimes.

In a totalitarian regime, on the other hand, an official who is faced with such cases will usually choose between two procedures. Since the organization, and to some extent even the utterance, of a deviating political opinion is excluded *a priori* by the conditions of the totalitarian establishment, the violator may be grabbed and handled without benefit of trial, by simple administrative procedure. But if public proceedings are indicated, whether for political or for propaganda reasons, the cases of the third level are invariably handled as if they implied sedition or treason.

Such a shift from the third to the second level is easier, of course, if the defendant has made some ascertainable, if only slight, preparations in the direction of the hypothetical circumstances. This is what seems to have happened, for example, to Cardinal Mindszenty, who, with other persons, discussed—and was careless enough to keep some documentary evidence—what steps might be taken if a *vacuum juris* were to arise, that is, if during a third world war, through circumstances beyond his power, his oppressors, the present Hungarian rulers, were overthrown.[2] But usually the task of projecting deviationist doctrine and presuming future action on the basis of past behavior involves more elaborate chores if, and this seems important, such charges are supposed to be taken at face value by the public at large.

This task requires what I would call prefabrication of an alternative reality. The prosecution must outline a concrete situation, blending

[2] See *The Trial of Jozsef Mindszenty* (Budapest, 1949), pp. 75, 76, 112–14.

elements of a universally known existing situation with fictitious happenings into projections of a dire future. The result is both prefabricated and alternative. It is prefabricated because its main elements have to be developed before the trial stage, as otherwise its various pieces might not fit into the total picture that the prosecution wants to create. Therefore the defendant and the prosecution must have agreed on the main theme, at least in its outline—be it collusion between Rajk and Tito for the overthrow of the Hungarian regime in 1948,[3] or the reestablishment of capitalism and the undermining of the Soviet regime by organizing sabotage and terrorist and diversionist acts on orders of Trotsky, as in the trial of the so-called Trotskyite center in 1936.[4] And the prosecution's case represents an alternative reality because the trial is conducted with a view to showing that the accused, but for the official action, would have had a good chance of success in carrying through his program. The element of alternativity necessitates a large amount of concrete substantiation, for the public must be directed toward accepting a dramatic channeling of all future contingencies into a battle between the present policies and the criminal alternatives identified with and pinned on the defendant.

Contrary to some beliefs, only a certain measure of collaboration from the defendant, not his full admission of everything charged, is necessary in order to fulfill the requirement that the prefabricated reality be concretely substantiated. Thus, for example, many important defendants in the Russian trials of the 1930s,[5] as well as Kostov in the postwar Bulgarian trial,[6] admitted their intentions of doing away with the existing regime yet stoutly denied espionage, drawing a sharp line distinguishing freely admitted sabotage, subversion, and general opposition from only very incompletely admitted political relations with the enemy. Such partial cooperation with the prosecution may be proffered for any number of reasons. Continued identification of the defendant with his party may cause him to accept the distortion of

---

[3] *Laszlo Rajk und Komplicen vor dem Volksgericht* (Berlin, 1949).

[4] *Traitors on Trial*, a verbatim report on the case of the anti-Soviet bloc of rightists and Trotskyites (Moscow, 1938).

[5] See *ibid.*, p. 432—Bukharin: "I never considered myself a spy, nor do I now"; Vishinsky: "It would have been more correct if you did"; Bukharin: "That is your opinion, but mine is different."

[6] See *Traitscho Kostoff und seine Gruppe* (Berlin, 1951), pp. 76–77, 639, 653.

facts as a means of reaching the party's aims, through dramatizing the external dangers and the mistaken strategy of the opposition. The defendant may also desire to utilize the only channel available to explain his stand before a wider audience, even if only in a devious and mutilated form.

Nevertheless, in the cases mentioned above the defendants' admissions allowed the prosecution to construe—from actual activities of former periods, interpreted in the light of the existing situation, and from the concretization of the projected plans—a picture of what would have happened if the defendant had been victorious. In order to obtain this alternative reality the proceedings followed what has been called "rules of translation." [7] Under the defendants' sometimes willing, sometimes grudging cooperation, certain of their thought and discussion patterns were translated into the realm of action, and they were debited with the hypothetical consequences of these nonexistent actions. Thus Vishinsky in his prosecutions led his victims close to admitting that foreseeing certain contingencies is tantamount to supporting their coming into operation. In doing so he took the defendants through the remotest possible consequences flowing from what he made them admit to be their plans for political action, always trying—in order to create the concrete image of the defendants which the prosecution wished to impress on the public—to force on them interpretations in line with the prosecution's theory of how they would have acted in these hypothetical contingencies.

In obtaining this effect, prosecution policy was clearly more successful during the Russian prosecutions of the 1930s than in the satellite prosecutions of the forties and fifties. It seems that the growing elimination of major intraparty policy controversies from public discussion, and consequently from the subject matter of the trial, and the concentration on characterizing the main defendants as spies and foreign agents have lessened the chances of creating something akin to a meaningful alternative reality. The low point seems to have been reached in the Slansky trials in 1952, where admissions were intentionally ambiguous because more often than not they concerned activities that were perfectly normal at the time they were undertaken.

[7] Nathan Leites and Elsa Bernaut, *Ritual of Liquidation: The Case of the Moscow Trials* (Glencoe, 1954).

Prefabrication of alternative reality did not play a major role among the Nazis. For this there were two simple reasons: there was little discipline in their own ranks for upholding a party ideal in the face of serious factional dissension; and disloyalty among the politically conscious part of the population was ever so omnipresent that fabrication was unnecessary.

It is obvious that under nontotalitarian conditions no such cooperation is obtainable from defendants. There is virtually no possibility of easily turning omnibus charges into treason and sedition trials. Only through the willing cooperation of the defendant, or through the presentation of evidence admissible under the standards of a Western type of court, is it possible to attain sufficient concretization for the creation of an alternative reality. Under such conditions experienced practitioners handling the prosecution of adherents of revolutionary organizations have never cared, in the absence of revolutionary action, to spell out the issue of the imminence of danger, preferring to reach a conviction on the basis of propaganda activities and doctrinal assertions. They have been satisfied with a stereotyped formula without feeling a need for elaborate discussion and justification.

In the United States this trend has been magnified in the shift from the "clear and present danger" formula, which would require some concrete justification in terms of the likely effect of group activities, to Learned Hand's "grave and probable" test, adopted with very slight variations by the majority of the Supreme Court in the Dennis case. Both the vigorous, if problematic, concurring opinion of Justice Jackson and the heart-searching and tortuous consent of Justice Frankfurter question the feasibility of spelling out the chances of communism.[8]

It would be difficult indeed to sort out, even retrospectively, the various causal strands in cases of past court action—and inaction. Would we agree with a recent historian about the significance, in the later misfortunes of the Weimar Republic, arising from the failure of the Munich People's Court and the Bavarian Minister of Justice to expel Hitler after the November putsch of 1923? Or, acting in reverse —and because we know that after 1923 the pseudo-revolutionary slogans of the German Communist party only hid their patent unwill-

[8] See 341 U.S. 494,517,570 (1951).

ingness and inability to create a revolutionary situation—would we reproach the *Reichsgericht* for having continuously applied to the German Communists what we have now come to call the "grave and probable" test, and bundled them off to prison in droves?

Yet if neither prospective nor retrospective considerations provide a court with much of a guide in determining how to strike the balance between freedom and community protection, what else remains but remembering that decisions of this nature are as much, if not more, an outcome of the prevailing psychological and institutional structure as of a rational choice? Perhaps future courts will find help toward making a rational decision in trying to analyze why the British political system has not created the same pressure for preventive repression as has the present system in the United States. I do not say that the decisions will therefore necessarily be different, but courts may become more conscious of all the elements entering into their decisions.

However that may be, whenever and wherever there are in a society potentially dangerous elements whose very existence carries a threat to the continuation of the current regime—be it the opposition within the ranks of the Russian Communist party in the early 1930s, or the semilegal residual source of opposition represented by the Catholic Church in Communist Hungary, Poland, or Yugoslavia, or the Communist parties throughout the non-Communist world, serving as self-appointed heirs to any regimes of patent social and economic disequilibrium—wherever there are such elements, decisions have to be taken by the existing powerholders whether to live with, harass, or destroy these potential threats to their existence.

Whether the courts in nontotalitarian societies are better equipped or more influential in shaping these decisions than those in totalitarian countries remains an open question. We are not here discussing court participation under totalitarian conditions, where courts play principally the role of auxiliaries of the prosecution, with interest concentrated and purpose directed exclusively on the propaganda effect of the trial, and with the main outline of judgment a foregone conclusion. To my mind the most precious thing about the courts' participation in such decisions in nontotalitarian societies is that they are participating at all.

This participation has the advantage that a decision for preventive repression on the basis of doctrine, association, or dangerous tendencies —level three of our classification, if you remember, rather than level two—can never be completely monolithic or fully coordinated. It is divided among different state organs, which may not respond in the same degree to the pressures of the moment. Moreover, court decisions may carry dissents—a now classic one is that of Justice Douglas in the Dennis case (pp. 494, 581)—and thus give the community the possibility of applying a legitimate yardstick to criticize its own actions. Apart from this there is another important advantage. Such decisions have to stand squarely on the need for preventive repression. The offender appears as exactly what he is: a potential danger to the present institutions, whose chances for survival depend on all the factors determining the history of the present generation, including the wisdom or foolishness of the policy of those in power, and not on lurid plots of murder, corruption, subversion, and espionage, perpetrated in our midst as prefabrications à la Vishinsky.

Communist states, as we have seen, have tried to create in their trials a perverted picture of alternative reality. Their indictments are formulated in terms sweeping enough to embrace the sum total of the defendant's career. The trial and the much less important skeleton-type judgments concretize and reinterpret this career as the prosecution envisages it, thus fabricating history for official use. With us, traditional procedural rules, the customs of the bench and bar, in short the sum total of our Western tradition, exclude such a course of action. Either we must find evidence of treason and sedition or we have to admit, shamefacedly or unabashed, openly preventive repression. Thus we never intentionally try to press the court to do the historian's job. According to standards of present-day Western society, it is the collective mind of the people which decides on the acceptability of an historical image. Our most effective political trials—which, however, were at the same time our most dubious—have demonstrated awareness of that fact.

Thus we arrive at the fourth and last level of political justice, comprising what may be called the artificially created political offense. This does not have its origin in the defendant's alleged intent to take away life or property, or to carry out real or imaginary assaults on the political order—attempts against which the state rushes in whenever they come to its attention. The offense on this fourth level is artificially created, dug out by the defendant's enemies, somewhere from the millions of facts that may be found in the files, depositions, and affidavits constituting the archives of contemporary government. From them the minute issue, the artifact, is distilled and prepared by counsel and pressed into the tight form of a libel or perjury suit. History seems to have been obliterated from the proceedings. The grandstand play becomes a thrilling detective story, with every member of the public invited to participate in the solution of the riddle, which is carefully reduced to simple true-false proportions.

Making a virtue out of procedural impediments and necessities, the proceedings minimize the usual front-page political stuff and concentrate instead on minute aspects of the defendant's past. These may or may not illuminate his character, acts, and desires. But once they have been chosen, dissected, prepared, and applied, the person who has been identified with them has to stand on them, affirm or deny them. They may concern the exact wording of a speech he gave on an occasion now long past; an isolated official act which formed only a segment in a whole chain of transactions; his membership in an organization that had meaning for him in bygone days; even the date of a long-ago dinner engagement.

At times, to be sure, these dredgings relate to a past that has a logical or necessary connection with the person's present situation or thought patterns, activities, hopes, and rejections; in a few cases the past patterns may be clearly related to an occurrence that remains important in the person's as well as the nation's life, and for technical reasons perjury or libel proceedings are considered the only means of evoking them before a court. Equally often, however, they remain isolated facts neither relevant to the individual's present life nor organically related to the public's legitimate concern. Produced by the legal technician, there they are, isolated from the time and circumstances that gave them meaning and purpose. Because of their apparent factuality they are easily understandable and reducible to the level of the detective story, with the contemporary public's conceptual apparatus furnishing the key to their interpretation.

It is not the jury or the court that makes the interpretation; the verdict of these bodies relates only to the narrow factual issue under scrutiny. Even during the trial, the carefully distilled artifact, the concrete issue, begins to disappear. The process of translation and transformation from fragmentary acts to a simplified picture of political reality has set in. It is a collective process, taking part simultaneously in millions of minds, and it is more intensive than the mere passive reception of the artificial reality prefabricated for the purposes of the totalitarian trial. Millions carry out a total identification of the Klieg-light-fixed episode with the political beliefs with which the defendant is presumably identified, though not charged.

In this process of collective translation from the isolated fact of yesteryear to the political reality of today, a sin of omission has been committed. Time, historical time, personal time, has been treated as if it were forever arrested. Accordingly, personal, historical, and collective meaning do not jibe. On the three other levels of political trials, defendants are at the same time victors and martyrs, sinners and criminals, and will remain so until history debunks or vindicates them. The hapless individual in the artificial political trial will be kept in limbo, because more often than not there is no meaningful tie between the order of facts from which the legal technicians have distilled the artifact and the order of human purposes.

The collective translation, with all its spontaneity, is a blind alley if employed as a key to the interpretation of history. Libel suits and perjury proceedings, the penny-arcade access to the realm of history and justice, are more powerful in the making of history than the Communist prefab. Yet, though they may create history, they rarely reveal its secrets.

III

Can the political prosecution be de-politicized? Can the prosecutor be released from the orders and suggestions of politically responsible officers—attorneys general or ministers of justice? After all, so goes the argument, it is the prosecutor's job to enforce the law, and it should lie within his discretion to determine the circumstances in which the machinery of repression should be set in motion. This discretion should be exercised with a view to the availability of evidence and the dictates of public interest, rather than with a view to the desires of those in power.

Before dealing with this argument it is important to emphasize that the prosecutor in our day is only one of a multiplicity of repressive agencies. He has to take his place with those who take away jobs or, as the case may be, low-cost housing from political unreliables, who cancel citizenship papers, reject passport applications, and refuse honorable discharges from the armed forces. Yet there has to be some coordination and some focal point in repression, even though it may sometimes seem that there is more competition in political repression than in any other line of business. And criminal prosecution, as a result of procedural guarantees and the assurance of fully adversary proceedings, is still the one method that sifts its material less with an eye toward the politically desirable than the legally attainable results.

The question is, then, whether political pressure becomes worse because it is channeled through an office like that of the ministry of justice or the attorney general. Its centralization has at least the advantage of fixing political responsibility on somebody above the bureaucratic level. Moreover, to what degree does the prosecutor's responsiveness to pressures depend on his civil-service or bureaucratic status? Is the European district attorney, the model of the old-fashioned ideal of status and *esprit de corps* and a conscious representative of what he himself likes to call the most objective office in the world, less impervious to pressures than the attorney of the United States Department of Justice and the elected or politically appointed American district attorney? On the other hand, is the American go-getter at subversion, with his reputation dependent on the number of convictions obtained, preferable to his European colleague, whose peers judge him more according to the number of cases disposed of without complications and within a certain time limit?

In any case, whatever the advantages and disadvantages of a specific institutional setup, there is one point that should be firmly kept in mind: the sheer multiplication of required contacts with officialdom has skyrocketed the chances that criminal prosecution can be brought against any one of a vast number of persons, for what appears to most as technical violations of the law, if only the required amount of energy and money is available—with the statute of limitations and, in some countries though not in the United States, periodic amnesties forming only an incomplete bar against such undertakings. Thus the concept of universal guilt becomes almost a social reality, which is no less shocking because it becomes ever more morally meaningless. It is this wide and ever increasing area of choice of possible criminal prosecutions, with the test of relevance and materiality inevitably judged by the political criteria of the day, which brings the prosecuting agencies forever into the danger zone of political justice.

Especially under the conditions of the Anglo-American legal system the judge plays a dual role in the administration of political justice. He presides over the trial as an arbiter of contending claims, and sums it up for the jury. After the verdict he turns around and engages in the business of sentencing. I have often marveled at how easily this transition from an umpire to an enforcement officer comes to most judges. The solution of the riddle seems to lie in the fact that the value structure embodied in the law enforced by the judge is not only his personal choice; what he expresses are the most cherished community values. This situation may change, however, if the political sovereign, manipulating law and administration alike, ceases to represent community values. Doctrines of the right to resistance have an odd habit of entering court opinions only under successor regimes.

As long as a complete estrangement persists between community values and the official public order, the judge must either obey that order or resign. Frequently, however, the community develops deep and lasting divisions as to the preferable scale of values. These divisions may have their origins in disputes over the forms of social, economic, or military organizations or over moral and religious systems; often the cleavages become so deep as to create formidable and composite total ideological structures. In the most auspicious circumstances judicial independence connotes impartiality in establishing the facts, or assisting the jury to establish them, and judging them according to the premises of the commonly agreed value structure. But in the absence of such common values the judge incurs the unavoidable danger of trying to create new community values by identifying his own predilections with the value structure of one segment of the community; in addition, he may become myopic in the establishment of the facts

themselves. He is thus in danger of forfeiting on both counts his claim
to obedience.

In the eyes of the defendant the situation will then arise which
Socrates in Plato's *Gorgias* (522) describes as follows (Jowett translation): "I shall be tried just as a physician would be tried in a court of
little boys at the indictment of the cook. What would he reply under
such circumstances, if some one were to accuse him, saying, 'O my
boys, many evil things has this man done to you: he is the death of
you, especially the younger ones among you, cutting and burning and
starving and suffocating you, until you know not what to do; he gives
you the bitterest potions, and compels you to hunger and thirst. How
unlike the variety of meats and sweets on which I feasted you!' What
do you suppose that the physician would be able to reply when he
found himself in such a predicament? If he told the truth he could
only say, 'All these evil things, my boys, I did for your health,' and
then would there not just be a clamour among a jury like that? How
they would cry out!"

Thus the absence of a commonly acknowledged value structure is
the basis of the defendant's attitude in most political trials. I intentionally say most, not all, political trials. In a society with an almost universally acknowledged value structure, a defendant may deny all intention
of disloyalty, completely submit to the accepted procedures, and with
maximum energy try to prove that he has always kept within the
society's bounds. This is the one configuration of a political trial where
the established society will invariably triumph. Even if the prosecution
loses its case, it has the satisfaction of seeing its rules and procedures
acknowledged as just and legitimate. But the great majority of defendants in political trials are unwilling to undertake this act of total submission. Unlike Socrates at his own trial, they will not only deny the
ideals for which the court stands, but negate its very authority.

Under such a configuration the defense strategy will be determined
by purely technical motivations. If the defense has the better witnesses,
and if the established procedures leave enough leeway for the defense
to press for acquittal—or, what may be more important, to impugn, for
propagandistic purposes, the methods of the investigation or the prosecution—then the defendant may be willing to acknowledge enough of
the court's authority to carry out these objectives. But the primary

object of the defendant is to maintain and if possible improve his status in his own group. It is therefore the political needs of the group and not his private predilections which decide his attitude in the trial. The aim of his group will vary according to the political circumstances. It may vary from trying to establish the perfect legality of the group's actions—perhaps even taking the form of an offer of future cooperation with the established authorities under freely agreed terms—to professing its revolutionary fervor. But in the mind of a political defendant the exploitation of the court proceedings for the propaganda purposes of his group, and the public manifestation of his loyalty to the ideals of that group, remain uppermost. According to the yardstick of his group it is Dimitrov who established the perfect defense record, and Torgler who established the negative record, for he "perverted" a political into a criminal trial by accepting the very system and premises under which it was held. From the viewpoint of the established order the evaluation would obviously be exactly the opposite.

The same consideration determines the choice of a defense attorney. In his own methodical way Lenin, during the 1905 revolution, thought this problem through from the viewpoint of a revolutionary group.[9] He started from the premise that a lawyer is bound to be a most reactionary and untrustworthy being who should be entirely restricted to collecting and criticizing evidence. In no circumstances should he be allowed to influence the political line of the defense, and especially he should not be permitted to make any statement that would detract from the full political or propagandistic effect of the attitude taken by the defendant in the interest of and in accord with the party. Little could Lenin foresee at that time that within a few decades there would be Communist lawyers working on both ends of the political spectrum.

In political trials in Communist courts the defense lawyer plays, indeed, not only a secondary but a pitiful role. He is allowed neither to organize nor to comment on evidence, tasks that are reserved to the defendant's terms of bargaining with the MVD and to the dictates of his revolutionary conscience, nor is the lawyer permitted to evaluate the trial as a whole in his summing up. When he appears at the very

[9] See his letter of January 19, 1905, to Helena Stassowa, reprinted in *Oeuvres complètes*, VII (Paris, 1928), 76.

end of the proceedings he enters what may be considered, at best, a plea for mitigation derived from the personal circumstances of the defendant.

On the other hand, lawyers in the Western system of courts who share the political affiliation of the defendant are bound to become a problem to the court. They function essentially as middlemen between the defendant and his free associates, and as executors of a policy determined primarily by political goals rather than by traditional trial objectives. The degree of incompatibility between these trial-transcending goals and the objectives of the court may be sufficient to culminate in expulsion of the lawyer or in declaring him in contempt of court.

If this happens, one of the main dilemmas of political trials becomes readily apparent: clothing political repression in judicial forms protects the community from the grave danger that repression may become unlimited and ubiquitous; at the same time it surrounds repression with as much legitimacy as it can ever obtain while retaining some degree of effectiveness and calculability. To whittle down these advantages of orderly political repression constitutes a major objective of the political defendant and his lawyer. He may cry victory if the court itself helps him toward revising the meaning of the trial in the verdict of history.

Thus, unless the defendant totally submits to both the procedures and the value structure which the court represents, the prosecution will never be able to proclaim a complete victory in a political trial. Exercise of authority without consent may at times become inevitable. Yet this very configuration engenders the everlasting process of revision. Therefore if I were asked whether there is any rewarding feature in political justice, my answer would be what is at the same time the most serious reproach against it: that it forever lacks the element of finality.

THE *RECHTSSTAAT* AS MAGIC WALL

I SHALL BEGIN with some remarks on the historical setting of the British Rule of Law and the German *Rechtsstaat*.[1] From there I shall proceed to show how these concepts have been transplanted and are still serviceable under conditions of present-day industrial society. Changes in the apparatus of government, and the substitution of executive and bureaucratic government for parliamentary government, bring about modifications of the rule of law without affecting the requirement that it serve the essential protective needs of the individual. The true yardsticks of legal devices, as of the regimes to which they belong, are their practices. It is the behavior of state officials, who along with their political elites are the creators and manipulators of institutions, that determines the effectiveness of available legal devices.

What types of claims is society willing to satisfy by putting legal machinery at everybody's disposal? How does society proceed when it is faced with the necessity of setting its course in uncharted or half-charted waters? What does it do with traditional formulas? Hide behind them, junk them, or try to adapt them to the purposes at hand?

"Ein Schelm gibt mehr als er hat." Questions are cheap and answers may be long in coming.

Reprinted, by permission of Beacon Press, from *The Critical Spirit: Essays in Honor of Herbert Marcuse*, ed. Barrington Moore, Jr. *et al.* (Boston, 1967), pp. 287–312.
   [1] Speaking of Western countries, I treat "rule of law" here as a generic proposition. Its specific cases of historic application include Germany's *Rechtsstaat* and the British Rule of Law, which will be capitalized.

The career of concepts resembles that of established trade names. The good will attached to them is too precious, too much in the nature of mental first-aid kits, to be cast aside lightly. What matters then is to hold the gloss added by successive generations against the original text, thus helping them to analyze and provide for their own situation. But is there an original text in the concept of Rule of Law in Britain or the related German *Rechtsstaat?* I think that for all the differences in historical roots and particular legal traditions [2] their common denominator lies in the simple thought that the security of the individual is better served when specific claims can be addressed to institutions counting rules and permanency among their stock-in-trade than by reliance on transitory personal relations and situations. Beyond that, a good part of their common success probably lies in the mixture of implied promise and convenient vagueness. Who would not breathe more freely if told that the law can rule and that state and law may march hand in hand? Yet, rule may mean different things to different men. It may imply that the legal rule dominates the scene with a firm hand, but it may also mean an indefinite type of overlordship entrusting the actual running of things to those who minister to the needs of the customers. Such a state of affairs would leave the rules somehow in the position of the God of eighteenth-century deism, providing those in need with a certificate of correct origin, but little more. What is the nature of the law which rules or which, in the German version, enters into an indissoluble partnership with the state? What transformations does it experience in this union? If the state fathers the law, how and under what circumstances does it become a force of its own? Is it a center that directs or at least forms the conscience of the state? How much will rule-of-law concepts help us to answer these questions?

The British Rule of Law is a token of gratitude to a political success story. When formulated in 1885 by Dicey it connoted a safely established level of political civilization and a career of constitutionalism nearly 200 years old. Constitutional continuity is by no means tantamount to social continuity. But the fact that the political establishment did not snap out of order during the bitter years of post-Napoleonic starvation and repression or during the years of Chartist agitation lends

[2] These differences are sharply emphasized in Ernst Fraenkel, *Das amerikanische Regierungssystem* (Cologne and Opladen, 1960), pp. 196–200.

some color to the asserted connection between the political success story and the constitutional underpinning. What Dicey did was to fuse the timeless elements of the story—the interest of all individuals to be hauled into court only for specific breaches of law established by general propositions (Parliament) and under regular procedure—with the particular concerns of a British Whig. Arbitrary power was thus not only the policeman's knock on the door but also what we might call the discretionary power of the administration to act in the interest of public welfare. Conferring of such powers should be maximally avoided and submitted to what Dicey, in a polemical way and with a side glance at the contemporary French situation, called "regular law courts." [3] Added to this was a somewhat myopic view of the meaning of equality before the law. It had nothing to do with the entry of new classes into the fold of the community but instead was another paean to the virtues of middle-class constitutionalism. The fact that a colonial governor, a secretary of state, or a military officer could be haled into court like any ordinary citizen was for Dicey both the necessary and the sufficient content of legal equality. (This is not to deny that Dicey was on firm ground when he established "equality before the law" in the formal sense as an integral part of his Rule of Law. What later generations criticized was the absence of any thought that the formal concept of the Rule of Law would need to be supplemented by an ever increasing body of legislative and correlative administrative action.)

But where does this law come from? As common law it is the judge's and his predecessors' own creation. As statute law it originates in Parliament, formally omnipotent but which, as a corporate body, is thoroughly reasonable and "does not interfere with the course of the law." [4] Dicey's *fin de siècle* formula mirrors both the constitutional tradition and a social ambience. In the absence of a written constitution Parliament has a theoretical omnipotence which, given the careful doses of nineteenth-century enlargement of the franchise, raised few problems. To the extent that law was statute law, a "popularly revered judiciary," [5] safely recruited from Oxbridge precincts, remained loyal

[3] See A. V. Dicey, *Introduction to the Study of the Law of the Constitution*, 7th ed. (London, 1908), p. 198.
[4] *Ibid.*, 10th ed., p. 415.
[5] *Ibid.*, p. 398.

to the emanations of Parliament. In case of need, however, the latter could be rendered harmless by a narrow interpretation of statutory intent.

In contrast to the placid career of the British Rule of Law throughout the nineteenth century, the German *Rechtsstaat* retained some elements of a snake charmer's performance, remaining an index of partly fulfilled and partly outstanding claims. How can a rising class, the bourgeoisie, gain entrance into the official setup without being able to make the requisite show of strength? In classical fashion, it will assert the universality of its demands. Thus, when the century was young, it protested against an eighteenth-century, police-state concept of individual freedom that would allow the state to busy itself with the personal happiness of the individual for which, according to Kant and Feuerbach, there was no general law. As long as the state apparatus was slated to stay in the hands of privileged groups, a *Rechtsstaat* concept featuring the state's limitation to legal purposes deriving from the moral freedom of the individual might provide the objective law which would miraculously bind ruler and ruled together in common observance. The *Rechtsstaat* idea might permeate the state apparatus and induce the state to observe as objective law what could not be postulated as subjective right.[6] A bureaucratic concept of duty might thus have to compensate for the absence of legally enforceable claims by individuals or groups. But what if the ruler were not willing to subscribe to the tenets of early constitutionalism? Kant could not find a right of revolution, though he would accommodate its results.[7]

When Bismarck undertook to fix the relations between army, bureaucracy, and bourgeoisie, he did not hand over full legislative power to the bourgeoisie but rather conceived it as a unifying bond between relevant social forces. For the administration the legislative power circumscribed, as Gneist put it, the discretionary space within which it could continue to operate.[8] For the bourgeoisie it safeguarded its primordial role in the legislative machinery, jointly to be operated by the federal and state bureaucracies and itself. If Bismarck granted the

[6] C. Welcker, *Letzte Gründe von Recht, Staat und Strafe* (Giessen, 1813), p. 95; see also L. Krieger, *The German Idea of Freedom* (Boston, 1957), p. 255.
[7] *Metaphysische Anfangsgründe der Rechtslehre*, par. 49a.
[8] Rudolf von Gneist, *Der Rechtsstaat* (Berlin, 1873), p. 159.

bourgeoisie at best an indefinite share in what Gneist had called the Archimedean point of the *Rechtsstaat*, participation in local self-government,[9] he gave it its full share of legislative power. But at the same time he made the bourgeoisie uncomfortable by the introduction of universal suffrage which, in the words of its spokesman Gneist, "produces average opinions which cannot maintain the stability of legal principle." [10] The people at large, besides being admitted to the precincts of the *Reichstag*, became beneficiaries of a system of administration based on law (*Gesetzmässigkeit der Verwaltung*). Administrative action was subjected to legal scrutiny by courts, civil and administrative, whose members were somehow not completely integrated into either the bourgeoisie or the reigning regime but managed to maintain their own *esprit de corps*.

II

When the battle of concepts was again joined after the two world wars, the European political scene had changed. In the beginning of the century, practice had been concerned with supervision of a limited number of state functions and with the techniques of guaranteeing individual freedom and property. The more or less efficient carrying out of these tasks now made it quite evident that in a number of countries individual freedom was threatened more by those who controlled jobs and the necessities of life than by the official authorities of the day. Hence there arose increasing demands for positive governmental action, whether pertaining to town and country planning or health and welfare legislation.

These demands were facilitated by the fact that everywhere in the West the electoral franchise had become universal. The last remnants of more limited forms of representative government had by the end of World War I given way to political democracy. But the appearance on the parliamentary scene of mass parties committed to the speedy fulfillment of the above-mentioned welfare demands raised a new problem: how to relate the rule of law to the new output of the legislative body. Since the beginning of the twentieth century a practice, recog-

9 *Ibid.*, p. 160.
10 *Ibid.*, p. 137.

nizable enough in its outlines even if not always tidily followed, had developed, requiring that general rules for identical case situations were to be issued by parliamentary legislation. Individual cases were to be dealt with by the administrative services on the basis of these statutory rules. Such cases were to be reviewed, upon application, by courts of law which scanned both the legal basis and, at least to some extent, the limits of discretion applied in administrative action. The criminal case and the civil claim continued to enjoy the benefit of direct access to the courts without need of prior administrative decision. Could the same general scheme which applied to the granting of professional licenses, building permits, etc., be transferred to the handling of an increasing body of legislation in the fields of city planning, health and welfare, agricultural subsidies, etc., which either conferred benefits on the individual or made some of his activities dependent on administrative agreement?

Attacks were now forthcoming in force, alleging that the extension of state activities to such an ever increasing number of fields was not compatible with the rule of law and would destroy its protective character. It was intimated that special legislation introducing numerous new administrative jurisdictions in the interest of a great variety of social and professional categories was incompatible with a concept of equality of law, which rested essentially on the existence of a body of common law to be uniformly applied by the judiciary to all groups. The French jurist Ripert had blazed the trail, and Swiss, Austrian, and Italian lawyers, economists, and social scientists followed suit.

Is not, for instance, legislation allowing the government to take away land for a compensation, fixed at prices substantially inferior to those prevailing on the free market, a violation of the rule of law? [11] This idea that the rule of law requires the state to restrict its activities to whatever is compatible with formal guarantees of legal equality, thus necessarily excluding the legislator from the welfare field, is a theorem which does not become more tenable by endless repetition. On the contrary, a more far-reaching measure of social equality, exemplified by some types of land legislation, while not required by the equality postulate of the rule of law, is in no way contradictory to it. Nobody will doubt the immense importance of land-use planning in densely

[11] See Bruno Leoni, *Freedom and the Law* (New York, 1961), p. 69.

settled areas after World War II. The almost uniform failure of the French, German, and Italian governments to deal comprehensively with the immense surplus profits accruing to proprietors of development land, and the consequent impossibility for the overwhelming majority of the population to acquire land of their own, has become one of the social characteristics of postwar Europe. Could it be seriously argued that the accident of physical proximity of land to urban agglomerations vests in the proprietor a right, attributable to the rule-of-law concept, to benefits toward which he has contributed nothing? In such cases remedial legislation, without doing violence to the concept of formal equality before the law, supplements it with a concept of social equality.

It has also been argued that any policy carrying out the substantive ideals of distributive justice must inevitably lead to the destruction of the rule of law as the impact of decisions becomes incalculable. Yet it is not intelligible why social-security rules cannot be as carefully framed and the community burdens as well calculated, as rules concerning damage claims deriving from negligence actions. As to the chances of the foreseeability of results in yesterday's and today's social system, one might safely ask a French peasant of the 1960s whether he prefers the old-age pensions and government-fixed wheat prices of today or his grandfather's competitive freedom under Méline.

Such arguments are quite dated by now. More far-reaching contentions are made to uphold the link between economic liberalism and the rule of law. Doubts have been raised whether the lawmaking process by central authorities and the core of the rule of law are mutually compatible. Downgrading the importance of central legislation, according to this opinion, is justified not only by the simultaneous prevalence of a free market economy and common law as the predominant source of law for private disputes in the nineteenth century, but also by the superiority of economic over political choice. At the basis of the whole argument is mistrust of unwelcome majority decisions and an attempt to seek refuge in the *fata morgana* of a society able to dispense with intermediary public organizations, those mediating between groups and between individuals and groups. A spontaneous lawmaking process through voluntary cooperation of individuals as loosely tied to each other as they were under the reign of the trusted nonexpert, the common-law judge, is recommended as an alternative. But this is at best romanticism, at worst sheer evasion of the administrative tasks to be faced in order to make the world a place worth living in for the majority of the population in our age. One does not wish away the reality of the administrative state in mass society by reminiscing on the judges' social role in bygone days.[12]

Economic liberalism's attacks on the compatibility of the rule of law and collectivist forms of society are rearguard skirmishes. The more intensively a particular state went through a period of massive economic and social dislocation and the resultant abandoning of constitutionalism, the more urgent thereafter the insistence that community planning for decent living not only has a political priority but constitutes a task postulated by the very constitutional order. The *Rechtsstaat* is transformed into the *Sozialrechtsstaat*. What previously might have been stated in purely permissive terms may now become elevated to the dignity of a constitutionally prescribed mission for the whole community.[13] Thus legal protection is no longer only an appanage of conflicts concerning personal freedom and property titles. It becomes available for other claims to which the individual may be entitled in his various status capacities, whether this status derives from his own initiative or is a consequence of a merger of societal guidance and personal response. If social services may be produced for the purposes of mass consumption, the accompanying procedures guaranteeing these rights must be producible too.[14]

But the doubts expressed about the legislature's role in the rule-of-law scheme come not only from the ranks of those who deprecate the extension of community interest from commercial and penal codes to land speculation and social insurance. It is asserted that parliaments have for a long time been covering up for a job which in fact is being

[12] R. Stevens, "Justiciability. The Restrictive Practices Court Reexamined," *Public Law*, 1961, p. 265, reports the astonished reaction of English legal circles when judges were recently called upon to sit in implementation of the vague policy concepts of the 1956 Restrictive Trade Practices Act. Their attitudes belie continued reliance on the judges as experts in non-expertise.
[13] Konrad Hesse, "Der Rechtsstaat in der Verfassungsordnung des Grundgesetzes," in *Staatsverfassung und Kirchenordnung*, Smend Festgabe (Tübingen, 1962), p. 78.
[14] H. W. Jones, "The Rule of Law and the Welfare State," *Columbia Law Review*, LVIII (1958), 155.

done by somebody else, namely the bureaucracy. Yet the relative weight given to the interest of the individuals in the forming of general rules does not depend on specific forms of representation. The individual's chances depend on organizational vigilance, multiplicity of points of access to respective decision-makers, and, closely connected, the existence of some form of intrabureaucratic competition. None of these requirements is necessarily tied to the parliamentary institution, which, as experience has shown, is as prone to manipulation as any other body. Some of the rules formulated by the still powerful American legislature have been like bills of attainder, legislation as inequitable as decrees occasionally produced by de Gaulle's government.

There has been a merger of the authorities who make the general rules with those who apply them to the individual case. What about the possible dangers that application of rules may represent in the context of this administrative practice of post-parliamentary society? Is the individual ruling the citizen receives from an administrative office now more aleatory because the bureaucracy is likely to have had a decisive hand in forming the general rule thereafter applied to his case? Most countries provide a layer of isolation between the rule-making activity and the decision of individual cases—possibly as much in the interest of the efficiency of the establishment as in the asserted welfare of the customer or in deference to the doctrinal claims of the constitutional lawyer. They cannot rearrange the applicable categories each time to fit the particular purposes of the case. Even de Gaulle experienced resistance when he repeatedly reshuffled extraordinary military courts in order to obtain desirable policy results.[15]

Moreover, the substantive ends of justice require that the individual be able to make effective use of its procedural weapons. This has recently led to a remarkable diffusion of an institutional device originally domiciled in northern European countries, the Ombudsman. As supervisor-extraordinary in the interest of both the aggrieved citizen and administrative efficiency, he has been allowed to lift some of the veil of intrabureaucratic case handling [16] which a judge may only

[15] See *Conseil d'État*, 19 octobre 1962, *Canal et autres*, and the remarks of François Mitterand in *Journal officiel* (Débats, Assemblée Nationale), 4 janvier 1963, p. 221.
[16] The emphasis lies on "some." Intraoffice memos made in preparation of a case, even in the country where the institution originated, become available to

pierce with the heavy weapon of subpoena of documents and records. It may well be that the Ombudsman—as a nonformalized half-insider able to penetrate somewhat further into the mysteries of administrative discretion than a court bound by strict rules of evidence—will become a blessing for the little, organizationally unattached fellow pursuing a pension claim or chasing after a change-of-residence indemnity. To that extent he fills in for the member of parliament of old. For the petitioner, the certainty of a thorough examination is enhanced by exchanging a high-level parliamentary letter-carrier for a semidetached bureaucratic representative; but the member of parliament by this token might lose his line of contact with the ordinary citizen.

Nevertheless the relative success of the Ombudsman—relative because only isolated success stories have been reported on inquiries of a more complicated nature pertaining to disputes involving larger socio-political complexes—brings only into sharper relief a large additional problem area. This area is exemplified by pension or overtime claims of former employees where the social situation and the antecedent relations out of which the claim originated are relatively simple and clear-cut. This could explain why the rate of compliance with the respective judgments may be quite high, why in this type of case the legal determination of the claim and its realization (*Recht* and *Rechtsverwirklichung*) have a tendency to converge. The near certainty that many types of claims once established will in due course be satisfied makes it reasonable for many legal systems to take such great pains to build up foolproof procedures to establish claims. If adjudication of a claim is tantamount to final settlement, it is certainly worth the effort to equip the parties with the best available means to get to the decision stage. But does the assumption of a unity between law and its realization hold true in all cases? If it did, our job would be finished. For Rule of Law and *Rechtsstaat* would be truly identical with the availability of generous and impartial procedures for obtaining legal protection or pursuing legal claims. To what extent does this proposition hold true? Is the concept of the rule of law exhausted by the availability of legal redress?

---

the Ombudsman and his staff only after they have been placed into the permanent record, which is to say after the case has long been closed. Cf. N. Herlitz, "Publicity of Office Documents in Sweden," *Public Law*, 1958, pp. 50, 65.

III

In 1956, during the trial of the German Communist party before the Constitutional Court, a discussion arose whether that party could claim a "right of resistance" against specific policies of the West German political leadership which in the Communist party's opinion were violations of the Basic Law. In answering this line of argument, the reasoning of the court decision [17] insisted on the fundamental difference between what the court called an intact constitutional order, in which isolated violations of the Basic Law might happen, and an order in which the organs of the state show no respect at all for law and justice and therefore corrupt the constitution, the people, and the state as a whole. Only in the latter case, so argued the court, would legal remedies be of no use to the people, so that resistance might be justified.

From this dictum we might assume that a clear-cut dichotomy exists in the mind of the German court between good and bad regimes. The good ones would provide effective and honest procedures of legal redress for any and all parties that might feel their position threatened by an abuse of public power. There is an implied premise that well-functioning means of legal redress, part of what we have recognized as the traditional armor of the rule of law, will always guarantee a balance between individual and public authority, thus arresting trends in a process of deterioration which would land the state in the "bad" column.

Is there such an easy way to sort out the good from the bad state? How does the problem of the "good" and the "bad" state present itself to the *homme situé*, the man trying to exist within the confines of modern society? Generally speaking, the state, "good" or "bad," remains an abstraction. People think in terms of subdivisions: politicians, tax collectors, welfare officers. Only in periods of turmoil does the day-to-day confrontation recede behind the expectations and fears directed toward larger entities. How do the men who constitute the state behave in the most acute and not infrequent situation when a break of continuity occurs and a new regime takes over?

For the officials or other dignitaries of the establishment, continuity, with its double sense of legal and social continuity, is the password.

[17] Vol. III, p. 737.

The first is elliptic and contains an element of necessary self-deception. The official is at one and the same time the witness to and the creator of this continuity. As a contemporary he watches the transition, the mixture of accidental or contrived emergency, of coercion and formal correctness, in the course of which the requirements theoretically set by the antecedent regime's constitutional documents are fulfilled. The official's continuing performance in his job constitutes the major certificate desired by the new regime to show that the fact of transition had all the hallmarks of regularity. The new regime thus hopes to earn the first credit toward transforming a shaky legality into legitimacy. Thus continuation in his job, immensely valuable for the incoming regime, both registers and by the same token creates the legality of the formal take-over. Yet the very nature of this transition also contains the official's absolution for his mode of acquiescence: passivity. Frequently the official in the exercise of his duties need not concern himself with the question of the legality of the regime. If he stopped running the trains or delivering the mail when the regime changes, he would be dubbed a partisan rather than an official. Insulation in correct jurisdictional grooves avoids such difficulties; yet the victims of extralegal violence that may accompany the change-over might still appeal to judicial officialdom, as did the bedraggled Prussian government after its ejection from office in 1932. But this appeal only proved that this particular government was not prepared to fight for its life. What could a judge do for a party unwilling to incur any risks in the service of its own cause? Its attitude only indicated that the cause was beyond rescue even before the chain of legality had snapped completely, and the case evaporated into thin air. Thus, when the chips are down, in the very process of maintaining or changing power the official must either join the fight, if there is anything or anybody to fight for, or, as he usually does, become a witness and passive but valuable co-creator of the new regime's legality.

But legality, whether representing true or barely contrived continuity, is a step, and no more than that, toward creating legitimacy. To behold legitimacy there must either be social continuity or the attractive promise of a new social system. This legitimacy is the business of the community as a whole, not only the official's. The official may have been instrumental in creating the penumbra of beneficial legality but, this job done, he steps back into the ranks and becomes a citizen, naïve or skeptical, enthusiastic or matter-of-fact, reticent or correct, scheming against or joyfully participating in the regime. In contrast to the official, the citizen at large, unless he is one of the few declared partisans in politics, need not take a position at all, as nothing is asked of him but to continue to pay his taxes and give an occasional cheer from the sidelines. His act of registering events is steeped in ambiguity and less consequential than the official's behavior with its precedent-building quality. It is both these things at the same time, because the social continuity which the citizen's passivity helps to create could be endangered, lacerated, or cut through by many manifestly contrary acts.

If the regime engages in foreign wars and imperialist conquest, the legitimacy problem reaches new dimensions. The citizen's total identification with both internal and foreign policy, which hitherto might have been evaded, may now become inescapable. Unless the foe of the regime has made a clear-cut choice of rejecting the official ideology, the daily necessities that are seemingly unconnected with the larger purposes of the regime may take precedence. Alienated, he may continue the daily routine. Court opinions dealing with negative choices, naturally written only under a successor regime, are not a very reliable guide, especially if the judges themselves have to realign and rationalize their own record in this process. But at least they elucidate the dimensions of the problem and show that behind the neat differentiation between "good" and "bad" regimes there may lurk a number of additional problems. Complications arise from the fact that even "bad" regimes must run the mails and feed their citizens, in short, pursue the millions of transactions without which the civilized existence of millions of people would rapidly come to an end. The citizen who refuses to lend a hand separates himself not only from the regime but perhaps also from his fellow citizens' intent to continue living as well.

Thus men's actions under any regime will have to be judged in the light of their own contribution. The record of the regime under which they serve establishes at best a rebuttable presumption as to their own behavior. There are few who will deny this truth when it concerns the record of what commonly is called a "bad" regime; indeed, much time has been spent in the courts of many a country to put the burden of a fallen regime on the broad shoulders of its principals if they are safely out of the way, thus by logical implication absolving all those acting in their and the regime's name. But the opposite contention is one which bears some additional inspection, i.e., that a regime which has some well-established and well-safeguarded channels for setting up general rules and universally accessible procedures to redress injustice is a perfect rule-of-law candidate.

There is no hard and fast line of separation between the formal remedies and the substantive goals of a social order. The availability of legal remedies for the citizens and the implantation of legal duties for the official world may, under favorable circumstances, lead to the attainment of individual or community goals. Whether available procedures are put in motion and whether legal rulings once obtained will be enforced or complied with has to be investigated for each category of cases. Without making such an effort, a rule of law, resting only on the theoretical availability of legal remedies, somehow resembles a modern house whose glass wall, the major attraction for all visitors, already stands, but whose wooden utility walls no one has so far bothered to build.

From the fact that, in some cases, finding the law is almost tantamount to executing its mandate, it is a big step to assuming that such a situation must invariably prevail. Let me develop a case whose interest centers not only on the psychology of the players but on the intermeshing of many levels of participants. Presumably all of them acted correctly within their understanding of the rules of the *Rechtsstaat* and yet never arrived at satisfactory results. What I have in mind are the antecedents of and the 1965 German debate leading up to what in effect amounted to a prorogation of the statute of limitations for National Socialist murders. Official statements, as well as the course of the public and parliamentary debate, have established beyond doubt that until more than eight years after the Federal Republic was established no one in a responsible official position took the initiative systematically to collect evidence and initiate proceedings against the multitude of Nazi murderers. This does not mean that no one against whom witnesses had preferred complaints, or whose anonymity was lifted by private or bureaucratic accident, was investigated and, if the evidence was sufficient, prosecuted by the competent local authorities. But, as an official German report puts it with unintentional irony—as if murder were something which is only followed up upon specific complaints—"the survivors were much too busy building up a new life to care to push criminal prosecutions in Germany." [18] As no agency coordinated these individual local efforts, collected evidence, and systematically searched through the mountains of documents dispersed over many places at home and abroad, the outcome of these chance proceedings was unsatisfactory. Of 12,882 persons indicted between May 8, 1945, and January 1, 1964, only 5,445 were convicted; 4,033 or 31.8 per cent were acquitted, whereas the highest acquittal rate in German courts for all types of proceedings in the 1950s was 8.5 per cent. The remaining persons were discharged without judicial proceedings.[19]

It is thus entirely clear that the German executive, administrative, and judicial authorities during the first decade of the new state did not perceive any connection between the *Rechtsstaat* concept and the need to look for ways of dealing effectively with the problem of the National Socialist murders. The relentless zeal which characterized the German federal government's handling of the reverse side of the Nazi criminal account, the energetic and successful pressure on the Western High Commissioners in 1951 for speedy release of war criminals sentenced by Western Occupation Courts, found no resonance in the field of settling accounts with Nazi murderers. It took eight years until in the wake of public pressure, following the revelations of the Ulm SS trial, the various federal and state administrations of justice founded an agency coordinating the collection of evidence and other documents. After another six years it became clear that the statute of limitations would run out before it became possible to start proceedings against all presumable participants in Nazi murder activities. Under the impact of new pressures from abroad, some of them mainly designed to embarrass the regime, the Bonn legislature then decided that the statute of limitations for murder, which had been presumed to have started running again in May, 1945, would be deemed to have come into operation

---

[18] *Die Verfolgung Nationalsozialistischer Straftaten im Gebiet der Bundesrepublik Deutschland seit 1945* (Bonn, Bundesjustizministerium, 1965), p. 49.
[19] *Ibid.*, p. 43.

only in December, 1949. Thus, sins of omission were followed by the sin of commission—depriving presumed, not yet adjudged, culprits of the mild type of protection which the statute of limitations furnishes against the abuse of bureaucratic routine and changing political pressures. Moreover, the new solution solves the problem as little as did the policy before 1958 of diffuse and hit-or-miss prosecution. Certainly the 750 proceedings, presently pending, with more than 7000 defendants which so far have not ripened into the trial stage, together with the new proceedings which may be opened in the next four years, would push the trials well into the 1970s. This not only would put a burden on the defendants called to task more than a quarter of a century after the incriminating acts, but also raises the question with what yardstick a new generation of judges, of jurors, and of the public, acting in a totally changed political situation, should measure the deeds of a previous generation.

The whole episode shows that the *Rechtsstaat* concept can be honored by scrupulous observance of all prescribed forms and proceedings while its spirit is constantly violated by an unwillingness to initiate steps commensurate with the magnitude of the problem at hand. In terms of the official rule books, the Law on the Administration of Justice, and the Code of Criminal Procedure, every German authority was proceeding correctly within its own jurisdiction. Many minor impediments to action (initial remnants of the few Allied reservations on jurisdiction; partial unavailability of records; access to records only under conditions not in accord with the goals of inter-German or German foreign policy, etc.) were allowed to stand in the way of facing the problem squarely, allowing it to be downgraded in this process to a series of interminable individual cases. There is no discernible individual to whom responsibility can be assigned. Who is to be blamed? The German Parliament, which in the fifties withstood right wing pressures to issue blanket amnesties for National Socialist crimes, but carefully refrained from checking up on the positive performance of the bureaucracies involved? The political and administrative heads of the federal and state ministries of justice who waited until 1958 to take the necessary coordinating steps? The untold numbers of individual prosecutors and judges who acted properly in terms of the cases before them, but never transmitted doubts to their superiors nor aroused the public as to the spotty and unsatisfactory results obtained?[20] They all acted bureaucratically correctly in terms of their individual jobs and yet eluded their responsibility when the occasion arose for showing that mass murder could be prosecuted in an administratively and morally difficult situation, yet well within the safety margin of the regime they were serving.

The example is instructive: not because it proves that the Federal Republic is not a *Rechtsstaat*—which obviously it does not—but rather because it shows that the implementation of the rule of law is a problematic affair and that the mere enumeration of available remedies and jurisdictions does not suffice. The case shows how compartmentalization of organizations, each of which acts correctly within its own jurisdiction, may lead to results which might satisfy the tactical needs of participants in the official game, but falls wide of the mark of what one might call a step toward solving the substantive problems involved. The German politicians, lawyers, and administrators must have been fully aware that buying four more years for initiating new criminal proceedings would take the spotlight off an unsatisfactory record while compounding old sins of omission by new iniquities. Quite probably a full parliamentary inquiry into the causes of failure, which, except for exculpatory arguments, were only evoked in the most cryptic terms, would have been more appropriate than the theorizing on the justifiability of proroguing the statute of limitations, a measure of which nobody knew the meaning in actual practice. An analysis of the shortcomings of case handling would have laid bare the need for a new approach to the problem of human dignity. Is the time of the subject at the unlimited disposal of the official, is it part of the suspect's preemptive punishment to be at the authority's disposal literally till his last judgment day? Or is an enforceable provision for "deliberate speed" part of the subject's inalienable legal rights? What comes to the fore, therefore, is the *Rechtsstaat*'s need to strive for the attainment of substantive justice through procedures which are not liable to negate the very goal of the *Rechtsstaat* itself. The admixture of complementary elements of mass democracy and bureaucracy may create distortions at both ends.

[20] Admittedly, however, the very change of role of the German judicial apparatus, from involvement in the legal politics of the National Socialist regime to the handling of the latter's criminal legacy, made such an expectation largely illusory.

IV

It is the title to glory of the *Rechtsstaat* and of the Rule of Law that remedies for all claims are provided. Implicit in the rule-of-law concept is the calculation that the mere availability of remedies will settle most claims out of court or enhance the chance of voluntary observation of the law, even though only a fraction of the offenders can ever be pursued. We ask more rarely whether a claim is always recognized where injury has been inflicted. Suppose the injury has occurred in an area where the individual concerned has established no business or employment relations with the agency involved. The jobholder who loses his employment through mistaken withdrawal of his security clearance may have avenues of redress; but the job seeker equipped with all necessary professional qualifications who for security reasons is not permitted to pass beyond the interview stage never has a chance to contest the report which deprives him of access to entire job categories.[21]

Would it help in this connection if we introduced a differentiation separating the roles of the rule of law in conflicts involving public law from those in private law? Recently an erstwhile official practitioner of international law has opined that the private sphere is eminently related to courts, whereas law as a system allocating public power is by no means the creation of judges and courts. If judges go beyond the limits in which they can effectively exercise power, the result will be evasion rather than vindication of legal authority.[22] The statement reflects experience in a field where the discrepancy between existing norms (above all, Art. 2, par. 4, Art. 51, and Art. 53 of the United Nations Charter) and the unwillingness of the major powers to comply with these norms makes it problematic how far the rule of law extends into the field of major power relations. Increasingly we meet attempts to deny that the rules in question are legally applicable to a specific situation or to reconstruct the meaning of the concept of compliance. In the place of judging a state's willingness to comply with a legal norm,

[21] For the most recent discussion of this problem, see J. Rottmann's review of H. U. Evers, *Verfassungsschutz im Rechtsstaat* (Tübingen, 1961), in *Archiv für öffentliches Recht*, LXXXVIII (1964), 227–44.

[22] A. Chayes, "A Common Lawyer Looks at International Law," *Harvard Law Review*, LXXVIII (1965), 1396–1413.

it is now proposed that we consider compliance as a "spectrum, . . . a matter of degree varying with the circumstances of the case." [23] But such an approach confounds the job of the lawyer with that of the sociologist. The latter may try to determine under what circumstances a rule is enforced or meets with resistance. The lawyer, however, cannot turn doubts and considerations antedating his opinion into some sort of statement like the following: "Because of original doubts as to whether my country is acting in self-defense or committing an act of aggression, I am recommending the landing of a limited troop contingent only." Limited or unlimited troop commitment, his country either acted in self-defense or committed an act of aggression, i.e., if the problem is considered as a proposition of law, the action can only be classified as either aggression or self-defense, compliance with or violation of the rules of international law.

In so far as the rule of law enters international relations, it exists only at the sufferance of the major powerholders and to the extent that the latter find it advantageous to submit to its working. Given the ever increasing importance of interpersonal and interorganizational exchanges on an interstate level, the absence of enforceable rules governing the behavior of the most powerful territorial units is fraught with the danger of a constant spillover into other fields. But while the spillover from international relations into the domestic field may be a constant threat in our times, it has relatively little to do with a differentiation between an acceptable rule of law for private violations and its unacceptability for the public sector.

Our world knows no magic wall separating the structure of private from that of public law. Nonjusticiability in the one sphere can easily spill over into the other. Witness the situation already mentioned concerning the activities of agencies protecting the security of the state. If anyone is in public business, then these agencies are; yet they interfere with the chances for a private life of untold multitudes of people. Or take the matter of race relations, where the finding of meaningful solutions has become a matter of critical public concern and where one of the major difficulties lies in the permanent intermingling of public objectives and private decisions. The effectiveness of new state or

[23] L. Gross, "Problems of International Adjudication and Compliance with International Law," *American Journal of International Law*, LIX (1965), 56.

federal policies is frequently predicated on a great variety of attitudes of private persons: the behavior of labor unions toward opening equal employment opportunities; the reaction of real-estate interests and their customers to fair housing regulations; or the degree of willingness of Negro parents to submit their children to the tormenting experience of serving as guinea pigs for integration. Are the busloads of SNCC students traveling south engaged in a private trip? What then about the reception they will receive from the local sheriff? Or do we have to await how the sheriff's actions will be characterized, first in the state courts and then in the federal courts? Semantics may help to rationalize a court decision one way or another, though to harmonize federal decisions and those of southern states is beyond human ingenuity. But one interesting observation can be made: the (until recently) official U.S. practitioner of international law would call "public" the area from which he wanted the courts to be excluded, whereas in the realm of race relations the argument would go the other way. The U.S. Supreme Court rationalizes the right to interfere with a certain institution by referring to its public character, while it calls private relations those areas in which it does not feel entitled to interfere. The private-public dichotomy is thus largely a matter of the different manipulative concerns of various agencies. It offers no clue to the problem of which relationships should be left to private arrangements and what form necessary cooperative arrangements should take.

One can hide the magnitude of the enforcement problem as one of the touchstones of the rule of law, as, e.g., in Llewellyn's variant of legal realism. Only those legal rules may then be considered meaningful which involve solutions acceptable to major forces in the community. From this viewpoint, few enforcement problems are likely to arise. First, lawmakers are psychologically conditioned to issue norms compatible with the wishes of major clienteles; and secondly, if the lawmakers have somehow failed to take such ground rules into account (the motto being "where reason stops, there stops the enacted rule"), the duty of restrictive interpretation takes over.[24] As Llewellyn puts it, "even the machinery of the rightest of right *jus* is subject to limitations of human inventiveness." [25] In other words, few occasions arise

[24] See K. N. Llewellyn, *Jurisprudence* (Chicago, 1962), p. 228.
[25] *Ibid.*, p. 486.

for conflict between the will of the legislator and grass-roots obedience to his mandate, because the intermediate level of interpreters takes care of accommodation and excludes what to the legal realist must be "meaningless" conflicts. No doubt this has happened often enough. One might even add the numerous cases where the legislator is of such uncertain or divided mind that the called-for interpreter, be he judge or, as is more frequent, administrative agency, will have full freedom to evolve substantive decisions of his own with only a minimum of legislative guidelines.[26]

Yet legislative efforts, sometimes braced up by the executive, are not always uncertain about what they want to achieve, nor do judges invariably function as harmonizers or eternalizers of the existing group equilibrium. In other words, there may be situations where the question of enforcement of a definite policy may be inescapable. This was the case, for instance, in the United States in World War II when the Office of Price Administration was set up to ration all scarce but essential commodities. They were to be distributed fairly among customers at prices within inflation-preventing ranges. The allocation part of the system somehow worked. The number of commodities available outside rationed channels was curtailed, but not to the extent that the ethically relevant part of the goal, equality of sacrifice, could be sufficiently realized. Enough commodities, like gasoline or meat, moving in parallel channels, remained available for those willing and able to pay. Yet, the risk of suspension orders, injunctions, civil-damage suits, and to a very minor degree fines was reflected in premiums of various sorts. Now one might say, in the fashion of legal realism, that the authorities had neglected to calculate the magnitude of organized pressures against the system, which were simply too great to allow for anything but hit-or-miss enforcement.[27] Thus, in the nature of things, people would understand that punishment, i.e., prison sentences, remained mostly reserved for those in the business of counterfeiting ration coupons, while all other visitations by the authorities were simply reflected in the size of the risk premium.[28]

[26] Cf. M. Edelman, *The Symbolic Uses of Politics* (Urbana, 1964), ch. 3.

[27] Whole regional production lines, like Del-Mar poultry or Southern lumber, worked outside the system. See H. C. Mansfield, *A Short History of the OPA* (Washington, D.C., 1948), p. 257.

[28] M. B. Clinard, *The Black Market* (New York, 1952) reports that 88 per cent of a sample of businessmen in 1945 simply did not understand the difference be-

The OPA case shows that the enforcement of legal sanctions is anything but automatic, even though in contrast to the German case it involved routine problems of a continuing political and social order—sanctions destined to keep goods out of undesirable channels and to further a reasonable price level and patriotic morale. Yet, enforcement not only presented the difficulty that businessmen against whom measures were to be taken were organized, in close contact, and therefore never broke ranks to help the prosecution; but the potentially much more numerous supporters of enforcement policy, the consumers at large, neither had an organization to speak of nor many voices to represent them in public. The outcome of the individual enforcement skirmishes may have been unpredictable. Trade associations, more often than not helped along by politicians, joined issue with the OPA staff. The latter was itself frequently split according to whether the division in question was more interested in the survival of the organization, with its important allocation function,[29] or in attempts to implement policies aimed at equality of sacrifice. If a conscious choice had ever been made, it would have been between symbolic enforcement as part of an educational bargaining drive and effective enforcement to obtain the goal of equality of sacrifice. Circumstances helped to avoid such a clear-cut choice. In essence, both sides, the government and the consumer, carried part of their points, because the concatenation of propaganda, compromise, and symbolic enforcement—and still more the reality of ample profits through a guaranteed mass market rather than through inflationary prices—kept price rises in bounds. And the chiseler won, in that attempts at enforcement, such as they were, were never able to stamp out the market in parallel-risk premiums. Seen from the viewpoint of legal organization and the rule of law, the outcome was at best dubious, for neither the substantive goal of equal sacrifice nor evenhandedness in enforcement procedure made a particularly strong showing. It demonstrates the difficulty of harnessing the legal system to the pursuit of nationally approved goals in the face of concerted resistance by major organizations in the Establishment.

The situations in law enforcement are too multifarious for even a

---

tween criminal fines and payments which had to be made as the result of triple damage suits (p. 235), and quite justifiably so, since this was all included in the same risk premium.

[29] See V. A. Thompson, *The Regulatory Process in OPA Rationing* (New York, 1950).

rudimentary attempt to catalogue them. Visualized as a continuum, at one end there would be adjudicated individual claims for wages or damages—reinstatement claims of employees being quite a different matter—deriving from contractual relations. At the opposite end would lie situations such as that presented in *Korematsu* v. *U.S.*, the case of Japanese exclusion during World War II.[30] Here the government, by expelling citizens from their homes and places of work and sending them into camps because of their Japanese ancestry, committed direct and acute injury; but the courts in trying to remedy the situation might have run head-on into difficulties in enforcing their judgment against the executive. They thus had to choose between covering up the impotence of the law by adducing a special wartime jurisdictional scheme allowing security questions to be decided by the military without outside interference; and—as done in Justice Jackson's well-known dissent—establishing a dichotomy between the judicial power, which applies the law and the Constitution and must judge accordingly, and the military power, telling the people at the same time not to rely on the exercise of judicial power in such circumstances.

A judgment first and above all renders a decision on the concrete situation which has been presented. To that extent the administration and the private litigant must fashion their attitude so as to bring themselves into line with the specific order of the court. But higher courts do not make their decisions merely with regard to the particular case before them. They may want to give directives to future actors in only partly charted fields or to weed out malpractices not in conformity with their notions of applicable law or constitutional rule. To what extent will they succeed? A look at wiretapping, search and seizure, and utilization of illegally obtained confessions gives rise to the following observations.

Courts have no direct supervisory power over the police—federal, state, or local—except in relation to the individual case under review. From the viewpoint of the administrator their decisions serve therefore primarily to introduce a new element of risk. Politicians can be expected to make declarations showing deference to the court; yet in the absence of continuous organized political pressure the situation in

30 323 U.S. 214 (1944).

the case directly under review will differ from the sum total of the practice falling under related headings. In the particular case under review, the Supreme Court in nine cases out of ten may be able to see its mandate through, even if the instrument through which it has to work is as unpromising as a state court in the deep South. But in later cases the lower courts, if they feel the urge or are exposed to sufficient pressure, may exercise the fine art of distinguishing some elements justifying a different outcome and, at the very best, requiring time-consuming new litigation in the higher courts. On the other hand, however, lower courts may also get tired of shielding police practices against criticism by higher courts that might possibly reflect a large segment of public opinion. In any case, from then on the administrators will have to face increased risks against which even legislative support is not invariably a permanent help.

Conformity of administrative practices with rules emanating from lawmakers and bodies interpreting the law has not the same meaning for administrative and judicial organizations. For the administrative organization, conformity to the law is one factor among many in its calculations. To obtain such conformity is essential, however, for courts, whose very impact is predicated on the community's willingness to abide by the rules set by courts. On the other hand, the fact that the courts are outside bodies which do not stand to the administration in a relationship of hierarchical superiority enhances the numerous factors of uncertainty in their relations to each other.

The facile idea that the availability of procedure for making claims or upholding the public order is tantamount to guaranteeing that these rules are effectively observed or put to work has little to recommend itself. Wherein then lie the benefits derived from rule-of-law concepts and from the institutions to which they correspond? For both procedural and substantive goals, rule-of-law concepts are best understood as yardsticks for performance. They connote law as observed regularities. Where the route is charted, and only there, there is a great advantage to drawing up formulas to be applied to both the object and the subject of power situations. The sheer need to avoid the eruption of chaos among the ever increasing masses of population, as much as the unheard of increase in the productive capacity of the advanced nations, puts a premium on satisfying the expanding needs of such multitudes. The efficient handling of the host of recurring problems which make up their daily existence, pertaining to job conditions, living quarters, health arrangements, and the easy translatability of such typical needs into corresponding money equivalents, makes the operations involved smooth and calculable—up to a point. To the extent that the rule of law furthers these ends, it contributes elements of personal security and even of substantive justice. It may well be, however, that the historian of the twentieth century will be less impressed by diverse propagandistic claims of various regimes as to the reign of law under their dominion than with the close cohabitation between wide stretches of certainty for mass man's daily living conditions with unheard-of areas of oppression, lawlessness, and rewards for maximum aggressiveness. A generation which has lived through Auschwitz and Hiroshima and was indifferent or powerless to prevent them, and which is prepared to see bigger Hiroshimas, has no cause for complacency about its preservation or even enlargement of some orderly forms of living. It may have forgotten the essential: there must be life for life to be worth living.

PRIVATE MAN AND SOCIETY

Der wirkliche Mensch ist der Privatmensch der jetzigen Staatsverfassung.
MARX, *Kritik der Hegelschen Staatsphilosophie*

How DOES THE INDIVIDUAL acquire the capacity to participate in the general affairs of the state? How does it become possible for all citizens to approach public affairs, not as particular individuals, but in such a manner that their assembled particular wills embrace the state as their common affair?

THE MIRAGE OF CONSENSUS

This alpha and omega of democratic theory would lose its explosive power if we substitute a theory of consensus for concentration on the difficulties of the individual in his capacity as a fundamental constituent of the state. Were we to hypothesize something like a national consensus, sometimes swelling to a mighty chorus, sometimes running underground, but always strong enough to drown out or interpose itself between the thousand individual conflict situations between the rich and the poor, the mighty and the small, we would not need to bother about the riddle of the common will. The individuals spontaneously at one with the state on their most vital common concerns

Reprinted, by permission, from *Political Science Quarterly*, LXXXI, No. 1 (March, 1966), 1–24.

may safely leave to the executive ranks the details of policy. But theorems of the nation as fundamentally one, despite their frequent use, have a fragile existence. In the face of religious, nationality, economic, and ideological cleavages they often are forced to beat a retreat in favor of more pragmatic tests.

If substantive agreement remains an elusive proposition in societies whose members often have widely disparate goals, consensus might still be saved, so it seems, on a narrower basis. Although difficult to agree on last principles, agreement might still be found on what to do here and now under the changing circumstances of the day. We might decide to emphasize civil rights or international peace, but still be willing, when acute danger threatens, to call out the police or build the arsenal of democracy. Who knows, perhaps we could all follow the Low Countries' *verzuiling* system, and erect our polity on some neatly built up fortresses of separate *Weltanschauungen*. We could then start negotiating endlessly with each other, provided we were reasonable enough to build up an ironclad codex about how to conduct our negotiations. To haggle endlessly over substance but keep the system going via sacrosanct ways of procedure may be one worth-while and well-known way out of our dilemma. The value of this procedure, however, may be circumscribed by a common-sense observation: to ride together in a bus while wanting to go to different places may be all right, provided that the destinations are not too different from each other.

Recently our quantitative brethren have uttered doubts. They indicate that what they are wont to call the influentials and the public at large show, as expected, little agreement on major premises of the political system. Moreover, if questioned closely, and not allowed to mouth conventional phrases, the public appers to be much less concerned over the necessity for procedural guarantees than their more genteel brethren.[1] We could play down this difference, as an American peculiarity, and point out that other industrial countries with a different historical and institutional record may be more universally conscious of procedural values. Or, we might surrender to the happy conscience of the technological elitist, and guess that as long as the

[1] Herbert McCloskey, "Consensus and Ideology in American Politics," *American Political Science Review*, LVIII (1964), 365.

going is good, the run of the mill of the citizenry will not enter the political market except in defense of their own specialized interest. Or, if they enter they will be guided by the common man's recognition of the superior workmanship of the more exalted community members in performing particular functional tasks.[2] Or, we could rejoice with the civic culture man over the fact that the citizens of this outstanding pilot democracy have such a high estimate of their own political subjective competence, and need not be concerned unnecessarily about the gap between the citizens' assertion of subjective competence and their ostentatious failure to make use of it.[3] Thus, consensus statements of any kind remain rather problematic.[4] Besides, as we have already mentioned, consensus statements might run into the barrier of quantitative inquiries. The less such inquiries are guided by images of desirable participant political structures, the more they are prone to cast doubts on the nature of the ties between the official political establishment and the underlying population.

THE MARKET DEFINITION OF FREEDOM

A closer analysis of the structure of man's mind in relation to the surrounding social universe may put the inquiry on a more secure footing than either consensus theories or selected opinion tidbits relating to a complicated structure of social reality can provide. This hiatus between asserted subjective competence and inability to use it connotes failure to connect official policies with man's fate. From the recent inquiries regarding the average individual's place in society and state, Lane's book seems to offer the best point of departure for our critical enterprise.[5] It accompanies the citizen, so to speak, in his engagement with social reality and watches how he internalizes his vari-

---

[2] Carl Joachim Friedrich, *The New Image of the Common Man* (Boston, 1950).

[3] Gabriel Almond and Sidney Verba, *The Civic Culture* (Princeton, 1963), p. 481.

[4] "Consensus is one of the more elusive and misleading concepts to have been introduced into recent political theory," Dankwart A. Rustow, *The World of Nations* (Washington, D.C., 1965), mimeographed, ch. I, p. 21. See also Bernard R. Crick, *In Defence of Politics* (rev. ed.; Baltimore, 1964), 24.

[5] Robert E. Lane, *Political Ideology* (New York, 1962).

ous experiences. Thus, society's apparatus appears not only as an outside agent to be avoided, resisted, managed one way or another, but
also as an element in his own personality structure. Instead of juxtapos-
ing, as the civic culture man does, individuals and institutions and
tabulating the former's relations to the latter on a preconceived scale of
integrative or disintegrative traits viewed through the eyes of the best-
available model of state organization, Lane tries to show us the results
of the individual's confrontation with society's ideologies and realities.
Thus the types of answers he receives are not predetermined by his
mode of analysis. We are presented with the individual curricula of
fifteen native-born white people, with quite divergent personality
structures, whose occupations run from various kinds of machine
operatives to truck drivers, policemen, bookkeepers, and supply clerks.
Variations in reaction patterns are as a result probably much broader
than if the author had studied people on a somewhat lower rung of the
social ladder and with a smaller degree of skill specialization or less
regular work habits. Despite these variations, and despite the existence
of an irreconcilable minority of four citizens who adopted irrational
explanatory schemes and viewed their surroundings with a cabalist's
belief in the presence of secret groups behind the scene acting as
creators of political reality, enough common themes run through
Lane's analysis to merit close attention. Only within their local environment is the political experience of these men an immediate one;
within these limits some possibility of access to local machines and
political figures exists, and, occasionally, the adjustment of a particular
grievance may take place.

Outside the strictly local sphere, the importance of which is dimmed
for the individual by the high frequency of interlocal mobility, political experience is mediated through other layers of the social system,
such as unions. As none of these upper-working-class groups has a wide
range of professional choice, there is little question of having conscious
options in social existence. Their liberty, then, is best described as the
possibility of foraging around within the confines of the system for a
rewarding job combination opening up maximum access to consumer
goods. These men's universal liberty is, then, the liberty of the consumer's market. But one would think that liberty must somehow be
related to the options in one's life: how to fill one's time after the

necessities are taken care of. It becomes readily apparent that in the time horizon of Lane's sample collective, images of nation, religion, or class have little part. One might think that there exist such things as working time and leisure time, individual time and group time, private time and public time, with as many variations in measurements as there are variations in intensity of pursuits and of intergroup and interpersonal relations. Yet, for Lane's men, only one universal equation seems to exist: the endless reversibility of two coordinates which are the men's primary resources, time and money.

This reduction of life into a time-money equation limits the horizon of the future. Not too many time units can be exchanged, as the human supply of time runs out rather quickly. In order to escape this natural limitation one would have to convert individual into collective time, switch from short- and middle-range consumer expectation to more universal entities, thus transcending the time-money equation. But Professor Lane is quite emphatic on this point: "the failure to extend their private range of interest and attention beyond their own generation tends to limit the social goals that have much appeal to them." [6]

How do Lane's men then see their relations to the surrounding world? Let us examine two aspects of this problem. The first concerns their notion of how to relate themselves to those on the lower and upper levels of society and through these relations to formulate their particular notion of equality. The answer is clear-cut again. They do not look at the quest for equality as a desirable postulate, but as an unwelcome agent of social destabilization. They have reached a certain plateau—with a slight overestimation of their individual contribution as against more general social conditions as the causal factor—and their psychological investment in this position must be defended against the more unfortunate classes. In order to get the maximum benefit from this form of ego defense, the misfortune of these lower-level groups will be ascribed to their shiftlessness rather than to causes beyond their control.[7] By the same token, their position seems to favor the recogni-

---

[6] *Ibid.*, p. 293.

[7] The inclination to emphasize individual rather than collective or accidental chances of personal success can be seen also in the data in Alfred Willener, *Images de la société et classes sociales* (Bern, 1957), pp. 111, 115. Sixty per cent

tion of a meritorious elite as the precondition for security in their own ranking. Thus the quest for equality disappears or is reduced to small increments of mobility allowing for a limited amount of advancement as a precondition for the smooth functioning of the social system. The status satisfaction of Lane's workers requires that the cleavage between their own ranks and the lower orders be upheld, and at the same time legitimizes the position of their betters.

If equality as a dynamic concept which abates intergroup distance meets with little comprehension, what about social relations in the worker's own world made up of factory, office, and colleagues? A wide variety of evidence would show, at best, a somewhat narrow range for initiative and autonomy, varying from oppressive to tolerable according to the job structure and form of authority. A half-hearted camaraderie may occur, resting on shared experience and limited by the continual presence of competitive elements; such camaraderie scarcely extends to the level of shared purpose and close friendship. In Lane's interpretation, the lessons of industrial discipline, punctuality, attention to detail, and avoidance of waste help to create the self-reliant man. The industrial citizen accepts responsibility for his own destiny, though in a more limited way than did his forefathers. While this knowledge has not yet been rationalized into a new belief system, the worker has come to rely on the helping hand of the state in an increasing number of situations in which his own willingness to do his stint would not suffice.

Yet with all his understanding for the world of the self-reliant industrial man who lacks a sense of shared purpose or evil, Lane has little confidence in man's political ability or judgment. With slightly condescending praise for their sturdy qualities, Lane turns toward the professional classes rather than the business and laboring classes for the realization of the major democratic values, liberty and equality. Given the picture he draws of his sample's distinctive qualities, I fail to see what else he could have done. Captives of their surrounding civilization in more than one sense, industrial jungle-dwellers and one-

of his Swiss sample emphasize factors relating to individual effort as preconditions of success; 21 per cent emphasize that success is socially conditioned; and 19 per cent emphasize pure chance. The same distinctions are made in a discussion of the causes of poverty: individual factors, 50 per cent; social factors, 24 per cent; chance factors, 25 per cent.

dimensional privates in the consumers' army, Lane's workers contribute little to the public enterprise beyond their presence as producers and consumers.

What do we need to add to Lane's description? That liberty from the viewpoint of the population at large is first and above all perceived in consumer terms is by now a well-accepted thesis. But what is the genesis of this freedom? Does it rest on the accidental juncture of mass production, higher wages, and some sort of communal care? Social security and medical services have allowed the lower strata, for the first time in history, to think in terms of consumer goods beyond the area of primary needs. The lower strata's initiation into consumer society required nothing but the exchange of their work time for desirable consumer goods. This initiation took place with a high degree of spontaneity and a marked absence of coercion, which was present in the previous major social experiences of this group.

Moreover, what was the alternative? How frequently has advanced industrial society offered these executants [8] the possibility of parlaying their earnings into enough power to work a radical transformation of their present occupational position? Whatever their chances for social mobility, such chances did not essentially depend on doubts about fully entering the consumer goods market. Yet, the restriction of freedom exclusively to consumer goods orientation may also be grounded in something like substitute satisfaction. It seems, therefore, to the point to look at the position of various working-class strata in the production process and to see to what extent their position offers an explanation for the shrinkage of freedom to the choice of consumer goods.

PRIVATIZATION, COMPETITION, AND ISOLATION

What strikes us first is the great variety of positions in the industrial process. The problem is to find a common denominator between the pre-industrial artisan, still abundant in many regions of southern Eu-

---

[8] The executant class comprises all positions, whether blue collar or white collar, where a job is narrowly circumscribed by strict hierarchical subordination and/or restriction to a single phase of a larger project.

rope, the often-analyzed automobile worker whose rhythm is set by the conveyor belt above him, the girl in the textile mill simultaneously supervising a dozen looms, the chemical operator watching his dials at regular intervals and adjusting instruments correspondingly, and his higher level maintenance colleague reading the funnies while waiting to hurry to some repair job. If one thinks primarily in terms of outlets for initiative and variation, there exists little common measure for their respective job experiences. Initiative would become a disturbing factor if the pace of work and the time allowed for it is exactly regulated by the rhythm of the performance required from the individual. A work group or an individual might petition a foreman, and through him the engineer, to change the rhythm; if either attempted to do so on his own, chaos would result. The girl watching the looms may determine in what order to examine the machines, and not much else. Nonetheless, the operator and the maintenance man in a fully automated enterprise can use their ingenuity and play around with alternative solutions to obtain the organizationally prescribed goals.

There is no reason, however, to expect automation will be introduced in the entire industrial field. Many industrial jobs are too marginal to warrant the necessary capital outlay for automation. Automation will also limit the workers' individual discretion in handling their particular problems. Frequently a new layer of office workers or plant engineers will appear; they are expected to calculate or lay out in detail the most economic performance for the workers' particular job. In many jobs educational requirements will increase drastically, not simply (as has often happened previously in times of growing unemployment and job insecurity) by upgrading job qualifications without corresponding changes in needed skills, but by raising the number of jobs combining a variety of skill elements. Skill group differentials may become increasingly important factors in determining how one conceives relations to the outside world. A recent inquiry in a New Jersey car assembly plant has shown, for example, that a threefold distinction between skilled, repair, and line workers with corresponding differences in initiative, security, and status is, without further mediating agencies, immediately translated into different attitudes toward a wide range of social phenomena. Confidence in the future, acceptance (with some reservation) of social, institutional, and state organizations

marked the higher group; so-called radicalism, mistrust of the surrounding world, and expectation of violence as a regulator of world
affairs marked the lowest skilled group.[9]

These differences appear as barriers to the formation of common
horizons and bonds of experience between workers, both within the
same enterprise and between various units. But a type of common
experience also exists. When Lane speaks of the self-reliant industrial
man as a prerequisite for the functioning of democracy, he makes a
political virtue out of common social necessity. Job risk is still individ-
ualized in the sense that society does no more than furnish a favorable
or an inhospitable climate for job hunting. The socialization process
which the worker undergoes when he enters the work group includes
acquiring a sense of balance between cooperation and the distance
necessitated by the universal fact of interpersonal competition. The
balance between cooperation and competition is quite different from
the specific role which goes with each individual job. Two processes
must be differentiated from each other: the specific role change, supposed to take place only at the time when a person steps up the ladder
from, say, worker to foreman, connotes a mask which can be slipped
on and off at will,[10] but, in addition, there is more universal and
constant behavior, the gyroscope activity of scanning the horizon for
yet undetermined pickups to improve one's position.

The model of fully competitive interpersonal relations may be subject to various gradations. At one end we find Crozier's model of fully
bureaucratized industrial state organizations.[11] Here there is a differentiated system of conditions for entrance into the organization, and
within the organization there is watertight compartmentalization allowing a minimum chance of moving upward on the hierarchy of
functional levels. Correspondingly, the cadres have only a minimal
right to interfere with the work and position of either the individual or
his functional group. Under such conditions there is a far-reaching
convergence of the horizons of individual and group expectation. The

[9] Lewis Lipsitz, "Work Life and Political Attitudes: A Study of Manual
Workers," *American Political Science Review*, LVIII (1964), 951-63.
[10] Harold L. Wilensky and Hugh Edwards, "The Skidder: Ideological Adjustment of Downward Mobile Workers," *American Sociological Review*, XXIV
(1959), 215-31.
[11] Michel Crozier, *The Bureaucratic Phenomenon* (Chicago, 1964).

incidence of submission to hierarchical discipline, frequently the most resented part of the worker's existence,[12] may not altogether disappear, but it loses much of its substance. Changes in the individual situation no longer derive from a mixture of individual accommodation and the discretion of a determinate superior, but appear to be the work of a *deus ex machina*, orders of an anonymous ministry without the participation of a proximate superior. Here the element of insecurity is transferred from dependence on the interest and evaluation of one's immediate superiors to the interference of unknown forces, the operation of which cannot be calculated in advance and consequently cannot be influenced by modifications of one's own behavior.

Of the two levels of insecurity, insecurity by virtue of a life situation's dependence on proximate superiors or by virtue of impersonal decisions deriving from major organizational changes, bureaucratic structure eliminates most of the former. Their distance from the fountainhead of authority prevents the lower strata from catching more than an occasional glimpse of decision-making; the missing link between high-level decision and individual fate shows up,[13] however, to the same degree in bureaucratic and competitive organizations.

To what extent upper-level decisions may be changed by low-level pressure depends as much on the cohesion of the lower ranks as on the form of organization in which the work takes place. Thus, protection, both against job risk and the weight of organizational structure, may be obtained through the introduction of bureaucratic rigidity, but such rigidity provides no guarantee against major organizational change. Hierarchical dependence is also mitigated in proportion to: (1) the complexity of the task performed, (2) the acquisition of a high degree of technical sensitivity in servicing machines, and (3) the extent that performance is intricately geared to and dependent on the individual effort of other group members. Hierarchical dependence is also miti-

---

[12] The point is scarcely controversial. See the instructive tabulation in Andrée Andrieux and Jean Lignon, *L'ouvrier d'aujourd'hui sur les changements dans la condition et la conscience ouvrières* (Paris, 1960), p. 81. Of ninety answers to the question, "What displeases you most at your enterprise?" forty-two named "subordination and dependence."

[13] See the typical workers' responses in Otto Neuloh, *Der neue Betriebsstil* (Tübingen, 1960), p. 101, and Heinrich Popitz *et al., Das Gesellschaftsbild des Arbeiters* (Tübingen, 1957), p. 227.

gated when automation substitutes the job of recurrent observation and possible modification of an uninterrupted production system for exactly-timed repetitious physical labor. A greater degree of work initiative, except under the conditions of Crozier's fully bureaucratized model, does not, however, exclude a certain amount of competition to improve one's position in relation to wages, job type, and work schedule.[14] It is through the agency of personal improvement that hierarchical dependency again enters working relations in automated industries, although it plays a somewhat smaller role in the work performance itself.

Could the consumer goods society ever have prospered without the notion of the supremacy of one's private existence within the bosom of the nuclear family over all other competing values? Whether we are dealing with Crozier's sheltered employee in the accounting office or the tobacco monopoly, or with Zweig's and Hoggart's British workers,[15] Popitz's German foundry workers, or Lane's self-reliant industrial men, the experience is everywhere the same, the increasing isolation of the working-class individual. Here we are dealing not only with the side effects of boundary lines between groups, the fact that each professional group tries to surround itself with an artificial barrier as a protective shield against erosion of its occupational basis by advancing production techniques. Nor are we merely dealing with the impact of isolation of work places in nonautomated industries. It is to the point that workers frequently prefer to work in isolation rather than as members of a group.[16] This attitude is in line with the tendency to reduce risks and avoid conflict situations potentially damaging to one's own prospects. Thus, projects for collective workers' action against management can run counter to the presumed interest of the members as individual parts of a hierarchically ordered factory organization.[17]

Self-isolation and withdrawal from participation in collective action, even at the cost of lowering the climate of the work place to a temperature which excludes the possibility of collective action, may be per-

[14] Robert Blauner, *Alienation and Freedom* (Chicago, 1964), p. 161.
[15] Ferdinand Zweig, *The Worker in an Affluent Society* (London, 1961); Richard Hoggart, *The Uses of Literacy* (London, 1957).
[16] See Neuloh, *op. cit.*, pp. 236–37.
[17] See Daniel Mothé, *Journal d'un ouvrier, 1956–1958* (Paris, 1959), a running account of such a situation.

ceived, at whatever psychological cost, as the best means to avoid immediate damage to a personal interest situation. But the problem may go deeper than the ambiguity inherent in a person's choice between upholding collective action on the basis of shared experience and the safety of prescribed correctness within the work organization. The climate of isolation is also part of a pseudo-bourgeois pattern of existence. Professional or commercial elements may continuously coalesce to explore situations affecting them, rally in defense of an acquired position, or battle those of others. After each short-lived combination, there may remain a nucleus of strong personal relationships to be recombined and reactivated at the spur of the moment. In contrast, for the executant, congeniality of environment and people [18] may seem desirable, but possibilities of controlling and manipulating the job environment are restricted; narrowly conceived economic necessity remains the primary consideration. Once "their social rights to a living wage" [19] have been secured by the evolution in production techniques, with some assistance from the state and from union representatives, the executant's interest in his position as an industrial citizen recedes. His reactions to the endeavors of official spokesmen to interest him in any kind of socialization or co-determination schemes are mildly enthusiastic, somewhat like a child's feelings toward a complicated gift which will bring more joy and excitement to the donor experimenting with it than to the recipient. The executant's interest leans more in the direction of intraorganizational rewards, enhancing his status, initiative, and salary.[20]

Would the experience of Crozier's fully bureaucratized organiza-

[18] Herbert H. Hyman, "The Value Systems of Different Classes: A Social Psychological Contribution to the Analysis of Stratification," in Reinhard Bendix and Seymour Martin Lipset, eds., *Class, Status and Power: A Reader in Social Stratification* (New York, 1953), pp. 426, 433, Table 5.

[19] T. H. Marshall, *Class, Citizenship, and Social Development* (Garden City, N.Y., 1964), p. 106.

[20] See Blauner, *op. cit.*, p. 206, Table 45. It should be especially noted that only 30 per cent of the workers gave cynical answers in regard to the factors determining advancement chances and that advancement chances are more favorable in automated industries. This is in contrast to previously prevailing opinions that workers expect more benefits from collectively granted awards, an opinion still upheld by Lipset in "Trade Unions and Social Structure: I," *Industrial Relations,* I (1961), 75–89. The same type of factory management organization orientation is reported in Neuloh, *op. cit.*, p. 205.

tions contribute major modifications to this picture of the worker's passivity and isolation? The competitive situation which creates ambiguous relations between personal interest and collective action may be absent in the fully bureaucratized organization. Since he is protected in his relations with his hierarchical superiors by the working of impersonal rules, the possibility of formal and informal pressures on the worker is at a minimum.[21] Could one not argue that with the existence of this universe of protective groups and individual positions the blossoming of personal friendships free from all impediments of interest and loyalty claims should be the order of the day? But the absence of competition as a major agent of instability in intragroup relations does not seem to have had the expected consequences. Crozier's explanations, which emphasize the continued isolation of individuals in their bureaucratic milieu, rest on reasons peculiar to the French psychological and social structure. We should prefer to look at this isolation and at the shallowness of interpersonal relations, which engulf human beings working in subordinate positions under different types of social arrangements, as a more generalized phenomenon in our society.

Lack of initiative, compartmentalization, feelings of dependence (resulting either from direct supervision, or from the decision of an anonymous ministry reaching down to the lowest-level executant) go hand in hand with an appreciable easing of both the physical burden of work and an increase in material benefits. It is on the basis of both the confining condition and the increase in material rewards that worker response must be considered. In a previous generation, when work was more arduous and material rewards less abundant, those workers who translated their personal experience into a larger social framework often espoused concepts of social equality. Vague ideas of a more just society were accompanied by more concrete images of what equality would mean in the context of work organization. These images included fraternal relations of mutual respect which would prevail between all ranks; hierarchical relations with strict subordination of the lowest rank were expected to fall by the wayside.

During the course of the last decades, workers have learned that

---

[21] Crozier, *op. cit.*, p. 286.

increasing material benefits and a much greater amount of social security were not accompanied by greater equality on the job.[22] Whatever may have been changed in the organization of the group in command of the enterprise, the workers' visions which had the least chance of realization were those colored by any type of egalitarian ideology. Expectations of more egalitarian working conditions faltered when faced with the realities of the industrial situation. In this respect it seems significant that, considering the great difference between various job situations described in this paper, a majority of American workers would not choose again the type of work in which they are engaged now.[23]

It is in this context that the question of equality and status consciousness takes on new contours. If work hierarchy is unavoidable, if "the horizon is closed and the chain is quite solid," [24] maintenance of social status becomes simply a matter of protecting one's own interest. This is all the more the case when the conditions leading to a better job in the work hierarchy are of purely accidental nature (seniority, business requirements at a certain date, etc.), and therefore require more rationalization and fortification, or, as the case may be, more cynicism. Yet, the workers' status consciousness, as distinct from that of their artisan predecessors, does not give rise to any special pride.[25] Their reaction may depend on the exact place they hold in the working hierarchy. Those who are able to maintain their status may at times chase away moods of self-flagellation by upgrading their own relative success and enhancing their self-esteem through thinking of their less fortunate brethren. Yet, such tendencies are quickly counterchecked by industrial man's interest in some of the material aspects of social equality, helping him toward construing a state obligation to provide for the essentials of life running parallel and being supplemented by his own efforts. The worker has had enough experience with the quirks of

[22] Until recently the exception would have been printers who were considered craftsmen rather than industrial workers.

[23] This is true, even though in the majority of cases the same workers had no objections to the specific enterprise in which they were working. See Blauner, op. cit., p. 202 Table 37.

[24] Worker quoted in Andrieux and Lignon, op. cit., p. 210.

[25] Mothé, op. cit., p. 15. For the opposite tendencies toward self-devaluation, see Andrieux and Lignon, op. cit., p. 192.

the economic system to want the state to put up both a permanent collateral to be drawn on in case of necessity and possibly some extras to be distributed unconditionally right now. While the existence of an insurance policy may enhance feelings of security, it does not change environment and style of living.

Many attempts have been made to develop typologies of how to relate executant class experience to the surrounding world. The predominance of family involvement will, especially in the case of female workers, displace the effect of work experience. The same work experience may lead to a variety of reactions according to the degree of intensity with which the particular job experience is internalized by the respective individuals. But there are relatively few ways to translate this reaction into specific attitudes toward the outside world: an executant may look at the relations between himself and management as an individual or as a collective conflict situation in which management holds most of the trump cards, and he or his group relatively few and weak ones.[26] There may be, on the other hand, a complete absence of any societal image and a complete refusal to consider what is going on in the stratosphere above him. Both ways of experiencing his job will frequently emerge as two often-overlapping escape routes, and give rise to a type of existence in which those conditions which he misses most take a preeminent place: greater degree of personal initiative, and independence from hierarchical orders. On the upper fringes, especially, of the white-collar workers, the executant may feel confident to take his own risks.

There is ample evidence throughout industrial society that many have considered attempting escape with varying degrees of intensity. The most frequent goal, the hope of building a small business, frequently serves as a psychological escape mechanism rather than an actual alternative.[27] If the conditions of personal existence cannot be changed, the individual can strictly compartmentalize his command performance at the workshop and his private life. It should not be said, however, that this renunciation and withdrawal come easily. There are

[26] Popitz, *op. cit.*, p. 233.
[27] The point has been discussed frequently. See, for example, Ely Chinoy, *Automobile Workers and the American Dream* (Garden City, N.Y., 1955), p. 86, and Andrieux and Lignon, *op. cit.*, p. 104.

a large number of workers who want to connect their activity meaningfully with the goals of the organization.[28] To the extent that these hopes of participation are fulfilled, the worker can internalize the enterprise as a system of participant order rather than as a grudgingly recognized, but psychologically resisted, necessity. There is also the more ambiguous situation of part of the white-collar group. To whatever small extent they participate in the command function while they are still at the bottom of a ladder, they are nevertheless on it, and take attitudes that are helpful in climbing it.[29]

In the majority of cases, however, such conditions are absent. This is due in part to the intrinsic difficulties of overcoming basic antagonisms in worker-management relations. In part it is also due to a policy barrier; the right to meaningful information and discussion can shade imperceptibly into the right to disagree and challenge, which so far neither public nor private enterprise wants to recognize.

Thus the main tendency is separationist. Job life and private life have no common denominator. There is a scarcity of private contacts between co-workers. Eighty-five per cent of Crozier's sample never socialize with their colleagues.[30] Such separationist tendencies may be reinforced by isolation at the work place or by a competitive work situation. Twenty per cent of the working force consists of so-called skidders, people who have been unable to hold on to their positions. In anticipation of the loss of a job, restriction of one's contacts may minimize the psychological damage caused by such a threat. At the same time, a policy of shunning deeper personal involvement might not stand in the way of upward mobility, but favor it by the lack of affective ties. Whatever the impoverishment of the individual's existence, isolation releases the individual for a vigorous participation in consumer society, thus increasing the chance for a more tolerant acceptance of his job, which may now be reinterpreted as a kind of precondition for his consumer existence. "To be socially integrated in

[28] The point comes out most succinctly in Neuloh, *op. cit.*, pp. 86 ff., who, however, owing to his constant "harmonizing" tendency, makes no attempt to assess the reasons militating against the fulfillment of the urge to participate.

[29] See Michel Crozier, *Le monde des employés de bureau* (Paris, 1965), p. 39, and his discussion of Kroner's Theory of Delegation.

[30] *Ibid.*, p. 114; Zweig, *op. cit.*, pp. 75–88.

America is to accept propaganda, advertising and speedy obsolescence in consumption." [31]

LIMITED INTERMEDIARIES

With privatization of existence synchronized with consumer goods orientation, where does this leave the executant's ability to make contact with the wider purposes of society? If we say that his contribution restricts itself to his consumer role of making planned obsolescence a success, we are asserting that acting out his private desires remains his only public contribution. The executant's problematic ties with the affairs of the wider polity have been the object of numerous discussions within the framework of pluralism and mass society schemes. This discussion has emphasized mainly the destabilizing political consequences of isolation, especially for members of the lower classes, and resultant easy accessibility to extremist politics. Executant elements, who in emergencies may be mobilized by extremist dynamism, are more likely to stick to minimal political engagement in more settled times. They may respond only in case they feel their immediate interest situation is threatened.

How do these various theories see the executant's position in the polity? In theories based on pluralistic models, emphasis lies in maximal voluntary participation in intermediate social organizations which are strong enough to operate autonomously, having access to the political elite, yet existing independently of it. At the same time, it is expected that the participation of members in a system of linked pluralism which rests on simultaneous membership in various organizations enhances the chance of maintaining group balance effectively.

How does such pluralism fit the life experience of the executant class? The most important organizations for the rank and file of the executant class are trade unions and religious groups. The qualifications of thousands of other organizations, from stamp collectors and glee clubs to antivivisectionists and beekeepers, are doubtful. Participation

[31] Harold L. Wilensky, "Mass Society and Mass Culture," *American Sociological Review*, XXIX (1964), 176.

may possibly be intensive, but I fail to see how these groups qualify as intermediary powers between the official state organization and the individual except on a very narrow front. The Germany of the Weimar Republic had an untold multitude of associations of this hobby type which quickly took to the prescribed brown coloring in 1933. Intensive participation in hobbies—often another form of escapism from political reality—left the people stranded in their political ignorance, just as it left the country without a government enjoying sufficient political backing by major intermediary social organizations.

Few members of the executant group will become involved in special *ad hoc* protest or promotion groups on a national level. A sharply delineated local situation—the change of or an exception to a zoning regulation, a hospital or school building program, a slot machine or a liquor license problem—may be a different story. People in the executant category who are both familiar with the issue and possibly have an active personal interest in it may bring their otherwise dispersed and isolated political resources to bear on the decision.[32] To the extent that a particular constitutional settlement (the U.S. and Switzerland, for example, as against France and Germany) favors participation of the local citizenry in the settling of local financial issues, *ad hoc* groups may arise and compete with the political influentials for actual decision-making, without entering the political arena in a more steady fashion.[33]

What, then, is the meaning of membership in the major organizations of the executant classes, the trade unions and religious bodies? Union membership is often a required passport for certain jobs. Under such circumstances, membership may imply only a remote or perfunctory participation in the union's activities. Correspondingly, the degree of acceptance of the union's decisions, closely analogous to that of governmental decisions, may relate mainly to factors having to do with

[32] For the by now classic description, significant for the description of both the possibilities and the limits of mobilizing individual resources for local action, see Robert A. Dahl, *Who Governs?* (New Haven, 1961), ch. 16.

[33] The manifold social, economic, and political variations of new group entry into and exit from the local political process are now unraveled in Robert E. Agger, Daniel Goldrich, and Bert E. Swanson, *The Rulers and the Ruled* (New York, 1964), The authors rectify the somewhat overoptimistic conclusions in regard to nonelite participation in the local political process which readers might draw if they were to generalize from Dahl's New Haven picture.

power rather than with loyalty, and therefore fit only moderately well into the pluralist scheme. But the nature of decision-making may shift and with it the nature of membership ties to the organization. In some categories of automated enterprises, closer relations within the work group may develop, including a greater amount of cooperation between operators and engineers. These closer relations may allow some successful localized collective action against a management more concerned with uninterrupted production and more willing to compromise on the wage claims of an increasingly smaller number of executants, at least among their working-class staff. The central union type of organization would be relegated to purely legitimizing bodies. Instead, decisions would be taken on the spot by decentralized types of worker organizations with firmer roots in the workers' consciousness, and consequently with a greater chance of membership participation.[34] Of course, opposite tendencies are as likely, if not more so. The stake of workers in the enterprise may be so high as to lead to clear-cut identification with the enterprise. This identification may engulf the existent elements of workers' representation. The workers might accept the enterprise fully as their intermediary for dealing with the outside world. Were this to occur, such conditions would create, instead of bureaucratic paper giants, dispersed centers of more firmly rooted authority for the participants.[35] Unions would become a more vigorous and promising candidate for the role of the major intermediary organization.

The possible role of religious organizations is still less easy to circumscribe without considering the particularities of case and country. In spite of a thorough secularization of industrial society, and a corresponding increase in purely nominal membership, religious bodies still

[34] This hypothesis is discussed in Serge Mallet, *La nouvelle classe ouvrière* (Paris, 1963), pp. 27–69.

[35] An extreme case of management-worker collusion against the state has occurred recently in Germany. Management and works council often agreed on the introduction of a private kind of court system for employees guilty of asocial conduct extending from infractions of factory rules to larceny and sexual misdemeanors. Fines meted out by a combined worker and management representation would settle problems, expeditiously preventing the wasting of scarce labor power of defendants and witnesses and the disturbance by outside interference of enterprise harmony. For some details, see Herbert Lederer, "Betriebsjustiz etwas ausserhalb der Legalität," *Gewerkschaftliche Monatshefte*, XVI (1965), 215–19.

reach potentially more members of the executant groups than any other organization. Yet, to qualify as an effective intermediary organization, such bodies need not only have an existence separate from the state, but also need to appear to their members as separate entities. This requirement certainly raises questions for a country such as Italy [36] and, to a somewhat minor degree, for West Germany. In both cases the major denominations today are official bodies.

The United States system, on the other hand, operates on the basis of separation between state and a multiplicity of religious bodies, none of which has a predominant position. In the mind of an optimistic sociologist,[37] this arrangement has been one of the sources of success of the United States establishment. According to this interpretation, disestablishment has been an incentive for turning churches into secular, utilitarian, and democratic establishments, with a high degree of "religious mobility." The very use of the expression denotes a late stage of development in commercial civilization where religion may be primarily viewed a a social promotion scheme.

Within this system, sects retaining elements of an apocalyptic theology continue to preach to their flock the promise of future glory. These sects render the social system another significant service by reconciling their flock to the notion that the social system's inequalities and iniquities are of strictly secondary importance. In exchange, the political system, in spite of the sects' refusal to join the bandwagon of consumer goods orientation, grants them the same type of protection and recognition given to the major church organizations which are more intent on transforming themselves into institutions providing social service and status satisfaction.[38] The difficulty of this position, if

---

[36] For Italy, see Joseph LaPalombara, *Interest Groups in Italian Politics* (Princeton, 1964), ch. IX. The author has coined a new concept, "parentela," for the interrelation between church, ancillary church bodies, political parties, and state administration. This state of affairs, however, is subject to changes—*vide* Austria—where the dominant Catholic Church has, in the last decades, and despite its character as a public institution, become independent from the political setup.

[37] Seymour Martin Lipset, *The First New Nation* (New York, 1963).

[38] Rodney Stark, "Class, Radicalism, and Religious Involvement in Great Britain," *American Sociological Review*, XXIX (1964), 698–706. The author shows that—with associational affiliation kept constant—differences between upper-class religious affiliation, 73 per cent, middle-class, 56 per cent, and working class, 39 per cent, are quite appreciable (p. 703).

looked at rather as an operative device within a pluralist society than as a description of previous development in the field of religious institutions, concerns the impact of those denominations which continue to play a role in confirming status while their social service function is atrophying.[39] By raising specific social and moral problems on the basis of revealed truth accepted as a binding norm by the community, the churches create an incomparably firmer position for formulating and pressing demands on government authority than were they to opine on a broad front of contemporary issues merely on the basis of the *Zeitgeist*.

In contrast, various sects which serve as institutionalized devices for the incapsulation of their members against the surrounding world exercise a much stronger hold on their members. Because they radically divert their members' interest from the hopeless affairs of this world,[40] they arrive—except for occasional clashes with the state authorities over compulsory participation of the sects' members in state-ordered functions—at easy coexistence through nonparticipation. This may be a welcome feature for a state authority hard-pressed by many demands, but it provides somewhat problematic support for the model of a society resting on the participation of independent intermediaries.

A more favorable candidate for the role of such an intermediary is offered by the experience of a predominant, yet independent type of church, as is presently found in France. The absence of any competition encourages experimentation, yet prevents fragmentation according to social status categories. These categories are a considerable barrier to moral effectiveness and to the claim to representativeness for any religious organization which has left the sect stage behind it. The French type of independent church tries to solve the problem of relating its core activities to various social subdivisions by encouraging a multitude of ancillary organizations with a certain amount of initiative in their respective fields of action. In this way, the church enhances its

[39] The facts are scarcely controversial. See, for example, Arthur J. Vidich and Joseph Bensman, *Small Town in Mass Society: Power and Religion in a Rural Community* (Princeton, 1958), p. 313. For the corresponding fading of religious consciousness see Lane's instructive case studies, *op. cit.*, pp. 129, 137. For the British material compare Zweig, *op. cit.*, pp. 146–53, and Hoggart, *op. cit.*, pp. 93–99.

[40] See, for example, Wilbur Cash, *The Mind of the South* (New York, 1941), pp. 291 ff.

legitimacy in its dialogue with the state, addressing the state either in the interest of special disadvantaged and underrepresented groups or as a spokesman for broader social objectives. Knowing that its effectiveness would not reach further than the active support of its members allows, the church tries the difficult experiment of combining forms fixed by tradition and dogma with a wider range of social and political choices. The church has an impact on both members and polity, which is the more pervasive and ubiquitous for only rarely mounting a direct challenge to the official state authority. Factors favoring the church's position are its independence and distance from the official state apparatus, some cohesion in its religious core, absence of a rigid political and social doctrine, and solutions of vexing decentralization problems through a multiplicity of semi-independent ancillary organizations.

MALLEABILITY AND DISTANCE

The associational balance sheet of the executant is a checkered one. The increasing thought and effort the official world gives to the improvement of his condition serves, to use T. H. Marshall's words, not only "to raise the floor-level in the basement of the social edifice," but "to remodel the whole building." [41] The offerings of the mass media, in short, the possibility of partaking in civilization's wares without the necessity of any active engagement, coupled with a heavy dose of skepticism toward the motivations of those doing the offering ("we are not buying it"), sap the executant's commitment to any of the various policy centers of society. He is their client, and thanks to the universalization of some political competition and industry's interest in any outlets, the executant's needs and reactions have become a matter of steady preoccupation for those centers which x-ray and analyze the needs and reactions of the executant as a precondition for carrying out their combined service and domestication job.

But the occasions when the executant enters into communication with these centers remain limited. Even during the work process, which provides his most vital, frequent, and direct contact with the world outside the shopping center horizon, the executant's social

[41] Marshall, *op. cit.*, p. 106.

communication is restricted to his peers and the next higher executant echelon.[42] Otherwise, vertical relations are conducted either on a purely ceremonial level or through a class of professional social middlemen: the clergyman, the labor politician, the personnel officer, who serve as links or, to put it differently, check up on, or orient, the world of the executant.

One might therefore turn around, as has recently been done, and contest the validity of the pluralist assumption altogether.[43] There are enough examples of how the channeling of intensive loyalty to cohesive and strong intermediary organizations of the movement or sect type may deprive the state or official participants in the political process of communication with the adherents of such movements or sects, while allowing such bodies to checkmate and atrophy the official machinery. To avoid such a misfortune, one might feel constrained either to put more reliance on the individual again, or resort to the beneficial equalizing tendencies of mass culture which will in time even out the differences between the various popular strata in the industrial uniculture. Meanwhile, the most resourceful individuals of the executant classes may have developed enough upward social mobility and found their way into the executive classes. Their self-reliance may be sufficient to allow them to find their way through the jungle of the industrial landscape; their contribution to the political process is likely to be more modest. The executant is unlikely to disturb the political process, but, if called upon, he makes his legitimizing gesture. Wilensky insists that mass culture will even out the apparatus of perception in use by different groups, and create, in the long run, consistent behavior between various groups, classes, and fields of activities.[44] To the extent that this contention makes the point that pluralistic man and mass man are not essentially different entities, it is well taken. Pluralistic organizations such as the media, the established churches, the *meneurs des masses* (as Raymond Aron calls the political as well as the industrial leadership), which channelize, indoctrinate, and amuse the masses, will

[42] See the figures given by Neuloh, *op. cit.*, pp. 88–89.
[43] Joseph R. Gusfield, "Mass Society and Extremist Politics," *American Sociological Review*, XXVII (1962), 19–30. See also Charles Perrow, "The Sociological Perspective and Political Pluralism," *Social Research*, XXXI (1964), 411.
[44] Wilensky, "Mass Society and Mass Culture," p. 180.

continue to speak in different tongues. Their message remains the same: You never had it so good, be friendly to each other, and, above all, do not upset the applecart.

But what will be the reaction among the executants? Or is even such a question illicit? Has not indoctrination in the ways of mass society produced a common way of experiencing reality? Would one not want to conclude that whatever differences do exist are due either to different people exercising different functions in line with their capacities, or to very personal deviations, that is, reactions to the common fare of civilization which can be explained by differences in personality? But is it true to assert that all classes perceive reality in the same way because they are all subject to the same leveling mass culture influences in after-working-hours? Does this way of looking at things not neglect the different role of media in the life of various classes? Is the perception of a different capacity to manipulate reality not a more constant and more powerful element in human behavior than the unifying mass culture theory? Is the phenomenon of isolation and withdrawal, conditioned as it is by the experience of the executant and his position in industrial society, not identical with the permanent helplessness which he feels because of the narrow limits within which he is able to manipulate reality? Yet the only thing which mass culture cannot do is to change these limitations in dealing with reality. To that extent the growing identity of consumer reaction in the field of political and economic consumption will not close the gap. It may well be that electoral response to Ike's personality can be closely correlated with responses to undiscussed gasoline ads.[45] Does this mean that the executant's vistas are infinitely malleable by all organizations working in the context of mass society? I think that the combined system of consumer goods orientation and withdrawal to one's privacy allows a different interpretation.

Most of what can be singled out as relevant behavior are reactions within the context of mass-consumer institutions. Which candidate of two competing catch-all mass parties the executant votes for, to which brand of gasoline he gives his temporary allegiance, what TV program he switches on, may have important consequences for the purveyor of the respective goods. But for the individual these decisions draw their

45 *Ibid.*

importance only from the fact that they create the illusion of a margin of initiative. For a fleeting moment he may enjoy this initiative and then become a victim of subliminal guidance by the purveyors of these articles. While he might care for the illusion of initiative, he cares for nothing else in this decision, because it does not constitute a meaningful contribution to his problem of how to enlarge his control over reality.

Thus, the privacy of mass civilization is at the same time privacy and protection against mass civilization. The mass man as a producer and as a consumer may overlap, but they are not identical. The fact that mass man escapes from the first role to the second does not give the second role complete control over him. Thus, from the viewpoint of mass civilization, the executant's withdrawal and isolation remains ambiguous. It makes him the customer of mass civilization, but as in the case of the associations which the mass man joins, he does not become their prisoner. Mass man's withdrawal is not related to self-confidence or coolness toward those agencies which guide his consumer and leisure time satisfactions. The reason is that these agencies are insufficiently related to the major problem of his existence: his purpose in life. Even if tomorrow's consumer society could fill his last desires, therefore, and do a still more perfect job in creating uninterruptedly new ones, mass man would still have a chance to escape. The consciousness of his inability to control his job is at the same time the measure of mass man's distance from being irrevocably engulfed by mass society.

SELECTED PUBLICATIONS OF

OTTO KIRCHHEIMER

BOOKS

Weimar—und Was Dann? Entstehung und Gegenwart der Weimarer Verfassung [Weimar—and What Then? The Origins and History of the Weimar Constitution]. Berlin: Laubverlag, 1930.

Grenzen der Enteignung [The Limits of Expropriation]. Berlin: W. de Gruyter, 1930.

Staatsgefüge und Recht des Dritten Reiches [State Structure and Law of the Third Reich] Hamburg: Hanseatische Verlagsanstalt, 1935. (There is very strong evidence that this book, which bears the name of Hermann Seitz as author, was written by Otto Kirchheimer during his years in France and smuggled into Nazi Germany through underground channels.)

With George Rusche. *Punishment and Social Structure*. New York: Columbia University Press, 1939.

A Constitution for the Fourth Republic. Washington, D.C.: Foundation for Foreign Affairs, 1947. (Published anonymously because of U.S. State Department regulations.)

Political Justice: The Use of Legal Procedure for Political Ends. Princeton: Princeton University Press, 1961. Paperback edition, Princeton University Press, 1968.

—— German edition: *Politische Justiz*. Neuwied: Luchterhand, 1965.

Politik und Verfassung. Frankfurt/M.: Suhrkamp, 1964.

Politische Herrschaft: Fünf Beiträge zur Lehre vom Staat. Frankfurt/M.: Suhrkamp, 1967.

ARTICLES

"Zur Staatslehre des Sozialismus und Bolschewismus" [The Socialist and Bolshevik Theory of the State], *Zeitschrift für Politik*, XVII (1928), 593–611.

"Eigentumsgarantie in Reichsverfassung und Rechtsprechung" [The Protection of Property in the Constitution and in Judicial Interpretation], *Die Gesellschaft*, VII (1930), 166–79.

"Legalität und Legitimität" [Legality and Legitimacy], *Die Gesellschaft*, IX (1932), 8–20.

"Die Staatsrechtlichen Probleme der Reichstagsaufloesung" [The Dissolution of the *Reichstag* as a Problem of Constitutional Law], *Die Gesellschaft*, IX (1932), 125–35.

"Die Verfassungslehre des Preussenkonfliktes" [The Constitutional Lessons of the Conflict between Prussia and the Reich], *Die Gesellschaft*, IX (1932), 194–209.

"Verfassungsreaktion 1932" [Constitutional Reaction in 1932], *Die Gesellschaft*, IX (1932), 415–27.

With N. Leites. "Bemerkungen zu Carl Schmitt's 'Legalität und Legitimität'" [Remarks on Carl Schmitt's "Legality and Legitimacy"], *Archiv für Sozialwissenschaft und Sozialpolitik*, LXIX (1932), 457–87.

"Verfassungsreform und Sozialdemokratie" [Constitutional Reform and Social Democracy], *Die Gesellschaft*, X (1933), 20–35.

"Marxismus, Diktatur und Organisationsformen des Proletariats" [Marxism, Dictatorship and the Organization of the Proletariat], *Die Gesellschaft*, X (1933), 230–39.

"The Growth and the Decay of the Weimar Constitution," *Contemporary Review*, No. 815 (1933), pp. 559–67.

"Zur Geschichte des Obersten Gerichtshofes der Vereinigten Staaten von Amerika" [Remarks on the History of the Supreme Court of the United States of America], *Zeitschrift für Öffentliches Recht*, XIV (1934), 445–58.

"Remarques sur la théorie de la Souveraineté nationale en Allemagne et en France" [Remarks on the Theory of Popular Sovereignty in Germany and France], *Archives de Philosophie du droit et de Sociologie juridique*, IV (1934), 239–54.

"Remarques sur la statistique criminelle de la France d'après-guerre" [Remarks on the Criminal Statistics of Postwar France], *Revue de Science Criminelle et de Droit pénal comparé*, I (1936), 363–96.

"Recent Trends in German Treatment of Juvenile Delinquency," *Journal of Criminal Law and Criminology*, XXIX (1938), 362–70.

"Decree Powers and Constitutional Law in France under the Third Republic," *American Political Science Review*, XXXIV (1940), 1104–23.

"Criminal Law in National Socialist Germany," *Studies in Philosophy and Social Science*, VIII (1940), 444–63.

"The Historical and Comparative Background of the Hatch Act," *Public Policy*, II (1941), 341–73.

"Changes in the Structure of Political Compromise," *Studies in Philosophy and Social Science*, IX (1941), 264–89.

"The Legal Order of National Socialism," *Studies in Philosophy and Social Science*, IX (1941), 456–75.

"Criminal Omissions," *Harvard Law Review*, LIV (1942), 615–42.

With A. R. L. Gurland and F. Neumann. "The Fate of Small Business in Nazi Germany." U.S. Senate Special Committee on Small Business. Washington, D.C.: U.S. Government Printing Office, 1943.

"In Quest of Sovereignty," *Journal of Politics*, VI (1944), 139–76.

"The Act, the Offense and Double Jeopardy," *Yale Law Journal*, LVIII (1949), 513–44.

With Arnold Price. "Analysis and Effects of the Elections in Western Germany," *Department of State Bulletin*, XXI (1949), 563–73.

"The Composition of the German Bundestag, 1950," *Western Political Quarterly*, III (1950), 590–601.

"The Government of Eastern Germany," in H. J. Morgenthau, ed., *Germany and the Future of Europe*. Chicago: University of Chicago Press, 1951. Pp. 131–41.

"The Decline of Intra-State Federalism in Western Europe," *World Politics*, III (1951), 281–98.

"Notes on the Political Scene in Western Germany," *World Politics*, VI (1954), 306–21.

"Parteistruktur und Massendemokratie in Europa" [Party Structure and Mass Democracy in Europe], *Archiv des öffentlichen Rechts*, LXXIX (1954), 301–25.

"Politics and Justice," *Social Research*, XXII (1955), 377–98.

"The Political Scene in West Germany," *World Politics*, IX (1957), 433–45.

"West German Trade Unions: Their Domestic and Foreign Policies," in Hans Speier and W. P. Davison, eds., *West German Leadership and Foreign Policy*. Evanston, Ill.: Row, Peterson, 1957. Pp. 136–94.

"The Waning of Opposition in Parliamentary Regimes," *Social Research*, XXIV (1957), 127–56.

"Franz Neumann: An Appreciation," *Dissent*, IV (1958), 382–86.

"The Party in Mass Society," *World Politics*, X (1958), 289–94.

"France from the Fourth to the Fifth Republic," *Social Research*, XXV (1958), 379–414.

"Majorities and Minorities in Western European Governments," *Western Political Quarterly*, XII (1959), 492–510.

"The Administration of Justice and the Concept of Legality in East Germany," *Yale Law Journal*, LXVIII (1959), 705–49.

"Asylum," *American Political Science Review*, LIII (1959), 985–1016.

"The Quality of Mercy: On the Role of Clemency in the Apparatus of Justice," *Social Research*, XXVIII (1961), 151–70.

"German Democracy in the 1950's," *World Politics*, XIII (1961), 254–66.

"Sachverstand und Politik im Bereich der Verwaltung" [Expertise and Politics in the Administration], *Gewerkschaftliche Monatshefte*, XI (1962), 670–76.

"Prinzipien der Verfassungsinterpretation in den Vereinigten Staaten" [Principles of Constitutional Interpretation in the United States], *Jahrbuch des öffentlichen Rechts der Gegenwart*, XI (1962), 93–109.

With C. Menges. "A Free Press in a Democratic State?: The *Spiegel* Case," in G. M. Carter and A. F. Westin, eds., *Politics in Europe*. New York: Harcourt, Brace, 1965. Pp. 87–138.

The Problem of the East German Republic," *Samalgundi*, I, No. 1 (Fall, 1965), 88–95.

"Confining Conditions and Revolutionary Breakthroughs," *American Political Science Review*, LIX (1965), 964–74.

"Germany: The Vanishing Opposition," in R. A. Dahl, ed., *Political Oppositions in Western Democracies*. New Haven: Yale University Press, 1966. Pp. 237–59.

"The Transformation of the Western European Party System," in J. LaPalombara and M. Weiner, eds., *Political Parties and Political Development*. Princeton: Princeton University Press, 1966. Pp. 177–200.

"Private Man and Society," *Political Science Quarterly*, LXXXI (1966), 1–24.

"The *Rechtsstaat* as Magic Wall," in Barrington Moore, Jr. *et al.*, eds., *The Critical Spirit* (Essays in Honor of Herbert Marcuse). Boston: Beacon Press, 1967. Pp. 287–312.

"Political Justice," *International Encyclopedia of the Social Sciences*, XII (1968), 246–48.

EDITORS' NOTE: With the exception of *Political Justice*, items published first in English and subsequently in other languages are listed here only in the English version. In the case of items reprinted in other periodicals or symposia, only the place of original publication is cited.

In addition to the items listed above, Otto Kirchheimer published a large number of book reviews and newspaper articles. He also wrote a number of papers, some of them consisting of lectures he delivered, which remained unpublished. These include the following:

"The Policy of the Catholic Church toward the Jews." Institute of Social Research, 1940.

"The Present State of European Parliaments." Address delivered to the Ninth National Conference of the United States National Commission for UNESCO, Chicago, October 23, 1963.

"Elite–Consent–Control in the Western Political System." Paper delivered at the Columbia University Faculty Seminar on the State, October 26, 1964.